FL Education

Your Curriculum Companion

**The Essential Guide to Teaching
the EL Education K-5 Language Arts Curriculum**

Libby Woodfin and Suzanne Nathan Plaut

EL Education
247 West 35th St., 8th Floor
New York, NY 10001
212-239-4455

Design by Mike Kelly

Entypo pictograms by Daniel Bruce — www.entypo.com

All other photos EL Education

FIGURE 5.1 COVER ART:

Brave Irene by William Steig. Text and illustrations © 1986 by William Steig. Reprinted by permission of Farrar, Straus & Giroux, LLC.

Weather (National Geographic Readers Series) by Kristin Baird Rattini. © 2013 National Geographic. Reprinted by permission of National Geographic.

One Hot Summer Day by Nina Crews. Text and illustrations © 1995 Nina Crews. Reprinted by permission of HarperCollins Publishers.

The Snowy Day by Ezra Jack Keats. Text and illustrations © 1976 Ezra Jack Keats.

On the Same Day in March: A Tour of the World's Weather by Marilyn Singer. Text © 2000 Marilyn Singer. Illustrations © 2000 Frane Lessac. Reprinted by permission of HarperCollins Publishers.

Come On, Rain! by Karen Hesse. Text © 1999 by Karen Hesse. Illustrations © 1999 by Jon Muth. Reprinted by permission of Scholastic, Inc.

Weather Words and What They Mean by Gail Gibbons. Text and illustrations © 1990 Gail Gibbons. Reprinted by permission of Holiday House.

Umbrella by Taro Yashima. Text and illustrations © 1958 Taro Yashima.

Table of Contents

Table of Contents

Video Table of Contents

All videos can also be accessed from our curriculum website (Curriculum.ELeducation.org)

Chapter 1

Chapter 2

Chapter 3

Video Table of Contents

Video Table of Contents

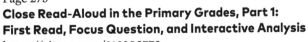

Video Table of Contents

Chapter 6

Chapter 7

Preface

When EL Education started 25 years ago, we would have never dreamed that we would become the creators of a comprehensive English language arts curriculum. We have spent two decades, in fact, standing shoulder to shoulder with teachers in their classrooms, supporting them to create their own curricula. This has been rewarding work—and we still engage teachers in this way every day in classrooms across the country—but it is deep, slow work and it hasn't allowed us to reach the number of teachers, and ultimately students, we need to reach to make a significant impact on education in the United States.

Curriculum design is also really hard work and, given the realities of classroom demands, is not always something to which teachers can devote the time they need. Our goal in creating this curriculum is to take the best of what we have learned from the teachers we work with—instructional practices that elevate student ownership and voice, structures for engaging students in meaningful and collaborative work, and the power of building curriculum around compelling topics, texts, and tasks—and weaving that into an explicit daily curriculum that can reach many thousands more teachers and students. We want to build teacher capacity to deliver great instruction, and accelerate their path toward that end.

There are many great frameworks for engaging students deeply in their learning, and we have promoted and used them since our inception. We have even developed our own. We have come to believe, however, that frameworks aren't enough to make deep and lasting improvements in the quality of classroom instruction. What we have done instead is to build a detailed, daily curriculum that breathes life into the innovative ideas and learning-centered practices of so many great frameworks, while at the same time helping students learn and master rigorous college- and career-ready standards.

We built our curriculum based on the research of experts in the field of literacy. It is a truly comprehensive approach, joining structured phonics with content-based literacy, providing explicit lesson-level support for English language learners, and weaving character development into every lesson. We joined this compelling research with the experience of practicing teachers who were with us every step of the way to help us create a curriculum that provides students with the great instruction they deserve.

Our curriculum offers a concrete and clear vision of instruction that challenges, engages, and empowers all students. It is a tool you can use to help your students be capable and confident readers, writers, thinkers, and communicators, and help you hone and sharpen your instructional practice. Though it is detailed and descriptive, the curriculum is not meant to be prescriptive—its best expression will come when your creative energy and decisions are poured into it. There are many inspiring examples from around the country of teachers who have used modules from our curriculum as a jumping-off place:

1. When a third-grade teacher in Denver taught the frogs module, she extended students' learning by including more independent research about bayous and species of frogs native to that region of the country, and then took her students on fieldwork to explore local frog habitats.

2. A teacher in New York state took advantage of the fact that all of her students had classroom Chromebooks and layered their close reading of the Universal Declaration of Human Rights with related multimedia pieces about human rights.

3. When teaching the first-grade module on birds, teachers in Chicago made the topic more relevant for students living in an urban setting by connecting with ornithologists at the Lincoln Park Zoo. They conducted fieldwork at the zoo and went bird-watching in the neighborhood.

4. Fifth-graders in Maine extended their learning from the rainforest module by conducting case studies on biodiversity in three different local ecosystems: forest, beach and dunes, and tidal pools. They researched, met with experts, and created pages for a magazine that explored human impacts on the ecosystems and what people can do to preserve them.

We hope this book will serve as your guide to not just implementing the curriculum, but also to truly delivering it to your students in ways that serve them best. By looking "under the hood" at the decisions that went into such things as the texts we chose, or the rationale for our use of discussion protocols, or why every lesson starts with unpacking learning targets with students, we hope to equip you with a sense of ownership of those practices so that you can make them your own and use them well.

Scott Hartl
President and CEO, EL Education
New York, NY
July, 2017

Acknowledgments

Before we thank those who helped make this book possible, we want to thank the real heroes of this project: the EL Education staff, the teachers, and the expert consultants in literacy, English language learning, universal design for learning, social-emotional learning, art, and science who wrote the EL Education K–5 Language Arts Curriculum, as well as those who help us bring it to teachers, schools, and districts across the United States. They are rarely publicly acknowledged, but they deserve our gratitude for creating and bringing to life a curriculum that is rigorous, joyful, and good for kids.

Curriculum Design

EL Education Curriculum Design Staff

Gwyneth Hagan
Kevin Jepson
Tere Peláez
Christina Riley
Casey Schultz
Katie Shenk

Teachers and Consultants on the Long-Term Curriculum Design Project

Margaret Beneke*
Rebecca Blum-Martinez*
Marijke Conklin
Rachel Coughlin
Stephen DelVecchio*
Genya Devoe
Krista Easton
Linnea Ehri*
Mary Ewing*
Ken Ferguson
Pat Fitzsimmons
Marisa Garcia
Amanda Hamilton Roos
Julia Handelman
Joey Hawkins*
Jolie Heath
Erika Hedin
Andrew Hossack
Jean Hurst
Staci Intriligator
Vaishali Joshi
Jessica Kauffman
Shyla Kinhal
Diana Leddy*
Steven Levy*
Kate Lewis Kelley
Farren Liben
Anna Loring
Pete Martinez
Auddie Mastroleo
Lauren Mayer*
Jessica Miller

Charles Newling
Teresa Ober
Reanna Patterson
Deb Porter*
Dave Roos
Adam Rothstein
Anne Simpson
Molly Siuty
Lynne Spewak
Chrissy Thuli
Yoo Kyung Sung*

Teachers, School Coaches, and EL Education Staff Who Participated in Our Curriculum Design Intensives

Marissa Austin
Thora Balk
Andrea Bander
Lauren Benjamin
Jessica Bernacki
Anne Brophy
Veronica Carrejo
Cyrene Crooms
Katie Daday
Megan DeRitter
Enid Dodson
Erin Doyle
Katey Edson
Jenny Elahi
Therese Ellsworth
Ananda Grant
Heather Gray
Whitney Griggs
Katie Hansen
Shannon Hillman
Kate Hilmershausen
Wendy Hodgson
Annie Holyfield
Kari Horn Lehman
Pat Jeffers
Wendy Kenney
Teresa Lewers
Emily Lichtenstein
Callie Lowenstein

Misty McDonough
Wanda McClure
Kristen McNeil
Sara Metz
Carrie Moore
Monica Osborn
Jaime Passchier
Romey Pittman
Traci Price
Jodi Rabat
Sisa Renie
Maria Reyes
Jennifer Schmidt
Kate Schultz
Emily Smith
Katie Smith
Laura Sparks
Dina Strasser
Susan Tesser
Jennifer Trople
Lisa Veteto
Emily Williams
Kate Wolff
Jen Wood

Production, Project Management, and Administrative Support

Ananda Grant
Kathy Klein
Karen Leavitt
Farren Liben
Rupa Mohan
Maria Reyes
Lloyetta Walls
Emily Williams

Curriculum Implementation

Amy Bailey
Sandra Calderon
Genya Devoe
Wendy Hodgson
Kari Horn Lehman
Dina Strasser

*National Expert/Advisor

We also want to thank those who contributed directly to this book—from teachers who allowed our videographers into their classrooms, to school and district leaders and EL Education staff who reviewed drafts of each chapter, to the schools who partnered with us to pilot the curriculum, to videographers and designers. The book is better because of the experience and expertise you shared with us and, of course, your kind, specific, and helpful feedback.

Reviewers

School and District Leaders

Tammi Bauschka
Annaleah Bloom
Carmen Castro
Kristel Foster
Courtenay Hammond
Julia Lindberg
Rebecca Ridge

EL Education Staff

Amy Bailey
Ron Berger
Cyndi Gueswel
Gwyneth Hagan
Kevin Jepson
Christina Lesh
Wanda McClure
Sharon Newman
Tere Peláez
Kate Palumbo
Jodi Rabat
Christina Riley
Meg Riordan
Casey Schultz
Katie Shenk
Colleen Stanevich
Karen Tylek
Anne Vilen

Teachers Who Contributed Quotes

Tammi Bauschka
Katie Benton
Richard Flynn

Elizabeth Freitag
Laurie Godwin
Dolly Higgins
Annie Holyfield
Kerry Meehan-Richardson
Sara Metz
Sarah Mitchell
Kady Taylor

Teachers Who Appear in the Book's Videos

Ron Berger
Katie Benton
Stacey Cicero
Katie Daday
Erin Daley
Kerry Meehan-Richardson
Sara Metz
Susan Preston
Brenna Schneider
Jason Shiroff
Anne Simpson
Sheela Webster
Jessica Wood

Schools and Districts That Piloted the Curriculum in 2016–17

Michael R. Hollis Innovation Academy, Atlanta, GA
Southwest Baltimore Charter School, Baltimore, MD
Boston Public Schools, Boston, MA
Kuumba Academy, Wilmington, DE
Centennial Elementary School, Denver, CO
Joe Shoemaker Elementary School, Denver, CO

Lead Academy Charter School, Greenville, SC
Manhattan Charter School, New York, NY
Manhattan Charter School 2, New York, NY
Mapleton Public Schools, Denver, CO
Polaris Charter Academy, Chicago, IL
PS 51M—Elias Howe, New York, NY
Lincoln Elementary School, Pittsburgh, PA
DC Scholars Public Charter School, Washington, DC
Sunnyside Unified School District, Tucson, AZ
Scintilla Charter Academy, Valdosta, GA
Gateway Lab, Wilmington, DE

EL Education Staff Who Supported Schools and Districts Piloting the Curriculum

Wendy Hodgson
Emily Lichtenstein
Wanda McClure
Jill Mirman
Kate Palumbo
Jodi Rabat
Jennifer Schmidt
Katie Smith

Videographers

Katie Schneider
David Grant
Rosa Gaia

Finally, a few special thank-yous. First, to Mike Kelly, who designed this book and worked tirelessly with us to get everything just right. Second, to Casey Schultz, who not only led the design of the K–2 Reading Foundations Skills Block, but also wrote Chapter 4 of this book. Third, to two of EL Education's leaders, Scott Hartl, our president and CEO, and Kemi Akinsanya-Rose, our chief operating officer, for championing both the curriculum and this book and doing everything in their power to fund and prioritize both projects.

And last, but certainly not least, the EL Education field staff—school coaches and professional development specialists—who are in schools every day helping teachers hone their practice so that they can give their students the learning experiences they need and deserve.

About the Authors

Libby Woodfin

Libby Woodfin is the director of publications for EL Education. She started her career as a fifth- and sixth-grade teacher at the original lab school for the Responsive Classroom in Greenfield, Massachusetts, and went on to become a counselor at a large comprehensive high school. Libby started with EL Education in 2007 while completing graduate work at the Harvard Graduate School of Education in Education Policy and Management.

Throughout her career, Libby has written articles, blogs, chapters, and books about important issues in education. Her previous books include *Management in the Active Classroom*; *Leaders of Their Own Learning: Transforming Schools through Student-Engaged Assessment*; *Learning That Lasts: Challenging, Engaging, and Empowering Students with Deeper Instruction*; *Transformational Literacy: Making the Common Core Shift with Work That Matters*; and *Familiar Ground: Traditions That Build School Community*.

Suzanne Nathan Plaut

Suzanne Nathan Plaut, former director of curriculum design for EL Education, is now the managing director of program for EL Education. She previously served as the vice president of education at the Public Education & Business Coalition in Denver, overseeing professional development, evaluation, and publications. Suzanne holds a doctorate from the Harvard Graduate School of Education, where she served on the editorial board for the Harvard Educational Review. Her previous books include *Transformational Literacy: Making the Common Core Shift with Work That Matters* and *The Right to Literacy in Secondary Schools*. She has also been published in EdWeek. Suzanne worked as a literacy coach and director of literacy in several Boston public schools and taught high school English in Colorado and New Zealand. She lives in Lafayette, Colorado, with her husband and two daughters who were fortunate to attend an EL Education elementary school.

About EL Education

EL Education (formerly Expeditionary Learning) is redefining student achievement in diverse communities across the country, ensuring that all students master rigorous content, develop positive character, and produce high-quality work. We create great public schools where they are needed most, inspiring teachers and students to achieve more than they thought possible.

Created over 20 years ago through the collaboration of the Harvard Graduate School of Education and Outward Bound, EL Education's research-based approach challenges and empowers teachers and students. We transform education in thousands of schools and districts across the country through a unique combination of rigor and joy in learning. Students' impressive results encompass high academic achievement and college readiness, pride in the mastery of complex, authentic work, and a passion and capacity to contribute to a better world.

As a mission-driven, nonprofit organization, we work with all kinds of schools: district and charter, from pre-K through 12th grade, serving populations that reflect the diversity of our country. We create powerful resources—including an open-access literacy curriculum downloaded by teachers over eight million times—provide masterful coaching and professional development, and share a portfolio of award-winning, educator-developed materials. Our curriculum is in use in more than 600 districts across 44 states. One reason for our success: Our work is informed by decades of learning in our national network of over 150 high-achieving public schools.

For more information, visit www.ELeducation.org.

Your Curriculum Companion

**The Essential Guide to Teaching
the EL Education K-5 Language Arts Curriculum**

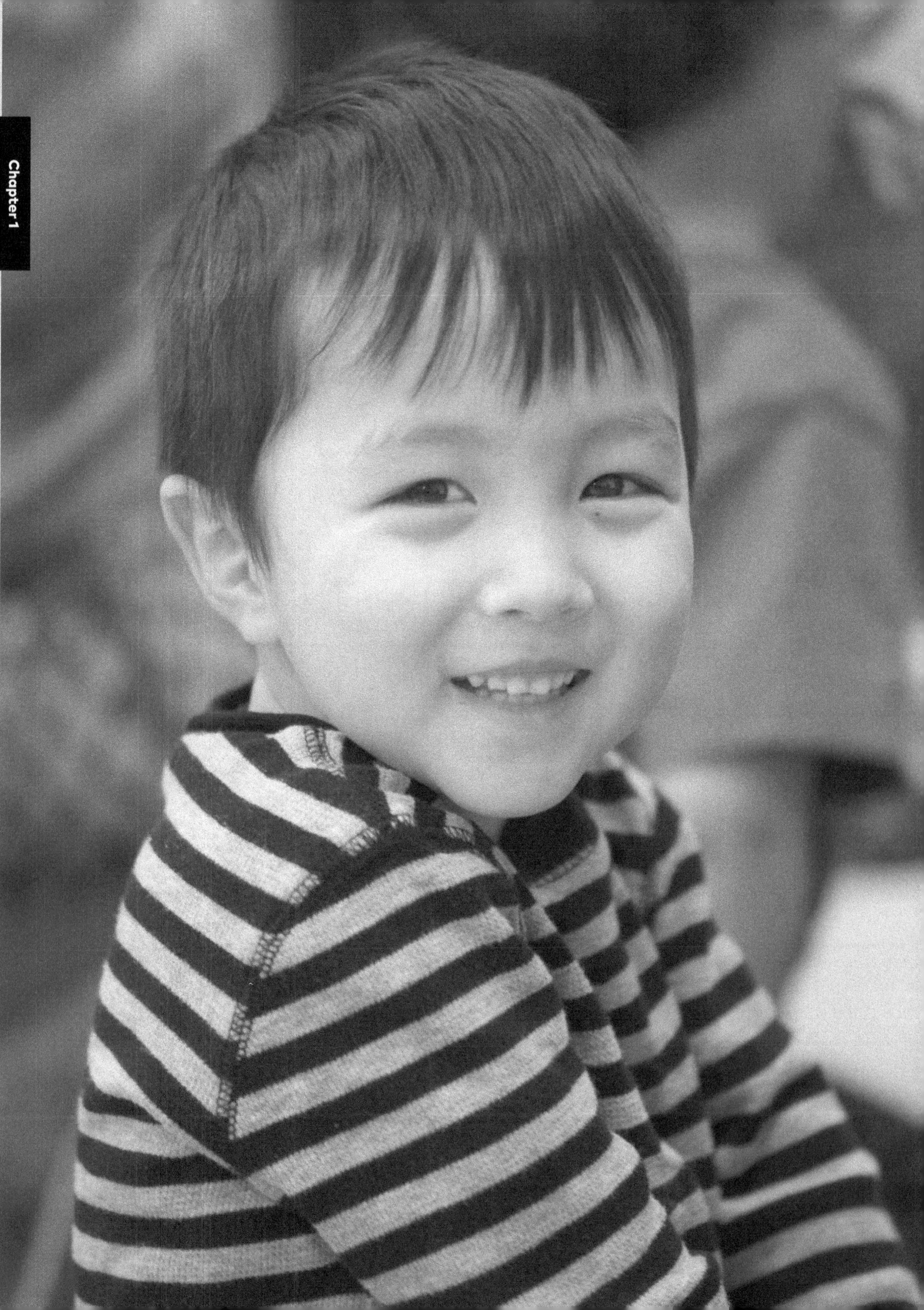

Chapter 1:
Before You Begin: The Foundations of the Curriculum

Chapter 1

Chapter 1A:
What Makes This Curriculum the Right Choice for Me and My Students?

By now you have probably encountered the EL Education K–5 Language Arts curriculum in some form or fashion. You may have found it online and downloaded modules or lessons to explore. Your school or district may have adopted it and delivered boxes of books and materials to your classroom. You may have attended school or district trainings to support you in using it, or even have had some experience teaching the first edition, which was published in 2012.

You may feel excited about its potential to help your students and be eager to get started. Or, you may feel overwhelmed.

For all of you, in all of these categories, this book is for you. It was written partly to provide you with an orientation to the curriculum, partly to be a guide to the instructional practices embedded in the curriculum, and, perhaps most important, partly to act as a coach. We hope it will alleviate your stress, address your questions, enable you to use the curriculum most effectively, and help you understand it deeply enough to decide whether, when, and how to make adjustments given your context and needs.

Our curriculum is fundamentally different from most published curricula. It was created to support your students to build skills and content knowledge, to meet college- and career-ready standards, and, at the same time, to become more confident and collaborative learners. It also was created to help you become a stronger teacher:

» **Our curriculum was written by teachers, for teachers.** It is not the product of a for-profit publishing company. Former teachers working at EL Education—a non-profit school improvement organization—and current teachers in public schools across the country joined together in this work. Many teacher-authors of this curriculum are practicing teachers who used their own classrooms to test and improve the practices and structures of the curriculum.

» **Our curriculum is offered as a free, open resource.** The complete first edition (Grades 3–8) of the curriculum (and soon all of the new K–2 and second-edition 3–5 curriculum) is hosted online. It is intended for you to "own" and make wise changes to once you understand the design fully. Our curriculum is not designed to be "teacher-proof" (a term that is disrespectful to the professionalism of teachers and represents a misguided and impossible goal).

If you need to make changes, this book provides the knowledge and tools to do so in a way that maintains the integrity of the purpose, principles, structure, and intended outcomes of the curriculum.

» **Our curriculum is designed to help teachers become even better in their practice.** We hope that using the curriculum will be a form of professional development for you, building instructional wisdom and providing strategies and tools that will help you hone your practice, whether you are a new or veteran teacher. Unlike most published curricula, which primarily consist of student-facing materials, ours consists primarily of teacher-facing materials. We provide extensive teaching notes, guidance for using new instructional techniques and protocols, suggestions for supporting English language learners (ELLs), and step-by-step training in practices such as leading students in close and careful reading of complex text or citing evidence in writing.

"The curriculum as a whole ... it's almost like this equal composition of learning how to become a better teacher ... and watching your students become better learners. I feel like this is the roadmap to being a good teacher."

Richard Finn

Teacher, Boston

Our curriculum has been judged by independent experts[1] to be the best in the country in its alignment to the new college- and career-ready English language arts (ELA)/literacy standards used in almost every state. It has also been a transformational learning experience for many teachers across the country, reinvigorating their passion for teaching, deepening their expertise, and making their classrooms more respectful, energized, and effective. *But none of that means anything if it doesn't work well for you.*

▶ How Will I Make This Curriculum My Own?

A curriculum is not effective on its own. It requires a teacher who understands it, trusts it, and teaches it with integrity, creativity, and professional judgment. This means both knowing the curriculum well and knowing your students well so that you can make decisions that serve them best: speeding up, slowing down, reviewing or skipping a step, adding a resource, or innovating with extensions. Our curriculum is not meant to be simply *delivered*. It is a tool to be used, with your professional expertise, to accelerate literacy learning and excellence for all of your students.

We designed our curriculum based on what teachers told us they needed: a curriculum that is comprehensive, that provides everything you need to teach and assess ELA standards; that engages students in meaningful content; that helps students become strong learners and people; that empowers them to create high-quality work that matters; and that is compelling, engaging, and joyful. We provide detailed lessons for almost every single day of the year that fit this bill, and we offer guidance for how to execute those lessons effectively.

When you first encounter our curriculum, you may incorrectly assume that it is prescriptive, since every lesson is described down to the smallest detail. It is *descriptive*, but it is not intended to be *prescriptive*. It is a *thinking teacher's curriculum*; it is not designed to be followed mindlessly.

---

[1] Edreports.org

Using Creativity and Professional Judgment

We encourage you to use your creativity and professional judgment to make the curriculum your own. You may wish to enrich a module by adding in local connections and resources, for example, or to slow down lessons to make sure all students understand the content. We also encourage you to weigh the pros and cons of any changes you are inclined to make. Because the various components of the curriculum are carefully constructed to ensure that students achieve mastery on every college- and career-ready ELA standard in the course of the year, any changes you wish to make should be done with care. This book will give you an "insider's" view into the *what, why,* and *how* of the curriculum's design so that you can make *informed* decisions about customization.

▷ This book will give you an "insider's" view into the *what, why,* and *how* of the curriculum's design so that you can make informed decisions about customization.

Counting on the Curriculum

For more than 20 years, EL Education has equipped teachers in our network schools across the country to design their own curriculum using an interdisciplinary project-based curricular structure we call *learning expeditions.* Thousands of teachers have used this structure to create powerfully engaging and effective curriculum for their students. From that work, we know that not all teachers, within and beyond our network, have the time, support, and expertise to design their own curricula while simultaneously attending to meeting the needs of every student with strong instruction and effective classroom management. As standards have gotten more challenging, it has been especially difficult to ensure that curricula support all students to meet those standards.

By creating this ELA curriculum, we provide you with a foundation of texts, lessons, and assessments that you can count on. We hope that those of you who have been creating your own curricula and struggling to meet all standards can now infuse this curriculum into your work. By giving you these resources, we empower you to spend more of your time thinking through the nuances of your instruction and how best to support your particular students. For those of you more accustomed to using published curricula, we hope that ours will give you all that you need to support your students to succeed and will also help you learn and grow as a teacher.

In the first year or two of using our curriculum, you may find that you adhere to it quite closely. Over time, we hope all teachers will learn to effectively customize and expand upon it to create powerful lessons and projects on their own. Designing curriculum is some of the most creative and rewarding work a teacher can do, but it's certainly not easy. We hope our curriculum, in combination with this book, will provide you with the tools you need to create powerful learning experiences that challenge, engage, and empower students equitably and hit standards sharply.

▶ What Are the Fundamental Questions about Teaching and Learning That This Curriculum Will Help Me Answer?

Our curriculum was created with founding principles designed to address *these fundamental teacher questions:*

» How can I motivate students to take on challenges and succeed?

» How can I ensure that *all* students have equitable access to high-level work?

» How can I elevate student achievement beyond just test scores?

» How will content-based literacy benefit my students?

» How do I help all students stay active, engaged, and excited to learn?

How Can I Motivate Students to Take On Challenges and Succeed?

In a number of urban public schools in the EL Education network, school begins in an unusual way. During the first month of school, students leave the building, sometimes for multiple days, to engage in a wilderness experience. The challenge for these students is to work together as a team to get every person to the top of the mountain. Many have never been in this kind of environment before, and there is a wide range of physical, emotional, and social abilities among students and teachers. But they have a few important things in common: They are all outside of their comfort zone; they are all facing a worthy challenge; and they all have to depend on each other and support each other if they hope to succeed.

The students and teachers will tell you right away that it isn't all fun. It's a long, hard journey. They get exhausted, sweaty, and filthy. They grow discouraged and overwhelmed. They argue sometimes and want to give up. But they stick together and eventually reach the summit—proud, exhausted, and amazed. They drop their backpacks and cheer and hug and drink cool water and sit down and take in the beautiful view together, on top of the world.

Back in school, "climbing the mountain together" is the memory and metaphor that guides learning. School may be overwhelming and discouraging at times, but the job of students and teachers is to work together as a team to make sure everyone gets to the summit. It won't be easy, but if they stick together and work hard, they can make it.

Though we are focused here on our K–5 curriculum, it is important to keep in mind that our goal is for students to leave high school college- and career-ready. Graduation and college acceptance is the looming peak. In many EL Education high schools in low-income urban communities, 100 percent of graduates have been accepted to college—every graduate, every year for almost a decade. That success is built on the strong literacy skills and habits of character students develop throughout their K–12 education.

A primary challenge for students in schools across America is building the literacy skills to succeed—not just during ELA/literacy lessons, but across all subjects. In the wilderness, the challenges may be rough weather, confusing trails, and steep climbs. In school, the challenges are likely to be difficult text to read and complex written tasks to complete. In both cases, the answer is the same: to embrace challenge, together; to not be afraid to stumble and fail at times; to take risks; and to push and support each other.

Providing Worthy Challenges

A founding principle of this curriculum is to provide worthy challenges for all students and to provide structures for them to work together as a team to support each other to succeed. If the curriculum feels daunting at first, to you and your students, that's by design. We believe that worthy challenges, carefully scaffolded and supported, lead to deeper learning.

By way of example, consider the story of how a middle school teacher in Boston skillfully walked her students up and over the mountain of a *very* complex text. The text, "Substrate Determinants and Developmental Rate of Claw Asymmetry in American Lobsters, *Homarus Americanus*," was first published in the *Journal of Crustacean Biology* (see Figure 1.1 for an excerpt). The students' initial reaction was similar to what you're likely thinking right now: "This is crazy! I'll never understand this!"

Figure 1.1: Excerpt from Lobster Text

SUBSTRATE DETERMINANTS AND DEVELOPMENTAL RATE OF CLAW ASYMMETRY IN AMERICAN LOBSTERS, *HOMARUS AMERICANUS*

Jason S. Goldstein and Michael F. Tlusty

(JG) Old Dominion University, Department of Biological Sciences, Hampton Boulevard, Norfolk, Virginia 23529 U.S.A. (jgoldste@odu.edu);
(MT, correspondence), New England Aquarium, Edgerton Research Laboratory, Lobster Rearing and Research Facility, 1 Central Wharf, Boston, Massachusetts 02110-3399 U.S.A. (mtlusty@neaq.org)

The North American lobster (*Homarus americanus* H. Milne Edwards, 1837) exhibits the largest chelipeds (claws) of any known crustacean. The ''Great Chelae,'' as published by Herrick (1909), exemplifies just one of many early studies examining the structure and function of American lobster claws (also see Smith, 1873, and Templeman, 1935). Although they may comprise less than 5% of the total contour containing faster responding muscles that yield a significantly reduced strength (Govind and Pearce, 1992). The fourth (post-larval) and fifth (early benthic phase juvenile) developmental stages are essential critical periods for determining claw asymmetry (Emmel, 1908; Govind and Pearce, 1989). Once a crusher claw has been determined, the asymmetric pattern becomes fixed for life

Source: Goldstein, J.S. & Tlusty, M.F. (2003). Substrate Determinants and Developmental Rate of Claw Asymmetry in American Lobsters, Homarus americanus. Journal of Crustacean Biology, *23(4), 890-896. By permission of Oxford University Press*

"Most students approach text expecting to understand it right away—they plow through and do their best to understand it after reading it once. If they struggle too much, they may begin to practice avoidance strategies, believing that the text is simply too hard for them. Too many experiences like these can affect students' confidence as readers" (Berger, Woodfin, Plaut, and Dobbertin, 2014, p. 85). But the teacher in this case approached the challenge with a different mindset, and she slowly but surely helped her students put one foot in front of the other to start making their way through the text.

Here's what she said:

> "This is a great scientific paper by one of the world experts on lobsters. It has important information that will inform our study of Boston Harbor. But almost no one in the world has read it, and few people can understand it. Even your parents may not be able to understand it. Some of the teachers here may not understand it. At least not right away. But together, we can make sense of it. We are in no rush. Today we are just going to tackle the first page. We will start with the words we know and the sentences that make sense to us. And we will keep going until it all makes sense. I'll bet there are many words you see right now that you understand, and parts of sentences, too. You will start alone, making sense of what you can, then you will work with two partners to share what you discover. Then all the triads will come together and share what they think. By the end of the period, we will understand this whole first page."

This teacher set a new expectation for students that disrupted their instinct to attempt to read quickly through something she knew would frustrate them and, ultimately, fail to teach them anything. She helped them see that they could each contribute to a shared understanding of a text they were unlikely to be able to read independently. She also chose an article that had information they wanted and needed for their research on Boston Harbor, so by the time she had reset their expectations about what their reading process would look like, they were eager to take on the challenge and poised to succeed. They left the class having learned a lot about lobsters, but most importantly, they left with a positive mindset about the challenge of complex text. They were proud, and they really did feel like they had climbed a metaphorical mountain together.

Fostering Students' Growth Mindset (and Your Own)

Most likely, if you are holding this book in your hands, the preceding example will have some resonance for you. Perhaps you have witnessed students feeling intimidated by challenging text, like that in Figure 1.1. You have also likely witnessed the pride that comes with overcoming a challenge like this. Perhaps more than any other challenge students and teachers face when striving to meet rigorous college- and career-ready standards, reading complex texts like this one is the greatest. The teacher who taught this lesson was not using our curriculum—this was many years ago—but she knew from experience that helping students climb the mountain together would allow them to succeed.

Fostering your students' growth mindset means encouraging and supporting them to take on meaningful challenges. Just as they would when reaching the peaks of mountains, students will feel pride in their success with challenging texts and tasks and build the muscles they need to push on and do more than they think possible. As you embark on your adventure with our curriculum, we urge you to consider your mindset as well; yours may be a figurative adventure, rather than a literal one, but that doesn't make the journey any less significant. You will encounter challenges, even if you are a veteran teacher, and your willingness to take them on with a spirit of growth and learning will help you and your students meet success.

> *"We have to believe that students can be successful with academic challenges the same way they are with character and physical challenges.... We can't wait until they are 'ready,' because what happens is that students in poverty and students at risk never even get to attempt that kind of work. All students need the same access to academics that will prepare them for college and beyond."*

Laurie Godwin

Principal, Aurora, Colorado

The metaphor of getting all students up the mountain is not meant to be intimidating. But it is meant to signal one of the key philosophical beliefs upon which our curriculum rests: All students deserve the opportunity and access to the tools they need to read and write proficiently. Equity for *all* students drives the EL Education curriculum.

How Can I Ensure That *All* Students Have Equitable Access to High-Level Work?

EL Education is fiercely focused on equity. All children deserve schools that foster their unique abilities, give them a real opportunity to achieve high academic standards, and help them take their full place in a society for which they are well prepared when they leave school. In our curriculum, all students are given the opportunity and the tools they need to read complex texts that are at or above grade level, compose high-quality writing, and engage in sophisticated high-level discourse.

Preparing students for the duties of work and citizenship has always been at the core of public education in the United States. Preparing students for the rigors of college, on the other hand, has historically been limited to a privileged minority. Despite centuries of restriction regarding who has access to college, the boundaries are beginning to crumble. More and more, college readiness is seen as a goal for all students. Certainly this doesn't mean that all students will go to college, but it does mean that all students must be prepared so that the choice is available to them when they graduate from high school. As author and activist, bell hooks, reminds us: "Being oppressed means the absence of choices."

K–5 teachers have a crucial role, particularly when it comes to building the literacy skills upon which students' entire academic lives will rest. New, more rigorous college- and career-ready standards are an opportunity, and a provocation, to think more expansively about the capacities of all of our students.

★ **A Word about the Common Core State Standards**

When the Common Core State Standards were first introduced in 2010, almost every state adopted them. At this point in 2017, most states have accommodated the changing political climate by customizing and renaming them. Despite new names, most states' college- and career-ready ELA/literacy standards closely resemble Common Core standards. We have built our curriculum around the Common Core standards because they allow us to have a common reference point in states across the country. If you teach in a state that doesn't use Common Core standards, this curriculum is still going to help you meet your state's standards. However, you may need to match the numbers or names of the Common Core standards to those in your state.

Students can and should be reading more challenging texts, presenting opinions and arguments with evidence, challenging ideas, and promoting divergent perspectives. They should be engaged in high-level thinking and discourse, analysis, and synthesis. This shouldn't be the aim of education only for elite scholars; all students deserve an education that gives them a chance to reach their full potential. Historically underserved populations of students have suffered from the "soft bigotry of low expectations," often experiencing less rigorous curricula and uninspired instruction, which has limited their educational opportunities. Our curriculum is designed to provide all students, from all backgrounds, with the skills and knowledge they need to be literate and confident students.

Leaning into the Highest Aspirations of the Standards

Ever since the Common Core standards were introduced, EL Education has leaned into them. Despite the controversy that has swirled around their implementation, we believe that they represent a real opportunity to create more equitable educational opportunities for students most in need. "We believe the standards invite us to build in our students critical skills for life—for career success and civic contribution. What is important is not just what the standards say, but how they are used. The standards can be used to build classrooms where students are active, reflective critical thinkers, not passive recipients of content. The standards can be used to build in students the dispositions and skills to do work that matters to them and their communities" (Berger, Woodfin, Plaut, and Dobbertin, 2014, p. 5). Our curriculum is built upon this expansive interpretation of the standards; if the standards were designed to level the playing field for all students, then our curriculum was designed to give all students the equipment they need to get in the game and win.

Honoring the Diversity of Learners

These aspirations are not always easy to achieve, or even imagine, when students come to school with such a wide variety of needs, but we believe strongly that students excel in diverse and inclusive settings. Students learn from one another—and learn to respect one another—when they learn together in the same classroom. At the same time, students sometimes have needs that require varied approaches. Our curriculum provides supports and resources for differentiated instruction, which allows teachers to provide for students with disabilities as well as those who may need academic extensions. Tools and scaffolding that support all learners and flexibility in the ways information is presented, the ways students respond, and the ways students are engaged are embedded throughout the curriculum based on Universal Design for Learning (UDL). (UDL is explored in Chapter 2C).

ELLs and language minority students also need their assets honored and their needs supported. These students bring a wealth of diverse experience and wisdom to the classroom. In our curriculum, these language learners are presumed to be fully participating members of a diverse and heterogeneous classroom structure. We also honor the fact that language learners need targeted instruction within each lesson and additional supports if they are to be successful. Specific scaffolds have been integrated into lessons so teachers can provide myriad supports for these students, particularly for those classified as "long-term ELLs." Additional designated time beyond that held by our curriculum may be needed for students who are new to learning English. (Supports for ELLs are explored in Chapter 2C).

Elevating Student Thinking, Voice, and Work

Our curriculum also prizes and elevates original student thinking, student voice, and student work. We ask students to grapple with worthy texts and tasks, participate in scholarly discourse, and engage in critique of their written work to build quality and ownership. We support them to become leaders of their own learning, rather than simply obedient task completers.

> ▷ Our curriculum also prizes and elevates original student thinking, student voice, and student work. We ask students to grapple with worthy texts and tasks, participate in scholarly discourse, and engage in critique of their written work to build quality and ownership. We support them to become leaders of their own learning, rather than simply obedient task completers.

Building these capacities in students has always been something we have believed in at EL Education and is what led us to rethink what student achievement really means. While we believe that new college- and career-ready standards represent an opportunity to address inequity, raise expectations, and increase opportunities and excellence for all students, we are also aware of the ways in which standards have polarized the debate about education in America. Reducing the success or failure of students and teachers to a single measure of mastery of standards does not allow anyone to live up to the promise of what standards *could* mean for students and communities. We have chosen to define student achievement more expansively, recognizing the fullness of what it means to succeed in school and life, and we have built our curriculum to reflect this more expansive definition.

How Can I Elevate Student Achievement beyond Just Test Scores?

We believe that our nation's schools are too narrowly focused on a single dimension of achievement, which can result in disengaged students and teachers and, often, poor student outcomes. The reality is that educators, parents, and students themselves care about much more than just the traditional view of what mastering knowledge and skills looks like on a test. We want students to also learn to be deep thinkers and good people who care about the quality of their work.

Promoting a Multi-Dimensional View of Student Achievement

We promote a three-dimensional view of student achievement—mastery of knowledge and skills, character, and high-quality student work—that offers a vision for education we would want for every child and provides the "north star" for all of our work (see Figure 1.2).

Figure 1.2: EL Education's Dimensions of Student Achievement

EL Education

Dimensions of Student Achievement

Dimension of Achievement	Students	Teachers and Leaders
Mastery of Knowledge and Skills	• **Demonstrate proficiency and deeper understanding:** show mastery in a body of knowledge and skills within each discipline • **Apply their learning:** transfer knowledge and skills to novel, meaningful tasks • **Think critically:** analyze, evaluate, and synthesize complex ideas and consider multiple perspectives • **Communicate clearly:** write, speak, and present ideas effectively in a variety of media within and across disciplines	• Ensure that curriculum, instruction, and assessments are **rigorous, meaningful, and aligned with standards** • **Use assessment practices** that position students as leaders of their own learning • Use **meaningful data for both teachers and students to track progress** toward learning goals • **Engage all students in daily lessons that require critical thinking** about complex, worthy ideas, texts, and problems
Character	• **Work to become effective learners:** develop the mindsets and skills for success in college, career, and life (e.g., initiative, responsibility, perseverance, collaboration) • **Work to become ethical people:** treat others well and stand up for what is right (e.g., empathy, integrity, respect, compassion) • **Contribute to a better world:** put their learning to use to improve communities (e.g., citizenship, service)	• **Elevate student voice and leadership** in classrooms and across the school • **Make habits of scholarship visible** across the school and in daily instruction • Model a **school-wide culture of respect and compassion** • **Prioritize social and emotional learning,** along with academic learning, across the school
High-Quality Student Work	• **Create complex work:** demonstrate higher-order thinking, multiple perspectives and transfer of understanding • **Demonstrate craftsmanship:** create work that is accurate and beautiful in conception and execution • **Create authentic work:** demonstrate original thinking and voice, connect to real-world issues and formats, and when possible, create work that is meaningful to the community beyond the school	• **Design tasks that ask students to apply, analyze, evaluate and create** as part of their work • **Use models of excellence, critique, and multiple drafts** to support all students to produce work of exceptional quality • **Connect students to the world beyond school** through meaningful fieldwork, expert collaborators, research, and service learning

Mastery of Knowledge and Skills

Mastery of knowledge and skills is the dimension of student achievement that most schools are already fairly familiar and comfortable with. Held within this dimension are state tests and other high-stakes assessments that are a required part of public schooling. High-stakes achievement tests have an important role to play in shining a light on inequities in public schooling. However, our nation's hyper-focus on these kinds of assessments in recent years has led to a reductionist view of what mastery of knowledge and skills means and how students should be taught.

When interpreted and applied as intended, the new standards are also asking teachers to focus on critical thinking, effective communication, and deeper learning. Our curriculum compels students to demonstrate deep understanding of concepts and content, analyze, evaluate, and synthesize their content knowledge, and demonstrate that they can transfer their understanding to novel tasks. When building knowledge of the world, students must consider multiple perspectives and viewpoints. They must present their thinking in multiple ways—informal and formal writing, conversation, and formal presentations—which builds strong communication skills. Our curriculum gives students opportunities to develop these skills, and the assessments and performance tasks are designed to evaluate them in authentic ways.

Character

A central goal of our curriculum is to give students the tools to become effective, ethical learners who work to make the world a better place. We have our own language and approach to fostering what we call "habits of character," which are a part of daily lessons at all grade levels. Our habits of character can and should complement, not replace, any existing frameworks, language, or routines for promoting social-emotional learning in your school. If another framework for character is in place at your school (e.g., Responsive Classroom; Caring School Communities; CASEL's five core competencies), it will be important for you to help your students make connections between that framework and ours. In practice, this means helping students understand the meaning of specific words (e.g., if "tenacity" is used at your school, help students see the connection to "perseverance," which is used in our curriculum). This unpacking is a great opportunity to teach academic vocabulary and for students to see how words that define character are connected to, not separate from, academic tasks.

Promoting character development is not new in schools. What makes our curriculum distinct is that it integrates an intentional focus on developing students' habits of character within the context of academic lessons (e.g., persevering as they work on multiple drafts of their performance task). Character is not "preached" through admonishments; rather, it is learned through authentic experiences and ongoing reflection on those experiences. *How* children learn and the environment in which they learn is as important as what they learn.

High-Quality Student Work

When students complete their formal schooling, with few exceptions they will no longer be assessed by tests. Instead, they will be assessed by the quality of their character and their work. Preparing students to be successful in these areas is one of the reasons we are so focused on a broader definition of student achievement.

High-quality student work—work that demonstrates complexity, craftsmanship, and authenticity—not only has the power to assess aspects of student learning that can be elusive, such as communication skills and conceptual understanding, but can also motivate students. Models of high-quality work give students something to aspire to and can answer some of their most timeless questions: *Why do we have to do this? How will we use this?* High-quality work, especially when modeled after real-world work and embedding the knowledge and skills students are currently learning, can engage students in ways that little else can.

In the curriculum, a commitment to quality shows up in all kinds of ways—from scaffolded, and often collaborative, high-quality performance tasks to the everyday craftsmanship of practicing just the right shape of the mouth when pronouncing the difference between an "a" and a "u." Helping students commit themselves to quality work and being leaders of their own learning is a thread throughout all components of the curriculum. (In Chapter 7A, we will explore how you can look at student work as one source of evidence to assess student progress.)

Of note, one key aspect of high-quality work—authenticity—was not always possible to build into our curriculum. Among other things, true authenticity can mean that student work is connected to a real community need. Within a nationwide curriculum like ours, it's a challenge to make local connections that will have relevance across the country. This is one area ripe for enrichment, where your experience and creativity as a teacher can bring greater authenticity to students'

Students persevere through multiple drafts to produce work they can be proud of, like this pollinator scientific drawing from Grade 2, Module 3.

work. For example, consider using your social studies time to reinforce your fifth-graders' literacy work on human rights by digging into a human rights crisis in your community. Allow students to see how what they study in school relates to (and can make a difference in) their own community.

How Will Content-Based Literacy Benefit My Students?

The design of our curriculum reflects compelling research showing that students learn best to become effective readers, writers, thinkers, and speakers when literacy instruction is content-based. Content-based literacy is an approach to helping students build literacy as they learn about the world.

Content knowledge and literacy skills are inextricably linked. The Common Core State Standards for ELA/literacy state: "Building knowledge systematically in English Language Arts is like giving children various pieces of a puzzle in each grade that, over time, will form one big picture. At a curricular or instructional level, texts—within and across grade levels—need to be selected around topics or themes that systematically develop the knowledge base of students" (National Governors Association Center for Best Practices & Council of Chief State School Officers, 2010, p. 33).

Research shows that the deeper the content knowledge a student has, the more she is able to understand what she reads, and the more she is able to speak and write clearly about that content. In fact, remarkably, research shows that she is even more able to successfully read about and understand *new* content. This proficiency and knowledge transfer to the next occasion for reading and learning, creating an upward surge that builds on itself and is both highly rewarding and motivating (Baldwin, Peleg-Bruckner, and McClintock (1985); Cervetti, Jaynes, and Heibert (2009); Kintsch and Hampton (2009); McNamara and O'Reilly (2009)).

Content-based literacy is similar to, yet distinct from, what many educators refer to as "reading to learn." The approaches are similar in that the goal is for students to learn about the world and build literacy skills; however, there are important differences. Reading to learn means that students first build strong literacy skills so that they can access texts, which allows them to build their knowledge of the world. By contrast, content-based literacy means students build their knowledge of the world by reading multiple texts on a topic—some with structured support and some independently—which allows them to read even more sophisticated texts and build more knowledge, which builds their literacy skills.

Turning on Students' Curiosity Motors

Content-based literacy is highly engaging for students and, often, inspiring for teachers. You are probably familiar with children, either in your classroom or your own family, who become "obsessed" with dinosaurs, trucks, horses, or princesses. Their interests push them into texts that may be much more complex than they would choose if their own curiosity weren't driving them like a motor. When students get into this zone, they can really dig in, even when the going gets tough. They read and read and can talk about their topics for hours.

Too often school isn't the place where these interests are nurtured. Texts are disconnected or treated shallowly, and topics may shift from week to week. In our curriculum, we walk students into the content with the intention of turning on those curiosity motors. We build curiosity through high-interest topics, texts, and collaborative tasks, and we find that once students are hooked, they engage much more deeply in both the content and the key literacy standards of reading, writing, speaking, and listening. For example, what follows is a sampling of some of the high-interest topics in the curriculum, which students are immersed in for eight to nine weeks:

» Toys and Play

» Birds

» Plants and Pollinators

» Adaptations and the Wide World of Frogs

» The American Revolution

» Stories of Human Rights

At the same time, students need skill-building to become fluent readers who can comprehend increasingly complex texts and communicate what they learn in writing. In the K–2 Reading Foundations Skills Block (Skills Block), students learn to crack the alphabetic code through a structured phonics program. This phonics work complements the strong focus on content-based literacy in the Module Lessons and K–2 Labs (Labs). The structured phonics program is not connected to the content-based modules, but neither is it "all work and no fun." We have built in "engagement texts" that will appeal to young children and motivate them to read harder and harder texts. In Grades 3–5, students build skills in the Additional Language and Literacy (ALL) Block. The ALL Block is connected to the content-based modules and provides additional practice with complex texts, writing, grammar, and vocabulary. (Each of these components of the curriculum will be explored in depth in Chapter 2.)

Our curriculum aims to prove that a *both/and* approach to content and skills is possible and preferable. Research and experience have shown us that students need both content *and* skills and, beyond that, both should be woven together in ways that turn on those curiosity motors that keep driving students forward. Students learn best when they are engaged, and it's hard to be engaged when learning skills in a vacuum. Building knowledge of the world is an important arrow in our quiver as we strive to accelerate literacy learning and excellence for all students.

How Do I Help Students Stay Active, Engaged, and Excited to Learn?

One of the fears for many teachers and parents in our test-centered educational world is that play and joy and creative pursuits in learning have been lost. In their place: tests, worksheets, and rows of disengaged students. These are well-founded fears and an unfortunate reality in far too many schools.

Our curriculum was designed with the needs of elementary learners in mind. We have balanced the need for students to be challenged academically and to advance on pace with grade-level peers with engaging instructional strategies and—yes—play, joy, and creative pursuits. Within the two or three hours per day of ELA instruction offered in our curriculum, your students will learn to read challenging texts and produce high-quality writing while at the same time building toys, dramatically re-enacting stories, collaborating with their classmates, and connecting their learning to issues of social justice and community need. Nearly every day, students will engage with protocols that allow them to work together, co-construct meaning, and take charge of their learning. We prioritize active learning, not passive listening.

We're committed to active, engaged, and purposeful learning at all grade levels, anchored by compelling, content-based modules. Our K–5 curriculum is divided into two grade bands to best meet the unique developmental and academic needs of students in Grades K–2 and 3–5, respectively. By the time students reach Grades 3–5, we build in more frequent opportunities for them to build independence and mastery, reflect on and take ownership of what and how they are learning, and connect their learning to real issues in the world related to social justice, human rights, and protecting the Earth.

We recognize that primary-age learners have a unique set of developmental needs, and we have designed the K–2 curriculum with those needs in mind. Our work in this area has been guided for many years by a document called "The Characteristics of Primary Learners." At EL Education, this document is the equivalent of your favorite book, dog-eared and softened by years of reading and rereading and sharing with friends. It's two pages of some of our best wisdom on what it takes to meet the needs of young children just starting out in school, and it has guided the design of all three components of our K–2 curriculum just as much as the new standards have.

Designing Curriculum with the Characteristics of Primary Learners in Mind

What follows are 11 key characteristics of primary learners—their ways of thinking and engaging with the world and their remarkable hunger for learning. Each of these characteristics is based on the writings of developmental psychologists and educators such as Lev Vygotsky, Maria Montessori, and Jean Piaget, as well as peer-reviewed research and the experience of primary educators in the EL Education network.

1. **Young children find security in rhythm, ritual, and repetition.** Primary students live in the present tense. They experience the flow of time in the rhythms of the day, the week, and the year. They do not relate to the abstract symbol of hands on a clock to know "when" they are. A feeling of order and independence is established in the consistent patterns of their schedule. Children love the predictability of repeating stories, songs, and activities. They delight in the rhymes, meters, and alliterations of language. They feel a sense of security and control as they live through the recurring rhythms of the school day, anticipate the special traditions of the week, and celebrate the annual festivals of the year.

2. **Young children learn through play.** Primary students are masters of play. One of the most important indicators of a species' intelligence is the behavior of its young—all intelligent animals play (Ackerman, 1999). Primary learners are at an age when learning capacity and brain development are at their peak, and nature has given them the drive to maximize that power with its best learning tool: play. It is no surprise that children prefer acting and interacting to listening passively. It's how they are designed. Play is the context within which primary students can develop vital skills that are harder to practice in more structured formats: complex decision-making, leadership, and executive functioning. It invites the "having of wonderful ideas." Play also builds the foundation for abstract representational thinking; a rag on a stick becomes a flag, just as a set of squiggles on a page stands for a word. Play encourages children to create and narrate their own worlds, grapple with the challenges most urgent to them, and gain experience negotiating alliances, roles, and strategies with their peers. Encouraging play in the classroom and strategically harnessing its power for specific learning purposes allows for authentic engagement and deep learning opportunities for our youngest students.

3. **Young children want to belong to a community that is safe, beautiful, and good.** Primary students seek to belong. More important than any curriculum or instruction is a

culture of love, warmth, and beauty. Children are keen observers of the environment and adult behavior. What they see when they walk into the classroom, how they are greeted by their teacher and classmates, and how they perceive social interactions all have a profound effect on their sense of belonging (Howard, 2006). A strong relationship with an adult in the classroom is especially critical for young students to feel safe. The teacher's love, care, and thoughtfulness are evident in the organization of the classroom, the display of beautiful student work, and the quality of the materials for expression, learning, and play. Classroom communities celebrating acts of kindness and respectfully resolving conflict reinforce a sense of justice and good will. Singing and dancing together create a language of unity that young children understand—a sense of safety in a community that is greater than any individual member. Feeling secure in a kind and beautiful classroom creates a strong inner foundation for the development of young children's academic and relational character.

4. **Young children explore the world with wonder.** Younger learners are always asking questions. They hunger to make discoveries, to find answers that will help them make meaning of the world around them. They ask questions not to annoy or interrupt, but to pursue their inherent drive to learn. Much like scientists, they develop hypotheses and test them, incorporating their findings and often retesting and modifying their theories over time—the foundations of logical reasoning. Children love to develop deep expertise, naming obscure dinosaurs, explaining the workings of a toy, or playing "teacher" with precision of gesture and speech. Guiding this relentless curiosity in the direction of students' academic growth without squelching it is a primary teacher's greatest challenge. By joining students in the inquiry process and creating rich opportunities for discovery, for building deep expertise, and for sharing that new knowledge, teachers are able to harness the "engine" of children's natural learning predispositions to power their success in the classroom.

5. **Young children "understand" the world first through their bodies.** Children are born to move. They explore the world with their bodies, particularly their senses, before they process it with their minds. They learn best when their bodies are fully engaged. Because of busy family schedules, limited access to the outdoors, and the allure of electronic devices, children need opportunities to develop their physical senses—the five we all know, plus others such as balance and proprioception (the sense of one's body in space). Occupational therapy researchers have documented the strong connections between sensory development and academic success (Flanagan, 2009). Cognitive skills and literacy are built on a foundation of sensory integration. Primary teachers find ways to develop the senses through playful movement and to link learning with physical activity. They invite children to explore complex concepts first through movement, then through feelings, and finally in thought.

6. **Young children seek independence and mastery.** Primary learners seek to assert power and gain control over their world (Erikson, 1959). They take great pride in accomplishing independent tasks: tying their shoes, building a tower, or caring for seedlings. Primary children look to adults to model the skills and attitude required to gain independence, imitating and practicing what they observe through pretend as well as "real" work. They long for challenging, meaningful, authentic work. When they find it, they engage with great perseverance, a sense of craftsmanship, and joyful purpose. They delight in sharing and celebrating their accomplishments with others, through speaking, writing/dictation, art, music, or drama. When teachers take children's work seriously and design environments and activities that promote autonomy and mastery, they allow their students to take ownership of their learning.

7. **Young children thrive in the natural world.** Children experience order, beauty, and diversity in the natural world. The outdoors beckons them with an endless variety of flowers, trees, and fascinating creatures—in the woods behind the school or in the cracks in the asphalt playground. Nature offers opportunities for the pre-literacy skills of close observation and detailed questioning. Students experience risk-taking adventure, from

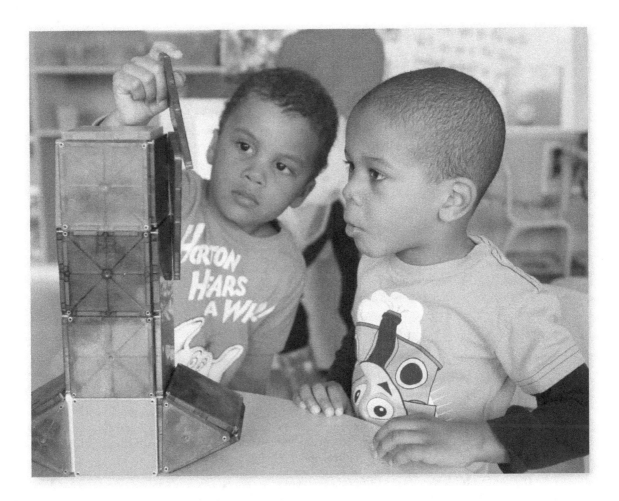

holding an earthworm to conquering a big hillside, and evaluate risk as they grapple with success and failure—can I climb that tree? Can I jump over that stump? Spending time in the outdoors creates a context for self-discovery. It fosters a sense of belonging to something greater than oneself and participation in the interdependent web of life. The natural world inspires reverence and wonder, an essential foundation for learning. Bringing nature indoors and children outdoors fills important developmental and human needs.

8. **Young children use stories to construct meaning.** In all cultures throughout history, humans have used stories to give meaning to events, to express their values, fears, and hopes. In the oral culture of young children, stories provide the cognitive structure to explore big ideas and express deep emotions. Telling their own stories helps children to organize and sequence information and communicate their thoughts and feelings, from the simple tale of what happened on the playground to the complex explanation of why it rains. Narrative development in the primary years is a strong predictor of success in reading and writing (Snow, Burns, and Griffin, 1998). Children develop moral imagination through the feelings generated by classic fairy tales and legends from around the world—a love for what is good and beautiful, empathy for the oppressed, loathing of the bully and the cheater. Children readily understand content when it is organized into story form. Primary students learn vocabulary and syntax through stories and create foundational schemas of organization, sequence, and causation. Their memory is stimulated by rhythm, rhyme, and repetition. Imagination is developed as children create vivid images of story settings and characters in their own minds. Story and metaphor clothe abstract concepts in developmentally appropriate "language," enabling students to explore big ideas and make meaning from experience.

9. **Young children seek patterns in the world around them.** Primary students search for patterns in everything they observe. Seeking order in their surroundings, they notice the angles in a brick walkway or the flowers that can be made from diamond-shaped play tiles. They sort and quantify and measure nearly everything around them—announcing the height of a block tower, separating the colors in a bag of M&Ms, comparing the size of their brownie to a sibling's, or counting the number of caterpillars fallen from the playground tree. Learning to communicate mathematical ideas visually and verbally is an inherently exciting challenge. Similarly, finding order in the structure of words and language delights young learners. They discover letters of their names in street signs, notice refrains in songs, and hear patterns of rhyme and alliteration in poetry and prose. Listening for and affirming pattern discoveries and helping students to name, create, and manipulate patterns is a key part of the work of the early primary teacher.

10. **Young children construct their identities and build cultural bridges.** Nearly all children travel between cultures when they travel from home to school. For some, the cultural differences are more dramatic than for others: different foods, different words, different unconscious patterns of body language, different fundamental values. Primary students are remarkably adept at learning the new culture of school but are also particularly vulnerable to unspoken negative messages about the values, language, and traditions of their home culture. At an age when identity as part of a family group and as a unique self are in transition, children need to see their home culture reflected positively in their school experience (Brooker and Woodhead, 2008). They also need affirmation of their developing gender identities (Park and Gauvaine, 2009), personal preferences, and unique strengths. Because children develop at different rates, skilled primary teachers find ways to affirm the abilities and preferences of each of their students, to celebrate diversity and encourage inclusion. Embracing the distinct cultural identities and individual differences of students creates a solid foundation on which students can build bridges between their school community and their cultural and individual selfhood.

11. **Young children express themselves in complex ways.** Primary students construct and express their understanding of the world around them in a variety of complex ways. They express their thoughts, emotions, questions, and needs through different modalities. A painting may describe a child's experience visiting a relative; stacked blocks may represent a hospital; sketches, scribbles, or wobbly letters may tell the story of sibling rivalry; and a song or dance may demonstrate a child's understanding of the seasons. Young children express their individuality and needs in the unconscious ways that they speak and move—in their posture, gesture, and tone of voice, in the way they walk or hold a pencil. By listening carefully to how children express themselves and encouraging them to represent their thinking in a variety of ways, we help them to build stronger foundations for literacy and mathematics and to deepen connections with one another and with the world.

These 11 unique characteristics have deep implications for primary teachers and certainly had a big influence on the design of all three components of our K–2 curriculum: Module Lessons, Labs, and the Skills Block. In some ways, the needs of primary students are no different from those of any age: the need to belong, to express themselves, and to engage in challenging, meaningful work. In others ways, our youngest students require an approach that emphasizes certain practices, adapts others in developmentally appropriate ways, or creates unique structures and tools to provide the foundation that will support cognitive and social flourishing as they mature. The caterpillar requires different nourishment than the butterfly. If we can harness primary students' natural strengths to develop their character, imagination, identity, and physical engagement, we are able to provide the optimal foundation for all students to become active contributors to building a better world and to succeed in school, college, career, and life.

Chapter 1B:
How Did Research Impact the Design of the Curriculum, and What Difference Will It Make to My Students?

Children enter kindergarten with varying levels of readiness for reading and writing, and those who start behind too often *stay* behind as they move through school. Our curriculum is driven by a simple mission: give *all* students access to a challenging, engaging, and empowering curriculum built on best practices in literacy instruction in order to accelerate their achievement.

The research on the literacy achievement gap is sobering. By the age of three, children from households in which the mother has less than a high school education have been exposed to 30 million fewer words than children from households in which the mother has a college education. This is known as the "30 million word gap" (Hart and Risley, 2003). More words, of course, mean more sentences; more sentences mean more questions; more questions mean more knowledge. Before entering school, learners from less affluent backgrounds suffer from a chain breaking at every link:

» They know fewer words.

» They have less knowledge.

» They hear and use less complex syntax.

» They are asked fewer questions (which means they are less used to making inferences).

These differences are exacerbated by what is known as the Matthew Effect (Stanovich, 1986, 1992; Stanovich and Cunningham, 1993): "The rich get richer; the poor get poorer." In school, this means that proficient readers start at a higher level than non-proficient readers and move faster each year relative to non-proficient readers. Given the reality of these deficits, research tells us that schools must stay laser-focused on certain elements of literacy instruction—vocabulary, knowledge-building, syntax, fluency, and decoding—to close the gap.

▶ How Will the Curriculum Help Me Accelerate Literacy Learning and Excellence for All of My Students?

Research has helped us learn a great deal about the problem of the literacy achievement gap. Thankfully, it also offers many strategies to attack the problem and find solutions. In Table 1.1, we look at the five elements of literacy instruction most critical for addressing the literacy achievement gap—vocabulary, knowledge-building, syntax, fluency, and decoding—and how our curriculum addresses each.

Table 1.1: Research and Strategies to Close the Literacy Achievement Gap[2]

Vocabulary
Students need to know a lot of words. In Grades K–2, they need to learn 1,000 to 2,000 words per year (Biemiller, 2010; Anderson and Nagy, 1992) to stay on track. They particularly need to learn academic vocabulary (or "Tier 2 words") (e.g., community, relate) that they'll encounter across contexts and content.

What We Know from the Research	How Our Curriculum Addresses It
Students don't know enough words: » Nearly a century of research shows that word knowledge is critical for reading comprehension (Whipple, 1925; National Center for Education Statistics, 2012). » When reading complex text, unfamiliar words are the feature with which students typically have the most difficulty (Nelson, Perfetti, Liben, and Liben, 2012). » Students' scores on first-grade vocabulary assessments predict 30 percent of Grade 11 comprehension (Cunningham and Stanovich, 1997). » Reading or listening to a series of texts on the same topic can yield as much as four times the vocabulary growth (Landauer and Dumais, 1997; Adams, 2009; Cervetti, 2015).	» Lessons at all grade levels feature a heavy focus on volume of reading and close reading of complex text (in Grades K–2 this is done primarily through teacher read-alouds and close read-alouds, which are equally critical for primary-age students' literacy development). » Students read multiple texts on a topic. At least half of the texts students read are related to the specific topic of study. » Students learn to analyze the morphology of words (i.e., roots, affixes, suffixes), which is taught explicitly in earlier modules and becomes a habit in later modules. This helps them learn word-learning strategies, rather than just learning specific words. » Explicit vocabulary instruction occurs in almost every K–5 lesson (e.g., unpacking academic vocabulary in a learning target, focusing on vocabulary words in text). » In addition to addressing specific standards related to vocabulary, we paid as much, if not more, attention to choosing rich texts and designing meaningful activities that build students' knowledge and academic vocabulary.

Cont.

---

[2] Based on a presentation by David Liben, Student Achievement Partners, July 2015; adapted with permission

Knowledge-Building
Students need not just "word" knowledge but also "world knowledge." They must develop knowledge about important topics in science, social studies, arts, and technology.

What We Know from the Research	How Our Curriculum Addresses It
» Reading or listening to a series of texts on the same topic can yield as much as four times the vocabulary growth (Landauer and Dumais, 1997; Adams, 2009; Cervetti, 2015). » Knowledge builds knowledge. The more one knows about a topic, the more one is able to read and understand about that topic (e.g., children who have been dinosaur fanatics from age two and who have read many increasingly complex texts on that topic over the years can read really sophisticated texts about dinosaurs by age six) (Adams, 2009). » In a research study, seventh- and eighth-grade students were asked to read a text about baseball. Students reading at "lower reading ability" (approximately third- to fourth-grade reading level) who had some knowledge about baseball did better than students with "high reading ability" but low knowledge about baseball (Recht and Leslie, 1988).	» The curriculum is based on topics (rather than "themes" or "skills"). Students read multiple texts on a topic. » Structures are built in for independent reading on the same topic. » Students study the same topic over many weeks in many ways (e.g., reading, writing, drawing, drama, investigations). » Students have many opportunities to talk about the topic.

Syntax
Syntax is the grammatical structure of a sentence. Research has shown that the ability to parse complex syntax is a critical skill for proficient readers to develop.

What We Know from the Research	How Our Curriculum Addresses It
» Hart and Risley's research (2003) showed that in addition to being spoken to with *more* words, students from high-income families were spoken to with *different types* of words, in particular more questions that invite students to think, talk, and make inferences. » Much research has shown that the ability to parse complex syntax is a critical skill for proficient readers to develop. For example, only students who obtained nearly perfect scores (35 out of 36) on the 2006 ACT tests did as well on complex text as they did on the less challenging text, indicating that a significant number of students who met the benchmark still scored relatively poorly on complex text (ACT, 2006).	» Students are exposed to complex sentence structures in written and spoken language. » Across Grades K–5, the amount of time students work with complex text increases. In Grades K–2, this happens primarily through read-alouds; by the second half of second grade, students are reading complex text increasingly independently, including scaffolded partner reading. » Students do close, careful reading of complex text; they don't just read it once. Students work not only with the text's meaning (basic comprehension), but also its vocabulary, syntax, and author's craft.

Cont.

What we know from the research	How our curriculum addresses it
» Text that students read in school has become less complex. Between 1963–1991, the average length of sentences in K–8 reading textbooks (basals) was shorter than in books published between 1946–62 (Hayes, Wolfer, and Wolfer, 1996); in seventh- and eighth-grade "readers" (usually anthologies, which are widely used), the mean length of sentences decreased from 20 to 14 words. Vocabulary also declined. The vocabulary level of eighth-grade basal readers after 1963 was equivalent to fifth-grade readers before 1963; 12th-grade literary anthologies after 1963 were equivalent to seventh-grade readers before 1963.	» Students engage in frequent Language Dives: 10- to 20-minute conversations between teacher and students about the meaning and purpose of a compelling sentence from a complex text, followed by frequent practice using the language structures from the sentence. (See Chapter 2C for more on Language Dives).

Fluency

Fluency is defined as reading grade-level, complex text accurately, at a rate appropriate to the text, and with proper expression (Rasinski, 2004). Over 100 studies have connected fluency to comprehension at all grades (see achievethecore.org).

What We Know from the Research	How Our Curriculum Addresses It
» Fluency does not guarantee comprehension, but lack of fluency guarantees lack of comprehension, especially with complex text. » Average scores of students not fluent were "below basic" on the Grade 4 National Assessment of Educational Progress (NAEP) (Chall, 2005). » 61 percent of urban ninth-graders are unable to read eighth-grade text fluently (Rasinski et al., 2005). » Fluency problems compound vocabulary and knowledge gaps. » Most vocabulary is learned by reading after second grade and especially after fifth grade (Nagy and Anderson, 1984; Nagy, Anderson, and Herman, 1987). » Reading is the most efficient way to grow knowledge. » If you comprehend less of what you read, you will gain less knowledge and will learn fewer new words. » Disfluent readers are less motivated to read.	» Students are supported in decoding with automaticity, since this is the greatest cause of disfluency. They learn to decode increasingly complex texts (e.g., reading the same text multiple times and reading decodable texts). » Students follow along in the text while a fluent reader reads aloud. » Students read the same text multiple times until they can read it fluently and with expression. » Students learn specific criteria for fluent reading. » Students practice reading a text fluently, receive peer or teacher critique, and then perform or record that text for a broader audience. » K–2 students hear the same complex text read aloud multiple times. In Accountable Independent Reading they may explore that text on their own and be able to "read" more of it, since they in effect have it memorized. » K–2 students recite poems and songs across multiple lessons. Repeated reading has been shown to dramatically improve students' fluency and confidence. » The K–2 Reading Foundations Skills Block (Skills Block) teaches and assesses the behaviors of a fluent reader: reading smoothly, with expression and meaning, and at just the right speed.

Cont.

What we know from the research	How our curriculum addresses it
	» The Skills Block builds students' automaticity with decoding words, leading to fluent reading of connected text.

Decoding
Decoding is the ability to recognize words automatically without effort. Failure to decode automatically hinders comprehension.

What We Know from the Research	How Our Curriculum Addresses It
» Students who come from language-rich homes, where they are frequently asked questions or encouraged to look for patterns in language and elsewhere, are more likely to make inferences about spelling-sound patterns in the early grades (Liben, personal communication, July, 2015). » Decoding skills help proficient readers retain words in memory and support the development of automatic word reading skills (Adams, 1990). » Hundreds of studies have shown the benefit of structured phonics programs. The report of the National Reading Panel reviewed the best of these studies. The research is so strong and so consistent that the IES (Institute for Educational Science, the research wing of the Education Department) has decided that there is no further need to review what the evidence shows about the effectiveness of structured phonics programs. They are convinced.	» In the Skills Block teachers directly teach letter recognition, phonological awareness, and a sequence of grapheme/phoneme patterns in and out of context, using phonetically controlled readers. » Decodable readers are paired with engagement texts (both/and) in the Skills Block. » In K–2 Module Lessons, students regularly apply the letter-sound patterns they have learned in the Skills Block as they work to read and comprehend grade-level text (e.g., "We learned the sound an 's' makes last week; do you see an 's' in this page we are reading about toys?") » Because phonics and fluency are necessary, but not sufficient, students also build knowledge, vocabulary, and syntax through complex texts, read-alouds, investigations, and play. » The 3–5 curriculum does not include explicit instruction on decoding. For struggling readers in this grade band, teachers may want to consider using aspects of the Skills Block as an intervention.

Addressing Decoding and Fluency with Structured Phonics

The research in Table 1.1 highlights the need for a "both/and" approach to literacy instruction: Students need *both* content-based literacy *and* explicit skills-based instruction on decoding and fluency. Curricula that provide both build students' ability to comprehend text and build knowledge of the world.

A compelling body of evidence indicates that a structured phonics approach is the most effective way to help students crack the alphabetic code. Simply defined, structured phonics directly teaches the spelling-sound patterns of English in a clear sequence. Not all students need a structured phonics approach, but many do, particularly those who enter school farthest behind. Our K–2 curriculum includes one hour per day—the Reading Foundations Skills Block (Skills Block)—when students learn to crack the alphabetic code. They read "decodable texts" that are controlled for taught spelling patterns and high-frequency words and engage in Accountable Independent Reading (during differentiated small group time) so that teachers can confer with them and track their progress.

Many educators, particularly veterans trained in guided reading, often ask us, "Where is guided reading in your program?" Our curriculum does not include designated time for a typical guided reading program, but it does address the *goals* of guided reading:

» Help students crack the alphabetic code

» Ensure that students have differentiated practice and support (with decoding, fluency, and comprehension)

» Track students' progress

» Accelerate students' skills

» Build comprehension (addressed partly in the Skills Block and partly in Module Lessons)

To learn much more about structured phonics and the Skills Block, as well as the similarities and differences between this approach and guided reading, see Chapter 4, which is devoted to these topics.

▶ How Will the Curriculum Help Me Address New College- and Career-Ready Standards?

Much of the research base on the critical areas of need explored in Table 1.1 informed the creation of new college- and career-ready standards and the identification of three big instructional shifts that focus teachers on addressing these needs, particularly for those students who have had fewer opportunities and therefore start school with deficits. The instructional shifts attempt to bring into balance a prevalent disconnect between the research on best practice and *common* practice in literacy instruction in the United States. In common practice, the majority of reading instruction involves fictional text; the majority of writing centers on personal narratives and personal opinions; and, in all subjects in school, too many students are not challenged to read complex text. Therefore, the three main shifts in English language arts (ELA)/literacy instruction focus on:

» Building knowledge through content-rich nonfiction

» Reading, writing, and speaking grounded in evidence from literary and informational text

» Regular practice with complex text and its academic language

Shift 1: Building Knowledge through Content-Rich Nonfiction

Common practice: The majority of reading instruction in elementary schools involves literary texts.

Instructional shift: Content-rich nonfiction (informational text) must be balanced with literary texts in Grades K–5. As students move through the grades, they should read a greater proportion of informational texts so that they are well-prepared for the kinds of reading that will be required of them in college, careers, and life. The content-based literacy components of our curriculum feature a mix of high-quality texts—both literary and informational—that deepens students' understanding of the content. Informational texts give students an opportunity to build world knowledge (e.g., about animal adaptations or human rights). And related literary texts—with engaging stories and characters—help them connect with the content more deeply.

Shift 2: Reading, Writing, and Speaking Grounded in Evidence from Literary and Informational Text

Common practice: The majority of writing in school centers on personal narratives and personal opinions.

Instructional shift: Reading standards require that students read for and write with evidence. Students must read texts with care so that they can understand a topic deeply and then present clear analyses, well-defended claims, and clear information based on evidence in the text. Rather than asking questions that students can answer from prior knowledge or experience, teachers should ask text-dependent questions that point students back to the text for evidence to support their opinions and claims. The questions should require not only literal comprehension, but also inferences based on careful attention to the text. Narrative writing is still called for by the standards, and students still write stories and poetry. But there is a greater focus on the sequence and detail that are so important in argument and informational writing. Our curriculum features frequent opportunities for students to gather and talk about evidence so that they can use it skillfully in all kinds of writing. We use the Writing for Understanding framework developed by the Vermont Writing Collaborative to ensure that students have plenty of opportunities to learn about a topic and strong scaffolding to communicate their learning, usually through writing.

Shift 3: Regular practice with complex text and its academic language

Common practice: In all subjects in school, too many students are not challenged to read complex text (or hear it read aloud in Grades K–2).

Instructional shift: The standards call for students to read texts of increasing complexity as they move through their K–12 schooling so that they are ready for college- and career-ready reading by the time they graduate. Our K–5 curriculum prioritizes high-quality, complex texts related to compelling content that students are eager to dig into. Close reading helps them unpeel the layers of text so that they can comprehend it deeply. In Grades K–2, most of students' work with complex text occurs through read-alouds (less so by the end of Grade 2). Also key to this shift is a greater focus on academic, or Tier 2, vocabulary: words that appear in a variety of content areas (e.g., ignite, commit). In our curriculum, students grow their vocabularies through a mix of structures and strategies that involve reading complex texts, engaging in academic conversation and discourse, and direct instruction. In addition to building students' knowledge and vocabulary, complex texts help students become more facile with syntax (the arrangement of words and phrases).

Addressing Specific Aspects of the Standards

The new college- and career-ready standards themselves, based in research on best practices in literacy, were a strong and steady guide when designing this curriculum. This was layered on top of our commitment to providing students with worthy challenges, elevating achievement beyond test scores, content-based literacy, and student engagement. Our focus on play, joy, and engagement is always in service of meeting standards and helping students be better readers, writers, and communicators. For every instance when we ask students to build a toy or observe a tree, we are clear about what standards they are working toward and how these experiences, combined with reading worthy texts, help students build their knowledge of the world. Table 1.2 describes how the curriculum addresses specific aspects of the new standards.

Table 1.2: Addressing College- and Career-Ready Standards

Reading	
Aspect of Reading	**How Our Curriculum Addresses It**
Text complexity	Frequent use of grade-appropriate complex text at all grade levels for all students; in Grades K–2, many close read-alouds are conducted with texts two to three grade levels above what students can read on their own to encourage high-level thinking and discourse; scaffolds so that all students are successful; Language Dives[3] for all students (more frequent for English language learners); Storytime to launch every K–2 Lab session

Cont.

---

[3] Language Dives are critical high-leverage supports in place for English language learners. More information about this practice can be found in Chapter 2C.

Vocabulary	Intentional vocabulary-building from content-based text; attention to figuring out words from context; decoding; emphasis on academic (Tier 2) vocabulary
Close reading	Teacher-led close reading or close read-alouds of content-based texts; carefully developed text-dependent questions; multiple reads for deepening comprehension; focus question that drives a series of sessions on a single text
Volume of reading	Daily Accountable Independent Reading at each individual student's level (or rereading complex text previously read with teacher support); reading to deepen and expand content knowledge and vocabulary; Storytime to launch every Lab session
Research	Gathering evidence for knowledge building before writing; Accountable Independent Reading; K–2 Research Lab
Fluency	Multiple reads of complex text; research reading; volume of reading; reading decodable texts (in the Skills Block)
Foundational skills (Grades K–2)	A dedicated hour per day to explicitly teach the letter-sound patterns of the English language (in the Skills Block)

Writing	
Aspect of Writing	**How Our Curriculum Addresses It**
Writing reflects content under-standing	All writing supports content knowledge: Students write both as they are learning content knowledge (e.g., note-taking) and as they synthesize that knowledge (e.g., in their formal writing); note-taking in the K–2 Research Lab.
Specific instruc-tion in aspects of writing	Writing skills (e.g., use of introductions, transitions) and approaches (e.g., gathering evidence to support a statement, as well as concepts of craft) are scaffolded specifically for particular writing in each module.
Writing fluency; ease with writing	Frequent "short writes" as well as more developed pieces; Grades K–2, almost daily writing in Module Lessons; goal-setting and reflection in Labs; handwriting and letter formation in Skills Block; writing practice as one specific component of the 3–5 Additional Language and Literacy (ALL) Block
Oral processing of ideas before writing	Frequent opportunities for students to "orally rehearse" ideas and thinking before writing, including structured conversations and Language Dives
Writing process (i.e., plan, draft, confer, revise, edit)	Instruction and scaffolding in each aspect of the writing process; emphasis on use of models, critique (kind, specific, and helpful), feedback, editing, and revision

Cont.

Language	
Aspect of Language	**How Our Curriculum Addresses It**
Standard grammar and usage	Short and fully developed writing (including emphasis on revising and editing skills); explicit instruction on specific language standards in K–2 Module Lessons (often involving analyzing or punctuating songs and poems) and in the ALL Block; Language Dives; embedded grammar and usage instruction (within performance task and often within other writing assignments)
Standard writing conventions, including spelling	Short and fully developed writing (including emphasis on revising and editing skills); focus on letter formation and spelling patterns in Skills Block; explicit instruction on conventions in K–5 Module Lessons and the ALL Block (grammar, usage, and mechanics component); Language Dives
Academic and domain-specific vocabulary	Multiple reads of complex text; short and fully developed writing; Language Dives; unpacking learning targets; explicit teaching of the language of habits of character (e.g., collaboration, perseverance)

Speaking and Listening	
Aspect of Speaking and Listening	**How Our Curriculum Addresses It**
Building knowledge through oral processing	Conversation to process reading and prepare for writing (i.e., the read-think-talk-write cycle)
Participation in discussion, building on others' ideas	Collaborative protocols; small group discussion; discussion norms; Conversation Cues[4]; sentence frames to scaffold productive discussion
Presentation of ideas in a style appropriate to audience	Presentation of students' work, both formally and informally, to an audience of their peers, families, or invited guests

▶ How Can Understanding the Backward Design of the Curriculum Help Me Teach It More Effectively or Adapt It If Necessary?

We designed this curriculum using the guiding principles of backward design, which require curriculum designers to consider three questions:

1. At the end of a sequence of instruction, what will students know and be able to do?

2. What will proficiency look and sound like?

3. How will we know when students are proficient?

We considered these three questions when we designed all of the components of the K–5 curriculum, though our approach varied depending on the component. Here we focus on our approach to backward design in the content-based literacy components of the curriculum, in particular the Module Lessons.

---

[4] Conversation Cues are critical high-leverage supports in place for English language learners. More information about this practice can be found in Chapter 2C.

Designing Curriculum with the Four T's: Topic, Task, Targets, and Text

When designing the K-5 Module Lessons, we employed the principles of backward design using a framework we call the Four T's. We started the process of designing every module asking ourselves the question: How can we best combine **topics**, **tasks**, **targets**, and **texts** to engage students with worthy content in a way that compels them to meet the standards? The Four T's interact dynamically at every level of a module—for the module as a whole, for each unit, and even for discrete lessons—to support students to learn about the world, master standards, become proficient and confident readers and writers, and produce work that matters. Table 1.3 describes each of the Four T's. Following the table, we describe in greater detail the decisions that went into each T when designing the Module Lessons.

Table 1.3: The Four T's: Topic, Task, Targets, Text

Topic:	Task:
The compelling topic that brings the content to life; almost always based on priority content standards that students are expected to meet	*The culminating task—a scaffolded product or performance task—and the on-demand assessments to gauge students' independent mastery of content and literacy*
The topic gives cohesiveness to the unit of study. It is the "what" students are learning about, often connected to specific content knowledge. Although students may be able to meet standards without an engaging topic, a compelling, relevant topic helps them develop their reading and writing skills more deeply as they engage with increasingly complex text. The best topics teach standards through real-world issues, original research, primary source documents, and the opportunity to engage with the community, and they lend themselves to the creation of authentic tasks/products.	The culminating task gives students the opportunity to read for and write with specific textual evidence and to meaningfully apply standards (targets). This is different from just writing "about" what one has read. The best tasks give students the opportunity to address authentic need and an authentic audience related to the topic. This task is always scaffolded and leads to high-quality work.

Also essential are on-demand tasks (assessments) so that students can demonstrate independent mastery of content and ELA/literacy standards. |
Targets:	**Text:**
The learning targets derived from the specific language and rigor of grade-level ELA/literacy standards that students are expected to meet; contextualized based on the topic	*The complex texts (e.g., books/articles) that students will read closely and additional texts to ensure students read a "volume of reading" on the topic at their independent reading level*
In the context of the Four T's framework, "targets" refers to the ELA standards. Attention to the specific language of the grade-level demands of the standards is paramount, as is an analysis of how a given standard is typically assessed. (Some say, "The standard is not the standard; the assessment of the standard is the standard.") The standards are then turned into long-term targets, contextualized to the topic, which prepare students for and guide the task and ensure proper, deep analysis of the text. The types of texts students would need to read to master specific standards is a highly interrelated consideration.	The text is the main vehicle through which the topic is taught. Carefully selected texts within the text complexity band for a given grade level give students access to the topic/content standards through close and careful reading. Attention to text selection ensures that students can practice specific ELA standards *and* learn content deeply. Text must be chosen judiciously to ensure that it is "worthy" in terms of the world knowledge it will help students build and the opportunities it presents for students to master specific standards (based on the text's content, language, or structure). Less is more.

How Will the Four T's Impact My Experience Teaching the Curriculum?

The Four T's is the framework that drove the design of the Module Lessons. This framework has a certain elegance in its simplicity. Considering each T elicits important questions for anyone designing curriculum, whether for a weeks-long module or a daily lesson. What compelling **topic** will students learn about? What standards (**targets**) will students work toward through their study of that topic? What worthy **texts** on the topic will students read to build knowledge and practice applying specific reading standard(s)? And what **tasks** will allow them to demonstrate mastery and deepen their knowledge and understanding of the topic?

Teachers working with the Four T's for the first time quickly realize that if you pull the thread of one T, it impacts the others. You can choose any old text through which students will learn about frogs, for example, but if you're working toward Grade 3 Common Core State Standard (CCSS) RI.9: *Compare and contrast the most important points and key details presented in two texts on the same topic,* the choice of text must be much more intentional. In this case, you'd better have at least two texts that will allow students to compare and contrast the information.

One of the reasons we want to give you a look "under the hood" of our design process is so that you understand the complexity of the process and appreciate the need to be thoughtful and careful if you wish to make any changes to the curriculum. The Four T's are highly interrelated and, when purposefully packaged together, create powerful learning experiences for students. Therefore, any changes you are considering in one T should be tested against the others. We also hope that this window into our design process will support those of you who are already designing curriculum or are ready to engage in that work.

▶▶ Video Spotlight

The accompanying video offers a window into the process that our curriculum design team used to build this curriculum. You'll also see how the Four T's allows a group of teachers in Rochester, New York, to break down the complicated work of their own curriculum design by focusing them on topics, tasks, targets, and texts.

https://vimeo.com/116564458

What follows is the process we took when designing our modules with the Four T's as a framework for backward design.

Topic

CONTENT STANDARDS

We began with content standards:

» We identified the compelling content that students will learn about (aligned to priority science or social studies standards). Is this topic central, enduring, and relevant?

» We unpacked the relevant content standards, focusing on big ideas. What do students need to understand?

» We built our own content knowledge, reading widely about the topic in order to identify the big ideas we needed to help students understand.

» We consulted with content experts to ensure that our understanding was accurate and to flag any potential student (or teacher) misconceptions with this content.

GUIDING QUESTIONS

We drafted guiding questions that drive the "So what?"/"Who cares?" for students:

» We structured time for students to return to guiding questions throughout a module/unit.

» Typically we crafted both a "content" guiding question and a "literacy" guiding question (e.g., Grade 2, Module 3: "How do pollinators help plants grow and survive?"; "How do we build our research skills and share our learning?").

KNOWLEDGE-BUILDING

We prioritized students building knowledge through a *volume of reading* (see the Text section):

» We moved students through multiple texts on the same topic, up the staircase of complexity.

» We were guided by the principles of content-based literacy (see Chapter 1A): Students build their knowledge of the world by reading multiple texts on a topic, some with structured support and some independently.

Task

THE PERFORMANCE TASK

We planned backward from a literacy-rich performance task (typically a writing task; sometimes a speaking and listening task):

» Across the year, we strove for a balance of performance tasks among the three types of writing: opinion/argument (CCSS W.1), informative/explanatory (CCSS W.2), and narrative (CCSS W.3). (See the Targets section.)

» We unpacked the relevant writing standard, considering what mastery would look and sound like, what thinking the standard requires, and what scaffolding would be necessary for students to be successful.

» We made sure that every performance task is based on the knowledge students build as readers and that almost every performance task requires and supports students to cite textual evidence (there are some exceptions for narrative writing).

» We focused on designing performance tasks for a clear purpose and authentic audience, integrating technology and real-world formats whenever possible.

» We drafted the focus question and then "test-drove" all tasks, trying to write it as if we were a student, thinking about implications for instruction.

» We built in time for students to unpack the academic language of the rubric and/or co-construct a list of criteria with teachers.

» We kept in mind that the performance task is not a formal "assessment" (since it is always scaffolded and often collaborative). The performance task drives the backward design, but it is not the only "task"—also critical are the assessments.

ASSESSMENTS

We designed standards-aligned assessments (other "tasks") as a structure or "through-line" of each module/unit (one assessment per unit in Grades K–2 and two per unit in Grades 3–5):

» We ensured that assessments require students to work with text-based evidence.

» For each assessment, we identified a strategic "bundle" of standards to address (e.g., standards regarding citing evidence, identifying main idea, or analysis of structure could all be assessed with a single text).

» For the three types of writing (see the Task section), we designed writing rubrics (based on our own expertise and strong models of high-stakes assessments).

» We used question formats that mirror typical high-stakes tests (e.g., on reading assessments, we included multiple choice, two-part evidence-based selected response, short constructed response, and open response).

» We created checklists for Speaking and Listening standards and Language standards that can be used during both formal and ongoing assessment.

» We built in opportunities for students to learn, practice, and get feedback on a standard before being assessed.

» Specifically for Grades K–2, we carefully considered how to assess standards for which students are expected to work "with support."

WRITING FOR UNDERSTANDING

We considered the interplay of writing opportunities, instruction, and assessment, remembering that "writing is not a subject—it's a way to build and show understanding about subjects." (Hawkins, personal communication, March, 2017):

» We adhered to the principles of "Writing for Understanding": On the lesson level, we used the read-think-talk-write cycle, which allows students to test out their understanding and organize their thoughts before writing. Before they can use writing structures and tools effectively, they must deeply understand what they are writing about.

» We ensured that students read enough, and carefully enough, to build real knowledge to use in their writing.

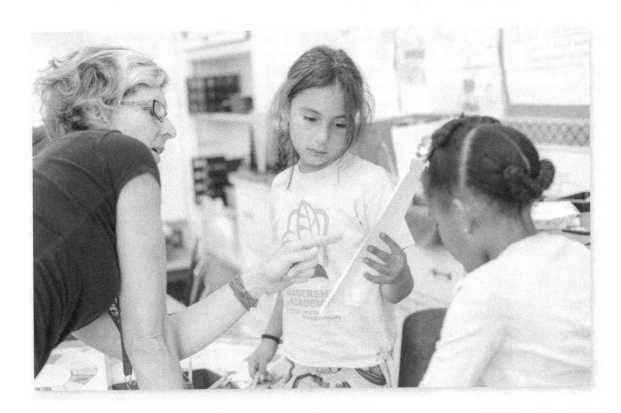

» We included frequent academic writing (e.g., short constructed responses, paragraphs, extended responses).

» We balanced scaffolded writing with "on-demand" writing assessments.

» We provided explicit writing instruction and scaffolding (e.g., graphic organizers).

» We included supports for students to effectively use working knowledge, revisit texts/notes, and integrate vocabulary.

» We built in time for students to read "like readers" (re: content) before reading "like writers" (re: craft).

ROUTINES

We built in established routines:

» We ensured that lessons integrate reading and writing (plus thinking and talking).

» We developed "types" or "patterns" of lessons that can be repeated (for efficiencies).

» We backward-planned and "test-drove" the scaffolding (e.g., anchor charts and graphic organizers aligned to a standard or bundle of standards; modeling).

» We included "writing to learn" and note-taking routines, including class notes for Grades K–2.

Targets

Note: In terms of the Four T's, the word "Targets" refers to the actual ELA standards (content standards are addressed in "Topic").

BUNDLED STANDARDS

With the topic and content standards already in mind, we strategically bundled them with ELA standards and mapped them out across the year:

» We unpacked all standards for a given module to identify what mastery would look and sound like.

» We were mindful of the broad instructional "shifts," not just individual standards.

STANDARDS-ALIGNED ASSESSMENTS

We then designed standards-aligned assessments. (Note: Assessments are structural walls or "through-lines" of modules and units. See the Tasks section.):

» We bundled both content and ELA standards strategically, grouping complementary standards together to create efficiencies.

» We aligned supporting materials to specific standards (e.g., this graphic organizer aligns with CCSS RI.4.2).

LANGUAGE STANDARDS

For Language standards specifically:

» We considered where/how a specific Language sub-standard would authentically fit with the reading, writing, or speaking students are doing (e.g., in first grade, teach CCSS L.1.1e: *Use verbs to convey a sense of past, present, and future* and CCSS L.1.1f: *Use frequently occurring adjectives* in the context of a module with a narrative writing performance task).

Text

ANCHOR/CENTRAL TEXTS

We carefully selected anchor/central texts:

» We addressed the instructional shifts of the new standards: building knowledge through content-rich informational texts; reading for and writing with evidence; regular practice with complex text and its academic vocabulary.

» We ensured that texts are "worthy"—they teach important information and build students' understanding.

» We ensured that texts are sufficiently complex (in both quantitative and qualitative measures) for the grade level/grade band.

» We paired informational and literary texts and toggled between them to build knowledge and engagement.

» We identified informational texts to serve as the conceptual framework for a module/unit.

» We attended to diversity and inclusion.

» We chose the appropriate type of text needed to address specific standards or "bundles" of ELA standards.

» We sought out provocative texts that offer multiple perspectives but stayed away from partisan politics.

» In rare cases, we wrote or modified texts, being careful not to simplify syntax or academic vocabulary.

SCAFFOLDS

We differentiated to meet students' needs through scaffolding so that all students have access to the same rich, grade-level complex texts:

» When designing lessons, we applied the Universal Design for Learning framework to consider multiple ways for students to engage with text and represent their understanding of text.

» We designed Language Dives to help students pay close attention to particularly rich sentences with compelling content and/or complex language structures.

» For English language learners, we sometimes prioritized excerpts of longer texts to focus on.

A VOLUME OF READING

We built in structures to ensure that students experience a volume of reading (see the Topic section):

» We built the K–5 Recommended Texts and Other Resources lists on the module topic (particularly focused on "research reading").

» We provided a range of texts at different levels of complexity, yet ensured that all students have access to complex text.

» We attended to standards specific to the integration of knowledge and ideas.

» We built in structures that foster research through expert groups (see the Topic section).

» We set up a yearlong structure to promote Accountable Independent Reading (within the Skills Block and in Grades 3–5 as a homework structure and within the Additional Language and Literacy (ALL) Block).

» In K–2 Labs, (Labs) we designated one Lab specifically for research (using text and images).

CLOSE READING/READ-ALOUDS

We built structures for the close, careful reading of complex texts (see the Tasks section):

» We kept in mind that designing close reading lessons requires skill with analyzing texts.

» We provided teacher support to help students deeply understand complex texts (e.g., through close reading/close read-aloud guides).

» We made time to go slow: time for less reading, deeper reading, and more analytical reading. In Grades K–2, close read-alouds stretch across as many as five lessons; in Grades 3–5, often two or three lessons.

» We built routines such as: reading first for the gist of the text (what it is mostly about); multiple reads; and a focus on academic vocabulary.

» We incorporated close reading/close read-alouds into almost every unit, typically at least every two weeks.

» We built in structures to help students be metacognitive (e.g., Close Readers Do These Things anchor chart).

» We incorporated Language Dives in every unit for all students and almost daily optional Language Dives for ELLs.

» In the ALL Block, we designated one component specifically for additional work with complex text.

» We kept in mind when NOT to go slow, keeping close reading in balance with building background knowledge, and volume of reading.

VOCABULARY ROUTINES

We established vocabulary routines (see the Targets section), which are critical for helping students transfer word-learning strategies across content and context:

» We built in Interactive Word Walls and vocabulary notebooks/personal dictionaries.

» We focused on word-learning strategies (CCSS L.4) such as defining based on context and using word roots.

» We made sure that writing and speaking and listening tasks require and support students to use the vocabulary they are learning.

» We incorporated unpacking learning targets into most lessons (focusing on academic vocabulary, which tends to be words from the standards, such as "determine" the main idea or "building on" each other's ideas).

» We seized opportunities in the flow of instruction to call students' attention to vocabulary.

» We included encouragement for teachers to help ELLs connect new words they are learning to words in their home language (e.g., "How would you say that in your home language?")

» In the ALL Block, we designated one component specifically for word study/vocabulary.

» In Grades K–2, we regularly incorporated movement when teaching vocabulary (e.g., "show me the word *slither* with your bodies.")

Note: Since the Labs and ALL Block are the second hour of content-based literacy (complementary to the Module Lessons), they necessarily reinforce and echo the Four T's of a given module. In the Labs, this looks mostly like students spending more time exploring the topic while building their oral language skills (and thus practicing Speaking and Listening standards). In the ALL Block, this looks like students rereading complex texts from the module, reading new texts on the module topic, and getting more practice and support meeting particular targets (standards).

The "Fifth T": Time

The truth about this curriculum, and any curriculum, is that no matter how good it is, its success relies heavily on the Fifth T: **time**. Without *your* time spent learning deeply about the purpose of the curriculum as a whole and the practices embedded within it, the potential of the curriculum to accelerate literacy learning and equity for all students may not be fully realized. We focus on time a lot in Chapter 3A. There we'll give you some tools and techniques for unpacking and analyzing each part of the curriculum to help you feel ready to teach it.

Chapter 1C:
What Will It Take to Lead Schoolwide Change?

Whether you are a district leader, principal, instructional coach, or teacher who is leading the charge with this curriculum in your school, you know that change of this nature is not easy. You may find yourself supporting new teachers who are already feeling overwhelmed by learning how to manage a classroom alongside veteran teachers who may feel that what they are already doing is working just fine.

In almost every school, there will be some who are eager to get started with new curriculum and some who are reluctant. This is a common dynamic in schools and districts; usually everyone can agree that they want students to succeed, but not everyone can agree on how to get there. This reality is actually quite healthy—neither teachers nor students are automatons, and our curriculum, like any curriculum, will root itself in the real conditions of your school and the people who interact with it. Helping everyone in your school community, including families, understand how the curriculum will accelerate literacy learning and excellence for all students is key to its success. For all of these reasons, strong and focused leadership is critical to the success of this work.

▶ As a School Leader, How Can I Maximize the Potential of the Curriculum to Help Students and Teachers Succeed?

No curriculum, no matter how comprehensive, is a panacea. Like a lot of things, you'll get out of it what you put into it. We feel confident that ours is a great curriculum; otherwise we wouldn't have published it. The principles it is built on and its focus on accelerating literacy learning and excellence for all will give students a strong foundation for success as readers, writers, and thinkers. It has been highly rated by independent reviewers and, anecdotally, we hear frequently from teachers that it is making a difference for their students.

That said, it doesn't really matter how we feel about it or what others say about it! What matters is how it takes root in your school. Your efforts to create the conditions for success can make the difference between the curriculum living up to all that it *can* be and the potential for it to be just one more change for teachers to adjust to. You have a pulse on the needs of your teachers and students and deep knowledge of both strengths and areas of needed growth among your staff. Experience tells us that at the heart of the work we do is a need to tend to the people who are most deeply impacted by the changes that are on the horizon:

» How will you support them and set them up for success?

» How will you make space for risk-taking?

» How will you ensure that teachers have time to talk and plan together to make sense of all that they are learning?

» How will you articulate your encouragement of them and assure them that they are on the right path?

At its best, this curriculum is about reimagining what learning can look like for students. You may find that you and your staff will need to examine your current thinking about long-held instructional practices or your approach to student engagement. At the same time, you will likely see how the deep study of compelling, relevant topics will start to transform your students. As teachers begin to examine their practice and take risks, you will see them grow and transform as well. But, like a lot of journeys, it won't necessarily be a linear process for everyone, and it will take time. In the pages that follow, we offer suggestions, specifically for those in leadership roles, for where to start, how to dig deep, and how to find additional resources from EL Education.

> *"As the instructional coach at my school, I made it my job to read the lessons each grade level was teaching in the upcoming week. This was a big commitment, but by doing this work up front, I was prepared to support the teachers at weekly team meetings, as well as familiarize myself with the curriculum across all grade levels. This allowed me to see how everything connected and built from grade to grade."*

Elizabeth Freitag

Instructional Coach and Testing Coordinator, Valdosta, Georgia

Managing Complex Change

There's no one right way to do things, because every school is different. The important thing is to find entry points that will be effective within the culture of your school.

Lay the Groundwork

» Be the lead learner. Though you may believe in the need for this change, it will be hard for you to help teachers navigate the implementation of the curriculum if you do not understand it well. We encourage leaders to lean in to the change as much as possible. Consider adopting a classroom or two as case study classrooms that you can visit often, or consider doing some teaching yourself so that you better understand the instructional practices in the curriculum.

» Form a team to help you lead this change and to maximize the support you are able to offer teachers.

» Build shared commitment to the need for change. In some schools, an examination of achievement data, combined with the research on the literacy achievement gap explored in Table 1.1, is a helpful place to start. In other schools, teachers may feel drawn to the compelling topics and active pedagogy in the curriculum. It's important that teachers see the curriculum as a solution to a problem they are having and not a top-down mandate. (See box for a few change management models we recommend.)

🔦 Tools for Managing Complex Change

Adopting our curriculum may mean a big change for your school. Consider using an existing model for managing complex change to guide you and your staff through this work. Here are a few that we recommend:

» The Beckhard and Harris Change Equation (Dissatisfaction x Desirability x Practicality > Resistance to change) may be a useful place for you to start to assess your school's readiness for change of this nature.

» The Knoster Model can help you assess the conditions and climate at your school against the five elements required for effective change: vision + skills + incentives + resources + a plan = sustainable change.

» The Concerns-Based Adoption Model (CBAM) can help you and your staff identify concerns as you progress through the stages of implementing something new. The seven stages of concern include awareness, informational, personal, management, consequence, collaboration, and refocusing.

» Include staff in the strategic planning. Work together to set goals, gather data (e.g., student work, teacher observations), and make clear the relationship between the actions of adults in the building and the expected outcomes for students.

» Seriously consider what you should *stop* doing. As a leader, you can see the big picture of all that is happening across the school and district. As you plan for implementation of this curriculum, look around at other changes and new initiatives and ask yourself, "What can we stop doing?" This process isn't easy, but what we know for sure is that you are unlikely to be able to continue all that you have been doing *and* add this curriculum into the mix. You may need to rethink your approach to the teaching of phonics, the practice of guided reading, and other long-held literacy practices. Importantly, you'll also need to include your teachers in these discussions and decisions so that they feel like changes are happening *with* and *in support of* them and not *to* them.

» Establish a schoolwide growth mindset. Acknowledge and celebrate that everyone is learning something new—administrators, teachers, and students—and no one has all the answers. Hard work and effort will make the difference.

» Attend to the language you use to message change to the school community. Messages that connote tackling a worthy challenge together will be supportive of teachers who may need inspiration and motivation.

» Be the lead listener. There will be bumps in the road along the way. It's important to listen to concerns and to approach each one with a collaborative, problem-solving spirit.

Be an Instructional and Operational Leader

» Be ready to support teachers with the learning required to teach the curriculum. There's a lot to learn, and you'll need a plan. You know your school best and have a sense of the amount of change affecting teachers in your building and, in some cases, across the district. Look carefully at the components of the curriculum and at current literacy curricula and programs in your school. Ask yourself honestly how much change will be required of teach-

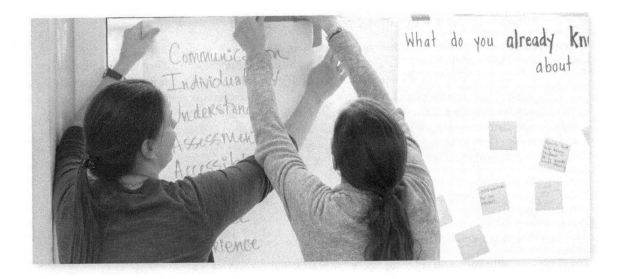

ers and how much you think they can handle. Is it best to begin all components at all grade levels at the same time, or should you consider a phased rollout?

» Set up a schedule and structures for professional learning. This may include whole-staff meetings, team meetings, professional learning communities, book groups, and the like. This book, along with many of the resources listed at the end of this section, are good resources for this professional learning. You may also consider bringing in staff from EL Education for professional development and/or coaching. Suggested topics for professional learning include:

- Managing change/coaching for change

- Growth mindset (addressing fears that "this is too hard")

- Character and social-emotional learning in the curriculum

- The Four T's of curriculum design (with a deeper dive into learning targets)

- Management in the active classroom (addressing an increase in student engagement and activity in the classroom)

- Protocols (addressing what they are and why they are important)

- Close reading/read-aloud

- Strengthening writing with models, critique, and descriptive feedback

- Supporting English language learners

- Universal Design for Learning

» Set up effective feedback loops. Teachers will benefit from coaching support and feedback from leaders as well as opportunities to observe and learn from each other. Gather real-time data and celebrate success, gains, and early wins. If you have a team to support curriculum implementation, distribute leadership for this work.

» Take care of the logistics so that teachers can focus on their instruction. Setting up the daily schedule, scheduling professional development for training and coaching, and communicating with families are all steps you can take that will shrink the change for teachers.

» Order (or designate someone to order) all of the materials teachers will need, including student texts. (If possible, support teachers even more by designating someone to organize and manage the materials.)

Assessing Your Readiness to Offer Support

Be open to change in your role as an instructional leader. Depending on existing practices in your school, what you see in classrooms using the curriculum may be different than what you are used to. Classrooms will buzz with activity. If your existing observation checklist rewards teachers with very quiet classrooms, for example, you may need to create a new one. Because you won't experience the same changes and eurekas that your teachers will on a daily basis, it's important that you learn as much as you can about the curriculum and the practices designed to help students be leaders of their own learning. It's also important that you spend as much time as possible in classrooms so that you are as close to the experience of your teachers and students as you can be.

As you think about your role in making the curriculum a success in your school, consider the following questions and assess your readiness to offer support to teachers.

» Consider the schoolwide logistical implications of adopting a new curriculum:

- What do you need to do *before you start* using the curriculum?

- Do you need to change your master schedule?

- Do you need to reexamine staffing?

- What do you need to *stop doing* to give yourselves the best chance of success? This may involve letting go of some existing programs to protect time for the curriculum.

» What data do you have or should you collect to understand teachers' needs in teaching this curriculum?

» How well do you understand the research behind new college- and career-ready standards and instructional shifts? How well-aligned is your school to standards?

» What professional development needs do you personally have to best support implementation of the curriculum? Where might you need the help of other teachers, leaders, or outside experts to provide quality support to teachers?

» How can you adjust your personal schedule to maximize your availability to support the teachers in your building? Do you have a system in place to put classroom walkthroughs and observations on your calendar as "sacred" time?

» How can you gather evidence and provide growth-producing feedback to teachers?

» How can you assist teachers in looking at student work and assessments to guide instructional decisions and plan for future professional development?

» How do you currently use time in the following areas? If it's not already, can any of this time be used for literacy-focused professional development?

- Early release days

- Grade-level meetings

- Team-level meetings

- Whole-faculty meetings

- Curriculum committee meetings

- District and school administrator meeting

- Other structures

» What would a plan for support look like? Try mapping out a schedule of professional development that meets your teachers' needs and takes advantage of structures already in place. Consider what additional structures could be put in place to offer greater support.

» What resources from EL Education can you use to support your work (see possible resources in the Instructional Leadership section at the end of this chapter)?

Proactively Addressing the Complexities You Will Encounter

As with any new curriculum adoption, you can expect complexities and challenges to arise. In Table 1.4, we highlight some of the complexities that you and your teachers will likely face. Proactively acknowledging these complexities with teachers is one way to build a sense that you are all working together to overcome challenges. This can go a long way in helping teachers not feel isolated with their struggles. In addition to highlighting several complexities and noting the reasons why they might occur, we also offer strategies that you might use to support problem-solving for this complexity.

Table 1.4: Implementation Complexities

Implementation Complexity # 1
Managing Complex Change: You may face resistance from teachers.
Reasons This May Occur
» Change is hard, and some resistance is normal, especially within schools, which are highly complex systems with many moving parts. » Teachers may not have enough information about the curriculum to see its value. » Teachers have not been included in the process and feel that change is happening *to* them and not *with* them. » The master schedule has not been adjusted to accommodate the various components of the curriculum, and teachers feel squeezed for time. » Teachers don't have enough time to learn the curriculum's practices and structures or to collaborate with each other.
Leadership Strategies to Support Teachers
» "Go slow to go fast." In other words, invest time in the process of change so that resistance doesn't slow it down or derail it. Spend time with staff analyzing student needs, learning about the curriculum, and identifying the ways that it can be a solution to a problem teachers are having. Build a vision and a plan for its implementation and hoped-for impact *together* with teachers. » Communicate with staff transparently about the process of adopting and implementing the curriculum. » Provide professional learning opportunities for teachers to learn the structures and practices in the curriculum, as well as time for them to collaborate and learn from each other. » Help teachers see that the curriculum is an opportunity for them to learn and grow as teachers—it is not a script to follow, but a tool to use. » Ensure that the master schedule supports implementation of the curriculum. » Consider using a tried-and-true model for managing change (see box: Tools for Managing Complex Change).

Cont.

Implementation Complexity # 2

Pacing: Teachers may struggle to match the curriculum's suggested pacing.

Reasons This May Occur

» Teachers are learning a new curriculum; effective and efficacious implementation takes time.

» Teachers are hanging on to existing practices that are comfortable and feel important to them and sometimes supplement or substitute these practices into lessons. This "mixing and matching" often slows the pacing.

» The curriculum promotes a higher ratio of student talk to teacher talk. Depending on current practices, teachers may need to work at not talking as much because it can slow pacing.

» There is a built-in intensity to the curriculum that requires students and teachers to work at a pace that may seem initially uncomfortable. Students have lots to do! Our experience tells us that in most cases, students and teachers rise, over time, to this level of rigor.

» Teachers may stretch one lesson out over multiple days because they are afraid students did not master the content.

» Teachers are not prepared ahead of time with the various materials needed in lessons, units, and modules (e.g., anchor charts, note-catchers).

Leadership Strategies to Support Teachers

» Offer empathy and encouragement to teachers. Saying, "Yes, pacing is an issue. You are learning something new" invites teachers to more safely engage in the productive struggle needed when they are first starting out.

» Remember that teachers are shifting their instructional practice. This happens to varying degrees and at different rates depending on multiple variables (e.g., a teacher's length of time teaching, the degree to which the curriculum requires teachers to shift their practice). Some teachers will need to unlearn old practices; as they embrace these changes, their pacing will improve and their confidence in the curriculum will grow. Newer teachers may not be as challenged by pacing as veteran teachers, as they have less to unlearn.

» Encourage teachers to ask, "When will students talk, and when will I talk?" as they prepare for lessons. This will help them be mindful of not talking too much.

» Ensure that teachers have common planning time to discuss pacing and other complexities of practice that emerge in the implementation of the curriculum. Looking ahead through lessons, units, and modules will also support them with materials management. Guidance on planning, including task cards for teachers, can be found in Chapter 3A.

» Remind teachers that the K–2 Labs (Labs) and 3–5 Additional Language and Literacy (ALL) Block often offer additional time to work with ideas or texts from the Module Lessons and have flexible time built into their schedules that can be used to extend lessons that run over time.

» Help teachers understand that the curriculum spirals through Reading, Writing, and Speaking and Listening standards over time; they are repeated in multiple lessons and various components of the curriculum. Reassure teachers that if students do not meet standards the first time around, they will have several more opportunities to do so. For this reason, encourage teachers not to stretch lessons over multiple days.

» Encourage teachers to use a timer.

» Emphasize that students are not expected to understand 100 percent of all complex texts, including every academic vocabulary word. They are refining their understanding of a topic *over time*. As they build content-related vocabulary and background knowledge, students' understanding of texts will increase.

Cont.

Implementation Complexity #3
Classroom Management: Teachers may struggle to adapt to managing an increased activity level in their classroom.

Reasons This May Occur

» The curriculum depends on students collaborating and becoming leaders of their own learning. This often means an increase in student activity and talk in the classroom.

» There are multiple student engagement strategies used throughout the curriculum, including protocols. Protocols can appear to be messy and unorganized at first.

» There are natural management issues in active classrooms.

Leadership Strategies to Support Teachers

» Promote active classrooms where students are collaborating, talking, and moving. Celebrate and honor teachers who are courageous in implementing new strategies; it can take multiple tries to feel comfortable.

» When teachers ask, "Can I just skip the protocols?" encourage them to keep at it. Protocols need to be rehearsed and reinforced multiple times; they are worth the effort because during protocols students are challenged, engaged, and empowered to learn more deeply. Protocols ensure equal participation and accountability in learning.

» Encourage teachers trying a new protocol with students to be very clear initially with their expectations by:

  • providing a model and unpacking success criteria with students

  • giving students real-time feedback during the protocol, based on success criteria

  • facilitating student reflection and goal-setting around success criteria for subsequent uses of the protocol

  • viewing together the videos Classroom Protocols in Action: Back-to-Back and Face-to-Face (https://vimeo.com/164447189) or Classroom Protocols in Action: Think-Pair-Share (https://vimeo.com/164455361) to see how students learn to effectively use a protocol. Debrief the video with teachers and help them plan for how to model, practice, and reinforce protocols in their classrooms.

» Encourage teachers to work together with their students to develop classroom norms. As the activity level increases in the classroom, student behavior will be guided by the norms. More on norms can be found in Chapter 3C.

» Use protocols in staff meetings and professional learning so you and your staff become more accustomed to them.

» For additional reading, see Chapter 3 of this book and the Classroom Protocols section of our curriculum website (Curriculum.ELeducation.org). You may also wish to purchase the EL Education book *Management in the Active Classroom* or view its accompanying videos, which can also be found on our curriculum website.

Cont.

Implementation Complexity #4
Mindset: Teachers and/or students may describe the curriculum as "too hard."

Reasons This May Occur

» Students and teachers are often engaging in new and unfamiliar tasks. Students are reading text that is complex in language, structure, and content. It is hard!

» Students are asked to write for multiple purposes, with higher expectations and in higher volumes than they may be accustomed to.

» Students may be asked to embrace greater levels of independence, perseverance, and personal ownership of learning than they are used to.

» The curriculum moves slowly in places to build deep conceptual understanding and encourage higher-level thinking. Occasionally teachers may feel that the curriculum is "easier" than what they have done in the past because some components don't move as fast as what they are accustomed to. In these cases, the hard work for teachers may be trusting the process of slowing down and going deeper.

Leadership Strategies to Support Teachers

» Remind teachers that getting used to the rigor of the curriculum will take time. Implementing the curriculum is a process of change that all are engaging in together over the course of the year.

» Remind teachers that as they raise expectations, students may find tasks and texts "too hard." Teachers will need to coach students on habits of character such as perseverance, collaboration, and productive struggle.

» Provide reassurance to teachers that they will begin to grow more confident and comfortable with each module.

» Talk to teachers about having a growth mindset about themselves as professionals and about their students as learners.

» Unify teachers around a central message that curricular choices are made to support students in building stronger literacy skills and more word and world knowledge and, ultimately, to prepare them for the world that awaits them. The curriculum is designed to compel and support students to work together to tackle challenging materials and solve difficult problems.

» Remind teachers that the Labs and ALL Block offer students additional time and practice to build skills and content knowledge.

» Highlight that this curriculum is a core curriculum for *all* students. Students should not be given less complex text as a replacement for grade-level text. More on scaffolding texts and tasks for students is provided in subsequent chapters of this book, and plenty of guidance is offered in the lessons themselves.

Cont.

Implementation Complexity #5
Grading: Leaders and/or teachers seek guidance on grading student work and reporting on student progress.

Reasons This May Occur
» The curriculum does not specifically provide guidance on how to assign grades on individual components of the curriculum (e.g., point value, letter grades).
» Student work is often assessed using standards-aligned rubrics, rather than letter grades (which may be unfamiliar for some teachers).

Leadership Strategies to Support Teachers
» Provide time for grade-level teams to calibrate regarding grading practices.
» Give teachers specific time to examine the Assessment Overview and Resources document (one per module for Grades K–5) and the benchmark assessments (for the K–2 Reading Foundations Skills Block). These assessments include sample student responses and scoring guidance (e.g., rubrics, checklists) that show teachers what proficiency looks like for a given standard or set of standards at a particular grade level. (See Chapter 7 for more information.)
» Give teachers time to analyze and calibrate the writing rubrics (opinion, informative/explanatory, and narrative) as well as various checklists (for Speaking and Listening standards, Language standards, and some ongoing assessment of reading) that are used in K–5 Module Lessons.
» Use a process or protocol that promotes looking at student work as a way to assess student progress on standards (see Chapter 7 for more details).
» Remind teachers that every lesson includes "ongoing assessment." Teachers need not collect or record all this data, but there are specific suggestions for formative assessment.
» Promote conversations about using learning targets as a way for students to self-assess progress toward standards. (Note: Learning targets are discussed in more detail in Chapter 3B.)
» Ensure that time is spent creating a common vision for how student achievement is measured. See the EL Education Dimensions of Student Achievement in Figure 1.2.

Chapter 1:
Instructional Leadership

Table 1.5: Chapter 1 Instructional Leadership[5]

Questions to Ask Yourself and Your Staff
» What do you already do to foster a spirit of equity in the school—that all students deserve and can be successful with challenging work? What more can you do to foster success?
» What steps have you taken to cultivate a growth mindset throughout the school—a belief that "being smart" isn't something we're born with, but "getting smart" is something we can achieve with effort, strategies, and support?
» How do you currently define student achievement? Now that you've read about EL Education's three Dimensions of Student Achievement (see Figure 1.2), what are your next steps as a school to identify and celebrate achievement in all three dimensions?
» How will you share the research behind the design of the curriculum to build understanding and support for its adoption in your school? Can you build a bridge between what the curriculum offers and areas of need identified by teachers or by school-level data?
» Do you and your teachers understand the "deep logic" of the curriculum's design (i.e., the Four T's) well enough to know when and how to customize it if necessary?
» Have you and your staff developed a vision for change and a plan for how to get there? Do teachers feel included in the vision (i.e., it's being done *with* them and not *to* them)?
» Have you proactively identified the complexities or challenges you will face? What is your strategy for managing change of this nature?
» How does your school cultivate a culture of risk-taking and trust?

Cont.

---

[5] At the end of each chapter of this book, look for this section on Instructional Leadership, where you will find a table, just like Table 1.5, that includes questions to ask yourself, evidence of progress, and further resources and suggestions related to each chapter. Though Chapter 1 already includes extensive guidance for leaders and some information in Table 1.5 may be repetitive, we have included it here for you so that you'll know what to look for in subsequent chapters.

» Have you analyzed your school schedule to accommodate the components of the curriculum? Are teachers clear about what they may need to stop doing as they start teaching the curriculum?

Evidence of Progress

» Teachers express a belief that all students deserve the opportunity to do challenging work and that they can provide them with the tools they need to do it.

» Professional development time is devoted to learning about the curriculum: its design, the research that supports it, and its potential impact on student learning and teacher growth. Teachers see the value of a curriculum that includes both content-based literacy and structured phonics.

» School staff feel that they have a voice in developing the vision and process for adopting the curriculum.

» Structures are in place for staff to share successes and voice concerns or questions, and they trust that they will be heard respectfully.

» The complexities and potential challenges teachers may face have been addressed through professional development and logistical support so that teachers can focus on quality instruction.

» The school schedule supports successful implementation of the components of the curriculum. Teachers have enough time for lessons and can focus on quality instruction.

Resources and Suggestions

» The curriculum itself, along with a full suite of companion resources and tools, can be found at: Curriculum.ELeducation.org. Resources include:

- Curriculum Plans

- Curriculum Maps

- K–5 Required Trade Book Procurement List

- K–5 Recommended Texts and Other Resources

- K–2 Labs Materials List

- Life Science Materials List

- Classroom Protocols

- Sample Schedules

- Videos

» Additional resources can be found on the main EL Education website (ELeducation.org):

- PD Packs

  ○ Culture of Growth

  ○ Coaching for Change

  ○ K–5 Language Arts Curriculum (second edition)

- Walkthrough Tools

Cont.

- Professional Development Opportunities (or email pd@eleducation.org)

» Books by EL Education that deepen understanding of practices in the curriculum:

- *Management in the Active Classroom*

- *Leaders of Their Own Learning: Transforming Schools through Student-Engaged Assessment*

- *Transformational Literacy: Making the Common Core Shift with Work That Matters*

- *Learning That Lasts: Challenging, Engaging, and Empowering Students with Deeper Instruction*

» Website: achievethecore.org (Common Core resources)

Chapter 1: Before You Begin: The Foundations Of The Curriculum

Chapter 1A: What Makes This Curriculum The Right Choice For Me And My Students?

Chapter 1B: How Did Research Impact The Design Of The Curriculum, And What Difference Will It Make To My Students?

Chapter 1C: What Will It Take To Lead Schoolwide Change?

Instructional Leadership

▶ Frequently Asked Questions

Chapter 1:
Frequently Asked Questions

I recognize that this curriculum has a lot to offer my students, but I'm going to miss designing my own. What opportunities are there to put my own stamp on it?

Depending on your teaching experience and your comfort level with the instructional practices embedded in this curriculum, you may feel ready to begin enhancing or customizing some elements of it right away. However, we strongly recommend that you spend at least a year teaching the various components of the curriculum and getting used to the rhythm and flow before making too many changes. Some components of the curriculum (like K–2 Labs [Labs]) are easier to put your stamp on than others (like the sequence in which letter-sound connections are taught in the K–2 Reading Foundations Skills Block [Skills Block]).

In terms of the Module Lessons, one of the best enhancements is to find local connections for your module topics. Is there additional fieldwork that students can do to deepen their learning? Can experts in the field visit your classroom? Can you provide a service learning component related to the module topic? You may be able to incorporate these kinds of enhancements during other parts of the school day (e.g., science time) so that they don't conflict with time needed to teach English language arts (ELA) lessons. If you are inclined to make changes to the Module Lessons themselves, such as changes to texts, tasks, topics, or targets (the Four T's), we urge you to use caution and to consider the implications of any changes you make on the overall goal of helping students achieve mastery of all grade-level standards.

K–2 Labs and the 3–5 Additional Language and Literacy (ALL) Block, by design, leave more room for adaptation and innovation over time. But even with those, we recommend that you "play the music as written" for a year before you make significant adjustments. By contrast, the Skills Block is quite technical and layered in its design; we recommend you approach significant adaptations cautiously. However, you can and should find ways to incorporate things like your own songs and activities once you understand the phases and the deep logic of the differentiated small group instruction (see Chapter 4 for more information).

I'm nervous that this curriculum is going to be too hard for some of my students. Are there ways I can adapt it for students who may struggle?

Our approach to supporting students who may struggle is not to adapt, but to scaffold. We want all students to have access to rigorous content, engaging texts, and opportunities for sophisticated thinking and discourse. Rather than denying students these opportunities, the curriculum offers scaffolds that give them the support they need to succeed. Throughout the curriculum, you will find extensive support for English language learners and guidance for meeting all students' needs through Universal Design for Learning (UDL). We urge you to nurture your own growth mindset as a teacher and to embark on this journey with a belief that your students can do it and that you can give them the support they need.

You talk a lot about content-based literacy. Does this mean there's less time for skills work?

Content-based literacy means that students are learning key literacy skills as they learn compelling science and social studies content. Content-based curriculum isn't in opposition to skills—it's more like a vehicle for skills. Learning literacy skills in the context of learning important content actually accelerates literacy learning (refer to the research in Table 1.1). In our curriculum, there's not *less* time for teaching skills, but time is used differently; skills work is woven into student learning about content. Instead of teaching discrete literacy skills (e.g., like practicing "determining the main idea in a text") with a random assortment of materials that aren't connected to one topic, we connect them through compelling content (e.g., as third-graders learn about how people overcome learning challenges in Module 1, they read an excerpt about Kenya, and then recount key details, explaining how those details support the main idea that people in Kenya use camels to overcome the challenge of accessing books). The only part of our curriculum that isn't content-based is the Skills Block, which targets foundational reading standards.

What about play? Is this curriculum going to have a lot seat work, or will my students have a chance to play and be kids?

We have designed the curriculum with the needs of K–5 learners in mind, incorporating movement, play, creativity, and collaboration wherever possible. However, we view play as frequently synergistic with, rather than in opposition to, rigorous academic work. Our content-based literacy curriculum helps students experience learning as fun and to find joy in the process of uncovering the mysteries held within texts, being able to explain their learning to their peers, or cracking the alphabetic code. In the chapters that follow, you will learn more about particular structures and practices in the curriculum—such as the Labs or protocols—that are intentionally designed to give students an experience that is quite the opposite of "seat work."

I know I'm going to have to answer a lot of questions from parents and guardians about why we chose this curriculum. What's the best resource for explaining the why behind the what?

There are different resources you can choose from based on the level of interest of your community. If families are eager to read more about the research, Table 1.1 is a good summary. In fact, all of Chapter 1B makes a compelling case for the design of the curriculum, based on research. For those who want a more general overview, we suggest directing them to our website (Curriculum. ELeducation.org) to explore videos and other resources and to learn more about the compelling content in the curriculum.

We don't use the Common Core State Standards in my state. Is this curriculum still going to work for us?

If your state is not using the Common Core State Standards, there's a good chance that it is using standards that closely resemble them. You or your school or district leaders may need to do some mapping of the standards we use onto yours. We can't speak for every possible context, but we are pretty confident that this curriculum addresses ELA/literacy standards in most locations. We have also chosen module topics that address science and social studies content that is commonly taught in states across the country.

We don't have time to implement the full curriculum at our school. What do you suggest we cut?

We certainly recommend teaching the entire comprehensive curriculum and feel that it is your best bet to help your students achieve mastery on college- and career-ready standards. However, we recognize that that's not always going to be possible, whether because your schedule is too restrictive or because you don't want to let go of certain elements of your existing curricula that are working well for you and your students. Before making those decisions, we urge you to get to know the structure of the curriculum more fully (see Chapter 2) so that you can make an informed decision.

I'm familiar with EL Education's curriculum for Grades 3–8. How does this new K–5 curriculum compare to the older 3–8 version? Are there overlaps, or is it all new?

EL Education has expanded its ELA curriculum offerings to include a brand-new comprehensive K–2 curriculum. We have also written a second edition of four of our 3–5 curriculum modules to broaden the curriculum's relevance to schools nationally and incorporate feedback from teachers across the country. The four second-edition modules for Grades 3–5 require the same one-per-student texts as the corresponding first-edition modules and, as a result, are focused on the same topics. The second-edition 3–5 curriculum also includes an additional hour of content-based literacy instruction, the ALL Block, to support and reinforce the learning in the Module Lessons. An additional optional companion Life Science Module is also offered for the second-edition 3–5 curriculum, which accompanies Module 2 for a third hour of instruction lasting eight to nine weeks.

The K–5 curriculum is comprehensive, meaning that it explicitly teaches and formally assesses all strands and standards of the Common Core ELA standards for each grade level. (With or without the Life Science Module, the two hours of content-based literacy for Grades 3–5 are considered comprehensive.)

In addition to adding new components to the 3–5 curriculum, we have also enhanced the modules themselves:

» All Language standards explicitly taught and formally assessed in Module Lessons

» Supports for a range of learners aligned to the UDL framework (multiple means of representation, multiple means of action and expression, multiple means of engagement)

» Unit- and lesson-level supports for English language learners

» Language Dives that allow students to study syntax and meaning at a deeper level

» More explicit vocabulary instruction (e.g., morphology, vocabulary notebooks)

» More explicit instruction on the writing process, including formatting paragraphs and essays

» Explicit instruction for grammar, usage, mechanics, punctuation, and spelling

» More explicit focus on students practicing habits of character as they work independently, collaborate with peers, and care for one another and their classroom

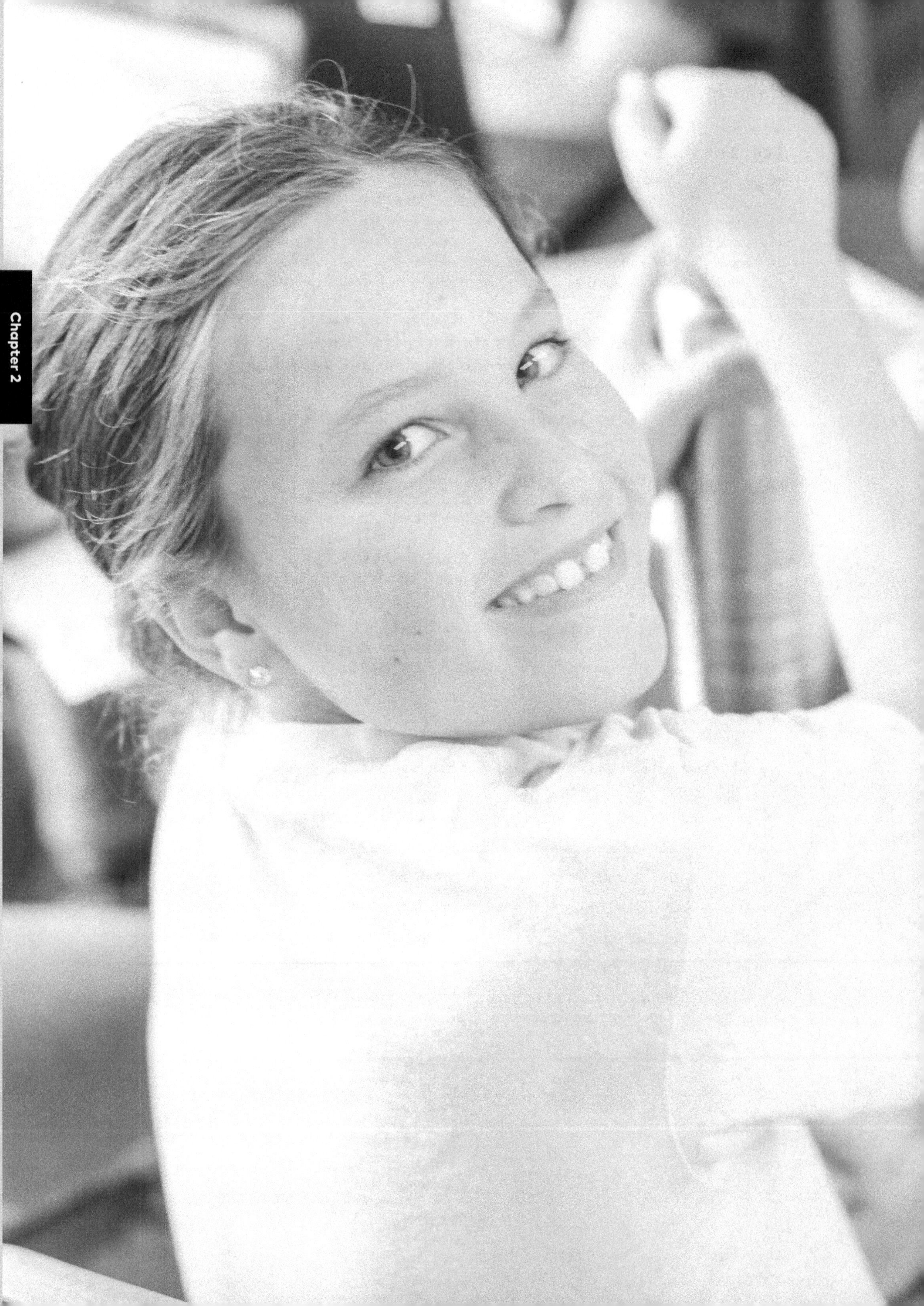

Chapter 2:
Getting Oriented: The Structure and Supports of the Curriculum

Chapter 2A:
How Do All the Parts of the Curriculum Fit Together?

Now that you have explored the foundations of the curriculum in Chapter 1, it's time to get your arms around the curriculum itself. The first part of this chapter, Chapter 2A, will orient you to the structure of the *entire* K–5 curriculum, which includes two hours of content-based literacy at all grade levels, plus one hour of structured phonics for Grades K–2 and a one-hour optional science module for Grades 3–5, which runs for eight weeks.

Chapter 2B will dig deeper into what it takes to implement the K–2 Labs (Labs) and the 3–5 Additional Language and Literacy (ALL) Block, which, along with the Module Lessons, make up the content-based literacy part of the curriculum. These complementary blocks allow students additional time to explore and dig deeper into the science, history, or literary content they are learning in the Module Lessons and build additional literacy skills. Both blocks have logistical considerations that need further explanation and detail than we provide here in Chapter 2A. Therefore, we have devoted Chapter 2B to detailing those logistics so that you will feel well prepared.

The hour of structured phonics provided by the K–2 Reading Foundations Skills Block (Skills Block) also has special logistical considerations and details. We have devoted an entire chapter—Chapter 4—to this component of the K–2 curriculum, which is designed to help young readers crack the alphabetic code.

The final part of this chapter, Chapter 2C, explores our frameworks for helping all learners succeed. We detail the supports for English language learners (ELLs) used throughout the curriculum, as well as the Universal Design for Learning (UDL) framework. UDL is a widely used framework for providing all students with curriculum and instruction that meet their unique learning needs. These frameworks will be broadly introduced here and then explored further in subsequent chapters in the context of specific instructional practices in the curriculum.

▶ What Will My Students Experience across the K–5 Continuum?

Our K–5 curriculum offers either two or three hours of literacy instruction per day, depending on your grade level. The K–2 curriculum offers two hours per day of content-based literacy (Module Lessons and Labs), plus one hour of structured phonics (Skills Block). All together, these three hours of curriculum are considered comprehensive, meaning that they explicitly teach and formally assess all strands and standards of the Common Core English language arts (ELA) standards for each grade level.

The 3–5 curriculum offers two hours of content-based literacy instruction per day (Module Lessons and the ALL Block), with an additional optional companion Life Science module, which accompanies Module 2 for a third hour of instruction lasting eight to nine weeks. With or without the Life Science module, the two hours of content-based literacy are considered comprehensive.

Figure 2.1: EL Education K–5 Language Arts Curriculum

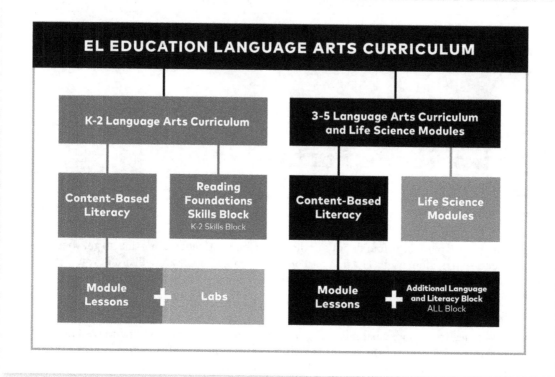

At the heart of the curriculum, at all grade levels, are the hour-long Module Lessons. Each grade level includes four modules, which span a full school year. The four modules allow students to build important content knowledge based on a compelling topic related to science, social studies, or literature. Each module uses rich, authentic text throughout. Figure 2.2 shows the progression of the four modules throughout the year. Table 2.1 summarizes the compelling content topic of each module at each grade level.

Figure 2.2: Year-long View of the Four Modules

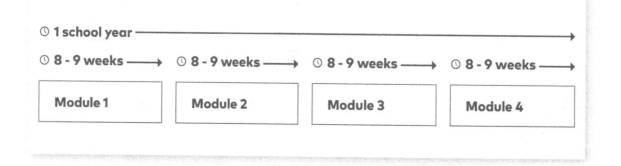

Table 2.1: Content Topics of the K–5 Modules

Grade	Module 1	Module 2	Module 3	Module 4
K	Toys and Play	Weather Wonders	Trees Are Alive	Enjoying and Appreciating Trees
1	Tools and Work	The Sun, Moon, and Stars	Birds' Amazing Bodies	Caring for Birds
2	Schools and Community	Fossils Tell of Earth's Changes	The Secret World of Pollination	Providing for Pollinators
3	Overcoming Learning Challenges Near and Far	Adaptations and the Wide World of Frogs	Exploring a Literary Classic	The Role of Freshwater around the World
4	Poetry, Poets, and Becoming Writers	Animal Defense Mechanisms	The American Revolution	Susan B. Anthony, the Suffrage Movement, and the Importance of Voting
5	Stories of Human Rights	Biodiversity in the Rainforest	Athletes as Leaders of Change	Natural Disasters in the Western Hemisphere

Hopefully these brief descriptions of the various components of the curriculum have given you a sense of what to expect. We'll delve deeper in the pages that follow, but before we get into the details, let's start by meeting some students so you can get a better feel for what a day in the life of the curriculum is like.

📷 Snapshot: Meet the Students

It is 10:15 a.m. on Wednesday, and first-graders Anna, Kristina, Elvin, and Omar are hard at work building together. Over the past few weeks in their Module Lessons, they have spent time every day immersed in *The Most Magnificent Thing*, a rich and complex text about a girl who creates a scooter, which their teacher, Ms. Sanchez, reads aloud. Now, later in the morning during Labs, Ms. Sanchez helps them learn about tools, and the students work and talk together about how to use various tools and materials to try out designs.

More than a month into this module, Anna, Kristina, Elvin, and Omar are collaborating on a "magnificent thing" for their classroom: a lovely box, decorated with their original design, that will hold colored pencils for the class to use. Once the box is complete, each of them will write a paragraph, explaining how they built the magnificent thing and how to use it. Now that they are comfortable with the letters and sounds of written language and can encode them—thanks to their hard work in their daily hour of the Skills Block—the first-graders are ready for this final supported task.

Down the hall, fourth-graders Nathan, Sergei, and Alma are working just as hard. Over many weeks in the Module Lessons, their teacher, Ms. Henderson, has immersed her students in a study of animal defenses and what it takes for animals to survive and thrive. She has helped her students successfully read complex texts about the topic. During her second hour of literacy instruction, the ALL Block, she also has ensured that students read a lot on their own about animal defenses and that her students received much-needed explicit skills instruction and practice.

Ms. Henderson has facilitated intense conversations among her fourth-graders about what might happen to specific animals without their defenses. Dividing the students into small, heterogeneous groups, Ms. Henderson facilitated as her fourth-graders researched three specific animals. Then she gave them specific instruction on narrative writing. Now Nathan, Sergei, and Alma are about to craft choose-your-own-adventure stories about how armadillos use natural defenses to survive and thrive. And during science time, they are using the Life Science module to explore the internal and external structures of plants and animals and how they function.

This snapshot reveals the realized goals that underlie our comprehensive literacy curriculum: engagement, perseverance, and mastery for Anna, Kristina, Elvin, Omar, Nathan, Sergei, Alma, and all of their elementary classmates.

Overview of the K–2 Curriculum

John Dewey, education icon, famously said, "Education is not preparation for life; education is life itself." Our curriculum for primary learners reflects that truth. Young children live in a world of activity, exploration, creation, singing, talk, and play. These ways of living—with the encouragement of loving and supportive adults—give young learners both meaning and joy. As they move, sing, explore new ideas, make stuff, talk endlessly about what they are doing, and repeat songs and poems over and over again, primary children are learning. Our curriculum is rich and academically challenging, and it is built with the needs of the primary learner at its core. (Note: The "Characteristics of Primary Learners" are described in detail in Chapter 1A.)

The K–2 curriculum offers three hours of rich ELA instruction per day:

» Two hours of content-based literacy

- One hour of Module Lessons

- One hour of Labs

» A third hour of structured phonics:

- One hour of the Reading Foundations Skills Block (addresses the Common Core Reading: Foundational Skills standards as well as Language standards 1 and 2)

These three hours of curriculum are considered *comprehensive*, explicitly teaching and formally assessing all strands and standards of the Common Core ELA standards for each grade level. Taken as a whole, this rigorous and joyful ELA curriculum is designed to ensure that all children have a genuine opportunity to grow and succeed.

Figure 2.3: EL Education K–2 Language Arts Curriculum

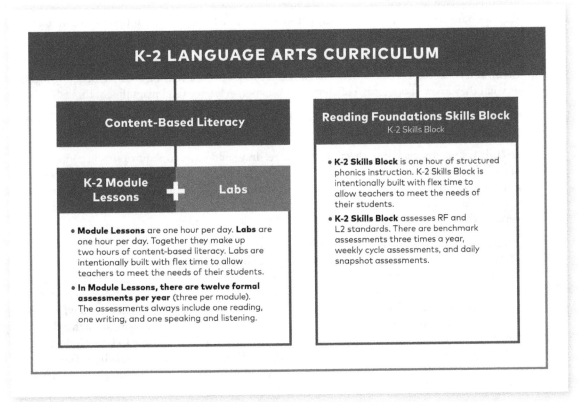

K-2 LANGUAGE ARTS CURRICULUM

Content-Based Literacy

K-2 Module Lessons **+** Labs

- **Module Lessons** are one hour per day. **Labs** are one hour per day. Together they make up two hours of content-based literacy. Labs are intentionally built with flex time to allow teachers to meet the needs of their students.

- **In Module Lessons, there are twelve formal assessments per year** (three per module). The assessments always include one reading, one writing, and one speaking and listening.

Reading Foundations Skills Block
K-2 Skills Block

- **K-2 Skills Block** is one hour of structured phonics instruction. K-2 Skills Block is intentionally built with flex time to allow teachers to meet the needs of their students.

- **K-2 Skills Block** assesses RF and L2 standards. There are benchmark assessments three times a year, weekly cycle assessments, and daily snapshot assessments.

K–2 Content-Based Literacy: Module Lessons and Labs

MODULE LESSONS

Across Grades K–5, students experience four modules per year. In Grades K–2, Module 1 is a bit shorter (six weeks rather than eight), so you have time to do the other important work of getting classroom routines and culture in place, which often takes more time and deliberate attention for primary age students. (For more on creating an active and collaborative classroom culture, see Chapter 3C.) Each module has a consistent structure of three units, each of which includes one formal assessment.

Figure 2.4: K–2 Module, Unit, and Assessment Structure

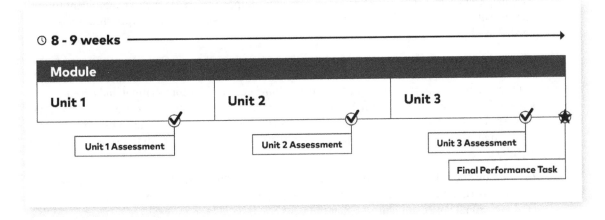

🕐 **8 - 9 weeks**

Module

| Unit 1 | Unit 2 | Unit 3 |

Unit 1 Assessment

Unit 2 Assessment

Unit 3 Assessment

Final Performance Task

The curriculum was built using the principles of backward design, meaning that we started by identifying what we wanted students to know and be able to do at the end of each module, and then we built each unit to intentionally get them there. Let's explore what that means in the first-grade classroom introduced in the Snapshot at the beginning of this chapter.

The last unit of each module, **Unit 3**, culminates with a performance task. This is where Kristina, Elvin, and Omar have created their "magnificent thing" and are writing about it, bringing together what they know about tools, collaboration, and perseverance (and magnificent things!).

What students learn in Units 1 and 2 helps them prepare for this performance task. (This is the principle of backward design in action.)

In **Unit 1**, students read, sing, discuss, dramatize, draw, and write to acquire strong content knowledge as well as the literacy skills that they need to do so. Ms. Sanchez's first-graders read informational text to learn about lots of tools and the jobs each tool does. They learn how to ask and answer questions about the many texts they work with. They learn to collaborate and converse with one another, capturing their thinking in pictures and words.

Several weeks later, in **Unit 2**, they begin work with "close reading" of a complex text, *The Most Magnificent Thing*. In primary grades, this close reading happens through hearing the text read aloud (i.e., a close read-aloud). Ms. Sanchez uses a close read-aloud guide to conduct a series of sessions (across multiple lessons) that invite students to analyze and discuss this rich literary text. Students become deeply familiar with what a "magnificent thing" might be and what sorts of habits of character (such as perseverance) the girl in the story needed to make such a thing. Few first-grade students can read the text independently, yet they all come to know it deeply and to internalize its language, syntax, and meaning—reading comprehension at its best. During the Module Lessons in this unit, students also do a series of design challenges that gives them hands-on experience with collaborative problem-solving.

As the lessons in each unit progress, Ms. Sanchez regularly checks in on her students' progress. Each unit has a standards-based assessment built in. Here, students read, write, or speak with increasing independence about the texts they have been working with. These assessments help Ms. Sanchez in two ways: They allow her to have a clear sense of what her students can do and cannot yet do, and they give her valuable information about how best to use the time in the Labs for her students' benefit.

Almost every day, K–2 students share songs and poems. These serve many functions: They give students cues about transitions from activity to activity, help build a positive classroom community, build fluency, give students opportunities to practice specific language standards, and give students a deep schema for rhythm and syntax. And, they are joyful.

This unfolding of the three units means that by **Unit 3**, when the performance task is introduced, Kristina, Elvin, Omar, and their classmates are fully equipped to create their "magnificent things" and to synthesize their understanding of what they accomplished through supported, standards-based writing.

K–2 LABS

Labs are an important feature of the K–2 curriculum because they complement and extend student learning from the Module Lessons. They are designed to help teachers ensure that *all* of their students get the time to play and explore, become immersed in oral language and content knowledge, and practice skills and habits of character that they need—both to live joyfully and to be fully successful and proficient.

Labs are one hour long and complement Module Lessons. These two hours of content-based literacy instruction are complementary, working together to accelerate the achievement of all students. You'll notice in Figure 2.5 that the Labs are designed for six weeks of instruction within an eight- to nine-week module. This design allows you to use your discretion to flexibly schedule the Labs to best meet the needs of your classroom. You may choose to spend that hour during those additional two to three weeks on such things as solidifying structures and routines, providing additional "spill-over" time to support Module Lessons, providing additional instructional time for ELLs, or for additional explicit language instruction.

Keep in mind, this is an intentionally brief description of the Labs; we'll provide much more detailed information in Chapter 2B.

Figure 2.5: K–2 Content-Based Literacy: Module Lessons and Labs

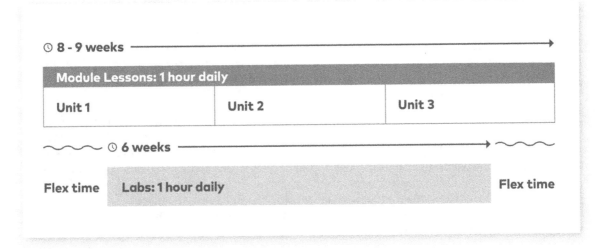

KEY FEATURES OF THE K–2 MODULE LESSONS AND LABS

» **Emphasis on habits of character**. Character is one of EL Education's three Dimensions of Student Achievement (see Figure 1.2). Collaboration, perseverance, a growth mindset, and being able to set goals and then reflect on them all are key aspects of strong social-emotional learning. They are critical to student success, in school and in life.

» **Emphasis on oral language development**. Interactive, conversational immersion in oral language in the early years is critically important for children's literacy development. Primary students build important oral language (vocabulary and syntax) and listening habits that will be key to their development of literacy. Module Lessons include explicit focus on the Speaking and Listening standards, and the Labs provide opportunities for students to use content-specific and academic vocabulary and apply the speaking and listening skills taught in the Module Lessons.

» **Daily work with rich, complex text and volume of reading**. The Module Lessons are built around close read-alouds of complex text. In addition, each day in the Labs begins with Storytime—a read-aloud chosen for its relationship to the content or character focus of the Labs—so students are consistently immersed in rich, meaningful, content-connected language. This frequent work with rich text builds comprehension skills, broadens content knowledge, and develops academic vocabulary.

» **Daily student goal-setting and reflection**. Module Lessons include learning targets, which are student-friendly "I can" statements that help students know where they are headed with their learning. Teachers help students check back in with their progress toward learning targets during lessons. Similarly, at the start of each Lab, students set personal goals. At the end of the Lab block, they have time to reflect on their learning. As they reflect, students are developing their executive functioning skills—their ability to think about what they are doing, name it, and begin to make more intentional decisions.

» **Culminating performance task**. Unit 3 of the Module Lessons culminates with a student performance task. Students get support to synthesize and transfer their knowledge and understanding from the module—in terms of both content and literacy—in an authentic and often collaborative task. This is scaffolded with models, drafts, critique, and revision to lead to high-quality work.

» **Assessment.** Both summative and formative assessments are integral. In each module, three formal summative assessments are built in (one per unit). Formative "ongoing" assessment happens frequently, as teachers observe, use checklists, and give feedback to students in Module Lessons and Labs.

Structured Phonics: The K–2 Reading Foundations Skills Block

Our curriculum is comprehensive. The Module Lessons and Labs immerse primary students in content-based literacy. These two components of the curriculum complement each other to give students strong, active literacy instruction grounded in compelling topics. And then the Skills Block gives K–2 students another hour per day of essential structured phonics instruction to help them crack the alphabetic code.

We know that to become fully literate, all children must acquire internalized, automatic knowledge of the building blocks of spoken and written language: letter names, sounds, and formation; the ability to break words apart and blend them back together; common spelling patterns; and decoding of words. In addition, students must develop automaticity with reading. They need to internalize predictably patterned words in context (so that the words become sight words) and smoothly and accurately read basic sentence patterns—and, increasingly, texts. Learning these building blocks of written language gives students the "mental bandwidth" to pay attention to the meaning of text and improves their reading comprehension.

The Skills Block is organized by cycles, most of which include five lessons. Each day:

» Students spend 15 to 20 minutes in whole group instruction.

» Students spend 40 to 45 minutes in differentiated small groups, based on their strengths and needs.

Students develop foundational skills in "phases" of reading and spelling development (see Table 2.2). Our curriculum is designed to help teachers identify what phase each student is in and then to give students specific instruction in mastering each phase. (This framework is based on the work of Dr. Linnea Ehri, an educational psychologist who has researched how learners crack the alphabetic code.)

Keep in mind, this is an intentionally brief description of the Skills Block; we'll provide much more detailed information in Chapter 4.

Table 2.2: The Phases of Reading and Spelling Development

Pre-Alphabetic (Pre-A)	Partial Alphabetic (PA)	Full Alphabetic (FA)	Consolidated Alphabetic (CA)
Reader is not yet making any alphabetic connections. May recognize some letters (e.g., letters in own name) and environmental print (e.g., "Stop" on stop sign).	Reader is making partial alphabetic connections. Beginning to decode and encode consonant/vowel/consonant and vowel/consonant words but frequently confuses vowels and vowel sounds.	Reader is making full alphabetic connections. Able to decode and encode all regularly spelled, one-syllable words and some multisyllabic words.	Reader uses knowledge of syllable types to decode and encode multisyllabic words. Continually growing bank of high-frequency and irregularly spelled words.

Overview of the 3–5 Curriculum

Just like primary age students, upper elementary age students are joy seekers. They crave collaboration with their peers and engagement in their learning through play, story, and games. They also have unique needs and characteristics. Their growing hunger for independence and mastery as learners makes them ready to put their hard-earned reading and writing skills to work.

Our 3–5 curriculum honors students' growing capacity to read complex text, write at length and with depth, and explore pressing issues in the world around them. The 3–5 curriculum comprises two hours of rich, content-based literacy instruction per day:

» One hour of Module Lessons

» One hour of the Additional Language and Literacy Block

These two hours of curriculum are considered comprehensive, explicitly teaching and formally assessing all strands and standards of the Common Core ELA standards for each grade level. (In Grades 3–5, the initial exposure to and formal assessment of standards happens in the Module Lessons; the ALL Block is for additional practice.) There is also an optional companion Life Science module that accompanies Module 2 and comprises eight weeks of instruction.

Figure 2.6: EL Education 3–5 Language Arts Curriculum and Life Science Modules

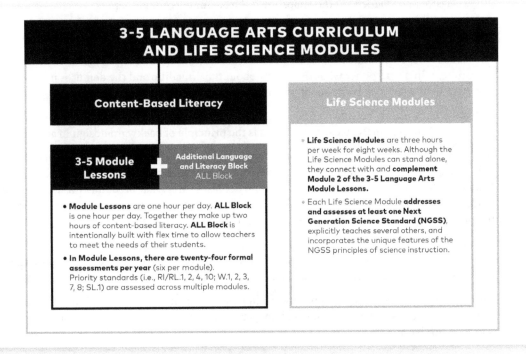

3–5 Content-Based Literacy: Module Lessons and Additional Language and Literacy Block

MODULE LESSONS

In many ways, the 3–5 curriculum is similar to the K–2 curriculum. The modules are based on compelling topics and use rich, authentic text throughout. Divided into three units each, the modules are designed to build important content knowledge and understanding, as they fully teach and assess all of the ELA standards at each grade level. As in Grades K–2, each module has a consistent structure of three units. But unlike Grades K–2, in Grades 3–5 there are two assessments per unit, which reflects the readiness of students this age to do more independent work and to practice with high-stakes testing formats.

Figure 2.7: 3–5 Module, Unit, and Assessment Structure

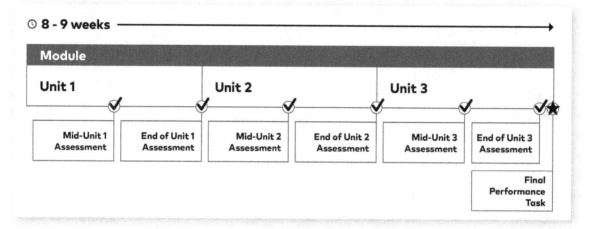

The curriculum was built using the principles of backward design, meaning that we started by identifying what we wanted students to know and be able to do at the end of each module and then built each unit to intentionally get them there. Let's explore what that means in the fourth-grade classroom introduced in the Snapshot at the beginning of this chapter.

The last unit of each module, **Unit 3**, includes the performance task: an extended, supported writing task or presentation in which students need to successfully bring together what they know about the topic. Students Nathan, Sergei, and Alma are writing choose-your-own adventure narratives, bringing together what they know about the armadillo and the defenses it has to help it survive (and what they know about writing).

If this is what students need to be prepared to do in **Unit 3** of the module, what they learn in Units 1 and 2 must help them get there. (This is the principle of backward design in action.)

In **Unit 1**, students read, discuss, dramatize, draw, and write so that they acquire strong and specific content and background knowledge, as well as the literacy skills that they need to do so. Ms. Henderson's fourth-graders learn what "natural defenses" are, what predators do, and the many kinds of defenses that animals have, depending on their habitat. In the process, the students learn to read closely, reread carefully for meaning, gather evidence, and develop a paragraph.

In **Unit 2**, they take this basic understanding to a deeper level. They do more research and discuss with one another what defenses specific animals might have. With close support, they respond to a prompting question to write a full multi-paragraph essay about animal defenses.

Throughout, for homework, students are reading independently at their own level. They are using research texts to gather deeper and deeper knowledge about how animals use natural defenses to survive and thrive.

As the lessons in each unit progress, Ms. Henderson has the opportunity to carefully check in on her students' progress. Each unit has two built-in assessments: a mid-unit assessment (usually reading) and an end of unit assessment (usually writing). These assessments help Ms. Henderson in two ways: They allow her to have a clear sense of what her students can do and cannot yet do, and they give her valuable information about how best to use the time in the ALL Block for her students' benefit.

This structure and sequence means that, by **Unit 3**, Nathan, Sergei, Alma, and all of their classmates are fully equipped to write their choose-your-own adventures about how the armadillo uses its defenses to survive.

EL Education | Your Curriculum Companion

THE ADDITIONAL LANGUAGE AND LITERACY BLOCK

The ALL Block and the Module Lessons are complementary, working together to accelerate the achievement of all students.

The ALL Block has three units, parallel to the three units of the module. Each module unit is accompanied by two weeks of ALL Block instruction (with one flex day built in every week). And when a particular unit of the Module Lessons runs longer than two weeks, the ALL Block hour during those days that extend beyond two weeks is flex time, used to meet the specific needs of students. For example, you might want to provide additional time for work started in Module Lessons, practicing literacy skills introduced there that students are finding particularly challenging, informally assessing reading foundational skills, or offering additional time for ELLs.

Figure 2.8: 3–5 Content-Based Literacy: Module Lessons and Additional Language and Literacy Block

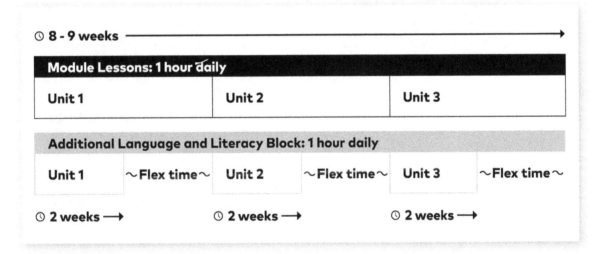

The ALL Block has five components:

» Independent reading

» Additional work with complex text

» Reading and speaking fluency/GUM (grammar, usage, mechanics)

» Writing practice

» Word study and vocabulary

Each component is built into the Module Lessons in various ways, and then is reinforced and practiced in the ALL Block. Over the course of two weeks, students work with all five components.

Keep in mind, this is an intentionally brief description of the ALL Block; we'll provide much more detailed information in Chapter 2B.

KEY FEATURES OF THE 3–5 MODULE LESSONS AND ADDITIONAL LANGUAGE AND LITERACY BLOCK

» **Regular close reading of complex texts**. Students in Grades 3–5 consistently read complex text to gain both deeper content knowledge of the topic and deeper familiarity with the structures, syntax, and vocabulary of complex text.

» **Writing for understanding**. As students write to show understanding of particular content, they both synthesize that content and acquire transferable skills and approaches to new writing situations, becoming more independent writers.

» **Habits of character**. Character is one of EL Education's three Dimensions of Student Achievement. Collaboration, perseverance, a growth mindset, and being able to set goals and then reflect on them are all key aspects of strong social-emotional development and are critical to student success, in school and in life. To help students become independent learners, the 3–5 curriculum continues to build in frequent opportunities for students to collaborate and reflect on their learning.

» **Robust instruction for English language learners**. Throughout the Module Lessons and the ALL Block, ELLs are provided with specific and differentiated instruction and support. In the Module Lessons, ELLs are usually part of the overall heterogeneous grouping in the class. In the ALL Block, there is a strategic mix of heterogeneous grouping and ELL-only grouping to meet specific needs.

» **Building knowledge and literacy skills through a volume of reading**. Students have many opportunities to read a lot on the module topic. This results in stronger vocabulary, stronger content knowledge, and greater ability to write in depth about content.

» **Daily student goal-setting and reflection**. Module Lessons and the ALL Block include learning targets, which are student-friendly "I can" statements that help students know where they are headed with their learning. Teachers help students check back in with their progress during lessons.

» **Sufficient practice of skills for students to demonstrate mastery**. In both the Module Lessons and the ALL Block, all students receive consistent, specific, and differentiated skills practice, in both reading and writing.

» **Culminating performance task**. Unit 3 of each module culminates with a student performance task. Students get support in synthesizing and transferring their knowledge and understanding from the module, in terms of both content and literacy, in an authentic and often collaborative task. This is scaffolded with models, drafts, critique, and revision to lead to high-quality work.

» **Assessment**. Both summative and formative assessments are integral. In each module, six summative assessments are built in (two per unit). Formative assessment happens frequently as teachers observe, collect homework, use checklists, and give feedback to students in Module Lessons and the ALL Block.

The Grades 3–5 Life Science Modules

Our 3–5 curriculum includes one optional Life Science module per grade level. If you choose to teach this optional module, it will represent three additional hours per week of instruction, but only during Module 2, which is approximately eight to nine weeks. Although the Life Science modules can stand alone, each one connects with and complements Module 2 of the grade-level ELA modules.

We will orient you to the Life Science modules here, but we won't provide any additional detail about them in this book. If you do choose to teach these engaging and interesting modules (which we heartily recommend), more instructional support is provided in the Teacher's Guide for each Life Science module. If you are not going to teach the science modules, you might want to skip ahead to the section on assessments.

Table 2.3: The 3–5 Life Science Modules

Grade	Life Science Module
3	Diverse life cycles and inheritance of traits in aquatic plants and animals: This module extends learning about frogs from the ELA module.
4	Ecosystems and specialized structures and their functions in terrestrial plants and animals: This module extends learning about animal defenses from the ELA module.
5	The cycle of energy and matter in a healthy forest ecosystem: This module extends learning about rainforests from the ELA module.

Science is about asking questions, observing carefully, investigating, reflecting, and then drawing conclusions based on evidence. Our Life Science modules for Grades 3–5 are designed to provide teachers and students with an inquiry-based approach to rigorous and authentic science instruction.

Each Life Science module is designed to last eight weeks, with about three hours of science instruction per week. Each addresses and assesses at least one Next Generation Science Standard, explicitly teaches several others, and incorporates the unique features of the NGSS principles of science instruction.

The Life Science modules have been designed for the elementary school generalist, like Ms. Henderson. Each module gives the regular classroom teacher the plans, the background content, and the resources she needs to provide strong, rigorous, literacy-integrated science instruction. For the classroom teacher, the goal of our science curriculum is the recognition that science can be fun—both to learn and to teach!

THE STRUCTURE AND STORY OF A LIFE SCIENCE MODULE

Like the ELA modules, each of the Life Science modules has been backward designed from the performance task and the summative assessment. Let's explore what that means in the fourth-grade classroom introduced in the Snapshot at the beginning of this chapter.

In Ms. Henderson's fourth-grade class, Nathan, Sergei, and Alma will be designing a fictional animal and creating an explanatory model to show how the animal's structures work together to help the animal survive in a specific ecosystem. Finally, they will each write a paragraph to argue that the animal they designed can survive well in a given habitat.

What will the instruction include, so that these fourth-graders have a genuine opportunity to be both engaged and successful?

» **Anchoring phenomenon.** Each module begins with an "anchoring phenomenon." This is an event set up by the teacher that raises an "I wonder" question for students (NGSS: Disciplinary Core Ideas). It is an "anchor" in the sense that the questions students generate drive the rest of the module for them.

• For example, Nathan, Sergei, Alma, and their classmates look at two pictures—one is a fictional, cartoon beetle, and the other is a beetle discovered *after* the cartoon was created. Students note the remarkable resemblance between the two and ask themselves: "How does someone imagine an animal that is so realistic that it really might exist? Could I do that? What would I need to know to create a realistic but fictional animal?"

» **Building background knowledge.** Students learn about structures in animals and plants and how they function to allow the organism to survive. They build/draw explanatory models and carry out original investigations (NGSS: Science and Engineering Practices). They explore the connections among the structural elements that allow the organism to survive (NGSS: Cross-Cutting Concepts).

- For example, our fourth-graders work with complex texts in close reading sessions, as well as a variety of other texts, as they build knowledge. They then speak and write about that understanding in clear, focused paragraphs (all important ELA standards). Throughout the lessons, students are brainstorming and revising the structures on their own fictional animal.

  » **Performance task**. In the final week, students put their deep knowledge and understanding of structures and their role in the survival of plants and animals to work as they design an animal whose structures help it to survive in a given habitat (which itself has key structures that allow it to flourish).

  - For example, Nathan, Sergei, and Alma create an explanatory model with labels on each structure that explain how the structures help the animal survive. They then present their model to an authentic audience to help them decide if what they have created is indeed an animal so realistic that it may, one day, be discovered.

THREE-DIMENSIONAL SCIENCE INSTRUCTION

The Next Generation Science Standards (NGSS) reflect a significant shift from earlier science instruction. Each of the NGSS standards is described in terms of a *performance expectation*: What should a student know and be able to do with that particular science concept at the end of instruction? In addition to naming a specific performance expectation, each science standard is described in terms of three dimensions. (These three dimensions are a key structure of the NGSS and shouldn't be confused with EL Education's three Dimensions of Student Achievement, introduced in Chapter 1 and referenced throughout this book.)

Table 2.4: The Three Dimensions of the Next Generation Science Standards

Science and Engineering Practices	Disciplinary Core Ideas	Cross-Cutting Concepts
Students ask questions and define problems related to the topic. They make explanatory models and revise them as they learn more. They set up investigations, gather evidence, and make thoughtful claims supported by reasoning, both orally and in writing.	This is the actual content and information that students are learning about a topic. In the EL Education Life Science modules, the content is some aspect of life science, which varies by grade level. This knowledge functions as the anchor of the module.	Students learn that there are ways of thinking and underlying "big ideas" that are not specific to a topic (or even to science) and extend across and through many topics. This includes ideas like systems, patterns, and cause-effect relationships. They are the "glue" that holds ideas together.

KEY FEATURES OF THE 3–5 LIFE SCIENCE MODULES

» **Science notebooks**. From the beginning of the module, each student keeps an interactive science notebook and uses it every day. Modeled after the way "real scientists" use notebooks, these are set up for students to include both a prompting question for the particular lesson sequence and space for students to think and work.

» **Scientists Meetings**. Scientists Meetings occur at least once a week. They give students the opportunity to translate their thinking into language that can be shared with others and revisited over time. Talking about ideas allows students to reconsider and revise their developing ideas as they listen to classmates.

» **Flexible time for lessons**. Unlike the ELA components of the curriculum, which are one hour long, the time allotted for each lesson sequence of the Life Science modules is flexible. You are encouraged to plan science instruction on a weekly, not daily, basis and adjust times for investigations as needed.

» **Self-coaching prompts for teachers**. Many elementary generalists may lack confidence teaching science. Every lesson includes questions for you to consider to help guide student inquiry, reflect on what students know and need, and anticipate classroom management needs.

» **ELA Standards**. The standards that are so central to the ELA modules are central to the Life Science modules as well. Students engage in close reading of complex texts and acquire and use key academic and domain-specific vocabulary. They discuss and process their understanding in frequent guided conversations in Scientists Meetings, and they write arguments and scientific explanations supported by accurate, reasoned evidence.

▶ Assessments in the K–5 Curriculum: I've Taught It— How Will I Know If They've Learned It?

Our K–5 curriculum explicitly teaches and formally assesses all strands and standards of the Common Core ELA standards. (Note: The optional 3–5 Life Science modules include assessments to address the NGSS.)

Key features of the assessment system include:

» All components emphasize formative (ongoing) assessment.

» All components emphasize daily learning targets and checking for understanding techniques.

» Three components include formal assessments: Skills Block, K–2 Module Lessons, 3–5 Module Lessons).

» Two components do not include formal assessments: Labs and the ALL Block.

It is important to note that Module Lessons at all grade levels feature performance tasks. These culminating tasks help students synthesize and apply their learning from the module, often in a real-world format. Performance tasks in the Module Lessons are highly scaffolded and collaborative, so they should not be considered summative assessments.

Table 2.5: Assessment System for Each Component of the K–5 Curriculum

Curriculum Component	Assessment System
K–2 Reading Foundations Skills Block *Hour-long explicit instruction in the alphabetic code, phonemic awareness, phonological awareness, concepts of print, and spelling; 15 to 20 minutes whole group instruction and 40 to 45 minutes differentiated small group work*	Explicitly teaches and formally assesses: » Common Core State Standards (CCSS) Reading: Foundational Skills standards (phonemic awareness, phonological awareness, decoding, fluency, and concepts of print) » CCSS Language standards associated with spelling and letter formation Assessments are based on phases of reading and spelling development, which determines whether students are in the Pre-Alphabetic, Partial Alphabetic, Full Alphabetic, or Consolidated Alphabetic phase: » Benchmark assessments (three times/year) to address all CCSS Reading: Foundational Skills standards (e.g., Phonological Awareness, Fluency, and Spelling) » Cycle assessments (weekly[1]) to assess targeted reading/spelling pattern (cycle assessments begin in kindergarten Module 4) » Daily snapshot assessments and exit tickets Student reflection and goal-setting (weekly)
K–2 Module Lessons *Hour-long whole group lessons in which students read, think, talk, and write about compelling science and social studies content*	Explicitly teaches and formally assesses: » CCSS Reading: Informational Text standards (comprehension) » CCSS Reading: Literature standards (comprehension) » CCSS Writing standards » CCSS Speaking and Listening standards » CCSS Language standards (Note: Language standards associated with spelling and letter formation are taught and assessed in the Skills Block.) Each module contains three formal assessments (one per unit): reading, writing, and speaking and listening: » Reading assessments based on the requirements of the standards and common formats of high-stakes tests (Grade 2) » Writing assessments based on K–5 writing rubrics EL Education has developed (a synthesis of PARCC, Smarter Balanced, and our own expertise) » Speaking and listening assessments based on checklists (used informally throughout the module and sometimes during a specific discussion or presentation that is formally assessed) » Language standards are bundled with reading, writing, or speaking standards. Priority standards are assessed in multiple modules: » CCSS RI/RL.1, 2, 4; CCSS W.1, 2, 3; CCSS SL.1 Often, standards are assessed in a variety of ways (e.g., drawing, writing, selected response). Each module also includes a culminating performance task. This is not a formal assessment (since it is always scaffolded), yet the performance task still offers rich data for teachers about students' mastery toward standards: » Heavily scaffolded, with models, critique, and revision » Often collaborative

Cont.

[1] Due to the length of Skills Block assessments in Grade 2, there are full cycle assessments provided only every two or three weeks. There are brief, optional cycle assessments provided for the weeks in between.

Curriculum Component	Assessment System
K–2 Labs *Hour-long small group inquiry-based learning aligned to science or social studies content of Module Lessons; a time to explore, play, apply, and develop speaking and listening skills*	No formal summative assessments » Labs checklists with targeted ELA standards are provided with recommendations for how to use them for formative assessment.
3–5 Module Lessons *Hour-long whole group lessons in which students read, think, talk, and write about compelling science and social studies content*	Explicitly teaches and formally assesses: » CCSS Reading: Informational Text standards (comprehension) » CCSS Reading: Literature standards (comprehension) » CCSS Reading: Foundational Skills standards » CCSS Writing standards » CCSS Speaking and Listening standards » CCSS Language standards Each module contains six formal assessments (two per unit). Usually the mid-unit assessment emphasizes reading and the end of unit assessment emphasizes writing, but this pattern may be inconsistent depending on the design of a specific unit: » Reading assessments based on the requirements of the standards, our own expertise, and common formats of high-stakes tests » Writing assessments based on K–5 writing rubrics EL Education has developed (a synthesis of PARCC, Smarter Balanced, and our own expertise) » Speaking and listening assessments (discussions, presentations, and performances), as well as opportunities to informally assess speaking and listening skills using checklists » Language standards are bundled with reading, writing, or speaking standards (rather than assessed discretely). Priority standards are assessed in multiple modules with progress tracked by students and teachers across the year: » CCSS RI/RL.1, 2, 4, 10; CCSS W.1, 2, 3, 7, 8; CCSS SL.1 Each module also includes a culminating performance task. This is not a formal assessment (since it is always scaffolded), yet the performance task still offers rich data for teachers about students' mastery toward standards: » Heavily scaffolded, with models, critique, and revision » Often collaborative

Cont.

Curriculum Component	Assessment System
3–5 Additional Language and Literacy Block *Hour-long small group work featuring extensive and differentiated practice and support with reading fluency and grammar, word study, additional work with complex text, writing fluency, and accountable independent reading; includes teacher directions and student task cards for independent work, with specific instructional guides for ELLs*	No formal summative assessments Speaking and listening checklists and writing process checklists are provided for formative assessment, with recommendations on when and how they can be used Independently completed student task cards

Chapter 2

Chapter 2B:
How Will the K–2 Labs and 3–5 Additional Language and Literacy Block Deepen and Enhance My Students' Learning?

The first edition of our curriculum, for Grades 3–8, which was published in 2012, offered only one hour of instruction. The Module Lessons were the entire curriculum. We certainly did our best to cover as much territory as we could in that one hour, but we were unable to claim that it was a comprehensive curriculum because it didn't explicitly teach and formally assess all college- and career-ready English language arts (ELA)/literacy standards.

In this second edition of the curriculum for Grades 3–5 and brand-new for Grades K–2, we have responded to feedback from teachers and leaders and added additional components that give you the opportunity to teach a curriculum that is comprehensive. In addition to explicitly teaching and formally assessing all of the standards, the curriculum also offers time to reinforce and give students additional practice with important skills, time for creativity and play, and time to help them be leaders of their own learning by developing strong habits of character.

We will cover the details of the K–2 Reading Foundations Skills Block (Skills Block) in Chapter 4. Here we will focus on the K–2 Labs (Labs) and 3–5 Additional Language and Literacy (ALL) Block. These hour-long blocks are designed to give students more time to deepen their content knowledge and literacy skills through exploration, play, and additional time for reading, writing, and speaking. These complementary blocks, when joined with the Module Lessons, comprise two hours of content-based literacy.

Though they are tightly connected to the Module Lessons, Labs and the ALL Block unfold a bit differently. Here in Chapter 2B, we'll explain the structure and purpose of each, as well as special logistical considerations, so that you are well prepared to challenge, engage, and empower students with this additional time.

▶ How Are the K–2 Labs Designed with My Students' Needs in Mind?

Primary learners need exploration (active learning, rather than passive), independence (a sense of mastery and accomplishment), wonder (an authentic need to answer a question or solve a problem), and collaboration (the ability to talk with, and learn from, their peers). This is why the Labs exist. One hour per day of content-based literacy instruction in the Module Lessons—even very strong literacy instruction—is not enough. The additional hour spent in the Labs is an important part of accelerating literacy learning and ensuring equity for all students. The Labs address a different, and complementary, way of accessing complex ideas, content knowledge, literacy skills, and habits of character than the Module Lessons can do on their own. This point of access is vital for the success of all primary learners.

> *"I have loved seeing how the Labs bring the curriculum to life. As a teacher who adamantly believes in the power of play, I have been thrilled to use a curriculum that celebrates play in such a meaningful way. My students have been deepening their content knowledge, academic vocabulary, and collaboration skills while having a blast every day. Labs are the highlight of their day, and it has been amazing to see them transform into content experts during this time!"*

Annie Holyfield

K–1 Teacher, Denver

Meeting the Developmental Needs of Primary Learners

Each of the components of our K–2 curriculum (Module Lessons, Labs, and the Skills Block) honors the characteristics and needs of the primary learner. But Labs in particular are designed to help you make sure that all of your students play and explore, become immersed in exploring content, develop oral language, and practice skills and habits of character that they need—both to live joyfully and to be fully successful and proficient. What follows is some of the research that points to the need for such focus.

» **Play and social behaviors**. Research shows that giving primary learners student-directed, collaborative spaces has a direct effect on their academic and social success. In a child-directed, play-based environment, children are more likely to "rise to the challenge" of negotiating complex social scenarios and exhibit levels of maturity greater than outside of these environments (Berk and Meyers, 2013). The Labs, which provide students with a large degree of independence, invite them to become their best selves, both in their own learning and in their interactions with peers.

» **Executive functioning skills**. Labs give students an authentic need to learn and practice executive functioning skills, including setting goals, controlling attention, self-monitoring, organizing, and reflecting, that translate to other aspects of their learning and social lives. The Labs do this by dedicating time, instruction, and practice to goal-setting and reflection and also by immersing students in authentic, compelling tasks with highly engaging materials. Research indicates that development of executive functioning skills in early childhood is a strong predictor of academic achievement through high school (Berk and Meyers, 2013).

» **Multiple intelligences**. Labs invite all students into the learning process through the use of multiple modalities and a variety of materials that may not be available in other parts of the curriculum. Children form their identities and identify their strengths by experimenting with a variety of activities and mediums, and they do this best in a playful and child-directed space (Eberle, 2011). As a result, a greater number of students are able to feel successful in their learning and, therefore, develop more positive attitudes about school, increase their engagement, and deepen their learning.

» **Building content knowledge**. Students make meaning about the world and the content they are studying in diverse ways. Studies have shown that students who are engaged in projects that provide a variety of entry points (e.g., art, music, drama) into a single topic make more connections and are better able to engage in content-connected discourse with their peers (Halvorsen, Duke, Brugar, Block, Strachan, Berka, and Brown, 2012). The Labs provide these multiple points of entry to the topic being studied in the Module Lessons. As a result, students deepen their content knowledge, are more likely to meaningfully engage in the topic, and have more spontaneous and authentic conversation about the topic with their peers.

» **Oral language**. Young learners love to talk. The Labs use this basic truth as a learning opportunity, harnessing student conversation as a learning tool to build content knowledge as well as foster language development. Research shows that when children are in control of an interaction, as they are in the Labs, they are more engaged. This engagement, which emerges from a sincere curiosity and personal stake in the conversation, leads to learning a greater number of words and more sentence structures. Students' acquisition of language in play environments is especially potent in "guided play," in which an adult has carefully created scenarios and provided materials to help lead students to pre-determined learning goals (Weisberg, Zosh, Hirsh-Pasek, and Golinkoff, 2013).

For ELLs, oral language is particularly important. It is the basis for reading with comprehension and writing fluency. Therefore, for ELLs, it is important to opt for more productive interactions and academically based conversations, such as those cultivated in the Labs. The Labs also provide opportunities for ELLs to participate in extended, task-based interactions with peers, with teachers present to provide guidance and feedback to support effective communication. This affords ELLs authentic opportunities to self-correct and to grapple with language to achieve specific goals. Second language development is enhanced when students negotiate meaning through collaboration on authentic tasks (Long, 1996).

Deepening and Enhancing Learning in Each of the Five Labs

There are five distinct Labs. Table 2.6 describes how each Lab is designed to promote student proficiency and growth.

Table 2.6: The Five Labs and How Each Promotes Proficiency and Growth

Lab	How This Lab Promotes Proficiency and Growth
Explore *Students build background knowledge and immerse themselves in a hands-on exploration of the content they are studying in the module.*	Young children are natural explorers and scientists. They learn first by doing. The Explore Lab gives them a space for this. Students wonder, handle authentic objects and tools, and experiment. They may try and fail, and then try again. The Explore Lab allows students to make meaning of abstract ideas and build content knowledge through hands-on, collaborative activities.
Engineer *Students represent their learning and/or attempt to solve a design dilemma by building or designing various types of two- or three-dimensional models related to the content of the module.*	In an ever-changing and quickly moving world, we cannot yet imagine some of the careers, opportunities, and obstacles of the future. We do know, however, that certain skills will be invaluable to our students: design thinking, problem-solving, and collaboration. In the Engineer Lab, students engage in the design process, independently and collaboratively, to solve problems and address wants and needs. Problem-solving, content knowledge, and play come together as students become scientists, engineers, designers, and inventors.
Create *Students use a variety of media to artistically expand and represent their content learning through visual arts.*	As young learners' literacy skills continue to emerge, the Create Lab gives students the opportunity to express a range of content understanding through another modality: the visual arts. This medium helps students develop their fine motor skills, a sense of craftsmanship in their work, and the perseverance required to take a product through multiple drafts.
Imagine *Students use their imaginations to engage in play through role-playing and make-believe. Students take on, interpret, and become immersed in the content they are studying as they play and perform. In Grades 1 and 2, in Module 4, students write and perform narratives.*	One of the most powerful learning tools at the disposal of primary learners is also one of the most obvious, yet most overlooked: play. Play provides a joyful context for students to build the vital life skills often more difficult to re-create in more structured learning environments: leadership, negotiation, decision-making, and executive functioning. Through content-connected play and storytelling, the Imagine Lab gives students the time and the tools (in both the concrete and abstract sense) to narrate their own worlds, grapple with complex ideas, and navigate social interactions.

Lab	How This Lab Promotes Proficiency and Growth
Research *Students expand their understanding and knowledge of content through a range of research activities: They study pictures and photographs, watch videos, and conduct original research based on their own questions. As students acquire greater literacy skills, they are able to read a variety of texts to build content knowledge and write to build fluency and stamina. At all grade levels, the Research Lab begins in Module 2. This gives students time to build strong reading and writing routines in other parts of the curriculum before expanding the volume of reading and writing in the Labs.*	Young learners have a lot of questions. Sometimes these questions are answered in the course of whole group learning, but often not. The Research Lab gives students the materials, the skills, and the space to pursue answers to questions. In the Research Lab, students have the space, time, and materials to answer teacher-generated questions or their own burning questions about the content they are learning in the Module Lessons. This pursuit of knowledge creates an authentic need for students to increase their volume of reading, build word and world knowledge, and communicate (in a variety of ways) their learning with others.

Reinforcing and Extending the Work from the Module Lessons

Labs are scaffolded experiences with specific learning related to literacy skills, content knowledge, and habits of character. Each Lab connects to and extends what students are learning during the Module Lessons.

For example, in Grade 1, Module 1, students are learning about tools. The literacy and content focus of the module revolves around reading and writing about tools, including the anchor text *The Most Magnificent Thing*. Students also spend time using tools. For the performance task at the end of the module, students design, build, and write about their own "magnificent thing" for classroom use. The four Labs for Module 1 support this work:

» **Create Lab**. Students use real-world tools, or pictures of tools, as models, as well as a set of skills in their "Artist's Toolbelt," to create realistic drawings of tools (e.g., construction tools, cooking tools). They practice perseverance as they grapple with drawing lines and texture, and craftsmanship as they create multiple drafts incorporating peer feedback.

» **Engineer Lab**. Students use a variety of materials to create their own "magnificent thing" like the character in one of the module's central texts. Students work with a partner to practice collaboration and working through a design process.

» **Explore Lab**. Students experiment with moving a material (e.g., water, rice, or beans) from one container to another using a variety of tools. Working with a partner, they time their work, eventually determining the "best tool for the job."

» **Imagine Lab**. Students use blocks, puppets, dress-up materials, and writing spaces to create imaginative play scenarios, independently and collaboratively. They explore ways to bring the stories of the module to life or create their own stories based on narrative structures and content they are learning.

Building Independence and Habits of Character with a Consistent Structure

For any given module, students will rotate through four of the five Labs. Each of the four Labs unfold in a similar way across the entire module. The hour-long Labs time is divided into four daily activities:

» **10 minutes: Storytime**. Students listen to a rich text read aloud (core instruction, aligned to CCSS R.10).

» **5 minutes: Goal-setting**. Students decide on and articulate what their individual goals are for the Labs for that day.

» **40 minutes: In the Labs**. Students work in the Labs. Depending on the stage, students may spend the whole time in one Lab or move between two Labs. (More information about the stages is provided in the pages that follow.)

» **5 minutes: Reflection**. Students discuss and reflect on how their time went in the Labs. What went well? What might they still need to work on?

Figure 2.9: The Labs Hour

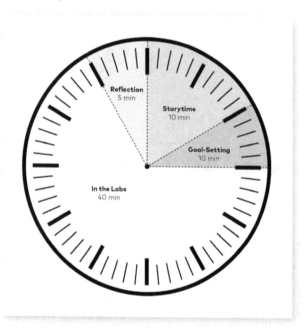

Promoting Growth: How the Labs Unfold over the Course of a Module

Labs unfold across an entire module. In any given module, however, just four of the five Labs will be used. This design helps to limit the number of materials and overall preparation required at any given time. It also supports students by limiting the number of learning targets and helping them track the purpose, expectations, and materials for the Labs with which they are engaged. Finally, some Labs are a more natural fit for certain modules. For example, when first-graders are studying light and shadow in Module 2, it makes more sense for them to explore these phenomena in the Explore Lab than in the Engineer Lab; therefore, the Engineer Lab is not a part of that module.

Each of the four Labs runs across the whole module and goes through stages: the Launch, Practice, Extend, and Choice and Challenge stages. The stages are designed to intentionally build students' learning experiences in a way that leads to a final product. Every Lab goes through the first three stages, but not every Lab goes all the way through the Choice and Challenge stage. Figure 2.10 and Table 2.7 will help you understand how the Labs progress through the stages.

For each module, Labs start a week after the module begins and end a week before the module ends. This design allows you to use your discretion to flexibly schedule the Labs to best meet the needs of your classroom. You may choose to spend that hour during those additional two to three weeks on such things as solidifying structures and routines, providing additional "spillover" time to support Module Lessons, providing additional instructional time for ELLs, or for additional explicit language instruction.

Figure 2.10: How Labs Unfold across a Module in Four Stages

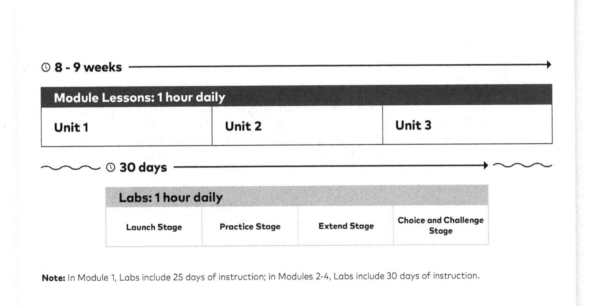

Note: In Module 1, Labs include 25 days of instruction; in Modules 2-4, Labs include 30 days of instruction.

The overarching intent of Labs is to build student independence. Therefore, they are structured to gradually release responsibility from the teacher and gradually increase independence of the student across the six weeks:

- » **Launch**. Students are introduced to each of the four Labs that will be used during the module, including learning targets, materials, and expectations.

- » **Practice**. Students continue to work toward the learning targets, explore materials, and practice the expectations that were established in the Launch stage.

- » **Extend**. Each Lab becomes more complex, in terms of the task, the materials used, and/or the level of independence in the student experience.

- » **Choice and Challenge**. Students choose one Lab to specialize in at this stage. This stage culminates in creating a Labs product.

In all four stages, Labs are an hour long, and much of the daily schedule remains the same: Students always start with Storytime and then set goals; they always end with reflection. But across the four stages, the "In the Lab" time looks different, as students gradually increase in independence across the six weeks. Table 2.7 will give you a better feel for what the daily schedule might look like during each of these stages.

Table 2.7: Labs Daily Schedule: Increased Independence during "In the Labs" Time[2]

Daily Activity	Description
Storytime (10 minutes)	The first 10 minutes of Lab time, no matter what stage, is Storytime. You have lots of flexibility in the texts you choose; suggestions for texts and structure of these 10 minutes are included in the EL Education K–2 Labs: Teacher Guide (Teacher Guide) that accompanies each module.
Setting Lab Goals (5 minutes)	Five minutes is spent on goal-setting during all stages. Specific learning targets and questions are offered in the Teacher Guide that accompanies each module.

In the Lab
(40 minutes)

Launch stage:	Practice stage:	Extend stage:	Choice and Challenge stage:
During the Launch stage, students are introduced to each of the four Labs for the module, one Lab per day. They learn the focus and routines so they are prepared for greater independence in subsequent stages.	During the Practice stage, students work in two Labs each day (for 20 minutes each). They have greater independence than in the Launch stage as they rotate through the Labs. Students will rotate through all four Labs during this stage. You can sequence the Lab rotations in whatever way you think is best for your students.	Students spend the first two days of the Extend stage in whole group lessons clarifying expectations for their work in each Lab before beginning a more independent rotation through two Labs per day. At this stage, the materials and/or the task change for added complexity. Students will rotate through all four Labs during this stage. You can sequence the Lab rotations in whatever way you think is best for your students.	Students choose one Lab to specialize in. In this Lab, students will complete a different task than they did the first time through the Lab. This task challenges them in a new way. Students work on a product, give and receive feedback, apply feedback, and share their final product.

Reflecting on Learning (5 minutes)	Five minutes is spent reflecting on learning and reinforcing habits of character every day during every Lab stage. Specific guidance on reflection questions and activities is offered in the Teacher Guide that accompanies each module.

Throughout the "In the Lab" time, students work on different tasks throughout the room. For the most part, you will be circulating and supporting students in all Labs. However, some Labs, due to the complexity of the task or the materials involved, will require greater support than others. You will need to use your best professional judgment as to where to focus your time and energy. We have also provided checklists that you can use as you circulate to collect individual student data regarding literacy skills and habits of character.

---

[2] Specific guidance on what students experience during the Labs and how to prepare the materials is offered in the EL Education K–2 Labs: Teacher Guide that accompanies each module (e.g., suggested text and structure for Storytime, learning targets and questions to support goal-setting, reflection questions, and activities). Teacher Guides do not provide day-to-day lesson plans, but a lesson plan is provided for the first day of a new stage when students are introduced to new tasks, materials, and expectations. Thereafter, students have ongoing tasks and goals for the remainder of the stage. A Labs Day-to-Day schedule is also included in the Labs Overview that accompanies each module. This is a recommended schedule for implementing the four stages of Labs over the course of the module.

In Chapter 3A, we will walk you through the process of analyzing the various overview documents that will prepare you to teach all parts of the curriculum, including the Labs.

Grouping Students during Labs

Your grouping strategy for Labs is an important part of your planning process. Since all of the Labs require varying levels of student collaboration, students will need to rely on each other to stay engaged and productive and to meet learning targets. Taking the time to create, support, and celebrate a collaborative learning environment will support your students in this work. (Note: Creating an active and collaborative classroom culture that is conducive to this work is the subject of Chapter 3C.)

During Labs, students should be grouped heterogeneously, including ELLs. Lab groups should be balanced in regard to students' abilities as readers and writers, their language development, their work styles, and their strengths and needs in habits of character. All students have something to offer, and all students can benefit from others in some way. Students may surprise you in terms of what they can handle when given explicit modeling and sufficient practice.

The Snapshot that follows describes a typical day for Ms. Sanchez and her first-graders.

📷 **Snapshot: A Day in the Labs**

On Wednesday morning, Ms. Sanchez worked on Unit 3, Lesson 2 of the Module Lessons. Today, after lunch, students begin work on Day 13 of the Labs (the second day of the Extend stage). Throughout the Launch and Practice stages leading up to this session, students met the learning targets and become familiar with the basic materials for each Lab. Now they are ready for the new challenges in the Extend stage.

Before the launch of the Labs, Ms. Sanchez divided her class into four Lab groups. She created these heterogeneous groupings by carefully balancing students' academic strengths and needs, language needs, and habits of character. Each of the four Lab groups has stayed together through the first three stages of the Labs experience (Launch, Practice, and Extend). Grouping during the final stage—Choice and Challenge—will largely be determined by student interests. Today's groups are as follows:

» Bears (Anna and five other students)

» Birds (Elvin and five other students)

» Butterflies (Kristina and five other students)

» Bees (Omar and five other students)

Ms. Sanchez has posted the Labs Daily Schedule so that each group knows which two Labs they will visit today.

Ms. Sanchez begins singing the Labs song, a familiar way to signal that Labs are beginning. As students join the song, they move to a designated spot in the whole group meeting area near their Lab group.

Once students are settled, Ms. Sanchez introduces the book for Storytime, a story about a boy baking birthday treats in his kitchen. Before she begins reading, she invites students to think about the questions: "What tools does the boy in this story use?" and "How does the boy collaborate, or work together with others, throughout the story?" Ms. Sanchez proceeds to read the story slowly and fluently, without interruption, pausing occasionally to clarify unknown words or remind students of the focus questions.

After reading the story, Ms. Sanchez directs students' attention to the Labs Daily Schedule. She invites students to find their Lab group on the schedule and then silently point to the Lab space in the room they will visit first. She reminds students of the learning targets and purpose for each Lab (both of which were introduced in previous Lab sessions). Then she asks students to turn to a partner and, using a familiar sentence frame, articulate their goal for their time in that Lab. She repeats this process for the second Lab students will visit. Ms. Sanchez invites students to dramatically put on their imaginary lab coats and their imaginary lab goggles before transitioning to their four separate Lab spaces.

The Bears' first Lab that day is the Create Lab. Anna and her Lab group head to the Create Lab space, which Ms. Sanchez has already prepared with paper, pencils, colored pencils, magnifying glasses, a variety of tools (or photographs of tools), a laminated card with different types of lines, and an anchor chart about drawing different textures. Anna and her group get to work drawing, or revising, realistic pictures of tools, many of which they have encountered in the Module Lessons.

The Birds are headed to the Engineer Lab. Elvin and his Lab group go to the Engineer Lab space, which is filled with a variety of building materials: cardboard, paper bags, paper, pipe cleaners, string, tape, and scissors. There are also a variety of real-world objects (or photographs of objects) that serve as models: boxes with hinges and clasps, picture frames, a matchbox car organizer. Elvin is working with his Lab partner today. They need to collaborate in a design process that Ms. Sanchez showed them during previous Lab sessions. Their design challenge: Use the materials of the Engineer Lab to re-create one of these real-world objects. Elvin and his partner get to work talking together to decide which object they are going to build, and then they begin choosing the materials they will need to build it.

The Butterflies begin in the Imagine Lab today. Kristina wants to use the puppets. She set a goal of re-creating one of the stories the class is studying in a close read-aloud. Another student in Kristina's Lab group wants to use the puppets as well. At first, the two cannot resolve who will use the puppets first. However, Ms. Sanchez, who is checking in with the Butterflies, reminds the students of their conversations about respect of materials and peers, as well as their practice with collaboration. Kristina and the other student decide to work together: They will first use the blocks to build a small stage and then create a puppet show together.

Meanwhile, the Bees are visiting the Explore Lab first. Omar and his team are exploring a variety of tools that help move materials. Ms. Sanchez has set up this space with two large bowls, one filled with beans; a funnel; measuring cups; spoons; tweezers; and a stopwatch. Omar and his Lab partner are trying to discover the fastest way to move the beans from one bowl to another and determine the best tools for the job. One student serves as the timer while Omar uses the measuring cup to start moving the rice. After they have finished, recorded their results, and talked about the process, they decide to try again. They decide that the funnel may help them get the rice in faster, so they try it again.

Throughout this first part of Lab time, Ms. Sanchez has been circulating through the room, supporting students in their work and using a checklist to monitor their progress toward the targeted standards for the Lab. She has ensured that students are clear in their goals and use of materials. She has discussed with students their thinking behind choices they are making. She has helped students make connections between this work and the learning from their Module Lessons. And she has given students specific, positive feedback for their displays of habits of character.

After about 20 minutes in the Lab, Ms. Sanchez gives the familiar signal to clean up Lab spaces. Students reset their Lab stations by putting materials back where they found them and storing their work in the designated storage space. Once Ms. Sanchez has determined that the Lab spaces are cleaned up, she invites students to point to their next

Lab space, think about their goal for that Lab, and then transition with their Lab group to the second Lab of the day. Students then begin work in their second Lab.

At the conclusion of the next 20 minutes, Ms. Sanchez once again gives the signal to clean up. She gives students specific, positive feedback on their organization and respect for materials. Once again, Ms. Sanchez begins to sing the Labs song. As students join in the song, they return to the whole group meeting area. Once students are settled, Ms. Sanchez invites students to quietly reflect on the question: "What is something you did in the Labs today that you are really proud of?" Students give her a silent signal—thumbs-up on their knees—when they have thought of something. When all, or the majority, of students have signaled, Ms. Sanchez uses a total participation technique for students to share their ideas. Kristina says, "I'm proud of how Marissa and I solved our problem when we both wanted to use puppets to act out the story." Ms. Sanchez then asks, "What is something you want to do better tomorrow?" Again, students reflect quietly before sharing their goals for the next day. Omar says, "The next time I visit the Explore Lab, I want to remember everything I have already learned about tools so I can make a better choice about which is best for the job."

▶ How Will the 3–5 Additional Language and Literacy Block Sharpen Skills and Build Mastery in My Students?

The ALL Block responds to upper elementary age students' need for greater independence and mastery as learners. Certain aspects of the literacy work in the Module Lessons require that students get more practice to achieve mastery. This is why the ALL Block exists. During this hour, students have additional time to work with texts, ideas, and skills that are initially introduced in the Module Lessons. They also have time set aside every day in the ALL Block to read—something that all too often gets lost in the shuffle of a busy school schedule.

Promoting Proficiency and Growth

To better understand the *why* behind the design of this hour of instruction, Table 2.8 describes each component of the ALL Block and describes how it promotes proficiency and growth.

Table 2.8: The Five Components of the Additional Language and Literacy Block and How Each Promotes Proficiency and Growth

Component	How It Promotes Proficiency and Growth
Accountable Independent Reading/Volume of Reading *Content-related reading at each student's independent reading level; free-choice reading*	In recent years, it has become clearer that one of the reasons strong readers are strong readers is that they read a lot. Research confirms what common sense might tell us: The more one reads, the more one knows—about the topic, about vocabulary, about syntax, even about related topics. With this firmly in mind, volume of reading has been intentionally built into our curriculum. In the ALL Block students' independent reading is most often independent research reading on the module topic. Through research reading, students build background knowledge and vocabulary—both domain-specific and academic. However, students also have time for free-choice reading to build their motivation and love of reading. The ALL Block gives students time for both of these kinds of reading.

Cont.

Component	How It Promotes Proficiency and Growth
  Additional Work with Complex Text *Rereading complex text from the module with a specific focus (e.g., making inferences)*	New college- and career-ready standards remind us how important it is for all students to be able to successfully read (and understand) complex text throughout the grades. We take seriously the fact that if we are going to truly prepare students for college and career, we need to make sure they can successfully navigate complex text. Deep knowledge, rich syntax, and strong vocabulary all come from frequent and successful immersion in complex text (Shanahan, Fisher, and Frey, 2012; Hiebert, 2012; Gomez, 2008; Liben, 2010). The ALL Block gives students additional time to work with the complex texts from the Module Lessons. Furthermore, a growing body of research suggests that instruction with increasingly complex texts within the study of a single topic (such as the American Revolution) can lead to significant gains in reading rate, vocabulary acquisition, and comprehension (Adams, 2009; Morgan, Wilcox, and Eldredge, 2000; O'Connor, Swanson, and Geraghty, 2010; Williams, Stafford, Lauer, Hall, and Pollini, 2009). Essentially, as students learn more about a topic, they can read more difficult texts on that topic and, if given support, improve their foundational reading and comprehension skills. In fact, they can even read more complex text on new topics.
  Reading and Speaking Fluency/Grammar, Usage, and Mechanics (GUM) *Practice with oral reading, speaking with expression, and grammar rules*	If students are going to read and write successfully and proficiently, they will need to read fluently (silently and orally) and speak and write competently in standard English. Practice with these literacy skills has been put together into one section of the ALL Block for two reasons: 1) convenience in scheduling, and 2) because understanding the standard conventions of written English helps students read more fluently. Reading and speaking fluency: When a student is reading fluently, he is reading smoothly, naming the words correctly and automatically, using appropriate phrasing, and attending to the punctuation. When one listens to a fluent reader, one is able to pay attention to the meaning of the passage. More important, the student who is reading fluently is able to pay attention to the meaning of the passage. He does not have to stop and take apart words to decode them; they have become sight words, and he can read with automaticity. GUM: When students write, the writing must make sense to other people. Thus, it is important that students learn the standard conventions of written English, including usage, mechanics, capitalization, and punctuation. Research tells us that the most useful way to teach these conventions is through the use of good models, as well as targeted mini lessons in the editing stages of writing.

Cont.

Component	How It Promotes Proficiency and Growth
Writing Practice *Writing fluency practice; QuickWrites; additional practice with specific skills*	Students need to write for different purposes; broadly, they need to write to learn for themselves, and they need to write to construct and communicate meaning for other people. Within this broad construct of "writing practice," students need to become fluent with writing, and they need specific skills of writing structure and craft. Writing fluency: Fluent writers are not stopped by any of the physical or cognitive aspects of writing. They are comfortable with the pencil and/or the keyboard and are not hindered by questions of where to begin or how to connect ideas in writing. Fluent writers also have writing stamina; they are comfortable with a grade-appropriate task and can sustain it for an appropriate amount of time. Writing to learn: Students need many opportunities to write brief summaries of what they think they know, reflect on the significance of an idea with which they've been working, or respond to a thought-provoking question. When students use writing in these ways, they are literally learning and discovering from the act of writing itself, and all students need these opportunities frequently. Writing to communicate: Ultimately, we teach students to write so that they can communicate their thinking to others clearly, accurately, and effectively. In addition to the huge, fundamental importance of knowledge and understanding in writing, our curriculum emphasizes the importance of teaching students clear structure and craft as tools to make their knowledge and understanding clear to others.
Word Study, Vocabulary *Structural analysis of specific words; vocabulary work from module content*	Word study: In the primary grades, students have an entire block (the Skills Block) devoted to decoding and syntax. In Grades 3–5, "word study" is still important but is approached differently. Research tells us that readers in intermediate grades benefit from a more contextualized approach to teaching phonics and word recognition (Bear, Invernizzi, Templeton, and Johnston, 2003; Bloodgood and Pacifici, 2004). Students in these grades still need phonics instruction about how words are built, including syllabication patterns and more complex spelling patterns, but they also need an increased focus on the morphology of words (i.e., affixes and roots) as it relates to word meaning. Therefore, the ALL Block gives students opportunities to practice with all of these aspects of word study in a variety of activities, including vocabulary games, vocabulary squares, and Frayer models. Vocabulary: Recent research also emphasizes the need for and benefit of a large vocabulary in terms of one's ability to read rich and complex text. When vocabulary is deficient, the achievement gap looms large; vocabulary is highly related to student achievement in every way. For these reasons, explicit vocabulary instruction is a key feature of our 3–5 curriculum. Besides this explicit vocabulary instruction, students get a great deal of implicit instruction in general academic and domain-specific vocabulary through exposure to many complex (and less complex) informational texts and some literary texts as well. In the ALL Block students have additional time to practice module-related word analysis through word study games and activities.

The Structure of the Additional Language and Literacy Block

Now that you have a better sense of *why* the ALL Block is so important for Grade 3–5 learners, we'll dig in more to the *what* and *how* of this hour. As noted previously, certain aspects of the literacy work in the Module Lessons require that students get more practice in order to achieve mastery. This happens in the ALL Block. These two hours of instruction are complementary, working together to accelerate the achievement of all students. The ALL Block is organized in units, just like the modules, and the three units of the ALL Block parallel the three units of the module. As a result, your preparation for teaching a unit will involve analysis of the unit-level documents for the module *and* unit-level documents for the ALL Block at the same time. That analysis (which we go into in more detail in Chapter 3A) will reveal the ways that skills and topics explored during Module Lessons are picked up again during the ALL Block, during which students have additional time working with you and working independently to achieve mastery.

As you can see in Figure 2.11, although a module is eight weeks, there are only six weeks of ALL Block lessons. This supports flexible pacing: Based on the needs of specific students, you can extend or add ALL Block lessons. Based on the needs of your students, you might want to provide additional time for work started in Module Lessons, practicing literacy skills introduced there that students are finding particularly challenging, informally assessing foundational reading skills, or offering additional time for ELLs.

Figure 2.11: 3–5 Modules Lessons and the Additional Language and Literacy Block

🕐 **8 - 9 weeks** ──────────────────────────────────→

Module Lessons: 1 hour daily		
Unit 1	Unit 2	Unit 3

Additional Language and Literacy Block: 1 hour daily

Unit 1	~Flex time~	Unit 2	~Flex time~	Unit 3	~Flex time~

🕐 **2 weeks** ⟶   🕐 **2 weeks** ⟶   🕐 **2 weeks** ⟶

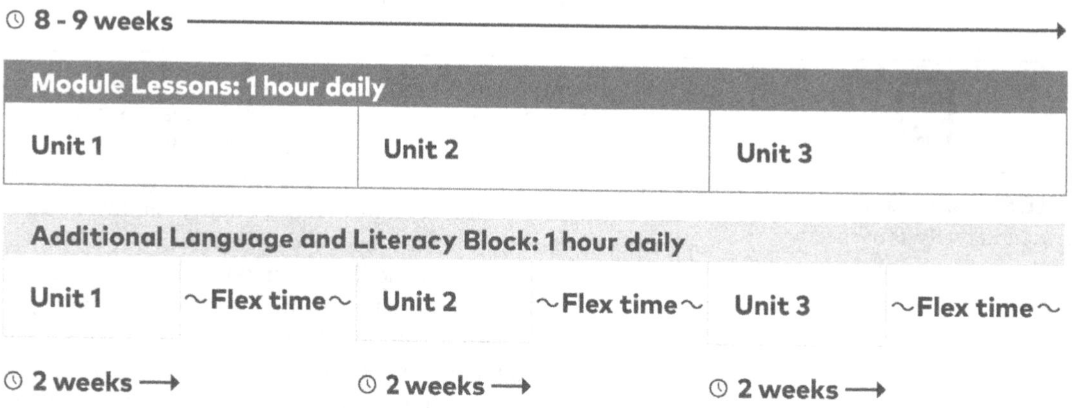

Reinforcing and Extending the Work from the Module Lessons

The ALL Block reinforces work from the Module Lessons by providing students with additional time and differentiated support to work with literacy skills they are learning in those lessons. During the ALL Block students work independently with task cards that bring them back to texts, word work, or writing tasks begun in the Module Lessons. Additionally, the teacher-guided mini lessons that are also a feature of the ALL Block each day make room for additional instruction that clears up misconceptions or deepens learning from the Module Lessons. (We will explain much more about how the grouping and rotations work in the pages that follow.) Table 2.9 details the relationship between the Module Lessons and the ALL Block.

Table 2.9: The Relationship between the Module Lessons and the Additional Language and Literacy Block

Accountable Independent Reading/ Volume of Reading in the Module Lessons	Accountable Independent Reading/ Volume of Reading in the ALL Block
» 20 minutes daily Accountable Independent Reading for homework at a range of levels; students respond to a prompt in their reading journal » Students are held accountable for their reading through discussion with their peers and teacher checks of their reading journals.	» Additional time for independent reading at a range of levels, building more content and domain-specific knowledge » Free choice reading (for one week, every other week) to build on students' motivation and interests
Complex Text in the Module Lessons	**Complex Text in the ALL Block**
» Read and reread complex text about the module's content » Frequent supported close reading » Figure out words from context	» Reread same complex texts from Module Lessons » Deepen comprehension of text and content
Reading and Speaking Fluency/GUM in the Module Lessons	**Reading and Speaking Fluency/GUM in the ALL Block**
» Reading and speaking fluency: Read aloud new and familiar excerpts of literary and informational text; speak to audiences during planned presentations » GUM: Work with models of accurate use of conventions and written syntax and grammar	» Reading and speaking fluency: Practice reading aloud texts from Module Lessons; set goals and monitor progress » GUM: Further practice (e.g., students practice revising sentences based on the grammar rules they have learned in Module Lessons)
Writing in the Module Lessons	**Writing Practice in the ALL Block**
» Frequent opportunities to "write to learn" (e.g., QuickWrites, reflections, assessment questions, exit tickets) » Writing structures: expository and narrative » Specific instruction on elements and craft of writing (e.g., focus statements, conclusions, linking words, organization of ideas, character development, narrative techniques) » Writing process: building content knowledge; planning, revising, editing, rewriting, or trying a new approach	» Continued practice to develop fluency; QuickWrites » Continued scaffolding of elements of writing (e.g., for "explaining evidence," thoughtful conclusions)
Word Study/Vocabulary in the Module Lessons	**Word Study/Vocabulary in the ALL Block**
» Work with words emerging from complex texts related to content and words of general academic value that cut across many domains with an emphasis on morphology, syllabication, spelling » Use of vocabulary protocols, routines, and tools to figure out meaning of new words; use of new words in writing, both domain-specific and general academic vocabulary	» Practice with word analysis of additional words from text » Work with two academic words per week; practice using the words in context » Work with additional domain-specific words found in research reading and independent reading » Word study games and activities

Strategizing for Rotations and Student Groupings

Over the course of a two-week ALL Block unit, students rotate through all five components in a mix of heterogeneous and homogenous groupings in consistent and predictable ways. Each day in the ALL Block, students rotate through three of the five components. In the pages that follow, particularly in Table 2.10, we detail how the rotations work over a two-week period. Each rotation is differentiated according to student need. There is also a specific strand for ELLs.

During the first two units of Module 1, students are introduced to each component gradually through whole group instruction, small group teacher-guided instruction, and independent work. They don't start working with all five components in a consistent two-week cycle, which will last for the remainder of the year, until Unit 3 of Module 1.

Each day in the ALL Block, students rotate through three components:

» Accountable Independent Reading (in heterogeneous groups) (20 minutes)

» Independent work in an ALL Block component (in heterogeneous groups, with a task card to guide their work) (20 minutes)

» Teacher-guided work in an ALL Block component (in homogeneous groups, including a separate strand for ELLs) (20 minutes)

The activities are differentiated based on student need:

■ = Below grade level

● = On grade level

◆ = Above grade level

▲ = English language learners

These are not four *static* levels. Rather, at the start of each week, you will plan student groups for the two weekly components based on student needs and the specific instruction they will engage in that particular week. Going back to our classroom Snapshot from the beginning of Chapter 2A as an example, for the Additional Work with Complex Text teacher-guided activities this week, Ms. Henderson may level Nathan below grade level (■) due to the demands of the texts and to provide the additional support she noticed he needed (based on his ongoing assessment in the Module Lessons). But she may level him above grade level (◆) for Reading and Speaking Fluency/GUM, since he has shown a clear understanding of modal auxiliaries (the GUM rule students will focus on this week).

Table 2.10 lays out the two-week cycle of the ALL Block. As you can see, during each two-week cycle students will have two sessions of teacher-led instruction and two independent sessions in each of the ALL Block components (except for Accountable Independent Reading, which happens every day). They will also have two flex days during the two-week cycle. The day of the week you assign as a flex day will depend on your schedule and the needs of your students. The sample calendar provided with each ALL Block unit also provides suggestions for when to take flex days. In Table 2.10, it is listed as the final day of the week, but it could also be the first day of the week so students can finish a significant piece of work from the previous week, for example, or in the middle of the week so students can practice a specific skill they will be assessed on in a module assessment on the final day.

Table 2.10: The Two-Week Additional Language and Literacy Block Cycle

Week 1			
Day	**Rotation (20 minutes)** *Teacher-Guided Homogenous Grouping*	**Rotation (20 minutes)** *Independent Heterogeneous Grouping*	**Rotation (20 minutes)** *Independent Heterogeneous Grouping*
Day 1	Reading Fluency and GUM	Additional Work with Complex Text	Accountable Independent Reading
Day 2	Additional Work with Complex Text	Reading Fluency and GUM	Accountable Independent Reading
Day 3	Reading Fluency and GUM	Additional Work with Complex Text	Accountable Independent Reading
Day 4	Additional Work with Complex Text	Reading Fluency and GUM	Accountable Independent Reading
Flex Day	Flex Day: Use according to student need. For example: Whole group instruction to practice the GUM rule students have been learning in GUM this week or to address an unanticipated confusion about a text.		

Week 2			
Day	**Rotation (20 minutes)** *Teacher-Guided Homogenous Grouping*	**Rotation (20 minutes)** *Independent Heterogeneous Grouping*	**Rotation (20 minutes)** *Independent Heterogeneous Grouping*
Day 1	Writing Fluency	Word Study and Vocabulary	Accountable Independent Reading
Day 2	Word Study and Vocabulary	Writing Fluency	Accountable Independent Reading
Day 3	Writing Fluency	Word Study and Vocabulary	Accountable Independent Reading
Day 4	Word Study and Vocabulary	Writing Fluency	Accountable Independent Reading
Flex Day	Flex Day: Use according to student need. For example: Finish the writing students have been working on in Writing Practice this week, or give more time for students to revise their final performance task.		

There is one teacher guide per component, per week. Symbols embedded in the instructions on the teacher guides indicate differentiation for four levels: *below, on,* and *above* grade level, and *English language learners.* Differentiated student materials, marked with the same symbols, are provided for students.

There is one student task card per component, per week. When working independently, all students work on the same task card, regardless of level, to support one another and to encourage academic discourse. Independent task cards have a "More Challenge" section for students who either finish quickly or need additional rigor. Figure 2.12 shows how students move from one rotation to another during the ALL Block.

Figure 2.12: Group Rotations during the Additional Language and Literacy Block

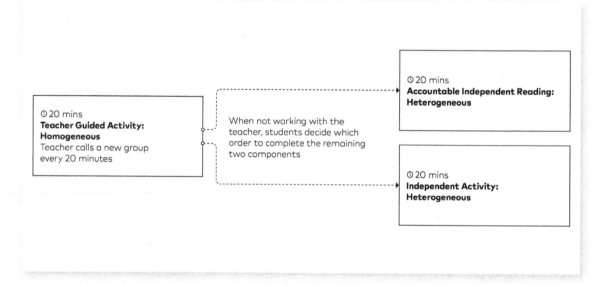

At first, learning to manage the rotations, groupings, and materials for the ALL Block will take some getting used to. Rest assured, everything you need is provided in the materials. Once you and your students go through one or two units, you'll get the hang of it. Creating a positive and collaborative classroom culture (the topic of Chapter 3C) will go a long way in supporting your students to take charge of the transitions and small group work they will engage in when they are not working directly with you. Building this culture will take time, practice, and frequent feedback to make it really hum.

The Snapshot that follows is a helpful illustration of how the rotations and groupings work. For example, you may be wondering how four differentiated groups of students rotate through only three stations each day! Read on about how this works in Ms. Henderson's classroom; the Snapshot will help you visualize and prepare for teaching the ALL Block in your own classroom.

📷 Snapshot: A Day in the Additional Language and Literacy Block

On Monday, Ms. Henderson leveled her students based on their strengths, challenges, and needs for the two teacher-guided components of this week's ALL Block: Additional Work with Complex Text and Reading and Speaking Fluency/GUM. To determine levels for teacher-guided work time, she read through the instruction for the week and considered the specific needs of each of her students and then decided which level of instruction each student would need for each component.

In this week's Additional Work with Complex Text component, students will navigate and read their animal expert group web pages. Sergei is an English language learner who reads accurately but struggles with comprehension and is easily overwhelmed by a lot of text. Ms. Henderson knows he will benefit from the specifically designed ELL instruction that focuses on comprehending the meaning of just a few key sentences about his expert group animal, so she puts him in the ELL group for Additional Work with Complex Text (▲).

In this week's Reading and Speaking Fluency/GUM component, students will analyze how modal auxiliaries such as *can, could, may, might, shall,* and *will* change the meaning of sentences. Although Sergei is an English language learner, Ms. Henderson knows from observing his work and discussion of this skill in the Module Lessons that he has a very clear understanding of this content, and that he will not be challenged by the instruction for ELLs. She thinks the instruction for students working below grade level (■) will be a better fit.

Ms. Henderson creates a list for her own reference showing which level each student will be working on for each of the two components this week. Below we show a sampling of this list. (Students do not need to know which level they have been assigned. When calling the groups Ms. Henderson can refer to her list and call students by name.)

Student Name	Additional Work with Complex Text	Reading and Speaking Fluency/GUM
Sergei	ELL	Below
Nathan	On	Above
Alma	On	On
Sara	ELL	Below
David	On	On
Juan	Below	ELL

Ms. Henderson now has mapped out the needs of her learners into four levels, but there are only three 20-minute blocks of time in each ALL Block hour for teacher-guided instruction. A recommendation for the three groups is suggested in the Unit Overview for each component. In this week's Additional Work with Complex Text component, Ms. Henderson sees the recommendation is:

» *Group 1:* ▲ *(English language learners)*

» *Group 2:* ■ *(below grade level)*

» *Group 3:* ● ◆ *(on and above grade level)*

Having looked at the instruction before leveling students, Ms. Henderson realizes that ELLs are working in a group on their own because they will participate in a Language Dive that other students might not benefit from.

In this week's Reading and Speaking Fluency/GUM component, Ms. Henderson sees the recommendation is:

» *Group 1:* ■ *(below grade level)*

» *Group 2:* ● *(on grade level)*

» *Group 3:* ◆ ▲ *(above grade level* and *English language learners)*

Ms. Henderson realizes that the grouping of students working above grade level with ELLs will allow ELLs to hear native speakers use modal auxiliaries and will give students above grade level increased responsibility as they practice peer support and coaching.

Tuesday morning, students worked on Grade 4, Module 2, Unit 2, Lesson 2. In the module, students are preparing to research a particular animal with a unique defense mechanism. They will work in expert groups to write an informational piece about their animal. They have closely read a complex text as a whole group and have been practicing using modal auxiliaries.

According to the sample calendar for this unit, the corresponding ALL Block work for this module lesson is Unit 2, Day 2. So now, after lunch, students are beginning their additional hour of literacy time with Unit 2, Day 2 of the ALL Block.

Ms. Henderson knows that Week 1, Day 2 always includes teacher-guided Additional Work with Complex Text (homogeneous groups). While she leads three 20-minute sessions of differentiated Additional Work with Complex Text instruction, students read independently or work independently on the Day 2 section of the Reading and Speaking Fluency/GUM task card for this week.

At the start of the ALL Block hour, she calls out the names of the students in Group 1: *English language learners* (▲), including Sergei, who makes his way over to her.

The other students have two choices about how to spend these first 20 minutes: either Reading and Speaking Fluency/GUM first or Accountable Independent Reading first. Each student makes a choice, and then heads over to the appropriate table/area for that component. They see the materials Ms. Henderson has organized for them, and they dig in.

In Ms. Henderson's teacher-led Additional Work with Complex Text group for ELLs, students participate in a Language Dive about one particular sentence about the armadillo—specifically on how the words *when* and *however* are used. They think of sentences about their expert group animals that include the words *when* and *however* and say them aloud to an "elbow partner." They then share them with the group and Ms. Henderson repeats them back and writes them on the chart paper. While Sergei knows students in other groups will read more than just one sentence, he is pleased that he now has a deep understanding of the sentence and will be able to apply it to read other sentences with similar structures.

After 20 minutes, Ms. Henderson gives the signal and calls the names of students in group 2 (*below grade level*) to go work with her. The ELLs choose a component to work on independently. Sergei chooses to work on Reading and Fluency/GUM first, and in that area of the room he picks up a task card. He knows he is expected to complete the Day 2 portion of the task card in the given time. After a reminder from Ms. Henderson, the students at the Reading and Fluency/GUM table focus their attention on the ALL Independent Group Work Protocol posted on the wall to allocate a facilitator and timekeeper and to begin.

After 20 minutes, Ms. Henderson calls the names of students in group 3 (*on* and *above grade level*) to go work with her. She invites the other students to move to their final component. For Sergei, this is Accountable Independent Reading. He retrieves his research reading book, independent reading journal, and vocabulary log and heads over to the independent reading area. He knows these task cards well, since he has used them many times before, so he and the rest of the group working on this component are able to get straight to work.

Chapter 2

Chapter 2C:
How Is the Curriculum Designed to Help My Diverse Group of Learners Succeed?

With your arms fully around the components of our comprehensive K–5 curriculum, you may find yourselves now starting to think about your individual students. In particular, you may be thinking about how you will best support students who may struggle with a rigorous English language arts (ELA) curriculum like this. Will the curriculum offer the necessary supports for English language learners (ELLs) or for those who are behind in reading?

This curriculum was designed for *all* of your students. As a central part of our mission, EL Education is focused on equity and ensuring that all students have the opportunity to learn and master rigorous content that prepares them for the future. This means that all students must be held to the same high expectations and given the supports they need to meet them.

Much of our curriculum is inherently supportive of students' varied learning needs. From highly scaffolded close reading lessons to discussion protocols that give students "oral rehearsal" before writing, all students have a real chance to succeed. That said, some students or groups of students may need additional scaffolds and supports. In this chapter, we take a close look at how the curriculum supports ELLs, as well as the Universal Design for Learning (UDL) supports in place for students who may struggle.

▶ How Will the Curriculum Support the Success of My English Language Learners?

English language learners are the fastest-growing population of students in the United States. Because these students are learning English, they will likely need additional support when working with our curriculum. It's important to remember, however, that not all ELLs need the same kinds of support. Just like any group of students, they bring a great diversity of language, skill, and educational background to the classroom. In the Snapshot that follows, we'll meet a few ELLs and then explore how our curriculum is designed to support them.

📷 Snapshot: Meet the English Language Learners

Bing-Shan is a six-year-old student in first grade whose family speaks Mandarin at home. Born in the United States, Bing-Shan came to school with some English that she learned from her older brother. She is generally quiet and does not always let the teacher know when she doesn't understand what the teacher or her classmates have said.

Marco is one of Bing-Shan's classmates; he attended preschool and kindergarten in his home country, Mexico. He spoke no English when the school year started but has begun using phrases that he has learned thus far, such as "tha's mine," "please help," and "please ba'room." Because he is more vocal and outgoing, Marco interacts more with his English-speaking classmates than Bing-Shan does.

Zaineb is an eight-year-old Arabic-speaking refugee student from Syria in third grade. She has had almost no schooling in her home country and has been in a refugee camp for three years. In the camp, she attended English classes only sporadically because she suffered and continues to suffer from posttraumatic stress disorder (PTSD). In her new school, she has been placed in a class where there are no other Syrian or Arabic-speaking children. Zaineb loves to draw and spends a great deal of time in class drawing pictures. She is shy around most of her classmates. She has begun to sit together and walk around the playground with one Korean-speaking girl.

Andrés is in the same class as Zaineb. He was born in Guatemala but came to the United States at age three. Andrés is very popular with his classmates because he is good at sports and makes his classmates laugh. However, although Andrés can communicate in English, he is rarely on task and struggles with the complex language in the texts his teacher is using.

Salvador, in Grade 5, has challenges similar to Andrés'. Although Salvador can speak English to his teachers and classmates, he has difficulty comprehending both the spoken and written English used in grade-level academic texts. Salvador was born in the U.S., and he and his family live in a Spanish-English bilingual community. The adults in this community speak only enough English to get by. However, Salvador and those in his age range mostly speak English because they have never had the opportunity to study in Spanish. Moreover, Salvador has not had access to a coherent and consistent English as a second language program, nor have his teachers known how to assist him in further developing his abilities in English. They have mistakenly diagnosed him as a "struggling reader" and placed him in remedial reading pull-out classes. The simple short sentences and words in the remedial readers have further curtailed his access to the kinds of language used in different genres and content areas, thus stunting his English language development.

Salvador is like the majority of ELLs across the country and in many school districts: "stuck" in the middle ranges of English language development. Too many students like them are assigned to remedial programs with little to no access to rich, varied, complex, and compelling material that ultimately would help them become fluent readers and writers. Our curriculum attempts to disrupt this pattern for this large population of students by targeting instruction to these "long-term English learners." At the same time, the curriculum attempts to honor and serve all ELLs, from newcomers to the more proficient speakers, by incorporating both heavier and lighter support.

Overall, the five students in the Snapshot represent the great variation in background, languages, and academic abilities found in ELLs. Not all ELLs are new to English like Marco or Zaineb; some, like Bing-Shan, Andrés, and Salvador, have heard English at home from older siblings or in their communities. Some ELLs have had some schooling in their home countries; others have attended only U.S. schools. This great variation makes it difficult to use a single set of strategies to assist ELLs in learning English (Bunch, Kibler, and Pimentel, 2012). For this reason, we have built in consistent instruction and support for ELLs at the lesson level that will help them gain access to the curriculum and suggestions to the teacher for those students who need heavier or lighter support.

Before we begin describing the supports that are in place for ELLs in our curriculum, it's important to start by describing the principles for supporting them upon which this curriculum was built.

What Principles for Supporting English Language Learners Underlie the Curriculum?

English Language Learners Deserve a Rich, Compelling, Challenging Curriculum

We believe that ELLs deserve the same rich, compelling, and challenging curriculum that other students receive. ELLs have developed age-appropriate concepts and understandings about the world—as they have experienced it. They have the same cognitive needs for an enriching and challenging curriculum and learning experience that any child does. Varying levels of support in using English are built into our curriculum so that ELLs have equitable access to this compelling and challenging curriculum.

Learning English Should Not Be Viewed as a Barrier to Learning

English language learning is not a disability. It is not a barrier. ELLs have a language; it is just not English. Lack of English is not perceived as a problem, but rather as an opportunity to add a second language. When appropriately supported, bi- or multilingualism is an asset and an indicator of intelligence and ability.

Our curriculum encourages teachers to honor and incorporate children's home languages as students learn English. Teachers can learn words and phrases in their students' home languages and publicly acknowledge them, for example, by adding the words and phrases to anchor charts and using them during various classroom routines.

To describe this process for the student learning English, we opt for the common term "English language learner" and "English language learning." Although "emergent bilingual" is an apt, asset-based term to describe students who are in the process of adding English to their linguistic repertoire, this term has some fundamental sticking points: Unfortunately, for those with less experience in this field, "emergent bilingual" is often confused with bilingual education, and our curriculum is designed for multilingual contexts for learning English. In addition, many state English language development (ELD) standards use "emergent" to describe only their lowest-proficiency students.

All Educators Are Responsible for the Success of English Language Learners

As educators, we all are responsible for educating ELLs. This includes administrators, counselors, assessment specialists, and teachers. At the school level, schedules, materials, and any additional support needs to be in place to support the work with ELLs in classrooms. As educators, how we interact with ELLs and plan for and enact learning opportunities can make a fundamental difference in their educational careers and their lives. Assessment specialists must ensure that the district assessments are fair and unbiased toward ELLs. All educators have the power to make it or break it for ELLs.

Our curriculum integrates high-leverage instructional approaches that can assist all learners, but especially ELLs. Two of the most important approaches are Language Dives and Conversation

Cues (these important practices will be detailed later in this chapter). By consistently incorporating these two high-leverage instructional approaches in particular, we hope that all educators will come to understand how to better assist their ELLs on a regular basis.

Second Language Development Reveals Itself in Various Ways

Understanding second language development is important. As demonstrated by the profiles of students in the preceding Snapshot, those who are developing a new language, in addition to their home language, are often in different places academically. As they embark on learning a new language, ELLs may vary in the speed and accuracy with which they use English. And not all language learning follows a linear path of progression. Often students will seem to regress, reverting to developmental errors they had demonstrated previously, and then jump ahead after a few months. In some cases, students may demonstrate understanding through gestures. Some students may learn a short phrase and overextend its use.

Other students who have more outgoing personalities may attempt to speak regardless of errors. Critical errors should be tracked and addressed, but always with the consideration that language errors are a sign of beneficial risk-taking and growth. It is important to be aware of a student's English level so the student can receive instruction and support that will foster language and academic growth. A newcomer student may need the support of visuals to participate in class activities. However, these initial kinds of supports would not be appropriate or sufficiently challenging for a student who is at a more intermediate stage, and might in fact hinder him or her from making greater progress. ELLs need to be assisted in ways that will allow them to continuously move to more proficient levels of English. For this reason, we must always combine the appropriate supports with rigor (Wong Fillmore and Fillmore, 2012; Staehr Fenner, 2013; Gibbons, 2010; García and Walqui, 2015).

Productive and Equitable Conversation Spurs Language Learning

Oral language is critical. It is the basis for reading with comprehension and for writing fluency. Therefore, for ELLs, it is important to opt for interactions that are more productive and conversations that are more academically based. Before students can write successfully, they must discuss the content they are to write and the precise language they will need to use to communicate through writing. Their conversations should be content-related but also metacognitive: Students should be able to explain why they are completing any given task and what they have learned from their work. They have to engage in academically productive conversations, guided by the teacher, that call out language structures that make for great complexity in literary and informa-

tional texts. In extended, task-based interactions with peers, with teachers present to provide guidance and feedback to support effective communication, ELLs encounter authentic opportunities to grapple with language to achieve specific goals, to self-correct, and to succeed. Indeed, environments in which ELLs have multiple opportunities to negotiate the meaning of content are most conducive to second language learning.

Language Dives, a high-leverage instructional approach for engaging students in conversation about how language is used to construct knowledge about content, and Conversation Cues, another high-leverage approach to help teachers and students have and maintain extended interactions around content, will be detailed later in this chapter. Other discussion protocols used throughout the curriculum, such as Think-Pair-Share, can complement these deep, extended conversations. In Chapter 6, we will explore in detail how all students—not just ELLs—read about, think about, and talk about text as preparation for writing. This practice is central to our curriculum at all grade levels and is highly supportive of language learning for ELLs.

New College- and Career-Ready Standards Offer a Strong Framework for Authentic Language Engagement

New college- and career-ready standards provide opportunities to help ELLs interact with challenging, complex, and engaging material. Our curriculum permits students to see how language is used in academic texts from different subject areas. By listening to, talking about, and reading and writing about literary and informational texts about compelling material, ELLs will be able to put this rich input to use for their own authentic purposes.

As described in Chapter 1, our curriculum is built around Common Core standards, and in each lesson specific standards are addressed. State ELD standards are a necessary complement to the Common Core. ELD standards help educators gauge language proficiency level and growth as students engage with content. While states across the country have adopted many different ELD frameworks, our curriculum designers consulted the California English Language Development (CA ELD) Standards to help guide the design of ELL instruction and supports in the curriculum. This framework was selected as a baseline because of its balance of specificity and practicality. Of all standards frameworks, the CA ELD Standards seem to provide the most useful framework, offering robust language standards and proficiency level descriptors that clearly describe what ELLs should know and be able to do across a variety of contexts and at specific benchmarks. An important benefit is that the CA ELD Standards were developed to connect to the Common Core and to encourage students to engage with rigorous academic content. The CA ELD Standards descriptors also draw upon other state and national ELD descriptors.

Each Module Lesson in our curriculum includes the CA ELD Standards that helped guide the design of the ELL instruction and support in that lesson. If your district uses a different framework, such as the World-class Instructional Design and Assessment (WIDA) ELD Standards or other state standards, you may wish to align those standards to the CA ELD Standards for comparison and accountability purposes.

Reading Level Is Not Necessarily Language Level

Some ELLs, like other students who are native English speakers, may face some reading challenges. However, it is important to remember that an ELL is faced with a different set of challenges. She must encounter new sounds, new vocabulary, new grammatical structures, and new meanings. For an ELL, decoding may not translate into meaning. Therefore, although phonics practice may assist beginning ELLs with the sounds of English, continuous practice in these skills actually may be counterproductive. To grow linguistically, ELLs must have access to rich and complex language as it is used in the different academic subjects. As they come to understand and use this kind of language, their English abilities will grow. The Language Dives and productive conversations around these kinds of language uses, which are key practices in our curriculum, are critical to their academic success (Abedi and Liquanti, 2012).

Home Language Should Be Developed and Honored in Tandem with English

All ELLs should have the opportunity to further develop their home language. Some have had the opportunity to develop literacy in their home language, but many have not. It may be beyond your ability to offer support in the home language, but it is important to encourage families to help their children develop literacy and other more complex and academic uses of their home language.

Although you may not speak a child's home language, you can highlight and incorporate the language into the classroom by asking your ELLs to teach phrases and words to their classmates (UNESCO, 1996; Garcia, 2009; Collier and Thomas, 2004). Throughout the curriculum, you will find specific suggestions for how you might acknowledge and honor students' home languages.

Diversity Is a Strength to Be Leveraged

Throughout the curriculum, we have included texts and activities that honor the knowledge, languages, beliefs, and skills that exist in the cultures and backgrounds of students and their families. Students are asked to reflect on how their own experience connects to content and are invited to bring books and objects from home to share and discuss. For this reason, we have included suggestions for asking students to use their home languages or to share the knowledge they have with you and their peers. In this way, ELLs have a chance to shine and their classmates have an opportunity to learn from them and their families (Gay, 2000).

⚠ A Caution Regarding Translations

Our curriculum encourages the use of each student's home language because it benefits students. However, for those with less experience with translation, some cautions are in order regarding extensive translation of the curricular materials themselves. Use of translations of informational texts dealing with science, mathematics, or social science materials may be helpful if students have had schooling in their home languages or if their family members are able to help them understand these texts and if the translation is performed by a professionally trained translator to ensure accuracy.

Literary translations, especially when dealing with children's literature, are not always as helpful because elements such as meaning, tone, beauty, and cultural nuance may shift or disappear. And translations of instruction, such as English discourse analysis and writing conventions, may have unintended consequences. The ways in which English expresses meanings can be ambiguous, which can result in translations that shift the meaning or use the home language in stilted, unnatural ways, robbing students of the opportunity to develop rich and expressive home language abilities.

Consider, for example, this imperative in English: "Put the books on the table where they belong." In this sentence, it is not clear whether the books are on the table, which is the wrong place, or they are somewhere else and need to be placed on the table. In translating to Mandarin, the translator cannot keep the ambiguity. Thus, these two meanings would be distinctly expressed:

Mandarin	Transliteration	Literal English translation	English translation
把桌子上的书放回原处	bǎ zhuōzi shàng de shū fàng huí yuán chù	take table-top book(s) place back original place	Take the books from the table and put them where they belong.

把书放回原来的桌子上	bǎ shū fàng huí yuánlái de zhuōzi shàng	take book place back original table-top	Take the books (from elsewhere) and place them back on the table where they belong.

The expert translator, unless given guidance by the original writer, would struggle to decide which is the correct translation to convey the ambiguous meaning of the original English sentence.

EL Education supports bilingual curricula that honor the beauty and literary traditions of all languages. In the meantime, our curriculum, as it is designed, is not meant to be translated for use in bilingual programs.

What Specific Instructional Strategies Will I Use to Support English Language Learners When Teaching the Curriculum?

The basic design of our curriculum is inherently and intentionally supportive of ELLs, incorporating many literacy practices that support their learning needs. Content-based language and literacy instruction, for example, which is the foundation of our curriculum, allows ELLs to engage with interesting and cognitively challenging material as they learn English. This is considered one of the best ways for students to learn a language (Tedick and Wesley, 2015; Walqui and Van Lier, 2010; Bunch, Lotan, Valdés, and Cohen, 2005). In the pages that follow, we detail some of the other key design elements, practices, and structures in the curriculum that support ELLs. (The ELL instruction and supports embedded in our curriculum are not designed to replace federal- and state-mandated ELL or bilingual instruction.)

Language Dives: Empowering English Language Learners to Understand and Use Complex Language Structures

A Language Dive[3] empowers students to analyze, understand, and use the language of compelling sentences, which can often seem opaque to students. During a Language Dive, the teacher and students slow down for 10 to 20 minutes to have a conversation about the meaning, purpose, and structure of a compelling sentence from a complex text. These structures can include the purposes for communicating, syntactical constructions, collocations, and idiomatic expressions. The classroom becomes a space in which students are assisted to figure out why the author chose a particular phrase.

Language Dives are not meant to be grammar lectures, nor do they follow the initiate-response-evaluate pattern typical of most teacher-student interactions. Rather, they are "wonderings" about the ways in which language is used to convey particular meanings, and students are encouraged to grapple with the meanings, supporting our general philosophy of building perseverance and self-efficacy. The conversations adopt a "deconstruct, reconstruct, and practice" routine as a necessary part of both language and building literacy and habits of mind:

» *Deconstruct:* Teachers guide students to deconstruct the sentence and discuss what it means and its purpose in the text by chunking a sentence into essential phrases. For example, in kindergarten, Module 3, students read the text *What's Alive?*. One key sentence is deconstructed into four main chunks:

They	bend	their stems and leaves	to follow the sun.

---

[3] The EL Education Language Dive is based on "Juicy Sentences": Wong Fillmore, L., and Fillmore, C. (2012, January) "What does text complexity mean for English learners and language minority students?" Paper presented at the Understanding Language Conference, Stanford, CA

» Students could wonder about the words *they* and *their*: What do they refer to? And then students could reflect on what it means to *follow the sun*. The teacher can call students' attention to the word *to* and ask what its job is: "Can you figure out why the author wrote this word? What if the word *to* were replaced with the word *and*?"

» *Reconstruct:* After unpacking the sentence through conversation, students put it back together chunk by chunk. For example, students could try to develop this one sentence into two, check to see if the meaning remains the same, and then figure out how the author made it into one sentence. They talk about how the Language Dive has added to their understanding of the meaning of the sentence and the big ideas of the unit.

» *Practice:* Students practice using one or more of the language structures as they speak about their own lives and write their own sentences. In the example above, students can focus on *to* + base verb as an infinitive to express the various purposes of plant functions using a sentence frame: "Plants ____ to ____."

» *Apply:* Later, students can draw on their discussions of these sentences when speaking or writing in subsequent tasks in the curriculum and in life.

Language Dives help students acquire language through analysis, conversation, and usage, which can be more effective than teacher lecture. Helping students understand how the English language works is ultimately important in sharing power and establishing equity.

A consistent Language Dive routine is critical in helping all students learn how to decipher compelling sentences and say and write their own. Proficient writers can use the routine to continue to grow as lifelong learners in the complex task of communication. The routine may hasten overall English language development for ELLs. For this reason, Language Dives are included an average of twice a week for all students and suggested daily for ELLs:

» At times, Language Dives are done with the whole class. All students benefit, and ELLs benefit from listening to and interacting with native English speakers. Native speakers also gain new insight into their native language. Language Dives may be discrete agenda items in a Module Lesson or embedded in close reading/read-aloud sessions for all students. Beginning in Module 3 of the 3–5 Additional Language and Literacy (ALL) Block, Language Dives are routinely incorporated into Week 1 Additional Work with Complex Text and revisited in Week 2 Writing Practice for all students. For ELLs only, Language Dives are integrated into the strategic grouping of the ALL Block. At other times in the Module Lessons, Language Dives are suggested for ELLs as an option in the Meeting Students' Needs section so that teachers can guide smaller groups of ELLs while other students are working on independent tasks, or English as a second language (ESL) specialists can pull out ELLs for short periods.

» When helpful, Language Dives can be divided into shorter sessions, with a focus on deconstructing the sentence on the first day, for example, and reconstructing and practicing it on the second. Alternatively, students can discuss the first part of a sentence one day and the latter part the next day.

In addition to the Language Dives provided in our curriculum, you are encouraged to strategically choose sentences and times for additional Language Dives that you design yourself. Ideally, the work of Language Dives eventually will go beyond ELA to science, mathematics, history, and social studies texts, offering conversation and practice across several days and subjects to meet the language needs of all learners, but particularly of ELLs.

Conversation Cues: Promoting Academically Oriented Conversations

Conversation Cues engage ELLs and their peers in thoughtful and extended academically oriented conversations. Conversation Cues are questions teachers can ask students to promote productive and equitable conversation, helping to gauge students' thinking. The questions can encourage students to have productive discussions and generate new ideas before they begin writing tasks. Conversation Cues are based on four goals[4] that encourage each student to:

» (Goal 1) Talk and be understood (e.g., "I'll give you time to think and sketch or discuss this with a partner" and "Can you say more about that?")

» (Goal 2) Listen carefully to one another and seek to understand (e.g., "Who can repeat what your classmate said?")

» (Goal 3) Deepen thinking (e.g., "Can you figure out why the author wrote that phrase?")

» (Goal 4) Think with others to expand the conversation (e.g., "Who can explain why your classmate came up with that response?")

Across the year, Conversation Cues are introduced one goal at a time. In this context, Conversation Cues are designed to slowly build the capacity of all students to engage in rich, collaborative discussions targeted at ELA and ELD standards, thus helping to level the playing field and establish equity. For example, some students who are shy, introspective, or have less knowledge or language ability in some contexts may respond more readily to a Goal 1 Conversation Cue: "I'll give you time to think and write or sketch," while other students may be willing and able to respond to a Goal 4 cue: "How is what Lupe said the same as or different from what Young Bin said?"

Conversation Cues help all students begin to think deeply about the material, to explain their thinking, and to learn to listen to various points of view as they consider the material. You can encourage students to gradually begin using appropriate Conversation Cues themselves, along with other discussion conventions, to expand their independent interactions with their peers. Table 2.11 includes the complete set of Conversation Cues that appear throughout the curriculum.

Table 2.11: Conversation Cues

Conversation Cues	
Cue	**Expected Response**
Goal 1: Help all students talk and be understood (introduced Module 1, Unit 1).	
Think and Process Language Internally	
"I'll give you time to think and write or sketch." "I'll give you a minute to think and write or sketch." "I'll give you time to discuss this with a partner."	
Elaborate upon or Expand	
"Can you say more about that?" "Can you give an example?"	"Sure. I think that ____." "Okay. One example is ____."
Clarify	
"So, do you mean ____?"	"You've got it." "No, sorry, that's not what I mean. I mean ____."

Cont.

───────────

[4] These goals are adapted from Sarah Michael's and Cathy O'Connor's *Talk Science Primer*, Cambridge, MA: TERC, 2012. http://inquiryproject.terc.edu/shared/pd/TalkScience_Primer.pdf. Based on: Chapin, S., O'Connor, C., and Anderson, N. (2009). *Classroom Discussions: Using Math Talk to Help Students Learn, Grades K–6. Second Edition.* Sausalito, CA: Math Solutions Publications.

Conversation Cues

Cue	Expected Response
Goal 2: Help students listen carefully to one another and seek to understand (introduced Module 1, Unit 3).	
Repeat or Paraphrase	
"Who can repeat what your classmate said?" "Who can tell us what your classmate said in your own words?"	"She said ____." "He was saying that ____."
Goal 3: Help students deepen their thinking (introduced Module 2, Unit 2).	
Provide Reasoning or Evidence	
"Why do you think that?" "What, in the (sentence/text), makes you think so?"	"Because ____." "If you look at ____, it says ____, which means ____."
Challenge Thinking	
"What if ____ (that word were removed/the main character had done something different/we didn't write an introduction)? I'll give you time to think and discuss with a partner." "Can you figure out why ____ (the author used this phrase/ we used that strategy/there's an -*ly* added to that word)? I'll give you time to think and discuss with a partner."	"If we did that, then ____." "I think it's because ____."
Think about Thinking (Metacognition)	
"What strategies/habits helped you succeed? I'll give you time to think and discuss with a partner." "How does our discussion add to your understanding of ____ (previously discussed topic/text/language)? I'll give you time to think and discuss with a partner."	"____ helped me a lot because ____." "I used to think that ____, and now I think that ____."
Goal 4: Help students think with others to expand the conversation (introduced Module 3, Unit 1).	
Compare	
"How is what ____ said the same as/different from what ____ said?"	"____ said ____. That's different from what ____ said because ____."
Agree, Disagree, and Explain Why	
"Do you agree or disagree with what your classmate said? Why?"	"I agree/disagree because ____." "I think what he said is ____ because ____."
Add on	
"Who can add on to what your classmate said?"	"I think that ____."
Explain	
"Who can explain why your classmate came up with that response?"	"I think what she's saying is ____."

To maximize Conversation Cues, particularly Goals 3 and 4, consider modeling productive and equitable conversations with a student volunteer before releasing students to have their own conversations. Reinforce the model conversation by displaying it, including possible questions and responses. Consider this sample kindergarten Goal 3 conversation from Module 2, Unit 2, Lesson 10. What follows is a transcript of what it might sound like:

» Teacher displays focus question and says to class: "Let's think about our focus question: How does this Language Dive sentence help us understand how the changing weather affects Tess and Mamma?"

» Teacher to class: "Before you talk with your partner, your classmate and I will model the conversation. This conversation frame can help us."

» Teacher displays conversation frame, which reads:

  • Person A: "How does this Language Dive sentence help you understand how the changing weather affects Tess and Mamma?"

  • Person B: "The sentence helped me understand the focus question because _____. How does the sentence help you understand how the changing weather affects Tess and Mamma?"

  • Person A: "It helps me understand that _____."

  • Person B: "I agree/disagree. I'd like to add that _____."

» Teacher and volunteer point to the conversation frame on display as they begin to model the conversation.

  • Volunteer to teacher: "How does this sentence help you understand how the changing weather affects Tess and Mamma?"

  • Teacher to volunteer: "The sentence helped me understand the focus question because I now know that the rain makes Tess and Mama feel happy. How does the sentence help you understand how the changing weather affects Tess and Mamma?"

  • Volunteer to teacher: "It helps me understand that rain made Tess and Mamma feel better because they were too hot and tired."

  • Teacher to volunteer (listening carefully): "Sorry, I'm not sure I understood that. Could you please repeat what you said?"

  • Volunteer to teacher: "Sure! It helps me understand that, before the rain, Tess and Mamma were so hot and tired. And then the cool rain made them feel better."

  • Teacher to volunteer: "Oh, yes. I agree. I'd like to add on that we know they feel better because they were jumping around."

» Teacher to class: "Now, I will give you time to think and discuss with a partner. You can use the conversation frame on display if you want help."

Offering Differing Levels of Support

Nationally, the majority of ELLs (between 45 to 60 percent) achieve intermediate to high-intermediate levels of English language proficiency, also known as the "Expanding" level in the CA ELD Proficiency Level Continuum. Keep in mind, as the name "Proficiency Level Continuum" suggests, that language proficiency shifts depending on content, task, and situation, and proficiency cannot be considered fixed. However, most students assessed as achieving intermediate proficiency levels get "stuck" there for a few years, and often for their lifetime. These students may be formally classified as "long-term English learners" (LTELs). To help break this pattern, our curriculum targets instruction for LTELs in particular, in large part through Language Dive instruction, to help them reach advanced levels of language proficiency and be reclassified as proficient speakers.

At the same time, in addition to the focus on LTELs, the curriculum honors and supports ELLs at lower and higher proficiency levels. Heavier and lighter levels of support are provided for different activities within each lesson to help learners at any language proficiency level in accessing content. Examples:

» **For heavier support**. For students who are new to English, the curriculum provides sentence frames they can use both orally and in writing, as well as suggested word and phrase banks and manipulatives to help them begin to construct their own sentences.

» **For lighter support**. For students who have moved beyond intermediate levels, the curriculum suggests strategic grouping, inviting students with more language proficiency to create sentence frames for students who need heavier support.

Additionally, while heavier support generally helps students at the "Emerging" level of the CA ELD Proficiency Level Continuum and lighter support generally helps students at the "Bridging" level, these supports may, at times, benefit students classified at *any* language proficiency level. A relative newcomer at the "Emerging" level may benefit from lighter supports in certain contexts, while a more proficient student at the "Bridging" level may benefit from heavier supports during some tasks. It is essential to observe student ability in various situations and select supports based on need, rather than seeing student ability as fixed at one level.

Knowing each of your students and their levels of English is critical in helping you to differentiate supports. Each lesson references relevant descriptors from the California ELD Standards; these, in coordination with your state ELD standards and proficiency continuum, can help you understand where your students are in their development of English and where you need to guide them in their growth. Although the curriculum has built in different levels of support, these may not meet your students' needs specifically at one time or another. For this reason, it may be important to modify these supports and seek further assistance.

Honoring Diversity and Inclusion

We encourage teachers to acknowledge, celebrate, and incorporate student experiences to promote equity. Throughout the curriculum, we have included texts and activities that honor the cultures and backgrounds of students and their families. For example, in the Grade 4 module Perspectives on the American Revolution, students are asked to consider not only the American and British points of view, but also those of Native Americans and African Americans. They are asked to reflect on how their own experience connects to the content and are invited to bring books and objects from home to share and discuss.

Students are encouraged to use their home language, when comfortable, to begin negotiating particularly challenging tasks or to bridge their understanding as newcomers. In addition, the curriculum includes possible cultural cautions, such as using particular hand gestures that are common in the United States but may be offensive in other countries or in national, family, or personal cultures. Teachers are invited to get to know students well, and, in turn, share their own national, family, and personal traditions, value systems, myths, and symbols.

The concept of culture is intricate; any given group is not monolithic and should not be stereotyped. Furthermore, each person may identify with several layers of culture—national, community, family, personal—that may shift with situation and time. Therefore, the cultural supports in the curriculum are intended to suggest the infinite possibilities of different student experience, not to essentialize or label any single student or group. For example, in Grades 3–5, teachers should be aware that the concept of plagiarizing may not be clear-cut for some students during some writing tasks. Teachers are encouraged to discuss and understand varied perspectives on using other people's work and to explain the cultural and legal aspects of citation as well as how citation is part of providing evidence in U.S. classrooms.

Strategic Grouping

Grouping ELLs strategically, in different configurations for different purposes, will allow you to provide targeted support to students and will give them a chance to support each other. Depending on the task, you may wish to group ELLs with other students who speak their home language, either in mixed-proficiency groupings or in homogenous groupings. In home language groups with a range of English proficiency, students with greater language proficiency can help their peers negotiate particularly challenging tasks. These students can also serve as models for their peers, initiating discussion and providing implicit sentence frames for them. Processes like these are ideal for language development. In home language groups with homogenous levels of English proficiency, students can help each other by grappling together with tasks, which also promotes English language development.

> *"In EL Education's curriculum, English language learners are supported not only by the teacher, but also by their peers. These peer interactions are very meaningful to students because they can learn from each other in ways they might not learn from the teacher."*

Tammi Bauschka

Literacy Program Specialist, Tucson, Arizona

For most tasks, you may wish to group ELLs with native and proficient English speakers, who can provide language models and help ELLs feel successful when they communicate clearly, or try out new language and help clarify the communication as necessary. The curriculum will provide suggested groupings, but depending on the makeup of your class, you may need to develop additional strategies to best meet the needs of your students. Overall, it is important that you don't use one static grouping strategy; just like any group of students, ELLs will benefit from working with a variety of students. Specifically, in terms of English language development, ELLs benefit from spoken and written interaction with other students who exhibit a range of language proficiency levels and communication styles.

Multiple Modes, Multiple Intelligences

Just like any group of students, ELLs have varied learning needs and styles. What follows are a few specific suggestions that will amplify language learning opportunities for ELLs, who, like any students, have greater success when instruction is delivered through various modes and maximizes various intelligences:

» Support visual learning by enlarging key portions of the texts, graphic organizers, note-catchers, and models.

» Promote collaboration and oral processing by facilitating "Information Gap" activities (e.g., complete half of a graphic organizer for half of your students, half for the other half, and allow students to talk to opposite groups to complete the organizer).

» Set up jigsaw reading activities in which students read different sections of the same text or different texts on a common topic and then share their learning.

» Identify and label familiar parts of complex content for students, including directions, learning targets, vocabulary, and key sections of text.

» Ask students to demonstrate their understanding of complex content through guided movement, sketching, and gestures.

» Have ELLs read shorter jigsaw texts with more proficient peers who can ask questions and help summarize the information.

» Engage students in the read-think-talk-write cycle, which allows for "oral rehearsal" before writing (see Chapter 6 for more information).

» Allow students to sketch as they plan their writing and consult more proficient students for language models before writing.

» Ask students to "say back" the purpose of completing a given task or what they have learned from their work.

The Meeting Students' Needs section in each lesson contains support for ELLs as well as Universal Design for Learning (UDL) supports. Some supports can serve a wide range of student needs, but ELLs have unique needs that cannot always be met with UDL support. According to federal guidelines, ELLs must be given access to the curriculum with appropriate supports, such as those that are specifically identified as "For ELLs" in the Meeting Students' Needs section.

Writing Practice

In addition to the read, think, talk, write cycle, which is an embedded design feature of the curriculum that gives all students ample writing practice in the Module Lessons, there are many additional structures and instructional practices that further support ELLs with writing:

» In Grades 3–5 in particular, as students begin to do more formal extended writing assessments, we provide additional writing practice for ELLs that is similar in structure (but not in content) to their writing assessments. For example, in Grade 4, Module 2, students are given the opportunity to complete a similar task twice: They practice reading and writing about one animal's defense mechanisms during lessons, and then they read and write about a different animal's defense mechanisms in the end of unit assessment. This helps ELLs become familiar with writing expectations.

» Writing scaffolds, such as teacher modeling and sentence and paragraph frames, may be offered for students who need additional support.

» Language Dives support both reading and writing fluency. After students learn to understand language structures through very focused reading at the sentence level, they practice those same structures that will give them greater confidence and skill as writers.

» In the K–2 Reading Foundations Skills Block (Skills Block), each letter of the alphabet includes a mnemonic device—an animal or object with the same beginning sound as a given letter—along with gestures and finger tracing that help students remember the most common sound associated with that letter and the proper formation of that letter. These visual, auditory, and tactile cues can help ELLs recall the letter in English that represents each sound.

In K–2 Labs (Labs), students do not do much formal writing. Yet the content knowledge they build and the oral language they develop ensure that they have more to write about in the Module Lessons.

Vocabulary and Phrases in Context

Teachers help students learn and practice vocabulary within the context of the topic and text they are using. Students learn and practice an unfamiliar word as it is commonly used with other words—in collocation. In Unit 2 of the Grade 2 module Schools and Community, for example, students read the learning target: *I can write about my observations after closely viewing pictures.* They discuss the meaning of *observations* in this sentence and then observe school communities through some mystery pictures. Afterward, students talk about what they observed before they write about it. ELLs can also compare shades of meaning (e.g., *observe, see, notice, spot*), use sentence frames to describe what they observe ("I see ____. One thing I observe is ____."), and contrast the observing and noticing process to the inquiring, evaluating, and wondering process.

All students use a Word Wall to track and learn selected vocabulary. Students in grades 3–5 also use a customized vocabulary log. In addition, 3–5 students and teachers can consult collocation and vocabulary references such as the following:

» Oxford Collocations Dictionary for Students of English

» https://prowritingaid.com/Free-Online-Collocations-Dictionary.aspx

» http://global.longmandictionaries.com

» http://www.learnersdictionary.com/

Language Usage: Celebration and Error Correction

Teachers and students explicitly and compassionately point out effective communication, especially when aligned to standards, and attend to language errors as part of the path to establishing equity and building content knowledge. Students can benefit from discussions as to why their communication is effective, or why it is inaccurate or incomprehensible, especially during the writing process.

At times, it can be helpful for students to discuss an error that is common to the group. At other times, giving one-on-one, individual feedback may be more respectful. Consider identifying, logging, and categorizing errors as follows, and practice correcting them over time (Ferris and Hedgcock, 2013).

» **Global:** errors that interfere with overall meaning. If writing can't be understood because of an error, students need to know right away. Correcting these kinds of errors should happen on any kind of writing that others will be using or looking at, whether it's a group note-catcher used during a protocol or a more formal essay used during a peer critique session.

  • Example from the preceding Language Dive sentence: "They bend their leaves following sun." (Here, a student has used a participle [*following*] instead of the infinitive [*to follow*] and omitted the article [*the*].)

» **Pervasive:** errors that are common. These kinds of errors won't necessarily impede understanding of meaning, so they may not be focused on for correction until the final stages of editing a more scaffolded piece of writing.

  • Example: "Bend they leaves, follow the sun." (Some students may omit the subject pronoun [*They*], use the subject pronoun [*they*] instead of the correct possessive pronoun [*their*], or omit the infinitive marker *to*.)

» **Stigmatizing:** errors that disturb more proficient speakers. Errors of this nature require varied approaches to correction. Most often a stigmatizing error will be corrected at the final editing stage, unless it is impeding meaning, in which case it should be corrected right away.

  • Example: "They bending their leaves to follow the sun." (Some students may overuse the present progressive. Although more proficient speakers may understand the communication, they are primarily critical of the learner's language proficiency because of the error.)

» **Student-identified:** errors that students notice themselves. These kinds of errors can and should be corrected at any time throughout the writing process.

  • Example: "Bend their leaves to follow the sun. The plants, they bend." (A student omitted the subject and attempted to clarify in a subsequent sentence.)

Giving kind, specific, and helpful feedback on successes and errors can help normalize the language learning process and put students "in the know," as well as mitigate the substantial risk students take on as they try out new language. We acknowledge that error correction may be ineffective when too much time is spent on less meaningful errors, when the correction is misunderstood, or when students feel targeted. The primary goals are to share power with students, to show them how you care about their language usage, and to help them communicate their message as intended.

Where and How Will My English Language Learners Be Supported throughout the K–5 Curriculum?

Table 2.12: Overview of English Language Learner Supports in the K–5 Curriculum

Curriculum Component	Support for English Language Learners
K–5 Module Lessons	ELL instruction is seamlessly integrated into lessons.
	Language proficiency standards, lesson highlights, and levels of support are provided at the beginning of each lesson in the Supporting English Language Learners section. Lesson-specific ELL supports also are added to the Meeting Students' Needs section.
	The instruction and supports are designed to provide ELLs with access to complex text, assessments and performance tasks, learning targets, peer and teacher interaction, and the expectations of the ELA and ELD standards.
K–2 Labs	In primary grades, rich oral language and exploration of content through multiple modalities is a hallmark of the Labs. Although Labs don't include formal scaffolds for ELLs, the focus of lessons and activities allows ELLs to focus on, practice, and play with language. Every Labs session also begins with Storytime (a read-aloud), which continues to expose ELLs to important content and complex text in English.
3–5 Additional Language and Literacy Block	ELL instruction is seamlessly integrated into lessons in the ALL Block.
	Separate lessons are also sometimes included to meet the linguistic and cultural needs of ELLs. These lessons focus on the same texts, tasks, and targets but make explicit the knowledge that may be innate for native speakers.
K–2 Reading Foundations Skills Block	The Skills Block includes notes for supporting ELLs in the Meeting Students' Needs section of each lesson. Also, overall, a structured phonics approach is a strong support for ELLs (see Chapter 4 for more details).

▶ How Will Universal Design For Learning Support The Varied Learning Needs Of My Students?

Our approach to supporting all students' learning needs is based on the principles of the Universal Design for Learning (UDL) framework, which is all about providing equal opportunities for *all* students to learn. This framework for learning emerged from a similar concept in architecture. Universal design in architecture means that buildings are designed to accommodate—from the outset—the physical needs of all people. Rather than retrofitting the staircase entry to a building with a wheelchair ramp, for example, architects employing universal design would use landscaping and other design elements to eliminate the need for stairs altogether. An entry without stairs helps people in wheelchairs, but it also helps all people access the building more easily (e.g., those with strollers, luggage).

Applying this concept to learning means that curriculum is designed from the outset to meet the learning needs of all students. This approach to curriculum design helps *all* students learn, not just those who may have learning disabilities or other learning challenges. This universal approach cuts down on (though doesn't necessarily eliminate) the need to retroactively re-teach or otherwise adapt learning experiences for those students who may struggle.

UDL, which was developed by David Rose, Anne Meyer, and their colleagues from the Center for Applied Special Technology, is based on the science of neurodiversity. Instead of focusing on learner deficits, UDL sees learner variability as a strength to be leveraged, not a challenge to overcome. Because there are many areas in which we know that learners will naturally vary, we can design curriculum to account for this variability. UDL consists of three broad principles, which are aligned with three networks in the brain that guide learning[5].

What is Universal Design for Learning and How Will It Benefit My Students?

Universal Design for Learning Principle 1: Provide Multiple Means of Representation

Learners differ in the ways that they perceive and comprehend information that is presented to them. For example, those with sensory disabilities (e.g., blindness or deafness), learning disabilities (e.g., dyslexia), language or cultural differences, and so forth may all require different ways of approaching content. Others may simply grasp information quicker or more efficiently through visual or auditory means rather than printed text. Also learning, and transfer of learning, occurs when multiple representations are used, because they allow students to make connections within, as well as between, concepts. In short, there is not one means of representation that will be optimal for all learners; providing options for representation is essential.

GUIDELINE 1: PROVIDE OPTIONS FOR PERCEPTION

» Offer ways of customizing the display of information.

» Offer alternatives for auditory information.

» Offer alternatives for visual information.

GUIDELINE 2: PROVIDE OPTIONS FOR LANGUAGE AND SYMBOLS

» Clarify vocabulary and symbols.

» Clarify syntax and structure.

» Support decoding of text, mathematical notation, and symbols.

» Promote understanding across languages.

» Illustrate through multiple media.

GUIDELINE 3: PROVIDE OPTIONS FOR COMPREHENSION

» Activate or supply background knowledge.

» Highlight patterns, critical features, big ideas, and relationships.

---

[5] This information on the three principles and their corresponding guidelines is reprinted with permission from The National Center on Universal Design for Learning.

» Guide information processing, visualization, and manipulation.

» Maximize transfer and generalization.

Universal Design for Learning Principle 2: Provide Multiple Means of Action and Expression

Learners differ in the ways that they can navigate a learning environment and express what they know. For example, individuals with significant movement impairments (e.g., cerebral palsy), those who struggle with strategic and organizational abilities (e.g., executive function disorders), those who have language barriers, and so forth approach learning tasks very differently. Some may be able to express themselves well in written text but not speech, and vice versa. It should also be recognized that action and expression require a great deal of strategy, practice, and organization, and this is another area in which learners can differ. In reality, there is not one means of action and expression that will be optimal for all learners; providing options for action and expression is essential.

GUIDELINE 4: PROVIDE OPTIONS FOR PHYSICAL ACTION

» Vary the methods for response and navigation.

» Optimize access to tools and assistive technologies.

GUIDELINE 5: PROVIDE OPTIONS FOR EXPRESSION AND COMMUNICATION

» Use multiple media for communication.

» Use multiple tools for construction and composition.

» Build fluencies with graduated levels of support for practice and performance.

GUIDELINE 6: PROVIDE OPTIONS FOR EXECUTIVE FUNCTIONS

» Guide appropriate goal-setting.

» Support planning and strategy development.

» Facilitate managing information and resources.

» Enhance capacity for monitoring progress.

Universal Design for Learning Principle 3: Provide Multiple Means of Engagement

Affect represents a crucial element to learning, and learners differ markedly in the ways in which they can be engaged or motivated to learn. There are a variety of sources that can influence individual variation in affect, including neurology, culture, personal relevance, subjectivity, and background knowledge, along with a variety of other factors. Some learners are highly engaged by spontaneity and novelty, while others are disengaged, even frightened, by those aspects, preferring strict routine. Some learners might like to work alone, while others prefer to work with their peers. In reality, there is not one means of engagement that will be optimal for all learners in all contexts; providing multiple options for engagement is essential.

GUIDELINE 7: PROVIDE OPTIONS FOR RECRUITING INTEREST

» Optimize individual choice and autonomy.

» Optimize relevance, value, and authenticity.

» Minimize threats and distractions.

GUIDELINE 8: PROVIDE OPTIONS FOR SUSTAINING EFFORT AND PERSISTENCE

» Heighten salience of goals and objectives.

» Vary demands and resources to optimize challenge.

» Foster collaboration and community.

» Increase mastery-oriented feedback.

GUIDELINE 9: PROVIDE OPTIONS FOR SELF-REGULATION

» Promote expectations and beliefs that optimize motivation.

» Facilitate personal coping skills and strategies.

» Develop self-assessment and reflection.

How Will Universal Design Impact the Way I Teach the Curriculum?

At EL Education, our approach to curriculum and instruction is, overall, already quite aligned with UDL. We believe in learning-centered classrooms that provide varied experiences and draw on an array of materials, methods, and assessments to keep all students challenged, engaged, and empowered. In addition, we took care to bake the three principles of UDL into every part of the curriculum and to call your attention to them in two places in the Teacher's Guide for every Module Lesson:

1. **Universal Design for Learning.** This section appears at the front of every Module Lesson, adjacent to the other sections meant to prepare you for each lesson (e.g., Teaching Notes, Materials, Supporting English Learners). The purpose of this section is to orient you to the ways in which the lesson was designed to provide multiple means of representation, action and expression, and engagement. What follows are two examples of the kinds of information you will find in this section of each lesson:

   • Example 1: Multiple Means of Representation (MMR): kindergarten Module 2, Unit 1, Lesson 3: *As students work on their Temperature page, provide visual access to the thermometer by placing it on a document camera. This will help students draw the shape and details of the thermometer from observation. (MMR)*

   • Example 2: Multiple Means of Action and Expression (MMAE): Grade 5, Module 1, Unit 1, Lesson 5: *Students who many need additional support with reading can benefit from engaging with the unfamiliar text in different ways. Consider pre-selecting important sentences or chunks for this section of the text and preparing scaffolded questions to help support comprehension (see the Meeting Students' Needs section). Also consider highlighting key portions of the text and asking students to identify how they are examples of threats to human rights. This relieves students from wading through large portions of text and allows them to more readily demonstrate their comprehension.*

2. **Meeting Students' Needs.** Within each Module Lesson, the Meeting Students' Needs section will direct your attention to specific supports and extensions you can provide during each part of the lesson. What follows are two examples of the kinds of information you will find in this section:

   • Example 1: Multiple Means of Action and Expression (MMAE): kindergarten, Module 2, Unit 2, Lesson 6: *To help students express their ideas in the weather journal, offer options for drawing utensils (examples: thick markers, colored pencils), writing tools (examples: fine-tipped markers, pencil grips, slant boards), and scaffolds (examples: picture cues, shared writing, extended time). (MMAE)*

   • Example 2: Multiple Means of Engagement (MME): Grade 5, Module 1, Unit 2, Lesson 14: *Students who need additional support with writing may have negative associations with writing tasks based on previous experiences. Help them feel successful with writing by allowing them to create feasible goals and celebrate when these goals are met. For instance, place a sticker or a star at a specific point on the page (e.g., two pages) that provides a visual writing target for the day. Also, construct goals for sustained writing by chunking the 25-minute writing block into smaller pieces. Provide choice for a break activity at specific time points when students have demonstrated writing progress. Celebrate students who meet their writing goals, whether it is the length of the text or sustained writing time.*

What If Some of My Students Need Additional Support?

Though we have tried to predict and proactively troubleshoot the places where we think students may need additional support, we don't know your students. You know best what will help them be successful and stay engaged. As you consider their needs and further differentiation strategies for any given lesson, consider the dos and don'ts in Table 2.13. Keep in mind that to make good decisions about any one of the dos and don'ts in this table, you will need to read the lesson carefully ahead of time. We will also provide you with more guidance on differentiation in subsequent chapters of this book, contextualized to the focus of each chapter.

Table 2.13: The Dos and Don'ts of Supporting Students' Needs

For Students Who Need Additional Support ...	
DO	DON'T
Chunk the text to make the amount of challenging text more manageable	Change the text to a less challenging text
Sparingly pre-teach vocabulary if student(s) are unlikely to figure out the meaning in context	Pre-teach too much of the vocabulary if student(s) can grapple with it productively and figure out the meaning in context
Provide sentence frames for conversation	Allow students to be silent or passive
Let students dictate text to you if they are working toward mastery of a reading standard	Let students dictate text to you if they are working toward mastery of a writing standard
Group students strategically	Allow stronger students to do all or most of the work in a group
Group flexibly based on assessments of progress (note: more information on flexible grouping follows)	Create static groups that are not responsive to assessments of progress

How Will Flexible Grouping Support My Students and Promote Their Growth?

Flexible grouping is a strategy for creating groups that is, by definition, temporary. Students are grouped for specific purposes—perhaps for a day, perhaps for a week or more—and then regrouped based on new needs or assessment data. The needs that determine groups may be learning needs or, sometimes, social-emotional needs. We consider flexible grouping an important practice because not all students progress at the same pace in all skill areas—the same student may be above grade level as a reader and below grade level as a writer—and because students don't necessarily progress on pace with peers. If a student progresses quickly, he or she should be assessed for readiness to move to a group that will offer greater challenge. And, conversely, if a student is struggling, he or she should be assessed for a group with additional scaffolding or support. Keeping students in static groups can inhibit their growth and, often, their confidence.

Flexible grouping is used throughout the curriculum, and suggestions are provided in the Teaching Notes of lessons. As you can see in Table 2.14, different components of the curriculum approach grouping in different ways.

Table 2.14: Approaches to Flexible Grouping in the K–5 Curriculum

Curriculum Component	What Is the Grouping Strategy?	What Evidence of Progress Is Used to Make Grouping Decisions?[6]
K–5 Module Lessons	Strategically pairing students for partner work, with at least one strong reader per pair. For ELLs: Strategically pairing or grouping ELLs with native and proficient English speakers, other ELLs, or by home language, depending on the purpose of the partner work. For example, pairing ELLs with partners who have more advanced or native language proficiency will allow the partner with greater language proficiency to serve as a model in the pair, initiating discussions and providing implicit sentence frames.	Ongoing assessment (e.g., student responses to text-dependent questions, hearing students read aloud, independently written introductions to a literary essay) Formal summative assessments (one per unit in Grades K–2; two per unit in Grades 3–5)
K–2 Labs	Students are grouped heterogeneously (including ELLs), with a balance of academic strengths and needs, language needs, and habits of character.	Teacher discretion
3–5 Additional Language and Literacy Block	Before beginning biweekly rotations, students are placed in one of four levels so that activities can be differentiated: ■ = Below grade level ● = On grade level ◆ = Above grade level ▲ = English language learners These levels are not static; rather, you will designate levels at the beginning of the two-week rotation based on need and the specific instruction students will engage with.	Decisions for leveling students in the ALL Block are made using evidence of progress from the Module Lessons: Ongoing assessment (e.g., student responses to text-dependent questions, hearing students read aloud, independently written introductions to a literary essay) Formal summative assessments (two per unit)
K–2 Reading Foundations Skills Block	Students are grouped homogeneously based on their current microphase of reading and spelling development (see Chapter 4 for more information). These groups may change, however, from week to week based on weekly cycle assessments.	Benchmark assessments (beginning, middle, end of year) Cycle assessments (weekly)

---

[6] For more information about assessing evidence of student progress, see Chapter 7.

Chapter 2: Getting Oriented: The Structure and Supports of the Curriculum

Chapter 2A: How Do All the Parts of the Curriculum Fit Together?

Chapter 2B: How Will the K–2 Labs and 3–5 Additional Language and Literacy Block Deepen and Enhance My Students' Learning?

Chapter 2C: How Is the Curriculum Designed to Help My Diverse Group of Learners Succeed?

▶ Instructional Leadership

Frequently Asked Questions

Chapter 2:
Instructional Leadership

Table 2.15: Chapter 2 Instructional Leadership

Questions to Ask Yourself and Your Staff
» If you and your staff have committed to teaching the entire curriculum, have you ensured that the master schedule provides adequate time (Grades K–2, three hours/day; Grades 3–5, two hours/day)?
» Have you given teachers guidance about what structures and practices they might need to give up to fully teach the curriculum (e.g., if teaching the K–2 Reading Foundations Skills Block [Skills Block], letting go of guided reading)?
» If you and your staff have decided not to teach a particular component of the curriculum (e.g., the Skills Block), are you clear on your rationale for why not? Do you have data that shows that your current program is successful and worth keeping?
» Have you provided teachers the support they need for effectively grouping students and for managing small group work and independent work effectively?
» What data are teachers using to strategically (and flexibly) group students? Have you provided grouping strategy support to teachers who may need it?
» Have you given teachers the guidance they need for when and how to pull students for small group interventions if necessary (e.g., during the Skills Block; during the Additional Language and Literacy Block)?
» What systems are in place for support specialists to become knowledgeable about the curriculum, both in terms of the scheduling requirements and the content, so they can best support students? How are they included in planning time with general education teachers?
» What additional knowledge- or culture-building among staff needs to happen so that all are supportive of the principles of inclusion for English language learners (ELLs) and students who struggle with grade-level work? What can you do to help them feel confident in their abilities to support these students?
» How can your whole staff get better at the practices designed specifically to support ELLs (e.g., Language Dives, Conversation Cues)?

Cont.

» How can you ensure that your staff has dedicated time to study and gain comfort with ELL and Universal Design for Learning supports that are woven into the curriculum?

» What kinds of words and phrases do you and your staff use when talking about students who are struggling? Is there any "unlearning" you or your staff need to do in order to support all students to succeed with this curriculum?

Evidence of Progress

» All staff can articulate the purpose and structure of each component of the curriculum and have redesigned their schedules to accommodate it.

» Teachers have made the shift to the new curriculum without trying to hang on to existing practices that make fitting everything in a challenge.

» If only using certain components of the curriculum, teachers can articulate how the needs the omitted components are designed to meet are being met by existing school structures and instructional methods. Teachers can show evidence of student outcomes tied to these existing approaches.

» Grade-level teams have clear grouping strategies in place.

» Teachers are using small group time during K–2 Labs, the Skills Block, and the 3–5 Additional Language and Literacy Block for students to receive intervention support if necessary.

» General education teachers and specialists (e.g., English as a second language teachers, special educators, interventionists) have time to collaborate and plan together to meet the needs of all students.

» Teachers are consistently implementing whole group Language Dives.

» Consistent use of "person first" language (e.g., "a student in the pre-alphabetic phase" or "a student who struggles with writing")

» Consistent use of asset-based language when describing ELLs

Resources and Suggestions

» The curriculum itself, along with a full suite of companion resources and tools, can be found at: Curriculum.ELeducation.org. Resources include:

- Curriculum Plans

- Curriculum Maps

- K–5 Required Trade Book Procurement List

- K–5 Recommended Texts and Other Resources

- K–2 Labs Materials List

- Life Science Materials List

- Classroom Protocols

- Sample Schedules

- Videos

» PD Pack: K–5 Language Arts Curriculum (second edition) (ELeducation.org)

Cont.

» Resources related to ELLs:

- Research and writing by Lili Wong Fillmore

- Research and writing by Rebecca Blum-Martinez

- California English Language Development Standards (http://www.cde.ca.gov/sp/el/er/documents/eldstndspublication14.pdf)

» Resources related to Universal Design for Learning:

- The Center for Applied Special Technology (cast.org)

- National Center for Universal Design for Learning (udlcenter.org)

Chapter 2:
Frequently Asked Questions

We're not yet clear that we have time to teach the entire curriculum (Grades K–2, three hours; Grades 3–5, two hours). What resources do you have that can help us make this decision?

The best way to know whether you have time to teach the entire curriculum is to learn as much as you can about what it has to offer. How does it compare to what you are already doing? How satisfied are you with the impact of your current curricula on student learning and habits of character? Are there holes you need to fill? Is there dissatisfaction you need to address? If you are still unsure, you should contact us for further support at pd@eleducation.org.

The K–2 Labs seem fun, but my schedule is so packed. Is this hour of instruction really necessary?

When time is tight and something has to give in your schedule, it may seem tempting to cut the time for the K–2 Labs (Labs). There are no new standards taught or assessed during Labs and, with the exception of the 10 minutes of Storytime, this hour is not considered core instruction. This can make the Labs seem like dispensable time. The Labs, however, are developmentally important for young children. They reinforce and deepen module content with a focus on play, creativity, oral language development, read-aloud, and executive function development (e.g., goal-setting and reflection). Young children need that time.

Instead of cutting Labs altogether, we recommend that you consider flexible approaches to the hour. You could choose to eliminate one of the Labs (e.g., the Engineer Lab) in favor of something else you have decided your students need more (e.g., writers' workshop). It's important not to cut a Lab that provides critical scaffolding for the module performance task, but there may be some that are less critical and can be cut. Or, you could do Labs three days a week instead of five, which would allow you to make time for other things you need but still allow students the time to deepen their module learning in the Labs. It's better to run Labs in their entirety (the full hour) a limited number of times per week (e.g., one hour three days per week) than to run just portions of a given Lab hour. This ensures that students experience all Lab components (Storytime, Setting Lab Goals, In the Lab, and Reflecting on Learning). Also, don't forget that the Labs are designed to run for six weeks per eight-week module. That means you have two extra weeks to play with.

It seems like the 3–5 Additional Language and Literacy Block offers time for extra practice with things that I like to do in different ways in my classroom. What will my students be missing if I opt not to teach this block?

There are many other stand-alone programs and curricula for teaching things like spelling, grammar, and word work. Making the switch from your existing practice for teaching these to the Additional Language and Literacy (ALL) Block will be beneficial for your students because the ALL Block is based on the same content as the Module Lessons. This synergy, as opposed to decontextualized approaches, is powerful for students and makes it much more likely that all students will reach mastery of standards. Learning is made stronger and more coherent for them, and more manageable for you, because the two instructional blocks speak to and reinforce each other.

I'm still not clear what the K–2 Reading Foundations Skills Block is all about. Where do I find more information about that?

Chapter 4! If Chapter 4 doesn't provide you with what you need, the K–2 Skills Block Resource Manual, will provide you with much more detailed support on everything from assessment administration to differentiated small group instruction.

How do the various components of the curriculum give students experience with a volume of reading?

Research confirms that the more one reads, the more one knows—about the topic, about vocabulary, about syntax, even about related topics. Students should be swimming in text. With this firmly in mind, volume of reading is an important part of every component of our curriculum. From close reading/read-alouds in Module Lessons, to Lab Storytime and research reading, to decodable readers in the K–2 Reading Foundations Skills Block (Skills Block), to structures for Accountable Independent Reading in Grades 3–5, including daily homework and ALL Block rotations, it's a high priority for us and is considered core instruction. Our curriculum includes lists of recommended texts connected to every module so that you can make your classroom a text-rich space that gives students plenty of opportunity to build their content knowledge and their reading muscles.

Throughout the curriculum, there are many times when some students work independently while teachers work with small groups. What are some strategies for managing a classroom full of students when teachers are busy with small group instruction? How will students stay productive and on task without teacher direction?

We believe strongly that not only can students handle productive academic work when they are working in small groups away from their teachers, but that teaching them strategies to do so should be considered a vital part of their classroom experience. Building their capacity to take ownership of their learning and to work both independently and collaboratively is how they truly engage with and deepen their academic learning and their habits of character. We offer many opportunities, through such instructional practices as protocols and debriefs, for students to have positive interactions that help them learn how to converse with each other, ask and answer questions, and reflect on their learning. These structures build their capacity to "self-manage." (For more on self-management and building an active and collaborative classroom culture, see Chapter 3C.)

In addition, the curriculum is designed so that you have time and support to introduce these structures and give students practice with them. For example, in the ALL Block, students work independently in heterogeneous groups following a protocol that guides them through the completion of a task card. This grouping structure enables students to use their strengths to support one another. During Module 1, students learn the routines for the ALL Block and how to work independently, including learning how to be an effective peer coach. This helps build student independence while leaving you free to focus on the small group instruction. For those times when they get stuck, students also learn to use Red Light, Green Light: They show a red, yellow, or green card to signal that they can work independently or need help.

What should I do to support students in Grades 3–5 who still have significant struggles with phonics and decoding?

Based on the standards, by third grade students are expected to have mastered the phonics and decoding skills described in the K–2 Reading: Foundational Skills standards. But realistically, not all students will have done so. The ALL Block is not designed for remediation, although skillful teachers certainly can differentiate for students who need it during this time. We highly recommend that students who are significantly behind on reading foundations receive targeted intervention and support based on resources provided in the Skills Block.

How important are the K–2 Labs and the 3–5 Additional Language and Literacy Block for my English language learners?

Labs are inherently supportive of English language learners (ELLs): Students explore compelling content through multiple modalities and have rich opportunities to talk with peers about what they are discovering and are curious about. In addition, a variety of supports for ELLs are embedded within the Lab lessons and the supporting materials. These include (but are not limited to) anchor charts, schedules and task cards with picture supports, time to process alone and with peers, and sentence frames to support common verbal interactions, such as goal-setting and reflecting.

The ALL Block has specific activities, such as Language Dives, vocabulary, and writing practice, that are focused specifically on ELLs and their needs.

When and where in the various components of the curriculum do English language learners receive targeted small group instruction?

ELLs, like all students, need to work in mixed groups to talk with and learn from their peers. It is also true that they have some specific language acquisition needs that are best served with targeted small group instruction. In the K–5 Module Lessons there are suggested Language Dives to conduct with small groups of ELLs. In the Labs students are grouped heterogenously, however, there are many opportunities for you to confer with students, and flex time to provide additional targeted support. During the ALL Block, students are grouped homogeneously for targeted teacher-guided instruction (20 minutes per day). However, students are grouped heterogeneously during their independent work on task cards (20 minutes per day) so that they have the support of peer coaches and the opportunity to speak with and learn from others.

How can I address the needs of newcomers to English?

While our curriculum will assist all ELLs in gaining academic English abilities, we provide some additional suggestions for teachers to use with students who are brand-new to English. One of the best supports for newcomers in the early days is a functional approach. This involves helping students learn how to use language for particular functions, such as requesting ("Can I go to the bathroom?" "Can you help me, please?" "How do I say ___?"); responding to simple questions ("Yes, I understand." "No, I'm not finished"); and using formulaic language for expressing things like gratitude, apologies, and requests for clarification. It is important to try to use the same phrasing of language and routines for newcomers every day (e.g., say, "Let's go to recess" consistently; don't vary it with alternate phrasing like "Time for recess"). Visuals/kinesthetics are also helpful. Short lessons with newcomers introducing this kind of language can be helpful when they are used in addition to our content-based curriculum. It will also be important to give the newcomer some special attention on a regular basis until he or she feels more confident and is better integrated into the class.

How can my school's English as a second language teachers best support students with this curriculum?

It is important to establish a close working relationship with English as a second language teachers and to meet regularly about ELLs' progress. Specialists can and should preview Module Lessons and Labs or ALL Block lessons and meet proactively with you to consider how to most strategically apply or enhance the written materials.

What about the other subjects I teach, such as mathematics, science, and social studies? How can I help English language learners in those subjects?

Explicit attention to the complex language in the texts—whether ELA, math, science, or social studies—is critical. We recommend that teachers use the math, science, and social studies texts to conduct Language Dives with their students in these subjects.

How does EL Education's curriculum address the California English Language Development Standards for English Language Arts for ELLs?

Our curriculum was designed using the California English Language Development (CA ELD) Standards to help guide ELL instruction and supports. This framework was selected for its balance of specificity and practicality. Of all standards frameworks, the CA ELD Standards seem to be the most useful, offering robust language standards and proficiency level descriptors that clearly describe what ELLs should know and be able to do across a variety of contexts and at specific benchmarks. An important benefit is that the CA ELD Standards were developed to connect to the Common Core in order to engage students with rigorous academic content. Each Module Lesson includes the CA ELD Standards that helped guide the design of the ELL instruction and support in that lesson. If your district uses a different framework, such as the World-class Instructional Design and Assessment (WIDA) ELD Standards or other state standards, you may wish to align those standards to the CA ELD Standards for comparison and accountability purposes.

Should I use the Universal Design for Learning supports for English language learners?

ELLs have unique needs that require targeted support. In the K–5 Module Lessons, the Meeting Students' Needs sections in every lesson contain support for both English language learning and Universal Design for Learning (UDL). Some supports can serve a wide range of student needs. For example, inviting students to explicitly discuss why they are completing a "noticing and wondering" task can help make explicit for ELLs the purpose and goals of noticing and wondering; this type of support also connects with multiple means of representation as part of UDL.

However, ELLs have unique needs that cannot always be met with UDL support. According to federal guidelines, ELLs must be given access to the curriculum with appropriate supports, such as those that are specifically identified as "For English Language Learners" in the Meeting Students' Needs sections. For example, ELLs also must discuss and practice the language (e.g., syntax, intonation) they will need to complete the noticing and wondering task, such as the language to help them ask noticing and wondering questions. This type of language information is often innate for native and proficient English speakers.

I understand the principles of Universal Design for Learning and that the curriculum was designed to be supportive from the start, but what if my students need more support? How can I further differentiate instruction to support the students who struggle?

The curriculum provides supports and resources for differentiation where needed, within the Module Lessons, the Labs, the ALL Block, and the Skills Block. The lessons themselves offer suggestions for how to support students who may be struggling as well as those who may need academic extensions. Differentiated tools and scaffolding that support all learners are also provided in the student materials. One of the most important things to remember about differentiating instruction for our curriculum is that some common practices you may have used in the past may need to be changed. For example, when students are reading complex texts, it's important for all students to work with the same text, even if it's very challenging for some. Instead of providing a different text, it will be important to provide scaffolds that lift students to the text (e.g., smaller chunks of text, pre-highlighted text). We offer more on differentiation strategies throughout the book.

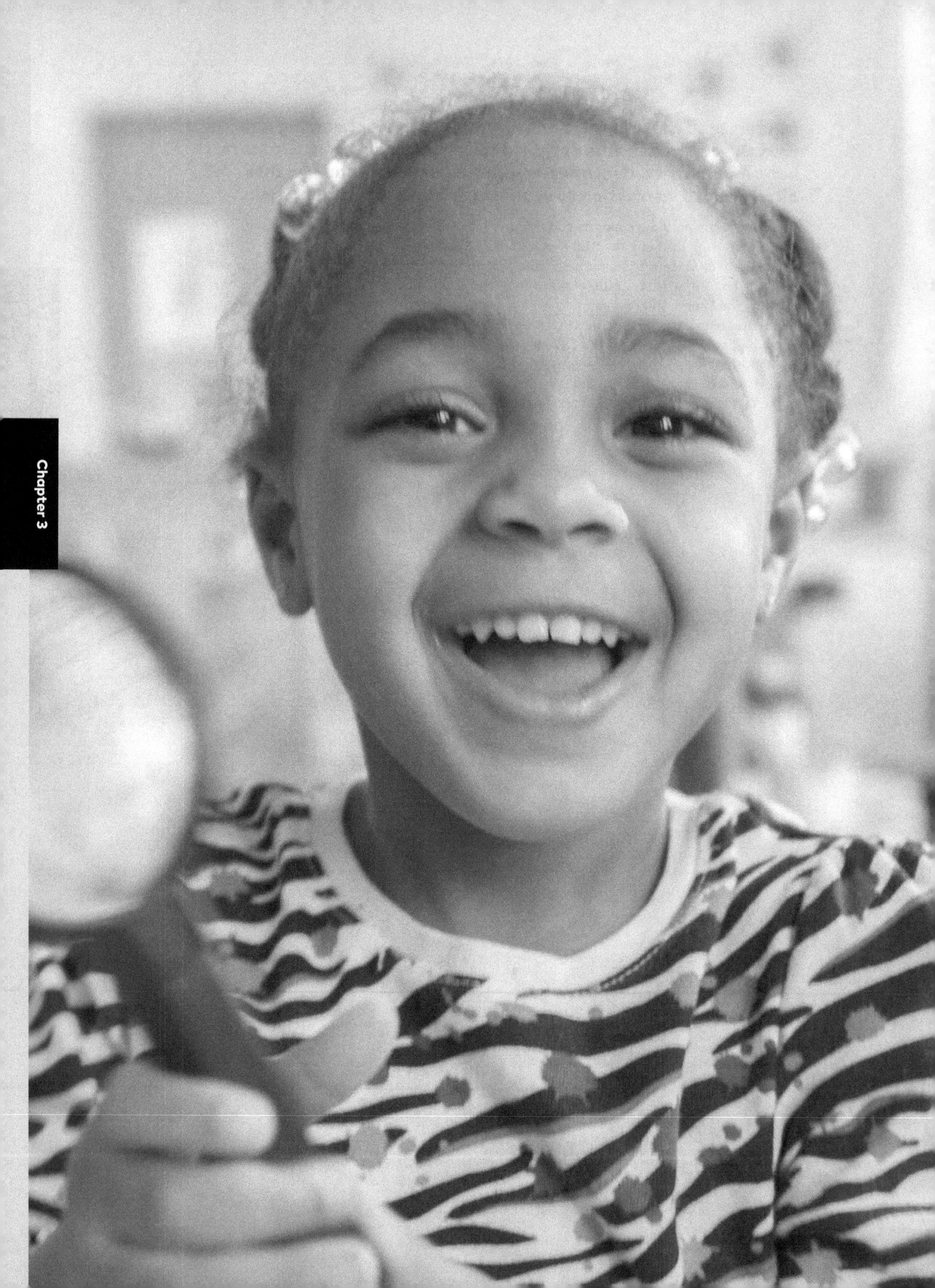

Chapter 3:
Preparing to Teach: Planning for Challenge, Engagement, and Empowerment

Chapter 3A:
How Do I Plan When the Planning Has Been Done for Me?

Chapter 2 has no doubt revealed to you that our K–5 curriculum is comprehensive. It includes everything you need to teach and assess new college- and career-ready English language arts (ELA) standards. It is also compelling, built around topics we know students will be interested in, full of books that are worth reading and proven strategies to help them become better readers, writers, speakers, listeners, and thinkers. As you and your students dig into and become accustomed to these new materials and practices, we feel confident that they will grow as readers, writers, and thinkers and that you will grow as a teacher too—you will undoubtedly learn new things, no matter how much experience you have in the classroom.

It may be tempting to think that such a comprehensive and detailed curriculum means that you won't have to do much planning. After all, hasn't the planning already been done for you? Yes and no. The answer to that question is more complex than you might think.

▷ This is a thinking teacher's curriculum. It is not a script. Our goal is for teachers to be less concerned with *fidelity* to the words on the page and more concerned with upholding the *integrity* of the purpose of the curriculum.

Teaching our curriculum will require a different kind of planning than you may be used to. You'll need to look out across units and modules to understand the flow of the year and the ways in which the K–2 Labs (Labs), 3–5 Additional Language and Literacy (ALL Block), and K–2 Reading Foundations Skills Block (Skills Block) fit within the big picture. And, although you won't need to plan a lesson from scratch, you will need to plan *for* each lesson to make it your own and the best it can be for your students. This is a thinking teacher's curriculum. It is not a script. Our goal is for teachers to be less concerned with *fidelity* to the words on the page and more concerned with upholding the *integrity* of the purpose of the curriculum.

Conducting lessons exactly as they are written and adhering strictly to the timing, language, and suggestions provided is possible, but it's not necessarily typical, nor is it recommended. This *fideli-ty* to the way the curriculum is written doesn't account for the dynamic and unpredictable ways in which a classroom full of students interacts with the material. A question from a student may take the class in an unpredictable, but worthwhile, new direction; students may struggle to find the an-swer you want them to find in the text; or the mundane realities of life in school—from fire alarms to snow delays—can disrupt, delay, or redirect a lesson. These "hiccups" to the best- laid plans are actually the most predictable part of teaching.

Knowing this, our goal is to help you teach the curriculum with *integrity*. This means understand-ing the deep logic of the design, as well as our commitment to challenging, engaging, and empow-ering all students, so that making changes to accommodate the living, breathing organism of the classroom still results in students meeting standards and achieving at high levels. Understanding, for example, that grappling with challenging text is a purposeful feature of close reading lessons and serves an important role in developing student's literacy muscles may help you consider how best to scaffold the lesson for particular students to ensure that they have access to the same chal-lenging text and can feel successful reading it. Similarly, understanding the purposes and benefits of protocols will help you avoid the temptation to skip them or, if necessary, to swap one protocol for another with a similar purpose. Just as students start each module by building background knowledge of their topics, this book is designed to help you build background knowledge of the curriculum so that you can make the most of it in your classroom.

▶ What Kind of Planning Will Help Me Teach the Curriculum with Integrity (Not Just Fidelity)?

Teaching this curriculum with integrity requires deep knowledge of it. Knowing where you are headed over the long term allows you to make more informed decisions in the short term. If you are not sure what's coming tomorrow or next week, you may find yourself feeling unsure of how to make informed decisions to best support your students' learning *today*. This can sometimes lead to an overreliance on fidelity to the words on the page of any given lesson, as if it were a script.

On the other hand, if you have looked ahead and understand how standards spiral in and out of lessons over days and weeks, and you have analyzed the assessments and the ways in which stu-dents prepare for those assessments, you'll be able to use your wisdom and experience as a teacher to be responsive to the needs of your students within your fast-paced, always changing classroom environment.

Zooming in: from Wide Angle to Close-Up

With teaching with integrity as the goal, it will be important for you to engage in both a yearlong "wide-angle" unpacking of the curriculum and a lesson-level "close-up" unpacking.

Wide-Angle Planning

Looking over the year with a wide-angle lens will help you get a feel for the flow of the four mod-ules, including how standards are taught and assessed across the year and how the Labs and ALL Block connect to and support the content, as well as the scope and sequence of the Skills Block. In addition to the wide-angle, yearlong view, it will also be important to engage in a slightly zoomed-in, midrange module- and unit-level analysis four times a year, well before you start teaching a new module.

Close-Up Planning

The close-up lesson-level view, which occurs weekly and daily, will ensure that you understand each lesson fully and that you have a chance to consider the needs of your particular students, including the supports and materials they may need above and beyond what's included in the lesson. This is your time to think through the logistics of each lesson. How will you make it your own? How will you keep your notes to stay organized? How will you prepare for the inevitable distractions or account for the fact that your students have lately needed extra time with things like transitions and paper management? For any given week and day, this lesson-level unpacking and prepping is necessary for the Module Lessons at all grade levels, alongside the Labs and ALL Block, plus the stand-alone Skills Block.

Refining Lessons

You might be starting to think that that's a lot of unpacking to do! It is; however, it's the kind of preparation that allows you to spend your time taking a lesson you know is already solid and making it the best you can for your students. It may help to think of the process more as refining than as planning. Rather than running around looking for a good text or being forced to improvise because you ran out of time to plan, you can instead spend your time considering the best grouping strategies for your English language learners (ELLs), for example. Or, perhaps you can spend time preparing the materials in such a way that your students, who have been struggling with transitions, will have them at their desks when they come in from recess. Reading ahead, taking notes, and making the lesson your own will help you attend to these kinds of small details because they matter a lot, especially to your students, and they can make a big difference in both what and how students learn.

> *"As a critical thinker, I'm compelled to adjust the lesson to meet the needs of my students.... The great thing about the modules is that the lesson plans, student work, and student texts are already prepared, so my planning time is spent planning the differentiated materials for students."*

Kerry Meehan-Richardson
Grade 3 Teacher, Rochester, New York

▶▶ **Video Spotlight**

In the accompanying video, see third-grade teacher Kerry Meehan-Richardson from World of Inquiry School in Rochester, New York, refining a Module Lesson. Meehan-Richardson attends to students' various readiness levels through her instructional decisions, the adaptation of materials, and classroom management strategies.

https://vimeo.com/84898604

For the remainder of this section, we're going to walk you through the process of unpacking the entire curriculum, starting with the wide-angle lens (the yearlong view) and working our way to the close-ups (the daily lessons). We will provide brief descriptions of the documents you'll need to reference, followed by task cards that will help you and your colleagues dig in. This chapter is focused on the content-based literacy components of the curriculum (Module Lessons plus the Labs and ALL Block). The Skills Block requires a similar unpacking process, but the details are so unique that we have saved them for Chapter 4. Look for Table 4.15: Preparing to Teach the K–2 Reading Foundations Skills Block, near the end of Chapter 4C.

★ **A Word about Using the Task Cards**

The task cards you will find on the following pages are extensive. It's perfectly reasonable to take one look at them and say, "Those will take me hours to fill out!" That's exactly right. They very well might. But that's by design. We think it should take hours to really internalize the purpose and flow of the curriculum over weeks and months, to understand the backward design, to feel fully prepared to teach the texts, and to see how the Labs and ALL Block deepen student learning and provide additional time to practice important skills.

The yearlong, module- and unit-level task cards are completed infrequently. We expect you'll work with these during summer planning time or periodic professional development days at your school. They are designed for a deep review of how the curriculum unfolds over the course of the year, and it's important to analyze them carefully.

▷ These task cards as well as other, more detailed planning templates can be found on our website. You can download them and either print them or work from digital copies.

It is really the lesson-level task cards that you will want to develop efficiencies with, because you'll need to unpack lessons frequently. You may start slow with those task cards and, over time, move more quickly, zooming in on the questions that represent your particular areas of need as a teacher. For example, it may take you longer to analyze the note-catchers and other student-facing materials and think through differentiation options for your students than it does to plan for transitions. If you are great at transitions and you have 10 strategies in your back pocket that work like a charm with your students, you can probably reliably skip that question.

As you get used to how the lessons work, you can judge what's most helpful to you and, if it makes your life easier, create your own task card that suits your needs best. You may find that 20 to 30 minutes gives you plenty of time to read the lessons, think through the needs of your students, and prep your materials.

These task cards as well as other, more detailed planning templates can be found on our website (Curriculum.ELeducation.org). You can download them and either print them or work from digital copies.

Orienting to the Year

There are two documents that will give you the widest view of the yearlong content-based literacy components of curriculum (Module Lessons plus the Labs and ALL Block): the **Curriculum Plan** (one for Grades K–2 and one for Grades 3–5) and the **Curriculum Map** (one for each grade level). These documents will orient you to the big picture of the skills and content focus of the modules.

The Curriculum Plan, which is the widest-angle lens, will orient you to how the four modules will unfold across the year at your grade level, as well as the grade levels that precede and follow. One thing you will notice when reading the Curriculum Plan is that the high-level focus of each module is the same for each grade in the respective K–2 and 3–5 grade bands. Students in each grade band will experience the same general flow in terms of the skills they will build in each module (e.g., Module 2: Learning through Science and Story), while the specific topics differ from grade to grade (e.g., kindergarten: "Weather Wonders"; Grade 1: "The Sun, Moon, and Stars"; Grade 2: "Fossils Tell of Earth's Changes").

The focus of the K–2 modules:

» Module 1: Building Literacy in a Collaborative Classroom

» Module 2: Learning through Science and Story

» Module 3: Growing as Researchers

» Module 4: Contributing to the School Community

The focus of the 3–5 modules:

» Module 1: Becoming a Close Reader and Writing to Learn

» Module 2: Researching to Build Knowledge and Teach Others

» Module 3: Considering Perspectives and Supporting Opinions

» Module 4: Gathering Evidence and Speaking to Others

The Curriculum Map zooms a little closer into the four modules for your grade level, detailing the texts, assessments, and standards across the entire year. This document is critical to your understanding of the flow of the modules, how each module builds on the preceding module, and when and how often each standard is assessed. As you read, consider how the modules connect to other requirements in your school or district. For example, if your school or district has curriculum maps in place for coverage of science and social studies content, how can standards covered in each module fit into that agreed-upon scope and sequence? The Orienting to the Year Planning Task Card on the following page will help you see the big picture of how the curriculum unfolds across the year.

Note: For Grades K–2 teachers, don't forget that guidance for unpacking the Reading Foundations Skills Block is found in Table 4.15 in Chapter 4C.

Orienting to the Year Planning Task Card

Step 1: Read the **Curriculum Plan** and **Curriculum Map.**

Curriculum Plan and Curriculum Map	Response
After reading through these documents, what benefit do you see in revisiting them multiple times throughout the year? **In what ways will the information guide your big-picture planning?**	
Look closely at the standards grid. How would you describe this grid? What do the check marks mean, and why is it important to pay attention to them?	
What implications does the standards grid have for your **pacing and planning?**	
How might you describe the literacy work in your classroom this year to your students or their families? **What are you looking forward to?** What do you think your students will most enjoy? How will they benefit from this curriculum?	
If you are a coach or a school leader, how will these documents help you plan for and talk about the literacy focus at your school and the **expected impacts for students?**	

Orienting to a Module

There are several key documents that will orient you to each module: the **Module Overview**; the **Assessment Overview and Resources**; and, for Grades K–2, the **K–2 Labs Overview** for the module and the **K–2 Labs Materials List**.

The module is the heart of the curriculum. It drives the content and skills students will focus on for approximately eight to nine weeks, before they move on to a new module. There are four modules per year, each with a different content and skills focus. A module is made up of more than just the Module Lessons, though you could argue that they are the main characters on this eight- to nine-week stage. Just as important are the "supporting characters": the Labs, the ALL Block, and the optional Life Science module that accompanies Module 2 in Grades 3–5. Just like in a play, these supporting characters are a critical part of how students experience the module. They help students explore the content in different ways and reinforce the skills they are learning. The Module Lessons plus these complementary blocks make up the content-based literacy component of the curriculum.

In each Module Overview, there is a small box called the Four T's (see Figure 3.1 for an example). This box will give you a quick snapshot of the topic, texts, targets, and tasks of the module. If you have time, we recommend covering this box up with sticky notes (no peeking!) and grappling with the Four T's on your own or as a team as you examine the documents. Grappling is good for students; it's also good for you. Searching for this information will likely make it stick a bit more than just reading it.

Figure 3.1: Sample Four T's Box from the Grade 3, Module 1 Overview

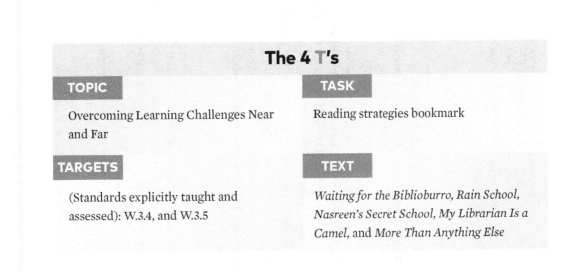

The Orienting to a Module Planning Task Card on the following pages will help you analyze the important overview documents for the module and make connections between the Module Lessons and the Labs and ALL Block. (Note: Although there are some connections to the ALL Block made in the Module Overview, the real unpacking of the ALL Block is best done at the *unit level*. You will find guidance for that work in the Orienting to a Unit section, which follows this section.)

Orienting to a Module Planning Task Card

Step 1: Read the **Module Overview.**

Module Overview	Response
Locate the **guiding questions and big ideas.** What's most exciting to you, and what do you think will be most exciting for your students?	
Read the summary paragraph closely. It describes students' learning across the three units of the module. **Describe in your own words what this module is mostly about,** in terms of both the content students are learning and the literacy skills they are building.	
Read the short paragraph that describes the performance task. **How will students be asked to synthesize and show their learning at the end of the module?** How would you describe how the three units build toward this performance task? What are options to modify or extend the learning or put your own stamp on it as a teacher?	
Depending on your grade level, review the brief description of the connections to the Labs and ALL Block. **How do these blocks connect to and enhance the content and skills focus of the module?**	
Locate the CCSS section, which list the standards explicitly taught and formally assessed in this module. What are the grade-level expectations for students? **Do you anticipate needing to provide any additional support for particular students?** Be sure to consider available language progressions for ELLs.	
Read the Habits of Character/Social-emotional Learning Focus for the module. How is this focus already reflected in your classroom? **What else can you do to make this focus permeate the school day and give your students a coherent experience?**	

Cont.

Step 2: Read the **Assessment Overview and Resources.**

Assessment Overview and Resources	Response
Read the description and standards for each assessment (one per unit in Grades K–2; two per unit in Grades 3–5). **What literacy skills are students focused on?**	
Read the other resources provided (e.g., rubrics, checklists, and sample student responses). What insight do these give you about the **support/scaffolding** students will need to be successful on the assessments?	
Consider what additional supports specific students may need to succeed with the assessments. How might support specialists (e.g., English as a second language teachers) work with specific students outside of literacy time to set them up for success in these areas?	
Take the assessments yourself, as a learner, to identify what students are going to need to be able to do. What literacy skills or knowledge does this assessment require? What do *you* need to do or know to be able to teach this module?	

Cont.

Step 3: Read all texts used in this module (listed in the **Module Overview**).

Texts	Response
Read the central text. What is this text about? What did you learn about this topic/issue/content? **What will your students like about this book?** What will you enjoy about using this book with them?	
What is intriguing, surprising, or confusing about the information in this text? **What do you anticipate might be challenging about this text for your students?**	
Consider specific students. **Who might struggle, and how can you support them?**	

Cont.

Step 4: Grades K–2 only: Read the **K–2 Labs Overview** for the module and the **K–2 Labs Materials List.** (3–5 teachers: Note that specific questions related to the Additional Language and Literacy Block Unit Overview are in the Orienting to a Unit section that follows.)

Labs Overview and Materials List	Response
Which four Labs are running during this module? What is the guiding question for each Lab that will drive students' inquiry? How does each Lab connect to students' learning in the Module Lessons? **What do you think will most excite (or challenge) your students?**	
For each of the four Labs, note how the learning targets get more sophisticated in each stage of the Lab. What does this signal about how students are **building independence and deepening their thinking** in each Lab across the entire module?	
Do you plan to use Lab time to offer interventions for particular students? If so, how will you structure Lab time? Will you run all four Labs? Will you do Labs every day? How can you think flexibly about the schedule to meet student needs?	
Are there any modifications you might make to the Labs for this module to better meet the needs of your students? If there are some Labs that are critical scaffolding for the module performance task, don't omit them. However, there may be others that are easier to omit for a variety of reasons. If you free up time by omitting a Lab or Labs, how will you use that time to meet your students' needs?	
Do you feel that your students would benefit from additional writing experiences in the Labs? If so, how will you structure these experiences? Consider having students formally write up their learning and notes from the Research Lab, adding more narratives in the Imagine Lab, or adding more formal written reflection, particularly during the Choice and Challenge stage.	

Cont.

Labs Overview and Materials List	Response
How might you use the flex time at the start to prepare for Labs? How might you use the flex time at the end to support students with their performance tasks or their products from Labs?	
What other **logistic considerations** are important to plan for before you launch Labs (e.g., developing Labs groups, supporting students with transitions, or materials use)?	
What materials will students need access to for each Lab? Which materials do you already have? How will you acquire what you need? How will you organize these so students are able to access them independently?	
What types of texts might you read during Storytime based on the content and character of the module? Do you have a sufficient set of texts in your classroom? See the Labs Recommended Book List.	
How will you protect time during Labs for goal-setting and reflection? Are there any tricks you can use to ensure that these important opportunities to develop executive function and build character don't get lost in the shuffle (e.g., setting a timer)?	

Orienting to a Unit

Each unit contributes to the story of the module by focusing instruction around the specific literacy skills necessary to holistically study the module topic. Reviewing unit-level documents—the **Unit Overviews** and the **Additional Language and Literacy Block Unit Overview** (for Grades 3–5 teachers only) will bring more of the details into focus as you continue the process of "zooming in" closer and closer to daily lessons.

It is important to read all three Unit Overviews to get a sense of the big picture of how the three units build on each other and how they fit together to tell the story of the module. The Unit-at-a-Glance charts are an especially important component of the Unit Overviews. Most teachers reference these charts frequently to understand the arc of each unit, how lessons build toward assessments, the recommended scaffolding (including key anchor charts), the protocols used across the unit, and when each text is introduced and how much time is recommended to spend on each. When reviewing the Unit Overviews, it is also a good idea to refer to the **K–5 Recommended Text and Other Resources List** to ensure that your classroom has the materials students will need to build their knowledge of the module topic.

You will want to analyze all three units of a module; however, you may opt to take a collaborative approach to this work. For example, with your grade-level team and/or other support specialists who are involved with your class (e.g., English as a second language teachers), you might consider a "jigsaw" structure to divide and conquer the analysis of the three units, with each teacher completing one of the Orienting to a Unit Planning Task Cards on the following pages. Build in time to share information with each other and revisit this information on your own before teaching. Whether reviewing the Unit Overviews on your own or as a team, if your time is limited:

» Prioritize analyzing how the units work together to create the arc of the entire module.

» For Grades K–2, consider how the entire unit scaffolds to the formal unit assessment and what additional assessment you might gather throughout the unit (e.g., through use of checklists).

» For Grades 3–5, chunk the unit into two halves and focus on how the lessons in each half scaffold toward the assessments: What is expected of students, and how do the lessons get them there?

For Grades 3–5, this is also the time to review the Additional Language and Literacy Block Unit Overview, as this block connects to Module Lessons at the unit level (as opposed to the Labs, which connect at the module level). In a unit of the ALL Block, students dig deeper into the texts introduced in the Module Lessons and practice the skills introduced.

Orienting to a Unit Planning Task Card

Step 1: Read all three **Unit Overviews,** considering the arc of the module.

Unit Overview	Response
Read the summary paragraphs. **What is the "story" of each of the three units?** How do they build on each other? What knowledge and literacy skills do students develop across all three units?	
In addition to the central text(s), what do students read? How do the content, skills, and texts connect to and build off one another across these three units? **What will your students like best about these texts?**	
Analyze the Unit-at-a-Glance chart. Based on the lesson titles, learning targets, protocols, and anchor charts, **describe the logic and scaffolding of the lessons leading up to each assessment.** Are any additional scaffolds needed?	
Review the section on Accountable Independent Reading. **Is your routine established?** Have you reviewed the K–5 Recommended Text and Other Resources List for suggested books, articles, and videos on the module topic? Is this material available in your classroom?	
Review the Supporting English Language Learners section. Which of the strategies are most needed for your students? **Are there any structures or routines that will require additional planning and/or support?**	
Consider the **optional extensions for the unit.** Would your students benefit from any of these suggestions? How will you plan for them?	

Cont.

Step 2: Grades 3–5 only: Read the **Additional Language and Literacy Block Unit Overview** and the sample calendar. (K–2 teachers: Note that specific questions related to the K–2 Labs Overview and the K–2 Labs Materials List are in the Orienting to a Module Planning Task Card.)

Additional Language and Literacy Block Unit Overview	Response
Overall, how would you describe how students' work in the ALL Block supports their work in the Module Lessons? **Are there additional areas of need or interventions for particular students for which you can use time in the ALL Block?**	
Which texts will students be rereading and digging into more deeply in the ALL Block? **Based on your reading of the texts in this unit, are there texts that you think your students will need more time with?**	
Given your formal and informal assessment of student achievement toward the standards they will be practicing in this unit of the ALL Block, **how will you level your students for each component?** There are four levels of groups (*above*, *on*, and *below grade level*, and *English language learner*), but only three rotations per session. How will you place your four levels into three groups for the instruction in this unit? How will you approach ongoing grouping and regrouping?	

Chapter 3

Orienting to the Module Lessons

The primary document you'll reference at this stage—the "close-up" stage—is the specific **Module Lesson** you are preparing to teach.

Like most teachers, your lesson planning process most likely involves toggling between looking out over the week or weeks ahead and then focusing in on what's right in front of you—tomorrow (or even today!). The process with our curriculum is no different. To prepare well for what's coming tomorrow, it's important to situate individual lessons within the module and unit, and it's *critical* to spend focused time understanding and preparing for individual lessons and the arcs of lessons that may occur over the course of several days.

Each lesson in our curriculum provides detailed descriptions of everything from the purpose of the lesson, as stated in the learning targets, to the materials you will need, to suggested language for introducing new vocabulary, text-dependent questions, and myriad other "moments" in the lesson. Extensive Teaching Notes are provided to help you think through the key parts of the lesson and how each connects to previous and future lessons.

> *"Because this was my first year implementing the curriculum, I spent a lot of time reading the material to really understand what I was teaching. The teacher guides are extremely helpful when thinking about the 'flow' of a lesson. I've done my own work around building instructional slides to help with my pacing. But other than that, a lot of the heavy lifting has already been completed, especially compared to last year when I was using a different curriculum and working incredibly hard to find materials to use."*

Kady Taylor

Grade 1 Teacher, Lead and K–2 Instructional Strategy Reading Lead
Wilmington, Delaware

As curriculum designers, we've put tremendous thought into every part of every lesson, and we hope that they will come alive as you apply your own wisdom and expertise to delivering them. But the lessons need your input to be the best they can be. This is why analyzing each lesson and understanding its greater purpose is so important. Because all the basics for a strong lesson are already there, you can spend your prep time really thinking through how to make it most effective and engaging for your particular students and, importantly, how you are going to deliver it. (We offer advice on delivering your lessons in the section titled "How Can I Stay on Track and on Target with My Pacing?" which follows the task cards.)

The Module Lessons Planning Task Card on the following pages will help you analyze and gain comfort with the Module Lessons. Use this task card often when you're first starting out. Over time, you may find that you need it less and less.

Module Lessons Planning Task Card

Step 1: Read the entire **Module Lesson**, considering how it fits within the arc of the module.

Module Lesson	Response
What cognitive work will students be doing during this lesson? (Hint: Look at the verbs in the learning targets.) Look through the supporting materials that accompany the lesson. What will your students most enjoy about the lesson? What might be challenging for them (or for you as a teacher)?	
Describe how each form of assessment throughout the lesson will help you know whether students are making adequate progress toward the learning targets. **How will you know if they need additional support?**	
Are there any suggested ongoing assessments that **require additional planning** for you to use them successfully? (Examples: If observation is suggested, what checklist should you use? Might it help to create additional recording forms?)	

Cont.

Step 2: Reread the **Agenda** and **Teaching Notes**. Together, these sections give you a snapshot of the flow of the lesson, the high-level purpose, and important things to consider and prepare before you begin teaching.

Agenda and Teaching Notes	Response
What is the purpose of this lesson? How does it connect to previous lessons and build to future ones?	
What does the agenda tell you about transitions in the lesson? **What planning is necessary to make these transitions successful?**	
Look specifically at the "In advance" portion of the **Teaching Notes** and at the **Multimedia and Technology** section. What do you need to prepare?	

Cont.

Step 3: Look through the **Supporting Materials** for the lesson.

Supporting Materials	Response
Look carefully at student note-catchers and graphic organizers. How are these designed to scaffold students toward learning targets? **Will they serve as effective formative assessments?**	

Step 4: Reread the **Materials** and **Vocabulary** sections.

Materials and Vocabulary	Response
Have you read all the texts and materials for this lesson? Will it be obvious to students how they help them meet their learning targets? What additional bridge-building might you need to provide so **students see these connections and understand the purpose of their work?**	
Examine the vocabulary words. Are there any additional words not listed in this section that you may need to teach?	

Cont.

Step 5: Reread the **Opening, Work Time,** and **Closing and Assessment** sections.

Opening, Work Time, Closing and Assessment	Response
How will you introduce the learning target(s) and **continually check for understanding** in the lesson?	
What kinds of collaborative work will happen in this lesson? What is your grouping strategy? How will you manage efficient transitions? If the flow doesn't make sense for you, **what changes can you make that maintain the integrity of the lesson?**	
What will you have in your hands as you are teaching? Will you reference the lesson itself? Will you create a "Cliff's Notes" version or a Power-Point to guide your instruction? What will help you teach it most naturally?	
How can you foster high-level discourse throughout the lesson and ensure that students have plenty of time to think and do? What suggested questions in the lesson (or additional questions) do you want to be sure to ask?	
How does the Closing and Assessment portion of the lesson explicit-ly or implicitly reinforce the Habits of Character/Social-Emotional Learning Focus of the module? How will you ensure that you protect time for this important reflection?	

Cont.

Step 6: Reread the **Supporting English Language Learners (ELLs)**, **Universal Design for Learning (UDL)**, and **Meeting Students' Needs (MSN)** sections.

Supporting ELLs, UDL, MSN	Response
Determine which of your ELLs may need lighter or heavier support in this lesson. As indicated in the notes in this section, which materials will you prepare for which students?	
The UDL section cues you to prepare specific materials to support students who may struggle in this lesson. Based on what you know of the lesson so far, **who is likely to need this support, and what preparations are necessary?** Consider: groupings, additional adult support, differentiated materials. (Also see the additional support section of the Teaching Notes at the start of the lesson.)	
Think through the logistics of supporting students. If there is a Language Dive in this lesson for ELLs, for example, where and when will that occur? If some students need a more scaffolded text, how will you get it to them in a respectful way? Consider all of your students: Will the suggested scaffolds for ELLs support the whole class?	

Chapter 3

▶ How Can I Stay on Track and on Target with My Pacing?

Maintaining the suggested pacing during many components of the curriculum is likely to be challenging, especially your first time through. It will take practice. The steps laid out in the preceding pages will help ground you in the big picture of where you're headed and can allow you enough foresight to adjust if necessary. After working through the Module Lessons Planning Task Card, consider the following steps to guide wise, carefully considered pacing decisions.

Before the Lesson

» Study the lesson in advance individually or with your grade-level team and complete the task card. The more familiar you are with the lesson, the easier it will be to move through the components with fluidity.

» As you analyze the lesson, ask yourself: "When will students talk?" and "When will I talk?" Consider inviting a colleague into your classroom to take note of when you are talking and when students are talking, or invite him or her to videotape you. Often it's too much teacher talk that leads to the lesson getting off track in terms of pacing. It takes practice to get the balance right.

» Consider one or more of the following strategies to prepare you to deliver the lesson fluidly:

- If you have a printed version of the lesson, use it as is but mark it up with a highlighter or use sticky notes to keep yourself focused and to aid a smooth delivery.

- Create a "Cliff's Notes" synthesized version of the lesson with the main chunks to cue you for the flow. Within each chunk, highlight in large text specific phrasing or instructions. Consider using one of the digital planning tools found on our curriculum website (Curriculum.ELeducation.org) to help you create these notes and customize your delivery of the lesson.

- Create a PowerPoint or Smartboard Notes that will guide you through the lesson with visuals of the learning targets, directions for protocols, text-dependent questions, images, vocabulary words, or other lesson elements that will be helpful cues for you and your students. You can also use the notes section of the PowerPoint to include specific questions and other things you want to remember to say in a particular way.

- Write the agenda out on the white board with key words to cue you about the contents of each part of the agenda. Use the lesson itself to reference as needed, with things you want to say highlighted or pointed to with sticky notes for easy visual reference.

» Talk to your colleagues. Is another teacher in your building a few lessons ahead of your class? Can you talk with him or her about successes and challenges? Are there any barriers to avoid? Make note of their suggestions and consider whether they would be helpful in your class.

During the Lesson

» Use a timer. Setting a timer sends a message to students that there is a sense of urgency and that staying on task is important. The timer is likely to help you maintain the pacing of the lesson; it will also be appreciated by many students.

» Stay on topic and aligned with the learning targets. Students may be interested in learning more, but before being led astray by their many questions, consider alternatives for exploring additional topics. Some teachers have offered students extra credit or offered individual research opportunities in areas of interest. Explain to students why it's important to stay on topic. Study the flow of the module ahead of you so you know if the things students have questions about will be the topic of a future lesson.

» Thoroughly unpack the learning targets. The lesson will offer specific suggestions for how to unpack the learning targets, which frequently include a focus on vocabulary. It's important to be thorough, but don't linger there too long. The average time you should spend unpacking the learning targets is 3 to 5 minutes. When more than the recommended amount of time is spent on the learning targets, this segment is likely to turn into a mini lesson, which is not the intention.

» Pay attention to when students will talk and when you will talk during the lesson. It's easy to unintentionally use up a lot of time explaining things to students. The lessons are designed to let students figure things out on their own. Try to keep your teacher talk aligned to the facilitation and guidance they need.

> *"For daily planning, I make sure I know where we are heading for the week and then I condense the lessons into my own personal planning document using trigger words from the curriculum to help me remember where to go next in the lesson. I always make sure I have the materials prepared the day before so that everything is on hand when I need it."*

Sara Metz

K–1 Teacher, Denver

» Catch students' attention to clarify misconceptions or answer questions and then release them back to the task as soon as you can.

» Plan for and practice transitions. Moving from one section of a lesson to another can be a time waster. Have materials ready in advance and spend time at the beginning of the year practicing with students. It will pay off to "go slow to go fast" with transitions—front-load students' attention on efficient transitions early in the year to save time later.

» When using protocols, maintain the recommended timing noted in the lesson. If you are running short on time, use your discretion—you may be able to substitute one protocol for another as long as it serves the same purpose.

» Be very cautious about cutting a portion of the lesson. Remember to maintain the integrity of the lesson and consider its greater purpose in terms of the intended content and skills students are meant to learn. It's also important to know where the lesson is leading; look at the "down the road" section of the lesson's Teaching Notes, the Four T's for the modules, and the mid- and end of unit assessments to understand if a missed lesson component will deny students an important learning opportunity.

After the Lesson

» Would some students benefit from the re-teaching of certain pieces of the lesson at another time? If so, when could this small group instruction take place?

» Jot down any thoughts or notes about streamlining the lesson for the following year. Save samples of student work to use as models next year.

Chapter 3B:
How Will the Curriculum Empower My Students to Own Their Learning?

On the surface, this curriculum might look like *just* an English Language Arts (ELA) curriculum. It certainly is that. *And* it's also full of powerful practices designed to empower students to own their learning that can be lifted out of our ELA curriculum and into all parts of the school day. From the learning targets that start every lesson, to protocols that engage students in academic discourse, to debriefs that ask students to reflect on their learning and habits of character, you can see our commitment to teaching much more than just literacy skills. This commitment is a part of our heritage and our work in schools over the last two decades.

Though this curriculum may be your first introduction to EL Education, we have actually been around for a long time—more than 20 years—working with schools and teachers. We have a K–12 whole-school model and network of schools focused on combining challenging work with the joy of discovery and pride in mastery, and on preparing students to become contributing citizens with both the skills and character necessary for success throughout college, work, and life.

To use our ELA curriculum requires no familiarity with EL Education, our model, or our network of schools. It stands alone and can be used in any school. That said, our experience working with schools and teachers has helped us develop a set of practices and approaches to teaching and learning that may be new to you. When you encounter high-leverage practices like discussion protocols or total participation techniques for the first time, for example, we think it will help to have a little background on why we use those practices, how they can be used in other parts of your school day, and, most important, their impact on student learning.

Table 3.1 describes high-leverage instructional practices that are not necessarily specific to literacy but that empower students to be leaders of their learning across the school day, building the skills they need to be engaged and self-directed learners. The practices are highly transferable; their consistent use in the curriculum will allow you to gain mastery with them so that they can be used throughout the school day. Following this table, each practice is detailed in greater depth.

Table 3.1: High-Leverage Instructional Practices That Empower Students to Own Their Learning

Instructional Practice	Impact on Student Learning
Using learning targets *Learning targets translate standards into student learning goals for lessons. They are written in student-friendly language that is concrete and understandable, beginning with the stem "I can." Learning targets are posted, discussed, and tracked by students and teachers.*	» Learning targets set a course for learning: Students know where they are headed during the course of the lesson. » Learning targets contain embedded vocabulary. Unpacking the targets with students is an opportunity to teach new words, particularly academic vocabulary. » When learning targets are used actively during lessons, students gain valuable skills in setting goals, taking ownership of their learning, and reflecting on their progress. » Beyond mastery of standards, student ownership of and engagement with their learning is a higher-level goal of the curriculum.
Checking for understanding *Checking for understanding goes hand in hand with using learning targets. Quick and frequent formative assessments allow you to adapt instruction quickly and respond to students' needs in real time so that you can move forward if they are ready and help them get back on track if necessary.*	» Frequent formative assessments of student progress allow you to adapt instruction to meet students' needs. » Getting students back on track quickly helps them sustain their confidence and effort, which leads to new learning. » Asking students to frequently self-assess their progress keeps them tuned in to their learning targets and further develops their ownership of their learning.
Employing total participation techniques *The total participation techniques in the curriculum are used to solicit answers to questions or prompts from a wide variety of students. Rather than just calling on those students who may have their hands raised, these total participation techniques (e.g., Turn and Talk) challenge and hold accountable all students.*	» Total participation techniques demand accountability and attention from all students because anyone can be selected to offer their ideas at any time. » Especially when a positive classroom culture has been established, students who otherwise may have remained quiet have the chance to share ideas with a peer, small group, or the whole class. » Total participation techniques establish a sense of fairness for students: Rather than the "smart kids" or the "struggling kids" always being prioritized to be called on, all students have the same chance, voice, and expectation of active engagement.
Fostering a culture of grappling *A culture of grappling is one in which students are supported to make meaning on their own or with peers, rather than being taught by a teacher first. In the curriculum, students often have a "first go" at something, particularly complex text, before teacher instruction or intervention. The idea is not to "give" students information or understandings that they can figure out on their own.*	» Students learn best when they can grapple with challenges that are within reach (i.e., productive struggle). If they are "spoon-fed" information, they won't experience the joy that comes from figuring things out on their own, and they often won't learn the concepts deeply. » Productive struggle supports students to build a growth mindset and take academic risks.

Cont.

Using questions to promote—not just assess—student learning *In the curriculum, we view questions as a way to help students learn, not just as a way to assess their learning. Strategic questions can help "lift" students to an understanding of a challenging text or make sense of a tricky concept.*	» Asking open-ended questions, rather than those with "right" answers, gives students a chance to come up with their own ideas, individually or in collaboration with peers, and defend them with evidence. » Strategic questions can engage students more deeply in the lesson content, help them make connections, and require them to articulate their learning in their own words. » Strategic questions demand that students think deeply and critically, not just that they remember or relate to their own experience.
Engaging students with protocols *The protocols in the curriculum are one of the key ways that students are engaged in discussion, inquiry, critical thinking, and sophisticated communication. There are a variety of protocols in the curriculum, and all offer a structure and a set of steps to help students talk to each other and dig deeper into text or ideas. Protocols can be used throughout the school day, in any classroom, to promote student engagement and discussion.*	» Protocols are one of the best ways we know to help students be leaders of their own learning. » Making meaning together enhances learning. Rather than looking to the teacher for answers and information, protocols help students learn to find those answers themselves and with the help of their peers. » Protocols are a great way for students to learn and practice speaking and listening skills and to build their habits of character.
Deepening student discourse *Perhaps the best measure of an effective classroom is the quality of student conversation. With teacher modeling, Conversation Cues, sentence frames, consistent use of academic vocabulary, and a commitment by the teacher to draw out and celebrate student ideas, students can learn to have powerful analytical conversations at all grade levels.*	» When students recognize that their ideas and opinions will be taken seriously by you and their peers—analyzed, critiqued, and built-upon—it lifts their commitment to sharing their best thinking. » Simple sentence frames can transform discussion in a classroom (e.g., "I would like to build on Chantelle's idea"; "I appreciate that idea, but I respectfully disagree"; "Can you offer some evidence?"). » Prioritizing discourse in the classroom elevates student voice, develops their oral processing skills, and deepens their learning.
Co-constructing anchor charts with students *Anchor charts make student thinking visible by recording content, strategies, processes, cues, and guidelines during the learning process. Students add ideas to posted anchor charts as they apply new learning, develop new understandings, and expand their knowledge of the topic. These charts reflect the current learning in the classroom, contain only the most relevant or important information, and are neat and organized, with simple icons and wording.*	» Posting anchor charts keeps relevant information easily accessible for all students, reminds them of prior learning, and enables them to add to their learning as it changes and expands. » Posting anchor charts provides students with support when answering questions, adding to discussions, and problem-solving in class. » English language learners and students who may need additional support with perception and information processing benefit from this kind of visual display as a varied means of representation. » Providing individual copies of anchor charts to students and/or customizing the display (e.g., enlarging the font; adding simple icons, definitions, or translations next to important words or ideas) also provides students with additional support.

▶ Using Learning Targets

We start here with learning targets because that's where we start nearly every lesson in our curriculum. Learning targets anchor students and teachers in a common understanding of where they are headed with their learning. When students know where they are headed, they can take more ownership of getting there.

I can describe what learning targets are and why they are important.

> "Learning targets are goals for lessons, projects, units, and courses. They are derived from standards and used to assess growth and achievement. They are written in concrete, student-friendly language—beginning with the stem "I can"—shared with students, posted in the classroom, and tracked carefully by students and teachers during the process of learning.

> "Rather than the teacher taking on all of the responsibility for meeting a lesson's objectives, learning targets, written in student-friendly language and frequently reflected on, transfer ownership for meeting objectives from the teacher to the student. The seemingly simple work of reframing objectives written for teachers to learning targets written for—and owned by—students turns assessment on its head. The student becomes the main actor in assessing and improving his or her learning.

> "The term 'target' is significant. It emphasizes that students are aiming for something specific. Learning targets are meant to focus students in this way, directing their efforts and attention, as would a physical target. Every day, students discuss, reflect, track their progress, and assess their work in relation to learning targets. Learning targets build investment in learning by giving students the language to discuss what they know and what they need to learn. As an eighth-grader at the Odyssey School (in Denver) remarked, 'The teacher will take time to break down the target, so we know where we're going with the learning'" (Berger, Rugen, and Woodfin, 2014, pp. 21–22).

In our curriculum, we use daily learning targets, which are reviewed with students during each lesson, often in the Opening following an engaging "hook." Sometimes learning targets are reviewed later in the lesson following a new chunk of cognitive work (e.g., the first part of a lesson may have a learning target related to speaking; later, when students dig into a writing task, there may be a second learning target related to writing). Often, we think of reviewing learning targets as *unpacking* or *dissecting* them. This should not take much time, but it is an important opportunity to look carefully with students at the words in the learning target and make sure they know what they actually will be learning (not just what activity they will be "doing").

Unpacking Learning Targets

Using the learning target that serves as the heading for this section as an example—*I can describe what learning targets are and why they are important*—let's start with the verb *describe*. The verbs in learning targets are important because they dictate what students will be doing and give an indication of the cognitive rigor of the lesson. *Synthesizing* will be more cognitively rigorous for students than *describing*; *evaluating* more so than *labeling*. No matter the verb or the rigor it signals, the first step is to make sure students know what the verb means and what it's going to look like and sound like for them to do that work.

Reviewing, or unpacking, learning targets is an excellent way to teach academic vocabulary: "What does it mean to *describe*?" Often—and we'll get to this later in this chapter—the curriculum will suggest a total participation technique, such as Turn and Talk, to give all students a chance to think and talk about what it will mean for them to describe (or synthesize or evaluate or label, or whatever the verb is). This engages all students in beginning to take aim at the learning target; it sets a course for their learning throughout the lesson.

But verbs aren't the only important words in learning targets. Using our example again, the next question might be: "What other words in this learning target seem most important to guide our learning today?" Students might come up with *learning targets* as the things they'll be learning about and *what* and *why* to indicate that there are two parts to what they'll be describing; first they'll describe *what* learning targets are, and then they'll describe *why* they're important.

All of this unpacking should happen quickly in the lessons in our curriculum, usually 5 minutes or less. The goal is to make sure that students know what they are aiming for and to set purpose, not to belabor every word. This is why vocabulary is so often the focus of this process. It will be hard for students to take aim at the target if they are not sure what it means. Though we offer lots of guidance on this process in our curriculum, it's something that you are likely to pick up quickly. There's no one right way to do it; what really matters is that students are crystal clear on their intended learning so they can take ownership of their progress.

I can actively use a learning target throughout a lesson.

Unpacking learning targets during the lesson opening is just the first step. It is critical that learning targets are used *throughout* a lesson. "Even well-written learning targets will contribute little to engaging, supporting, and holding students accountable for their learning if they are not referred to and used actively during the lesson. For this reason, teachers must use techniques to check for understanding and mark progress toward learning targets. Students must have the opportunity to reflect on their progress; this is key to student ownership of their learning" (Berger, Rugen, and Woodfin, 2014, p. 29).

Going back to our example, *I can describe what learning targets are and why they are important*, how will you know how students are progressing on their efforts to describe what learning targets are and why they are important? The lessons in our curriculum will cue you to check for understanding in a variety of ways. Sometimes you will listen in to student conversations to assess progress; other times you might stop the class, read the learning target, and ask students to give you a self-assessment, such as a thumbs-up, thumbs-sideways, or thumbs-down, so that you know who you might need to spend extra time with to help them reach the target. Other times students may write an "exit ticket" that you will collect and assess. (We will explore many more checking for understanding techniques in the next section.)

There are numerous ways to keep the learning target alive during the lesson and to check for understanding. And, just as with the process of unpacking learning targets, there's no one right way to actively use them throughout a lesson. What's important is that you find ways to do so that are appropriate to the target. Not every assessment of progress is appropriate to the target. For example, if students are labeling a diagram, you won't be looking for progress in a written paragraph. If they are *collaborating* with partners, you won't be looking for individual responses.

Our curriculum will give you plenty of good strategies to check for understanding and keep the learning target front and center in students' minds. Based on the way your students respond and your assessment of their needs on any given day (e.g., they need more movement), you will likely find your own favorite ways to keep the learning targets alive during lessons.

I can analyze learning targets so that I am clear on what the intended learning is for my students.

First and foremost, learning targets must help students understand what their intended learning is, which is driven by standards. This is something we took deeply to heart when crafting the learning targets you see in the curriculum. We always started with what the standards require, what mastery will look and sound like, and what scaffolding students will need to get there. This drove all of the downstream creation of daily learning targets.

"A common mistake that many teachers make when learning to write quality learning targets is writing a learning target that describes the task rather than the learning. For example, to say 'I can make a poster about the ideal habitat of a polar bear' is much different than 'I can describe the ideal habitat for a polar bear using a poster format.' The emphasis in the first learning target is on making the poster. In the second, the emphasis is on learning about polar bear habitats. The choice of verbs is critical for identifying the intended learning for students" (Berger, Rugen, and Woodfin, 2014, p. 26).

When using our curriculum, there is no need for you to create your own learning targets. They are "baked in" to every lesson. However, learning to analyze the learning targets that are provided will help ground you in the greater purpose of any given lesson. If a target states, for example, that students will determine a character's motivations *using details from the text*, you and your students have some clues about the work of the lesson. Know, too, that all of our targets were carefully derived from the Common Core standards; if you are ever in doubt about the intent of a lesson, go back to the language in the standards themselves.

We have already pointed to the importance of the verbs in learning targets. The framework of knowledge, skill, and reasoning as three types of learning targets—which are largely determined by what verbs are used—can offer further precision for your analysis. Table 3.2 describes each type, along with a sampling of accompanying verbs that will make it clear to you and your students what the intended learning is. Throughout the curriculum, you will notice all three types of learning targets. Attending to a balance of all three types is one way to ensure that the cognitive rigor of student tasks is varied.

Table 3.2: Attending to Cognitive Rigor: Knowledge, Skills, and Reasoning Learning Targets

	Knowledge	**Skill**	**Reasoning**
Explanation	Knowledge, facts, concepts to be learned outright or retrieved using reference materials	Use of knowledge to perform an action; demonstration is emphasized	Thinking proficiencies—using knowledge to solve a problem, make a decision, plan, and so on
Sample verbs	explain, describe, identify, tell, name, list, define, label, match, choose, recall, recognize, select	observe, listen, perform, conduct, read, speak, write, assemble, operate, use, demonstrate, measure, model, collect, dramatize	analyze, compare and contrast, synthesize, classify, infer, evaluate

Source: ETS (Educational Testing Service), Stiggins, Rick J.; Arter, Judith A.; Chappuis, Jan; Chappuis, Steve, Classroom Assessment for Student Learning: Doing It Right—Using It Well, 1st Edition, © 2008, Reprinted by permission of Pearson Education Inc., New York, NY.

I can derive my own quality learning targets.

The learning targets in the curriculum are derived from multiple sources. The primary source is the Common Core State Standards (CCSS).

Other sources include the Next Generation Science Standards and the National Council for Social Studies 3C framework. While we have strived to select a variety of content topics that meet grade-level content standards in states across the country, we know that we haven't met them all. Depending on your school, district, or state, you may be compelled to adapt or enhance the curriculum further to meet your local context.

Further, once you see the power of learning targets to empower your students to take more ownership of their learning, you may feel motivated to create learning targets for other parts of the school day, beyond ELA lessons. We wholeheartedly endorse this. Using learning targets is truly a high-leverage instructional practice that can be lifted out of the curriculum and into mathematics, science, physical education, and any other part of the day in which students will benefit from being grounded in where they are headed in the lesson (i.e., *all* parts of the day!). For this reason, we offer some guidance here on how to create your own learning targets.

Making Learning Targets Student-Friendly

One of the first things to remember about creating quality learning targets is to avoid the temptation to tack the words "I can" onto a standard. Learning targets must be written in student-friendly language that students will understand and can take ownership of. "For example, in

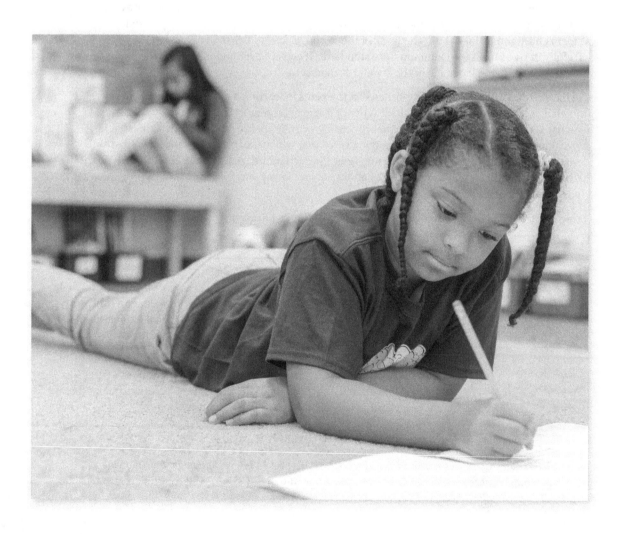

one first-grade classroom in Massachusetts, a state standard called for all students to 'understand the monetary value of standard US coinage.' This is a reasonable and useful standard, but putting the words 'I can' in front of that sentence would not make it understandable or motivating to any first-grader. The teacher in this classroom used the learning target: 'I can make change for a quarter in many different ways.' This was exciting for the students. They all got good at it and could demonstrate it to their friends and families. When they were done, they had met the intent of the state standard beautifully" (Berger, Woodfin, and Vilen, 2016, p. 24).

Another key to quality learning targets is that they focus on one thing at a time so that students can focus on the intended learning and monitor their progress most effectively. Let's look at an example from a Grade 1 module in our curriculum. The standard that guides this particular lesson (Module 3, Unit 3, Lesson 10) is CCSS W1.5: *With guidance and support from adults, focus on a topic, respond to questions and suggestions from peers, and add details to strengthen writing as needed.* This standard requires students to demonstrate mastery of two skills: 1) listening to and responding to questions/suggestion from peers and 2) applying the feedback from peers by adding details to improve writing. These two skills are combined in the standard because students have to engage in a conversation with their peers before they can effectively apply feedback; however, leaving the skills together in one learning target would be a lot for first-graders to take aim at. As a result, we created two learning targets to help students focus on one skill at a time:

1. I can actively participate in a feedback conversation with my classmate.

2. I can use feedback from my classmate to strengthen my writing.

Now let's look at an example from a Grade 4 module in our curriculum. The focus of this lesson is on CCSS RL.4.3: *Determine a theme of a story, drama, or poem from details in the text; summarize the text.* This standard requires students to demonstrate mastery of two skills: 1) determining a theme of a literary text from details and 2) summarizing the text. The two skills are together in one standard because an effective summary will include the themes of a literary text with supporting details.

Once again, tacking the words "I can" onto this standard will not make it student-friendly. In this case, we created two daily learning targets in Module 4, Unit 1, Lesson 6, to help students focus on one skill at a time. Each learning target is addressed, and assessed, at a different time in the lesson, but when writing summaries, students make the connection between the two:

1. I can determine themes of *The Hope Chest* using details from the text.

2. I can summarize Chapter 5 of *The Hope Chest*.

As opposed to the example regarding "monetary value of standard U.S. coinage," with the teacher making the decision to use different terms to describe money in the learning target, the language of this fourth-grade standard has largely been retained in the learning targets. Words like *theme* and *summarize* are precise, grade-appropriate, and frequently used when analyzing literary texts. It is difficult (and not necessary) to use alternate terms for these words. And using these terms appropriately builds students' understanding of central aspects of ELA.

Assessing Student Progress toward Meeting Their Learning Targets

A final key to creating strong learning targets is being clear on how they will be assessed. A learning target that states, "I can understand how the prefix 'anti' changes the meaning of a word" might seem okay at first, but when you think about how to assess it, you should start to see that it has a problem. Ask yourself how you and your students will assess *understanding*. Perhaps *describe* is a better verb? Or perhaps what you really want is for students to be able to use this prefix. In that case, a better target might be: "I can effectively use the prefix 'anti' to change the meaning of words." It's also important to develop assessments that are well-aligned to the cognitive work described by the learning target. Table 3.3 shows how different kinds of assessments align with knowledge, skills, and reasoning learning targets.

Table 3.3: Selecting Assessment Methods Based on Type of Learning Target

	Selected Response	**Extended Written Response**	**Performance Assessment**	**Personal Communication**
Knowledge	**Good match**—for assessing mastery of elements of knowledge	**Good match**—for evaluating understanding of relationships among elements of knowledge	**Not a good match**—too time-consuming to cover everything	**Match**—can ask questions, evaluate answers, and infer mastery, but a time-consuming option
Skills	**Not a good match**—can assess mastery of prerequisite knowledge but do not tell the evaluator that the student can use the skill itself		**Good match**—can observe and evaluate skills as they are	**Good match**—when skill is oral communication proficiency
Reasoning	**Match**—only for assessing understanding of some patterns of reasoning	**Good match**—Written descriptions of complex problem solutions provide a window into reasoning proficiency	**Good match**—can watch students solve some problems and infer reasoning proficiency	**Good match**—can ask students to think aloud or can ask follow-up questions to probe reasoning

Source: ETS (Educational Testing Service), Stiggins, Rick J.; Arter, Judith A.; Chappuis, Jan; Chappuis, Steve, Classroom Assessment for Student Learning: Doing It Right—Using It Well, 1st Edition, © 2008, Reprinted by permission of Pearson Education Inc., New York, NY.

We know from experience that creating quality learning targets is not easy. Astute readers may have noticed, for example, that several of the learning targets we offered as examples in the previous pages are focused on skills. If these learning targets were used for three days in a row with students, we might find ourselves in a rut without enough variety in the cognitive work with which students will engage. Often when we look back on learning targets, we find these kinds of imbalances or notice ways the targets can be clarified or streamlined. We're all learners, honing our craft. It takes practice.

If you decide to dive into this yourself for other parts of the school day, be aware that there many common challenges to the practice, including:

» Learning targets that are actually *doing* targets (e.g., *I can make a poster* vs. *I can describe in poster format*)

» Learning targets that are too complex

» Learning targets that require all lower-level cognitive work

» Learning targets that are mismatched to assessments

If you want to start creating your own learning targets, we encourage you to collaborate with other teachers and help each other critique and revise the targets. Table 3.4 is a rubric for quality learning targets that should help. You can also find more information in our 2014 book *Leaders of Their Own Learning: Transforming Schools through Student-Engaged Assessment.*

Table 3.4: Learning Targets Rubric

	Accomplished	**Developing**	**Beginning**
Standards-based and rigorous	They are derived from national or state standards and school or district documents such as curriculum maps and adopted program materials. Targets fall across multiple categories in a cognitive rigor matrix.	They are derived from general academic tasks but not grade-specific standards, or they describe learning or tasks that do not meet proficiency standards. Targets fall across limited categories in a cognitive rigor matrix.	They are not derived from standards and do not clearly reference academic tasks. Targets fall primarily in one or two columns/rows of a cognitive rigor matrix, or learning targets are not rigorous enough.
Student-friendly	They are written in student-friendly language (accessible vocabulary and from a student perspective) and begin with the stem "I can."	They begin with the stem "I can" but may not use student-friendly language (i.e., they sound like "objectives").	They do not begin with "I can" and/or are simply reiterations of state objectives.
Measurable	They are measurable and use concrete, assessable verbs (e.g., identify, compare, analyze). The verb suggests the way in which the target will be assessed (e.g., *analyze* suggests a writing or problem-solving assessment, not a multiple-choice quiz).	They are measurable but may contain two verbs or have too broad a scope in content (e.g., "I can draw a raccoon and describe its habitat").	They are not measurable (e.g., "I can understand" or "I can commit").
Specific and contextualized	They are specific, often referring to the particular context of a lesson, project, or case study.	They articulate only long-term targets that can be generalized for any similar academic task (e.g., "I can write a persuasive essay").	They are too broad for students to see progress (e.g., "I can read") or too narrow for students to own their learning (e.g., "I can put my name on my paper").
Learning-centered	The verb following the "I can" stem clearly identifies the intended learning, articulating what the students will learn rather than how they will demonstrate their learning.	The verb following the "I can" stem focuses on the academic tasks students will do rather than what students will learn (e.g., "I can complete a graphic organizer").	The targets are focused only on compliance and completion (e.g., "I can retake my test").

▶ Checking for Understanding

Checking for understanding goes hand in hand with using learning targets. Many checking for understanding strategies are used throughout the curriculum to formatively assess students' progress. The Ongoing Assessment box in every K–5 Module Lesson and K–2 Reading Foundations Skills Block lesson will orient you to the kinds of data you can collect on student progress in the lesson (e.g., observing students using their drawings to support their discussion; using the Reading Informational Text Checklist). These quick and frequent assessments allow you to adapt instruction quickly and respond to students' needs in real time so that you can help them get back on track if necessary. And, importantly, checking for understanding helps students check in with themselves as they self-assess their progress and take ownership of their learning.

There are many ways to check for understanding, including summative assessments like tests, essays, and performance tasks. These more in-depth checks for understanding are certainly a part of our curriculum, but we will explore them fully in Chapter 7. Here we focus on techniques used during the flow of daily lessons throughout the curriculum:

- » Writing and reflection
- » Quick checks
- » Strategic observation and listening
- » Debriefs

Writing and Reflection

Writing—or sometimes drawing, with primary learners—is an effective way for students to articulate and reflect on their developing understanding of a topic. Writing is often overlooked as a quick formative assessment technique, perhaps because it's not as quick as eliciting verbal responses. However, many writing techniques, especially once students grow accustomed to them, can be done quite quickly, and they appeal to students' diverse learning styles. Writing also requires that students commit to a response, revealing evidence of progress that is quite useful as a formative assessment. In general, the written response techniques we're talking about here are short, informal assignments that are completed and checked quickly. Table 3.5 describes some, but not all, of the techniques that you may find in the curriculum.

Table 3.5: Checking for Understanding: Writing and Reflection Techniques

Technique	Description
Shared writing (Grades K–2)	A group of students, sometimes the whole class, composes their writing together, but the teacher does the actual writing.
Drawing with labels or captions	Students communicate their understanding of a concept or knowledge of content through a simple sketch with labels or captions. This strategy is particularly useful in Grades K–2.
Read-Write-Pair-Share	Students read or watch something, write a short response, and share their written responses with a partner. A teacher circulating the room and listening in on the conversations can pull out key ideas to bring back to the whole class, as well as surface any misconceptions that need to be clarified.
Summary writing	Students summarize what they have learned. This technique gives them valuable practice in condensing information and provides you with a window into student learning.
Note-catchers	Students record facts, observations, and insights on a note-catcher template as they work.

Cont.

Technique	Description
Journals	Students keep a journal to capture their ongoing reflections, observations, and responses to prompts.
Entry and exit tickets	As an opening or closing activity, students write a reflection on their learning in the class that day or the previous day in response to a specific prompt. The writing serves as evidence of student understanding to help shape subsequent lessons.

Quick Checks

Quick checks are used in nearly every lesson of our curriculum. They may take anywhere from a few seconds to a few minutes, often involving physical movement and interaction, and serving a variety of purposes—from checks of factual knowledge, to monitoring confusion, to deeper probes of understanding and opinion. As you gain familiarity with the techniques, you and your students may develop favorites, which can often be swapped for those suggested in the curriculum. If your students are bursting with energy, you may opt for a technique that gets them out of their chairs for a few minutes. Alternatively, if they've just come in from recess and need help settling down, you might opt for a technique that involves quiet reflection. It's okay to make changes; just keep in mind the purpose of the quick check. Table 3.6 describes some, but not all, of the techniques that you might find in the curriculum.

Table 3.6: Checking for Understanding: Quick Checks

Technique	Description
Factual or brief-response checks	
Go-around	When a one- or two-word answer can show understanding or readiness for a task, teachers ask students to respond to a standard prompt one at a time, in rapid succession around the room.
Do Now	This is a brief problem, task, or activity that immediately engages students in the learning target for the day. It enables the circulating teacher to monitor students' readiness to move on and judge their grasp of necessary background knowledge.
Monitoring confusion or readiness	
Explain It Back	Ask students to repeat or summarize instructions or content to the group or a partner in their own words to check for misconceptions.
Red Light, Green Light	Students use red, yellow, and green table tents, cards, or plastic cups to indicate their comfort with a learning target or readiness for a task. They show red, yellow, or green as a signal that they can work independently or need help.
Thumb-O-Meter or Fist-to-Five	To show degree of agreement, readiness for tasks, or comfort with a learning target or concept, students can quickly show their thinking by putting their thumbs up, to the side, or down. Or students can hold up a hand with a fist for zero, or disagree, or one to five fingers for higher levels of confidence or agreement.
Glass, Bugs, Mud	After students try a task or review a learning target or assignment, they identify their understanding or readiness for application using the windshield metaphor for clear vision: glass—totally clear; bugs—a little fuzzy; mud—I can barely see.

Cont.

Technique	Description
Status checks	
Sit, Kneel, Stand	Students reflect on progress toward a learning target or respond to a prompt. They sit if they still have a lot of work to do, kneel if they have made some progress, or stand if they feel fully satisfied with their progress.
Learning Lineups	Identify one end of the room with a descriptor such as "novice" or "beginning" and the other end as "expert" or "exemplary." Students place themselves on this continuum based on where they are with a task or learning target. Invite them to explain their thinking to the whole class or the people near them.

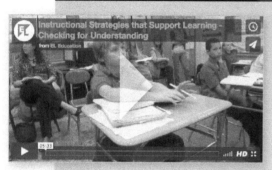

In the accompanying video, Jessica Wood from the Springfield Renaissance School in Springfield, Massachusetts, uses a variety of checking for understanding strategies to keep her students focused on their learning target throughout the lesson.

https://vimeo.com/43990520

Strategic Observation and Listening

Circulating and listening in while students are engaged in conversation and group work is an effective and efficient way for you to assess progress and confer with students. In fact, in nearly every lesson in our curriculum you will find something like this: "As students work, circulate and look/listen for...." Also, throughout the curriculum we use parentheses to cue you to what you should listen for after asking a question or giving a prompt. For example, from Grade 3, Module 1, Unit 1, Lesson 4:

> "Use your note-catcher to think about what happened in this story. What message or lesson do you think the author wants you to learn and take away from this story? What details make you think that?" *(Responses will vary, but may include: Education and learning is important enough for students to build a school to be able to learn.)*

Of course, this means that students must have plenty of opportunities to work with and talk with each other. In our curriculum, protocols are often used to give students this chance for discourse. (Protocols will be discussed later in this chapter.)

At times throughout the curriculum, we will prompt you to use a specific checklist as you observe and listen in. These checklists will allow you to keep track of individual students' progress on specific standards. For example, in kindergarten Module 2, Unit 2, you find this note in Lesson 4:

> *As students talk, circulate and listen in. Take note of the ideas students are sharing and target a few students to share out whole group. Consider using the Reading Informational Text Checklist to document student progress toward CCSS RI.K.1, RI.K.2, and RI.K.4.*

The checklist will not only help you stay focused on particular standards, which are tied to daily learning targets, but it also helps you track how many and which students you have observed or conferred with, make decisions about any further support that may be needed, and determine next steps for instruction. (Using checklists as formative and summative assessments is explore in Chapter 7).

Debriefs: Reflecting on Learning

"An effective debrief is the last chance during a daily lesson for a teacher to check for understanding, help students synthesize learning, and promote reflection so that students can monitor their own progress. It is an essential component of each lesson" (Berger, Rugen, and Woodfin, 2014, p 74). Each Module Lesson in our curriculum includes a Closing and Assessment, which typically lasts for 5 to 10 minutes. This is when the debrief occurs. During this time, students often reflect on the content they learned (e.g., "What interesting things did we learn about weather today?"), on their growing literacy skills (e.g., "How is our narrative writing improving?"), on their collaboration (e.g., "How did we follow our discussion norms today, and how did that support our learning about frogs?"), and on their habits of character (e.g., "How does using empathy help us give our writing partner better feedback?"). Other components of the curriculum have similar structures:

» The K–2 Labs end with a reflection on the goals students set for themselves that day.

» The 3–5 Additional Language and Literacy Block doesn't include a formal closing in every session, though it does allow for students in independent groups to discuss how their learning connects to the work they are doing in the Module Lesson.

» The K–2 Reading Foundations Skills Block includes a closing during which students revisit the learning target or respond to a question like, "How did our work today help us become even better readers?"

During the debrief, and at any point in a lesson, you can build students' ability to be metacognitive by helping them analyze their thinking and the logic of their reasoning, or giving them opportunities to apply their learning to novel situations. Probing questions may include the following:

» Why do you think this?

» How do you know?

» What evidence supports your thinking?

» How has your thinking changed, and what changed your ideas?

» How might your thinking change if...?

It's hard to fit everything in when you're teaching. When time is short, as it often is at the end of a lesson, resist the temptation to skip the debrief. You can save time by inviting students to answer synthesis or reflection questions in pairs, trios, or quads rather than speaking them out to the whole group. Or you may be able to employ a quick written check for understanding that can save you time.

Also, remember that giving students the chance to reflect on *what* and *how* they learned keeps them tuned in to their progress and builds ownership in their learning. Character is one of our three Dimensions of Student Achievement (Figure 1.2). It was a priority for us to build habits of character into the curriculum, and we hope it will be a priority for you too. This is something you can build into lessons throughout the day, not just during ELA lessons, to equip your students with powerful tools for learning. Chapter 7 will provide you with more information about using formative and summative assessments to monitor student progress.

▶ Employing Total Participation Techniques

In many ways, total participation techniques, from the book *Total Participation Techniques: Making Every Student an Active Learner* (2011) by Persida Himmele and William Himmele, are similar to checking for understanding techniques. In our curriculum, we use a slice of the total participation technique pie specifically to guide you in how to engage *all* students—not just your "frequent fliers"—in responding to questions and prompts.

> *"With total participation techniques, I really try to have them in my back pocket, like a handful that I know I can pull out at any time. That way when I get to a question that I know I'm going to ask, I can gauge the room. Do they need to move?"*

Sara Metz

K–1 Teacher, Denver

In the curriculum, each total participation technique is introduced in Module 1; thereafter, you will be invited to use a total participation technique of your choice. You may find that your class develops a favorite or that one is more effective than another with your students. You may use techniques from the curriculum or develop your own. Table 3.7 describes some, but not all, of the total participation techniques that you will find in the curriculum.

Table 3.7: A Sampling of Total Participation Techniques

Technique	Description
Turn and Talk	Turn and Talk is one of the easiest, quickest, and most efficient total participation techniques. It can be used practically at any time, anywhere, in a lesson in any content area. 1. When prompted, students turn to an elbow partner. 2. In a set amount of time, students share their ideas about a prompt or question posed by the teacher or other students. 3. Depending on the goals of the lesson and the nature of the Turn and Talk, students may share some key ideas from their paired discussions with the whole class.
Think-Pair-Share	This practice promotes productive and equitable conversations, in which all students are given the time and space to think, share, and consider the ideas of others. It ensures that all students simultaneously engage with the same text or topic, while promoting synthesis and the social construction of knowledge. 1. Move students into pairs and invite them to label themselves A and B. 2. Pose the question and give students time to think independently and silently about their answer to the question. 3. Invite partner A to ask partner B the question. 4. Give partner B a specified time frame (e.g., 30 seconds, 1 minute) to share his or her response. 5. Have partners reverse roles and repeat Steps 3–4. 6. Using another total participation technique (e.g., cold calling, equity sticks), invite students to share their responses with the whole group. 7. Repeat this process with remaining questions.

Cont.

Technique	Description
Write-Pair-Share	This is a variation on Think-Pair-Share in which students think *and* write before they share with their partner.
Cold Call	Cold Call serves as an engaging and challenging, yet supportive, way to hold students accountable for answering oral questions the teacher poses, regardless of whether a hand is raised. Cold Call requires students to think and interact with the question at hand, even if they're not sure of the answer. It also promotes equity in the classroom; students who normally dominate the discourse step back and allow other students to demonstrate their knowledge and expertise. 1. Name a question before identifying students to answer it. 2. Call on students regardless of whether they have hands raised (often using equity sticks). 3. Scaffold questions from simple to increasingly complex, probing for deeper explanations. 4. Connect thinking threads by returning to previous comments and connecting them to current ones; model this for students and teach them to do it too.
Equity sticks	Equity sticks are true to their name: They ensure academic equity by allowing teachers to physically track who they have called on or interacted with during the course of the class. This is especially useful during whole class discussions or while working with large groups of students. Using Popsicle sticks or something similar—one per student: 1. Pose a question to the class. 2. After giving students some think time, pick an equity stick and call on the student whose name is on the stick for an answer. As you do so, move the equity stick from one location to another, indicating that the student has participated in class that day.

▶ Fostering a Culture of Grappling

"Never help a child with a task at which he feels he can succeed." There are two important messages embedded in this quote by Maria Montessori. The first is that students should have the opportunity to try things and to puzzle through challenges independently or with peers. In other words, they shouldn't always be "taught" how to do things before they try them, and they shouldn't be bailed out at the first sign of struggle, because engaging in a productive struggle is how we learn.

The second is the message about the importance of getting the level of challenge right. Students must be able to see a path to success—they must grapple with something within their reach. This doesn't mean that they won't need scaffolds and support to help get them there, but those must be skillfully employed. Some of the most intricate work of designing this curriculum was finding this sweet spot with the level of challenge. What are the texts and tasks that will give students an opportunity to grapple productively and to see that they can succeed by persevering through something difficult? What scaffolds can we predict students will need to find success?

The close reading/close read-alouds that are woven throughout the curriculum, which are explored in great depth in Chapter 5, often involve grappling as students have a first go at reading complex texts. The process is carefully scaffolded so that students have the experience of pushing through challenging material in a way that leads to success, not to frustration. Close reading is also carefully introduced to students at the start of the year, in Module 1, in a way that builds in them a sense of playful exploration and academic courage.

It is important to note that often lesson arcs of two to three lessons might feature a period of grappling in the first lesson, with students reaching greater clarity over the course of a few days. They won't always push through and reach those "aha" moments during one lesson. This is why it is so important to look out ahead with lessons so you have a feel for these rhythms and can help students stay in the zone of the productive struggle without being tempted to "rescue" them.

Building Academic Courage

A sense of academic courage, which allows grappling and productive struggle to thrive in the classroom, can be fostered in all parts of the school day. The following list provides an overview of strategies you can use to create a class culture in which challenge or struggle is viewed as a way to learn, not as a barrier to learning:

» Build common language in your classroom for "grappling." You don't have to call it grappling, but label it for students. Make grappling a class routine with specific strategies (e.g., anchor charts for what to try when we feel stuck).

» Give students tangible successes early in the year by designing tasks you know they can be successful with and supporting them to do the tasks with quality. Give students lots of individual feedback to help them grow and regularly point out their growth.

» Talk explicitly about the importance of taking on challenges in order to learn. When appropriate, read and discuss with students short pieces of research about having a growth mindset and its impact on learning.

» Use group initiatives to practice grappling with a challenge, tenacity, and problem-solving; discuss application to classroom lessons when debriefing the initiative.

» Engage students in discussions that make the link between character traits and the grapple phase of your lessons (e.g., "What does perseverance look like? What are tips for helping yourself keep going when the going is hard?")

» Create meaningful metaphors for instilling a growth mindset (e.g., the mind is a muscle that can get stronger).

» Do a "zones of comfort" activity: Draw concentric circles for the comfort, stretch, and panic zones. Students identify the types of experiences they have that fall into the different zones. Point out that the stretch zone is our learning zone—we learn best when we are a little uncomfortable.

While our curriculum, particularly at the beginning of the school year, goes slow with grappling activities, this is an area that benefits from a holistic approach in your classroom. Building a culture of grappling throughout the day—from morning meeting to recess to mathematics lessons—will support students to build a growth mindset, persevere through challenging material, and take academic risks in an emotionally safe and supportive environment.

▶ Using Questions to Promote—Not Just Assess— Student Learning

One of your best tools for nurturing a culture of grappling and playful intellectual exploration in your classroom is questions. Asking open-ended questions, rather than those with "right" answers, gives students a chance to come up with their own ideas, individually or in collaboration with peers, and defend them with evidence. Such questions engage students more deeply in the lesson content, help them make connections, and require them to articulate their learning in their own words. In this way, questions are used to promote learning, not just assess it.

In our curriculum, each lesson contains suggested questions that are designed to intentionally scaffold student learning, often moving students toward more complex thinking. However, given the reality of life in the classroom, it is often the case that you will need to think on your feet with additional follow-up questions if students seem off track. Developing your own "question-asking muscles" will help you be more strategic about what you ask (and when), while still maintaining the integrity of the lesson. It will also help you prepare for ways to probe for deeper understanding or to encourage students to build off of their peers' responses to questions so that the focus isn't always on you asking a question, students responding, and you evaluating the answer.

> *"Every time we ask students, 'What was the name of the town in which the characters in this story lived?' we leave less time for questions like 'Why do you think the characters never left home?'"*

Alfie Kohn, "Who's Asking?"
Educational Leadership, September 2015

Understanding the considerations that went into our development of questions will help you ask additional questions that give you the information you really need from students. It is also important to remember that asking too many questions and following students' lead in too many new directions has a big impact on the pacing of your lessons and can get you off track. The best questions drive at learning targets, stimulate and assess powerful thinking, and ensure that all students are engaged in thinking and supporting their ideas with evidence. Figure 3.2 illustrates strategic questioning strategies along with accompanying examples.

Figure 3.2: Pre-Planning Strategic Questions

Strategy:	Example:
Design questions to provide a clear vision of the learning target(s). Use questions to clarify the meaning and connections between learning targets, connect prior lessons, establish criteria for success, and track learning along the way.	Near the end of kindergarten Module 2, students prepare to write a narrative about an imaginary character that teaches their readers about the weather. Students have already planned their "weather stories" and created drawings. In this lesson, they think about and write their weather stories. *From the lesson:* Direct students' attention to the posted learning targets and read the first one aloud: I can tell the story of my character and the weather using pictures and words. After reviewing the definition of character, direct students' attention to the phrase *tell the story* in the learning target. » "What does *tell the story* mean? What does this learning target tell you about what you will do today?" » "What are the elements of a story?" Direct students' attention to page 1 of their My Weather Story booklet at their seats. » "What elements of the weather stories are on page 1 of the My Weather Story booklets?" Invite students to turn to an elbow partner and take turns sharing the ideas about the character and setting from their drawings. Circulate and probe further as necessary: » "Who is your character? Describe him or her." » "What type of weather will your character experience?"

Strategy:

Scaffold questions from basic to complex. Ask questions that start at the knowledge and comprehension levels and move quickly to reasoning and critical thinking. This helps students practice thinking skills, make connections between ideas, align and evaluate evidence, synthesize information, and apply learning to new situations. These questions are generative, eliciting multiple correct answers.

Example:

After Grade 2 students read an Aesop's fable in Module 4, they answer a series of increasingly challenging text-dependent questions related to the learning targets: *I can recount the fable "The Ants and the Grasshopper" using the story elements* and *I can determine the central message of "The Ant and the Grasshopper" based on how the characters respond to the problem/challenge.*

From the lesson:

» "Where or when does this fable take place?"
» "Why is it important to know that this fable takes place in the autumn and the winter?"
» "What actions did the ants take that showed responsibility?"

Strategy:

Ask questions that are text-dependent. To check for understanding and comprehension of complex texts, ask questions that are text-dependent rather than drawn from the students' personal opinions or past experiences. This questioning strategy compels students to read carefully and cite evidence, which in turn raises the quality of student thinking. Carefully crafted questions serve as a scaffold to "lift" students to the text and build higher-order thinking skills and new perspectives. (Note: Text-dependent questions are explored in greater depth in Chapter 5.)

Example:

In Grade 4, Module 1, students closely read the author's note from the text *A River of Words* (about William Carlos Williams). The questions consistently invite and challenge students to dig back into this complex text. The examples that follow focus students on just one paragraph of the text, helping them think about what inspired Williams. For each question, the teacher prompts the students to draw specific evidence from the text and defend their answers.

From the lesson:

Invite students to reread from the sentence beginning with "But perhaps his most ..." to the end of the paragraph. Ask:

» "What was the focus of Williams's poems?"
» "Reread the last sentence. What was unnecessary?"
» "What did Williams do with these unnecessary details?"
» "Think about Williams's writing style. What does the phrase stripping away unnecessary details mean?"
» "Think about these details. What does this help you to understand about Williams's writing style?"
» "Why did Williams try to strip away the unnecessary details?"

Strategy:

Clarify expectations. Use questions to clarify criteria for success and help students check their own understanding to determine their next steps.

Example:

Grade 1 students learn all about birds' amazing bodies in Module 3; then, as their final performance task in Module 4, they create a "Feathered Friends Saver," a realistic portrait of a local bird that attaches to a window to help prevent birds from flying into the window. As part of the process to create this authentic product, students analyze a model of a scientific drawing of a bird.

From the lesson:

Review the Feathered Friends Saver Criteria anchor chart, reading aloud criteria:

» "Scientific drawing of a bird includes attention to: size, shape, placement, details"
» "Coloring should be: inside the lines, covering all the space, layered"

Focus students on the phrase "coloring should be" and tell them that there is one new criterion that they need to help figure out.

Students work with a partner to examine the Model Feathered Friends Saver and answer questions to try to figure out what the new criterion on the chart is. They consider these three questions:

» "What is one thing that is new on this scientific drawing that was not included on the expert bird drawing for the riddle cards?" (done previously)
» "Do the colors match the colors in the bird photograph?"
» "Why is it important for the colors to match?"

Through this questioning, students become clear that when creating their own Feathered Friends Saver, the colors they use in their scientific drawing should match the colors of the actual bird they are drawing.

"If the questions are not causing students to struggle and think, they are probably not worth asking," says Dylan Wiliam (Berger, Woodfin, and Vilen, 2016, p. 51). In Chapter 3A, we explored the steps necessary to prepare for each lesson, which include reading through the entire lesson carefully and preparing for your delivery of the lesson. This is the best time to make decisions about questions that may need to be added or tweaked to best meet the needs of your students. Keep in mind that any questions you develop should advance the discussion of a text, the understanding of a topic, or the synthesis of the lesson's activities. They should demand that students think deeply and critically, not just that they remember or relate to their own experience.

▶ Engaging Students with Protocols

Protocols are an important feature of our curriculum because they are one of the best ways we know to engage students in discussion, inquiry, critical thinking, and sophisticated communication. A protocol consists of agreed-upon, detailed guidelines for reading, recording, discussing, or reporting that ensure equal participation and accountability in learning. Importantly, protocols allow students to talk to *each other*, not just to you. As a result, they build independence and responsibility. Protocols in the curriculum range from very quick protocols like Back-to-Back and Face-to-Face to longer lesson-length protocols like Science Talks.

Speaking and listening protocols are especially useful for scaffolding the learning experience for students with learning challenges and those are who are learning English. These students, who may struggle with reading grade-level texts, will likely be able to contribute to conversations and discussions when using an appropriate discussion protocol. The repeated academic and procedural language of protocols also facilitates language acquisition.

Committing to Teaching the Protocols

Since the first edition of our curriculum came out in 2012, we have heard from some teachers that they often skip the protocols. They do this usually for one of three reasons:

» *They don't think their students can handle the activity level of the protocol (or they're not sure they can handle the classroom management aspect of the protocol).* This is a real concern, and there's no doubt that classroom management is one of the hardest things about teaching, especially in an active, collaborative classroom. Chapter 3C is dedicated to this topic, so keep reading!

» *They don't feel they have time to do the protocol and choose instead a more traditional method for "delivering" the content.* Just because you deliver the content doesn't mean students have learned it. They need time to *think* and *do* to make the learning stick. Protocols give students a chance to synthesize and communicate knowledge and to practice important skills. Protocols don't always take more time; once you and your students learn the protocols, they should run quite efficiently.

» *They don't place as much value on Speaking and Listening Standards (usually because they aren't assessed on high-stakes tests) and skip the protocols, thinking that they are only about speaking and listening.* Protocols are about much more than speaking and listening. They serve as an important scaffold for reading and writing. Discourse is a way for students to make meaning and rehearse their ideas.

We urge you not to skip the protocols! They are too important. The most important thing about the protocols in the curriculum is that they deepen learning experiences for students. They give students a chance to play with ideas and to engage in oral rehearsal before writing. They help students synthesize their understanding and learn to have academic conversations with each other. They take the focus off you and let students take charge of their own learning.

Key to the success of any protocol is practice. It will take time, especially for students who have never been a part of a classroom protocol, to get used to their structure and "rules" for participation. Spending a little more time on the front end modeling the procedures and expectations of protocols will go a long way toward their efficient use throughout the year. Also important for you to take into consideration is that protocols involve many transitions—from independent work to partner work, from partner work to group work, from one part of the room to another. Looking ahead throughout a series of lessons and planning for these transitions will help the protocols run smoothly. But once you've got it and the students have got it, protocols will be a powerful tool for learning in your classroom.

Learning the Routines

When a protocol appears for the first time in the curriculum, it is described fully; thereafter, a shortened version appears. If you skip a protocol the first time it appears, you may wonder how you will ever find it again. Each protocol is described fully in the Classroom Protocols section of our website, Curriculum.ELeducation.org, and in our book *Management in the Active Classroom*. You can access them there at any time. These are also good resources if you decide you want to explore new or different protocols that you might want to use with your students.

▶▶ **Video Spotlight**

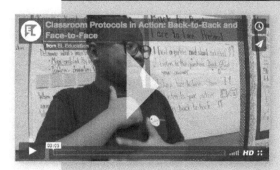

In the accompanying video, see first-graders practice the steps of the Back-to-Back and Face-to-Face protocol and how to be safe doing it. They first practice taking turns talking and listening about an easy question—*What is your favorite thing to do in the summer?*—before moving on to questions about their text.

https://vimeo.com/164447189

The Purposes of Protocols

The protocols in the curriculum serve a variety of purposes:

» **Reading, writing, and annotating.** Protocols for reading, writing, and annotating hold all students accountable for building background knowledge about a topic and for analyzing what they read by annotating the text with questions, comments, or summary language. Protocols are not text-specific; instead, they provide students with tools to dig deeper into any text. These protocols also allow you to assess which students are struggling with the text and may need further support for comprehension. Finally, they allow students to gather and organize their thoughts before discussion or writing.

» **Building vocabulary.** Protocols for building vocabulary make domain-specific and general academic vocabulary come alive for students through creating meaningful context, connecting new words to previous schema, and repeating shared use of the words. Vocabulary protocols and strategies help students understand that acquiring new words is an active process requiring interaction and application.

» **Collaboration and discussion.** Protocols for collaboration and discussion invite students to value different perspectives and new insights. They make room for listening as well as contributing to discussion: guidelines for timekeeping, turn taking, and focusing help students develop the skills they need for productive discussions. Sentence stems for academic conversation and asking questions, norms for honoring diverse perspectives, and procedures for synthesizing contributions to a discussion hold individuals and groups accountable for pushing their thinking further. Discussion protocols and strategies can be embedded into a daily lesson, or they can be the entire lesson.

» **Sharing and presenting.** Protocols for sharing and presenting focus on fairness and equity. They enable all members of a group to see or hear the work done by individuals or small groups in an efficient way. Timekeeping and turn-taking norms are emphasized to maximize equity of sharing.

» **Critique.** Protocols for peer critique are essential for teaching students how to offer and receive kind, helpful, and specific feedback. They allow students to navigate the tricky social terrain of giving constructive criticism, while keeping them focused on sharing and supporting rigorous content.

▶▶ Video Spotlight

In the accompanying video, first-graders in Anne Simpson's class at Two Rivers Public Charter School in Washington, D.C., do the work of real scientists. Students are focused on the question: *How does a spider's body help it survive?* They have prepared for the Science Talk by researching spiders, drawing diagrams, and learning academic and disciplinary-specific vocabulary so that they are prepared to share their ideas and back them up with evidence. (See box: The Science Talk Protocol for a full description of the protocol).

https://vimeo.com/169909161

▶ Deepening Student Discourse

There is no better indicator of the quality of learning taking place in a classroom than the quality of student discourse. Over the past few years, Harvard researcher Jal Mehta has traveled across the United States to visit exemplary classrooms looking for examples of high-level work—"deeper learning"—for an upcoming book. He quickly found that regardless of the reputation of the school or the teacher or the stated outcomes of the lesson, what really mattered was *what students were discussing and how they were discussing it*. In the best classrooms, students were taking the lead in offering ideas and analysis of deep topics, were responding to the comments of other students with respect and interest, and were insightful in the questions they asked of each other and of the teacher.

Students *can* learn the skills for powerful discourse. Regardless of grade level and academic background, students will change their behaviors to fit into the culture of a high-level classroom when they are guided and supported to do so. Once students have made this shift and developed these skills, it can spill over into all of their academic and personal life: They learn that they have the courage and ability to speak up with clarity and eloquence.

Modeling Discourse

The first step in students learning the skills of strong discourse is modeling. When you listen carefully to the ideas and questions of students and unpack and analyze them in front of the class, students learn that their own ideas and those of their peers have value. Formalizing student ideas by naming them by that student (e.g., Kara's hypothesis; Carlos's approach) helps students take pride in themselves as intellectuals and thinkers. When you direct students to ask questions and make responses to each other, rather than keeping the dialogue just between you and the students (e.g., "Brianna, why don't you address that question to Simeon? He has strong opinions

THE SCIENCE TALK PROTOCOL

Purpose

Science Talks are discussions about big questions. They are appropriate for any grade level, but they are particularly useful for elementary school. Like a Socratic Seminar, Science Talks deal with provocative questions, often posed by students themselves. Science Talks provide space for students to collectively theorize, to build on each other's ideas, to work out inchoate thoughts, and to learn about scientific discourse. Most importantly, they allow all students to do exactly what scientists do: think about, wonder about, and talk about how things work. These talks provide a window on student thinking that can help teachers figure out what students really know and what their misconceptions are. Armed with this insight, teachers can better plan hands-on activities and experiments.

Materials

» Guiding question for the Science Talk, determined beforehand

Procedure

1. Choose the question. The best questions are provocative and open-ended, so as to admit multiple answers and theories.

2. Often, students generate great questions for Science Talks. Teachers can also generate questions based on their own wonderings.

3. Introduce Science Talks to students. Gather students into a circle on the floor. Introduce the first Science Talk by discussing what scientists do.

4. Then ask, "What will help us talk as scientists?" Record the students' comments, as these will become the norms for your Science Talks. If the students don't mention making sure that everyone has a chance to talk, introduce that idea, as well as how each person can ensure that they themselves don't monopolize the conversation. Stress how each student's voice is valued and integral to the success of a Science Talk.

5. Set the culture. Students direct their comments to one another, not to the teacher. In fact, the teacher stays quiet and out of the way, facilitating only to make sure that students respectfully address one another and to point out when monopolizing behavior occurs. In a good talk, you'll hear students saying, "I want to add to what Grace said ..." or "I think Derek is right about one thing, but I'm not so sure about...."

6. Another good question to pose is: "How will we know that what we've said has been heard?" Students will readily talk about how they can acknowledge what's been said by repeating it or rephrasing before they go on to add their comments. This is a great place to add (if the students don't) that talking together is one way scientists build theories.

7. A typical talk lasts about 30 minutes. Take notes during the talk about who is doing the talking and to record particularly intriguing comments.

Variations

» With young students, do a movement exercise that relates to the Science Talk. For a talk on how plants grow, students may be invited to show, with their bodies, how plants grow from bulbs. Not only does this give students a chance to move before more sitting, but it also gives them a different modality in which to express themselves. Sometimes the shyer students also find acting something out first helps them to verbalize it.

» Have students prepare for a Science Talk by reading and annotating pertinent texts. Combining Science Talk with a Jigsaw or another text-based protocol could work well.

» Pair a Science Talk with a writing activity on the same topic.

» Record the talks. Replaying the tapes later helps to make sense of what at first can seem incomprehensible. Students also love hearing the tapes of Science Talks.

about that"), students get in the habit of building student-to-student discussion in class. It may be helpful to think of this as a volleyball match, with ideas bouncing from student to student before going back over the net to you, rather than a ping-pong match, with the discussion passing back and forth between you and individual students.

Using Sentence Frames

For students of all ages, sentence frames can be powerful in shifting the quality of conversation. Simple phrases can become the norm in classrooms and elevate the level of conversation, making it more respectful and productive. In Anne Simpson's first-grade classroom, shown in the Science Talk video, students are reminded of a few key sentence frames before they begin the Science Talk protocol: "I agree with _____ because _____"; "I disagree with _____ because _____"; "I made a connection with _____"; and "I want to add on to _____." Sentence frames are a consistent structure used throughout the curriculum, designed to foster discourse and support productive and equitable conversation among students. Supported discourse of this nature is an important part of the process of acquiring literacy skills for all students, and for ELLs it plays a key role in language acquisition.

Additionally, when students build new vocabulary through their reading and their studies, that vocabulary will become a part of the discourse when you model its use and when you celebrate students who include it in their arguments (e.g., "Anthony, I'm impressed that you used the word theme in your argument. Can you remind us what that word means in this case?").

Assessing Yourself

It may be difficult for you to judge the level of student discourse during a lesson while you are teaching. Consider enlisting the help of an observer—a fellow teacher, coach, or administrator—who can take notes or record the lesson, not for an evaluation, but for learning. If the observer makes a diagram of who speaks to whom, and what they say, it is likely to surprise you to see this data after the lesson. How much did boys speak versus girls? Which students spoke a lot or very little? How much conversation was teacher-student versus student-student? What kinds of questions were asked? These data can be analyzed non-judgmentally to support your efforts to deepen classroom discourse, a powerful tool for student learning.

▶ Co-Constructing Anchor Charts with Students

By recording content, strategies, processes, cues, and guidelines from their learning on anchor charts and posting them in the classroom, teachers are able to help students make their thinking visible. Anchor charts empower students to own their learning because they are a place for students to look to for support when answering questions, contributing to discussions, processing their ideas, and writing. When students know where to look for help independently, they don't always have to ask you. Anchor charts also give students a chance to process their thinking and hear the thinking of others before or during writing, close reading, or other activities that may be challenging for them without such support.

Building Anchor Charts

There are many ways to build anchor charts. In the curriculum, there are some places where you will be cued to create anchor charts in advance of the lesson, others where you will co-create them with students during the lesson, and others where students will create them together in small groups. Sometimes students might work together in small groups to record their ideas on an anchor chart, come back together, present it to the class, and then contribute to one combined class version of the chart. Alternatively, you might work as a whole class to clarify and capture the most important ideas or questions on one anchor chart before students work independently or in small groups.

Generally, anchor charts are living documents that are clarified and added to by you and students. By adding to anchor charts throughout a unit or module or across an entire year, students are able to clarify, update, and expand their growing knowledge. In this way, the charts remain relevant and supportive over time and ensure that all students have access to the same information. There are other times when anchor charts support specific lessons or arcs of lessons and will be created and taken down in short order.

Supporting Students with Anchor Charts

Anchor charts are supportive of students' varied learning needs and play a valuable role in their learning. This is especially true for ELLs and students who may need additional support with perception and information processing. The very nature of anchor charts allows them to be easily customized based on students' needs, and they offer an alternative to providing only auditory information. And, unlike text written on a white board, anchor charts can live on in the classroom long after a lesson has ended.

We recommend that you add visuals, definitions, or translations to anchor charts to support ELLs' language acquisition and ability to access the information on the chart. Anchor charts will provide them with concrete examples as they try to apply the content, strategy, or process represented on them. You can also manipulate the display of information by using larger font or highlighting certain words or phrases. In addition to customizing the charts themselves, you may also want to provide individual copies to students who may need additional support to help them maintain focus, monitor progress, sketch or take notes about their thinking, and access important information as they work independently.

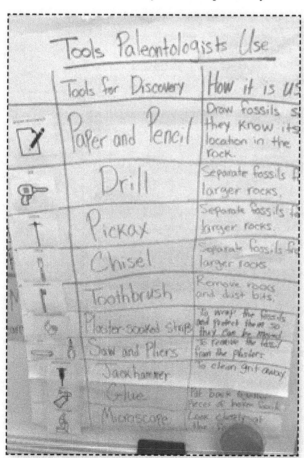

Visual aids and predictable ways of organizing information make anchor charts supportive of students' learning needs

Chapter 3C:
How Can I Create the Kind of Active and Collaborative Classroom Culture the Curriculum Requires?

Instructional practices like those described in Chapter 3B, which permeate the curriculum, result in classrooms that are active and collaborative, alive with energy and movement. This hum and buzz will be familiar and comfortable for some of you. For others, it may be new and potentially a little unsettling. Classroom management is one of the hardest parts of being a teacher, and the truth is that our curriculum may require a few changes, depending on your current approach. If you are accustomed to a classroom that is always quiet, where your students sit up straight with their eyes on you for the majority of the time, or one where students work mostly independently, you may need to stretch a little out of your comfort zone.

Learning to teach a new curriculum is a lot for any teacher; learning new classroom management strategies on top of that may feel overwhelming. Rather than thinking of this as "layering on," however, we encourage you to reframe the work of creating an active and collaborative classroom culture as a deepening or enriching of our curriculum. The truth is that all of the work you do to teach your students to read and write and comprehend complex text with this curriculum will be easier for you and more effective for them if you spend some time on the front end cultivating the soil of your classroom culture.

Managing an active classroom full of students doing collaborative work is different from managing a quiet classroom full of students doing independent seat work, and you may need to learn a few new techniques. Those we offer here are really just a start to get you on your way to making the most of this curriculum.

Much of what follows comes from our 2015 book *Management in the Active Classroom*, which describes self-managed classrooms and our approach to 23 classroom management practices. These practices cover topics ranging from "Transitions" to "Giving Clear Directions" to "Restorative Practices," and everything in between. The book also includes videos showing students and teachers in action, which can be viewed on our curriculum website (Curriculum.ELeducation. org).

We start here by describing what we mean by self-management and then move on to highlighting and summarizing some of the classroom management practices described in *Management in the Active Classroom* that will be most supportive when teaching the curriculum.

▶ What Is Self-Management, and How Will It Help My Students Be Successful?

Chapter 3

There's a certain instantly recognizable energy present in a high-achieving classroom. You can see it in the faces of the students: lighting up as they make new connections between their background knowledge and their reading, or settling into deep concentration on an entry ticket. You can hear it in the respectful but warm conversations that occur between student and teacher, and in the way students take control of their classroom routines and procedures with only the gentlest of reminders. You can touch it: the poster of jointly written classroom norms, the materials organized and ready for students when they enter.

A successful classroom is obvious to all our senses. But the steps to take to create that classroom often are not. Ironically, a robust body of research has identified effective classroom practices: We know what works. However, few educational researchers or teacher preparation programs in the United States address effective classroom management (Emmer, Sabornie, Evertson, and Weinstein, 2013).

As a result, teachers can be at a loss, particularly as novice educators, as to what "magic" is needed to keep students engaged, on task, accountable, compassionate, and safe. It can seem to be a kind of "secret sauce," or perhaps something only certain teachers are born with. Teachers who have the magic often have a difficult time explaining what their magic is—and yet they will also tell you that the most brilliant, creative lesson plan in the world will not work without it.

> *"They like taking responsibility and ownership for their learning and realizing 'I'm in charge of my learning now, I'm in charge of my own behavior, I'm in charge of my management.' That's a very empowering position for a second-grader to be in."*

Katie Benton

Grade 2 Teacher, Greenville, South Carolina

In fact, effective classroom management is not magic, secret, or a lucky gift given to a chosen few. It is this: the teacher, with his or her students, taking full responsibility for developing thoughtful, proactive, foundational management structures that are implemented and reinforced throughout every learning experience. It starts with the belief that students can and will succeed with effective support, and it is one of the most valuable investments of time you can make. The best news of all is that it is something every teacher can learn, practice, and master.

Good classroom management practice comes under many names: "the orderly classroom," "the rigorous classroom," or "the focused classroom." We invite you to think of it as "the self-managed classroom." A self-managed classroom is respectful, active, collaborative, and growth-oriented.

By using the term "self-managed," we don't mean to imply that classrooms will run themselves or that students don't need the authority and support of their teachers—academically and behaviorally. Rather, self-management is an ethos and a belief system that permeates the classroom and says students have the power, within themselves, to make wise choices that best serve them as learners and people and maintain a respectful classroom culture. Self-discipline is the end goal of all management structures. Students and teachers in the self-managed classroom are people who have self-knowledge, self-compassion, and self-control.

Figure 3.3 The Self-Managed Classroom

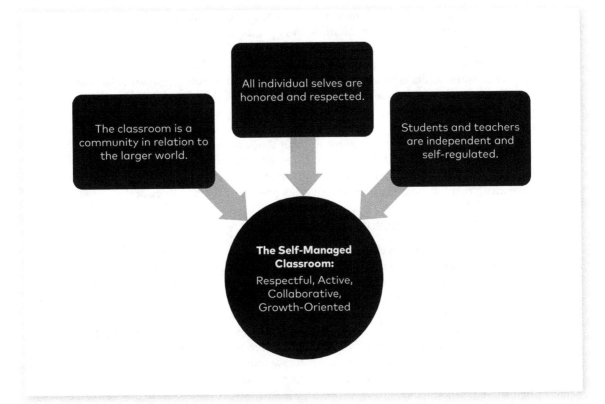

As a result, students in a self-managed classroom do not constantly need authority figures to compel them to exhibit correct behavior; ultimately, with guidance and practice, they own and enact that behavior themselves. Students reach this point through the consistent implementation of the formative assessment practices of modeling, practice, and reflection.

Finally, students in a self-managed classroom also understand that a "self" does not stand alone. A healthy sense of self necessarily includes a strong sense of community. Self-managed class-rooms know and nurture their place as a learning community unto themselves and alongside other classrooms with their own identities within a broader school community.

A Closer Look at the Self-Managed Classroom

Self-managed classrooms share basic characteristics, no matter the age of the students. These characteristics are rooted strongly in high behavioral and academic expectations, which in turn positively reinforce and support each other.

A Self-Managed Classroom Is Respectful

Respect is the bottom line for all academic and social interactions in the classroom. The teacher explicitly leads and models for students an unwavering disposition of respect in the way she interacts with the class and with her colleagues. Students are held to impeccable standards of respect toward each other and toward adults. Norms for respectful communication are set, modeled, and enforced without compromise. Cultural differences in the classroom are honored and respected. Students are not simply directed to "be respectful," however. They discuss respect every day; they hold themselves and each other accountable for respectful behavior. They are considered partners in the learning process, deserving the respect and expectations given to adults: engagement, support, and accountability. As a result, students feel safe and trust one another.

A Self-Managed Classroom Is Active

In a self-managed classroom, all students contribute to the learning experience and are held accountable for that contribution. Multiple entry points are evident, honoring different learning styles, strengths, comfort levels, and development. Self-managed classrooms help students learn about their own social and academic strengths and contribute to the class in significant and varied ways. Students and teachers shift through multiple configurations of learning (whole class lessons, group work, independent research, guided work) with grace and speed, with the ultimate goal of student independence in mind. Self-managed classrooms are silent and still at times, when that fits the nature of the work. Students can sit up straight when needed, following the speaker with attention and courtesy. At other times, self-managed classrooms are alive with movement and a productive "buzz" of discussion, problem-solving, critique, and creation when the work demands activity and collaboration. Like a real-world workplace, the classroom is often busy with a range of focused and productive independent and group work at the same time.

A Self-Managed Classroom Is Collaborative

A self-managed classroom is committed to collaborative, social construction of knowledge—a community of learners pushing each other's thinking and building each other's understanding—in whole class, small group, and paired work. Students are impelled and compelled to share their ideas and understanding with different groups and analyze and critique each other's ideas. Students often take leadership roles in classroom discussions and protocols, particularly at the secondary level. Students work together to maintain a classroom climate that is physically and emotionally safe and positive, keep their classroom space neat and organized, and produce high-quality individual and group work. They have individual and collective responsibility for the quality of the classroom culture and learning. It is not just the teacher's responsibility—it is their shared responsibility.

A Self-Managed Classroom Is Growth-Oriented

In a self-managed classroom, making mistakes is part of the territory. In fact, students and teachers understand that mistakes are not only normal but a necessary sign that learning is occurring. To that end, students demonstrate, analyze, and celebrate academic courage, taking risks to speak up in class, ask questions, pose ideas, and try out new concepts and vocabulary. They are not afraid or embarrassed to show that they care about learning. They understand and discuss the concept of growth mindset—that practice makes you stronger, that engaging in harder work and more challenging problems "grows your brain." They thrive on embedded cycles of practice, feedback, and documented growth in academics, communication, routines, and procedures.

Our library of Management in the Active Classroom videos includes 30 videos. Here we'll highlight just a few to give you a glimpse of what a self-managed classroom looks like and sounds like.

▶▶ **Video Spotlight**

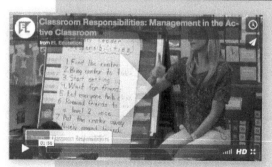

In the accompanying video, see how the principles of self-management allow students to take charge of taking care of their classroom. Students take on leadership roles and even conduct "staff meetings" with their classmates to reflect on quality control.

https://vimeo.com/142645382

In the accompanying video, see the power of a teacher's voice to set the tone in the classroom. Calm and measured tones support students to regulate their own voices and behaviors.

https://vimeo.com/123124604

In the accompanying video, see how your choices about how to set up your classroom—including multiple configurations for whole group, small group, and independent work—promote learning and self-management.

https://vimeo.com/124453007

Effective Classroom Management Is Built on Relationships

Every student wants to be known and valued—by their teachers and their peers. The better you know your students, the more effective you can be. It's possible to run a classroom without knowing students particularly well through stern and rigid, or entertaining and clever, teacher-centered lessons. It's even possible to keep students engaged much of the time through ritualized, fast-paced practices that keep eyes on the teacher. But to build a self-managed classroom where students are engaged, self-motivated, and self-disciplined while working actively and collaboratively, fostering good relationships with those students is the foundation of success.

Classroom management often breaks down when a student is struggling academically, socially, or emotionally. If you have built trust with that student, you have a foundation to intervene, subtly or demonstrably, to support and redirect him or her. It is especially important to be able to cite specific positive attributes of students when working with them—especially when their behavior is challenging—so that there can be a genuine basis for your faith in them to succeed. This doesn't guarantee an easy solution, but without this foundation, there is little to build on to help the student grow.

We believe that great teachers teach from the heart: They have a love of their subject areas, and, beyond this, they believe in and care deeply about their students. They genuinely feel that their students are capable of more ambitious success than their students themselves imagine. Because the purpose of this book and our curriculum is to support great teaching, we join what we know about classroom management to the positive belief in the capacity of students to succeed at high levels—independently and collectively.

Classroom Management for All

One of the greatest challenges for any teacher is finding strategies that work for all students. Just as academic instruction must be differentiated to meet the needs of diverse learners, often classroom management must be differentiated to meet the needs of the diverse young people in our classrooms. One-size-fits-all approaches may work some of the time, but they rarely work all of the time.

Responding to students' varied needs is an essential ingredient in any inclusive approach to classroom management. It starts with relationships: knowing students well, building trust, and listening to and responding to their needs. It also must include *learning* about the individual realities that students bring into the classroom with them. If, for example, you have a new student with an autism spectrum disorder, *learn* about that diagnosis. Read, ask questions, and collaborate with colleagues, specialists, and especially families to identify strategies that will make your classroom just as productive and supportive for that student as it is for other students. Understand the cultural differences among your students (and you) and what that means when building an active and collaborative classroom culture. Ask questions, be open to change, and don't assume that your way is the right way.

The Relationship between Classroom Management and Student Engagement and Motivation

The best management tool is creating engaged and motivated students. When schoolwork is personally meaningful, appropriately challenging, and invites creative and critical thinking, it brings out the best in student behavior. The same group of students who may be considered "behavior problems" or "unfocused" in one classroom may be "model students" in another classroom where the work is compelling. On the flip side, effective classroom management also creates the conditions that allow all students to engage in their academics.

Classroom management is most successful when students are not only academically motivated, but also motivated to be their best selves. This is most effective when students are primarily motivated not by compliance to rules (though compliance is necessary) or by external rewards and tracking systems (though for some situations or students, those may be helpful). The most effective management comes when students are primarily motivated by their aspiration to be good and positive members of a classroom community that they respect and value.

The most powerful engagement and motivation is not created by clever structures. It is created by a sense of belonging to a positive academic community. In our curriculum, students are grounded every day in their habits of character. Based on our three Dimensions of Student Achievement (see Figure 1.2), our habits of character are designed to help students be effective learners and ethical people who contribute to a better world. Working together toward these goals and reflecting on them frequently creates the sense of belonging students need to be most successful academically.

It is easy to see where this approach to classroom management is different. Traditionally, classroom management conceives of students as needing to be guided and controlled for the smooth, orderly operation of a school. Management is something done *to* students. Although we recognize the essential need for adult guidance, the self-managed classroom is created *with* students, promoting self-discipline and self-guidance, and thrives within classroom and school cultures that promote habits of character and intentionally work to help students become their best selves.

Self-Managed Classrooms in Support of College- and Career-Ready Standards

The way you choose to structure and run your classroom sends a powerful message to students about their capacity and responsibility and helps define the nature of the learning process. When management structures align with the cognitive demand of new college- and career-ready standards—demanding individual responsibility and independence, critical thinking, and collaborative work—then students can thrive in a coherent academic culture that promotes real-world skills. In simple terms, the classroom can promote college, career, and civic readiness through responsible self-management, rather than constrain student growth in a classroom that is exclusively teacher-driven and compliance-based.

When you succeed in sending messages that support the highest aims of new college- and career-ready standards, a synergy results that makes the standards not only meaningful and accessible, but also attainable. In this way, both classroom instruction and classroom management can and should be aligned to standards.

Consider these seven descriptors of college- and career-ready students from the introduction to the Common Core English language arts/literacy standards:

» They demonstrate independence.

» They build strong content knowledge.

» They respond to the varying demands of audience, task, purpose, and discipline.

» They comprehend as well as critique.

» They value evidence.

» They use technology and digital media strategically and capably.

» They come to understand other perspectives and cultures.

Our experience has taught us that a self-managed classroom—one that is respectful, active, collaborative, and growth-oriented—is one where this vision of a college- and career-ready student not only lives but thrives.

The section that follows highlights and summarizes some of the classroom management practices described in *Management in the Active Classroom* that are most salient to our curriculum.

▶ What Structures and Strategies Will Be Most Effective in Helping Me Build an Active and Collaborative Classroom Culture?

At EL Education, we believe that classrooms should be lively and learning-centered, where students feel a sense of independence and responsibility for their learning and are interested and compelled by the work at hand: reading, writing, talking, playing, singing, moving, creating, acting, and contributing. In such an environment, classroom management works because students feel a sense of ownership over their work and behavior.

We aspire for students to be delighted and engaged, not quiet and compliant. Our curriculum both requires and promotes a self-managed learning environment that is *respectful, active, collaborative,* and *growth-oriented* so that students can create authentic, high-quality work, tackle real life problems, and take charge of their own learning within a collaborative setting. Taking steps to build a classroom culture of trust, challenge, and joy for students to draw upon is an important foundation as they take on the challenges in the curriculum.

Building and strengthening such a classroom culture happens throughout the year, but it is critical to the start. For students, the first few weeks of school are the first steppingstones to becoming successful—opening wide the school door and beckoning them to come in and begin.

In this section, we highlight two areas that you can focus on to build a strong foundation:

1. Creating the Conditions for Success:

- Teacher presence

- Classroom spaces that teach

- Building community

2. Structures and Strategies for Building an Active and Collaborative Classroom Culture:

- Crafting classroom norms together

- Making expectations clear: problem-solving and consequences

- Establishing routines through modeling and think-aloud

- Introducing classroom materials through guided practice

- Setting the stage for shared learning and discussion

For more information about these practices, and many others, we encourage you to read our 2014 book *Management in the Active Classroom*, which we wrote specifically to support the kinds of classroom management practices that make our curriculum most effective.

Creating the Conditions for Success

Teacher Presence

Researchers Carol Rodgers and Miriam Raider-Roth (2006) describe a teacher's presence this way: "(We view) teaching as engaging in an authentic relationship with students where teachers know and respond with intelligence and compassion to students and their learning. We define this engagement as 'presence'—a state of alert awareness, receptivity, and connectedness to the mental, emotional, and physical workings of both the individuals and the group in the context of their learning environment" (p. 149).

Your attitude and mindset form the foundation for your presence: knowing and valuing yourself as a teacher, knowing and valuing your students for who they are, acting as your authentic self, and knowing that your ability, like your students', grows with your effort.

Considerations:

» Develop your own mindset by thinking about who you are as a teacher; your strengths, weaknesses, passions, and values; and the things that you want to learn.

» Develop relationships with students that let them know who you are and that you are interested in who they are.

» Check any biases and assumptions you may hold (consciously or unconsciously) about your students, given your background and theirs. Be aware of how students from different backgrounds may have experienced school, interpersonal relationships, and interactions, and commit to making your classroom welcoming for all.

» Get to know your students not just by previous test scores, but also by what they care about and what brings them joy. Know their cultures, backgrounds, and needs, perhaps through an interview with them or their families. Likewise, share what you care about and what brings you joy, along with stories from your culture, background, and challenges you've faced (as appropriate). This helps students respect your authenticity and feel respected in return.

» Attend to language. In Table 3.8, we offer examples of teacher language that conveys a trust in students' ability to think deeply and share about something of importance.

Table 3.8: How Language Conveys Teacher Presence

Language	Example
Language of inquiry *Conveying curiosity and inviting conversations*	In introducing Grade 2, Module 1, teachers ask the questions: "What is school? Why is it important?"
Language of observation *Describing without judging*	In the first lesson of Grade 3, Module 1, the teacher says, "I noticed many of you persevering with your planning process even when it was challenging."
Language of focusing *Inviting students to think about something of note rather than looking to the teacher for answers*	During a K–2 Reading Foundations Skills Block (Skills Block) spelling lesson, a Grade 2 teacher might focus on common errors, asking: "This is how you spelled the word *cuts*, and this is how I spelled it. It looks like we made some different choices. What do you notice about the choices we made?"
Language of choice *Giving options; opportunities and practice for making decisions; inspiring ownership*	"Jonathan, I see you are having a hard time settling down this morning. I can give you a choice: Take a quick stretch and try again, or get a drink of water and try again."
Language of access *When critical, repeating and rephrasing questions and answers and providing think time to give students greater access to understanding*	After a Skills Block reading and spelling assessment, the Grade 2 teacher gives a student feedback: "It looks like you and I made some different choices in how we spelled these words. What do you notice about the choices each of us made?" She repeats herself and rephrases what she said as well: "Think about the way we each spelled this word. Can you tell me what's the same and what's different?"

Classroom Spaces That Teach

The physical classroom space sends a potent message to students about how to behave and learn. The wall space, seating, work areas, and materials not only support instruction, but also support strong habits of scholarship, independence, and responsibility central to the curriculum. If the physical classroom works against these principles (e.g., desks in rows), much time and energy will be spent "fighting" the space rather than teaching and learning.

By contrast, if the space is organized to encourage collaboration, to showcase student work, to meet the physical and learning needs of all students, with resources easily accessible, the form of it will fit the function of the classroom and enhance the learning and teaching that takes place there.

Considerations:

» Create a respectful, personalized space where students feel welcomed, peaceful, and at home.

» Set up a collaborative space that has enough room and flexibility for various configurations: independent work, group work, and whole class work. Our curriculum uses all of these configurations daily.

» Organize the space so that students can easily access and care for materials. Provide enough room for students to store both their work and their personal belongings. Find manageable ways for students to help in the arrangement of the classroom by creating labels, sorting books, making charts, or arranging classroom tools.

» Create a growth-oriented space that prioritizes effort and promotes goal-setting and reflection. Make space for charts of classroom norms, academic anchor charts, module guiding questions, and documentation panels that show both students' finished work and their growth through multiple drafts.

» Display student work. Expand the definition of high-quality work to include work that shows high growth (e.g., work that a struggling student may have completed that is concrete evidence she achieved more than she thought possible).

» Involve students in discussions about the care of the classroom and create classroom jobs around that care.

» Set up and use anchor charts, learning targets, and other strategies for setting and reflecting on goals. These are used throughout the curriculum to focus students' attention and engage them in learning. Anchor charts often stay on display throughout a unit or module, so you will need to find a place where they can stay up for the long haul.

Building Community

The desire for love and belonging are basic human needs. Children arrive on the first day with pressing questions: "Where are the bathrooms?" "When is snack?" "Will we go outside?" "Am I safe here?" And, most importantly, "Do I belong here?" Though many of these questions are unspoken, children look to you for answers. On day one, it is important to take the role of a gracious host, inviting children in. But it's also important to quickly address students' basic questions and move them toward a sense of "ownership" of the classroom.

> *"Classroom culture is so important when implementing this curriculum. Students need to learn how to trust one another, how to respect a high level of vulnerability, and how to give and receive feedback that is purposeful, but most importantly, how to love one another and push each other through some potentially tough times when learning. I spend a lot of time with students on growth mindset and positive interaction, really drawing on the habits of character throughout the curriculum."*

Kady Taylor
Grade 1 Teacher, Lead and K–2 Instructional Strategy Reading Lead, Wilmington, Delaware

Nothing is more important in fostering students' growth than the degree to which they care about their own work and the success of the classroom community as a whole. And nothing fosters caring more than feeling that one is a valued member of a community. Creating positive relationships with students and families lays the foundation for a self-managed classroom, which in turn lays the foundation for success with the curriculum.

Considerations:

» Use purposeful play for students to get to know each other and build group identity. Invite participation through songs and noncompetitive games. Often, play is viewed as in opposition to serious learning. But experience and research show the opposite: Play is the natural way children learn and a joyful way to build the group cohesion that is so necessarily for collaborative deeper learning.

» Take time to get to know students personally as well as academically. Share your personal and academic stories when appropriate. Be aware of differences that may exist between your own background and experiences and that of many of your students, and how those differences shape your interactions.

» Give students time to get to know you and their classmates through daily greetings, noncompetitive group activities and challenges, and focused sharing. Throughout the curriculum, students work in diverse groupings. By learning about each other and playing together, children become more comfortable with the give and take such work requires.

» Encourage families to share their excitement and concern about the classroom and curriculum and integrate these considerations. Invite them into the classroom to convey their excitement and care and to serve as experts on particular topics.

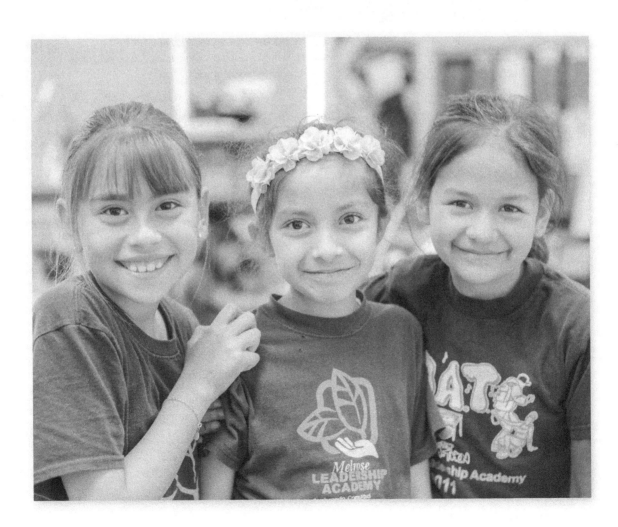

Structures and Strategies for Building an Active and Collaborative Classroom Culture

Crafting Classroom Norms Together

Rules, constitutions, guidelines, expectations—the behaviors we wish students to exhibit have many names. We call them "norms." Norms are the foundation for respectful behavior among students, between students and teachers, and among teachers.

Through a process of co-creating norms, students appreciate immediately that they are not being asked to regurgitate your thoughts, but are genuinely included in the process of governing themselves and their classroom. Co-creating norms is a great opportunity to raise awareness of how individual students are comfortable interacting interpersonally at home, socially, and academically, and to then integrate these routines into the classroom. Because they have authored the guidelines themselves, students understand clearly the intent behind them and are invested in respecting them. The key when creating norms is to generate a positive, thoughtful discussion and to distill student suggestions into a clear and effective list. Norms are then discussed often and used daily to guide interactions and behavior.

Our curriculum promotes student self-assessment. Even the youngest students learn how to reflect upon and articulate their own growth and then set goals for themselves. Creating and reflecting on norms is a vital first step in the yearlong process of setting and reflecting on goals.

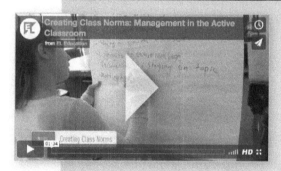

▶▶ **Video Spotlight**

In the accompanying video, students develop class norms and reflect on their use. Classroom norms for communication and respect help students feel safe and focused.

https://vimeo.com/124448656

Considerations:

In *Teaching Children to Care* (1992), Ruth Charney describes how to create norms by first asking each student to reflect on hopes for the coming year:

» Charney starts by modeling. She states her own hopes and dreams, translating them into concrete behaviors children can understand: "I hope that our class will work together and learn from each other" or "I hope our class helps the whole school be a friendly place to learn."

» Next, students generate their own hopes and dreams in writing or in pictures.

» From this list, students, with teacher guidance, create norms that reflect their hopes and dreams. (The teacher may start by using the class brainstorm of norms on chart paper.)

» Then, the teacher consolidates and simplifies the ideas into the positive norms the students will use throughout the year. She turns all the "don'ts" into "dos" (e.g., "Don't call each other bad names" becomes "Be kind to each other" or "Treat each other with respect").

» The norms are then "published" and posted prominently in the classroom.

» If your school has schoolwide codes of conduct, the last step is to connect the classroom norms to the schoolwide ones. Both documents should be a living part of the school culture and understood by students.

Making Expectations Clear: Problem-Solving and Consequences

In creating the norms with students, you are not abdicating your authority for classroom management; rather, you are making a promise to uphold what is most important to the students. Perhaps nothing you do carries more weight than how you manage misbehavior. All your norms, circles, advice, morning meetings, and advisory periods mean nothing if you don't deliver on what you say when it really counts.

> *"Where did we ever get the crazy idea that in order to make children do better, first we have to make them feel worse?"*

Jane Nelsen

Positive Discipline

Your approach to problem-solving and consequences should be in service of helping students self-manage within an active, collaborative community. Fair and logical consequences make students feel supported and help strengthen the classroom community. To take full advantage of our curriculum that teaches collaboration, perseverance, and initiative, students must be able to depend on this level of emotional safety. In the curriculum, students are regularly asked to take risks academically. They need to feel emotionally safe to do so. If students violate the norms, that must be addressed directly, specifically, and with compassion.

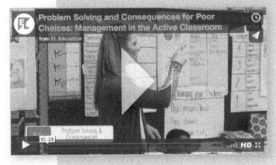

▶▶ Video Spotlight

In the accompanying video, see the importance of teacher voice and body language for helping students get themselves back on track after making poor choices. The way you handle poor choices sends a powerful message to students.

https://vimeo.com/124448651

Considerations:

» Carefully choose your words and tone. Students should hear, "You made a bad choice," not "you are a bad person." Deliver consequences firmly and gently.

» Use reminders or quick redirections. Rather than a long lecture, give a quick, subtle gesture that is culturally appropriate for all students. Fewer words frequently bring the best results because little attention is taken from the flow of the class.

» Consequences should be:

- **Relevant.** A consequence must be relevant to the deed (e.g., if a student writes on a desk, then he or she should clean it up).

- **Respectful.** A consequence is not a punishment; it is feedback from which a student can learn (e.g., rather than taking away recess for unsafe play, have a student stay close to you for a short period of time until he is able to say and demonstrate that he is ready to play safe). No consequence should be forever, or delivered out of frustration.

- **Realistic.** A consequence must be doable for the student and for you and not overly harsh (e.g., if a child writes on a desk, then she should fix her mistake by cleaning the desk, not cleaning *all* the desks).

» Introduce the concept of consequences and problem-solving through discussions and modeling. Question the idea that all students are familiar or comfortable with a consequences-driven approach to problem-solving. Discuss your approach and rationale with families.

» Discuss the *positive* consequences when students *do* follow the norms: "What happens when you choose to cooperate with your classmates? Why might that be important?"

» When students violate a norm or feelings get hurt, have set guidelines for fixing the mistake that repairs the harm done. Use restorative questions (rather than accusations) to find out what happened and what can be done to fix it (e.g., "What were you thinking at the time?" or "Tell me what you think happened").

Establishing Routines through Modeling and Think-aloud

Inviting students to feel welcome in and responsible for the classroom requires taking time to teach and practice daily routines. This is best done through modeling, think-alouds, and guided practice, just as with all new academic routines that are introduced in the curriculum.

Modeling is a way to scaffold learning. It is a participatory strategy that goes beyond just telling students what you expect; it *shows* students what is expected, invites them to reflect, and allows them to practice, leading them to ever more independence. Students who are learning to self-manage require a growth mindset so that they view routines and transitions as skills to practice and improve upon. Modeling is effective to teach start-of-the-year routines (e.g., lining up for lunch, responding to teacher signals for attention, handwashing, transitions). These routines need to be efficient, practiced, and purposeful. Combine modeling with think-alouds, which show students the internal and external language that supports decision-making and thinking processes.

Considerations:

» Model routines just as you would model academic work. Begin with an exemplar or ideal behavior, deconstruct the parts so students understand, and finally put it back together to practice. Suggested steps for modeling routines:

- Model the routine, including thinking aloud if appropriate.

- Ask the students what they noticed about what you did (e.g., "When you raised your hand, other students did too").

- Summarize the routine and have students repeat the steps.

- Call on one or two students to demonstrate.

- Ask again what students notice.

- Have everyone practice until it is 100 percent correct for all students. Don't settle for less.

» When practicing, consider aspects of teacher presence, such as body language and voice, to convey the message that you know students can succeed.

Introducing Classroom Materials through Guided Practice

Guided practice is much like modeling but is used specifically to introduce materials that students will use in more open, creative ways throughout the year. For example, using a three-hole punch should be modeled because it has one basic use, but paints are better introduced through guided practice because they can be used with endless possibilities.

A critical aspect of guided practice is to first generate excitement about the possibilities that a given material offers and secondly to think about the care and placement of the materials in the classroom so that everyone can use them throughout the year. Guided practice directly promotes equity, since it lets everyone have experience with materials before using them (rather than assuming students' have prior experience with a given material). Knowing how to use materials effectively and creatively will be important as students begin work in the K–2 Labs and the 3–5 Additional Language and Literacy Block, during which they will be working both collaboratively and independently.

Considerations:

In *Teaching Children to Care* (1992), Ruth Charney highlights five steps to Guided Discovery:

» Introduce the material. With younger students, this may mean sitting in a circle on the rug with a box of crayons in the middle. With older students, it may mean "fieldwork" at the computer lab. Bring students' focus to what material or space you want them to "discover."

» Ask students what they notice about the material or the space (e.g., "It looks sharp," "You can't see it from the teacher's desk," "It might spill").

» Let students explore the material or area. This may mean passing it around from student to student or letting them mill about a particular area of the room.

» Once they have explored, ask them to share anything else they notice. Help them generate ideas about possible ways to use the material (including unintended uses or possible safety concerns).

» Have students try a few of the ideas they generated.

» Ask students to suggest and come to agreement on the "rules" they want to set up for using that material or area. Young students may benefit from signs around the room that remind them of proper use. To support their sense of ownership of the classroom, consider assigning different materials or areas of the room to individual students or small groups. They can create signage and help you monitor how things are going throughout the year and determine if the class needs a refresher discussion about using that material or space.

Setting the Stage for Shared Learning and Discussion

In the first few weeks of school, when students are just getting to know one another and learning how to work together, the focus is on sharing about oneself in a clear and concise way and on active listening and supportive responses. Sharing of this nature, which on the surface may look like traditional "show and tell," is the underpinning for building working relationships that are positive and participatory. Sharing things that are important to the sharer engenders feelings of belonging and, for the listener, connection and empathy.

Sharing provides a format for respectful interaction that will later be built upon as students begin to critique each other's work, and it is the basis for using the many protocols throughout the curriculum. Protocols are rooted in the culture of respect and participation that is built initially in learning how to share and listen to each other.

Considerations:

» Use the same steps to model sharing as you do to model routines (see previous).

Chapter 3

» Teacher sharing should feel routine, not sensational, showing students that everyone has something to share.

» As with any routine, establish transparency. Invite students to ask questions and explain why sharing is important in your classroom and to learning.

» Set a routine that includes ways for the "audience" to respond. For example, the student who is sharing is the one to signal that he or she is ready for questions and comments.

» Keep the interactions positive and safe by tightly controlling the experience in the beginning. Then, slowly give over more control to students. For instance, on day one you might cue the student who is sharing to signal the audience that he is ready to begin; on day 15 he should be able to do so independently, and the rest of the class should respond to him without cues from you.

» Uphold the norms by setting firm expectations for the care with which students interact. Be willing to stop any situation that is not friendly for everyone.

» Once a sharing routine is established, introduce other protocols. For the start of the year, consider these: Back-to-Back and Face-to-Face, Think-Pair-Share, and Turn and Talk. These protocols require students to work with various classmates rather than just a best friend.

» Take time to explicitly teach, practice, and reflect on how well students are using the protocols. "Go slow to go fast" in terms of establishing routines that will show up frequently.

» Plan the introduction of sharing and protocols to accommodate individual students' specific needs. For instance, Back-to-Back and Face-to-Face might be intimidating to a student on the autism spectrum, so you might have to change it to Back-to-Back and Side-to-Side so that the student isn't required to look anyone straight in the eye.

» Build your own expertise with Conversation Cues and sentence frames that promote productive and equitable conversations (e.g., "Can you say more about that?").

Chapter 3:
Instructional Leadership

Table 3.9: Chapter 3 Instructional Leadership

Questions to Ask Yourself and Your Staff
» What system is in place to ensure that teachers have time to plan and prepare for daily lessons?
» What structures exist that can support teachers in long-range unit, module, and yearlong planning?
» What planning paradigm guides teachers in their planning and preparation process?
» How will you and your staff make use of the task cards and digital planning tools? Or do you have a different plan for how to analyze curriculum documents with teachers (e.g., Module Overviews, Curriculum Maps, Assessment Overview and Resources)? How will you engage, support, and hold teachers accountable for instructional decision-making based on careful planning?
» What structures exist for classroom teachers to collaborate with support specialists (e.g., reading interventionists, English as a second language teachers)?
» What is your school's vision for what teaching and learning should look like in all classrooms?
» How do you engage, support, and hold teachers accountable to that vision?
» Are you prepared to make practices that promote student engagement and ownership of learning (e.g., learning targets, protocols) as much of a priority as more traditional literacy-focused practices? How will you support teachers to also make them a priority?
» How does the configuration of classrooms (e.g., desks, work areas, supplies) reflect the vision for teaching and learning?
» What are your expectations regarding classroom management? Are you supportive of the collaborative, active learning in the curriculum? How will you support teachers? How might you need to adjust your expectations for what classrooms will look like and sound like when teachers are teaching the curriculum?
Evidence of Progress
» The master schedule reflects regular collaborative planning time for grade-level and department teams, and all critical support specialists are able to consistently engage.

Cont.

» Planning time is protected for teachers, coaches, and specialists to both look out across units and modules and to plan for daily lessons.

» Teachers report clarity around the school's accountability system for lesson preparation and planning.

» Teachers, coaches, and specialists begin long-range and daily lesson preparation and planning with the "end in mind." They begin with high-level documents and aim for a deep understanding of the Four T's within a module, unit, and lesson.

» Structures are in place for learning walks and other opportunities for teachers to learn best practices from you and each other.

» Coaching and professional development is in place to help staff learn and master new instructional practices. Staff know when it's okay to make adjustments and when it's not and to ask when they need help.

» Classrooms are configured in a way that allows students to easily move in and out of small groups.

» Teachers set clear expectations and enact classroom routines that support students in assuming the responsibility for their learning.

» Students are clear on classroom expectations and contribute to an engaging and joyful learning experience for themselves and others.

» Staff receive coaching and support for classroom management that elevate respectful, active, collaborative, and growth-oriented classrooms.

Resources and Suggestions

» The curriculum itself, along with a full suite of companion resources and tools, can be found at: Curriculum.ELeducation.org. Resources include:

- Digital/Printable Versions of All Task Cards from Chapter 3A

- Digital Planning Templates

- Videos

» Resources available on the main EL Education website (ELeducation.org):

- Screencasts (overviews, grade-level specific, and K–2 Reading Foundations Skills Block)

- Walkthrough Tools

- PD Packs:

  ○ Leaders of Their Own Learning

  ○ Collaborative Culture

» Books by EL Education that deepen understanding of the practices in this chapter:

- *Leaders of Their Own Learning: Transforming Schools through Student-Engaged Assessment*

- *Management in the Active Classroom*

» Book: *Total Participation Techniques: Making Every Student an Active Learner*

» Resources on Protocols:

- Classroom Protocols collection at Curriculum.ELeducation.org

Cont.

- National School Reform Faculty website (nsrfharmony.org)

- School Reform Initiative website (schoolreforminitiative.org)

» Article: "Habits Improve Classroom Discussions" by Paul Bambrick-Santoyo

» Article: "Collaborative Conversations" by Douglas Fisher and Nancy Frey

Chapter 3: Preparing to Teach: Planning for Challenge, Engagement, and Empowerment

Chapter 3A: How Do I Plan When the Planning Has Been Done for Me?

Chapter 3B: How Will the Curriculum Empower My Students to Own Their Learning?

Chapter 3C: How Can I Create the Kind of Active and Collaborative Classroom Culture the Curriculum Requires?

Instructional Leadership

▶ Frequently Asked Questions

Chapter 3:
Frequently Asked Questions

Those task cards seem helpful, but when will I ever have time to do them?

Some of the task cards—those that look out across the year and across modules and units—take some significant time to complete. Since you won't need to spend your planning time *designing* your English language arts (ELA) curriculum, we advise that you spend that time carefully analyzing ours so that you can make it the best it can be for your students. That means looking ahead and planning backward from assessments, noticing how lessons build students' skills and knowledge. It means understanding how the K–2 Labs (Labs) and 3–5 Additional Language and Literacy (ALL) Block will deepen learning and reinforce skills from the modules. It means understanding how the Four T's—topic, task, targets, and texts—interact with each other at the module, unit, and lesson level. It means reading the texts before using them with your students.

The process will take some time—it has to. We hope that the lesson-level task cards will be the ones that you learn to move quickly with. Over time, you'll probably find that they take less and less time or that you have favorite questions that you like digging into and others that you skip. That's okay. The point is for you to feel well prepared, and there's no one right way to achieve that.

I know I'm encouraged to prioritize the integrity of the curriculum over strict fidelity to the way it is written in order to best meet my students' needs, but what are the things I really shouldn't change?

The answer to this question has a few layers. There are a few common adaptations we have seen teachers make within lessons that seem like they may be small and insignificant changes on the surface but actually have a big impact on students. For example, as we discussed earlier in this chapter, teachers are sometimes inclined to skip the protocols. Although this adaptation to the lesson is not necessarily going to impact students' progress toward a particular learning target, it might have a big impact on the quality of discourse in the classroom or on students' growth in habits of character. Similarly, we find that sometimes teachers don't ask the questions written in the lesson, but instead ask questions on the fly. Each question in our lessons has been labored over and serves a very specific purpose. We urge you, until you really build your question-asking muscles, to ask questions as they are written. If you need to adapt the questions, we would suggest prioritizing a smaller set and asking fewer high-leverage questions, as written, versus making up new ones.

There is also a deeper layer to this question that involves the design of lessons and assessments that lead to students meeting standards. In the Module Lessons, the assessments themselves should not be changed at all.

If you are a skilled curriculum designer who can backward-design learning experiences from assessments, you may be able to make some changes to the lessons leading up to an assessment that don't change the outcomes for students. But we urge you to be thoughtful about your choices. As you know from the exploration of the Four T's in Chapter 1, if you change a text or a learning target, it can unravel other components of a module. Instead, what we recommend is enhancements: make local connections or incorporate service learning but maintain the spine of the module as is. In the K–2 Reading Foundations Skills Block (Skills Block), we strongly recommend that you not change the sequence of taught spelling patterns. The Labs and the ALL Block offer you more flexibility overall (for more, see Chapter 2B).

What are the best tips and tricks for managing the pacing of lessons?

This question is certainly not unique to our curriculum. Any teacher who walks into a classroom full of 20 or 30 young children with a wide variety of personalities and needs, lesson plan in hand, knows that everything is not going to go as planned. *Some* things will, but not everything. Like most things in life, you will get better with experience. In this chapter, we offer many suggestions to help with pacing, including creating a "Cliff's Notes" version of the lessons or PowerPoint presentations to aid with delivery. You will need to figure out what you are going to hold in your hands during the lesson and how it will cue you to the purpose, structure, and hoped-for outcomes. Remember, the lessons are not scripts. You know your students best, including what kinds of instructions, questions, and routines they will respond to best. Once you gain familiarity with the curriculum, you will get better at customizing it and staying on pace. Also, don't forget that there is built-in flex time within the curriculum (e.g., Labs, ALL Block, and Skills Block "flex days"), which can be used as "spillover" time for lessons that you are not able to get through in the time allotted. At the lesson level, we also have found that many teachers benefit from teaching with a timer to help them stay on track during lessons. It's also helpful, as part of your preparation for teaching a lesson, to notice which activities in a given lesson are allotted more time. This should help you prioritize. For example, if "Reviewing Learning Targets" says 5 minutes, know that it is intended as a brief touchpoint for students. Don't get bogged down.

I know learning targets are important, but how can I make them come alive more in my lessons? Sometimes I feel like we're just going through the motions.

One of the best ways to make learning targets come alive is to ensure that you yourself really understand what the intended learning is for the lesson. This involves analyzing not only the agenda and materials, but also spending time processing the Teaching Notes. Once you are clear, then you need to ensure that students also really know not just what they will "do," but what they will *learn*. The lessons in the curriculum will cue you to teach the vocabulary of the learning targets and to engage students in thinking about what the learning target means, but it's up to you to *really make sure* they know what it means for them and how it will guide the lesson. If they seem puzzled or like they are just going through the motions, take a minute to have them turn and talk or ask them to restate the learning target in their own words. It's critical that they take ownership of meeting the learning targets and deeply understanding them in the first step.

Also critical is that you come back to the learning target(s) throughout the lesson. Look for opportunities to reference them and to check for understanding frequently. Help students see the learning target as a steady guide and grounding checkpoint on their progress, not just a routine or a bunch of words on the white board.

What should I do if I check for understanding and it's obvious that my students just aren't getting it? How can I stay on pace with the lesson?

It's important to take both a long-term and short-term view of this question. Having a good, solid sense of the longer-term scope of a series of lessons, units (or cycles for the Skills Block), and modules and how standards are addressed over time is the first step. If your students haven't mastered a standard in one lesson, it doesn't mean that they won't have another opportunity to master it. But you may not realize this if you haven't looked ahead at how standards cycle in and out of lessons. As a result, you may find yourself getting hung up on re-teaching materials you didn't realize would come back around in a few days or next week. This can throw off your pacing, and it's one of the reasons we urge you to engage in the planning process described in Chapter 3A. Use those task cards to look ahead and get a feel for the focus and flow over the long term.

In the short term, you can help students reach mastery in numerous ways during the course of daily lessons. Among the possibilities: pulling small groups for short mini lessons during Work Time; using flex time in Labs, the ALL Block, or the Skills Block for re-teaching either to the whole class or to small groups as needed.

How can I encourage students who talk infrequently to contribute more, and students who talk too much to listen more?

One of your first steps should be ensuring that you have established norms in your classroom that help all students feel that they belong and that what they have to say has value. Once that culture has been established, there are specific practices that permeate the curriculum that will give students practice (and confidence) contributing to discussions.

A great way to foster equitable and productive discourse is through protocols. A protocol consists of agreed-upon, detailed guidelines for reading, recording, discussing, or reporting that ensure equal participation and accountability in learning. We use protocols a lot in the curriculum because they get students talking; importantly, protocols allow students to talk to *each other*, not just to you. As a result, they build independence and responsibility. In addition to protocols, the curriculum also features the frequent use of total participation techniques, which give *all* students the opportunity to share their thinking with a partner or the whole class, and Conversation Cues, which promote productive and equitable conversations. These three instructional strategies are powerful ways to allow you to hear from *all students*, not just your "frequent fliers." As you gain comfort with these practices, we hope that you will consider using them even more, beyond where you are cued to do so in the curriculum and in other parts of your day.

My students don't seem that excited about the protocols anymore. Are there any others I can swap in to keep things fresh?

We definitely recommend that you build your own library of favorite protocols. If you find any that we have recommended have gone stale or just aren't working well with your students, you should feel free to swap them out. Before doing this, however, be sure that whichever new protocol you choose will serve the same purpose. You can view and download the full suite of protocols used in our curriculum in the Classroom Protocols section of our website (Curriculum. ELeducation.org). This same set is included in our book *Management in the Active Classroom*. The websites of the National School Reform Faculty and School Reform Initiative also have excellent libraries of protocols available for free download.

How can I find time to build an active, collaborative classroom culture and still have time to teach the lessons in the curriculum?

The curriculum has a fair amount of flex time built in to give you time to build the structures and routines you need. In Grades K–2, for example, Module 1 is designed for six weeks (as opposed to eight) so that you have a couple of weeks at the start of the year to establish routines and expectations about collaborative work. This is especially important for primary-age students. Flex time during the Labs, ALL Block, or Skills Block may also be used to "refresh" expectations when needed throughout the year. That said, this curriculum will be most effective when structures and routines that are used during ELA time are used throughout the day. Consider, for example, practicing protocols during morning meeting or helping students use sentence frames during mathematics (two videos referenced in this chapter, "Think-Pair-Share" and "Back-to-Back and Face-to-Face," show students practicing protocols). The more holistic your approach, the smoother things will go for your students.

I'm still pretty shaky on classroom management. What do you recommend to help me get up to speed?

We recommend that you read our 2014 book *Management in the Active Classroom*. Though this book can help any teacher, we wrote it specifically to support teachers using our curriculum, especially those for whom an active, collaborative classroom will require some getting used to. You may also want to observe a colleague in your building who has strong classroom management or ask a trusted colleague to participate in a peer coaching session with you. Classroom management is one of the hardest parts of being a teacher—it takes time and practice to build confidence—but there are techniques and practices you can learn. Set goals for yourself and make a plan for reaching them.

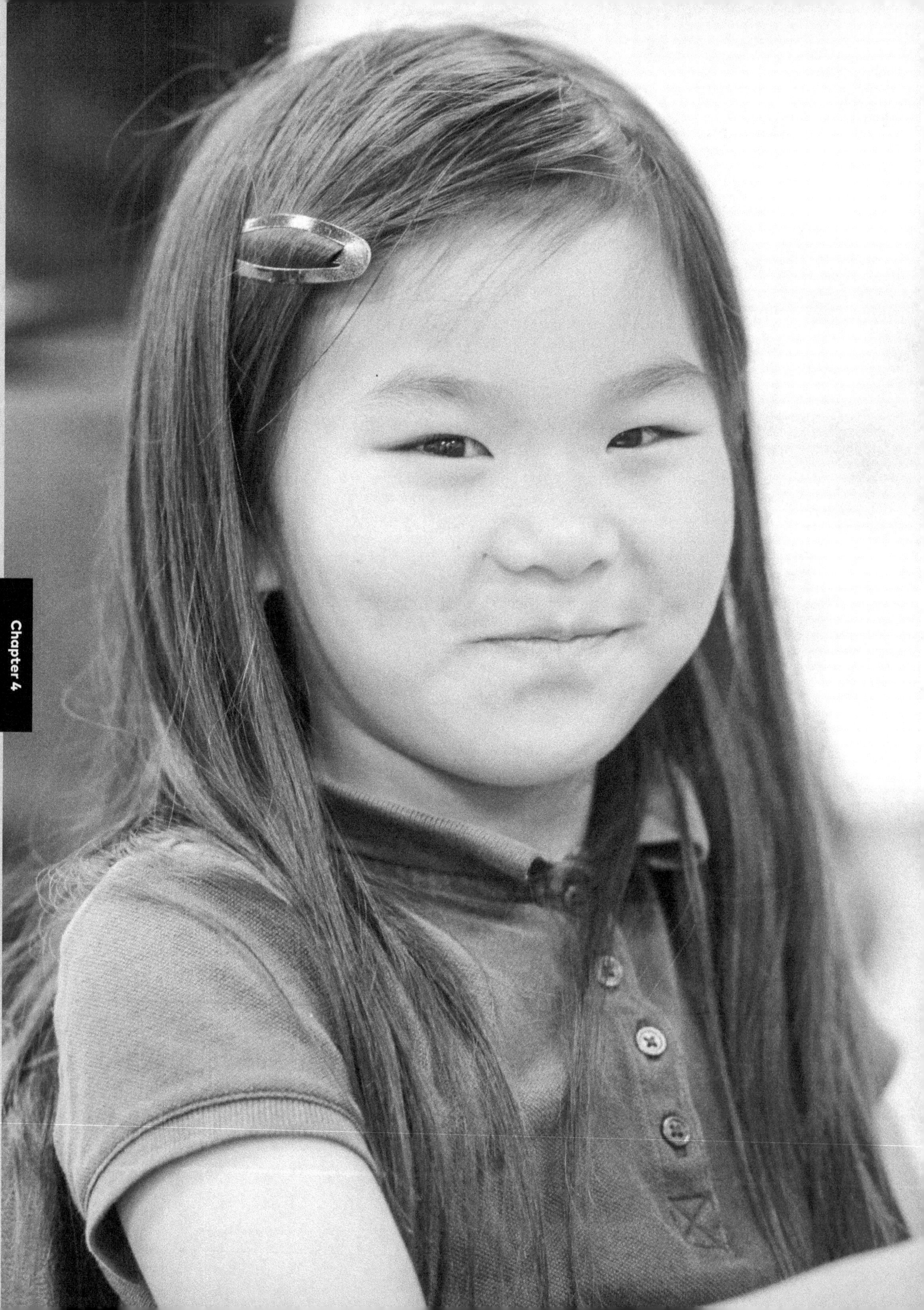

Chapter 4:
Structured Phonics: The Why, What, and How of the K–2 Reading Foundations Skills Block

Chapter 4A:
Why Should I Change My Approach to Teaching Reading?

Some of you may be approaching this chapter with trepidation. You may even find that your hackles are raised. "What is this new phonics curriculum, and why should I teach it?" you may be asking yourself. Others of you may feel curious, intrigued, or even eager, yet still daunted by what you may need to learn (or unlearn). You may be concerned that your teacher education program did not give you a solid understanding of phonics. Perhaps you have been teaching guided reading for years, or maybe you have your own unique approach that combines basals with leveled texts and other elements that are held together with the glue of your extensive experience in the classroom.

There's a saying you may have seen that appears on bumper stickers, T-shirts, and mugs, often in the possession of teachers of primary-age students: "I teach little people to read. I'm sort of a big deal." And it's true. It is a big deal. You are a big deal!

Your experience matters, and any hesitancy you may be feeling about changing your approach also matters. We get it. And, as curriculum designers, we want you to know that we've been there. Most of us, like many of you, taught guided reading and loved it. There's a lot to love: working with differentiated small groups, tracking individual students' progress, and ensuring that students have time reading texts they can read on their own. However, when choosing the "big rocks" behind the design of our entire comprehensive curriculum, after our own extensive analysis of the research and inquiry with master teachers, we turned to structured phonics as one critical component. Our research and analysis has convinced us that structured phonics empowers teachers to more systematically address the literacy achievement gap and to "catch" those students falling through the cracks.

With our commitment to equity and accelerating literacy learning for *all* students as our driving force, we designed a structured phonics curriculum called the K–2 Reading Foundations Skills Block (Skills Block). The Skills Block is designed to ensure that by the end of second grade, students acquire the depth of skills they need in the foundational reading standards to be able to read with fluency and, most importantly, comprehend grade-level text independently. And it is designed to work in concert with the content-based literacy components (K–2 Module Lessons and Labs) of our comprehensive K–2 English language arts (ELA) curriculum, so students get the "both/and" of precise phonics instruction and deep comprehension work.

Much of this book is focused on the content-based literacy components of our curriculum. In Chapters 5 and 6, in particular, we focus on reading and writing instruction connected to the compelling content of the modules. Here we zoom in on the structured phonics component, which rounds out our comprehensive ELA curriculum for Grades K–2.

▷ It is important that a comprehensive program emphasize both deep comprehension (held in our Module Lessons) and the foundational skills of phonemic awareness, phonological awareness, and fluency (held in the Skills Block).

It is important, as you read this chapter, to remember that the Skills Block is just one piece of the bigger puzzle of everything primary learners need in terms of literacy. Just as strong mathematics programs include a focus on students both developing a strong conceptual understanding and having a solid grasp of their math facts, so too with a literacy program. It is important that a comprehensive program emphasize *both* deep comprehension (held in our Module Lessons) and the foundational skills of phonemic awareness, phonological awareness, and fluency (held in the Skills Block). Thus, in this chapter we will explore structured phonics as one key aspect of teaching early literacy.

This chapter won't give you all the information you need to teach the Skills Block; there are numerous resources that accompany the curriculum that will do that in greater depth than we will here. Instead, we hope this chapter will give you the information you need to feel grounded in what structured phonics is, the research that supports it, and the features that make it most effective, especially for those students furthest behind. We will also spend considerable time in Chapter 4B describing the similarities and differences between guided reading and structured phonics and the ways that your current practice may be able to stay the same and the ways that it may need to change.

▶ How Will Structured Phonics Meet the Needs of My Students?

Reading and writing are ultimately about understanding. To gain and show that understanding independently, students need to be able to "crack the code" of written language. In the primary years, they need systematic and specific instruction in the basics of reading and writing so that they acquire strong and automatic knowledge of how letters and sounds work to form words in the English language. This foundation forms the basis for their success in school and, in many ways, in life.

Unfortunately, too many students are still falling through the cracks. Sixty-four percent of all fourth-graders in the United States scored "below proficient" (below grade level) on the 2014 National Assessment of Educational Progress (NAEP) reading assessment (The Nation's Report Card, n.d.). Even more alarming is that among students from low-income backgrounds, 79 percent scored below proficient. The relationship between mastery of foundational skills (e.g., phonemic awareness, phonological awareness, decoding, encoding, fluency) before third grade and subsequent success in school is supported by a significant body of research. Five essential studies highlight this research:

» Students who are not proficient in third grade are four times less likely to graduate on time (Hernandez, 2012).

- » Third-grade scores are predictive of eighth-grade and high school scores, and college enrollment (Lesnick, George, Smithgal, and Gwynne, J., 2010).

- » Seventy-four percent of third-graders who read poorly will still be struggling in ninth grade (Fletcher and Lyon, 1998).

- » A person who is not at least a modestly skilled reader by the end of third grade is quite unlikely to graduate from high school (Snow, Burns, and Griffin, 1998).

- » First-grade reading scores are a "reliable predictor of later reading scores" (Juel, 1998).

All primary-age educators have the same goal in mind: to teach students to read with automaticity and fluency and, ultimately, understanding. These sobering studies underscore the vital importance of strong reading instruction in the primary grades. Without this strong foundation, too many of our students will be denied the "keys to the kingdom," missing out on the chance to develop strong literacy skills and realize their full potential.

Unfortunately, despite all of the hard work and good intentions of educators, the achievement gap persists. It is more important than ever to find solutions for students who are the farthest behind. And it is equally important to ensure excellent instruction and outcomes for all students.

What Makes Structured Phonics a Good Solution for Helping Students Crack the Alphabetic Code?

Phonics is a method of teaching reading by correlating sounds with letters or groups of letters. *Structured* phonics is a method of teaching the spelling-sound patterns of English in a clear sequence so that students move systematically through the phases of reading and spelling development. All structured phonics programs are based on the Alphabetic Principle, which means, in a nutshell, that there are systematic and predictable relationships between letters and sounds. Reading and spelling (or decoding and encoding) are taught together because of the strong reciprocal relationship between written letters and the sounds they make when spoken.

Most structured phonics programs—ours included—focus on understanding how letters and sounds work in words. This includes phonological awareness (i.e., identifying and manipulating all units of oral language) and phonemic awareness (i.e., the ability to hear and manipulate individual sounds, or phonemes, in words), to varying degrees. Structured phonics programs follow an explicit, set sequence of instruction (e.g., "Today we are going to work on the 'ck' sound"). By contrast, other approaches, such as guided reading, rely more on implicit or incidental exposure (e.g., "Here is our book about ducks. There's a 'ck' in the word *duck*. Does anyone know what sound the 'ck' makes?").

A structured phonics approach is systematic and proactive in teaching spelling-sound patterns, whereas many other approaches are more reactive, teaching spelling-sound patterns as needed to decode words in texts.

Because structured phonics relies on a *systematic* and *sequential* approach to teaching spelling-sound patterns, the choice of texts that students use is paramount. In most structured phonics programs, the words in the texts are restricted to the spelling-sound patterns and high-frequency words that have already been taught. These kinds of texts are called phonetically controlled readers, or decodable readers. For example, if short vowel sounds have been taught but long vowel sounds have not, then only short vowel sounds will appear in the texts students read. Just as a mathematics teacher would give students problems that focus only on the specific skill they had just learned, decodable readers "control" for spelling-sound patterns students have been taught in a previous lesson. Simply put, a decodable reader gives students a chance to immediately apply what they have just been taught.

By contrast, programs that do not use decodable readers use texts that are controlled by every *other* feature of the text: repetition, context, illustrations/picture cues, shorter sentences, shorter paragraphs, and larger font. Such texts are usually called "leveled readers" or "leveled texts," since they are placed into complexity levels by this array of text features, or "predictable texts," since the array of supports makes what happens predictable and students use this to help them read the words. Typically, guided reading programs use these types of texts.

Table 4.1 highlights a few of the key differences between a structured phonics approach and other approaches. We'll come back to these key differences in Chapter 2B, when we focus on implications for your classroom practice, specifically what will stay the same and what may need to change, depending on your current approach to teaching reading.

Table 4.1: Comparison of a Structured Phonics Program to Other Programs

Area of Focus	Structured Phonics Program	Other Reading Programs (e.g., guided reading or basals)
Phonological awareness	Usually directly teaches phonological awareness skills	May or may not teach phonological awareness skills
Phonemic awareness	Directly teaches phonemic awareness skills	May teach phonemic awareness skills, often through incidental or implicit exposure (i.e., as spelling-sound patterns happen to appear in a text)
Spelling patterns	Directly teaches spelling patterns in a clear sequence	Rely on implicit or incidental exposure to spelling patterns
Texts	Uses texts that are controlled by taught spelling patterns ("decodable" texts)	Use texts that are controlled for sentence length, context, repetition, etc., but not for taught spelling patterns

What's Unique about Our Approach to Structured Phonics: The K–2 Reading Foundations Skills Block?

The Skills Block explicitly addresses the Common Core State Standards (CCSS) Reading: Foundational Skills standards (RF), as well as some Language standards associated with spelling and letter formation (CCSS L2 and L1a). Although this focus is consistent across many structured phonics programs, two things make ours unique:

1. It is based on the research of Dr. Linnea Ehri, one of the nation's foremost experts on how the brain maps sounds and letters.

2. It deeply honors and addresses the needs of primary learners.

Dr. Linnea Ehri is a Distinguished Professor in the Ph.D. Program in Educational Psychology at the City University of New York (CUNY) Graduate Center. Her phases of reading and spelling development help us determine students' progress with decoding and encoding:

» **Pre-alphabetic:** Reader is not yet making any alphabetic connections; may recognize some letters (e.g., letters in own name) and environmental print (e.g., "Stop" on stop sign).

» **Partial-alphabetic:** Reader is making partial alphabetic connections; beginning to decode and encode consonant/vowel/consonant (CVC) and vowel/consonant (VC) words, but frequently confuses vowels and vowel sounds.

» **Full alphabetic:** Reader is making full alphabetic connections; able to decode and encode all regularly spelled, one-syllable words and some multisyllabic words.

» **Consolidated alphabetic:** Reader uses knowledge of syllable types to decode and encode multisyllabic words; continually growing bank of high-frequency and irregularly spelled words.

Additionally, we worked with Dr. Ehri to develop "microphases," which are a further breakdown of the phases of reading and spelling development into *early, middle,* and *late.* This precision gives teachers a more detailed progression of reading and spelling behavior. The phases and microphases will be referenced throughout this chapter, and more information about what they mean in practice in the Skills Block will be provided in Chapter 4C.

Also unique to our structured phonics program is our commitment to honoring "The Characteristics of Primary Learners" (see Chapter 1) through movement, music, and joy and developing students' habits of character through goal-setting and reflection. We do this because learning to read is fun, and we want students to feel the joy that comes from persevering with something that is challenging and worthwhile.

▶ What Are the Key Features of Structured Phonics That Will Make It Effective for My Students?

Every teacher can agree it is paramount that all students learn to crack the alphabetic code. Letters need to move from just scribbles on a page to symbols that carry meaning and combine to make words, which ultimately is a powerful gateway to learning about the world.

Structured phonics programs have long been shown to be highly effective in teaching the foundational skills (specifically phonemic awareness, phonological awareness, and fluency) necessary for reading comprehension (National Institutes of Health, n.d.). In fact, the research is so strong and so consistent that the IES (Institute for Educational Science, the research wing of the Education Department) has decided that there is no further need to review what the evidence shows about the effectiveness of structured phonics programs. It is convinced.

Learning letters (their formation, name, and sound) and segmenting words into individual phonemes, or sounds, are the two most important contributors to learning to read words (Adams, 1990). Structured phonics programs systematically teach each letter and its corresponding formation and sound, as well as phonological and phonemic awareness, guiding students to hear units of oral language, including individual phonemes, or sounds (see Table 4.2 for key terms). The ability to hear each phoneme in a word, along with knowledge of each letter and its sound, will eventually translate to reading and spelling words. When a student can look at the letters c-a-t, sound out "k/a/t," and realize that makes the word *cat,* they are on their way as readers.

> *"My students love going to Skills Block. They love being challenged, and that brings them joy."*

Katie Benton

Grade 2 Teacher, Greenville, South Carolina

To read with comprehension—the ultimate goal—students need to read with fluency. Fluency is defined as reading accurately, at a rate appropriate to the text, and with proper expression (Rasinski, 2004). The first step in fluent reading is to accurately and effortlessly recognize the words in the text. A proficient reader reads a word in about 0.23 seconds (Larson, 2004). Students who stumble or hesitate in recognizing too many words are prevented from reading text fluently. By continually assessing and addressing students' progress in mastering spelling-sound patterns, structured phonics programs assure that all students can decode with automaticity, without which fluent reading is not possible.

Table 4.2: Key Terms

Term	Definition
Decode	Ability to apply knowledge of letter-sound relationships in reading
Digraph	Two graphemes used to represent one phoneme
Encode	Ability to apply knowledge of letter-sound relationships in writing
Grapheme	A letter or a number of letters that represent a sound (phoneme) in a word; one letter usually, though not always, represents one sound
Phoneme	Any of the perceptually distinct units of sound in a specified language that distinguish one word from another; for example, *p*, *b*, *d*, and *t* in the English words *pad*, *pat*, *bad*, and *bat*
Phonics	A method of teaching reading by correlating sounds with letters or groups of letters in an alphabetic writing system

To help students become fluent readers who can ultimately comprehend text and build their knowledge of the world, all structured phonics programs share commonalities that help students crack the alphabetic code:

» Teaching spelling-sound relationships separately and explicitly

» Proactively teaching and assessing the most common spelling patterns

» Targeting text choice and instructional activities

Teaching Spelling-Sound Relationships Separately and Explicitly

A structured phonics program introduces students to spelling-sound relationships separately and explicitly. Students learn the patterns using isolated words, and then practice with a decodable reader. In these decodable readers, students will encounter only spelling-sound relationships that they have been taught—this is what makes it phonetically *controlled*. Structured phonics programs do not use texts that require students to infer spelling-sound patterns by things like context (e.g., prior knowledge or picture cues) or repetition. Contextual exposure is important for students and can help them become more nimble readers; however, this kind of reading should *supplement* a structured phonics approach so that students learn spelling-sound relations individually and sequentially.

To make this distinction more clear, let's start with a counterexample: guided reading with leveled readers. Many primary teachers are familiar with and use leveled readers. As we noted earlier, leveled readers depend on context, pictures, short sentences, clear patterns, and repetition. Leveled readers include texts that are sometimes referred to as "predictable texts." Take, for example, a sample of text from *Mrs. Wishy Washy*:

» Mrs. Wishy Washy has a mop. [with accompanying picture of a mop]

» Mrs. Wishy Washy has a broom. [with picture of a broom]

Unlike with a decodable reader that is controlled for spelling-sound patterns, with *Mrs. Wishy Washy*, students can simply memorize the words and sentences because of the repetition and predicted words, thanks to the pictures and the context. They do not have to focus on the spelling-sound patterns of the words. As texts get more complex (even in these early grades), it becomes progressively more difficult for students to read the words by using contextual clues like this. In fact, it has been estimated that only one in four words can be predicted using context clues (Gough, Alford, and Holey-Wilcox, 1981). And this number decreases when talking about content-area words, which can be predicted only about 10 percent of the time (Gough, 1983). See Table 4.3 for a summary of the differences between decodable readers and leveled texts.

Table 4.3: Decodable Readers Compared with Leveled Texts

Decodable readers are controlled for:	Leveled texts are controlled for:
» Decodable words » Irregularly spelled, high-frequency words (taught) » Sentence length and complexity	» Predictability » Illustration support » Knowledge demands » Word count » Sentence length and complexity » Ratio of high- to low-frequency words

A decodable reader has less repetition, few pictures, and is less predictable. Students must focus exclusively on the spelling-sound patterns of the words that have been taught through structured phonics instruction. Consider the example below from an early first-grade decodable reader:

» I am Beth. I am ten. I am at camp. Camp is fun.

» Mom and Dad went on a trip to the camp. All of us were at the camp.

As you can see in these examples, students are expected to read only common high-frequency words and words that include short vowel sounds (such as *mom* and *ten*) and some initial and final blends (such as *trip* and *camp*). In sum, the major difference between teaching students to read with leveled texts (or "predictables") versus decodable readers concerns what knowledge or skills we ask students to draw on to read the texts. With leveled texts, we are asking students to predominantly use context clues to learn to read. With decodable readers, we are asking students to first and foremost use the spelling-sound patterns of the English language that they have been intentionally and sequentially taught.

Figure 4.1: Pages from a Grade 1 Reading Foundations Skills Block decodable reader.

The pan is a hat!

The hat is on the cat!
Two hats!

Proactively Teaching and Assessing the Most Common Spelling Patterns

A structured phonics program introduces spelling-sound patterns and high-frequency words in a sequence, one at a time. This lets you more easily assess which students have mastered which patterns and words. In turn, this makes it easier to provide more support for those who need it. If you don't introduce, teach, and reinforce the patterns in a clear sequence, then the only alternative is to address problems reactively as they become apparent in whatever texts students are reading. Just like in mathematics instruction, for example, when students likely get to learn and then practice their times tables for multiples of two on a separate day (or week) than working on multiples of three, in structured phonics students get time to learn and apply long "e" spelling patterns such as "ea" in a different week than the long "o" spelling patterns such as "oa."

If the texts are leveled like *Mrs. Wishy Washy*—written with no specific spelling-sound patterns in mind—then addressing problems becomes far more difficult to do. It also makes it far more difficult (but not impossible) for you to know which patterns specific students have learned, which students need more support, and how to provide activities to support these students.

In a structured phonics program, the assessment of which students have mastered patterns and words, and subsequent differentiation, is easier to do. Through frequent and regular check-ins and assessment of decoding and encoding of taught spelling-sound patterns, teachers *and students* are aware of which spelling-sound patterns have been learned and which need more work.

Targeting Text Choice and Instructional Activities

Since you know exactly which spelling-sound patterns have been taught in a structured phonics program, you can select the most appropriate texts and activities for your students: those that contain the spelling-sound patterns you are currently teaching, as well as those that students have already learned. For example, if a student needs more support with consonant blends such as "bl," "cr," and "dr," then working with a decodable reader that has these blends can provide this support. If books are chosen on some other basis (think *Mrs. Wishy Washy*) and are not controlled for spelling-sound patterns, this becomes far more difficult.

In addition to targeting texts to focus on specific spelling-sound connections, you also can target other activities. In the above example, you might choose a sort that contains words beginning with "bl," "cr," and "dr" or a writing activity using a list of these words. Conversely, if chosen activities have students practice spelling-sound patterns more broadly (e.g., having students play a memory game with a variety of one-syllable words), the practice becomes diluted and less impactful.

Again, going back to the mathematics analogy, if students have just learned and practiced how to multiply by twos, you'd want to be sure they then got word problems that required them to apply that new knowledge: "Andrea gets paid $2 each day that she walks her neighbor's dog. She walks the dog five days a week. How much money does she earn in a week?" It would be both unfair and inefficient to give students practice problems that required and presumed they knew how to solve for threes or how to divide if they hadn't been taught those skills.

▶ Is Structured Phonics Important and Appropriate for *All* of My Students, Even More Advanced Readers?

Even those of you who already understand the effectiveness of a structured phonics approach may still question whether it is appropriate for your whole class. Why use it as one component of core instruction for all students? Why not use it only as an intervention for below-grade-level readers?

It is true that some students require less explicit phonics instruction to learn to read, but a strong foundational skills program should encourage, challenge, and engage *all* students. Most programs typically include approximately 20 to 30 minutes per day of on-grade-level instruction on foundational skills. This can benefit all students in these crucial ways:

» Capitalizing on the reciprocal relationship between reading and spelling (decoding and encoding)

» Strengthening all students' vocabulary and comprehension

» Encouraging the use of cueing systems, particularly visual cueing

Capitalizing on the Reciprocal Relationship between Reading and Spelling (Decoding and Encoding)

When elementary teachers hear the word *spelling*, they often think about a memorized, weekly spelling list. But in fact, because decoding and encoding (reading and spelling) are so deeply interconnected, a strategic emphasis on spelling is a powerful tool for strengthening reading skills.

When a reader learns to write the correct letters that represent each sound in a word, it helps the reader to "glue" the printed form to the pronunciation of the word in memory. Repeated practice helps build reading and writing automaticity with that word. And the more words that are automatic, the more new words a student will be able to read and spell.

For more advanced readers, the act of spelling words (orally and in writing) is equally beneficial. Strong readers can be poor spellers (we all know a brilliant person who is an awful speller). When a fluent reader encounters an unknown word in a text, he or she may be able to quickly figure it out based on the meaningful context and/or the word's function in the sentence; the reader does not need to consciously look at every letter in the word to do this, so may not internalize the word's correct spelling. However, when readers encounter words in text, if they attend to the visual information in the word (i.e., the actual letters that make up the word) and take time to pronounce the word aloud or silently, they are more likely to compute connections between letters and sounds in the words, internalize the correct spelling, and recall it subsequently to read or write that word.

In the Skills Block, there are many tools that help students understand the interconnectedness of spelling and reading. For example, in the Spelling to Complement Reading instructional practice, used in kindergarten and first grade, readers analyze spoken words, listening for each individual sound, and then use "Sound Boards" (also known as "Elkonin Boxes") to write the letter or letters to match each sound (e.g., "sh" is a digraph made up of two letters that make one sound). Each sound is written in its own separate box, signifying the distinct phonemes of the word. After practicing with the boxes, students then write the word from memory.

Strengthening All Students' Vocabulary and Comprehension

As noted previously, the central focus of structured phonics is building students' skills with phonemic awareness, phonological awareness, decoding, and fluency. Yet through that work, there are many rich opportunities to develop and support students' vocabulary and comprehension as well.

For example, most structured phonics programs teach first-grade students how to read and spell words with common affixes such as -*ing* and -*ed*. They also likely teach how the affixes change the meaning of the words (e.g., when you add -*ed* to *work*, it changes the meaning to past tense). Therefore, as the affixes become more complex, students learn more about how words work and how the different word parts can give clues to the meaning of the word. For example, if a student has learned to read and spell words with the prefix re- and understands that "re" means "again," then when the student encounters an unfamiliar word with that prefix (e.g., *rework*), he or she will be able to read and spell the word more easily and will also know that it means to "work again."

For more advanced readers, analysis of word parts can be extended to more complex affixes and base words. Exposure to these base words and affixes can help the reader decode, spell, and understand the meaning of a variety of unfamiliar, multisyllabic words. For example, if an advanced reader picks up a Harry Potter novel and encounters an unfamiliar word such as "quidditch" or "Dumbledore," he or she can use knowledge of syllable types to decode this unknown word.

In the Skills Block, an example of this type of instruction is the Word Parts instructional practice, which begins in second grade. Students learn how to read and spell words with different base words and affixes and also learn and create new words with these word parts. They then discuss how the affixes change the meaning of each root word. For example, the students might work with the suffix -*s*, beginning with a list of root words like *book*. Once they have created new words (*books*) and talked about how the suffix changed the meaning of the root word (made the word plural), in small groups they might add -*s* and other taught affixes to a list of root words to analyze on their own.

Encouraging the Use of Cueing Systems, Particularly Visual Cueing

Almost all primary teachers are familiar with the three different "cueing systems" that students can use to process text:

» **Visual.** Sometimes called "graphophonic" cues, this cueing system helps readers attend to the visual information of the actual word on the page (e.g., the letters, spelling patterns, affixes in the word).

» **Meaning.** This cueing system helps readers predict a word based on what they already know about the topic—the story. Clues from the illustrations are also based on meaning.

» **Syntax.** This cueing system helps the reader predict what word might come next in a sentence based on knowledge of sentence structure in the English language.

It may seem counterintuitive to many of us that research indicates that rather than focusing students on meaning first (as many of us learned to do in our teacher training), the most efficient way for readers to solve an unknown word is to notice the letters or word parts in the word and decode based on knowledge of the sounds that match each letter (i.e., visual cueing).

Of course, the other two cueing systems—meaning and syntax—are invaluable as a way to confirm decoding of a word based on visual cueing. Readers can also use context clues such as background knowledge and illustrations (i.e., meaning) and can think about what the word might look or sound like in a sentence (i.e., syntax) to better understand the meaning of a word or sentence. Readers should be encouraged to attend to these cueing systems explicitly. In fact, this is a central focus of the Module Lessons in our curriculum. And teachers can point out to readers when they are using these cueing systems and how they are beneficial.

These common cueing systems can help readers *confirm* whether a word was decoded accurately or confirm the meaning of a word—"does it look right/sound right?" Yet these approaches are not the most efficient way for readers to *decode* an unfamiliar word. In fact, relying too heavily on meaning and syntax may impede students' ability to solve unknown words in more complex text if they do not have strong foundational skills.

Helping Students Know When to Use Each Cueing System

Although students should be encouraged to first attend to the visual cues of a word (the actual letters and spelling patterns in the word), there is no need to abandon the other two cueing systems. They will be helpful when students are reading a text that is not controlled for decodable words, such as a leveled text. Particularly in the lower levels of leveled texts (e.g., approximately Fountas and Pinnell levels A–H and Developmental Reading Assessment levels A–18), there are a large number of non-decodable words with very strong picture clue support. So, you can encourage students to *first* look at the visual cues of the word, but if they determine that it is "undecodable" (either because the spelling patterns are irregular or haven't been taught yet), *then* they can attend to the meaning or syntax cues available to them.

For more advanced readers, the long-term risk is that if they have ample knowledge about the world and strong vocabulary, they may over-rely on meaning and syntax cueing systems and fail to attend to the visual information in a word. Although that may work in the short term, these crutches will not be available to them as texts become more complex, with few or no pictures and increasingly unfamiliar vocabulary and word parts.

Consider this fictional, yet typical, example many of us might recognize: Marissa is a native English speaker and wants to be a veterinarian when she grows up. Her parents buy her fiction and nonfiction books about animals (and many other topics) and regularly read aloud to her at home.

She also learns more about animals (and other topics) at home from educational videos and trips to the museum with her grandmother. So she is building lots of word and world knowledge (which is a key focus of the content-based literacy components of our curriculum).

But at school, she is not receiving any structured phonics instruction. Therefore, when Marissa encounters a text, she can frequently rely on her knowledge base and her strong vocabulary to read many unfamiliar words (using meaning cues), especially if it is on a topic she's learned a lot about at home or at school and if there are illustrations and diagrams to support. So, even if she ignores most or all of the visual cues of an unknown word, her strong background knowledge and understanding of English sentence structure (syntax cues) give her a solid strategy for essentially guessing an unknown word in a text. And it works. Marissa is reading on grade level, according to the Developmental Reading Assessment and her teacher's monthly running record, by the middle of first grade.

> *"I could go on all day about the Skills Block. It is our favorite part of the day here at Lead Academy. It has been an absolute game-changer for us, especially in terms of closing the achievement gap."*

Sarah Mitchell
Instructional Coach, Greenville, South Carolina

But toward the end of first grade, something shifts. Because she relies so heavily on meaning and syntax cues to guess unknown words, which we know is only reliable between 10 percent and 25 percent of the time, her teacher has not noticed that she is still uncomfortable decoding words with affixes, vowel teams, r-controlled vowels, and multisyllabic words. As the texts used for assessments and instruction become more complex and have fewer illustrations, Marissa begins to struggle, especially if the text is about an unfamiliar topic. She has been relying on her strong background knowledge but actually has holes in her ability to decode. This is why a comprehensive approach to literacy instruction (e.g., content-based literacy joined with structured phonics) is so valuable. Marissa needs both.

In the Skills Block, students are initially taught new spelling patterns using words in isolation, not in "connected" text, to ensure that they are using the visual cueing system (not meaning or syntax) to solve the word. This means that they might just see the word *hive*, rather than seeing it in a sentence like "The bee is in the hive" with a picture showing bees buzzing around a hive. They are assessed with words out of context for the same reason. They learn the new spelling pattern (on the first day of a cycle). Only then do they apply the new knowledge to read words that contain this pattern (and other taught patterns) in connected text via the decodable readers.

▶ Is Structured Phonics Appropriate for My English Language Learners?

As we continue to emphasize, a strong structured phonics program is just one critical component of a comprehensive literacy program. It needs to be paired with content-based literacy. This is particularly important for English language learners (ELLs), who, unfortunately, are often not given access to rich content in school.

Having said that, the characteristics of a strong structured phonics program that benefits all students applies to ELLs as well, although sometimes in more significant or slightly different ways. The following are especially important for ELLs:

» **Visual cueing.** When attacking an unknown word in a text, ELLs may have strong background knowledge on the topic of the text but may not know the English word or words that represent a certain idea. So, the use of meaning cues is especially ineffective for ELLs. Similarly, many ELLs may have limited knowledge of English sentence structure, or syntax, so they may not be able to draw on this cueing system to "guess" an unknown word in the sentence like some of their native English-speaking classmates. As is true for native English speakers, attending to the visual, or graphophonic, features of a word is the most efficient and effective way for ELLs to decode an unknown word. Especially because they may not yet be as strong in the other cueing systems, visual cueing is particularly critical for ELLs.

» **Phonemic awareness.** For students whose native language does not include all of the same phonemes as English, a strong focus on hearing the individual sounds, or phonemes, in words and noticing how the pronunciation of the sound feels in their mouth can be extremely helpful. For example, though the visual representation is the same, most of the vowels in English are pronounced differently in Spanish. Teaching students whose native language is Spanish how to isolate and pronounce the vowels in an English word is the first step in teaching them how to translate this knowledge into reading and spelling words that include these vowel sounds.

» **Vocabulary acquisition.** As is true with native English speakers, when ELLs begin to learn affixes and base words through a structured phonics program, it not only helps them decode words with these affixes and roots, but also supports vocabulary development. By learning the meaning of each word part and how attaching those word parts can change the meaning of words (e.g., *-ed* added to *walk* makes it past tense) ELLs can better understand the meaning of more words and can more effectively identify discrete units of meaning (morphemes).

In addition to the benefits of structured phonics for ELLs, we have incorporated additional structures within the Skills Block that are supportive for ELLs (and all students) in other ways:

» **Teaching letter names and sounds through the context of stories and mnemonic devices.** Each letter of the alphabet (upper- and lowercase) includes an animal name beginning with the same sound (also called "keyword") and an accompanying read-aloud story. The engaging story provides background knowledge about the animal while the keyword provides a mnemonic device for both the sound and the shape of the letter. For example, *alligator* is the keyword for A, reminding students of the most common, short sound for that letter. And the image of the alligator's open mouth reminds the students of the shape of the uppercase A, while an illustration of a baby alligator curled up in an egg represents the shape of the lowercase letter.

» **Use of music and movement.** Music is a proven, effective tool for supporting ELLs (Christison, 1999; and Pinter, 2006). The Skills Block includes suggested transition songs, with lyrics that help students better understand the purpose of the upcoming activity. Other suggested songs help students remember spelling generalizations and other skills. For example, in kindergarten Module 4, students learn the song "Vowels Have Something Important to Say," which reinforces the role of vowels when spelling words. Movement is incorporated through skywriting of letters and words, explicit work with articulatory gestures (i.e., how a phoneme feels and looks in the reader's mouth), and other developmentally appropriate movement opportunities throughout the curriculum.

» **Repetition.** The design of an instructional cycle includes repeated instructional practices used from week to week and sometimes from module to module and across grade levels. Once ELLs have initially learned the routine for an instructional practice, they will be able to focus their attention on the more difficult work of the new skill or content.

▶ How Will the Skills Block Meet the Needs of My Students with Reading Disabilities?

Many students with reading disabilities have weak connections between speech and print, a foundational language skill that supports reading development. Students with reading disabilities, such as dyslexia, need explicit, repetitive, structured instruction to support the neurological connections linking the sounds of spoken words (phonemes) to the print code or letters that represent these sounds (graphemes) (Shaywitz, 2003).

Dr. Samuel Terry Orton, one of the first to recognize dyslexia in students, suggested that teaching the "fundamentals of phonic association with letter forms, both visually presented and reproduced in writing until the correct associations were built up" would benefit students of all ages (International Dyslexia Association).

Thus, the characteristics of a strong structured phonics program that benefits all students applies to students with reading disabilities as well, although sometimes in more significant ways. The International Dyslexia Association has identified the following as critical for students with reading disabilities:

» **Systematic and cumulative curriculum design.** Students with reading disabilities benefit from a structured phonics program that is designed in a way that follows the logical order of language. The scope and sequence begins with the easiest concepts and continues methodically to the more difficult, with each step building upon the concepts previously learned.

» **Explicit instruction.** Students with reading disabilities benefit from a structured phonics program that includes explicit instruction, in which the teacher continually engages with students in an intentional manner. The responsibility rests on the teacher for explicitly teaching the concepts, rather than assuming that students will naturally deduce these on their own.

» **Diagnostic teaching.** Students with reading disabilities benefit from a structured phonics program that includes diagnostic instruction, based on careful and continuous assessment. This assessment cycle supports the teacher in providing targeted, individualized instruction that meets a student's needs.

Specifically, the Skills Block curriculum provides instruction that supports students with reading disabilities in the following ways:

» **Phonemic awareness.** The foundation for all reading instruction is phonemic awareness, as students develop an understanding of the sounds of language. Students begin developing these skills with recognition of rhyme. In noticing that words rhyme, students become aware of word parts (such as the shared ending in *cat, mat, hat*). This recognition supports students in the ability to manipulate phonemes in words, such as blending, segmenting, and substituting, as their phonemic awareness skills progress.

» **Mapping phoneme to grapheme.** Establishing the association between sounds (phonemes) and symbols, or letters (graphemes), is required for mastery of the alphabetic code, and therefore for reading development. Students are supported through repetitive and systematic instruction as they develop this association from visual to auditory (reading) and from auditory to visual (spelling).

» **Multisensory techniques.** Engaging students through multisensory techniques supports development of the pathways that map phonemes with graphemes, a common weakness in students with reading disabilities. Multisensory techniques embedded in the Skills Block curriculum include visual, auditory, and kinesthetic learning of language. For example, students are invited to use a mirror to "see" and feel the sounds their mouths are making.

▶ Will Some Students Still Need Interventions?

All the benefits of a structured phonics program, described in the previous pages, lead to two key points:

1. A structured phonics program—when taught skillfully with attention to differentiation—serves *all* students (even advanced readers and those farthest behind).

2. A structured phonics program, which by definition is both proactive and systematic, ensures that students who struggle the most get more of what they need upfront.

When all students regularly receive strong instruction on foundational skills, fewer students will need interventions. Some students who are identified as needing interventions simply may not have received the systematic instruction necessary to learn and apply knowledge of common spelling-sound patterns.

Certainly, not all students require the same depth of phonics instruction. This is the case in all subject areas. Yet in other subjects, like mathematics, teachers still devote time to teaching critical skills to the whole group. For example, some students will enter first grade with a conceptual understanding of addition (because of strong instruction in kindergarten, rich exposure to mathematical thinking at home, or a strong aptitude for mathematics). But just because a few students have already mastered basic addition, this does not mean that a teacher skips teaching foundational mathematics skills in whole group lessons. Instead, the teacher teaches these skills to the whole group and then provides differentiated activities or materials for the more advanced students. Or she partners a more advanced student with a less advanced student as a way to solidify and extend the advanced student's learning and support the learning of the struggling student. The same should be true for teaching foundational reading skills: 15 to 20 minutes of whole group, on-grade-level instruction of reading foundations will ensure that *all* students learn *all* of the skills they need to become proficient readers and will deepen their understanding of how the English language works.

In the Skills Block, all students systematically work with all of the CCSS Reading: Foundational Skills standards (and Language standards associated with spelling) for each grade level during whole group instruction, which includes all of the necessary foundational skills. Letter sounds and spelling patterns are taught in a logical sequence, aligned with the progression of the standards and the phases of reading and spelling development, and covering all of the most common patterns used in the English language.

As with a mathematics scope and sequence, this systematic coverage ensures that teachers know what has been taught to *all* students. And the built-in assessments (both the three-times-a-year benchmark assessments and the weekly cycle assessments) help teachers determine which of the taught skills each student has mastered and which skills each student might still need more support with.

Structured Differentiated Instruction

You will learn more about the structure of the Skills Block later in this chapter; for now it's important to know that the one-hour block consists of 15 to 20 minutes of whole group instruction and 40 to 45 minutes of differentiated small group instruction. In many cases, the Skills Block's systematic instruction for all students, followed by differentiated small group instruction, eliminates the need for additional interventions for struggling readers. However, some students may still need additional support. Although not every student will meet with you in small group every day, the Skills Block is structured so that those students farthest behind *will* meet with you every day in small group. There is also enough flexibility in the structure of the hour to allow for reading interventionists to work with students who need it during this time.

For the more advanced students, activities or materials can be differentiated to meet their needs as well. In the Skills Block lesson plans, the Teaching Notes, Meeting Students' Needs section, and differentiated small group suggestions offer guidance for extension. And, similar to the previous mathematics example, more advanced readers can be part of a mutually beneficial partnership with readers who need more support. This partnering can help the more advanced reader consolidate his or her learning, build confidence, encourage collaboration, and foster leadership skills.

Chapter 4B:
What Are the Similarities and Differences between Structured Phonics and Guided Reading?

We believe, based on a large body of research, that pairing a structured phonics approach with content-based literacy is the most effective way to teach reading. But it is not the only way. Guided reading is an effective practice for some readers, and many educators have had great success using this approach; however, our comprehensive curriculum does not set aside time for traditional guided reading. We made this choice for three main reasons:

» **Weight of cueing systems.** Typical guided reading programs place equal weight on three cuing systems—visual, structural, and meaning—when students are learning to read (see Chapter 4A for more information). By contrast, based on the research of Dr. Linnea Ehri, the K–2 Reading Foundations Skills Block (Skills Block) emphasizes visual cueing. Syntax and meaning cueing systems are seen as "confirmatory" (i.e., a reader uses these to confirm a word she has decoded if she is still unsure). The other two cueing systems then show up more prominently in the two hours of content-based literacy within our comprehensive K–2 English language arts (ELA) curriculum, as students work with complex text.

» **Text type.** Texts used in a typical guided reading program are not controlled for taught spelling patterns. When learning a spelling pattern—a central focus of our Skills Block—students need opportunities to read text that lets them apply that spelling pattern. In the Skills Block, students practice and apply what they have learned using a decodable text, instead of leveled readers, to ensure that they get to immediately practice the specific patterns they have just been taught. Students read authentic texts that are *not* controlled for spelling patterns during the Module Lessons.

» **A focus on automaticity and fluency.** In a typical guided reading program, small group instruction includes a focus on comprehension of leveled texts. Within our comprehensive curriculum, much of this comprehension work (aligned to the standards for reading informational text and reading literature) is addressed in the Module Lessons and K–2 Labs (Labs), not the Skills Block. In the Skills Block, although all decodable texts include basic comprehension questions, instruction is focused on automaticity and fluency. Although these skills do not necessarily demonstrate comprehension, they tend to be strong indicators of whether a student is reading with meaning. As students' alphabetic skills become more automatic and consolidated (making more complete and automatic connections between letters and sounds), they are then freed up to focus on comprehension.

Despite these reasons for moving away from traditional guided reading, the Skills Block doesn't necessarily throw the baby out with the bathwater. For example, we include a Reader's Toolbox routine that encourages teachers to use non-decodable texts with small groups once per week to teach new word-solving strategies (e.g., "look at the picture"). This routine acknowledges that when students are not reading decodable texts, they will certainly encounter unfamiliar words. We want to be sure to give them strategies for approaching these words as well.

Table 4.4 highlights some of the differences between structured phonics and guided reading but also notes similarities in the two approaches. There are still plenty of things that will feel familiar to those of you who teach guided reading. Throughout the remainder of Chapter 4B we will highlight what might stay the same and what might need to change based on your current practice.

Table 4.4: Comparing The K–2 Reading Foundations Skills Block Approach to Small Group Instruction with a Traditional Guided Reading Approach

What's the Same?	
» Differentiated small group instruction » Flexible groupings based on assessment results/data » Use of text to teach reading skills	
What's Different?	
K–2 Reading Foundations Skills Block	**Traditional Guided Reading**
» Students are grouped based on phases of reading and spelling development. » Teachers use texts controlled for decodable spelling patterns (based on a specific sequence of taught spelling patterns) and high-frequency words that have been explicitly taught. » Instruction focuses on visual cueing system for decoding, with meaning and syntax cueing systems used to confirm or to comprehend. » Word work is specific to the needs of the group (based on their phase). » Students learn spelling patterns systematically and explicitly. » Teachers ask basic, text-based comprehension questions about decodable texts and engagement text[1], but the majority of comprehension is explicitly taught and assessed during the Module Lessons; no focus on comprehension strategies. » Other activities such as word sorts, songs, and manipulatives (not just work with text), based on a student's phase, are used to teach spelling patterns and skills.	» Students are grouped based on Developmental Reading Assessment, Lexile, or Fountas and Pinnell reading level. » Teachers use texts controlled for background knowledge, sentence length, font size, repetition, etc., but not for decodable words. » Instruction focuses equally on all three cueing systems (sometimes more on meaning and syntax than on visual). » Word work is based on the words in the chosen text. » Students learn spelling patterns on an implicit or inferential basis. » There is explicit instruction of comprehension strategies.

---

[1] An engagement text is a text read aloud before introducing the decodable readers to students. It provides some backstory and helps students get to know the characters or topic better, since the decodable readers have a limited number of words.

▶ What Are the Implications for My Teaching Practice? What Will Stay the Same? What Might Need to Change?

Implementation of the Skills Block likely will align with some of what you're already doing when teaching reading. That said, there will also be some things that may need to change if you are currently teaching guided reading or even if you are teaching another structured phonics program. In this section, we describe what will stay the same and what may need to change for each of the following:

» Classroom setup

» Assessment

» Framework (used to describe students' strengths and needs)

» Whole group instruction

» Small group instruction

» Independent work

» Planning

Classroom Setup

Typical Current Practice

If you are like most primary teachers, your classroom environment is probably really important to you. From the cozy nooks for reading, to the rug for whole group instruction, to the instructional tools and student work lining the walls, you've put a lot of thought into what students will experience in that space. Most primary classrooms have a few features in common:

» A whole group meeting area with a carpet and a white board or blackboard

» A kidney-shaped or round table used for small group instruction

» Student work areas such as clusters of desks or tables

» Designated areas and a management system for accountable independent work

» Letters of the alphabet posted for student reference

» A Word Wall for student reference, which may include high-frequency words, student names, or possibly content-area vocabulary

» A library of student-friendly texts organized in any one of a variety of ways (e.g., Fountas and Pinnell level; theme)

WHAT WILL STAY THE SAME?

The good news is that the basic physical setup of your room can likely stay the same. We suggest just a few refinements.

WHAT WILL CHANGE?

There are a few things that will probably need to change in your classroom library. Your current method of housing your library (e.g., book baggies, tubs) will likely not need to change, or at least not very much. However, since a structured phonics program uses texts controlled for decodable words, the books themselves may need to change, or at least be reorganized. Your classroom library will need to include more decodable texts (our curriculum includes these for every cycle of

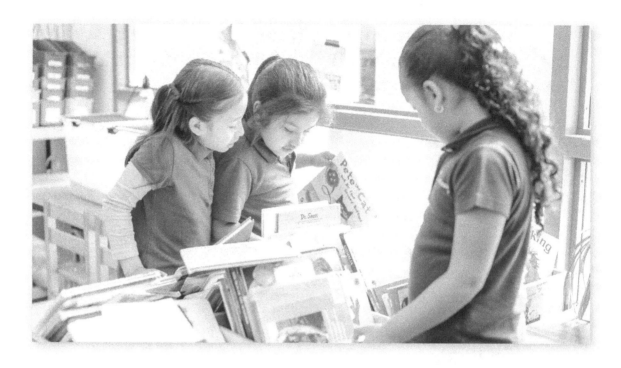

instruction). Leveled texts, which likely make up most of your current library, are not controlled for decodable words. They are still a useful resource, but they will probably need a new organizing system. Table 4.5 describes the "big buckets" for organizing texts in your library as well as suggested language for introducing these types of texts to your students.

Table 4.5: Types of Texts Needed in Your Classroom Library

Types of Texts Needed in Your Classroom Library	How You Might Introduce the Various Types of Books to Students
Decodable texts (sorted by phase, cycle, or spelling pattern)	"These books only have words with spelling patterns that you have learned or high-frequency words that you have been taught. So you should be able to read all the words."
Leveled texts (sorted by level and/or by approximate phase)	"These books have some high-frequency words and some words with spelling patterns you have been taught. They also have some words with spelling patterns you have not been taught yet. When you come to a word that you are unsure how to read, you can look for the spelling patterns that you know and then look at other clues to help you predict the word. You can look at the pictures or the other words in the sentence."
Research texts (sorted by topic)	"These are books that you might choose based on a topic we are learning about together or a topic you are interested in on your own. Many of the words in these books might be difficult for you to read. You can still try to read the words or you can 'read' the pictures and focus on the text features."
Other texts (sorted by author or genre)	"These are books that you might choose based a topic you are interested in, a genre you like, or a character you like. Many of the words in these books might be difficult for you to read. You can still try to read the words or you can 'read' the pictures and focus on the text features."

Another change to your classroom setup involves keyword cards used to form the class ABC line. The Skills Block provides keyword cards, which are printable cards (found in the K–2 Reading Foundations Skills Block Learning Letters book) that include words and pictures of animals that serve as a keyword for each letter of the alphabet, plus digraphs "ch," "sh," and "th." The Skills Block requires that you use these cards to form the class ABC line, headers for the Word Wall, and letter sound or letter sorting activities. Consistent use of the same keywords for each letter and letter sound will provide a common language for you and your students to use when referencing each letter and its sound and will help to effectively reinforce the name, sound, and formation of each letter.

As for the Word Wall, most classrooms likely have only one. If you are using our comprehensive curriculum (including Module Lessons and Labs), two Word Walls will be needed: one for high-frequency words and one for content-area vocabulary (from Module Lessons).

▶▶ **Video Spotlight**

In the accompanying video, first-graders in Anne Simpson's class at Two Rivers Public Charter School in Washington, D.C., experience the Engagement Text to Decodables instructional practice. This practice engages students in a read-aloud of an engaging complex text before they work with a decodable text on the same topic. First the teacher reads the engagement text aloud. Then students analyze high-frequency words in the engagement text that they likely would not be able to decode independently. Next students work with a partner to search for those same high frequency words in the decodable text. Students then read the entire text with a partner to develop automaticity with the new high-frequency words and apply the letter-sound patterns they have already learned in the Skills Block. Students add any new high-frequency words to the Word Wall and reflect on their learning. This instructional practice is used in kindergarten (starting in Cycle 13) and throughout Grades 1 and 2.

https://vimeo.com/168991756

Assessment

Typical Current Practice

Assessment tools can vary greatly across states, districts, and even schools within a district. Despite this variation, most schools administer:

» Some sort of foundational skills assessment, such as AIMS Web, STEP, or a district-created assessment

» Some sort of reading fluency and comprehension assessment, such as Fountas and Pinnell Benchmarking System or Developmental Reading Assessment.

These assessments are usually administered at the beginning of the year (diagnostic), at the end of the year (summative), and sometimes one or two more times throughout the year to check progress.

WHAT WILL STAY THE SAME?

The general scheduling of assessments (e.g., beginning, middle, and end of year) will remain. And the same assessment tools *can* continue to be used if they are mandated by your district or if your school simply chooses to keep using them. If possible, we recommend making strategic choices about which assessments to keep and which to let go of so that students don't feel too fatigued by them and you don't lose too much instructional time administering them.

WHAT WILL CHANGE?

Ideally, all Skills Block benchmark assessments will be administered at the beginning, middle, and end of year. However, if your school is mandated to or chooses to use other assessments that measure the same things, it is not necessary to do both. There are some grade-level priority assessments that are required if teaching the Skills Block. These priority assessments are identified in Table 4.6. (Note: More information about these assessments can be found in the Assessment Overview within the K–2 Skills Block Resource Manual). These priority assessments are essential because they help determine and track each student's microphase, which guides grouping, planning, and tracking of student and class progress throughout the year.

Table 4.6: Priority Assessments in The K–2 Reading Foundations Skills Block

Kindergarten	Grade 1	Grade 2
Letter Name and Sound Identification	Spelling Decoding	Spelling Decoding

Framework

Typical Current Practice

Schools and districts tend to "name" learners with language based on a stated or implied framework. Unfortunately, these descriptors often risk becoming labels that categorize students, rather than serving as descriptors that help teachers determine what students can do and what they need next.

For example, many teachers may group and describe students based on assessment data from their most recent Developmental Reading Assessment (DRA), saying things like "This group is DRA Level 6." Or schools might identify a learner's reading and spelling behaviors and the group he or she is placed in for differentiated instruction by using Fountas and Pinnell, Lexile, or Words Their Way stages, saying things like "These are my Level B readers" or "He is 70 Lexile" or "She is a Transitional Speller."

Even though labeling students in this way may seem like a useful shorthand, it risks conveying a fixed mindset about reading, implying that students "are" something, rather than "are working to become" stronger with particular skills. Instead, using the phases of reading and spelling development helps you clearly describe what students *can* do and what they need next. Importantly, it also helps instill a growth mindset in students: "Your ability grows with your effort."

WHAT WILL STAY THE SAME?

If your school or district is required to or chooses to continue using your current assessment system (e.g., DRA) alongside the Skills Block benchmark assessments, then you may still choose to use that system as a framework for data analysis or to communicate to parents.

However, we caution any school against layering on too many assessments or frameworks. If you are required to maintain your current system, that's one thing, but if you have a choice, it's important to be very clear about why you would choose to hang on to an existing framework or assessment system versus making the change to the Skills Block framework. Being clear about the pros and cons will help everyone in the school community get behind the decision one way or another.

WHAT WILL CHANGE?

The framework and its associated language is likely one of the biggest changes that comes along with adopting the Skills Block. The phases of reading and spelling development drive the design and all of the assessment and differentiated instruction in the Skills Block, so it will be important to internalize the concepts and the language held in Phase Theory (more detail will be provided in Chapter 4C).

One of the great benefits of the Skills Block framework is that the phases of reading and spelling development detail specific skills and behaviors related to letter-sound connections (e.g., a reader in the Partial Alphabetic phase is making only partial connections) and provide descriptive language and a framework for understanding the strengths and needs of a particular reader. Many other frameworks describe the level of text as a proxy for a student's overall reading proficiency.

Although our framework will require some new learning and language, it will ultimately help teachers and parents better understand each student as a reader. It will also help students better understand themselves as readers. Overall, the framework will help everyone be more targeted in measurement, tracking, and goal-setting. Take, for example, a student whom a teacher might label a "Level C reader" using the Fountas and Pinnell framework. This same student in a classroom using our Skills Block curriculum would likely be in the middle Partial Alphabetic phase, which is similar to Level C.

"Our teachers who have seen the most growth are the ones who were willing to fully and completely dive into the Skills Block. They had to have an open mind, be willing to try something new, and be ready to put things that may have worked okay in the past behind them. Their classes have soared."

Sarah Mitchell

Instructional Coach, Greenville, South Carolina

The descriptors for students in the middle Partial Alphabetic phase of the Skills Block offer a different kind of information for teachers compared to descriptors for Level C students. For example, in the Skills Block a student in the middle Partial Alphabetic phase may "frequently confuse short vowel sounds." This provides teachers with very specific information about the types of connections a student is making between letters and sounds. This behavior indicator could help a teacher understand why a student misreads the word *met* for *mat* and what sort of work he or she can do with that student to move forward as a reader. Conversely, a Level C indicator that notes that a student is developing a larger core of high-frequency words does not provide teachers with strong guidance about what to focus on instructionally with a student described as "Level C."

Although the phases undoubtedly provide more targeted information than a level, there are realities to consider when adopting a new framework like this. Teachers might ask, "What will I tell students? How will they know their reading level?" Or school leaders might ask, "What will I tell parents? How will they understand their child's reading level?" We might ask in response: Do students and parents need to know a number or a letter? Or do they need to know what their child is able to do and what they need to work on next? We would argue that the latter is much more important and that the phase indicators (based on microphase identification from Skills Block benchmark assessments) will give teachers, students, and parents rich information about the reading behaviors a student is exhibiting and the behaviors we want to work toward.

Whole Group Instruction

Typical Current Practice

When it comes to whole group instruction, what's typical in current practice is a little harder to pin down. Some schools may use a structured phonics approach, but only for intervention, while others might use a phonics program for whole group lessons but use guided reading for small group instruction. There is a wide variety of possible configurations. For these reasons, we'll articulate the possible changes for whole group instruction in fairly broad terms.

WHAT WILL STAY THE SAME?

There will be some kind of mini lesson, typically lasting 10 to 20 minutes. This is likely similar to your whole group lesson approach currently in use, no matter the reading program.

WHAT WILL CHANGE?

The focus and purpose of the mini lesson will be on letters and letter sounds, phonological and phonemic awareness skills, or spelling patterns and is part of a carefully sequenced progression.

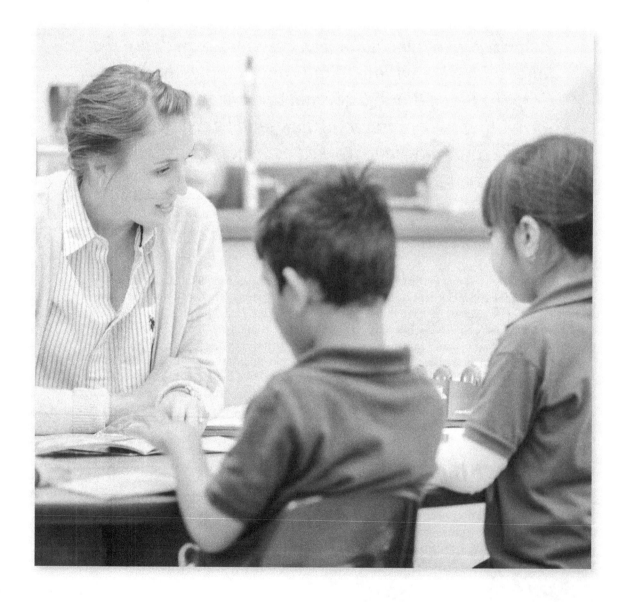

Small Group Instruction

Typical Current Practice

Many primary teachers use the bulk of their small group time on guided reading instruction (homogenous groups, taught using a set of leveled texts within the readers' instructional range). The sequence of instruction during small groups might go more or less like this:

» Picture walk and/or book introduction, usually to build necessary background knowledge, identify text type, etc.

» Students whisper-read independently; teacher might support with prompts such as "Would ___ fit there?" or "Check again. Does that look right or sound right to you?"

» Teacher and students return to the text for a teaching point based on the content of the text and/or something that students struggled with during independent reading (possibly word attack strategy, a comprehension strategy, or pointing out characteristics of the text to identify text type).

» Teacher asks some basic comprehension questions about the text.

» Students might conclude with a written or drawn response about the text and/or some sort of word work at the end.

WHAT WILL STAY THE SAME?

What will stay the same can be divided into three main categories:

» **Grouping.** You will still create homogeneous, flexible small groups and call groups over to meet at your classroom kidney table (or other designated meeting area) for about 10 minutes at a time. It will still be important to meet with the most struggling readers more frequently and allow the more advanced readers to work with greater independence.

» **Texts.** Texts will still be used in teacher-led small group—primarily decodable readers—though once a week, in Grades 1 and 2, students work with leveled texts during the weekly Reader's Toolbox routine.

» **Ongoing assessment.** Frequent quick checks, such as running records (probably used currently) and snapshot and weekly formative assessment should still be administered to keep a pulse on the progress of each individual and group.

» **Cueing systems.** Teachers should still encourage students to use all three cueing systems (visual, meaning, and syntax) and use whatever information is available to them to solve an unknown word (within text or in isolation), though the "weight" of each cueing system will change (see next section).

WHAT WILL CHANGE?

What will change also aligns to these three main categories:

» **Grouping.** Your homogenous groups should be based on microphase rather than level (e.g., Fountas and Pinnell, DRA). This will allow you to best use the guidance provided in our curriculum regarding the most appropriate materials to use for differentiated small group instruction for students in particular microphases.

» **Texts.** You will use decodable texts much more heavily so that students have ample opportunities for practice, teacher feedback, and teacher guidance with taught spelling patterns and skills. Leveled text may still be used for independent reading and for the weekly Reader's Toolbox routine.

» **Cueing systems.** Instruction heavily emphasizes the visual cuing system, which is the most efficient way to attack an unknown word. This should be students' "default" cueing system (as opposed to meaning or syntax cueing). This might be a significant shift for you (and your students): The visual features of the word should always be the first thing to which students attend when solving an unknown word. Students will need the other cueing systems, however, when they encounter words that are *not* decodable for them. Students will certainly encounter words that are not easily decodable for them, either because they are multisyllabic (readers in the Pre- and Partial Alphabetic phases are likely not ready to decode these words yet), or because they include an irregular or untaught spelling pattern. When students encounter words like this in a text (likely in a leveled text rather than a decodable text), they should then use one of the other cueing systems (e.g., look at the picture, read the sentence and guess what might make sense). This will be important for students as they encounter texts in the content-based components—Module Lessons and Labs—of the curriculum as well.

Independent Work

Typical Current Practice

The systems in place for independent work vary greatly among primary classrooms. Regardless of the system or the type of activities, students are usually given some sort of independent work, hopefully differentiated for the needs of each group or individual, to complete while the teacher works with small groups.

A veteran teacher might have the experience and confidence to employ a choice-based system in which students choose from a menu of independent options to complete throughout the week. Or a teacher might provide a weekly folder for each group or individual that includes an explicit sequence of worksheets and/or sorting activities to be completed.

WHAT WILL STAY THE SAME?

Students should still be given purposeful, differentiated independent work to complete while you work with small groups.

As for the actual work completed by students, the suggested rotations during the Skills Block are probably very similar to current practice in many primary classrooms (more details about each of these rotations can be found in Chapter 4C and in the K–2 Skills Block Resource Manual):

» Accountable Independent Reading (AIR)

» Fluency

» Word work

» Writing practice

And because the rotations will likely stay the same (or similar) to your current practice, the materials will not necessarily need to be overhauled. That said, it will be important to ensure that the work students are doing is intentionally aligned with their microphase. The curriculum provides materials to help you plan for this. But this shift will require that you adjust to these new materials and planning related to the materials. We discuss this in the next section.

WHAT WILL CHANGE?

Most importantly, you will need to ensure that all activities are chosen based on student or group microphase and cycle assessment data.

Our Skills Block curriculum provides three main resources for small group instruction: Suggested Re-teaching activities (for the whole group), Activity Bank activities, and the K–2 Reading Foundations Skills Block: Differentiation Pack (Differentiation Pack). For more details on each, see "Independent and Small Group Work" (found in the K–2 Skills Block Resource Manual).

You may also choose to use some existing materials, but *only* if it is clear how they align to students' microphases and the specific letter sound you are teaching that week. For example, if a group of readers in the late Partial Alphabetic phase is having trouble decoding and spelling long "e" vowel terms from the whole group lesson, you might pull an "ea" vs "ee" Words Their Way word sort. The students' microphase should drive the planning and material choices for their independent work. You will need to be strategic with your choices.

Accountable Independent Reading is another activity that has some aspects that will stay the same, but some that will require refinement because the practice holds particular importance in the Skills Block. Because students primarily use decodable texts in whole and small group Skills Block instruction, Accountable Independent Reading is an important time for them to read books that are not necessarily controlled for letter-sound connections. This lets them apply their skills to a variety of different texts. This is critical, since the end goal is not for students to fluently read and comprehend decodable texts, but rather to fluently read and comprehend a variety of texts.

Accountable Independent Reading is also an important time for you to confer with individual students to listen to their reading, provide specific feedback, and go over their phase-specific response sheets (found in the "Independent and Small Group Work" document).

Planning

Typical Current Practice

To prepare for a week of small group instruction, a typical primary teacher might visit the school book room, filled with sets of leveled texts, and check out a set of guided reading texts for each student group. He or she might then create a mini lesson for each of those groups, crafting a picture walk and teaching point and possibly planning a short word work activity. He or she might also designate one group for monthly running records as a way to track their reading progress and afterward potentially regroup some students.

In preparation for whole group, the teacher might consult a phonics curriculum or create lesson plans based on a scope and sequence of standards to be taught.

WHAT WILL STAY THE SAME?

For whole group instruction, the Skills Block lessons provide explicit instructional guidance. Teachers will still need to preview the lesson plans and prepare materials and, overall, determine whether the lesson/cycle is appropriate for the majority of their class.

For differentiated small group instruction, the lessons provide suggested rotations and activities. It will still be necessary to plan ahead for each small group, based on students' strengths and needs, and to continue to track progress and regroup as necessary. A text will still be used for teaching and practice.

WHAT WILL CHANGE?

Your weekly visit to the book room to gather sets of leveled texts might not be necessary, or at least not as frequent. Decodable readers will be used much more heavily than leveled texts so that students have ample opportunities for practice, teacher feedback, and guidance with taught spelling patterns and skills. You might use the decodable reader introduced during the current cycle and/or pull from previous or later cycles or grades to better meet the needs of the group.

For whole group instruction, planning will not revolve as much around the text, but rather around students' microphases and the skills necessary to move them forward. For differentiated small group instruction, a more significant shift in planning is in the choices of resources available to you. More detail on the planning process necessary to prepare to teach the Skills Block is provided in Chapter 4C. Look specifically for Table 4.15

Chapter 4C:
What Does It Take to Implement the K–2 Reading Foundations Skills Block?

We hope that by now we have made a compelling case that structured phonics is an effective and efficient approach to teaching the foundational reading standards. And, we hope that those of you who have been using a different approach to reading instruction, such as guided reading, have a better idea of what can stay the same and what might need to change to teach structured phonics as one component of our comprehensive literacy curriculum. Our effort in describing these similarities and differences is to try to "shrink the change" for you as you embark into what might feel like new territory.

In this section, we get more concrete about what it will take to implement the hour of daily instruction in the K–2 Reading Foundations Skills Block (Skills Block). Following the details about the structure of the Skills Block, we offer strategies for how to prepare to teach the Skills Block lessons, including guidance for unpacking lessons as part of your lesson planning process.

Before we begin, it's important to note that we're not going to be able to describe *all* of the ins and outs of implementing the Skills Block in this chapter because it's fairly technical and there

▶▶ Video Spotlight

In the accompanying video, see the Skills Block in action in Brenna Schneider's and Katie Benton's kindergarten and second-grade classrooms at Lead Academy in Greenville, South Carolina. The teachers prepare, assess and group students, select and manage materials, and foster students' self-management and smooth transitions during differentiated small group time. This video addresses common questions and challenges teachers face when implementing the Skills Block, in particular how to make the most strategic use of the differentiated small group time.

https://vimeo.com/220269148

are many moving parts. We'll cover the basics and direct you to look for further information in the key resources detailed in Table 4.7, which will either come bundled with your printed curricular materials (if you order print copies) or which you can locate on our curriculum website (Curriculum.ELeducation.org). Most of the resources listed here are found within the K–2 Skills Block Resource manual. Please note, Table 4.7 is not an exhaustive list of resources; we have chosen to highlight key resources.

Table 4.7: K–2 Reading Foundations Skills Block: Key Resource Documents

Document	Where It Is Found
"Phases and Microphases": Details Dr. Linnea Ehri's phases of reading and spelling development and how they inform the design of the curriculum. Also details EL Education's microphases (the phases broken down into "early," "middle," and "late" reading and spelling behaviors)	K–2 Skills Block Resource Manual
Assessment	
"Assessment Overview": Provides guidance for assessment administration and next steps	K–2 Skills Block Resource Manual
"Benchmark Assessments": Includes all assessment materials, teacher guidance, and scoring sheets for each benchmark assessment	K–2 Skills Block Resource Manual
"Assessment Conversion Chart": Guides teachers to use microphase information from benchmark assessments to determine appropriate cycles of instruction for small group instruction for each student/group of students	K–2 Skills Block Resource Manual K–2 Reading Foundations Skills Block: Differentiation Pack
Differentiated Small Group Work	
"Independent and Small Group Work": Provides suggested structures and activities for planning independent and small group work	K–2 Skills Block Resource Manual
"Activity Bank": Includes activities teachers can use in small group and independent rotations; activities are organized in alphabetical order and can also be searched by skill and standard	K–2 Skills Block Resource Manual
"Grade Level Differentiation Pack": Includes a word list, cycle overview information, an assessment conversion chart, and student decodables (or poems and handwriting sheets in kindergarten Modules 1 and 2) for each cycle of that grade level; along with suggested instructional practices provided in the introduction, this pack can be used as a resource for planning differentiated small group instruction for students whose microphase aligns with work from a different grade level	K–2 Reading Foundations Skills Block: Differentiation Pack
Teaching Letters, Sounds, and Words	
"Learning Letters": Includes keyword letter charts, letter stories, keyword cards, handwriting sheets, and handwriting formation charts	K–2 Reading Foundations Skills Block Learning Letters Book
"K–2 Word List": Includes a list of words for each spelling pattern taught in the Skills Block	K–2 Skills Block Resource Manual

Cont.

Chapter 4

Document	Where It Is Found
Grade-Level Specific Documents	
"Scope and Sequence: Year-at-a Glance": An overview of the sequence of skills and spelling patterns taught across a school year.	Modules 1–4 Teacher Guide and Supporting Materials
"Grade Level Overview of Instructional Practices": Describes each instructional practice used in each grade level	K–2 Reading Foundations Skills Block: Differentiation Pack Grade Level Differentiation Packs
"Module Overview": An overview of the module content, including the focus of each cycle and standards covered	K–2 Skills Block Teacher Guide and Supporting Materials

▶ What Will My Instruction Look Like during the Skills Block Hour?

The Skills Block, like the Module Lessons and K–2 Labs (Labs), is divided into four eight-week[2] modules that span a full year. In the Skills Block, each module is divided into seven five-day "cycles" of instruction. These cycles include an intentional sequence of instructional practices (simple routines such as Chaining or Spelling to Complement Reading), each of which builds off of the learning from the previous lesson and connects to the next lesson's learning.

Every eight-week module includes a flex week of five days. These days can be used at your discretion at any time throughout the cycle for such things as re-teaching or making up for a short school week. Each Module Overview includes suggestions for these days based on the content of the module. Table 4.8 shows the breakdown of an eight-week Skills Block module.

Table 4.8: Eight-Week K–2 Reading Foundations Skills Block Module

Week 1: Cycle 1	Each five-day cycle includes:
Week 2: Cycle 2	» Four days: repeated instructional practices, one per day
Week 3: Cycle 3	» One day: assessment and goal-setting (end of cycle)
Week 4: Cycle 4	
Week 5: Cycle 5	
Week 6: Cycle 6	
Week 7: Cycle 7	
Flex Week	The days in this flex "week" should be used throughout the module at the teacher's discretion.

The Skills Block is one hour long, divided into two major chunks:

» 15 to 20 minutes of whole group instruction

» 40 to 45 minutes of differentiated small group instruction (including independent work)

---

[2] Note: Module 1 of each grade level is only six weeks long, with five weeks of instruction and one flex week.

EL Education | Your Curriculum Companion

Figure 4.2 The K–2 Reading Foundations Skills Block Hour

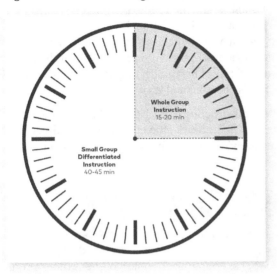

Table 4.9 summarizes the full hour of the Skills Block, with approximately 15 to 20 minutes spent in whole group instruction and 40 to 45 minutes spent in differentiated small group instruction. Whole group and differentiated small group instruction are described in greater detail following Table 4.9.

Table 4.9: Instruction during the K–2 Reading Foundations Skills Block Hour

Grouping	Instruction
Whole group instruction *15 to 20 minutes*	Opening (3 to 5 minutes): Students engage in a brief and familiar instructional practice that provides connections to prior learning and/or warms students up for the Work Time instructional practice.
	Work Time (10 to 15 minutes): Students engage in a familiar instructional practice routine, through which they practice newly introduced phonemes, graphemes, spelling patterns, or skills.
	Reflection and Goal-Setting (2 to 3 minutes): Each module includes a character focus (e.g., collaboration). Students make and/or reflect on personal goals connected to their growth as readers and the current character focus of the module.
Differentiated small group instruction *40 to 45 minutes*	Teacher meets with two or three differentiated small groups, based on phase. Each group meets with the teacher for approximately 10 to 12 minutes while other students do purposeful independent work.

Whole Group Instruction

In the Skills Block, whole group instruction is divided into three parts: Opening, Work Time, and Reflection and Goal-Setting. During the Opening, students engage in a familiar instructional practice that connects to prior learning or warms them up for the Work Time. In the Skills Block, an instructional practice is a routine used consistently over one or more modules that addresses grade-level standards, ensuring that all students have access to grade-level instruction as a whole group.

Work Time is the heart of whole group instruction. This is when students use instructional practice routines to practice newly introduced graphemes (letters), phonemes (sounds), spelling patterns, or skills. For example, in both kindergarten and first grade, there is an instructional practice called Phonemic Blending and Segmentation. It's a simple routine in which students use thumb tapping as they segment a word into its phonemes, and then slide their fingers to blend the phonemes back into a complete word. Students learn this instructional practice early in the year, practice it, and then apply it every time they learn new phonemes or words. So in a cycle early in first grade, they might be tapping out the phonemes in the word *nut*: n/u/t, and then blending it back together to pronounce *nut*. By the middle of first grade, they might be using this same instructional practice with more difficult words, like *shut* and *gasp*.

What follows are just a few of the many examples of instructional practices in the Skills Block. There are more than 20 instructional practices in the Skills Block—too many to list and describe here. We have chosen to highlight those that we have video of so that you can see them in practice. A picture is worth a thousand words:

▶▶ **Video Spotlight**

In the accompanying video, first-graders in Susan Preston's class at Polaris Charter Academy in Chicago use Phonemic Blending and Segmentation, an instructional practice that helps students understand letter-sound combinations and how those combinations help them read and spell words. Students first tap out the sounds in a word on their fingers, and then blend the sounds together. Next, they review what each sound looks and feels like in the mouth (i.e., "articulatory gestures"). Finally, they analyze the oral and auditory connections in the word they began with. This instructional practice is used in both kindergarten and Grade 1.

https://vimeo.com/159245835

▶▶ **Video Spotlight**

In the accompanying video, first-graders in Anne Simpson's class at Two Rivers Public Charter School in Washington, D.C., use the Interactive Writing instructional practice, which helps them apply their growing knowledge of letter-sound connections to write sentences using familiar spelling patterns and high-frequency words in a shared sentence. First, Simpson reads aloud an intentionally designed sentence and students tap out each word. Then students analyze the sounds in each word. Finally they reread the complete sentence. This instructional practice is used (with slight variations) in kindergarten, Grade 1, and Grade 2.

https://vimeo.com/168991757

In the accompanying video, students in Stacey Cicero's primary classroom at Genesee Community Charter School in Rochester, New York, use the Chaining instructional practice, which gives them targeted instruction for analyzing and decoding words with particular spelling patterns. One grapheme is changed in each successive word. Students analyze the first word to determine how it has changed as they decode the next word. Cicero then has students spell the words from memory, which reinforces letter-sound connections and lets her check for understanding. There are optional extensions. This instructional practice is used in kindergarten and Grade 1.

https://vimeo.com/169277923

In the accompanying video, first-graders in Stacey Cicero's class at Genesee Community Charter School in Rochester, New York, use the Spelling to Complement Reading instructional practice, which helps them examine the reciprocal relationship between spelling and reading. Students listen to a word read aloud and then repeat it and segment it into phonemes. They use sound boxes to analyze each word for the number of phonemes and graphemes. Finally, students hear the words read aloud again and write them from memory. This instructional practice is used in Grades 1 and 2.

https://vimeo.com/169252541

Meeting the Needs of Primary Learners

Building a set of familiar practices supports students as they apply those practices with increasingly complicated content. Primary learners thrive on a sense of rhythm and ritual. And the instructional practices also help you as a teacher: It will be slow going early in the year learning each practice, but then you will find you can use them with increased comfort and automaticity later in the year.

The instructional practices in the Skills Block are designed with the characteristics of primary learners in mind, incorporating music, movement, and flexibility. For example, instead of being asked to raise their hand when they hear a set of rhyming words in the Rhyme Time instructional practice, students are encouraged to stand up and jump when they hear the rhyming words. Teachers model the practice, and then students join in. What follows are a few additional examples:

» The **Mystery Word instructional practice** is a fun way to introduce new high-frequency words. The practice engages students by providing clues, such as the number of letters, in a new word and encouraging inquiry as they work together to guess the word.

» The **Silly Sentences instructional practice** in Grade 2 encourages students to use their imagination to come up with the silliest sentence they can, using words that include the spelling pattern(s) taught in that cycle.

» The Cycle Assessment review activities include the **Spelling with Style instructional practice**. Students practice spelling words aloud that follow the taught spelling patterns of the cycle, but they do it "with style." For example, they might do it "opera style" and sing with a silly opera voice or "ketchup style," pounding one hand into the other (like they are trying to get the ketchup out of a bottle) as they spell the words.

As students become more familiar with a particular practice, less teacher modeling and explicit instruction are needed. All of the instructional practices used in the Skills Block, such as Phonemic Blending and Segmentation, are detailed in the Module 1 Teacher Guide and Supporting Materials for each grade level.

During the Reflection and Goal-Setting portion of whole group instruction, students set goals for their growth as readers. Throughout our comprehensive K–2 curriculum, we focus on students' habits of character. The Skills Block is no different. The lesson closing often emphasizes growth mindset, asking students: "How did our work today help us become even more proficient readers?"

Differentiated Small Group Instruction and Independent Work

Differentiated small groups are determined after administering the grade-level benchmark assessments, which help you determine each student's microphase (a more detailed breakdown of each phase—see Tables 4.10 and 4.11—which denotes "early," "middle," and "late"). During differentiated small group instruction, you will work with a group of students to teach new material, re-teach, or extend, based on students' needs. (For more information about independent and small group work, see the K–2 Skills Block Resource Manual.)

Table 4.10 details the phases of reading and spelling development based on Dr. Linnea Ehri's Phase Theory (Metsala and Ehri, 1998). Phase Theory describes behaviors related to the types of letter-sound connections students are able to make as they learn to read and write.

Table 4.10: Dr. Ehri's Phases of Reading and Spelling Development

Pre-Alphabetic (Pre-A)	Partial Alphabetic (PA)	Full Alphabetic (FA)	Consolidated Alphabetic (CA)
Able to identify very few letters, if any	Able to identify many upper- and lowercase letters	Able to identify all upper- and lowercase letters and their associated sounds	Able to identify all upper- and lowercase letters and their associated sounds
Not yet able to identify letter sounds	Able to identify some letter sounds	Able to blend and segment sounds in a word	Has built a large bank of sight words, including multisyllabic words; learns words more quickly
Able to identify some environmental print	Has limited phonemic awareness	Has memorized a growing number of sight words (mostly shorter words)	Able to use context to confirm reading of a word in a text
If tries to spell words, may use a random string of letters or shapes	Has limited decoding ability	Growing ability to decode words and non-words	Has proficient memory for correct spelling; able to draw from alphabetic principles to spell new words
	Predicts unknown words by identifying beginning sound	Able to use context to confirm reading of a word in a text	
	Able to produce some invented spelling; weak memory for correct spelling	Has a growing memory for correct spelling; some invented spelling	

Small group differentiated instruction, based on students' microphases, lasts for 40 to 45 minutes per day and features the following:

» On average, you will meet with three groups per day.

» Students reading below grade level meet with you every day.

» Students reading at or above grade level meet with you one or two times per week.

» For each group, you refer to the suggested activities and instructions provided in the lesson, which may include:

- Suggestions for re-teaching or extending the whole group lesson (found in the Differentiated Small Group section of the lesson)

- Activity Bank activity (suggestions found in the Differentiated Small Group section of the lesson; Activity Bank found in the K–2 Skills Block Resource Manual)

- Differentiation Pack (found in the grade-level Differentiation Pack book for each grade level)

Each day, students who are not working with you will engage in purposeful independent rotations. Students will engage in a combination of the following each day:

» **Accountable Independent Reading.** This is a time for students to choose from a variety of texts based on interest and/or reading goals. You can use this time, possibly during a rotation or between rotations, to observe and/or confer with students on their reading proficiency goals and to monitor fluency and comprehension.

» **Word Work.** This is a time for students to analyze words and word parts. You may use materials from the Skills Block (e.g., suggested word sorts and Activity Bank activities) or other existing classroom materials (e.g., games, letter tiles).

» **Writing Practice.** Writing practice builds students' ease with the skills and habits needed to generate ideas on paper—everything from letter formation to spacing to knowing how to begin a sentence and continue a thought. In a primary classroom, students can practice writing and letter formation using a wide variety of mediums; you can use your creativity to design ways to help students practice these skills, build stamina as writers, and write about topics of interest in creative ways.

» **Reading Fluency.** Fluency involves lots of rereading. You can use a variety of familiar texts from the Skills Block or from existing classroom libraries for fluency work. You should give students texts that are familiar and/or easily decodable for a given phase. For example, readers in the Pre- or Partial Alphabetic phases are not yet able to decode, so they should "read" familiar classroom poems or songs that they have memorized.

► How Is Skills Block Instruction Aligned with Grade-Level Reading and Language Standards?

The Skills Block is designed as a seamless Grades K–2 continuum with three years' worth of lessons from the beginning of kindergarten to the end of Grade 2. The sequence of instruction progresses at a pace that aligns to grade-level Common Core State Standards (CCSS) Reading: Foundational Skills standards, some Language standards, and the four phases of reading and spelling development.

Because the Skills Block Grades K–2 continuum is tightly connected to the phases and the standards, teachers gain a clear picture of what a student is able to do at a given microphase, how it aligns to grade-level expectations, and the instructional steps that can be taken for differentiated small group instruction and meeting students' needs during whole group instruction. Table 4.11 shows how the four microphases, the lesson content of the Grades K–2 continuum, and the CCSS grade-level expectations align.

Table 4.11: Grades K–2 Continuum

Key:

Light gray = kindergarten lessons	Mid gray = Grade 1 lessons	Dark gray = Grade 2 lessons

Micro-phase	Pre- Alphabetic Phase	Partial Alphabetic Phase	Full Alphabetic Phase	Consolidated Alphabetic Phase
Early	Not applicable[3]	**Kindergarten, Module 3, Cycles 12–18:** digraphs, decoding CVC words, comparing short vowel sounds	**Grade 1, Module 3, Cycles 12–17:** syllable types: closed-syllable, open-syllable, and CVCe syllable-type words	**Grade 2, Module 2, Cycles 7–12:** new vowel teams and spelling generalizations; contractions; affixes: -ed suffix (three ways), -*tion*, and -*sion*
Middle	Not applicable[3]	**GKM4, Cycles 19–22:** decoding CVC words and beginning to decode CVCC; comparing long and short vowel sounds	**G1M3, Cycle 18:** two-syllable, CVCe syllable-type words **G1M4, Cycles 19–20:** introduction r-controlled vowel sounds **G1M4, Cycles 21–24:** long vowel patterns	**G2M3, Cycles 13–19:** consonant-le (C-le) word endings, other word endings, new vowel teams, and contractions
Late	**GKM1, Cycles 1-4:** ABC sounds and recognition, syllable and rhyme identification, concepts of print **GKM2, Cycles 5–11:** ABC sounds and recognition, syllable identification, rhyme identification and production, concepts of print	**G1M1, Cycles 1-4:** kindergarten review **G1M2, Cycles 5–6:** continued review of phonemes taught in kindergarten **G1M2, Cycles 7–11:** initial and final consonant clusters, "y" as /ī/	**G1M4, Cycle 25:** two-syllable words with long vowel patterns **G2M1, Cycles 1–6:** review vowel patterns by learning spelling generalizations, syllable types, and r-controlled vowels from Grade 1	**G2M4, Cycles 20–26:** "y" generalizations with plural endings, schwa, homophones, compound words, new word endings, and contractions

▶ How Will Assessment Structures in the Skills Block Help Me Pinpoint the Needs of My Students?

Primary teachers are deeply and rightfully committed to ensuring that all students are progressing as readers. Toward this same end, most schools and districts tend to heavily emphasize assessments, assessment systems, and reporting on data to the school community and parents. So,

---

[3] Students in the early and middle Pre-Alphabetic phase cannot yet identify letters. In the Grades K–2 continuum of whole group lessons, there are no lessons that explicitly address the needs of these students. Instead, in the kindergarten lessons, the differentiated small group instruction includes suggestions for Activity Bank activities and some possible differentiation of the whole group content.

understandably, teachers using the Skills Block curriculum always have significant and specific questions regarding assessments. In Table 4.12, we summarize the three major types of assessments in the Skills Block. (For much more detail, refer to the Assessment Overview found in the K–2 Skills Block Resource Manual.)

The results of these assessments, particularly the benchmark assessments, are so tightly aligned with the phases and microphases that each one helps teachers pinpoint and track students' progression through the phases toward mastery of taught skills. This targeted information empowers teachers (and students, parents, and leaders) with common language to discuss, plan, and set goals around students' strengths and areas of need.

▶▶ Video Spotlight

In the accompanying video, first-graders in Susan Preston's class at Polaris Charter Academy in Chicago participate in the end-of-cycle reading and spelling assessment. Preston administers the assessment with a small group, evaluates their responses, and confers with each student to set an individual goal.

https://vimeo.com/159828967

Table 4.12: Assessment Types in the K–2 Reading Foundations Skills Block

Purpose	Administration Frequency
Assessment Type: Benchmark Assessments	
Depending on the time of year you administer these assessments, they can be used to: » Provide diagnostic information to help you determine a student's current phase » Provide guidance for choosing lessons from the Grades K–2 continuum to best fit a student's instructional needs » Gauge whether the student is approximately on grade level (as defined by the CCSS) » Track students' progress and measure mastery of end-of-year goals (as determined by the Skills Block grade-level Scope and Sequence)	» Beginning, middle, and end of year
Assessment Type: Cycle Assessments	
Cycle assessments are used to: » Assess students' progress toward mastery of skills taught up to a given point in the curriculum » Give you information to help students set personal goals for reading proficiency	» Kindergarten: every cycle, starting in Module 4 » Grade 1: every cycle, starting in Module 1, Cycle 2 » Grade 2: full cycle assessment one or two times per module; optional, brief cycle assessments available for cycles in between

Cont.

Purpose	Administration Frequency
Assessment Type: Daily Assessments	
In kindergarten and Grade 1, optional daily assessments are called snapshot assessments, and in Grade 2 they are called exit tickets. In both cases, they are used to: » Track progress toward mastery of daily learning targets	» After every daily lesson

▶ How Will the K–2 Reading Foundations Skills Block Complement My Students' Learning in the Module Lessons and Labs?

As we've continued to emphasize, and primary teachers know, the ultimate goal of reading is comprehension. For students to reach this goal, to comprehend text with increasing independence, they need to be able to "crack the code"—to decode more and more complex words and to acquire automaticity with those words. As any parent or teacher of a primary-age student can attest, there is nothing more exciting than seeing this really click; young readers feel more confident and empowered, and their reading really takes off from there.

One way of thinking about this relationship between reading comprehension (the goal) and decoding and automaticity (the tools) is the Five Components of Reading, as defined by the National Reading Panel.

Figure 4.3: The Five Components of Reading

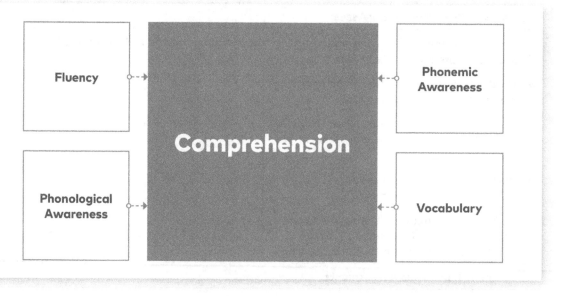

The End Goal: Comprehension

Comprehension is certainly the end goal. Yet we know that readers cannot independently comprehend a text if they can't actually make sense of the letters and sounds. And primary readers, especially those who are reading below grade level or learning a second language, need extra practice with these skills, specifically phonological awareness, phonemic awareness, and fluency. As readers become more secure in these skills, their reading can become more automatic and they can ultimately read independently and with meaning.

Skills Block instruction sharply focuses on these skills. Explicit instructional practice guides students to read with automaticity and fluency, ultimately freeing up their brains to focus on the end goal—comprehension—rather than laboring over every word and losing track of the meaning. The Skills Block focuses on just three of the Five Components of Reading: fluency, phonemic awareness, and phonological awareness. Comprehension and vocabulary are explicitly taught in the K–2 comprehensive curriculum (Module Lessons plus Labs), primarily through read-alouds of rich, complex texts in the Module Lessons.

Table 4.13 illustrates the five components, where each is taught within the three-hour K–2 comprehensive curriculum, and the Common Core standards associated with each.

Table 4.13: Where the Five Components of Reading Live in Our K–2 Comprehensive Curriculum

Component of the Big 5	Common Core State Standards	Where It Is Explicitly Taught and Formally Assessed
Comprehension	Reading: Informational Text Reading: Literature	K–2 Module Lessons
Fluency	Reading: Foundational Skills	K–2 Reading Foundations Skills Block
Phonemic awareness	Reading: Foundational Skills	K–2 Reading Foundations Skills Block
Phonological Awareness	Reading: Foundational Skills	K–2 Reading Foundations Skills Block
Vocabulary	Language	K–2 Module Lessons

The preceding table gives you a big-picture sense of where the five components of reading live in our K–2 comprehensive curriculum. Hopefully, this helps you "connect the new to the known" in terms of mapping our curriculum onto what you already know or do. And it should reassure you that everything you care about in terms of literacy is formally "held" somewhere in the three hours that make up our comprehensive curriculum.

But it's not so simple. For example, even though comprehension is taught and assessed in the Module Lessons, that does not mean that there is no comprehension work happening in the Skills Block. So Table 4.14 gets a bit more specific, showing you more concretely how different strands of the standards show up across the three hours of instruction.

Table 4.14: Addressing the Standards: The Interconnections between the K–2 Reading Foundations Skills Block and the K–2 Module Lessons and Labs

Aspect	How It Is Addressed in the K–2 Reading Foundations Skills Block	How It Is Addressed in the K–2 Module Lessons and Labs
Comprehension (CCSS Reading: Informational Text; Reading: Literature)	Assessment of basic comprehension in the Fluency Benchmark Assessment and Fluency Cycle Assessments (aligned to CCSS Reading: Foundational Skills standard RF.4) Optional assessment of basic comprehension in the decodable student reader routine Optional comprehension conversations (text-dependent questions tied to the engagement texts)	Read-aloud and independent reading paired with discussion and writing in response to text-dependent questions Assessment of deeper comprehension in unit assessments and using the Reading Literature and Reading Informational Texts checklists (aligned to CCSS reading standards for informational text and literature)

Cont.

Aspect	How It Is Addressed in the K–2 Reading Foundations Skills Block	How It Is Addressed in the K–2 Module Lessons and Labs
Fluency (CCSS Reading: Foundational Skills standard RF.4).	Fluency instructional practice and fluency independent rotation Fluency assessment	Modeled fluency through read-aloud and fluency practice through shared reading
Grammar, usage, and conventions	Language standards associated with spelling and letter formation (CCSS L.2) are explicitly taught and practiced. Language standards associated with handwriting (CCSS L.1.a) are also formally incorporated through explicit instruction and repeated practice with letter formation. Other language standards associated with writing and composition are echoed in the Interactive Writing instructional practice and Writing Practice (suggested independent rotation)	Read-aloud and analysis of songs, poems, and other texts, paired with practice and authentic application tasks, including shared writing and independent writing Assessment of CCSS Language standards L.1 (with the exception of L.1.a) and L.3 are embedded in unit assessments and using the Language Standards Checklist.
Writing	Conventions (letter formation and spelling) and Writing Practice independent rotation (CCSS Language standards L.1.a and L.2)	Composition of shared writing, individual scaffolded writing tasks, and individual on-demand writing tasks (CCSS Writing standards) Assessment of writing standards in unit assessments using writing rubrics (for opinion, informative/explanatory, and narrative) and ongoing assessment with writing checklists
Vocabulary (CCSS Language standards L.4, L.5, and L.6)	Word structure/word parts—explicit instruction of how affixes change the meaning of words	Direct vocabulary instruction before, during, and after reading with vocabulary selected from texts. Instruction focuses on determining the meaning of words and using new vocabulary in speaking and writing tasks. Assessment of vocabulary standards (CCSS R, W, and L.4, 5, and 6) are embedded in unit assessments and using reading, writing, and speaking and listening checklists.

The snapshot that follows describes a typical day for first-grade teacher Ms. Sanchez and her students (including Kristina, Elvin, and Omar, whom we first met in Chapter 2).

Soundboard with white board marker and eraser

It is Wednesday morning, and students are starting the third day of Cycle 4, which is part of Module 1. Before the students arrived this morning, Ms. Sanchez stacked all the soundboards (a horizontal row of three boxes on one side and four on the other, printed and laminated) and gathered the white board markers and erasers next to the class meeting area. She is ready for the Skills Block Work Time. But first, the class will warm up with an opening instructional practice called High-Frequency Word Fishing.

Ms. Sanchez leads the class in a transition song, the students singing together as they move from their seats to stand in a circle on the carpet (sung to the tune of "The More We Get Together"):

"Gather around together, together, together. Gather around together, together, let's go. Stand up in a circle to think about what we've learned. Let's make some great connections with letters and sounds."

The students stand excitedly around the "pond," eyeing the "fish" (high-frequency word cards) as they wait for Ms. Sanchez's cue to begin the practice: High-Frequency Word Fishing. These cards include review words that were introduced in Cycles 1–3 and some new high-frequency words introduced on the second day of this cycle.

Ms. Sanchez says, "Remember, learning high-frequency words helps us be more proficient readers. They are words we see a lot when we read and use a lot when we write. Okay, now let's all catch our fish!"

Each student, familiar with the routine and management expectations, holds up his or her (pretend) fishing pole and gets started. Kristina reels in (picks up) a card with the word *did* on it. Ms. Sanchez calls on her to read her card aloud.

"Did!" she reads aloud proudly, then "releases" it back into the pond. Ms. Sanchez calls on Omar, who has trouble reading the word *she* on his card. He has been working on identifying the sounds of digraphs *sh, ch,* and *th* but still mixes them up sometimes. Ms. Sanchez points to the keyword card posted on the wall with a picture of a person holding a finger up to her lips and saying "Shh." This helps Omar remember the /sh/ sound. He looks at the word again, remembering that *she* was one of the words they learned yesterday. Beaming, he exclaims, "She!"

Students sing another transition song as they sit down and prepare for the Work Time instructional practice: Spelling to Complement Reading.

In the days leading up to this in the cycle, students reviewed a list of letters and letter sounds they had learned in kindergarten, including /t/, /n/, /u/, /s/, and /sh/. These letters and sounds were introduced and practiced through a variety of instructional practices on the first day of the cycle. Students engaged with the letters and sounds in various ways, such as skywriting the letters and blending and segmenting words containing those letters. On the second day of the cycle, the new high-frequency words were explicitly introduced, as were the engagement text and decodable reader for this cycle.

Now Ms. Sanchez begins today's Work Time by passing out the sound boards and white board markers, one set to each "row captain." The row captain then distributes the materials to the other students in his or her row.

Once all the students have their materials, Ms. Sanchez begins the practice by saying a word aloud: *shut*. Students say the word after her, pronouncing each sound in the word slowly. Students then point to the boxes on their soundboard, pointing to one box for each sound that they hear in the word, moving from left to right. Then they write the letters that represent each sound of the word in one box each.

Ms. Sanchez watches the students and notices that Omar needs a bit of help. She signals for the students to erase their boards and do the next word (quit), walking over to Omar and stopping him from erasing his board. She says, "Omar! I see that you remembered that *sh* makes the /sh/ sound. Wonderful. Now I want you to say the word aloud for me one more time and use your fingers to tap out the sounds. Omar taps out /sh//u//t/ on his fingers, as he learned to do in the Phonemic Blending and Segmentation practice. He counts the sounds he hears and says, "Three!"

"That's right. There are three sounds in this word, Omar. How many boxes did you use to write the word?"

"Four," he says.

"So, let's erase your first try. Can you try again?"

Omar uses the soundboard option with three boxes, writing sh in the first box and u and t in the second and third boxes.

Ms. Sanchez gives the class two more words, and then closes the practice by saying each word once more as the students write each from memory on the back of their soundboards. This is her quick check for understanding, which will help inform some of the work she will do in differentiated small groups in a few minutes.

The class closes out Work Time with a short reflection. Ms. Sanchez has defined the word *proficient* with the students in past lessons and asks: "What have you done today that helped you become a more proficient reader? Think about your personal goals that we set after our cycle assessments last week. Turn and talk to a partner about it."

She walks around and listens in on the brief partner conversations, noticing that Elvin says, "I need to work on listening for the middle sound in words. I did that when we wrote the words on our sound boards. It was still kind of hard for me when I tried to spell the words on the back without the boxes, though."

Ms. Sanchez signals for the group to turn back to the front and finish their conversations. She asks Elvin if he would share out his reflection with the group. She then sends students off to their independent work rotations, calling the late Pre-Alphabetic group, which is named the "Mallard Group" (all groups have been named after ducks as a connection to the topic of the Module Lessons), to meet her at the kidney table to begin their differentiated small group work together.

▶ How Can I Prepare to Teach the K–2 Reading Foundations Skills Block?

Teaching the Skills Block will require a great deal of planning and preparation on the part of teachers and school leaders, particularly if this curriculum represents a big change from your current practice. This section will empower you and your colleagues to understand the "deep logic" of the Skills Block modules so that you can make the curriculum come alive for students. Careful analysis and preparation are the keys to success.

Similar to the process of preparing to teach the content-based components of our curriculum, described in Chapter 3A, analyzing the Skills Block module resources by "zooming in"—from the module level, cycle level, and finally to the lesson level—will help you understand the backward design of each module (i.e., planning with the end in mind, and then thinking through the scaffolding required to get students to that end goal). Understanding the logic of what students are learning and the structure of how the module scaffolds them toward mastery of the standards will empower you to make instructional decisions that best meet all students' needs and bring your own ideas and creativity to the activities.

Table 4.15 will walk you through the necessary preparations, starting six weeks to two months before beginning to teach the Skills Block (likely during the summer) and leading all the way to the weekly preparations necessary before starting each new cycle of instruction. We know that not all of you will be able to follow these guidelines for how soon to begin your planning; however, we do hope to signal the importance of starting early and looking far enough ahead that you are clear and confident about where you and your students are headed.

▷ We know that not all of you will be able to follow these guidelines for how soon to begin your planning; however, we do hope to signal the importance of starting early and looking far enough ahead that you are clear and confident about where you and your students are headed.

Once you begin reading through Table 4.15, you will no doubt notice that the planning requiring the earliest start involves assessments. To give you the timely and vital information you need to determine your students' needs, the assessment structure in the Skills Block is necessarily complex. Learning how it works and ensuring that your materials are ready and that your schedule can accommodate these changes requires early planning.

In Table 4.15, we have included boxes you can check off once a step is complete, as well as a space for notes. This planning tool can be found with the other digital planning tools referenced in Chapter 3A on our website, Curriculum.ELeducation.org.

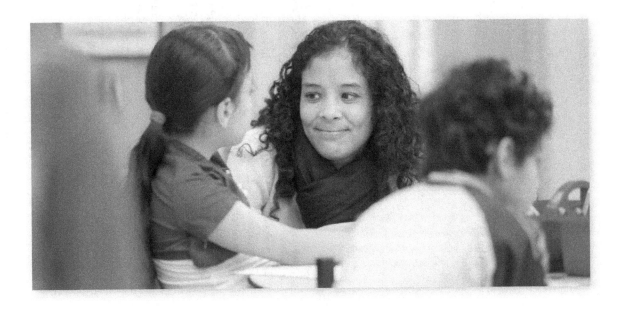

Table 4.15: Preparing to Teach the K–2 Reading Foundations Skills Block

Understanding the Why of the Skills Block		Notes
Six weeks to two months before teaching the Skills Block[5]	This preparation may be done individually if teachers are not able to meet together due to summer schedules, but it is strongly suggested that the following steps be coupled with discussion among school teams and/or grade-level teams. ☐ Understand why structured phonics is an effective way to teach students how to read ☐ Read this chapter for starters. ☐ Read the article "Why a Structured Phonics Program Is Effective" by David Liben (found at Curriculum.ELeducation.org). ☐ Understand the research: Dr. Linnea Ehri's Phase Theory ☐ Read the "Phases and Microphases" document (found in the K–2 Skills Block Resource Manual).	

Preparing to Administer and Score Skills Block Assessments		Notes
Six weeks to two months before teaching the Skills Block	Orient to assessments, phases, and overall structure of the Skills Block: ☐ Orient to the structure of the Skills Block hour either by studying this chapter closely or by reading the separate document "Implementing the K–2 Reading Foundations Skills Block," which can be found on our curriculum website (Curriculum. ELeducation.org). ☐ If applicable to your school/district, identify all other assessments that you must administer or have chosen to administer in addition to the Skills Block benchmark assessments. ☐ Read our Assessment Overview, with a strong focus on benchmark assessments. ☐ If your school or district requires that you administer other assessments, identify the priority assessments for the Skills Block for each grade level (refer to the Assessment Overview). ☐ Reread and discuss the "Phases and Microphases" document.	

Cont.

[5] The timing here is suggested; it may not be realistic for you. The important thing is to start early enough that you get the big-picture before zooming in on specific lessons.

One month to three weeks before teaching the Skills Block	Make a plan for administering assessments:
	
	☐ Create a schedule, keeping in mind that some assessments can be administered whole group (e.g., Spelling assessment) and some must be administered to individual students (e.g., Letter Name and Sound Identification).
	
	☐ Identify additional staff and/or space needed for assessment administration.
	
	☐ Decide how and where to record results (e.g., hard copy and/or electronic copy) and create necessary systems and materials as needed (e.g., spreadsheet, file folders).
	
	☐ Manage/organize materials:
	
	    ☐ Find all benchmark assessments and materials in the K–2 Skills Block Resource Manual.
	
	    ☐ Print all necessary paper materials and procure any other necessary materials (such as pencils and file folders).	

Two to three weeks before teaching the Skills Block	Administer assessments (over a one- to two-week period): ☐ During assessments, begin to set up classroom management expectations specific to Skills Block work and materials. For example, you can establish norms for management of small group work and rotations as you administer assessments to a small group and other students work on something independently. Similarly, you might practice procedures and expectations for the use of white boards and white board markers as students work on an independent activity. ☐ Score assessments and identify the microphase of each student (on each assessment, see the Scoring Sheet in the K–2 Skills Block Resource Manual for guidance in identifying the microphase of each student).	
One week before teaching the Skills Block	☐ Based on students' microphases, create groups for differentiated small group instruction. Note: Benchmark assessments should be readministered (and microphase growth monitored) at least once more in the middle of the school year and again at the end of the year.	

Cont.

Chapter 4

Preparing to Teach a Skills Block Module		Notes
One to two weeks before beginning the Skills Block	Orient to the Skills Block lesson materials: ☐ If using hard copies of the curriculum, ensure that you have all necessary books and materials. ☐ If using an electronic version of the curriculum, decide if you want to make hard copies of some materials. Make copies and distribute.	
	For whole group instruction: ☐ Orient to the sequence of instruction across the year by reading the grade-level Scope and Sequence (found in the front of the grade-level Module 1 Teacher Guide or on our curriculum website [Curriculum.ELeducation.org]). ☐ Orient to the instructional practices used in your grade level by reading the instructional practices (found in the front of the grade-level Module 1 Teacher Guide or on our website).	
	For small group instruction: ☐ Orient to the structure and purpose of this time by reading the "Independent and Small Group Work" document. ☐ To get ahead on creating and managing materials, consider looking ahead to the differentiated small group instruction time and preparing materials for Cycle 1 (or more cycles). ☐ Consider making master copies of all Activity Bank activities for a given grade-level team or K–2 team so that team members can pull activities as needed.	

Cont.

Chapter 4

One to two weeks before teaching each module	Orient your team to the Skills Block Module Overview:
	☐ Convene a planning meeting that involves teachers and specialists (e.g., general education teachers, special education co-teachers, reading specialists, English as a second language teachers) to analyze the focus and goals of the Skills Block module.
	☐ Read the goals of the module (usually in the second paragraph of the introduction, starting with: "By the end of the module students should ..."). The whole group lessons have been backward-planned from this goal; students reading on grade level (or slightly above/below) should be able to do this by the end of the module.
	☐ Read the Cycle Details section. Do you have any questions about the content of these cycles? Are any of the new skills being taught unfamiliar (e.g., maybe teachers have never taught about syllable types before)? If so:
	☐ Look for any resources in the K–2 Skills Block Resource Manual that will provide additional information (e.g., the Syllabication Guide if teaching syllable types is a concern).
	☐ Read the Module Pacing section. Consider:
	• Are there any new instructional practices being introduced? If so, will flex days be used to ensure that students understand the new procedure?
	• Are there any school calendar issues to consider? Will flex days be used to make up for a holiday or teacher work day?
	• Based on student data (either from the previous year or previous module) and the end goal of this upcoming module, are most students on track to meet the goals of the upcoming module (e.g., if first-graders should be able to decode CVCe words by the end of Module 3, are most of them decoding CVC words with automaticity near the end of Module 2)?
	○ If the answer is no, what are the implications for the use of flex days and/or small group differentiated instruction planning?

- If the majority of your students are behind, consider how this will affect whole group instruction. (For example, you might choose to use a few flex days to re-teach some whole group lessons from the previous module to catch students up before diving into the new skills. Or you might choose to shorten the whole group time and focus mostly on differentiating the whole group lesson's learning targets in small groups.)

☐ Read the Habits of Character/Social-Emotional Learning section. Does the focus align with your school's current focus? If not, will they work together well, or will you need to tweak this focus?

☐ Closely read lessons that include new instructional practices or new, more challenging content. This will ensure that you internalize the new practice or skills, understand and can find any related materials, and ask questions as needed.

Preparing to Teach a Skills Block Cycle

	Notes
Approximately one week before teaching a cycle of lessons	Ideally, grade-level teams should meet at least one week before each cycle begins, to examine and plan for the upcoming cycle. ☐ Teams are encouraged to think of efficient solutions to materials management and planning. For example, one teacher on the team might make copies of all of the supporting materials for the whole team while another makes all of the anchor charts. And/or one teacher might manage all of the differentiated small group planning and materials for a given microphase (e.g., early Partial Alphabetic) and share the plans and materials with the rest of the team. How can you and your team distribute this work? Whole group lesson: Orient your team to the Cycle Overview: ☐ Read the Cycle Overview to identify the skills introduced and new high-frequency words, and to take stock of any new instructional practices, assessments, etc. ☐ Look through the Materials section to determine whether any new anchor charts or other materials need to be created or copied. Copy and create materials for the week in advance if possible, working together with teammates, volunteers, and paraprofessionals.

Cont.

Differentiated small group instruction: Plan for small group instruction. Groupings should already be established, but also should be flexible based on cycle assessment results and mid-year benchmark assessment results.

Note: You will need to make choices based on the strengths, needs, and structure of a given classroom, so a specific set of steps might vary. What follows is a suggested sequence.

☐ Decide which of the following options you will use for each group:

- Lesson-specific suggestions: This is best for students slightly above or below grade level and is found in the Differentiated Small Group section of daily lessons.

- Differentiation Pack: This is best for students significantly above or below grade level. Use the Assessment Conversion Chart to identify an appropriate cycle (or cycles) of lessons, and then use the Differentiation Pack materials for that cycle or pull full lessons from other grade levels.

  ○ Note: If students are significantly above grade level and their needs extend beyond the Grades K–2 continuum of lessons, consider having them work on the extension words suggested in the Differentiated Small Groups: Work with Teacher section but focus on the meaning of the affixes and root words and other related vocabulary words. Or consider setting up a literature circle, providing additional work with complex text, or following the 3–5 Additional Language and Literacy Block lesson plans if your school is already familiar with this structure.

- Activity Bank: This option is best for students significantly below grade level.

☐ Once the appropriate option has been identified for each group, record the plans for each group for each instructional day. Keep in mind that the lowest group should meet with the teacher every day if possible, while those reading above grade level might need to meet with the teacher only one or two times per week.

Cont.

☐ Once plans have been recorded, gather or copy any necessary materials for each group for each day. Consider sharing the copying and preparation responsibilities with other teachers who have groups in the same microphase.

Plan for independent rotations (see the K–2 Skills Block Resource Manual, specifically the "Independent and Small Group Work" document):

☐ Will new rotation activities be introduced? If so, plan for explicit teaching of the activity and management expectations.

☐ Should groups or partnerships be updated based on behaviors, microphases, or type of activity? If so, regroup as necessary.

☐ Do any materials need to be prepared in advance (e.g, make fresh copies of response sheets for Accountable Independent Reading)? If so, prepare the necessary materials.

Chapter 4:
Instructional Leadership

Table 4.16: Chapter 4 Instructional Leadership

Questions to Ask Yourself and Your Staff
» Have you and your staff analyzed the similarities and differences between your current practice and the practices of the K–2 Reading Foundations Skills Block (Skills Block)? What will be the same? What will be different? How will you support staff to lean in to any necessary changes?
» Are you and your staff clear that structured phonics is just one critical component of a comprehensive literacy curriculum?
» Based on any changes in practice you and your staff need to make, is there anything you need to stop doing to make space (in terms of time and energy) for the Skills Block?
» Have you analyzed the assessments in the Skills Block? How will the assessment structure fit within your existing structure? Which of your current assessments might you be able to stop administering?
» Will any teachers need support managing the small group structures of the Skills Block? What structures can you set up to support them?
» How can you set up the Skills Block and its related planning structures so that reading specialists and other specialists can push into the classroom to best support students?
» Have you communicated with families about how structured phonics will be one critical aspect of reading instruction in your school? Have you provided them with a rationale for why the Skills Block will be beneficial for their children?

Evidence of Progress
» Teachers and leaders can identify the phases and microphases of reading and spelling development and are starting to feel comfortable using this language to describe learners.
» Staff is clear that the phases/microphases drive whole group and small group instruction and that lessons from any grade level can be used to best meet the needs of a student or group of students (i.e., all students will be exposed to grade-level content, but some students will likely work on something quite different in small groups based on their needs).

Cont.

Chapter 4

» Schedules: Assessment schedules, daily schedules, and planning time have all been created with the structure of the Skills Block in mind.

» Room arrangements and materials have been adjusted to meet the needs of the Skills Block (e.g., books sorted by decodable and non-decodable in the student library).

» Staff can articulate the shift from an equal focus on all cueing systems when teaching students how to read to a stronger focus on the visual cueing system, with the other two as confirmatory or as a supplemental strategy.

Resources and Suggestions

» Resources available on our curriculum website (Curriculum.ELeducation.org):

• All of the documents listed in Table 4.7: K–2 Reading Foundations Skills Block: Resource Documents, especially the K–2 Skills Block Resource Manual

• Videos

• Article: "Why a Structured Phonics Program Is Effective" by David Liben

» Research and writing by Dr. Linnea Ehri

Chapter 4:
Frequently Asked Questions

Is there a conversion chart that aligns the decodable readers with Fountas and Pinnell/A–Z leveling systems?

Yes and no. Fundamentally, comparing the K–2 Reading Foundations Skills Block (Skills Block) to programs that are not based on structured phonics is an "apples to oranges" comparison. However, in the Assessment Overview, the "Approximate Alignment of Phases and Grade with Levels of Common Reading Assessments" chart shows an approximate correlation (see the K–2 Skills Block Resource Manual). This chart can offer a sense of the approximate range of leveled texts that align with a given microphase and help identify appropriate books for students to use during Accountable Independent Reading.

What if the whole group lesson takes longer than 15 minutes?

When first implemented, the whole group lessons may take a little longer to complete as you and students familiarize yourselves with the instructional practices. Because the instructional practices repeat, it will gradually become easier to finish within the allotted 15 to 20 minutes. That said, each Skills Block module includes five "flex" days. These days can be used any time throughout the module. If a lesson takes longer than anticipated, you might choose to use a flex day to make up for the time lost in small groups as a result of an extended whole group lesson.

During differentiated small group instruction, can I use materials from other programs?

Yes. However, note that the purpose of this time is for students to have reinforcement with particular patterns: the same letters, letter sounds, and spelling patterns suggested in the differentiated small group instruction section of the particular lesson. So, for example, if you choose to use Words Their Way sorting materials, be sure to use words that contain relevant spelling patterns and/or word features. For further details, refer to the "Independent and Small Group Work" document within the K–2 Skills Block Resource Manual.

What if I am already doing district-mandated benchmark assessments? Do I still need to administer all of the Skills Block Benchmark Assessments?

It is not necessary to duplicate all assessments. But it is strongly suggested that "priority assessments" (i.e., Letter Name and Sound Identification for readers in the Pre- and Partial-Alphabetic phases; and Decoding and Spelling for readers in the Full Alphabetic and Consolidated Alphabetic phases) are administered. These assessments tightly align with the design of the Grades K–2 continuum and provide important information necessary to determine lessons within the continuum that may need re-teaching or extension. Refer to the Assessment Overview and Assessment Conversion Chart in the K–2 Skills Block Resource Manual for more details.

What about students who are way, way behind?

The beginning-of-year benchmark assessments provide valuable information about how far behind a student might be. Using this information, you can consult the Assessment Conversion Chart to identify lessons within the Grades K–2 continuum to best meet the student's needs (or specific instructional practices if students are below the earliest lessons of the continuum). In addition, the Meeting Students' Needs section (in the whole group lesson) and the Suggested Differentiated Small Group section provide suggested accommodations and activities to meet the needs of every phase.

Tell me again why I need to do structured phonics with students who can already read and spell?

Remember, based on your own professional experience and on the research behind Phase Theory, "reading" is not just binary. It's not as if students can't decode and then suddenly they can. More advanced readers are still solidifying their understanding of letter-sound connections. Based on the research behind the Phase Theory, students benefit from explicit phonics instruction as long as they are below the Consolidated Alphabetic phase; before this time, students are still working toward decoding of multisyllabic words and building their bank of irregularly spelled words.

Chapter 5

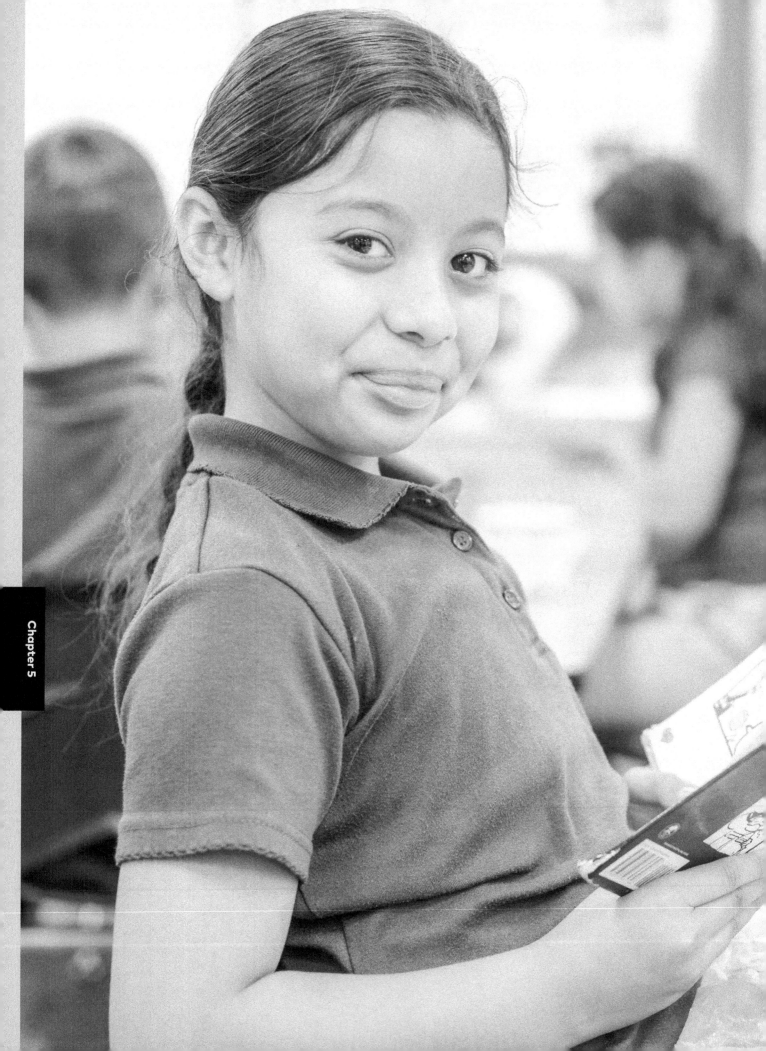

Chapter 5:
The Mighty Text: Worthy, Compelling, and Complex

Chapter 5A:
What Makes a Text Worthy and Compelling?

The decodable texts you learned about in Chapter 4 were selected with one central criterion in mind: spelling-sound patterns. These "phonetically controlled" readers are an important tool for Grades K–2 teachers using our structured phonics program, the K–2 Reading Foundations Skills Block (Skills Block). In the content-based literacy components of our curriculum—the Module Lessons plus K–2 Labs (Labs) and 3–5 Additional Language and Literacy (ALL) Block—text selection is no less important, but the range of texts and the criteria for their selection are much more expansive.

We have heard time and again from teachers around the country that one of the greatest gifts our curriculum gives them is a collection of rich, compelling, and worthy texts. And, as they learn to teach these texts in new ways, they learn more about what makes a text high-quality and what makes it worth their time to teach and their students' time to read, analyze, and draw meaning from. This experience teaching the high-quality texts in our curriculum often carries over into other parts of the school day, and teachers report greater confidence selecting worthy texts for their students. One teacher told us that the texts in the curriculum were a "gift that just keeps giving."

As you no doubt already know, pulling any fourth-grade book about the American Revolution off the shelf is not enough. When there are literally hundreds to choose from, how do you know where to begin? For us, the Four T's: topic, task, targets, text (see Table 1.3 in Chapter 1) were our steady guide. We asked ourselves what opportunities a text provides to teach students about the *topic* and to be a resource for the *tasks* we are asking them to complete. In turn, these questions were always tied tightly to the standards (*targets*). Will the text allow students to meet the standards? Is it sufficiently complex?

And then, of course, there is the intangible aesthetic element: beauty. Is it beautifully written? Is it compelling? Does it motivate students to read closely and investigate the topic deeply? Is it a good model of the author's craft? Will students enjoy looking at it and holding it in their hands? Does the book's quality give students the energy they need to persevere through challenges?

Because texts are one of the four key pillars that hold up our curriculum, it is important to spend some time understanding why and how we chose the ones we did and, more generally, why text selection is so vitally important to student achievement. What follows is an excerpt from a list introduced in Chapter 1; it's worth repeating some of the criteria for how we selected the texts for the curriculum:

» We addressed the instructional shifts of the new standards: *building knowledge through content-rich informational texts; reading for and writing with evidence; regular practice with complex text and its academic vocabulary.*

» We ensured that texts are "worthy" in terms of the content: They teach important information and build students' understanding.

» We ensured that texts are sufficiently complex (in both quantitative and qualitative measures) for the grade level/grade band.

» We paired informational and literary texts and toggled between them to build background knowledge and engagement.

» We identified informational texts, which often serve as the conceptual framework for a module/unit.

» We attended to diversity and inclusion in the texts.

» We chose the appropriate type of text needed to address specific reading standards.

» We sought out shorter texts from reputable sources (e.g., Readworks.org, Library of Congress, awesomestories.org).

» We sought out provocative texts that offer multiple perspectives but stayed away from partisan politics.

» We studied texts closely and aligned them to specific standards or "bundles" of English language arts (ELA) standards that arose authentically from the tasks students were being asked to do.

» In rare cases we wrote or modified texts, being careful not to simplify syntax or academic vocabulary.

One of the things you'll notice from this list and from studying the standards themselves is that, often, one book can't do *all* of the work you need a text to do. Most of the time, it is a carefully chosen set of texts that gives students a full and rich opportunity to explore the topic, complete the tasks, and meet the standards (targets).

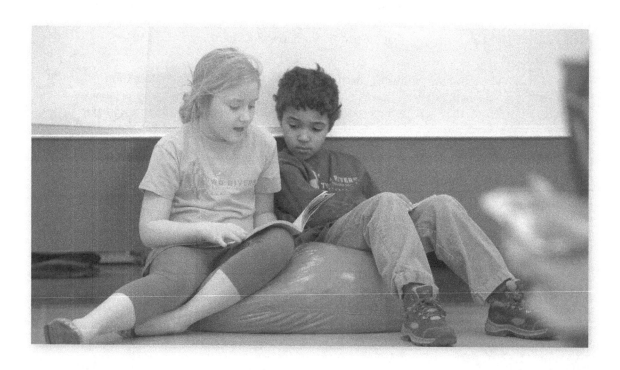

▶ How Will Rich Sets of Informational and Literary Texts Accelerate Literacy Learning for My Students?

"By asking students to read both informational and literary texts with shared topics and themes, we offer many more opportunities to experience big ideas in profound ways. Informational text suddenly becomes personal in the way that we've always understood literature to be. The elegant interplay—the movement from stories and poems that are personal to information that is convincing—gives students tools for taking a personal stand on challenging, real-world topics."

Dolly Higgins

Grades 5 and 6 Teacher, Boise, Idaho

There are a few phrases from the preceding quote that stand out: the opportunity to experience *big ideas in profound ways* and an *elegant interplay* of informational and literary texts. These phrases beautifully state why sets of texts are so powerful. Finding five texts on the American Revolution, even ones that you feel are strong texts and have taught before, is not the same as looking specifically for an *elegant interplay* among texts that will allow students to experience *big ideas in profound ways*. The former suggests a utilitarian purpose for the texts; the latter suggests something deeper.

One of the three big instructional shifts of new college- and career-ready standards is *building knowledge through content-rich nonfiction* (see Chapter 1 for more information). Our content-based literacy approach in the Module Lessons plus Labs and ALL Block responds to this shift by focusing on building students' literacy skills *and* their knowledge of the world with a balance of informational and literary texts that are representative of diverse people and cultures around the world.

When and How Do Students Read in the Curriculum?

Students interact with texts in two main ways in the curriculum: There are some texts that are complex, which students will read closely; and there are additional texts on the topic that ensure that each student experiences a volume of reading at his or her independent reading level.

We have built rich sets of texts around the topics in the modules that allow students to build the skills and knowledge they need to meet standards and complete meaningful tasks—the Four T's in action. Students build knowledge of the world by reading multiple texts on a topic—ranging from novels to scientific articles to speeches—and the more they read and build knowledge, the more challenging texts they can read, thus building their literacy muscles.

Pairing texts around a compelling topic is a strategic move that improves students' reading comprehension. The well-known "Baseball Study" by Recht and Leslie (1988) showed that students with low reading ability but high knowledge of baseball were able to outperform students with high reading ability but low knowledge of baseball on a test of reading comprehension related to a challenging text about baseball. The authors of this study concluded that knowledge of the topic had a much bigger impact on reading comprehension than did generalized reading ability.

Strategies for Pairing and Sequencing Texts

Within each set of informational and literary texts in the curriculum, there are a variety of ways they are introduced and woven together that help students draw meaningful connections. In the curriculum, you may find the texts sequenced in any one of the following ways[1]:

» **From mystery to understanding.** This sequence starts with a text that is intentionally dense or obscure so that students may initially struggle to make sense of it. Students are engaged in the "mystery" of figuring it out and will likely generate many questions that they become increasingly eager to answer. The main strategy for solving the mystery is reading other related texts on the same topic. For example, in the first lesson of Grade 2, Module 2, students read a "mystery journal entry" by a paleontologist. This mysterious text begins their exploration of fossils. Over the course of the module, students eventually build a great deal of knowledge about this topic by reading related texts.

» **From literary to informational text and back again (and vice versa).** In this back-and-forth relationship of texts, literary texts with relatable characters and stories help students engage more deeply with the content they read about in informational texts. Similarly, the knowledge gleaned from the informational texts helps students better understand and persevere with complex narratives or story structures in literary texts. The two types of text work together to deepen students' learning about a topic. This strategy also appeals to students with different preferences for the types of reading they enjoy best. In kindergarten, Module 2, for example, students learn about the weather first through a fictional character named Sofia, then through informational texts, and then they return to narrative texts such as *The Snowy Day*, which also serve as mentor texts for when they write their own weather stories (see Figure 5.1 for the full set of texts from this module).

» **From personal to universal.** Texts grouped in this way help students develop interest in a universal concern or topic. Starting with fiction helps students understand how a particular issue affects people (the personal side of an issue) through the characters in the book. This builds their motivation to read informational texts that help them explore the issue more broadly. In fifth grade, for example, students begin Module 1 learning about a fictional character in the novel *Esperanza Rising*, which leads them into a broader study of human rights. They then read excerpts of the Universal Declaration of Human Rights.

» **From universal to personal.** Conversely, students might begin their journey through a set of texts by starting with a framing document that provides universal concepts or ideas to think about, followed by reading something else that shows how the ideas or concepts affect people. For example, Grade 5 students read a variety of nonfiction texts to learn about the physical impact of natural disasters. Then they read the children's book *Eight Days: A Story of Haiti* by Edwidge Danticat, along with songs and poems written by people who have survived natural disasters, in order to understand the human impact. Finally the issue becomes personal when they consider how to prepare for a natural disaster in their own community and the items that should be included in an emergency preparedness kit. Students are asked to choose personal and practical items for the kit, considering how to address both the health and safety needs as well as the emotional needs of someone affected by a natural disaster.

---

[1] Much of the information in this chapter about text sets and central texts is drawn from our 2014 book *Transformational Literacy: Making the Common Core Shift with Work That Matters*.

Figure 5.1: Set of Informational and Literary Texts from Kindergarten, Module 2

Finding Just-Right Texts

When designing the curriculum, and for any teacher designing his or her own curriculum, one of the most important considerations is not whether we are including *enough* informational texts, but whether we are including informational texts that are worth reading. Textbooks are informational texts and are readily available in most schools, but they are not sufficient for meeting college- and career-ready standards; they don't typically represent multiple perspectives on complex subjects or engage students and motivate them to persevere with their reading. "The greatest benefit for students—in terms of their development as readers, their engagement with and ownership of their learning, and their ability to think critically—will result from teachers approaching text selection with a 'beyond the textbook' mentality" (Berger, Woodfin, Plaut, and Dobbertin, 2014, pp. 30–31).

Nested within the search for compelling and worthy texts, of course, is the search for texts that also ensure students have the opportunity to meet the reading standards. Texts must offer clear and compelling opportunities to learn and practice each standard. The fit between the standard and the text should never feel forced. Each text must lend itself to the type of thinking we want students to do.

Often the standards themselves offer helpful guidance. Common Core State Standard (CCSS) RI.5.6 states: *Analyze multiple accounts of the same event or topic, noting important similarities and differences in the point of view they represent*; the text must therefore give students the opportunity to analyze multiple perspectives. Or, if a single text can't be found, additional texts can be brought in to create a set of texts that will allow students to meet the standard. In Grade 5, for example, students read several texts about Jackie Robinson, including one written by Robinson himself, that offer differing perspectives on the factors that enabled him to be an effective leader of social change in the mid-1900s. Students then use the knowledge they have built by considering multiple perspectives to develop their own opinions about the topic.

Determining Text Complexity

It is easy to think—especially for those who are not teachers—that text complexity boils down to a number. If the Lexile measure says it's a third-grade text, then it must be a third-grade text. Right? Well ... not necessarily.

Teachers know that determining text complexity is itself a complex process. What makes a text complex? Three main factors determine a text's complexity: quantitative measures, qualitative measures, and reader and task considerations. The Lexile measure considers only quantitative factors such as word frequency and sentence length, and that's not enough to truly determine how your students will experience a text.

We're not going to delve into all of these factors in any comprehensive way in this book; however, we do want to provide you with some detail on how we assessed texts along qualitative measures because we think this will be the most transferable for you in your own efforts to select appropriate texts for your students beyond our ELA curriculum.

QUALITATIVE MEASURES OF COMPLEXITY

Once a text has been assessed for complexity using quantitative measures (e.g., Flesch-Kincaid, Lexile), which is easily determined using computer programs or online searches, we use a simple tool that we call the Four Quadrants of Qualitative Text Complexity (see Table 5.1) to help us determine qualitative complexity. At any given grade level, most texts will be complex in one or more of the following areas: meaning, structure, language features, and knowledge demands.[2] These "Four Quadrants" help us assess the specific ways in which a text is complex. Once we have determined how the text will challenge students, we can focus instruction to offer support in those areas as they read.

Table 5.1: The Four Quadrants of Qualitative Text Complexity

Meaning: Consider the layers of meaning in the text, as well as the purpose and the complexity of ideas/concepts in the text.	**Structure:** Consider the organization of the text, including factors like text features, genre, and how the ideas or events in the text build on each other to make meaning.
Language features: Consider factors like vocabulary, sentence structure, figurative language, and variety of English (e.g., dialect) used in the text.	**Knowledge demands:** Consider students' background experiences and knowledge with the topic of the text. What "outside" information or experiences will they need to understand the text?

Using the sample pages from *Come On, Rain!* in Figure 5.2, we have analyzed the text in Table 5.2 using the Four Quadrants of Qualitative Text Complexity. With this example, it becomes easier to see how the complexities within a *particular* text emerge by looking closely at these qualitative factors.

---

[2] These four factors are derived from Appendix A of the Common Core State Standards.

Figure 5.2 Sample Pages from Come On, Rain!

Source: From Come On, Rain! *by Karen Hesse. Text ©1999 by Karen Hesse. Illustrations ©1999 by Jon Muth. Reprinted by permission of Scholastic, Inc.*

Table 5.2: Sample Four Quadrants Analysis for Four Pages of Come On, Rain!

Meaning: The text has multiple layers of meaning. Connections between the weather and the character's activities and emotions must be inferred.	**Structure:** The storyline is clear, chronological, and fairly easy to predict. Illustrations support and enhance the reader's understanding of the story, showing characters' emotions as well as their actions and reactions.
Language features: The language includes a mix of conversational words and phrases ("Come on, rain!") and fairly abstract figurative language ("A creeper of hope circles 'round my bones.") This book uses rich, complex words and phrases with multiple meanings. The style is almost poetic. Many sentences are complex, with subordinate phrases or clauses and transition words.	**Knowledge demands:** The experience of being extremely hot and/or waiting for it to rain will be common to many readers. Some cultural elements related to living in a warm climate and living in a city may be unfamiliar to students, but most important context is available through the text and illustrations.

Cont.

WHAT ABOUT READER AND TASK CONSIDERATIONS?

With the reader and task layer of determining text complexity, we consider what students are being asked to do with the text, as well as the potential needs of specific groups of learners. What is the purpose of the text in this module? What are students being asked to do? How much support is provided in working with this text? What experiences have students had that might make working with this text easier (or more difficult)?

Once a text has been chosen, "Reader and Task" is the area over which we have the most control. In our curriculum, challenges that emerge when we analyze a text using the Four Quadrants of Qualitative Text Complexity are always addressed by the instruction and tasks we plan. Considerations about what may make a particular text challenging for certain groups, such as English language learners (ELLs) or students whose life experiences make the content or context of a text unfamiliar (like students who live in rural areas in the case of *Come On, Rain!*), are addressed either within the design of the task itself or in the Teaching Notes that accompany the lesson.

▷ Students deserve to read beautifully written and worthy texts. If it is literature, let it be great literature. If it is informational text, let it teach students new words and new ideas in sophisticated ways. Let it, always, be worth their time and effort to read.

WHY ALL THE FUSS OVER TEXT COMPLEXITY?

The end goal is for students to be prepared to read and learn from college-level texts when they leave high school. Therefore, the work of K–12 educators is to guide students up the ladder of complexity so that they are ready for the literacy demands of college and career when they graduate. Texts that are at the right level of complexity—taking into account both quantitative and qualitative measures as well as reader and task—are key to ensuring that students are able to meet the standards that will prepare them for life after high school.

The Common Core reading anchor standard R10 outlines this ladder of complexity explicitly. But for each grade level, reading standards 1–9 also offer signals about the complexity of the text needed to support the kind of *thinking* required by the standards. For example, CCSS RI.5.2 requires students to identify two or more main ideas in a text. This implies that the text needs to be complex enough to have two main ideas. In the younger grades, most standards require deep thinking. For this reason, a large portion of the texts used in the Module Lessons are above the quantitative complexity of text students can read themselves. It is difficult to do deep thinking with the short, controlled texts that most kindergarten and first-grade students can read on their own; therefore, much of the core instruction in Grades K–2 is done through active and engaging read-alouds with rich, complex text.

The considerations for text complexity are important. Equally important for us are the more nuanced considerations that come from looking at the quality of the texts. Students deserve to read beautifully written and worthy texts. If it is literature, let it be great literature. If it is informational text, let it teach students new words and new ideas in sophisticated ways. Let it, always, be worth their time and effort to read.

▶ How Will the Central Texts in the Module Lessons Maximize My Students' Opportunities to Meet Standards?

In our curriculum, the central text (sometimes known as the anchor text) is the centerpiece of students' reading. This text is one that all students will read in order to build content knowledge and literacy skills. "In the universe of all the rich resources students will read in a given unit, the anchor text is like the sun: All the other articles, poems, maps, charts, and other forms of text circle around this one text" (Berger, Woodfin, Plaut, and Dobbertin, 2014, p. 38). Although no single text is perfect, the following criteria and related questions helped our curriculum designers focus on the work a text needs to do and what additional texts might be necessary to fill in the gaps.

» **Content.** Is the text aligned to grade-level content standards? To what extent will this text help students learn something important and enduring about the big ideas of an academic discipline? How can the text help to build students' knowledge about the world? In a literary text, what understandings about the human experience can students draw from it? To what extent does this text provide sufficient information, so students can successfully respond to an evidence-based writing task?

Example (Grade 2): *Stone Girl Bone Girl: The Story of Mary Anning* by Laurence Anholt, the story of a little girl who became one of the world's best-known fossil hunters, offers an opportunity for students to connect with a real-life character similar in age to them as they learn about paleontology. The book weaves together science, history, and art to teach children that they are never too young to make a contribution to the world.

» **Interest.** Is the text compelling for students? Will students love digging into this text? Why? Is the text developmentally appropriate—will it sing to students of this age and background? Is it high-interest in terms of content or format? Is it particularly beautifully written or illustrated?

Example (Grade 5): *The Most Beautiful Roof in the World* by Kathryn Lasky (about rain forest researcher Meg Lowman) has rich scientific information about biodiversity and the rain forest and includes gorgeous photographs of her in the canopy and stories about her son's adventures in the rain forest that will hook kids.

» **Complexity.** Is the text appropriate in terms of qualitative and quantitative measures of complexity? What makes this text challenging? Based on qualitative measures, in what ways will the concepts, structure, language, and meaning give students something worth grappling with? Based on quantitative measures, is this text sufficiently demanding in terms of syntax and academic vocabulary? Does this text provide sufficient complexity to ensure that students have to work hard to build their literacy muscles as they work through it? How will this text be paired with others of greater or lesser complexity?

Example (Grade 5): *Esperanza Rising* by Pam Muñoz Ryan has a Lexile measure of just 750, somewhat low for fifth grade. Yet it provides quite a challenge for fifth-graders based on qualitative measures. The concepts addressed in the novel (identity formation of the main character and human rights violations experienced by migrant farm workers in the 1930s), a set of recurring metaphors that run throughout the book, and several main characters with very different perspectives make working with this text rigorous and challenging.

» **Reading standards.** Does the text offer opportunities to teach grade-level standards at a specific level of rigor? If the reading standard requires students to infer, is the text sufficiently rich to require such inferring, or are the ideas all right on the surface? If the reading standard requires students to interpret information presented visually, orally, or quantitatively, does the text include the types of diagrams and charts that would make this work possible? Usually, a complex text will provide opportunities to address many of the reading standards at once. But some texts provide a particularly elegant fit for addressing a given standard at a given grade level.

Example (Grade 1): *Birds* (*Scholastic Discover More*) by Penelope Arlon and Tory Gordon-Harris is an informational text that introduces young readers to the world of birds and is a great vehicle for addressing several Grade 1 reading standards. The text teaches interesting information about birds using rich content vocabulary (CCSS RI 1.4 *Ask and answer questions to help determine or clarify the meaning of words and phrases in a text*). The book uses text features and vivid images to support comprehension (CCSS RI.1.5 *Know and use various text features [e.g., headings, tables of contents, glossaries, electronic menus, icons] to locate key facts or information in a text*). Also, because of the way the authors present the information in the text, students are able to make connections among the ideas presented (CCSS RI.1.3 *Describe the connection between two individuals, events, ideas, or pieces of information in a text*).

» **Writing standards:** Does this text offer specific information that students can synthesize in their own written arguments, informative writing, or narrative writing? Can this text—or sections of this text—serve not only as a context for students to build knowledge, but also as an example of author's craft that students can emulate in their own writing?

Example (Grade 1): *What the Sun Sees, What the Moon Sees* by Nancy Tafuri. In Module 2, students read *What the Sun Sees, What the Moon Sees* first to more deeply understand the patterns of day and night, and then again as a mentor text to study the author's craft. Students work with one another to draft their own class poem titled "What the Moon Sees," which brings together what they have learned about the moon, its position, and what is happening to animals and people at night. Then, in the second half of the unit, students plan and write their own individual narrative poem, "What the Sun Sees," using the content from the module and concepts of craft learned from this mentor text.

▶ Using Text to Build Vocabulary

Texts of all kinds play an important role in building students' vocabulary, which is one of the highest-leverage instructional moves we can make in our effort to accelerate literacy learning and excellence for all students. Word-learning strategies transfer across content and context, and word knowledge is critical for reading comprehension. Simply put, students need to know a lot of words! In Grades K–2, they need to learn 1,000 to 2,000 words per year (Biemiller, 2010; Nagy and Anderson, 1992) to stay on track. They particularly need to learn academic vocabulary (or "Tier 2 words" such as *community* and *relate*) that they will encounter across contexts and content. (See box: Three Tiers of Vocabulary for more information about the vocabulary tiers.)

★ **Three Tiers of Vocabulary**

Tier 1: Basic Vocabulary

» Words found in everyday speech

Tier 2: Academic Vocabulary

» High-frequency words found in academic texts across a variety of domains

Tier 3: Discipline-Specific Vocabulary

» Low-frequency words specific to a particular field of study and often found in informational texts about that subject

---

Why Is Academic Vocabulary So Important?[3]

It is simple to recognize the importance of teaching discipline-related vocabulary within a particular topic of study. For example, if you and your students are studying the importance of protecting a watershed, you know that students need to know and be able to use science words such as *habitat*. But what is less clear and more central to building students' literacy skills is the need to address the academic vocabulary found in watershed-related texts. Consider the following short passage from the website of the nonprofit Center for Watershed Protection:

> "During the land development process, forests are cleared, soils are compacted, natural drainage patterns are altered, and impervious surfaces, such as roads, buildings, and parking lots, are created. These changes increase the amount of polluted runoff that reaches our local waterways. As a result, stream banks begin to erode, critical in-stream habitats are washed away or filled in with sediment, downstream flooding increases, and water becomes too polluted to support sensitive fish and bugs or recreational activities." (Center for Watershed Protection, n.d.)

To fully comprehend this passage, students must know the contextualized meaning of words like *development*, *process*, *altered*, and *sensitive* (Certainly the author of this passage does not mean to suggest the fish are crying!). These words are likely to appear again and again in different texts and across several disciplines. Knowing these "academic" vocabulary words will strongly support students as they continue to read all kinds of text. Therefore, college- and career-ready standards emphasize the teaching of Tier 2 (academic) vocabulary in addition to Tier 3 (discipline-specific) vocabulary.

"In the past, if I was reading aloud a text with complex vocabulary, I would change the vocabulary to be more 'kinder-friendly.' I thought that using complex language would only confuse my students and slow us down. However, after using the complex texts in this curriculum and seeing how my students' vocabulary has blossomed, I no longer skip tricky words. Instead, I see them as opportunities to invoke curiosity from students, ask meaningful questions, and build vocabulary."

Sara Metz
K–1 Teacher, Denver

Vocabulary learning can be incidental—the result of reading closely, using morphology, using context clues, and writing about and discussing complex texts—or it can be explicitly taught. Both are valuable in terms of addressing students' vocabulary development needs (and both are built into the design of our curriculum).

Our curriculum takes every opportunity to emphasize vocabulary; it is taught in every lesson, any time students work with text. From unpacking learning targets, to working with an Interactive Word Wall before writing, to close reading lessons, students learn strategies to explore the mean-

---

[3] This section is informed by our 2014 book *Transformational Literacy: Making the Common Core Shift with Work That Matters.*

ing of words they read and put them to use in their writing. What follows are some highlights of our approach to teaching vocabulary throughout the curriculum:

» Lessons often begin with teachers guiding students through a process of reading (or hearing read aloud) the learning targets, and then "unpacking" them. Typically this focuses on academic vocabulary related to the standards (e.g., "determine" the main idea; "build on" each other's ideas). The targets themselves serve as text and often signal how students will work with text in the lesson.

» Frequently, lessons include prompts for teachers to explicitly call students' attention to vocabulary before or during their work with the text. What follows are some questions teachers can ask themselves that influence when to explicitly teach vocabulary:

- What words are critical to students' understanding of the texts?

- What words are students likely not to know?

- Which words should I teach students before reading (be cautious here—don't rob them of the opportunity to practice learning words from context)?

- Which words can students learn by inferring from context?

- Which words present the opportunity to teach word parts (prefixes, root words, suffixes)?

- Which words can just be mentioned, and which should students store through a strategy for long-term use?

- Which words can I use to help students develop webs of word meaning (e.g., teaching the word *altered* provides the opportunity to teach *alternate* and *altercation*)?

» Students and teachers together build Interactive Word Walls of academic vocabulary (Tier 2) and domain-specific vocabulary connected to the content of the modules (Tier 3). They return to these Word Walls over and over as students read more texts and build knowledge.

» Vocabulary is always a strong component of close reading/read-alouds. The process walks students deep into text and brings their attention to the meaning of words and to questions about how individual words may affect the meaning of an entire text. (Close reading/read-aloud is the focus of Chapter 5B.)

▶▶ Video Spotlight

In the accompanying video, first-graders in Anne Simpson's class at Two Rivers Public Charter School in Washington, D.C., use the Interactive Word Wall protocol with words related to the module topic (both domain-specific and academic vocabulary). Students manipulate the words as they discuss relationships among the words and ideas. There are many ways to use an Interactive Word Wall; this video shows students doing concept mapping. First, Simpson restates the guiding question: *How does a spider use its body to survive?* She then reviews with students the purpose of concept mapping: to articulate how the words are related to each other. Next, students work in small groups, manipulating vocabulary cards and symbols (e.g., arrows, equals signs) that help convey the relationships. Simpson circulates to check for understanding, clarify misconceptions, and push student thinking. She ends the class with students reviewing other groups' concepts maps to give specific feedback on the strengths of each.

https://vimeo.com/174709417

» In Grades 3–5, students build and consistently use vocabulary notebooks and personal dictionaries based on the texts they read.

» Lessons prompt teachers to help students define words that they encounter in text based on context when possible, and to use word roots and affixes; these word-learning strategies focused on morphology become a habit for students as they progress through the year. Such practices develop a habit of mind of being "word detectives" and applying what one already knows when encountering new words.

» Writing, speaking, and listening tasks require and support students to use the vocabulary they learn based on their reading and discussions. Students engage with and apply new vocabulary in a variety of ways, which helps the meaning of words stick.

» One component of the ALL Block is designated specifically for word study/vocabulary. This often draws on text from the Module Lessons.

» In Grades K–2, teachers regularly incorporate movement into teaching vocabulary in a text (e.g., "The text says 'the rain soothed' them. Show me how it feels to be *soothed*.")

» Scaffolds for ELLs frequently help students connect new words they are learning from text, or from instruction, to words in their home language (e.g., "How would you say this word in your home language?"; "What word would you use to describe this in your home language?").

▶ How Will the Curriculum Ensure That My Students Experience a Volume of Reading With a Variety of Text Types?

New college- and career-ready standards challenge students to read complex texts to build content knowledge, literacy skills, and academic vocabulary. At all grade levels, our content-based curriculum includes one or more central texts: complex texts that all students read with support from teachers and peers. It is important that all students have access to, and support with, reading text at the appropriate level of complexity for their grade level.

But they also need to read a volume of texts—in other words, students need to read both complex text and *a lot* of text! Before focusing on complex texts in Chapter 5B, here we will focus briefly on other kinds of reading students do in the curriculum to give them the volume of reading they need at their independent reading level, which may be on, above, or below grade level. We want students to be swimming in text, in classrooms full of books, on the rug being read to, and nestled in beanbag chairs reading independently for as much time as possible during every school day. Table 5.3 summarizes the types of text found throughout the curriculum that support a volume of reading, and the purpose of each.

Table 5.3: Types of Texts throughout the K–5 Curriculum That Support a Volume of Reading

Types of Texts	Where They Live in the Curriculum	Purpose
Decodable student readers	K–2 Reading Foundations Skills Block	To offer an opportunity to apply and practice decoding skills; contain only the spelling-sound patterns and high-frequency words that students have been taught

Cont.

Types of Texts	Where They Live in the Curriculum	Purpose
Complex texts on module topic	K–5 Module Lessons K–2 Labs (Storytime) K–2 Reading Foundations Skills Block ("engagement text" read aloud to introduce decodables)	To allow students to learn and practice comprehension strategies with texts with rich content, diverse structures, and increasingly sophisticated vocabulary and syntax
Additional texts on module topic	K–5 Module Lessons	To build reading comprehension skills and knowledge on the module topic
Poems and songs	K–2 Module Lessons	To build content knowledge and fluency and to teach language standards in a meaningful context
Research texts (for independent reading on the module topic)	K–2 Labs (Research Lab) K–2 Reading Foundations Skills Block (Accountable Independent Reading) 3–5 Additional Language and Literacy Block (Accountable Independent Reading)	To build fluency, knowledge, and engagement using texts on the module topic at a variety of reading levels
Complex text aligned to the character focus of a module	K–2 Labs (Storytime)	To connect to and reinforce the habits of character or aspects of social-emotional learning students are working on (e.g., growth mindset)
Choice texts (on any topic)	3–5 Additional Language and Literacy Block (Accountable Independent Reading) K–2 Reading Foundations Skills Block (Accountable Independent Reading)	To build fluency, knowledge, and engagement using texts of the students' choice

To give students the amount of reading practice necessary, they need reading opportunities that are varied in purpose and type of text. Ensuring that students are given ample opportunity to read a variety of materials in a variety of ways increases their motivation—you will have a better chance to tap into students' interests and give them enough practice for reading proficiency to develop.

Reading development does not occur in a linear fashion, and students' reading proficiency occurs at different rates. Students need opportunities to be challenged while reading, as well as to read texts that provide for easy, fluent reading (National Governors Association Center for Best Practices, Council of Chief State School Officers, 2010). These experiences can occur when students read a range of texts within a given topic of study (e.g., Grade 3, Module 2, about frogs' adaptation). They also may occur during independent reading when students choose books based on personal interest.

Reading to Systematically Build Knowledge

Engaging students in reading a variety of texts on the module topic helps to build their knowledge of that topic and the world, as well as crucial academic vocabulary that they can carry with them to another text in the same or a different domain. This focus builds the knowledge and skills students need to read increasingly complex texts—this is content-based literacy in action.

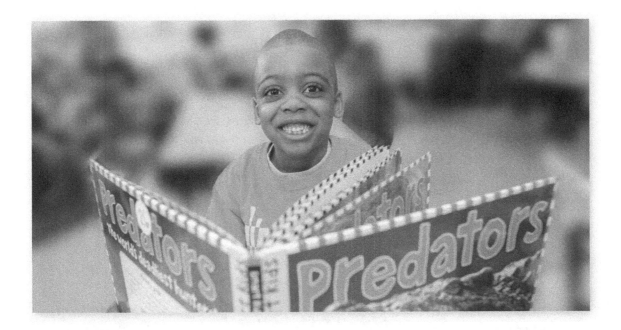

You may recall from Chapter 1 our desire to turn on the "curiosity motors" in students by systematically building their interest in compelling topics. As they are guided through experiences with texts through highly scaffolded close reading/read-alouds and delicious sets of texts that engage their hearts and their heads, they go deeper and deeper into these topics and become engaged with more and more texts. They view text as a way to learn more, to build knowledge, and to feed their growing curiosity.

Our content-based curriculum is designed to build this interest in systematic ways. Teachers generally lead students in a close reading/read-aloud of the central text early in the module to begin building background knowledge and vocabulary, and also to spark their interest for inquiry. Students then read a variety of texts to answer a guiding question and build expertise on the topic. These texts are pre-selected to complement the central text and often can be read independently or with minimal teacher support. Grappling with a variety of text types and sources pushes students to expand their vocabularies and repertoire of text structures, as well as their understanding of a topic.

Throughout the process, students write to record the information most relevant to their inquiry. They learn to organize the information they gather in journals, researcher's notebooks, and graphic organizers. Short text-based projects throughout the curriculum offer multiple opportunities for reading variety and practice with integrating content, reading, and writing. (For more on the relationship between reading and writing in the curriculum, see Chapter 6).

In the K–2 curriculum, the Research Lab provides additional time for topic-based reading and the other four Labs provide time for students to explore, engineer, create, and imagine, all related to the topic they are studying in the module. Similarly, in the 3–5 curriculum, the ALL Block allows students additional time for independent reading about the module topic.

Independent Reading

Independent reading is an opportunity for students to enlarge their world and find joy in learning new things. This may mean that students read additional texts on the topic of a module; the K–5 Recommended Text and Other Resources List provides options for the module topics at all grade levels. This also may mean that students choose books on topics of their personal interest; these books are likely to bridge a range of complexity. Both kinds of independent reading are worthy and important.

According to Clark and Rumbold (2006), "Reading for pleasure refers to reading that we do of our own free will, anticipating the satisfaction that we will get from the act of reading. It also refers to reading that, having begun at someone else's request, we continue because we are interested in it" (p. 6). New college- and career-ready standards have brought a great deal of focus to the cognitive aspects of reading: word recognition and comprehension of complex texts. It is important for us to keep in mind, however, that even if students *can* read, it does not mean they will choose to do so. Allowing students to choose texts for independent reading helps them discover what they want to read, as well as uncover new knowledge and connect with their world. Teachers and library media specialists can play a vital role in fostering a rich reading life for all students.

The curriculum's focus on content-based literacy and strategic sets of texts designed to build students' literacy muscles and knowledge of the world means that students will experience a great volume of reading in the modules. Table 5.4 describes additional structures at all grade levels to ensure that students have plenty of time to choose books at their independent reading level and experience an even greater volume of reading.

Table 5.4: Independent Reading Structures in the K–5 Curriculum

Component of the Curriculum	Independent Reading Structure
K–2 Reading Foundations Skills Block	Students work in differentiated small groups during the Skills Block. During Accountable Independent Reading, students can read decodables or something from the K–5 Recommended Text and Other Resources List (connected to the module topic), or they can try to independently read the "engagement text," which is a slightly more challenging text used in the formal lessons of the Skills Block and typically read aloud by the teacher. Teacher check-ins are built in to the structure to assess comprehension.
K–2 Labs	Starting with Module 2, students read independently during the Research Lab to build their knowledge of the module topic.
3–5 Module Lessons	Module 1 in Grades 3–5 features a kickoff for Accountable Independent Reading. Students learn the systems and structures of this program, which includes independent reading assigned almost every night for homework.
3–5 Additional Language and Literacy Block	In the ALL Block, students read every day for 20 minutes. They alternate the focus of their reading from week to week: One week is research reading on the module topic, and the next they can choose whatever they want to read for pleasure. Students keep a log of their reading.

Chapter 5B:
How Will the Curriculum Support My Students to Read Complex Texts?

Regular practice with complex text and its academic language is a big—and important—instructional shift of the new standards. We want to acknowledge from the outset, however, that reading complex text through close reading (or close read-alouds in the primary grades) is not a universally loved practice. Many teachers complain that it is tedious or boring for their students. Others feel that it is rigid and doesn't account for students' individual needs.

We hear you, and we agree that close reading/read-aloud *can* be all of those things, but it doesn't have to be and certainly shouldn't be! Close reading/read-aloud *should* be about helping students read texts that are stimulating and exciting because they are challenging and sometimes mysterious (think about the lobster text in Chapter 1, Figure 1.1) and because the texts contain information that students really want to understand. It *should* be about building students' skill to read with greater independence. Often students need help unlocking complex text because it is too complex for them to read on their own.

The purpose of close reading/read-aloud is not to march students through a tedious set of steps, but to hand over the keys so that they can unlock the texts on their own. That is the ultimate goal.

▶ Why Is Close Reading/Read-Aloud So Important for My Students?

Giving students the opportunity and the strategies to tackle complex text builds their independent reading skills and their belief in themselves as readers. And, importantly, it gives them access to the curriculum. It is difficult to build knowledge of the world—whether in first grade, twelfth grade, or college—if the ability to read and make meaning from text is a barrier.

Becoming a capable and confident reader opens many doors for students. A special educator supporting teachers using our curriculum in Cabell County, West Virginia, summed up the power of giving students the tools they need to read complex text: "They would go to their general ed. classroom, and they started participating and raising their hands. I had students actually say, 'I feel like a real fifth-grader. I'm doing grade-level work.'"

Whether students are listening to complex text read aloud or learning strategies to read complex texts on their own, we're committed to close reading because it's an effective practice that accelerates skill- and knowledge-building. As we emphasized in Chapter 5A, we certainly don't want close reading to be the only kind of reading students experience. We still want to see them

Chapter 5

nestled in beanbag chairs devouring books like *Diary of a Wimpy Kid*, and our curriculum makes plenty of room for independent reading of that nature. We also make plenty of time for research reading so that they can dig into a variety of engaging texts on their own on the topic being studied in the modules (e.g., toys in kindergarten or frogs in Grade 3).

But we also need to carve out space for students to push into new territory and build up their reading muscles. If *Diary of a Wimpy Kid* is the fifth-grade equivalent of a leisurely stroll through the park, let's be sure to vary the workout with occasional vigorous hikes with more challenging texts, such as selected articles from the Universal Declaration of Human Rights. Just like a varied physical workout is good for the body, a varied reading workout is good for the mind.

▷ ## Just like a varied physical workout is good for the body, a varied reading workout is good for the mind.

Although students don't read (or hear read aloud) complex texts every day in our curriculum, they do it frequently enough that they are able to develop a rhythm of close, attentive reading and get the "regular practice" they need. Students learn to internalize many of the strategies used while reading closely, which usually takes them back into the text over and over across multiple days. We refer to close reading "sessions" rather than close reading lessons because close reading makes up only a portion of the time over an arc of lessons (e.g., 20 minutes of a 60-minute lesson each day for five days). These "exposures" to complex text are often paired with other kinds of texts; for example, students may toggle back and forth between close reading of a complex informational text and independent reading of a related literary text that helps them make greater meaning of the complex text.

Close Reading Is an Equity Issue

Students should experience a "staircase of complexity" in the texts they read Grades K–12 so that they are prepared for college- and career-level reading by the time they leave high school. If we deny students the opportunity to learn the skills they need to read complex texts, they'll never catch up. They'll stay behind, caught in a vicious cycle. In the pages that follow, we hope you'll see that, yes, they can do it, and yes, you can help them.

We often hear a concern from teachers that the close reading of complex texts is too difficult for their students. Many find themselves "rescuing" students who struggle. This is a natural instinct, but keeping in mind our commitment to equity and excellence for all students, as well as the value of productive struggle, we encourage you to let the practice take hold and give your students a chance to surprise you.

The first key to success with close reading, for teachers, is to check in with yourself about your mindset. Do you harbor doubts that your students can read complex texts? Or, for Grades K–2, do you harbor doubts that they can do rigorous thinking about complex text that you read aloud to them (even if they can't yet read it on their own)? Do you find the prospect intimidating? Do you worry that close reading will take the joy out of reading for your students?

These are all legitimate questions, and we take them seriously. We are committed to making close reading collaborative, purposeful, and engaging for students and to helping you feel empowered with this critical literacy practice.

And, by showing you how we made decisions about the texts students read in our curriculum in Chapter 5A, we hope we have counteracted your fears that close reading means *boring* reading. Rest assured that we don't ask students to read dry texts about nothing just for the sake of reading complex texts. We chose the texts we did because they help students explore compelling topics and characters, which motivates them to persevere when the going gets tough. All students deserve this opportunity, not just those who already have strong reading skills.

▶ What Exactly *Is* Close Reading/Read-Aloud?

Close reading is a process of careful, analytical reading. It involves repeated reading, text-based discussion, and (often) written analysis of complex text. In Grades K–2, this process usually means a close read-aloud by the teacher; students draw or write simple words in response to the text, leading to full sentences and paragraphs as they move toward third grade.

At all levels, the purposes remain the same: to gain a deeper understanding and appreciation of the specific text, to build world knowledge, to learn academic vocabulary, to build analytical reading skills, and to foster perseverance and passion for deep reading of worthy texts. The close reading/read-aloud you'll find in our Module Lessons (and in one component of the 3–5 Additional Language and Literacy [ALL] Block) helps students build these skills through collaborative (and we think joyful) interaction with rich and compelling texts that help instill a spirit of courageous exploration.

▶▶ Video Spotlight

In the accompanying video, see a close reading session in action. This video is from our first-edition curriculum, so there are some elements that we have updated for our new K–5 curriculum. You will still see that teacher Kerry Meehan-Richardson, from World of Inquiry School in Rochester, New York, and her students understand that multiple reads with strategic text-dependent questions help them "conquer complex text." Meehan-Richardson is clear that she doesn't want to feed students her understanding; she wants them to construct their own (in this instance, about the scientific concept of adaptation). You will also see a nice example of how a simple protocol engages students in creating collaborative understanding of the text.

But, in hindsight, there is a bit too much focus in this lesson on "reading over and over" so students "won't forget the key details." What you will see more of in our new K–5 curriculum is an emphasis on questions driving toward a deepened understanding, with clear synthesis at the end. Look for the video on close read-alouds later in this chapter for an example that shows those details.

https://vimeo.com/89001348

What *Isn't* Close Reading/Read-aloud?

It's important to note at the outset that close reading isn't only one thing—it's not a protocol to be followed exactly every time students read complex texts. Sometimes students will need to reread (or hear read aloud) an entire text three times to unpack all of the layers of meaning. Other times, one time through the whole text is enough, with short passages chosen for further rereading. It is really the text and the task that dictate the approach in a particular close reading/read-aloud—not every text needs the same treatment. To further demystify close reading, Table 5.5 summarizes what close reading/read-aloud is and what it isn't.

Table 5.5: What Close Reading/Read-aloud Is and What It Isn't

What Close Reading/Read-aloud Is	What Close Reading/Read-aloud Isn't
A way to level the playing field by making complex text accessible to all students through carefully planned instruction	An unfair practice that forces struggling readers to read text they can't possibly understand
Exciting and enlightening, as students unlock the mystery of complex and often beautiful stories and poems, as well as rich informational text	Boring, dry, and dull
Crucial in a time when so much information is available through text and reading complex text is a prerequisite for success in college and careers	Unnecessary
A way to introduce developmentally appropriate strategies that support students in developing the kind of deep understanding of text that may have previously been available only to older students and excellent readers	A watered-down version of high school reading for younger students
A way to help students do the cognitive work of the Common Core reading standards that focus on deep comprehension (Reading: Literary Text and Reading: Informational Text)	A way to teach comprehension strategies (e.g., "asking questions" or "drawing inferences")

▶ How Is Close Reading Different with Primary Students?

Before we go on any further to describe the design of close reading/read-alouds in the curriculum, we need to pause and talk about how close reading works with students in the primary grades. Students who are still learning to crack the alphabetic code clearly won't be able to read complex texts independently. But that doesn't mean they can't think and talk about text in sophisticated ways. Many parents and kindergarten teachers, for example, read *Charlotte's Web* aloud to 5- and 6-year-olds. Children this age are unlikely to be able to read this classic on their own, but they can still do great thinking about the text.

In the curriculum, most close reading in the K–2 grade band happens through close read-*alouds*, which allow students to listen to and discuss more complex texts than they can read independently. This exposes them to more sophisticated concepts, content, academic vocabulary, and complex language than they would otherwise be able to access. As we referenced in Chapter 1B, the research tells us that, particularly for students who enter school behind in terms of their vocabulary, syntax, and world knowledge, this exposure is vital. This is why close read-alouds are an important component of Module Lessons in our K–2 curriculum. (Keep in mind that the K–2 Reading Foundations Skills Block is when K–2 students learn to crack the alphabetic code through a structured phonics program.)

Close read-alouds typically unfold over a series of short sessions (20 to 25 minutes each) that are part of the longer 60-minute Module Lesson, which includes other learning activities. Students may return to the text over the course of as many as five lessons, each time listening to parts of the text for a particular purpose. The sequence starts with students listening to the entire text read aloud without interruption, which helps them get immersed in the content and language while also modeling fluency and expression. In subsequent sessions, a focus question sets the stage for analysis of smaller chunks of text. This focus question drives inquiry across the entire series of sessions and helps students understand "why are we reading this?"

In each session, students are lifted to greater understanding of the text through purposeful text-dependent questions and activities. Keeping in mind the characteristics of primary learners, students engage with the text using a variety of modalities throughout the close read-aloud, including drama, art, movement, discussion, and writing. Students also use a variety of note-taking strategies to help them collect evidence that will enable them to answer the focus question, which may include drawing pictures or writing words to fill in sentence frames. In the final session, students synthesize their learning through a culminating writing or speaking task.

Just as with close reading in Grades 3–5, each close read-aloud in the curriculum is accompanied by a Close Read-aloud Guide. In Chapter 5C, we will walk you through a sample kindergarten close read-aloud and annotate the key components for you.

▶▶ Video Spotlight

This two-part video series features Sara Metz and her kindergarten class at Explore Elementary in Denver. Using a Close Read-aloud Guide, Metz and her students engage in analysis of the text, *Come On, Rain!*, as part of a module on the topic of weather. Sara strikes a balance of rigor and joy as she guides her students through a carefully crafted sequence of text-dependent questions that drive toward a focus question, total participation techniques to engage all learners, and a culminating task.

https://vimeo.com/213202773

https://vimeo.com/213193741

"Close read-aloud is really different from how I did read-alouds in the past because I rarely used to read a text more than once unless it was a class favorite. [I love] … diving deep into one or two high-quality, complex texts like we do now with close read-alouds. The benefit I've seen for my students is a more thorough understanding and a deeper level of text comprehension (and therefore content), which enhances their ability to ask and answer questions and engage in substantive conversations, especially my English language learners. As a result, they are better equipped to demonstrate their learning through drawing, writing, and oral language."

Sara Metz
K–1 Teacher, Denver

▶ How Are Close Reading/Read-Alouds Designed to Help My Students Build Deep Understanding and Literacy Skills?

As we have done in other parts of this book, we want to spend some time "looking under the hood" at what goes into the design of close reading/read-aloud sessions. Understanding the important decisions that go into creating these sessions will help you teach close reading/read-alouds with greater nimbleness and authority. As we stated in Chapter 1, we hope that teaching our curriculum will be its own form of professional development for you. Learning the ins and outs of these practices may positively impact the way you and your students approach reading across all subjects.

Three main ingredients contribute to the design of close reading/read-aloud sessions:

1. The first ingredient is the *text*, which must be carefully chosen so that it is at the right level of complexity for students. The close reading/read-alouds in our curriculum were designed to support students in navigating the complexities of a text, which we identified using the Four Quadrants of Qualitative Text Complexity analysis (see Table 5.1). Not every text is complex in the same ways. Once the specific complexities of a text are identified, close reading/read-alouds can be designed to address *some of* those specific complexities with students. The challenge for curriculum designers is to first identify how a particular text is complex, and then to determine which of those complexities to focus on, given the larger purpose of the module.

2. The second ingredient is the *purpose*. Why are students reading this text closely, given the larger context of the module? How will understanding this text help them understand the module topic more deeply?

3. The third ingredient is the *process* by which students read the text. "Rather than reading to merely learn 'about' the text, students must be able to read texts analytically, gathering information for a particular purpose and synthesizing it to create deeper understanding" (Berger, Woodfin, Plaut, and Dobbertin, 2014, p. 180). Along the way, students should be interacting with the text and each other to help deepen their understanding.

Close reading/read-aloud as an instructional strategy for tackling complex text will represent a shift in reading instruction for many teachers (see Table 5.6).

Table 5.6: What's In and What's Out for Teaching Complex Texts

In	Out
Regular encounters with complex texts	Leveled texts (only)
Texts worthy of close attention	Reading any old text
Mostly text-dependent questions	Mostly text-to-self questions
Mainly evidence-based analysis	Mainly opinion-based analysis
Accent on academic vocabulary	Accent on literary terminology
Emphasis on reading and rereading	Emphasis on pre-reading
Reading strategies (as a means)	Reading strategies (as an end)

The Planning behind a Close Reading/Read-aloud

Close reading sessions are like an iceberg; what the student experiences above the waterline is built on careful planning below the waterline. And, just like an iceberg, the planning and foundational work is actually much larger than the series of sessions themselves. Before students begin reading a complex text, there are many decisions to make (and remember that if you are a primary teacher, these decisions are made in the context of a close read-aloud, with your beginning readers likely acting as close *listeners*, who will often read silently in their heads as you read). As curriculum designers, the following steps were a part of our planning process:

Step 1: Evaluate the Context

» Determine the purpose for reading. What will students understand or do with the information they acquire?

» Look ahead. Where is this heading? Why do students need this information?

» What is the assessment? How will students write about what they read? What is the performance task?

» Choose compelling texts and be able to explain why a particular text was chosen.

  • What makes it worth reading?

Step 2: Analyze the Text

» What excerpts are particularly critical (in terms of the content students need to learn or make sense of)? Of those, which will need to be read slowly, deeply, more than once, and with support? (See Table 5.2 in Chapter 5A for an example of an analysis of the book *Come On, Rain!*)

» Specifically, what challenges will students need to overcome in terms of the text's meaning, requisite background knowledge, structure, and language?

» Attend to syntax and vocabulary. Determine what vocabulary students might be able to learn in context and what words will need to be defined for them.

» Should students first hear a particularly critical or difficult passage read aloud? (If so, students need to follow along.) Or can students first have a go on their own and then hear the text read aloud after?

Step 3: Prepare Questions, Engagement Strategies, and Scaffolding

» Which text-dependent questions will lead students through the text to the big ideas? The questions are really the heart of the lesson. See the "Lifting Students to Greater Understanding of the Text through a Carefully Crafted Series of Text-Dependent Questions" section later in Chapter 5B for more on text-dependent questions.

» How will students engage with the questions, the text, and each other during the close reading/read-aloud? See the "Engaging Students in Discourse about the Text" section later in Chapter 5B for more on engagement strategies.

» Are there students who will need a differentiated approach? What scaffolds can be put in place that will lift them to the text and not take away their opportunity to read and make meaning independently? See the "Supporting English Language Learners and Others Who May Need Additional Scaffolding" section later in Chapter 5B for more on scaffolding and differentiated instruction.

What Happens during a Close Reading/Read-aloud Session?

In our curriculum, we include Close Reading/Read-aloud Guides that walk you through the sequence of sessions on a particular complex text from beginning to end. These guides are backward-designed from a clear understanding of what knowledge and skills students should build as a result of reading the text and of the challenges the text presents. The primary goal of close reading/read-aloud is deep understanding of the text (or a particular part of the text) and how it relates to the module topic as a whole. Remember, we don't ask students to read closely just for the sake of reading closely; we do it to give them access to knowledge.

Close reading/read-alouds include certain elements that are the same, no matter the text:

» Setting purpose for the close reading/read-aloud (often through a focus question that drives students' thinking as they read/listen)

» Giving students an initial sense of the text through a "first read" (or read-aloud)

» Lifting students to greater understanding of the text through a carefully crafted series of text-dependent questions

» Working with vocabulary in context during close reading/read-alouds

» Engaging students in discourse about the text

» Supporting English language learners and others who may need additional scaffolding

» Synthesizing understanding of the text

Let's take a closer look at each of these elements of a close reading/read-aloud.

Setting Purpose for the Close Reading/Read-aloud

It is important for students to know why they are going to read a complex text before they begin reading it. One common misconception about close reading/read-aloud is that it is merely close reading for the sake of close reading (which implies that the purpose is only to develop a reading skill, such as annotating a text). Yet that is far from the case. Setting a greater purpose for students will engage their curiosity and their motivation. In our content-based curriculum, doing the hard work of reading a complex text is in service of building knowledge of the world. Students also learn skills (e.g., annotating), but comprehension and knowledge-building is paramount.

With their curiosity motors in high gear, we want students to be ready and willing to dig into the text. Connecting it to their desire to learn about the world is key. Think back to how the teacher introduced the lobster text (Figure 1.1) to her students in Chapter 1: "This is a great scientific paper by one of the world experts on lobsters. It has important information that will inform our study of Boston Harbor. But almost no one in the world has read it, and few people can understand it. Even your parents may not be able to understand it. Some of the teachers here may not understand it. At least not right away. But together, we can make sense of it." This teacher made an extremely complex text something these students suddenly couldn't live without reading.

In the kindergarten close read-aloud that we unpack in Chapter 5C, students begin their close read-aloud of *Come On, Rain!* with a reminder of how they have been studying weather from around the world and its impact on people. The story they are about to hear will help them learn more deeply about how the weather is affecting one place and one group of people. Two focus questions orient students to their purpose before the close read-aloud and then guide the progression of text-dependent questions and the culminating task for the whole sequence of five close read-aloud sessions with this one rich text:

» How does the heat/lack of rain affect the characters?

» How does the rain coming affect the characters?

In the fifth-grade close reading that we unpack in Chapter 5C, students pull out their copies of the Universal Declaration of Human Rights for a close reading session that helps them answer some of the central questions in the novel *Esperanza Rising*. The reason for reading the Universal Declaration of Human Rights is to know more about how the characters who they have come to care about through the novel have had their human rights threatened and how they responded to those challenges. They read to more deeply understand a complex social issue.

Giving Students an Initial Sense of the Text through a "First Read"

The first read of a complex text is almost always a read-aloud, even with older students (although sometimes in Grades 3–5, students may first read the text silently and then hear the teacher read it aloud). For this first read, teachers read the text all the way through without stopping. Despite its simplicity, the first read of a complex text is challenging for many teachers. It may require some unlearning of the way you have always done things. In the past, read-alouds have often involved frequent pauses to ask students questions about the text, to think aloud about the text, or to explain things to students: "Why do you think she said that? What do you think will happen next? How does this idea connect to what we learned yesterday? So in this part of the text, the author is really saying such-and-such." During the first read in a close read-aloud, we want you to resist this urge and to keep reading the whole piece.

There will be plenty of time for students to answer questions about the text. But the first read is not that time. It is important for students to hear the text read fluently and with expression. Hearing the text read as the author intended it to be read helps students enjoy the text, connect to its message, and get a sense of the flow and meaning of the whole piece. It's totally fine if students don't understand everything; we wouldn't expect them to. Think about the first time you read a dense poem, a contract, or an explanation of new science discoveries in a magazine or newspaper. You get something, but you know you'll need to keep digging in. The same is true with close reading/read-alouds. After the first read, subsequent close reading/read-aloud sessions devote time to helping students drill down into certain words, sentences, and paragraphs to make sense of the deeper meaning of the piece.

In the curriculum, certain texts have compelling audio files available that give students an even richer experience of the first read. Hearing Jackie Robinson read his "This I Believe" essay for NPR; or a Haitian poet read his reflection on the earthquake that destroyed his home deepens the experience for students.

Lifting Students to Greater Understanding of the Text through a Carefully Crafted Series of Text-Dependent Questions

Strong text-dependent questions are the foundation of close reading/read-alouds. The questions are not just for assessment of understanding; they ground the purpose of the reading for you and your students, they are the basis of class discussion and inquiry, and they shape how the text will be used in the lesson, including what parts of the text will be unpacked, individually and together, and to what depth. Unlike questions we often ask, this carefully crafted set of text-dependent questions is not designed to assess students' understanding of text. Instead, the questions draw attention to key ideas in the text and model strategies for unlocking meaning in complex text. The questions act as a scaffold to lift students to greater understanding of the text.

Any worthy complex text, by nature, invites many rich questions. When reading closely, it is important to ensure that the questions serve the larger purpose. When creating the text-dependent questions in close reading/read-alouds, we ruthlessly prioritized; we sought not to distract students (or teachers) with questions that would send them on tangents. Where is it crucial to slow down and take more time with a sentence? What concepts, themes, and issues are most important? What vocabulary and language learning is best served by the piece?

It is important to help students move through the text in a logical sequence; the series of questions should help students build a holistic understanding of the text, rather than creating a fragmented experience (another reason it is important that students read/hear the entire text first). (Note, however, that sometimes the lesson focuses students on just selected passages, not an entire text.) The best questions span a range of complexity, including concrete questions of recall and basic understanding, as well as questions that require critical thinking: inference, analysis, application, and transference. In practice, the questions are generally not planned in a simple sequence of increasing complexity; instead, purpose and understanding shape the order of questions used for discussion or written prompts. The challenges of making meaning within the text itself, rather than the specific standards to "cover," drive the sequence of questions, though typically a strong sequence of text-dependent questions will inherently hit many of the reading standards.

QUESTIONS AS A TOOL FOR ANALYSIS OF TEXT

As the name suggests, text-dependent questions must drive students back to the text, requiring them to read and often reread the specific text closely to answer them. Although questions must require analysis of the text and compel students to focus sharply on the language of the text itself, students may inevitably connect the text to their own experience, background knowledge, and other texts they have read. Indeed, this is how readers integrate new texts into what they already know to expand their schema for understanding the world.

Text-dependent questions should require students to look sharply and analytically at the text itself—not just the general ideas in the text, but the specific structure, language, and meaning of the text and the decisions that the author made to use particular words, phrases, and images. The questions can require students to make connections to broader themes, current issues, and even personal experiences but are always strongly grounded in the text itself. One simple test for whether a question is text-dependent: Would students need the text in hand, and eyes on the text, to answer it? If not, the question may be "about" the text but not "dependent on" the text. Typical text-dependent questions ask students to perform one or more tasks, which are highlighted with examples in Table 5.7.

Table 5.7: What Is the Work Text-Dependent Questions Ask Students to Do?

Task	Example
Paraphrase to convey basic understanding	In Grade 4, Module 3, as students read a text about the American Revolution: "How would you say the sentence 'Boston was the center of opposition to Britain's tax policies' in your own words?"
Analyze paragraphs sentence by sentence and analyze sentences word by word to determine the role played by individual paragraphs, sentences, phrases, or words	In Grade 5, Module 3, as students read Jackie Robinson's "This I Believe: Free Minds and Hearts at Work" essay: "In Paragraph 7, what two words repeat throughout this paragraph?" (*I believe.*) Students are invited to underline the things the author says he believes in, clarifying word meanings as needed (*human race, warm heart, man's integrity, goodness of a free society, that society can remain good only as long as we are willing to fight for it.*)
Probe each argument in an opinion/argument text, each idea in informational text, and each key detail in literary text, and observe how these build to a whole	In Grade 1, Module 2, students explore why authors write about the sun, moon, and stars. They engage in a close read-aloud of *Summer Sun Risin'*. In the final session, they review what happened in the beginning, middle, and end of this narrative. Then they consider two big questions: 1. "What is this story mostly about?" (*the boy and his day and what he and his family do; the sun and how it moves across the sky during the day*) 2. "What are the big ideas we learned from reading this story?" (*The boy and his family did certain things when the sun was in certain places in the sky.*)

Cont.

Task	Example
Note and assess patterns and structures in a text and what they mean; to illuminate these patterns, close reading/read-alouds often incorporate anchor charts	In kindergarten, Module 1, students consider what toys others prefer and why. They participate in a close read-aloud of *Have Fun, Molly Lou Melon,* in which Molly Lou's grandma talks about toys from long ago, and then Molly Lou creates her own versions of those toys. During each session of the close read-aloud, students are encouraged to notice this pattern in the structure of the text, considering: "What did grandma say?" "What does Molly Lou Melon do?" (see an example of this anchor chart on the next page). This leads to an understanding of the central message of the book, that fancy toys aren't needed to have fun.
Question why authors choose to begin and end when they do	In the same kindergarten close read-aloud of *Have Fun, Molly Lou Melon,* students notice that Molly Lou and her friend Gertie are looking up at the sky and imagining various shapes. Early in this session, the teacher asks some basic comprehension questions about this chunk of the text: "What do Molly Lou and Gertie see in the sky? Use pictures and words to help you." (*a butterfly, penguin, and refrigerator*) Then the teacher probes: • "Do Molly Lou and Gertie see a real butterfly, penguin, and refrigerator? Share your idea with a partner." (*Molly Lou and Gertie used their imaginations.*) • "How does this part of the text show you how Gertie has changed?" (*Gertie is not watching TV this time. She is using her imagination to watch the clouds.*) The teacher then reads the last two sentences aloud and defines the word *wink.* Then she shifts to a more challenging question about author's purpose (implied) and about text structure: "Why does Molly Lou wink at the Grandma-shaped cloud?" (*to show their special secret about using imagination to play*). This series of questions helps students notice that the author chose to end the story in a way that shows that Molly has learned the power of imagination from her grandma.
Consider what the text leaves uncertain or unstated	In Grade 4, Module 1, students closely read Robert Frost's poem "Stopping by Woods on a Snowy Evening." They consider what they know about the narrator in the poem (*the narrator has a horse and has stopped between the woods and a frozen lake*) and what is not as clear (*why the narrator has stopped*) and discuss the impact this has on the reader.

Working with Vocabulary in Context during Close Reading/Read-alouds

As we have emphasized, teaching vocabulary extends far beyond close reading/read-alouds; we take every opportunity to build students' vocabulary banks (see Chapter 5A for a fuller description of the various ways vocabulary is taught). Specifically during close reading/read-alouds, we focus on key vocabulary, often toggling between instances when we need to define a word for students, if it can't be figured out in context, and instances when we ask students to grapple with the meaning, based on context, morphology, or past learning. This toggling also supports the pacing requirements of the curriculum. In the annotated lessons in Chapter 5C, you will see plenty of examples of this dance, back and forth, between helping students figure out vocabulary on their own and providing definitions when necessary.

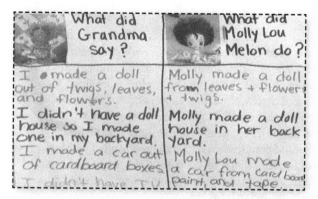

Anchor charts like this one from kindergarten, Module 1 are almost always structured to help students notice patterns in a text.

Vocabulary is often the subject of text-dependent questions. Exploring the meaning of words is one way to help students be evidence-based readers—by understanding the meaning of a word and how it affects the meaning of a piece overall or by exploring an author's choice to use a particular word, students are pushed to comprehend a text based on what the text actually says. In a progression of text-dependent questions, vocabulary is often a low-stakes place to start, to warm students up to looking closely at the text before they move on to syntax and structure and toward the big questions of the themes and central ideas of a text.

Engaging Students in Discourse about the Text

Text-dependent questions are not necessarily answered by students putting pencil to paper in order to independently answer each question or by teachers asking the class and calling on students ready to answer. You will find that at all grade levels, all close reading/read-alouds are designed so that students engage in some kind of discourse about the questions in each session. Often brief protocols, like Back-to-Back and Face-to-Face, are used as the structure for that discourse.

Brief protocols that have the same purpose as total participation techniques (i.e., to get all students thinking and talking) are used frequently to engage *all* students in responding to text-dependent questions. What follows are a few common brief protocols used during close reads/read-alouds in the curriculum:

» Think-Pair-Share: This protocol promotes productive and equitable conversations in which all students are given the time and space to think, share, and consider the ideas of others. It ensures that all students simultaneously engage with the same text or topic, while promoting synthesis and the social construction of knowledge.

» Back-to-Back and Face-to-Face: This protocol provides a method for sharing information and gaining multiple perspectives on a topic through partner interaction. It can be used for reviewing and sharing academic material, as a personal "ice breaker," or as a means of engaging in critical thinking about a topic of debate.

» Pinky Partners: This protocol is a fun way for students to find a partner to engage with concerning a question. They raise their pinky in the air and find another student to link pinkies with.

▶▶ Video Spotlight

In the accompanying video, primary students learn and practice the Think-Pair-Share protocol, which is a simple way for all students to get a chance to think, talk, and learn from others. Students first practice with an easy question from personal experience, and then move on to one that is text-based. This video is narrated by students and can be shown to students to help them learn this simple routine for productive conversations.

https://vimeo.com/164455361

Brief protocols like these promote greater engagement from students. They are also highly supportive for English language learners (ELLs) or for those who might struggle with complex text. Close reading/read-aloud is by design highly scaffolded and supportive, as students move slowly and deliberately through text. And the use of brief discussion protocols gives them plenty of opportunities to talk about the text with their peers, which helps students to solidify their understanding of vocabulary, syntax, and meaning and to articulate their ideas.

Note that more in-depth protocols, such as Science Talks or Socratic Seminars, may be used to bring students deeper and deeper into a text; however, these protocols are not frequently used during close reading/read-alouds. This is because protocols are designed so that teachers can use them with *any* text. And because close reading/read-alouds are *text-specific*, asking students to look closely at words and sentences in the text itself, protocols may be a useful early step but overall have more limited use. (Note: More in-depth protocols will be explored in Chapter 6 when we explore the read-think-talk-write cycle.)

In addition to brief protocols and total participation techniques, there are myriad other ways to increase students' engagement with complex text. Many of these are suggested in the Close Reading/Read-aloud Guides. Others you may choose to add based on the needs of your students.

» Movement: Physically "showing" understanding of vocabulary words (e.g., "show me *slither*"), circulating to analyze text excerpts or images, standing in groups to chart their analysis of the text

» Drama or role-play: Acting out events or ideas in a text in small groups or as a class

» Physical manipulation of text: Manipulating excerpts of the text (e.g. mystery quotes, sorting evidence into more or less relevant)

» Sketching: Making a quick drawing to show a key idea in the text or communicate ideas

» Annotating text: Writing in the margins or placing a sticky note with a note or visual to answer a question or explain the gist of a section of text

» Text-coding: Using symbols to indicate reactions to the text (e.g., a question mark for questions, a check mark for connections)

» Color-coding: Using various colors to indicate different aspects of a text's structure (e.g., highlighting key details in yellow or painting the focus statement in a model essay green)

Close reading/read-aloud will be a challenge for many students. It is rigorous cognitive work. There are a few things about the design of our close reading/read-aloud sessions that will help make these important literacy-building experiences effective and engaging for all of your students:

» Students are reading compelling and worthy texts that they will *want* to dig into.

» The sessions are short (20 minutes), and they don't happen every day.

» Students are not just reading independently, they are talking to each other and, especially with primary-age students, they are drawing, role-playing, and otherwise creatively and actively interacting with the text.

» The questions and activities in the close reading/read-aloud represent a line of inquiry that leads students to an understanding of the text most would not have come to on their own. Close reading offers *all* students access to the kind of experience those of us who love to read often take for granted. For many, this will be the first time they know the excitement and satisfaction of unlocking the deeper meaning and beauty of the words on a page.

Supporting English Language Learners and Others Who May Need Additional Scaffolding

Although close reading/read-alouds can seem intimidating to students because of the complexity of the text, the design of close reading/read-aloud sessions in our curriculum is actually quite supportive of ELLs and students who may struggle with reading. Because students are walked carefully through text, slowly and deliberately parsing words and unpacking layers of meaning, they learn essential reading strategies and have opportunities to build knowledge of the world.

Though the texts are challenging, the process of close reading/read-alouds, which happen regularly at all grade levels in the curriculum, gives students who may need additional support with reading new skills and strategies for tackling complex text. For ELLs in particular, this practice also honors the fact that though they may be learning a new language, ELLs deserve access to challenging texts and sophisticated ideas.

▷ Close reading offers all students access to the kind of experience those of us who love to read often take for granted. For many, this will be the first time they know the excitement and satisfaction of unlocking the deeper meaning and beauty of the words on a page.

PLANNING APPROPRIATE SCAFFOLDS

Like everything you do in the classroom, close reading/read-aloud sessions, which typically span three to five lessons, will require planning and forethought to meet the needs of your diverse group of learners. Because these sessions are designed to challenge students with complex texts, it is important that all students read the *same* challenging text. With that in mind, scaffolding strategies can then be applied to lift all students to the text, though we offer a word of caution when applying them: It is important not to *over-scaffold* the reading experience for students. Too much front-loading will take away their opportunity to figure things out on their own.

The curriculum already offers you many specific scaffolds, which you can find in the following sections of Module Lessons: Teaching Notes; Supporting English Language Learners; Universal Design for Learning; and Meeting Students' Needs. Taking the time to read and understand the lesson well ahead of time so that you can see how scaffolds are intentionally woven into the close reading/read-aloud will help you avoid too much front-loading. Among the suggested scaffolds, you will find some that should happen before the lesson and some that should happen during the lesson. The list of options in Table 5.8 should help you understand the types of supports you'll find in close reading/read-aloud sessions, as well as additional strategies you might consider to meet your particular students' needs.

Table 5.8: Scaffolding Options for Close Reading/Read-alouds

	Scaffolding Options
Lesson calls for reading chunks of the text independently	» For students who might get overwhelmed by seeing the whole text on a page, format the text in "bite size" pieces (e.g., one paragraph at a time on index cards or one page as a separate handout). » Have students read with a buddy. » Have small groups read with you or another teacher (or via technology). » Provide structured overviews for some sections of text. » Reformat texts to include more embedded definitions or even picture cues. » Provide the text to students in a clear format, either on a handout or displayed clearly via technology. » Though Grades K–2 students will not be reading the text independently during close read-alouds, it is still important to chunk the text for them to follow along with as you read. These chunks of text should be displayed for all to see or students should have their own copies.
Lesson calls for answering questions	» Start with concrete text-dependent questions before moving to the abstract. » Tackle small sections at a time. » Once students have tried the task, provide additional modeling for those who need it. » Provide sentence stems or frames. » Highlight key ideas/details in the text. » Modify graphic organizers to include picture cues or additional step-by-step directions. » Post directions and anchor charts. » Provide "hint cards" that give students more support with text-dependent questions (students access these only when they get stuck). » Indicate where students may find key information in the text or on an anchor chart by marking with sticky notes or highlights. » Give options for responding to questions with drawing, drama, or discussion before writing. » Make time for guided work with the teacher.
Lesson calls for writing	» Modify graphic organizers to include picture cues or additional step-by-step directions. » Provide sentence starters and sentence frames. » Use discussion, including Conversation Cues, to help students orally rehearse their answers before responding in writing. » Model writing using a similar prompt or a different section of the text. » Make time for small group guided work with the teacher. » Make time for more frequent conferring.

Cont.

Chapter 5

	Scaffolding Options
Lesson calls for collaborative work	» Review norms for collaboration in advance and after group work. » Have small groups work with a teacher. » Form heterogeneous pairs (strategic partnerships). » Monitor specific students more strategically (e.g., seat them closer to a teacher). » Provide (and model) structured roles for group members.
Other literacy or intervention time	» Offer additional practice with fluency (e.g., oral reading, speaking with expression) and grammar rules. » Offer additional writing practice. » Offer additional work with structured phonics. » Pre-read with students the text used in the Module Lesson. » Have students read additional (easier) texts on the same topic or theme. » Have students reread texts used in Module Lessons. » Provide additional quality read-alouds, including via technology. » Pre-teach critical vocabulary. » Engage students in word study (e.g., structural analysis of specific words from the text).
Homework	» Provide students with read-alouds via technology (e.g., audiobooks). » Provide picture cues or additional directions. » Provide sentence starters or sentence frames. » Provide video or slides of class examples on a website. » Modify expectations of quantity.

Synthesizing Understanding of the Text

As a bookend to setting purpose at the start of the close reading/read-aloud, students also need an opportunity to synthesize their understanding of the text once they are done. Often a short writing task or, in Grades K–2, a "culminating task" gives students a chance to step back to think about what they understand about the text.

In the kindergarten close read-aloud example we unpack in Chapter 5C, the culminating task is directly related to the focus questions that set purpose for the five close read-aloud sessions:

» How does the heat/lack of rain affect the characters?

» How does the rain coming affect the characters?

Students complete an independent writing task in which they draw a picture and write a word in a box about how a character feels before and after the rain. In the fifth-grade close reading we unpack in Chapter 5C, students synthesize their understanding of the text by writing on their note-catcher what nickname they would give to the article of the Universal Declaration of Human Rights they read to help them remember its main idea.

Synthesizing their understanding of a text at the conclusion of a close reading/read-aloud is a form of debrief that not only builds students' understanding of the module topic, but also builds their capacity to track and take ownership of their learning. And, connecting the synthesis to the purpose for reading set out at the beginning of the close reading/read-aloud deepens students' motivation to dig into challenging texts.

Chapter 5C:
What Does Close Reading/Read-Aloud Look Like in Action?

Module Lessons that include close reading feature Close Read-aloud Guides (Grades K–2) or Close Reading Guides (Grades 3–5), which are found in the supporting materials of the first lesson of the particular close reading sequence. Each guide walks you and your students through a complex text. Close reading/read-alouds typically make up 20 minutes of a 60-minute lesson. Lessons that include close reading/read-alouds will look like typical lessons, but when it's time for the close reading/read-aloud, you will be directed to the supporting materials for the Close Reading/Read-aloud Guide.

Here in Chapter 5C, we unpack and annotate two lessons that include close reading/read-aloud—one for kindergarten and one for fifth grade. In each case, we will start by orienting you to the entire 60-minute lesson and then zoom in on the Close Reading/Read-aloud Guide. Throughout, we will draw your attention to instructional strategies that are described previously in this chapter or previous chapters.

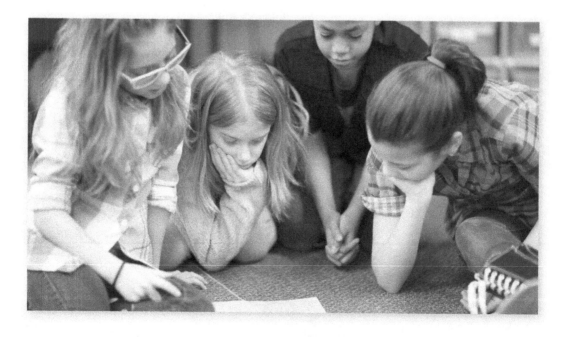

▶ Sample Lesson 1

Grade K: Module 2: Unit 2: Lesson 7

Lesson Title: Reading, Writing, and Speaking: Close Read-aloud, Session 2, and Coloring Carefully in Weather Journals

Examining a Close Read-aloud for *Come On, Rain!*

Let's look "under the hood" and examine a kindergarten close read-aloud. The series of five 20-minute close read-aloud sessions that span Lessons 6–10 in Module 2, Unit 2, supports students in deeply understanding the central text, *Come On, Rain!* by Karen Hesse in a unit about weather. *Come On, Rain!* is a narrative text about a little girl, Tess, who is waiting for rain to come on a hot summer day. The book contains rich descriptive and figurative language and vivid illustrations that support the meaning of the text with detailed depictions of how the weather affects the lives of the main characters.

In the lessons preceding work with this text, students read the picture book *On the Same Day in March* and considered how different kinds of weather affect people around the world. In *Come On, Rain!,* students read about local weather and its effects on a particular family. Through the close read-aloud, students strengthen their ability to understand and converse with their peers about the text as they hear it read aloud multiple times and engage actively with it through the use of a Before the Rain anchor chart, After the Rain anchor chart, and text-dependent questions. At the end of the close read-aloud, students participate in a culminating task by completing the Before and After the Rain response sheet. On this sheet, students draw and write to show how one of the main characters, Mamma, feels and acts before and after the rain.

(Note: This close read-aloud (all five sessions) is featured in the two-part video featured in Chapter 5B: Close Read-aloud in the Primary Grades).

Agenda

1. **Opening**

   A. Engaging the Learner: Making a Rain Shower Activity (5 minutes)

2. **Work Time**

   A. Close Read-aloud, Session 2: Come on, Rain!, Pages 1–6 (20 minutes)

   B. Independent Writing: High-Quality Work in Weather Journals (20 minutes)

3. **Closing and Assessment**

   A. Pair-Share: Weather Journals (10 minutes)

   B. Reflecting on Learning (5 minutes)

How Is the Close Read-aloud Integrated within the Lesson?

Close read-alouds are embedded within lessons. The agenda for the lesson shows where the close read-aloud we are using as an example fits within this particular lesson.

We'll start with the full lesson. As you review the lesson, notice how the close read-aloud of *Come On, Rain!* integrates with other parts of the lesson to build knowledge and understanding about weather. As you orient to this lesson, which includes a close read-aloud, it may help you to go back to Chapter 3B and refresh your memory regarding some of the high-leverage instructional practices used in the curriculum to empower students to own their own learning (Table 3.1 in Chapter 3B offers a useful summary). You will see many of those practices in the lesson that follows.

Note: We have excluded the prefatory material for this lesson, such as the Teaching Notes and materials list; instead, we start with the Opening section and go through the Closing and Assessment section. Immediately following the main lesson, we begin unpacking and annotating the Close Read-aloud Guide.

Lesson 7: Reading, Writing, and Speaking: Close Read-aloud, Session 2 and Coloring Carefully in Weather Journals

Opening

A. Engaging the Learner: Making a Rain Shower Activity (5 minutes)

▪ Invite students to stand in a spot around the edge of the whole group gathering area. As needed, remind students to move safely and make space for everyone.

▪ Review the definition of shower (a period of rain that lasts a short time), reminding students that they made a rain shower with their bodies in the last lesson. Today they get to do it again!

▪ Ask:

"In Come On, Rain! what is Tess waiting for?" (rain, a rain shower)

Select a few students to come to the middle of the circle and model the motions as you perform them together.

▪ Before beginning, make sure the class is quiet.

▪ Initiate the process, taking 10–15 seconds for each step:

1. Rub your fingers together softly.

2. Rub your hands together, continuing to make a soft sound.

3. Clap your hands softly.

4. Snap your fingers (if students struggle to snap, hitting their thumb and forefingers together also works well).

5. Clap your hands again, a bit more loudly.

6. Slap your thighs with both hands.

7. Slap your thighs and stomp your feet.

8. Reverse this process until the class is quiet and still again.

Refocus students whole group.

Work Time

A. Close Read-aloud, Session 2: Come on, Rain!, Pages 1–6 (20 minutes)

▪ Direct students' attention to the Unit 2 Guiding Questions anchor chart and read the second question aloud:

"How does weather affect people?"

▪ Review the definition of affect (to cause a change in). Remind students that the weather might affect the clothing people wear, the plans people make, or how people travel from one place to another.

▪ Invite students to turn and talk to an elbow partner:

"What is one way that the weather affected you today?" (Responses will vary, but may include: how students traveled to school, what clothing students wore, or what plans students made)

Chapter 5 *(side tab)*

Lesson 7 (side tab)

Activating schema: The teacher activates students' background knowledge with a brief review question.

Characteristics of primary learners: The "make a rain show" honors the characteristics of primary learners. Students learn through play, rhythm, and their bodies as they simulate the sounds of a rain shower (by rubbing their hands together, snapping, clapping, and stomping their feet).

Setting purpose: The teacher connects this text to the broader module topic and guiding question.

Note: Lessons are for example only. They may look different than actual curriculum materials.

- Refocus students whole group and select a few students to share out.

- Share that the two main characters in the text Come On, Rain! are also affected by the weather.

- Direct students' attention to the posted learning targets and read the first one aloud:

  "I can describe how the hot, dry weather affects Tess and Mamma in the text Come On, Rain!"

- Above the target, draw a simple picture of a mouth over the word describe, a sun over the words hot and dry, and two stick figures over the words Tess and Mamma.

- Using a total participation technique, invite responses from the group:

  "How do these pictures help us understand this learning target?" (The pictures mean students will talk about the hot, dry weather and Tess and her mamma.)

- Invite students to take out their magic bows and take aim at the target while you recite the "Learning Target" poem aloud.

- Guide students through the close read-aloud for Come On, Rain! using the Close Read-aloud Guide: Come On, Rain! (Session 2; for teacher reference). Consider using the Reading Literature Checklist during the close read-aloud (see Assessment Overview and Resources).

- Refer to the guide for the use of the Before the Rain anchor chart.

Meeting Students' Needs

- When preparing students for the close read-aloud, provide options for physical action and sensory input by differentiating seating. Some students might benefit from sitting on a gym ball, a move-and-sit cushion, or a chair with a resistive elastic band wrapped around the legs. (MMAE)

- For ELLs: Practice using the present simple tense for habitual actions using the verb affect. Invite students to share about when the weather affects them using the sentence frame: "The weather affects me when ____." (it snows and I need to wear boots; it is hot and I feel like swimming; it rains and I don't want to get out of bed)

Work Time

B. Independent Writing: High-Quality Work in Weather Journals (20 minutes)

- Remind students that in the last lesson, they recorded the daily weather on their own. Today they will complete this task again.

- Direct students' attention to the posted learning targets and read the second one aloud:

  "I can use high-quality words and pictures to describe what I observe about the weather."

- Invite students to take out their imaginary bows and take aim at the target.

- Direct students' attention to the High-Quality Work anchor chart and define:

  – quality (degree of value or excellence)

  – excellent (extremely good)

- Share that high-quality work means work that is excellent, or extremely good. It is work that students would be proud to share with others. Tell students that since they completed a weather journal page in the previous lesson, now they will complete one again and focus on

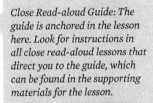

Unpacking learning targets: The teacher unpacks the first learning target to engage students in knowing where they're headed with their learning, uses pictures to give all students access, and uses a total participation technique to engage all learners.

Close Read-aloud Guide: The guide is anchored in the lesson here. Look for instructions in all close read-aloud lessons that direct you to the guide, which can be found in the supporting materials for the lesson.

Meeting Students' Needs: Multiple means of action and expression supports ELLs to focus on language acquisition (present simple tense verbs).

Unpacking learning targets: After the close read-aloud, students engage with the second learning target. Introducing one target at a time helps students focus on that target for a chunk of the lesson.

Characteristics of primary learners: In addition to unpacking the target to make sure all students know what they're aiming for, students literally and playfully "take aim."

Chapter 5

Note: Lessons are for example only. They may look different than actual curriculum materials.

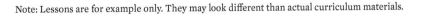

making the work look really excellent, or high-quality.

▪ Referring to the High-Quality Work anchor chart again, read the first criterion aloud:

"Color carefully."

▪ Repeat the word carefully, inviting students to listen for a word they know inside of the word.

▪ Ask:

"What word do you hear inside the word carefully?" (care, careful)

▪ Share that carefully means you take care, or are careful, in your work.

▪ Using a total participation technique, invite responses from the group:

"What do you think it looks like to color carefully?" (color inside the lines, fill the space with color, choose colors that show what something really looks like)

"Why do you think 'color carefully' is a criterion of high-quality work?" (It is listed because coloring neatly makes your work look excellent, or extremely good.)

▪ Display the Weather Journal: Page 2 Model and Weather Journal: Page 2 Non-Model side by side.

▪ Invite students to compare the model and the non-model.

▪ Pointing to the non-model, ask:

"What do you notice about this weather journal?" (The coloring is messy; it doesn't look neat or good; the colors are out of the lines; the colors don't look like the real thing.)

▪ Pointing to the model, ask:

"What do you notice about this weather journal?" (The coloring is neat; it looks good; the colors are in the lines; the colors look like the real thing.)

▪ Share that today students will again complete Steps 1 and 2 of page 2 of the weather journal. Today the challenge is to color carefully in Step 1.

▪ Display page 2 of the weather journal.

▪ Model completing Step 1:

1. Read the sentence aloud: "Today the weather is _____."

2. Choose one weather picture, looking outside to observe the weather. (Example: "The sky is bright blue today. I'll choose sunny.")

3. Color the selected weather picture using a crayon. Choose an appropriate color (e.g., yellow for a sun) and color inside the lines, filling the space with color.

4. Read the completed sentence aloud. (Example: "Today the weather is sunny.")

▪ Model completing Step 2:

1. Read the sentence aloud: "It is _____ outside."

2. Think aloud about a word that describes the weather. (Example: "I remember on the way to school, it felt windy so I put my hat on. It is windy outside.")

3. Write the word, saying the sounds aloud as you record them. (Example: "w-i-n-d-y")

4. Read the completed sentence aloud. (Example: "It is windy outside.")

▪ Point out the pencils, crayons and weather journals at students' workspaces. Invite them to turn to page 2 and begin working on Step 1.

▪ Give students 5–7 minutes to work on page 2 of their weather journal. As they work, circulate and engage with them about their work. Reread the sentence frame in Step 2 and refer students to the Weather Word Wall as needed. Consider prompting students by asking:

Total participation techniques: The teacher chooses a total participation technique so that all students can think and talk about what success with the learning target will look like.

Co-constructing anchor charts: Students work with the teacher to create a new anchor chart, defining key terms (e.g., quality) and identifying the first criterion of their own high-quality work: "color carefully."

Sentence frames: The teacher models each step of the writing, using sentence frames to scaffold student thinking.

Classroom resources: The teacher refers students to the Weather Word Wall to help them apply what they learned from their reading (knowledge and vocabulary) to their writing.

Note: Lessons are for example only. They may look different than actual curriculum materials.

"Can you show me how you color carefully?"

"What color would be the best to use for this picture?"

"Why did you choose this picture/word to describe today's weather?"

"Could you read your sentence aloud to me?"

▪ After 5–7 minutes, signal students to stop working through the use of a designated sound, such as a chime or whistle. Model cleanup, keeping directions clear and brief. Invite students to walk safely to the whole group gathering area, bringing their weather journals with them for the Closing.

> *Questioning: Prompts are included (e.g., "What color would be the best?") to help students continue to focus on today's criterion for quality work (color carefully).*

Meeting Students' Needs

■ When modeling how to complete the journal entry, emphasize the importance of process and effort by discussing how even when you try your best to color inside the lines, you can sometimes make a mistake and that is okay. (Example: "High-quality work means that I've tried my best to color carefully. But sometimes, even when I'm being very careful, mistakes happen. I might accidentally bump the table and color outside the lines. That is okay, and my work is still good because I tried my best to color carefully.") (MME)

■ For ELLs: After defining high-quality work, ask students to put the learning target in their own words now that they know what it means to do high-quality work. (Example: I can color carefully to write about the weather today.")

■ For ELLs: While discussing Part 2 of the weather journal entry, explicitly discuss the differences between the meanings of the words. (Example: "What is the difference between cold and chilly? Who can act like they are cold? Who can act like they are chilly? If it is snowing, do you think it is just chilly, or is it cold?")

■ For ELLs: After modeling the activity, consider completing it once more as an interactive writing experience to bolster confidence before independent work.

■ For ELLs: Some students may have trouble reading their work aloud. Help them identify key elements of their journal and allow them to repeat words and phrases. (Example: "It looks like you wrote 'It is warm outside.' Watch me point to the words. It. is. warm. outside. Now you try.")

> *Meeting Students' Needs: Suggestions are offered to further check for understanding of terms and the learning target (e.g., asking students to put the learning target in their own words).*

> *Meeting Students' Needs: Suggestions to scaffold student writing by giving them oral rehearsal help students practice and elaborate on their ideas before writing them down.*

Closing and Assessment

A. Pair-Share: Weather Journals (10 minutes)

▪ Direct students' attention to the Things Meteorologists Do anchor chart.

▪ With excitement, remind students that in the last lesson they shared a weather report with a classmate like a real meteorologist! Today, they will share a report of the weather again.

▪ Direct students' attention to the posted learning targets and read the third one aloud:

"I can share a report of the weather with others."

▪ Review the definition of report (a statement or story about something that has happened).

▪ Invite students to take out their imaginary bow and take aim at the target.

▪ Referring to the Conversation Partners chart, invite students to pair up with their predetermined talking partner and sit facing one another. Make sure students know which partner is

> *Unpacking learning targets: Students again unpack the learning target "just in time" for their new chunk of learning.*

Note: Lessons are for example only. They may look different than actual curriculum materials.

...ders

Structures for collaboration: Students discuss answers to questions with a partner before sharing with the whole group. The Ways We Share Our Work anchor chart supports total participation and helps students self-manage (teachers do not have to figure out transitions every time; students know expectations).

A and which is B.

■ Direct student's attention to the Ways We Share Our Work anchor chart and briefly review it.

■ Remind students that when they share, they will share the weather like a meteorologist. (e.g., use weather words, point at the weather picture).

■ Invite a student to come to the front of the whole group and model sharing Steps 1 and 2 with the class. Give the student specific, positive feedback. (Example: "Leonor, you pointed to the weather picture while you told me what today's weather is like.")

Deepening student discourse: The teacher models how to share with each other.

■ Tell students they will now share with their partner.

  – Invite partner A to begin sharing. Remind students to make a bridge with their arms after partner A has shared.

A simple Pair-Share protocol ensures total participation.

  – As students share, circulate and offer guidance and support as necessary. Re-model reading Steps–2 aloud if necessary.

  – Refocus students whole group.

Characteristics of primary learners: Simple routines (e.g., partner A shares first) honor young learners' desire for repetition and ensure equitable participation for ELLs and other language minority students.

  – Repeat the sharing process with partner B.

  – Refocus students whole group.

Meeting Students' Needs

■ For ELLs: Introduce language to empower students to ask their partners for help if they get stuck while sharing. (Example: "I forget how to say this word. Could you please help me?")

Closing and Assessment

Habits of character: Students reflect on perseverance, the character focus for this module. Co-constructing this new anchor chart engages students in this important new concept and academic vocabulary.

B. Reflecting on Learning (5 minutes)

■ Direct students' attention to the posted Perseverance anchor chart and read it aloud while tracking the print:

  – "I challenge myself."

  – "When something is hard, I keep trying."

  – "I ask for help if I need it."

■ Explain that this is the meaning of a new character trait: perseverance.

■ Invite students to say the word perseverance aloud several times with you.

■ Define challenge (an interesting or difficult problem).

Multiple means of engagement: The use of pictures supports all learners.

■ Pointing to each corresponding icon on the Perseverance anchor chart, explain that the mountain shows a big challenge, the mountain climber shows a person who keeps going, and the helping hand picture shows someone getting help when it's needed. All are important parts of perseverance: to try challenges, to keep going, and to ask for help.

■ Share that when people show perseverance, they persevere.

■ Model using the word in a sentence: "I persevere to finish all my work."

■ Show students the Weather Word Wall card for perseverance.

Note: Lessons are for example only. They may look different than actual curriculum materials.

- Point to the picture icon and ask:

  "How does this picture show perseverance?" *(Responses will vary, depending on the picture selected.)*

- Place the Word Wall card and picture for perseverance on the Weather Word Wall.

- Invite students to turn and talk to a partner:

  "How did you persevere today when you were completing your weather journal?" *(Responses will vary, but may include: trying hard to color neatly or write a word; asking for help to locate a weather word.)*

- Provide a sentence starter:

  – "I persevered today in my work by _____."

- If needed, remind students that perseverance means when you try a challenge, you keep going or ask for help.

- Refocus the group and invite several students to share their responses. Refer to the Perseverance anchor chart (for teacher reference) as needed to help students connect their actions to the aspects of perseverance listed on the chart.

- Tell students that during the next several lessons, they will be thinking about how they and their classmates can persevere to create high-quality work.

Meeting Students' Needs

- When adding perseverance to the Weather Word Wall, customize the display by including a printed photo or photos of children in kindergarten persevering as they learn about weather. (MMR)

- For ELLs: To illustrate the meaning of perseverance, tell a story about a time when you or a student in class persevered to do something challenging. (Example: "I noticed that Kendra was having such a difficult time writing her name. She tried and tried again. She didn't think she would ever be able to do it! But guess what? She kept trying. She persevered, and now she can do it! Perseverance really helped her succeed!")

- For ELLs: Provide alternative sentence frames for discussing perseverance to illustrate different ways the word can be used in a sentence. (Examples: "I show perseverance when I _____," "I persevere to _____," and "I persevere when I _____.")

Reflection: Students reflect on perseverance and how it connects to high-quality work. This reflection supports executive function and helps students continue to internalize the habit of character that is the focus for this module.

Deepening student discourse: The teacher provides a sentence frame ("I persevered today in my work by _____") and models how to complete that frame. The Meeting Students' Needs section provides additional frames.

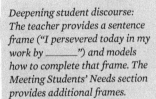

Note: Lessons are for example only. They may look different than actual curriculum materials.

Chapter 5

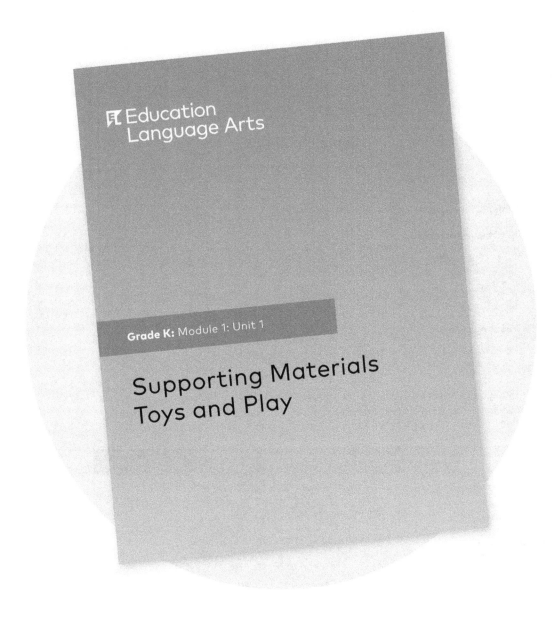

Grade K: Module 1: Unit 1

Supporting Materials
Toys and Play

The Close Read-aloud Guide

For each close read-aloud, there is a Close Read-aloud Guide (found in the Supporting Materials book for the module) that will support you as you help students move through all of the sessions, navigating the complexity of the text to form a deep and lasting understanding of both the text and the skills needed to read it. Remember that one of the main purposes of close reading/read-aloud is to help students deeply understand a text so that they can learn about the world. Like all texts in our content-based curriculum, *Come On, Rain!* was chosen to help students learn about the topic of the module, which in this case is Weather Wonders.

What follows is Session 2 of the Close Read-aloud Guide for *Come On, Rain!* In Session 1, students heard the full text read aloud, without interruption, and briefly discussed the gist of the story, identifying the setting and main characters. In this session, students begin to work through pages 1–6, a page at a time, focusing on the words used to describe the weather and on their focus question: "How does the heat/lack of rain affect the characters in the book?" This session has been annotated to highlight some of the questions and strategies to actively engage students in deeply understanding the text.

Close Read-aloud Guide

Come On, Rain!

(For Teacher Reference)

Time: 100 minutes (five 20–25 minute sessions)

Key Understanding:

- The heat and rain affect how Tess, Mamma, and the other characters feel and what they do. (Weather affects people's lives.)

- Living things (people, plants) need water to survive. Without water (in a drought), living things struggle.

Focus questions:

- How does the heat/lack of rain affect the characters?

- How does the rain coming affect the characters?

Culminating Task: This will be an independent writing culminating task. On the **Before and After the Rain response sheet**, students will draw and write to show how one of the main characters, Mamma, feels and acts before and after the rain.

Lesson 7

Chapter 5

Characteristics of primary learners: In this session, students participate actively by chorally repeating sentences in the text. Close read-alouds often incorporate movement, drama, role-play, and drawing. This allows young children to interact and make meaning of the text though a variety of modalities.

Strategic vocabulary: In this session, students are introduced to key vocabulary using their bodies. Vocabulary is selected for instruction in a close read-aloud based on two main criteria:

- *Supporting the key understanding (e.g., parched helps students understand how the hot weather affects the characters)*

- *High-leverage academic vocabulary that supports students' overall literacy development (e.g., descend helps students understand words that can be used to describe movement)*

Session 2: No Rain	
...ad	**Questions/Activities**
	• Read the sentence on page 1 aloud.
	• Reread the sentence, inviting students to join in to read the little girl's words as you read aloud ("Come on, rain").
	• Ask:
	"What does it mean to squint?" *(to partly close the eyelids)*
	• Explain that Tess, the little girl, is squinting because the sun is bright.
	• Invite students to pretend to squint while looking up at the sun.
	• Introduce the **Before the Rain anchor chart**.
	• Explain that in this text, the weather affects the characters in the story. On this chart, the class can record words the author uses to describe the hot, dry weather in the left-hand column. They can record how the weather affects what people do and how they feel when it is hot and dry in the other column.

Note: Lessons are for example only. They may look different than actual curriculum materials.

*Co-constructing anchor charts:
In this session, an anchor chart,
which is used throughout their
work with this book, helps
students record specific details
from the text to show how
the weather affects the main
characters. Anchor charts are
designed to capture students'
key understandings related to
the focus question(s). It helps
the class collect textual evidence
that students can easily access
through visuals and keywords.
Students typically reference
this chart when they do their
culminating task (written or
spoken) in the final session.*

Add "Tess squints in sun" to the How This Affects Characters column of the chart.

Before the Rain Hot and Dry	
Hot and Dry Words	How This Affects Characters
	Tess squints in sun

Read the first sentence of page 2 aloud.
Ask:

> "What has not happened for three weeks?" *(no rain)*

> "Not a drop of what?" *(rain, raindrops)*

- Explain that parched means to make very dry by heating.
Ask:

> "Why are the plants parched?" *(The plants are very dry because there has been a lot of sun or heat.)*

> "What does sagging mean?" *(to bend, to grow weak)*

> "Why is Mamma sagging?" *(the heat is making her feel weak)*

> "How do you know?" *(Mamma's shoulders are sagging in the illustration.)*

Add "parched" and "Mamma sags" to the chart.

Before the Rain Hot and Dry	
Hot and Dry Words	How This Affects Characters
Parched	Tess squints in sun **Mamma sags.**

*Text-dependent questions: In this
session, the teacher is cued to
ask text-specific comprehension
questions to ensure that students
notice and understand key details
in the story. Students are asked
to support their answers using
words and illustrations in the
book (e.g., "How do you know?").
Text-dependent questions are
designed to support the four
aspects of qualitative text
complexity:*

- *Meaning (the purpose and
complexity of ideas in the
text): Note that the structure
of the anchor chart itself helps
students notice the weather
(Hot and Dry Words) and
how that weather impacts the
characters.*

- *Structure (the organization of
the text and text structure):
"What is the weather like on
this page?"*

- *Language features (vocabulary,
figurative language, and
dialect): "'What does it mean
to squint?' Invite students to
pretend they are squinting into
the sun."*

- *Knowledge demands
(background knowledge this
text presumes readers will
possess): "Explain to students
that parched means to make
very dry by heating. Ask: 'Why
are the plants parched?'"*

Invite students to stand up and quietly show with their bodies how Mamma sags over her parched plants.
Refocus whole group.
Model a sentence frame to connect the weather to characters' actions and feelings:

- "What is the weather like on this page?"
"The weather is <u>endless heat</u> ..."

- "SO, what does Mamma do?"
"SO Mamma <u>sags</u> ..."

- "AND how does Mamma feel?"
"AND <u>feels tired</u>."

*Modeling discourse and using sentence frames: Students
are guided in constructing a sentence that summarizes
their understanding of how the weather is affecting the
characters in the book, using the new vocabulary they
are learning.*

Note: Lessons are for example only. They may look different than actual curriculum materials.

Chapter 5

Chunking complex text: Students work through this text one page at a time.

Lesson 7

Chapter 5

- Read the first section of page 3 aloud.
- Read the sentence "I am sizzling like a hot potato" aloud.
- Ask:

  "What does sizzling mean?" (the crackling sound of hot oil)

  "Is Tess really making a crackling sound?" (no)

  "What do you think Tess means when she says she is sizzling like a hot potato?" (She is really hot, like a cooked potato.)

- Read the rest of page 3 aloud.
- Ask:

  "What is Mamma wearing?" (a straw hat)

  "Why do you think she is wearing a straw hat?" (It's sunny and hot.)

- Ask:

  "What should we add to the chart?" (add "sizzling" and "Mamma wears a hat" to the chart)

Before the Rain Hot and Dry	
Hot and Dry Words	How This Affects Characters
Parched **Sizzling**	Tess squints in sun Mamma sags. **Mamma wears a hat.**

Page 4	<ul><li>Read the first sentence on page 4 aloud.</li><li>Reread the phrase "cats pant" and explain that to pant means to breathe in quick, short breaths. Cats and dogs pant when they are hot and need to cool down.</li><li>Invite students to pretend to pant like a dog or cat. Add "pant" to the chart.</li></ul>

Characteristics of primary learners and ongoing assessment: Students use their bodies to show their understanding of the text and of new vocabulary. Observing students also offers an opportunity for informal assessment.

Before the Rain Hot and Dry	
Hot and Dry Words	How This Affects Characters
Parched Sizzling **Pant**	Tess squints in sun Mamma sags. Mamma wears a hat.

- Reread the second section of page 4 aloud: "Not a sign of my friends Liz or Rosemary, not a peep from my pal Jackie-Joyce."

- Ask:

  "Why do you think her friends are quiet and not outside playing?" (too hot)

Note: Lessons are for example only. They may look different than actual curriculum materials.

- Add "kids are inside/quiet" to the chart.

Before the Rain Hot and Dry	
Hot and Dry Words	How This Affects Ch
Parched Sizzling Pant	Tess squints in sun Mamma sags. Mamma wears a ha **Kids are inside/quiet**

> *Co-constructing anchor charts: Students continue to work with the teacher to record information on their anchor chart that addresses the focus question. This anchor chart allows them to see patterns and can be accompanied by pictures so that students can "read back" what the class has recorded.*

- Invite students to Think-Pair-Share with an elbow p
    "*Think back to what we have learned about the*
    What science clues make Tess believe it will rain
    (clouds rolling in, gray clouds, purple sky)

    "*How do you know?*" *(illustrations show gray clou*
    sky)

- Read the last section of page 4 aloud.

- Invite students to join in as you read, "Come on, rc
    in a whisper voice.

- Ask:
    "*What is the weather like on this page?*" *(gray clouds,*
    clouds rolling in, hot and dry)

- Invite a student to use the frame to tell the weathe
    "*The weather is _____.*"

- Ask:
    "*So, what does Tess do?*" *(She looks for her frien*
    street, watches the sky in her neighborhood, and
    rain to come.)

- Invite a student to use the frame to tell something Tess does:
    "*So Tess _____.*"

- Ask:
    "*And how does Tess feel?*" *(excited, hopeful)*

- Invite a student to use the frame to tell how Tess feels:
    "*And Tess feels _____.*"

> *Total participation techniques:*
> - *The teacher invites students to whisper-read a key line from the text.*
> - *Students also stop to orally process with a partner at key points. Here they are also asked to draw on information previously learned in class to make an inference about the weather.*

> *Sentence frames: Sentence frames help students develop academic language and use more complex syntax. They are supportive of language development for all learners and are particularly supportive of ELLs or language minority students.*

> *Characteristics of primary learners: The close read-aloud includes repetition (e.g., using the same sentence frame taught earlier to summarize the effect of the weather on another main character).*

Note: Lessons are for example only. They may look different than actual curriculum materials.

Chapter 5

Pages 5-6	• Read pages 5–6 aloud.
	• Invite students to add words and phrases to the chart; clarify definitions as needed. (crackling-dry, stuffy)
	• Reread the line: "playing the same notes over and over"
	• Ask:
	    "How do you think the music sounds to Tess?" (boring; the same)
	
	    "Why do you think the music might sound boring?" (because Tess feels so hot and tired)
	
	• Stop reading for this session and briefly review the phrases posted on the chart.
	• Invite students to Think-Pair-Share with an elbow partner:
	    "How do the characters feel because the weather is hot and dry?" (They feel tired, bored, sad; they don't want to play outside.)
	
	    "What in the story makes you think so?" (They sag; they don't want to play outside; the music sounds boring.)
	
	• Help students use the chart and pictures in the text to support their inferences about how the characters feel.

Sentence frames: Students are invited to use the same sentence frame to deepen analysis and discourse.

Synthesis: Students go back to the focus question and summarize how the weather is affecting the main characters. They support their thinking using details from the text that have been recorded on the chart. Note: Students will synthesize their learning from all five close read-aloud sessions at the end of Session 5, when they complete the culminating task.

Where Does This Close Read-aloud Go Next?

As part of the next lesson, students continue working through *Come On, Rain!* using similar activities and familiar routines to understand each page. They learn new weather vocabulary and track the effect of the weather on the main characters, both before and after the rain comes. To finish the close read-aloud, students complete an independent writing culminating task: On a Before and After the Rain response sheet, they draw a picture and write in each box to show how one of the main characters feels and acts before and after the rain. They then share their thinking orally. Because of their intensive work with the text, their responses not only show insight, but they also demonstrate the new vocabulary and complex sentence structures students have learned and practiced throughout the close read-aloud.

Note: Lessons are for example only. They may look different than actual curriculum materials.

▶ Sample Lesson 2

Grade 5: Module 1: Unit 1: Lesson 5

Lesson Title: Esperanza Rising "Las Papayas" and Article 23 of the UDHR

Examining a Close Reading of One Article of the Universal Declaration of Human Rights

In this unit, students read Pam Muñoz Ryan's novel *Esperanza Rising*, a complex coming-of-age story set in Mexico and rural California during the early 1930s. They simultaneously read about human rights, and then apply this learning as one lens through which to interpret the characters and themes in the novel. Throughout the unit, students closely read selected articles from the Universal Declaration of Human Rights (UDHR) related to specific events in *Esperanza Rising*. Through close reading, interpretation, and making connections between fiction and informational texts, students build their understanding of the complex issues that arise when human rights have been threatened. In this sample, students closely read Article 23 of the UDHR.

> ### Agenda
>
> 1. **Opening**
>   - A. Reviewing Learning Targets (5 minutes)
>   - B. Engaging the Reader: "Las Papayas" of Esperanza Rising (20 minutes)
> 2. **Work Time**
>   - A. Making Connections between the UDHR and "Las Papayas" (10 minutes)
>   - B. Guided Close Reading: Article 23 of the UDHR (20 minutes)
> 3. **Closing and Assessment**
>   - A. Strategies to Answer Selected Response Questions (5 minutes)

How Is the Close Reading Integrated within the Lesson?

Close readings are embedded within lessons. The agenda for the lesson shows where the close reading we are using as an example fits within this particular lesson.

We'll start with the full lesson. As you review the lesson, notice how the work with the UDHR is integrated with other parts of the lesson to build knowledge and understanding about human rights and to deepen students' understanding of the characters and themes of *Esperanza Rising*. As you orient to this lesson, which includes a close reading, it may help you to go back to Chapter 3B and refresh your memory regarding some of the high-leverage instructional practices used in the curriculum to empower students to own their own learning (Table 3.1 in Chapter 3B offers a useful summary). You will see many of those practices in the lesson that follows.

Note: We have excluded the prefatory material for this lesson, such as the Teaching Notes and materials list; instead, we start with the Opening section and go through the Closing and Assessment section. Immediately following the main lesson, we begin unpacking and annotating the Close Reading Guide.

Opening

A. Reviewing Learning Targets (5 minutes)

- Move students into pairs and invite them to label themselves A and B.

- Direct students' attention to the posted learning targets and select a volunteer to read them aloud:

    "I can describe how pages 23–38 of Esperanza Rising contribute to the overall structure of the story."

    "I can answer questions about an article of the Universal Declaration of Human Rights by referring to the text."

- Tell students that in this lesson they will read a new chapter of Esperanza Rising, make connections to the UDHR, then dig into an article of the UDHR that is connected to this chapter of Esperanza Rising.

Meeting Students' Needs

- For ELLs and students who may need additional support with memory: Ask students to recall and describe one way that they worked toward the first learning target in Lesson 3. (MMR)

- For ELLs and students who may need additional support with comprehension: Check student comprehension of the second learning target by asking them to refer to page 4 of Esperanza Rising to answer this question: "When does the chapter 'Las Uvas' take place?" ("six years later," after Esperanza and Papa listened to the earth's heartbeat) (MMR)

- When reviewing the first learning target, refer to the text structure chart that you have been using so far to activate prior knowledge. (MMR)

B. Engaging the Reader: "Las Papayas" of Esperanza Rising (20 minutes)

- Invite students to retrieve their copies of Esperanza Rising and to turn to page 23, "Las Papayas."

- Begin by pointing out the title of this chapter and select volunteers to share:

    "What does 'Las Papayas' mean in English? How do you know?" (papayas; it says so underneath "Las Papayas")

- Add Las Papayas to the Spanish/English Dictionary anchor chart.

- Invite students to follow along, reading silently in their heads as you read aloud pages 23–38, adding words to the Spanish/English Dictionary anchor chart as they come up. Invite Spanish speakers to provide the translation and to record the Spanish on the anchor chart.

- After reading, invite students to reflect on the following question by thinking, writing, or drawing. Students must be silent when they do this:

    "What did this part of the story make you think about?"

- After 3 minutes, refocus whole group.

- Focus students on the Working to Become Ethical People anchor chart and remind them of the habit of character recorded: respect, as some students may be sharing out things that are very personal and meaningful to them.

Making learning targets student-friendly: Students are familiar with these targets and the lesson routine, since they unpacked similar learning targets in previous lessons. Therefore, to support effective pacing, the teacher just briefly restates today's learning targets.

Unpacking learning targets and Meeting Students' Needs: ELLs are given extra support to refer back to the text and prior learning to make sure they know where they are headed with the learning targets.

Home language honored in tandem with English: Spanish speakers are invited to provide and record translations; their assets as emergent bilinguals are elevated during whole group instruction.

Read-aloud of complex text: The teacher reads the chapter of Esperanza Rising aloud as students follow along. This ensures that all students have access to the text and models fluent reading. Even with students who are able to decode, read-aloud is used strategically throughout the curriculum to promote comprehension.

Habits of character: Students continue to work on showing respect when peers share their thinking, which may include significant personal connections.

Note: Lessons are for example only. They may look different than actual curriculum materials.

- Invite volunteers to share out what this part of the story made them think about. Do not force anyone to share their ideas with the group.

- As students share out, capture any threats against human rights they share on the Experiences with Threats against Human Rights anchor chart.

- Focus students on the Structure of Esperanza Rising anchor chart. Invite them to turn and talk to their partner, and then cold call students to share out:

  "What is the gist of this chapter?" (Esperanza's father had left the land their house is on to Esperanza's uncle, who now wants to marry her mother.)

  "Looking at the key, where do you think this part of the story fits into the structure? Why?" (rising action; we know that more things are going to happen to Esperanza and her mother because of what her uncle wants)

- Add this to the anchor chart. Refer to Structure of Esperanza Rising anchor chart (example, for teacher reference) as necessary.

- Distribute red, yellow, and green objects.

- Tell students they are now going to use the Red Light, Green Light protocol to reflect on their progress toward the first learning target. Remind them that they used this protocol in Lesson 3 and review as necessary. Refer to the Appendix for the full version of the protocol.

- Guide students through the protocol using the first learning target.

- Note students showing red or yellow objects so you can check in with them in the next lessons when this learning target is revisited.

Meeting Students' Needs

- For ELLs and students who may need additional support with memory: Before reading, invite students to turn to an elbow partner and summarize the first two chapters of Esperanza Rising in 30 seconds or less. Have them share out and give them feedback on their language use and summarizing skill. Then, after reading, invite them to turn to their partner and summarize once again, this time in 15 seconds or less. Repeat the feedback process. (MMR, MMAE)

- For ELLs and students who may need additional support with reading: Ask students about the meaning of chunks from a key sentence of this chapter of Esperanza Rising. Write and display student responses next to the chunks. (MMR, MMAE) Example:

  "Place your finger on this sentence: As you know, it is not customary to leave land to women and since Luis was the banker on the loan, Sixto left the land to him." Read the sentence aloud as students follow along.

  "What is the gist of this sentence?" (Responses will vary.)

  "Place your finger on leave land. What does leave land mean? What did Papa leave Mama?" (Before someone dies, he or she may write a document saying whom they want to give their property; the house)

  "Place your finger on left the land. What is the difference between leave and left?" Invite students to draw a timeline illustrating their responses. (infinitive verb to express an everyday, general truth; past tense verb to express a completed action)

  "Why did Sixto leave the land to Luis?" (When he died, Sixto was still paying a mortgage loan for his house, and Luis was in charge of that loan at the bank.)

Co-constructing anchor charts: Myriad anchor charts are used to help make students' thinking permanent and public.

Focusing on text structure: The instruction helps students not only think about meaning, but also about the structure of the novel and the role of the chapter titles, placing this chapter in the arc of the larger narrative.

Engaging students with protocols and checking for understanding: The teacher uses a simple Red Light, Green Light protocol to have students self-assess on their progress toward the first learning target.

Strategic vocabulary and Meeting Students' Needs: Focusing on specific words (leave and left) ensures that students understand the key events in the chapter.

Note: Lessons are for example only. They may look different than actual curriculum materials.

Chapter 5

"Place your finger on it is not customary. What does this phrase mean? What is not customary in your home culture?" (It is against tradition or practice.)

"Place your finger on since. I wonder why the author wrote the word since. What word can we replace since with in this sentence and keep the same meaning? Are there other meanings for since? How can we use since in our writing?" Tell students you will give them time to think and discuss with their partner. (Since joins two independent clauses and signals that the author will introduce a reason. It links two complete sentences into one more sophisticated one that shows a reason. Because. Since can also mean 'from a specific time or event until now,' e.g., since 2013. We can use since to join two independent clauses and signal that we will give a reason. We can also use it to signal a time span.)

"Can you complete this sentence with something from your life? 'Since learning a new language is hard work, _____.'" Tell students you will give them time to think and discuss with their partner. (Responses will vary, but may include: Since learning a new language is hard work, I try to read a lot.)

"Now what do you think is the gist of this sentence? What do you think about the ideas expressed here?" (People believed women shouldn't own property, so Luis, who managed the mortgage, got the land.)

"What connection can you make between your understanding of this sentence and your understanding of human rights?" (Mama's right to ownership was taken away—Article 17.)

- For ELLs and students who may need additional support with comprehension: Ask:

  "What are the series of conflicts and crises in this chapter leading toward climax? What do you think will happen next?" (the papaya delivery for the canceled fiesta, Papa's land being left to Tío Luis, Tío Luis' proposal to Mama and her refusal, Tío Luis' threats, Miguel's family's plan to leave for the U.S., the class divide between Miguel and Esperanza) (MMR)

- For students who may feel uncomfortable sharing their progress on meeting the learning targets publicly: Minimize risk by providing students with a sheet of paper on which they can select a color for each learning target in private. This provides you with useful data for future instruction and helps students to monitor their own learning. (MME)

Technology & Multimedia

- Work Time B: "Workers' Rights." Video. Youth for Human Rights. Youth for Human Rights, n.d. Web. 20 Apr. 2016. <http://www.youthforhumanrights.org/what-are-human-rights/videos/workers-rights.html>. Note the available translations of both the videos and accompanying website text.

- Work Time B: For students who will benefit from hearing the texts read aloud multiple times, consider using a text-to-speech tool like Natural Reader (www.naturalreaders.com), SpeakIt! for Google Chrome (https://chrome.google.com/webstore/detail/speakit/pgeolalilifpodheeocdmbhehgnkkbak?hl=en-US), or the Safari reader. Note that to use a web-based text-to-speech tool like SpeakIt! or Safari reader, you will need to create an online doc, such as a Google Doc, containing the text.

- Work Time B: Students complete their note-catchers online—for example, in a Google Form.

- Closing and Assessment A: Create the Strategies to Answer Selected Response Questions anchor chart in an online format—for example, a Google Doc—to share with families to practice skills at home.

Note: Lessons are for example only. They may look different than actual curriculum materials.

Work Time

A. Making Connections between the UDHR and "Las Papayas" (10 minutes)

▪ Invite students to retrieve their simplified version of the UDHR.

▪ Ensure students understand that each of the numbered items on their list is an article of the UDHR.

▪ Post the following question and tell students that they are going to have 5 minutes to work with their partner to look over the simplified UDHR text and "Las Papayas" in Esperanza Rising to answer it:

"Which human rights have been threatened in 'Las Papayas'?"

▪ Focus students on the How Were the Human Rights of the Characters in Esperanza Rising Threatened? anchor chart.

▪ Remind students of what the word threatened means.

▪ Tell students that when they find an instance of this, they need to record the number of the article that it goes against on a sticky note and stick it in their book to remind them. Model an example.

▪ Distribute sticky notes and invite students to begin working.

▪ After 5 minutes, refocus whole group.

▪ Cold call students to share out. As they share out, capture their responses on the anchor chart. Encourage students to provide you with accurate quotes from the text and mark those quotes using quotation marks. Refer to How Were the Human Rights of the Characters in Esperanza Rising Threatened? anchor chart (example, for teacher reference) as necessary.

▪ Focus students on the Quoting Accurately from the Text anchor chart and then underline the quote(s) from the text recorded on the anchor chart.

▪ Invite students to turn and talk to their partner, and then cold call students to share out:

"I have quoted accurately from the text here. What do you notice about quoting accurately from the text?" (You used quotation marks at the beginning and the end of the words from the book and made sure the quote is exactly what the text says word for word.)

▪ As students share out, capture their responses as criteria on the anchor chart. Refer to Quoting Accurately from the Text anchor chart (example, for teacher reference) as necessary.

Meeting Students' Needs

▪ For ELLs: To provide heavier support, when the learning target requires students to make connections between Esperanza Rising and the UDHR, display a note that symbolizes the learning target and say the learning target. Example:

"Las Papayas" <-> Articles 17, 23

▪ For ELLs and students who may need additional support with comprehension: Consider marking key sections of the chapter and asking students why these sections illustrate threats to human rights. (MMAE)

▪ For ELLs: Say: "Quoting sources is an important academic and career skill in the United States. In the United States, you can borrow important ideas from the original text, but you must use your own words to explain the ideas when you write and you must place quotation marks around the quotes you borrow. In addition,

Co-constructing anchor charts: The How Were the Human Rights of the Characters in Esperanza Rising Threatened anchor chart helps students notice a key pattern in the text that they have worked with across lessons: connecting Esperanza Rising to key ideas in the UDHR. This anchor chart makes students' thinking permanent and public and promotes the culture of an evidence-based classroom.

Total participation techniques: Students are all given think time and support; then the teacher uses cold calling, which holds individual students accountable to answer the question after they have had time to think and talk about it with a peer.

Meeting Students' Needs: ELLs are given information regarding how to quote sources in English. This explicit instruction regarding academic conventions honors cultural differences while also giving them access to college- and career-ready literacy skills.

Note: Lessons are for example only. They may look different than actual curriculum materials.

you must tell your reader where the ideas and quotes came from. Otherwise, you might get into serious trouble."

B. Guided Close Reading: Article 23 of the UDHR (20 minutes)

▫ Reread page 36 beginning with "My father and I have lost faith in our country" to "... we have a chance to be more than servants."

▫ Ensure students understand that in this chapter, Miguel explains that Esperanza's uncles would treat his family like animals if they stayed and that this threatens their human rights and goes against many of the articles of the UDHR.

▫ Play the "Workers' Rights" video.

▫ Invite students to turn and talk to their partner, and then cold call students to share out:

"From this video, what do you think you will see in this article of the Universal Declaration of Human Rights?" (being paid the right amount for the work you do)

▫ Distribute and display Article 23 of the UDHR.

▫ Distribute the Close Reading Note-catcher: Article 23 of the UDHR.

▫ Guide students through the Close Reading Guide: Article 23 of the UDHR (for teacher reference). Refer to the guide for how to integrate the Close Reading Note-catcher: Article 23 of the UDHR, Close Readers Do These Things anchor chart, and Affix List.

▫ Also refer to Close Reading Note-catcher: Article 23 of the UDHR (example, for teacher reference) as necessary.

▫ Refocus whole group and remind students that the Universal Declaration of Human Rights is also something we should follow in our behavior and actions toward one another, as we should all respect each other's human rights. Invite students to turn and talk with their partner, and then cold call students to share out

"From watching the video and reading this article, what have you learned about how to treat others?" (When working, everyone should be treated equally and is entitled to good working conditions.)

▫ If productive, use a Goal 1 Conversation Cue to encourage students to expand the conversation about how to treat others:

"From watching the video and reading this article, what have you learned about how to treat others?" (When working, everyone should be treated equally and is entitled to good working conditions.)

▫ Ensure students understand that this also applies at school as well as in the workplace.

Meeting Students' Needs

■ For ELLs: Consider creating home language groups and inviting students to watch the video or read the text in one of the many home languages provided at the Youth for Human Rights website.

■ For ELLs and students who may need additional support with expressive language: To provide lighter support, invite intermediate students to create sentence frames to bolster participation during the turn and talk. Invite students who need heavier support to use the frames. (Example: "The video made me think I should treat others _____ because _____.") (MMAE)

Multiple means of engagement: Students watch a video as a bridge between Esperanza Rising *and the UDHR.*

The Close Reading Guide: The guide is anchored in the lesson here. Look for instructions in all close reading lessons that direct you to the guide, which can be found in the supporting materials for the lesson.

Deepening student discourse: Conversation Cues are used during the discussion (Goal 1: "to talk and to be understood").

Strategic grouping; home language honored in tandem with English: The Meeting Students' Needs section suggests home language groups and texts (which, given this particular topic of human rights, fortunately are available in many languages).

Note: Lessons are for example only. They may look different than actual curriculum materials.

Closing and Assessment

A. Strategies to Answer Selected Response Questions (5 minutes)

- Refocus whole group.

- Tell students that the questions they answered with multiple options throughout the close read are called selected response or multiple choice questions.

- Select volunteers to share strategies they used to answer the selected response questions. As students share out, capture their responses on the Strategies to Answer Selected Response Questions anchor chart. Refer to Strategies to Answer Selected Response Questions anchor chart (example, for teacher reference) as necessary.

- Tell students they are now going to use the Red Light, Green Light protocol to reflect on their progress toward the second learning target. Refer to the Appendix for the full version of the protocol.

- Guide students through the protocol using the second learning target.

- Repeat, inviting students to self-assess against how well they showed respect in the lesson.

Engaging students with protocols and checking for understanding: The teacher again uses the simple Red Light, Green Light protocol to have students self-assess their progress, continuing to build student ownership of their learning.

Chapter 5

Note: Lessons are for example only. They may look different than actual curriculum materials.

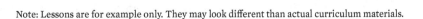

The Close Reading Guide

For any close reading, there is a Close Reading Guide (found in the Supporting Materials book for the module) that will support you as you help students navigate the complexity of the text to form a deep and lasting understanding, both of the text and of the skills needed to read it. Remember that one of the main purposes of close reading/read-aloud is to help students deeply understand a text so that they can learn about the world. This text, the Universal Declaration of Human Rights, like all texts in our content-based curriculum, was chosen to help students learn about the topic of the module, which in this case is Stories of Human Rights.

What follows is the Close Reading Guide for Article 23 of the UDHR. Students are already familiar with the purpose and structure of the UDHR. In this session, they work through all four parts of Article 23:

1. Everyone has the right to work, to free choice of employment, to just and favorable conditions of work, and to protection against unemployment.

2. Everyone, without any discrimination, has the right to equal pay for equal work.

3. Everyone who works has the right to just and favorable remuneration ensuring for himself and his family an existence worthy of human dignity, and supplemented, if necessary, by other means of social protection.

4. Everyone has the right to form and to join trade unions for the protection of his interests.

For each part, students first determine the gist (their initial sense of what the text is mostly about), and then focus in on key vocabulary (e.g., focusing on the prefix *un* in the word *unemployment* and using dictionaries and their Affix List to help them determine the meaning of *favorable* in this context). In a series of read-think-talk cycles, students dig into chunks of the text, discuss with a partner, and then share out to check for and deepen understanding. (For more information about the read-think-talk-write cycle, see Chapter 6). Simultaneously, they are practicing test-taking strategies by answering multiple choice questions about the text. At the end of the close reading, students "nickname" the article as a simple way to synthesize their understanding. This session has been annotated to highlight some of the questions and strategies to actively engage students in deeply understanding the text.

Close Reading Guide

Article 23 of the UDHR

(For Teacher Reference)

> *Structures for collaboration: Students discuss answers to questions with a partner before sharing with the whole group. Total participation techniques and protocols are used to ensure engagement from all students.*

Time: 20 minutes

> *Meaning: Students first determine the gist, then dig deeper, and finally are asked to paraphrase*

Directions and Questions	
1. What is the gist of this article? What is it mostly about?	• Throughout this close read, students work in pairs to discuss answers to the questions you ask. Use different strategies to have them respond, such as cold calling, selecting volunteers, or responding chorally as a group.
2.	• Refer to the Close Readin̲g̲ ̲N̲o̲t̲e̲s̲ for Article 23 of the UDHR (example as students share out an̲s̲ group.
a. Break up the word unemployment into root and suffix on the chart below.	*Read-aloud: Students hear this complex text read aloud before rereading on their own.*
b. Use your Affix List to determine the meaning of the prefix and suffix and a dictionary to determine the meaning of the root, if you need to. Complete the second row of the chart. (RI.5.4, L.5.4b, L.5.4c)	• Invite students to follow along, reading silently in their heads as you read the entire article aloud.
	• Point out the use of the w̲o̲r̲d̲ ̲h̲e̲ ̲i̲n̲ the article and explain that on offici̲a̲l̲ ̲d̲o̲c̲u̲m̲e̲n̲t̲s̲ he is often used to mean ̲a̲n̲y̲o̲n̲e̲,̲ when it says he, it is referring to al̲l̲ ̲p̲eople.
	Chunking the text: Students focus on one part of the complex text at a time.
	• Ask Question 1. Give students 3 minutes to work in pairs to find the gist of Article 23 and record it on their note-catcher.
c. What does unemployment mean? (RI.5.4, L.5.4b)	• Cold call students to shar̲e̲ ̲o̲u̲t̲ ̲w̲i̲t̲h̲ ̲t̲h̲e̲ whole group.
a. the state of working	• Focus students on Part 1̲.̲ ̲I̲n̲v̲i̲t̲e̲ students to follow along, r̲e̲a̲d̲i̲n̲g̲ ̲i̲n̲ ̲t̲h̲e̲i̲r̲ heads as you read it aloud.
	Strategic vocabulary: Students complete vocabulary work to specifically address CCSS L.5.4b in the same format they will be exposed to on the assessment.
b. the state of being paid money	• Invite students to circle unfamiliar vocabulary and to use the strategies recorded on the Close Readers Do These Things anchor chart to find the meaning of the words they don't know.
c. the state of not	• Focus students on the word unemployment at the end of this part of the article

> *Text-dependent questions: In this session, the teacher is cued to ask text-specific comprehension questions to ensure that students notice and understand key details in Article 23. Students are asked to support their answers using evidence and inferences. Text-dependent questions are designed to support the four aspects of qualitative text complexity:*
>
> • *Meaning (the purpose and complexity of ideas in the text): Note the heavy emphasis on paraphrasing the dense language.*
>
> • *Structure (the organization of the text and text structure): "Which statement best represents Part 2 of this article?"*
>
> • *Language features (vocabulary, figurative language, and dialect): Note the heavy emphasis on affixes, aligned to CCSS 5.L.4b: "Use common, grade-appropriate Greek and Latin affixes and roots as clues to the meaning of a word (e.g., photograph, photosynthesis)."*
>
> • *Knowledge demands (background knowledge this text presumes readers will possess): "Tell students that conditions are the things that affect the way we do something. For example, the conditions at school are the things that affect the school environment and the way things are at school." (The teacher then focuses them on the word favorable and has students turn and talk: "So what are favorable conditions of work?")*

Scaffolding student thinking: The teacher asks questions listed in the left-hand column of the guide, which are also on the student note-catcher.

| 3. How would you say Part 1 of the article in your own words? | • Invite students to popcorn out any other words that begin the prefix -un. (Responses will vary, but may include: unhappy, unreliable, unlikely.)
• Focus students on the phrase "protection against unemployment."
• Invite students to turn and talk with their partner. and then cold call students to share out:
  "You know what unemployment is, so what is protection against unemployment?" (job security—things in place to prevent you from becoming unemployed)
• Focus students on the words "free choice of employment." Remind them that by finding out the meaning of unemployment using affixes and root, they should know the meaning of employment (having paid work).
• Invite students to turn and talk with the ner, and then cold call students to share
  "What does free choice of employm mean?" (They get to choose where to work.)
• Focus students on the words "to just an vorable conditions of work" and read th aloud.
• Tell students that conditions are the things that affect the way we do something. For example, the conditions at school are the things that affect the school environment and the way things are at school. How clean the classroom is might affect how we work.
• Focus students on the word favorable and ask them to turn and talk. They can refer to dictionaries and their Affix Lists if they need to. Then cold call students to share their responses with the whole group:
  "What does favourable mean?" (good or suitable)
  "So what are favorable conditions of work?" (the way things are at work being good or suitable)
  Say: "So a clean classroom would be considered a favorable condition."
• Focus students on the word just and tell them that in this context, it means fair and right. |
| | |

Pacing: The lesson features a balance of telling students the meaning of words and having them determine the meaning of words independently. This keeps things moving forward at a productive pace.

Oral rehearsal: Students are given the opportunity to orally process before recording answers.

Relevance: The lesson provides examples that are relevant to students.

Chapter 5

Note: Lessons are for example only. They may look different than actual curriculum materials.

> *Text-dependent questions: Questions are designed to enhance students' understanding of text by pointing them back to the text in strategic locations.*

	• Invite stud[...] and then cold call students to share out: *"So what are just and favorable conditions of work?"* (the way things are at work being fair and suitable) *"What examples might you give of work being fair and suitable?"* (Responses will vary, but may include: safe, no favoritism) • Ask Question 3. Give 30 seconds of think time. Invite partner B to say it aloud to partner A, and then invite partner A to say it aloud to partner B. • Invite students to record their response on their note-catcher. • Select volunteers to share out.

4. Who has the right to equal pay for equal work? Quote accurately from the text. (RI.5.1)
 	
5. Which statement best represents Part 2 of the article?
 	
  e. a. Choose where they want to work and be paid whatever they want
 	
  f. b. Choose where and when they want to work and be treated fairly
 	
  g. c. Have a job, but they shouldn't be able to choose their job
 	
  h. d. Choose where they want to work and should be treated fairly
	• Focus students on Part 2 of the article. Invite them to follow along, reading silently in their heads as you read it aloud.
	• Invite students to put their finger on the word *discrimination*. Invite them to work in pairs to determine the meaning of this word. Remind them of the strategies listed on the Close Readers Do These Things anchor chart.
	• Cold call students to share the definition of the word in th[...] and the st[...] different [...] unjust tre[...] allowed to ha[...] the land in Esperanza Rising)
	• Invite students to turn and talk to their partner, and then cold call students to share out:
	  "What does equal mean?" (the same)
	  "What is equal pay?" (the same pay)
	  "What is equal work?" (the same work)
	• Ensure students understand that this means people who do the same job and the same amount of work should be paid the same.
	• Ask Question 4. Invite students to discuss with their partner before recording a response on the note-catcher. Remind them to use quotation marks and the exact words from the text to quote accurately.
	• Ask Question 5 and read the options. Invite students to cover the options on their note-catcher.

> *Student discourse: Students have frequent opportunities to converse with peers about their understanding of the text. This strategy is especially supportive of ELLs.*

Note: Lessons are for example only. They may look different than actual curriculum materials.

	• Give students 30 seconds of think time. Invite partner A to say it aloud to partner B, and then invite partner B to say it aloud to partner A. • Invite students to underline the response that is most like the one they just described in ⌐swer to their partner on their note-catc⌐ • Select volunteers to share with the who⌐ (Responses will vary, but may include: P⌐ have the right to choose where they wa⌐ work and should be treated fairly.)
6. Which statement best represents Part 3 of the article? i. a. paid as much as they want to make sure they and their family have a life worthy of respect j. b. paid as much or as little as their manager decides they are worth k. c. paid fairly and equally for work to make sure they and their family have a life worthy of respect, and where necessary have additional help l. d. paid less than the others but have help from other places to live a life of dignity	• Focus students on Part 3 of the article ⌐ it aloud for the group. • Remind them of what just and favorabl⌐ and invite them to put their finger on th⌐ remuneration. Invite them to work in pa⌐ termine the meaning of this word. Remi⌐ of the strategies listed on the Close Re⌐ These Things anchor chart. • Cold call students to share the definitio⌐ word in their own words with the whole ⌐ and the strategy they used. (pay for wo⌐ • Focus students on the phrase "an existe⌐ thy of human dignity." • Invite students to work in pairs to determine the meaning of the words existence and dignity. Remind them of the strategies listed on the Close Readers Do These Things anchor chart. • Cold call students to share the definition of the words in their own words with the whole group and the strategy they used. (Existence is the state of living, and dignity is being worthy of respect.) • Tell students that the rest of this part of the article means that if necessary, this pay can be added to or supplemented from other sources, such as food stamps to help people buy food. • Ask Question 6 and read the options. Invite students to work in pairs to read all of the answers and to eliminate any they know are incorrect. • Invite students to refer to the text to underline the correct response on their note-catcher. • Select volunteers to share out.

Anchor charts: The Close Readers Do These Things anchor chart is referenced in this close reading session (and throughout the curriculum). Two types of anchor charts in the curriculum support close reading. One, like this one, is general and cuts across all close reading/read-aloud lessons. Others are text-specific and help students track their analysis of a particular text as a scaffold for understanding things like patterns and text structures. Anchor charts should hang prominently in the classroom so students can reference them if they feel stuck and need a strategy for moving forward.

Note: Lessons are for example only. They may look different than actual curriculum materials.

Chapter 5

> *Pacing: As with vocabulary, finding the balance between making students work to find the meaning and telling them the meaning keeps the close read moving forward.*

7. What nickname would you give this article?	• Focus students on Part 4 [...] it aloud for the group. • Tell students that trade unions are groups that protect workers, so this article is saying that people should be free to form and join groups like this to protect them in their work. • Ask Question 7. Invite students to discuss with their partner before recording a response on the note-catcher. • Select volunteers to share out.

> *Text-dependent questions are designed to support the four aspects of qualitative text complexity:*
>
> • *Meaning (the purpose and complexity of ideas in the text): "What nickname would you give this article?"*
>
> • *Structure (the organization of the text and text structure): "Focus students on Part 3 of the article and read it aloud."*
>
> • *Language features (vocabulary, figurative language, and dialect): "'Focus students on the phrase 'an existence worthy of human dignity.' Invite students to work in pairs to figure out the meaning of the words existence and dignity."*
>
> • *Knowledge demands (background knowledge this text presumes readers will possess): "Tell students that trade unions are groups that protect workers...."*

Chapter 5

Where Does This Close Reading Go Next?

As part of the next lesson, students determine the main ideas of Article 23 of the UDHR and write a summary of the text. Throughout the rest of this half of the unit, students continue to closely read articles of the UDHR that connect with events in *Esperanza Rising* in preparation for reading and summarizing a new article of the UDHR for the mid-unit assessment. Ultimately, connecting articles of the UDHR with events in *Esperanza Rising* prepares students to participate in a series of text-based discussions about the evidence of threats to human rights in the novel.

Note: Lessons are for example only. They may look different than actual curriculum materials.

Chapter 5:
Instructional Leadership

Table 5.9: Chapter 5 Instructional Leadership

Questions to Ask Yourself and Your Staff
» Have you created time and support for teachers to read, discuss, and analyze the texts they use with students? What tools can you provide to help them structure this important work?
» What support do teachers need to create print-rich environments in their classrooms where students are "swimming in texts?" Are additional resources needed? How can you ensure that teachers have what they need?
» Do your teachers have a solid understanding of the research behind the literacy achievement gap and understand the critical role that both content-based literacy and close reading of complex text play in students' literacy development?
» Do teachers understand and see the value in all students doing regular work with complex text? How can you help them debunk any misconceptions they may still have about close reading/read-aloud?
» What do your teachers know about complex text: what it is, why it matters, how to help all students access it through close reading/close read-alouds?
» What systems and structures are in place to help teachers analyze and prepare to teach the close reading/read-alouds in the curriculum?

Evidence of Progress
» Professional learning time is devoted to helping teachers read and analyze texts. They practice doing Four Quadrants of Qualitative Text Complexity analyses and consider the challenges a text may pose for particular students.
» Practice reading and analyzing the texts leads teachers to consider the additional scaffolding that may be necessary to help all students succeed.
» Time for students to read, including Accountable Independent Reading, is considered crucial and is held sacred throughout the school.
» School and classroom libraries are filled with books—complex texts and texts at students' independent reading levels—that help students explore module topics.

» Teachers help students approach complex texts with a spirit of courageous exploration.

» Teachers never express to students that a text will be too hard for them or swap in an easier text in an effort to "protect" students from challenge. Instead teachers use scaffolding techniques to "lift" students to complex texts.

» Teachers approach teaching close reading/read-alouds as a skill that they can practice and hone.

» Structures are in place for school leaders and/or peers to observe close reading/read-alouds and offer feedback that helps everyone improve.

Resources and Suggestions

» Common Core State Standards: Appendix A

» Website: Achieve the Core (achievethecore.org) offers numerous resources:

- Understanding Text-Dependent Questions

- Qualitative Complexity Resources

- Read-Aloud Project (includes professional development on creating close reads for Grades K–2 as well as teacher-created read-alouds that align with common science and social studies topics)

- Reading between the Lines: What the ACT Reveals about College Readiness in Reading

» Website: Fisher & Frey Literacy for Life (fisherandfrey.com)

» Website: Shanahan on Literacy (shanahanonliteracy.com)

Chapter 5:
Frequently Asked Questions

I realize the text sets for each module have been carefully selected, but is it okay to swap out some of the texts? I have a lot of old favorites that I don't want to stop teaching.

It's true that the text sets have been carefully constructed to build knowledge and skills. It would be difficult to swap out texts without affecting the coherence of the module or interrupting the progression of learning. However, depending on the length of some of your old favorites, you could consider adding those in during a different part of the school day (e.g., during morning meeting for a short read-aloud). Or, for a longer text, you could consider using some portion of the flex time that is built into the curriculum if it is not needed for other things. You might also look for windows of time when 10 minutes of "storytime" can help students focus or transition, such as immediately following recess. Strive for coherence in the topic of the texts and the module topic.

I want to give my students more time for independent reading. Where can I fit that in?

Independent reading time is already built in to the 3–5 Additional Language and Literacy (ALL) Block and the K–2 Reading Foundations Skills Block. If you are still looking for additional time for Accountable Independent Reading, you may need to be creative with your schedule. After recess or lunch is often a good time to help students settle down and refocus; a consistent independent reading structure supports literacy development and self-management.

I understand that close reading/close read-aloud is a highly scaffolded process, but I still think it's going to be too hard for my students. How can I modify those experiences for my students who struggle?

It is critical that all students have access to the same complex texts; our stance on this is grounded in our commitment to equity for all students. If we deny some students the opportunity to read the same complex texts as their peers, because we fear they can't do it, they will never catch up. The key is to scaffold the experience for these students so that they can access the text. Table 5.8 offers many scaffolding strategies (e.g., providing the text to students in smaller chunks; writing the gist of each paragraph in the margin; providing sentence frames). Also, get in the habit of carefully reviewing the following sections of each Module Lesson, which will provide you with specific, targeted suggestions for scaffolding in that lesson: Teaching Notes; Supporting English

Language Learners; Universal Design for Learning; and Meeting Students' Needs. For students in Grades 3–5, the ALL Block has a specific component called "Additional Work with Complex Text," with teacher-guided sessions as well as independent work tailored to student readiness. Reviewing all of the materials for that component each week will help you think about how best to support students.

My students are getting bored reading the same thing over and over during close reading/read-aloud. Can we skip some of the rereading?

Rereading is a crucially important strategy for comprehending complex text and should become a lifelong habit. If started as a standard practice in younger grades, most students will comfortably and purposefully reread for meaning. Try to make multiple readings an expectation—part of the culture of your school—starting in kindergarten. Close reading/read-alouds have been designed to include *purposeful* rereading. Students won't be asked to reread just for the sake of rereading. Be sure to explain the purpose of each rereading to your students so that they understand why they are doing it. And, use the strategies for active engagement included in the close reading/read-alouds so that the work is collaborative (and more fun). And be sure that in your tone and body language, you convey your own sense of curiosity about the text and your sense of excitement that each time you dig in, you notice more.

How is a close read-aloud different from a typical read-aloud, or reading aloud during a guided reading lesson? What's the difference between close read-alouds and focused read-alouds in Grades K–2?

Close read-alouds go deeper than a typical read-aloud—usually students spend up to 100 minutes across five lessons digging into a single text. Close read-alouds slow the process way down to really support students' comprehension and ability to build knowledge from the text. Close Read-aloud Guides support teachers in focusing the reading, asking text-dependent questions that help students build vocabulary and knowledge, and helping students synthesize their learning from the text through a culminating task.

Focused read-alouds include a focus question and text-dependent questions, but students may work with the text across only one or two lessons and do not do a culminating task related to the text. The questions used during a focused read-aloud are in the body of the lesson itself, rather than in a separate guide. The main difference between the two types of read-alouds has to do with the depth with which students work with the text (which was determined based on how the text "serves" the overall arc or design of the module and builds students' knowledge on the module topic).

The biggest difference between guided reading and both close read-alouds and focused read-alouds is that in our curriculum the latter are situated within a content-based literacy curriculum. They are designed to build knowledge on a compelling topic. As a strategy for phonics instruction, guided reading also differs from our structured phonics approach. The similarities and differences between those approaches are described in great detail in Chapter 4.

I know that part of the reason we do close read-alouds is because students can think about complex texts that are read aloud even if they can't read them on their own, but what if my students' listening comprehension is lower than the level of this text?

The repeated purposeful reading, discussion, note-taking, and synthesis that define close read-alouds will build comprehension. And the questions you ask during the close read-alouds model the kinds of questions and thinking students need to eventually do on their own, which builds their comprehension skills. As a scaffold, you can also spend time frontloading vocabulary that will support comprehension. It is important to be strategic here: Frontloading too much vocabulary can overload students' working memory, but a strategic set of words can get them over a hump and build their comprehension.

What if I'm not comfortable reading aloud?

It is crucial for students to hear you regularly model fluent reading. If you are not yet a fluent reader yourself or find some texts in the curriculum particularly challenging, you are not alone. Consider finding audio recordings of the texts to listen to, as a scaffold for yourself. But challenge yourself to read aloud in front of your students, so you can pause and ask questions. If it is hard for you, this is another opportunity to model growth mindset for your students: Our ability grows with our effort. Use audio recordings with your students as well, so they can hear a variety of fluent readers (e.g., let them hear Jackie Robinson's own voice when they read his "This I Believe" essay in Grade 5, Module 3; or let them hear someone with a British accent reading aloud a chapter of *Peter Pan*).

When do students shift away from hearing complex text read aloud toward reading the complex text themselves?

Because close reading/read-aloud is done with complex text, it is a necessarily scaffolded experience across Grades K–5. Starting in the latter part of Grade 2, students more often read the text on their own rather than hear it read aloud, though even in Grades 3–5 teachers read certain sections (or sentences) aloud. Every complex text requires a different treatment, depending on the ways in which it is complex, and read-aloud remains an important strategy throughout the K–5 curriculum.

How does the Additional Work with Complex Text component of the ALL Block relate to the close reading in the 3–5 Module Lessons?

In the Additional Work with Complex Text component of the ALL Block, students sometimes reread texts that they have read closely in the Module Lessons in order to gain a deeper understanding of the text. They may focus on a specific key sentence with a Language Dive or answer additional questions about the text. Work in the ALL Block is differentiated to provide for a wide range of needs; the structure makes it easy for students to participate in targeted small group instruction and independent practice with a variety of texts used in the Module Lessons.

I can't seem to keep pace with the close reading/read-aloud guides. Do you have any tips for pacing so that I don't get behind?

The questions in a close reading/read-aloud are scaffolded to follow a line of inquiry. The questions support students in making connections between the words and ideas in the text. Often these connections are clearer if the questions move at a crisp pace. Understanding is built throughout the process, so don't worry if student understanding isn't crystal clear at every step. The culminating task will help you assess whether you need to return to key sections or concepts. Try to avoid stopping to answer too many questions, engaging in long discussions, or offering too much explanation during a close reading/read-aloud. Let student understanding ride on the wave of the carefully constructed set of questions and check for understanding by evaluating the culminating task.

The close reading/read-aloud guides are very detailed. Am I allowed to modify them based on students' needs? Are there certain things that are important not to change?

Before making any changes, it is crucial to understand the big picture and purpose of the close reading/read-aloud, including what the writing or speaking task entails. Given that purpose, consider what your students already "get" and omit steps or questions that feel redundant (e.g., my students already showed me they know what *slither* means, so I can skip that question). If you decide to omit a step or a question, do it to support pacing, not because you are concerned that your students can't do the cognitive work. Be sure to maintain the synthesis or culminating task as a check of students' understanding; this will help you know if anything you have omitted has impacted students' ability to achieve the goals of the close reading/read-aloud. Depending on your students' needs, you may also choose to add in more movement or swap out protocols or total participation techniques as long as they achieve the same purpose.

Chapter 6:
Reading for and Writing with Evidence: Deeper Learning in Literacy

Chapter 6

Chapter 6A:
How Does Evidence-Based Reading, Writing, Thinking, and Talking about Text Deepen Student Learning?

A focus on evidence is one of the key instructional shifts of new college- and career-ready standards. This shift brings together the paired practices of reading for and writing with evidence. Students need to be able to use evidence in their writing, but they also need to have enough evidence, through reading, that they have something to say when it's time to write. A focus on evidence is not new in classrooms, but it has taken on a certain urgency in schools across the country.

There's much to celebrate in this instructional shift. Learning to read for and write with evidence will better prepare students for college and careers, where unsupported views matter less than well-reasoned arguments based on evidence. And, importantly, a focus on evidence supports equity and excellence for all students. As noted in Chapter 1, the goal of college readiness for all students is relatively new in the United States. In the past, students from language-rich households with background knowledge that most aligns with what is taught in school (and how) were privileged with many advantages in school, particularly when considering the common practice of writing personal narratives and persuasive essays.

All students bring valuable assets with them to school. Yet many carry additional significant advantages with them, based on what they have had the opportunity to learn at home (e.g., word knowledge through a print-rich and discourse-rich environment, or world knowledge through opportunities to travel or go to museums). This disparity is often called the "opportunity gap," since it has nothing to do with students' intelligence or abilities, but rather with what they have had access to before entering the schoolhouse doors.

Importantly, a focus on reading for and writing with evidence allows us to level the playing field to some degree. With text as *the* source all students are working from, rather than experience or previously built schema, all students have a chance to build new knowledge together. Even with the youngest learners, everyone is grounded in the text and can make a contribution. For example, in kindergarten Module 3, students consider the important question: "How do we know that something is living?" But rather than just depending on students' home knowledge about living vs. nonliving things, students participate in a read-aloud of the text *What's Alive?* to research living and nonliving things. If they didn't already know, the text teaches them. And if they did already know, the text extends their understanding of this critical concept.

The focus on writing with evidence represents a similarly significant shift in writing instruction. In the past, as part of the "personal engagement" paradigm for literacy, schools of education have promoted the idea that if we simply got students writing about what interested them and reading "high-interest literature," they would "catch" good writing skills. In an article in the *Atlantic*, education professor Steve Graham says, "Research tells us some students catch quite a bit, but not everything. And some kids don't catch much at all. Kids who come from poverty, who had weak early instruction, or who have learning difficulties," he explains, "can't catch anywhere near what they need" to write an essay [or read a complex text] (Tyre, 2012, p. 5). Students need to build knowledge as readers if they are going to be empowered to then convey that knowledge as writers.

At EL Education, we are focused on equity. The literacy achievement gap is a symptom of societal inequities; the opportunity gap is the cause. We must do everything we can to ensure that all students have the opportunities they need and deserve. Our curriculum is designed to challenge and support students in equal measure. They all deserve the challenge of higher-order reading, writing, and thinking, and they all deserve the scaffolds and supports necessary for success.

▶ What Do the Reading and Writing Standards Require of My Students?

The Reading Standards

The Common Core State Standards (CCSS) include reading standards for literature (RL), informational text (RI), and foundational skills (RF)[1]. In this chapter, we focus on the 10 RL and RI anchor standards, which are designed to promote deep comprehension, a grasp of key ideas and details, an appreciation of structure and author's craft, and an ability to integrate knowledge and ideas—and all of this with appropriately complex texts.

These 10 anchor standards for reading focus on students' ability to read carefully and grasp information, arguments, ideas, and details based on evidence in the text. The "anchor standards" articulate the intent of each standard by describing what students should know and be able to do as readers by the time they finish high school. Sitting beneath the anchor standards are the grade-level standards, which go into much greater detail about the skills and understandings students must demonstrate at each grade level. Guidance for teachers on how to scaffold students toward the ultimate goal of college and career readiness is embedded in the very specific language of the grade-level standards themselves.

Using two anchor standards as an example, CCSS R.1 and R.10, Table 6.1 shows how the skill of reading for evidence becomes increasingly sophisticated as students get older. For students to truly meet the CCSS R.1 standards, the texts they read must be sufficiently complex, as indicated by CCSS R.10. Students, especially as they get older, should dig deep into texts and come back to them over and over to analyze them and draw inferences. As you know from Chapter 5, in the primary grades, particularly kindergarten and Grade 1, work with complex texts comes through read-alouds.

---

[1] The Reading: Foundational Skills standards are the topic of Chapter 4: Structured Phonics: The Why, What, and How of the Reading Foundations Skills Block.

Table 6.1: Common Core Reading Anchor Standards R.1 and R.10 across Multiple Grade Levels

Anchor Standard CCSS R.1: *Read closely to determine what the text says explicitly and to make logical inferences from it; cite specific textual evidence when writing or speaking to support conclusions drawn from the text.*			
Kindergarten	**Grade 1**	**Grade 3**	**Grade 5**
With prompting and support, ask and answer questions about key details in a text.	Ask and answer questions about key details in a text.	Ask and answer questions to demonstrate understanding of a text, referring explicitly to the text as the basis for the answers.	Quote accurately from a text when explaining what the text says explicitly and when drawing inferences from the text.
Anchor Standard CCSS R.10: *Read and comprehend complex literary and informational texts independently and proficiently.*			
Kindergarten	**Grade 1**	**Grade 3**	**Grade 5**
RI.10: Actively engage in group reading activities with purpose and understanding.	RI.10: With prompting and support, read informational texts appropriately complex for Grade 1.	RI.10: By the end of the year, read and comprehend informational texts, including history/social studies, science, and technical texts, at the high end of the Grades 2–3 text complexity band independently and proficiently.	RI.10: By the end of the year, read and comprehend informational texts, including history/social studies, science, and technical texts, at the high end of the Grades 4–5 text complexity band independently and proficiently.

The Writing Standards

There are 10 Common Core anchor standards for writing. There are three official "types" of writing, two of which have a heavy focus on writing with evidence: CCSS W.1 (argument writing) and W.2 (informative/explanatory writing). For CCSS W.3 (narrative writing), the third type of writing emphasized in the standards, writing with evidence is not particularly germane, except in the case of writing historical fiction, when students will need to draw on details and evidence from text to create historically accurate characters or scenes. CCSS W.7 (research) and W.9 (which focuses on drawing evidence from multiple texts to support analysis and research) also heavily emphasize writing with evidence. (In our curriculum, even the narrative stories and poems students write are based on knowledge they have built on the module topic. For example, in kindergarten Module 2, students read literature about how weather affects characters in stories such as *A Snowy Day*, and then write their own weather story.)

Table 6.2 shows how students are expected to write arguments with evidence (CCSS W.1) with increasing sophistication as they progress through the grades. For example, in kindergarten students must state an opinion; in Grade 1, an opinion with reasons; and by Grade 5, reasons and information. Eventually, in higher grades, students will supply *relevant* evidence and *sufficient* evidence.

Chapter 6

Table 6.2 Common Core Writing Anchor Standard 1 across Multiple Grade Levels

Anchor Standard CCSS W.1: *Write arguments to support claims in an analysis of substantive topics or texts using valid reasoning and relevant and sufficient evidence.*			
Kindergarten	**Grade 1**	**Grade 3**	**Grade 5**
Use a combination of drawing, dictating, and writing to compose opinion pieces in which they tell a reader the topic or the name of the book they are writing about and state an opinion or preference about the topic or book (e.g., My favorite book is ...).	Write opinion pieces in which they introduce the topic or name the book they are writing about, state an opinion, supply a reason for the opinion, and provide some sense of closure.	Write opinion pieces on topics or texts, supporting a point of view with reasons.	Write opinion pieces on topics or texts, supporting a point of view with reasons and information.

Just like CCSS W.1, shown in Table 6.2, W.2 (*Write informative/explanatory texts to examine and convey complex ideas and information clearly and accurately through the effective selection, organization, and analysis of content*) also becomes more rigorous as students progress through school. In kindergarten, students are supplying "some information about the topic," but by Grade 2 they "introduce a topic, use facts and definitions to develop points, and provide a concluding statement or section," and by Grade 5 there's greater focus on details such as providing quotes and using precise language and domain-specific vocabulary. CCSS W.2 encompasses quite a broad range of evidence-based writing: to inform, to explain, and often to share research findings. In the Module Lessons, many of the shorter pieces of writing students do align to CCSS W.2 (e.g., entrance or exit tickets, reflections, summaries of text, explanation of research). Students also write to inform or explain in more extended writing pieces, such as scaffolded tasks or formal unit assessments. One of the keys to writing in the era of the new standards is that students write regularly, for multiple purposes and audiences.

Research is the focus of CCSS W.7: (*Conduct short as well as more sustained research projects based on focused questions, demonstrating understanding of the subject under investigation*). In many ways, research is the nexus of reading and writing, and is therefore a strong example of both the read-think-talk-write cycle and the more big-picture Writing for Understanding framework, both of which will be explored in depth later in Chapter 6A. Students closely read and analyze texts to identify the information and evidence they need to answer a research question. They often do some form of shared research as a class, and then do a related research project with increasing independence.

In our curriculum, students learn skills and gain practice in all of these forms of writing. What follows are a few examples:

» In Grade 1, Module 3, students participate in a research cycle in which they study a specific bird to learn about how its body parts help it survive in its habitat. Within expert groups, students use the National Geographic Kids text *First Big Book of Birds for Little Kids* by Catherine D. Hughes to answer the unit guiding question: "How do specific birds use their body parts to survive?" Throughout the expert group research process, students take notes using words and pictures. Students then use their notes to write an informational riddle about their expert bird's body parts.

» In Grade 4, Module 2, the class builds background knowledge on animal defense mechanisms generally, and then together research the millipede. Then in expert groups, students follow the same process as they research the three-banded armadillo, the springbok gazelle, or the ostrich. All students keep their own research notebook to support them as they read, think, talk, and write about their animal with their small group. Finally, students write a choose-your-own-adventure narrative about their animal as part of their performance task for this module.

» In Grade 5, Module 3, after reading about Jackie Robinson and identifying the factors that supported his success in being an effective leader of social change, students research another athlete who was a leader of social change in expert groups. They determine the factors that supported his/her success in being an effective leader of social change, and in an informational essay, students compare and contrast the two athletes.

The Special Place of Argument

Of the three types of writing represented in the Common Core standards—argument writing (CCSS W.1), informative/explanatory writing (CCSS W.2), and narrative writing (CCSS W.3)—the standards reserve a special place for argument writing because of its critical importance in college, careers, and civic life and because of its relative neglect in K–12 education in recent years.

The world of college and work is a culture in which individuals influence attitudes, beliefs, and practices by making cogent evidence-based arguments for change. "Theorist and critic Neil Postman (1997) calls argument the soul of an education because argument forces a writer to evaluate the strengths and weaknesses of multiple perspectives. When teachers ask students to consider two or more perspectives on a topic or issue, something far beyond surface knowledge is required: students must think critically and deeply, assess the validity of their own thinking, and anticipate counterclaims in opposition to their own assertions." (National Governors Association Center for Best Practices, Council of Chief State School Officers, 2010, appendix A, p. 24).

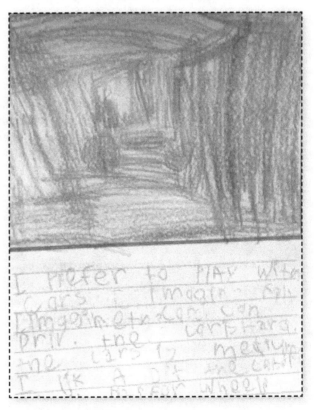

Our curriculum reflects this focus on argument writing, which demands that students use evidence to support their claims and prove the validity of their position. In Grades K–5, the standards refer to argument as "opinion," since the authors of the Common Core view it as a more teacher- and student-friendly term. This has led to some confusion in the field. However, the underlying emphasis is the same: a focus on evidence-based reasoning. In kindergarten, that begins as the seed of stating one's preferences.

As is evident in Table 6.2, even by Grade 1 the expectation is that students will provide reasons for their opinion. For example, in Grade 1, Module 4, when students write an opinion paragraph about birds, the prompt reads as follows: "We have read about Pale Male, the hawk who nested in New York City. His nest caused problems for some people, who had it taken down. Others liked having a hawk in the neighborhood and asked that the nest be put back up. You have already written about why the nest should stay. Now you will have a chance to write about why the nest should be taken down. Be sure to explain the reasons for this opinion."

Later in this chapter, you will learn more about

In kindergarten Module 1, students talk, write, and draw about the classroom toy they "prefer." By Module 4, they begin actually working toward the Grade 1 expectation for CCSS W.1: providing reasons for their preferences.

Writing for Understanding and the read-think-talk-write cycle, two related frameworks that allow students time to find, evaluate, and communicate evidence in support of their arguments/opinions and claims.

How Does Our Curriculum Address These Standards?

Overall, this focus on evidence has the potential to be quite positive for students. However, like many changes born from the best intentions, the devil is in the details. Many curricula have implemented this instructional shift by mistakenly doing away with personal narratives and poetry, and teachers and students have felt this loss acutely. Still others have narrowly focused on teaching students to identify evidence in sentences and paragraphs and state it back through simple writing tasks that may not be connected to any larger purpose beyond practicing this discrete skill. In the first scenario, students would not even be able to master the standards, as narrative writing is valued as a part of the Common Core. And in the second scenario, while students could technically master the standards, there are ways to deepen the experience for them, and that's what we are after with our curriculum.

Our focus is on the deeper challenge of students gathering evidence on a compelling topic over several weeks (weaving in stories and poems to text sets whenever possible), analyzing and synthesizing it, and then presenting it, often in writing, to answer a compelling question or serve a meaningful purpose. Our modules are designed strategically to scaffold this work:

» Unit 1 tends to emphasize **building background knowledge** about the topic, which usually means an emphasis on the close and careful reading of a complex text (or hearing it read aloud) that anchors students' learning about the topic. Students also often write with evidence.

» Unit 2 can play out in a number of ways. Students are always **going deeper on the topic**. This often includes more extended reading and research as students widen their reading to a greater variety of informational and literary texts and "write to learn" about the module topic. In Grades K–1 in particular, this may come through shared research projects. Again, since reading and writing are so interrelated, students typically write with evidence as well.

» Unit 3 is unique in that it almost always includes **extended writing** of the performance task, in which students complete a high-quality, scaffolded writing task and engage in a feedback and critique process to strengthen their writing (note, however, that performance tasks sometimes focus more on speaking than writing).

Along the way, during Module Lessons and in the K–2 Labs (Labs) and 3–5 Additional Language and Literacy (ALL) Block, students use various tools and protocols to help them make sense of evidence and use it to support their claims. What follows are some of the key curricular and instructional features of our content-based literacy curriculum that build students' capacity to read for and write with evidence.

Evidence-Based Curricular Structures

» Module Lessons focus on building students' content knowledge, related to a compelling aspect of science or social studies standards for that grade level. Students read and reread and engage in multiple experiences with that topic.

» Lessons are sequenced to ensure that students deeply understand the content before they begin writing about it. Students prepare to write about the topics and content they have studied deeply through reading, discussion, and other activities that scaffold toward effective writing.

» Throughout the curriculum, students do both "on-demand" writing tasks to show what they can do independently (e.g., assessments) and more scaffolded writing tasks to show what they can do with support (e.g., performance task).

- » The majority of writing tasks require students to write from sources.

- » Writing tasks at each grade level become increasingly complex over the course of the year.

- » In the Labs, students explore the module topic through multiple modes. They learn to work with evidence through such tasks as engaging in careful observation or experimenting.

- » In the ALL Block, three of the five components directly relate to evidence:

    - Additional Work with Complex Text: Students continue reading texts from the module to build word and world knowledge.

    - Writing Practice: often, though not always, is focused on evidence-based writing

    - Accountable Independent Reading: Students alternate between a week of research reading to build knowledge of the module topic and a week of free choice reading.

Evidence-Based Instructional Strategies

- » Often students will engage with a protocol, which offers detailed guidelines for reading, recording, discussing, or reporting that engages all students and gives them a chance to process evidence and talk about its importance (see box: Close Viewing Protocol for a sample evidence-based protocol).

- » Students read to research, learn more about topics, and answer compelling questions. They sort, sift, and weigh evidence, rather than simply "report" on a topic. In Grades K–2, in addition to gathering evidence from written text, students often spend time observing images or the natural world as ways to gather evidence. The sample protocol, Close Viewing (see box), offers a nice example of bringing a greater sense of purpose and structure to simply "looking" at things.

- » Students use graphic organizers and note-catchers to help gather information and plan their writing. They are exposed to a variety of tools—such as sketching, text-coding, marking evidence with sticky notes, and completing structured note-catchers—and especially in Grades 3–5 are empowered to analyze which tools work best for them.

- » Many lessons make use of class anchor charts, which are a way to collaboratively collect evidence, make inferences, and synthesize thinking. Anchor charts make the thinking permanent and public. These charts then serve as a critical scaffold for students' writing. Students can use the anchor chart for ideas or as a source of evidence that the class has gathered that they can then use in their writing.

- » In almost every lesson that involves working with text, the teacher questioning emphasizes evidence, with questions like: "How do you know?" "What evidence did you see in the text that supports your claim?" "What in the text helps us define/ explain/understand xx?" "Where do you see xx in the text?"

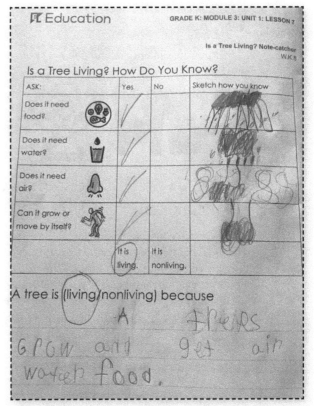

Students learn to use note-catchers and graphic organizers as tools to help them gather information and plan their writing.

» Focused mini lessons and activities help students analyze the use of *effective* evidence and apply this learning to their writing.

» Students write in multiple modes: They support opinions with evidence, use evidence to explain their ideas, and write or tell narratives informed or inspired by prior learning.

CLOSE VIEWING PROTOCOL

Purpose

This protocol helps students focus on the details in a picture, photograph, or illustration in an effort to add to their growing understanding of a given text or topic. It is designed to provide time for students to talk through their ideas with a partner before writing or drawing about them independently.

Materials

» picture, photograph, or illustration

Procedure

1. Direct students to zoom in on one part of the image.

2. Have students look closely at the details in that part of the image.

3. Invite students to think about what they can learn or infer from these details.

4. Have students turn to an elbow partner and talk about the details they noticed and what they have learned or inferred from these details.

5. Invite students to draw and/or write a note about the details they noticed.

6. Repeat Steps 1–5 with additional images.

Variations

» To focus pair interaction or to stimulate a specific type of thinking, consider providing a sentence stem for Step 4.

» Use this protocol as a kickoff to a module to spark student interest.

» This protocol can also be used with artifacts/realia.

▶ How Can I Build a Culture of Evidence in My Classroom?

Beyond the three hours per day (for Grades K–2) or two hours (for Grades 3–5) that you may spend teaching the lessons that are a part of this curriculum, there is much to be gained from building a culture of evidence in your classroom that permeates all parts of the school day. This consistency will further develop students' college- and career-ready habits so that they can think critically and independently and write for a variety of audiences, purposes, and disciplines.

What follows are some instructional techniques and classroom practices that help build a culture of evidence throughout the day:

» Ask students to reference specific page numbers, paragraphs, and exact phrases in text to support their points. Hold yourself to this same standard.

» Use Conversation Cues to probe for more information from students in ways that invite, challenge, and support them to cite evidence (e.g., "Why do you think that?" "What, in the (sentence/text), makes you think so?"). Conversation Cues are described in detail in Chapter 2C, in particular in Table 2.11.

» Give students specific, positive feedback when they cite evidence (e.g., "I noticed that Alma told us what page number she got her quote from. Great work, Alma.").

» Get students in the habit of coming to discussions prepared, with notes, annotated text, note-catchers, or sticky notes that mark and organize key evidence. For primary learners, this may be something as simple as a sketch.

» Use protocols throughout the day that require students to use evidence from text to support their opinions and claims.

» Emphasize how useful it is to reread a text to identify or analyze key details.

» Connect the idea of citing evidence to the more concrete skill of using context clues to determine unfamiliar words.

» Build students' academic vocabulary related to citing evidence.

» Have students sort evidence (e.g., before/after, stronger/weaker).

» Ask questions that favor textual evidence rather than background knowledge.

» Teach students to use sentence frames, such as "I hear you saying X, but the text says Y" or "I think you are saying X; here is another example to support…." Also teach them to use the same kinds of sentence frames in their writing (e.g., "According to the text X…."). Create class anchor charts with these sentence frames so that students have a "lifeline" if they get stuck. (See the box: Sentence Frames to Support Collaboration and Discussion for examples).

SENTENCE FRAMES TO SUPPORT COLLABORATION AND DISCUSSION

Agreement

» "I agree with _____ because _____."

» "I like what _____ said because _____."

» "I agree with _____; but on the other hand, _____."

Disagreement

» "I disagree with _____ because _____."

» "I'm not sure I agree with what _____ said because _____."

» "I can see that _____; however, I disagree with (or can't see) _____."

Clarification

» "Could you please repeat that for me?"

» Paraphrase what you heard and ask, "Could you explain a bit more, please?"

» "I'm not sure I understood you when you said _____. Could you say more about that?"

» "What's your evidence?"

» "How does that support our work/learning target _____?"

Confirmation

» "I think _____."

» "I believe _____."

Confusion

» "I don't understand _____."

» "I am confused about _____."

Extension

» "I was thinking about what _____ said, and I was wondering what if _____?"

» This makes me think _____."

» I want to know more about _____."

» Now I am wondering _____."

» "Can you tell me more about _____?"

Review

» "I want to go back to what _____ said."

▶ What Structures Will Help My Students Read, Think, And Talk about Text?

Ultimately, our goal for students, as they learn about the world through the compelling topics in the curriculum, is first that they deeply understand and then that they effectively communicate what they know. There are many layers to this work, which are addressed systematically in our curriculum.

The K–2 Reading Foundations Skills Block helps students crack the alphabetic code so that they can access texts, which are the gateway to everything else they will experience in school. The Module Lessons engage them with compelling topics and deepen their understanding of those topics through a careful sequence of building background knowledge, research, and extended writing. (Module Lessons are where deep comprehension of complex text lives.) Along the way, students "rehearse" their communication about these topics through play, the arts, short writing tasks, and many, many opportunities to talk to each other about what they are learning. This "rehearsal" happens during the Module Lessons and in the Labs and the ALL Block.

▷ Ultimately, our goal for students, as they learn about the world through the compelling topics in the curriculum, is first that they deeply understand and then that they effectively communicate what they know.

Writing for Understanding

We designed the curriculum with the principles of Writing for Understanding at its core. This approach (see Table 6.3), developed by the Vermont Writing Collaborative, is based on the premise that students need to deeply understand the topic they are writing about to use writing structures and tools effectively. After examining Table 6.3, you may recognize certain parallels between the Writing for Understanding approach described here and the basic flow of the units that make up each module of our curriculum. We start with a focus on building background knowledge about a compelling topic, move on to extended reading and research, and finally end with students communicating what they know, most often through writing. This structure allows students to gain the deep understanding they need to write purposefully and effectively.

Table 6.3: Writing for Understanding

Enduring Understanding/Big Idea What understanding about the content will this writing show? What understanding about the craft of writing should it show?	
Essential focusing question	What question will I (as a teacher) pose so that students can see how to approach this work in a specific, appropriate, manageable way?
Building working knowledge	How will students gain the content knowledge they need to be able to work with this?
Processing the knowledge	How will students select from and analyze the knowledge through the lens of the essential focusing question, and then capture it in notes so that they can use the ideas in their writing?
Structure	How will students know how to construct this piece of writing so that their thinking is clear, both to them as writers and to the readers of their work?
Writing process	How will students use the writing process (draft, confer, revise) so that their final writing is clearly focused, organized, and developed to show understanding of the big idea?

Source: Adapted with permission from Writing for Understanding: Using Backward Design to Help All Students Write Effectively *by the Vermont Writing Collaborative*

The Read-Think-Talk-Write Cycle

While the Writing for Understanding approach guides our overall curriculum design, when we talk about daily lessons we often use the organizing principle of the read-think-talk-write cycle. It may be helpful to think of this cycle, which lives dynamically in many of the lessons in our curriculum, as a microcosm of Writing for Understanding in action. The read-think-talk-write cycle gives students an opportunity to synthesize evidence, play with ideas, develop arguments, and "rehearse" various forms of communication during lessons (or sequences of lessons). It is highly supportive of students learning English, who benefit from oral processing and the social construction of knowledge, and, in general, of the varied learning styles represented in classrooms.

Note: A lesson featuring the read-think-talk-write cycle is annotated for you in Chapter 6B.

Figure 6.1: Reading, Thinking, Talking, and Writing about Worthy Text

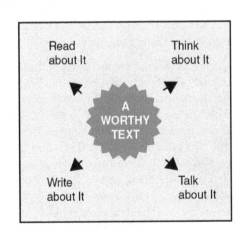

Source: Transformational Literacy: Making the Common Core Shift with Work That Matters. *Copyright 2015 by John Wiley & Sons, Inc. All rights reserved.*

Read about It: Let the Text Do the Teaching

Letting the text do the teaching may sound simple, but in reality it can be quite difficult. As teachers, we often have an instinct to preview for students what they are about to read, or to engage in a think-aloud with them to support them as they read (common in a traditional Readers' Workshop). Sometimes, after students have read a text, we will lead a whole class discussion about it, asking questions that fish for details about the information in the text, in effect summarizing its contents. In each of these cases, it's not the text that's doing the teaching; it's primarily the teacher.

Our approach is different. We position the text as the "expert" in the room. We structure lessons so that students are active readers, annotating as they go, using note-catchers to organize information and ideas, engaging in discussion protocols, and completing short writing tasks that bring them back into the text over and over.

This approach takes practice for teachers because, for many of us, it goes against our instincts to guide students toward the answers they are looking for or to help them when the going is tough. But, harkening back to Chapter 3B, where we discussed the benefits of grappling and productive challenge, students build their literacy muscles when they are given opportunities to figure things out on their own. In the curriculum, lessons scaffold this process for students as they learn strategies to find answers and evidence directly from the text. Key to this practice is that students are reading worthy texts that give them plenty to dig into (see Chapter 5A).

Think about It: Set a Purpose for Reading and Provide Time for Students to Think about the Text

Students need time and a focal point to comprehend what they read. Often what focuses students is a question, which is followed by a structure that gives them time to think about their response and ultimately to talk and write about it. These structures are often simple, like brief protocols or total participation techniques (e.g., Think-Pair-Share), and sometimes the structures are more complex (e.g., a Socratic Seminar). In either case, they are designed so that *all* students are thinking and talking, not just those who are already most inclined to do so.

During close reading/read-alouds, this focal point often takes the form of a focus question, which is introduced at the beginning of a close reading/read-aloud and sets the purpose for students as they read or listen (e.g., in the example in Chapter 5C of the close read-aloud of *Come on, Rain!*: "How does the hot, dry weather affect the characters?"). Text-dependent questions, which cannot be answered without reading and referencing a specific text, then direct students back to portions of the text for a particular purpose (e.g., "What science clues make Tess believe it will rain soon?"). As the Close Reading/Read-aloud Guides in Chapter 5C show, each time the teacher asks a question, students work together in pairs to grapple with the question and discuss their responses.

Questions that are prepared before the lesson will ensure that they point students back to the text in a way that builds their understanding of the text and their literacy skills, which is why you will find questions written right into the lessons in the curriculum. Asking deep questions—higher-order thinking questions on Bloom's taxonomy—that ask students to think about the text in ways that deepen their understanding is difficult to do on the fly. If you do find yourself needing to ask different questions than what you find in the lesson, it's important to keep in mind the purpose of each question and plan in advance whenever possible. It's also a good idea to plan follow-up questions in case students get stuck with a question or move in an unproductive direction. Developing good questions takes practice. As you gain familiarity with the curriculum, the way that questions are asked, and the structures in place for students to think and talk about them, you will likely feel more confident with this practice. (See Figure 3.2 in Chapter 3 for further guidance).

One important feature of the questions in our curriculum is the *way* that they are asked. Rarely do we recommend that teachers ask a question and call on volunteers to answer it. Instead, we usually suggest a total participation technique or a brief protocol so that *every* student can think about his or her answer and then talk to a peer about it, which deepens and extends students' thinking. Or we suggest a short writing task, such as a particular kind of annotation, a note-catcher, or an exit ticket, that gives students a chance to think and write independently. Brief writing like this may or may not be followed by a time for sharing with peers.

It's also important that questions be asked in an inviting tone that says, "Let's dig in together." The way you ask the question should set a tone of curiosity (i.e., "I can't wait to figure this out!") versus a tone of compliance (i.e., "I have to answer this question.").

Talk about It: Help Students Deepen Their Understanding of Text through Discourse

If you have read this book from the beginning, you have by now probably caught on to how important student discourse is in our curriculum. We subscribe to the idea that "learning floats on a sea of talk" (Barnes, 1976). At every grade level, in every lesson, we have built in structures that promote productive and equitable conversation among students. For example:

» Conversation partners: strategically assigned pairs to make partner talk both efficient and effective (e.g., pairing an English language learner with a more proficient English speaker). Note that these pairs should be varied, not static, so students have a wide range of interactions and language models.

» Triads (especially in Grades 3–5): similar to conversation partners, but groups of three, to add more variety of perspective, voice, and language to the peer conversations

» Expert groups: a small group of students assigned to research and become "expert" in one aspect of the topic (e.g., in Grade 2, Module 2, the class investigates "How do pollinators help plants grow and survive?" First they research bees as a whole group. Then, in small groups, students research and become experts in butterflies/moths, flies/wasps, or beetles.)

» Writing buddies: strategically assigned pairs so students can orally rehearse their ideas before writing or give each other kind, specific, and helpful feedback on their drafts

» Protocols: routines that offer a structure and a set of steps to help students talk to each other and dig deeper into text or ideas. Protocols allow students to talk to *each other*, not just to you.

» Total participation techniques: Rather than just calling on those students who may have their hands raised, total participation techniques (e.g., Turn and Talk) hold all students accountable.

Talking to each other about what they are reading gives students a chance for "oral rehearsal" of their ideas. It also allows students to hear the ideas of their peers, build off of them, and clarify their own misconceptions. Opportunities for student discourse are especially important for

Chapter 6

English language learners (ELLs). They thrive on interaction with a wide range of peers. Before writing about text, students think about and talk to each other about such things as what the text is about, what evidence from the text supports their opinions and claims, the meaning and purpose of academic structures, writer's craft, and the organization of ideas. This process gives ELLs a structure for simultaneously trying out their ideas and the language they need to express those ideas, learning about and clarifying the ideas of their peers, and deepening their understanding before writing. Furthermore, this oral rehearsal provides ELLs with the time they need to formulate what they want to say and communicate their thoughts, and then reformulate their speech if necessary, based on any confusion from their peers.

Strategic grouping can also help you support ELLs in specific ways. For example, a home language group might be a good place for ELLs to get oral rehearsal before writing, whereas a heterogeneous grouping of ELLs with native speakers or more proficient ELLs might be a better way for them to clarify misconceptions and fine-tune their own ideas.

Many lessons and sequences of lessons in the curriculum are designed to bring students through the read-think-talk-write cycle. Often, students engage in conversations with each other using a specific protocol with predictable steps and rules. Protocols are a great way for all students to hear from others and add to or change their own developing ideas. Because students follow set "rules" for discussion during protocols, everyone has an equal opportunity to talk, listen, and respond. The process helps students develop their growth mindset, learning and contributing to the learning of others, and not getting "stuck" believing that their ideas or answers are the only correct ones. "By following rules for talking (rather than rules that ban talking) students learn to listen first to understand and then speak to be understood; to use evidence from the text to support their opinions or inferences; and to respond with appropriate focus, tone, and equity of participation" (Berger, Woodfin, Plaut, and Dobbertin, p. 101). This social construction of knowledge helps students stay nimble and flexible with their thinking. (See box: Back-to-Back and Face-to-Face Protocol for an example.)

Also, not inconsequentially, engaging in productive and equitable conversation with peers is a great way to help students master the Common Core Speaking and Listening standards, such as anchor standard CCSS SL.1: *Prepare for and participate effectively in a range of conversations and collaborations with diverse partners, building on others' ideas and expressing their own clearly and persuasively.* Throughout the curriculum, Speaking and Listening Checklists are used to scaffold students' speaking and listening skills and, in Grades K–2, are also used to gather formal assessment data (see Figure 6.2 for an excerpt from a sample Grade 3 Speaking and Listening Checklist). Speaking and listening are critical scaffolds for reading and writing. But they are also crucial literacy skills in their own right.

Figure 6.2: Excerpt from a Sample Grade 3 Speaking and Listening Checklist

Student Name:							Grade 3 Date:
CCSS	**Criteria**	**4**	**3**	**2**	**1**		**Notes**
	Comprehension and Collaboration						
SL.3.1a	Comes to discussions prepared, having read or studied required material.						
SL.3.1a	Explicitly draws on preparation and other information known about the topic to explore ideas under discussion.						
SL.3.1b	Follows agreed-upon rules for discussions.						
SL.3.1c	Stays on topic.						

Note: Checklist is for example only. It may look different than actual curriculum materials.

BACK-TO-BACK AND FACE-TO-FACE PROTOCOL

Purpose

This protocol provides a method for sharing information and gaining multiple perspectives on a topic through partner interaction. It can be used for reviewing and sharing academic material, as a personal "ice breaker," or as a means of engaging in critical thinking about a topic of debate.

Materials

» Questions to be asked between student partners, prepared in advance

Procedure

1. Have students find a partner and stand back-to-back with him or her, being respectful of space.

2. Have students wait for the question, opinion, etc., that they will be asked to share with their partner.

3. Have students think about what they want to share and how they might best express themselves.

4. When you say, "Face-to-Face," have students turn, face their partners, and decide who will share first if you have not indicated that a certain person should go first.

5. Have students listen carefully when their partner is speaking and be sure to make eye contact with him or her.

6. When given the signal, students should find a new partner, stand back-to-back, and wait for the new question, opinion, etc.

7. This may be repeated for as many rounds as needed/appropriate.

Variations

» Partners may be assigned.

» Partners may also stay together for the length of the protocol.

» The protocol may be repeated several times in a row with the same partners, to give students multiple opportunities to check their understanding and receive information from their partners.

Write about It: Writing to Learn and Learning to Write

The final component of the read-think-talk-write cycle is writing; however, writing doesn't happen only at the end of the learning process. Instead, writing is an integral part of the learning process. When we ask students to annotate text by writing the gist in the margin, to complete a graphic organizer as they are reading or discussing a text, or to write short paragraphs in response to a prompt, writing is a way for them to crystallize their thinking. They are "writing to learn."

Writing is also a way for students to communicate their learning, and they must learn to do so effectively. In the curriculum, students read, think, and talk as a way to prepare themselves to write. And the writing itself serves to deepen their learning. Writing takes many forms in the curriculum, from letter formation and spelling, to note-taking, to collaborative, highly scaffolded writing and everything in between. These examples and more will be explored in the section that follows, which describes writing structures across the K–5 curriculum.

▶ What Are All the Ways My Students Will Write in the Curriculum?

Students do a great deal of writing in the curriculum, even though there isn't a standard "writing time" or "Writers' Workshop." Instead, the read-think-talk-write cycle calls for a more deep and fluid integration of writing with reading, thinking, and talking. The full range of the kinds of writing students do in the curriculum is explored in the pages that follow.

Writing Structures in the K–2 Curriculum

The K–2 Reading Foundations Skills Block

» **Conventions.** Students learn to print all upper- and lowercase letters and how to use conventional spelling, based on learned letter-sound connections, for regularly spelled words and many common irregularly spelled words.

» **Interactive writing.** Students work together to craft a shared sentence from the decodable text or from content in the Module Lessons. Students spell words, including high-frequency words, by segmenting the sounds (in sequence) of spoken words and matching them to their letter(s). They use rules of capitalization, spacing, and punctuation as they construct the sentence.

» **Writing practice (independent rotation).** Students apply skills they are learning by writing a variety of texts (e.g., free writes, letter formation, writing to prompts), developing stamina, perseverance, and overall writing fluency through this repeated practice.

The K–2 Module Lessons[2]

» **Independent writing.** This kind of writing often takes the form of note-taking in response to text, and students typically use a graphic organizer with a place for a drawing and a place for writing. Depending on their age and/or learning needs, sentence frames may be used to scaffold the writing and their understanding of the structure of sentences and paragraphs. In Grades K–2, note-taking often consists of just words or phrases, but it is critical "pencil to paper" thinking time.

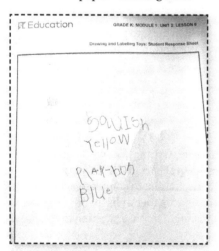

In kindergarten, putting "pencil to paper" is important thinking time for students.

» **Composition of shared writing.** Students do the thinking while the teacher does the actual writing. Generally this work is done as a whole group. First students talk together about the contents of what they want to write, often with a Turn and Talk, and then they decide together what words they want you to write. As students progress through the year, they transition from talking about what they want you to write to doing some draft writing and bringing it to you for the final draft. The nature of the writing changes by grade level: In kindergarten, students might just draw a picture and add a few words; in Grade 1, they may add a sentence; and by Grade 2, they may draft two or three sentences.

» **Writing assessments.** In each module, one of the three formal unit assessments addresses one of the writing types held in the standards: CCSS W.1 (opinion), W.2 (informative/explanatory), or W.3 (narrative). In Grades K–2, often this "assessment writing" has been scaffolded through partner talk; sketching, note-taking, graphic organizers; and peer feedback. Each module

---

[2] Of note, by Grade 2, students begin transitioning away from K–2 writing structures and toward 3–5 writing structures (e.g., less shared writing and more individual on-demand writing).

also contains writing checklists, which can be used on an ongoing basis to track students' progress toward writing standards during daily lessons. (For more on assessments of all kinds, see Chapter 7.)

» **Scaffolded high-quality writing.** For performance tasks that involve writing, students use sentence frames or models to craft their writing (often with accompanying sketches) to form well-developed sentences (kindergarten) and paragraphs (Grades 1 and 2) with a beginning, middle, and end. (For more information, see the following Scaffolded High-Quality Writing section.)

The K–2 Labs

» **Writing in the Labs.** There is no formal writing instruction in the Labs; however, students do put pencil to paper through other structures. For example, students set goals and reflect on them, make design plans, and take notes on their observations or research using note-catchers. And in Module 4, Grades 1 and 2 students do some narrative writing during Labs.

Writing Structures in the 3–5 Curriculum

The 3–5 Module Lessons

» **Independent writing.** After reading and discussing texts, students are often required to independently capture their thinking or demonstrate their understanding about what they have read by writing about the text. Depending on the grade level and where students are in the year, this writing may take the form of notes on a graphic organizer or note-catcher, for example, or writing short answers to questions on an exit ticket, or writing a paragraph. Depending on their learning needs, sentence frames may be used to scaffold the writing.

» **Writing assessments.** In each module, at least two of the six formal on-demand assessments address one of the writing types held in the standards: CCSS W.1 (opinion), W.2 (informative/explanatory), or W.3 (narrative). In Grades 3–5, this is a moment for students to show what they can do on their own as writers, although assessments are often supported with graphic organizers as a part of the assessment itself. (For more on assessments of all kinds, see Chapter 7.)

» **Scaffolded high-quality writing.** In Grades 3–5, for performance tasks that involve writing and for some other writing tasks, students begin to spend more time on scaffolded high-quality writing tasks, with particular focus on expository and narrative writing structures, the elements of writing (e.g., focus statements, conclusions, linking words, character development, narrative techniques), and the writing process. (For more information, see the following Scaffolded High-Quality Writing section.)

The 3–5 Additional Language and Literacy Block (Writing Practice Component)

» **Continued practice to develop fluency; QuickWrites.** During the independent activity, students are often given an uninterrupted block of time to independently respond to writing prompts relevant to the writing they are doing in Module Lessons. Sometimes they have a choice of prompts, and these prompts may require students to write opinion, informative, or narrative pieces of varying lengths. Often, students apply a specific language structure they learned during Language Dives.

» **Continued scaffolding of elements of writing.** During the teacher-guided activity, students often review language skills, learned through Language Dives, and elements of writing introduced in the Module Lessons (e.g., for "explaining evidence," thoughtful conclusions). They then analyze their own writing against models, checklists, and criteria generated in Module Lessons and revise it accordingly.

Scaffolded High-Quality Writing Tasks

Shared writing, independent writing, writing assessments, and other writing structures described previously are essential for teachers to assess individual students' progress toward mastery of standards. But this isn't the only kind of writing students should do. More scaffolded writing tasks that lead to high-quality work are important for building students' formal writing skills and their sense of purpose, audience, and the impact of their writing.

The combination of individual independent writing tasks and scaffolded high-quality writing tasks allows you to get a holistic picture of student progress toward standards. Providing opportunities for both kinds of writing also supports students to develop confidence as writers, building their skills but also their *belief* that they can succeed through clear expectations, a structured process, frequent feedback, and multiple opportunities to revise. Scaffolded high-quality writing allows students to take real pride in their work and to see that they can do more than they may have thought possible.

★ Defining High-Quality Work

You may recall that high-quality student work is one of the three Dimensions of Student Achievement at EL Education, first described in Chapter 1 (along with mastery of knowledge and skills and character; see Figure 1.2). As a result, opportunities for students to produce high-quality writing appear consistently throughout the year at every grade level. Our definition of high quality is further broken down into the following aspects:

Complexity

» Complex work is rigorous; it aligns with or exceeds the expectations defined by grade-level standards and includes higher-order thinking by challenging students to apply, analyze, evaluate, and create during daily instruction and throughout longer projects.

» Complex work often connects to the big concepts that undergird or unite disciplines.

» Complex work prioritizes transfer of understanding to new contexts.

» Complex work prioritizes consideration of multiple perspectives.

» Complex work may incorporate students' application of higher-order literacy skills through the use of complex text and evidence-based writing and speaking.

Craftsmanship

» Well-crafted work is done with care and precision. Craftsmanship requires attention to accuracy, detail, and beauty.

» In every discipline and domain, well-crafted work should be beautiful work in conception and execution. In short tasks or early drafts of work, craftsmanship may be present primarily in thoughtful ideas, but not in polished presentation; for long-term projects, craftsmanship requires perseverance to refine work in conception, conventions, and presentation, typically through multiple drafts or rehearsals with critique from others.

Authenticity

» Authentic work demonstrates the original thinking of students—authentic personal voice and ideas—rather than simply showing that students can follow directions or fill in the blanks.

» Authentic work often uses real work formats and standards from the professional world rather than artificial school formats (e.g., students create a book review for a local newspaper instead of a book report for the teacher).

> » Authentic work often connects academic standards with real-world issues, controversies, and local people and places.
>
> » Authenticity gives purpose to work; the work matters to students and ideally to a larger community as well. When possible, it is created for and shared with an audience beyond the classroom.

Scaffolded High-Quality Work in the K–2 Curriculum

One of the key purposes of scaffolded writing in the curriculum is to teach students about the structure of organized, formal writing. We have separated our description of scaffolded writing in Grades K–2 from Grades 3–5 because the approaches are so different. In the primary grades, students are still working on letter formation. And the writing standards in Grades K–1 call for student writing to be done "with support." This requires a different kind of scaffolding.

In Grades K–2, scaffolded writing is often organized into booklets; students are cued to write one sentence per page, along with a drawing, with the full booklet following the structure of a paragraph. Shorter or longer sentence frames are used, depending on the age and/or learning needs of the students. The sentence frames cue students to craft sentences and drawings that form a well-developed paragraph with a beginning, middle, and end. In Grades 3–5, the critique and revision process for paragraphs and essays often takes place after a full draft has been written, but in Grades K–2, students engage in critique and revision of scaffolded writing sentence by sentence.

Scaffolded High-Quality Work in the 3–5 Curriculum

The writing process in Grades 3–5, as in K–2, is built on the principles of Writing for Understanding—reading to build knowledge is a big part of how students get ready to write. In Grades 3–5, the writing process includes building content knowledge, planning, revising, editing, and rewriting or trying a new approach. Students participate in multiple rounds of peer critiques, using peer feedback to revise and edit their writing. (Much more on how models, critique, and descriptive feedback help students improve their work can be found in Chapter 6C.)

When it is time to write about their reading, students in Grades 3–5 use the Painted Essay structure developed by Diana Leddy at the Vermont Writing Collaborative (see Figure 6.3). The Painted Essay helps students visualize the parts of an essay using colors that help them organize their information. During Painted Essay writing lessons, students start by analyzing a model essay for content (e.g., "What is this essay about?" "What is the author trying to communicate about the topic?"). They then analyze that same model essay for craft, using watercolors to literally paint the components of a strong essay that they find in the model (e.g., red for the introductory "hook," yellow

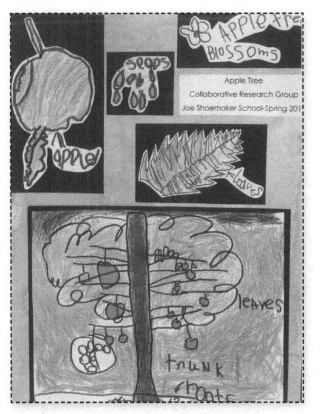

Models, critique, and descriptive feedback help students produce high-quality work like this (from kindergarten, Module 4).

Figure 6.3: Painted Essay Template

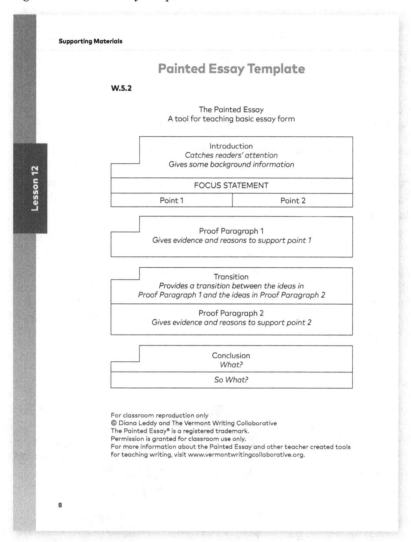

Supporting Materials

Painted Essay Template

W.5.2

The Painted Essay
A tool for teaching basic essay form

Introduction
Catches readers' attention
Gives some background information

FOCUS STATEMENT	
Point 1	Point 2

Proof Paragraph 1
Gives evidence and reasons to support point 1

Transition
Provides a transition between the ideas in
Proof Paragraph 1 and the ideas in Proof Paragraph 2

Proof Paragraph 2
Gives evidence and reasons to support point 2

Conclusion
What?
So What?

For classroom reproduction only
© Diana Leddy and The Vermont Writing Collaborative
The Painted Essay® is a registered trademark.
Permission is granted for classroom use only.
For more information about the Painted Essay and other teacher created tools
for teaching writing, visit www.vermontwritingcollaborative.org.

Lesson 12

8

for body paragraph evidence, green for the conclusion, etc.). They then work with their own arguments and evidence to complete an essay template and write their formal essay.

As students write essays, teachers provide critical scaffolding, instructing students on elements of writing (e.g., focus statements, conclusions, linking words, character development, narrative techniques). This scaffolding begins with careful analysis of the specific parts of the model, using the Painted Essay structure to determine the function and purpose of each part of an opinion or informative essay and determining the content and structural features that make it successful. Students also have the opportunity to practice saying parts orally before writing them. All of this work is supported further in the ALL Block, when students receive additional scaffolding for the elements of writing.

★ **Before You Assign Writing Tasks: Test-Drive Them Yourself**

You know your students best, and only you can identify what might trip them up as they embark on any given writing task. It is crucial to test-drive major writing tasks before you assign them. This will give you a chance to be metacognitive about the task, noticing the kinds of thinking and writing students will need to do to succeed. This knowledge will not only help you support students as they write, but it will inform your instruction

Chapter 6

throughout the module as students learn about and gather evidence they will need down the road. You can then more effectively plan backward to scaffold student success. Knowing where students need to be at the end of a module will add urgency to lessons in which they are gathering, organizing, and synthesizing evidence.

Discovering and overcoming the same obstacles that students are likely to encounter is an opportunity to revise the task or plan for additional scaffolding throughout the learning process. As you write your own response to the writing task, ask yourself:

» To what extent is the task clear, doable within the timeframe, and connected to the big ideas of the module?

» Does the focus question require me to use evidence from the research/reading?

» What content knowledge do I need to successfully complete this task?

» What writing skills do I need to successfully complete this task?

Writing Supports for English Language Learners: Structures K–5

One of the most effective supports for ELLs completing writing tasks of all kinds is talking about their ideas before writing. The read-think-talk-write cycle is inherently supportive, since it affords students rich interaction and opportunities to orally rehearse their ideas. For example, the process of identifying and synthesizing evidence from text by engaging in a Fishbowl conversation protocol gives ELLs a structure for trying out their ideas, learning about the ideas of their peers, and deepening their understanding before they are faced with what can feel like an intimidating task when learning a second language: writing. Many of the structures that support student discourse used throughout the curriculum at all grade levels support this cognitive process.

The read-think-talk-write cycle is a good example of how the curriculum was designed from the outset to be supportive of students' varied levels of language. Rather than responding to ELLs' struggles with reactive approaches, we have designed lessons to predict and proactively plan for the kinds of instruction that will be most effective for students learning English, which includes learning to become more effective writers in English. What follows are additional supports and considerations in place for ELLs:

» **Levels of support.** Each Module Lesson includes a section called Supporting English Language Learners. There, we not only signal how the lesson itself is inherently supportive of ELLs, but also signal specific scaffolds (including but not limited to writing scaffolds) for students who may need lighter or heavier support.

» **Targeted support.** In the Meeting Students' Needs section of each Module Lesson, you will find suggestions for light, medium, and heavy levels of support for specific activities within the lesson. For example, for those who are new to English (heavy support), we often provide sentence frames that students can use both orally and in writing.

» **Language Dives.** This practice not only supports students as readers, but it also supports them as writers and speakers. As they analyze sentence-level "models" to learn the language structures that show up in the complex texts they are reading, they can apply them to their own speaking and writing. For example, in Grade 4, Module 2, students research how animals use their bodies and behaviors to protect themselves. In the Language Dive, they play with the sentence: *Over many generations, they have developed both physical and behavioral defense mechanisms **that allow them to survive***. Then, they practice using the relative clause structure (*that* + verb + object + infinitive) to describe their own expert group animal's defense mechanisms: *Over many generations, the three-banded armadillo has developed a defense mechanism that allows it to protect its underparts.*

» **Additional practice.** Throughout the curriculum, you will find recommendations for ELLs to receive additional practice with writing leading up to assessments and performance tasks. For example, students may be asked to write about one animal's defense mechanisms in their writing practice, and then in the assessment write about a different animal and explain why these mechanisms are helpful. This helps ELLs become familiar with expectations for writing tasks.

» **Models.** Reading and analyzing a model of writing that is similar to the writing they are doing helps ELLs not only build knowledge (since they always first analyze the model for its content), but also understand expectations for structure and syntax. It is common to find Language Dives throughout the curriculum that use key sentences from the model for further analysis.

» **Error correction.** Teachers are often the primary source for pointing out errors in student writing; however, structures in our curriculum, such as the read-think-talk-write cycle and peer critique, also help students give each other feedback on errors. In either case, the goal is for students to move to independent error correction. Error correction can be bucketed as follows: global (interfere with overall meaning), pervasive (common), stigmatizing (disturb more proficient speakers), and student-identified (ones students notice themselves) (Ferris and Hedgecock, 2013). (For more information on these "buckets" of error correction, see Chapter 2C.)

When thinking about error correction, it is important to help students understand that people speak many varieties of English (i.e., systematic dialects), and those can and should be honored. But then teachers should talk with students about language used in writing: "How you write has to be in classroom or academic English, in a way we have agreed to in this classroom and in a way that is often expected for college and career, for a broader audience, unless you're writing for a specific audience."

Consider, for example, when a student writes: *The armadillo curling up to protect itself.* A teacher might begin by saying: "You're absolutely right. That's how armadillos protect themselves!" She then might ask: "How is '*The armadillo curling up to protect itself*' the same as and different from writing '*The armadillo is curling up to protect itself*'?" This would help students notice that classroom English requires the present progressive form *is curling up* to state an ongoing action in the present. Then the teacher might create a comparative language T-chart to honor both the variety of English ("curling up") and the classroom or academic English version ("is curling up") and ask students what they appreciate about both versions. The teacher also should be explicit that the classroom English version—using "is"—is what's expected for the writing task and in most college and career settings.

It is important to remember that ELLs in your classroom are not just learning English, they are often also learning the academic norms of American classrooms. When it comes to the writing process, we offer the following considerations:

» **Considerations regarding peer feedback.** Giving and receiving peer feedback is a common practice in our curriculum. Sometimes this practice is unfamiliar to ELLs. Depending on their academic backgrounds, this may be a new and different experience for them. It will be important to acknowledge that this practice may be new to them and help them approach the experience with an open mind by asking questions like, "What are some of the positive things you experienced when you tried this for the first time?"

» **Considerations regarding plagiarism.** Depending on their academic background, some ELLs may have different ideas about what it means to plagiarize. In many classrooms in China, for example, students are taught to learn and memorize important pieces of writing and use them in their own writing without citations. When they come to school in America, these students sometimes inadvertently learn hard lessons about this practice. Our curriculum includes lots of emphasis on citations, but it will be important for you to continually reinforce this message, particularly with ELLs.

Chapter 6B:
What Does the Read-Think-Talk-Write Cycle Look Like in Action?

The read-think-talk-write cycle is a central feature of our curriculum. It is a part of nearly every lesson, but it isn't a step-by-step process that looks the same from lesson to lesson. It may be useful to think of the cycle as more of a philosophy than an instructional practice. The main tenet of this philosophy is that when students interact with text in dynamic and collaborative ways, they comprehend the text more deeply and can communicate their learning from the text more effectively.

What this looks like in practice varies. There are myriad lessons we could have chosen to highlight for you here. The one we chose, from Grade 3, Module 1, features quiet reflection time before sharing and a protocol called Say Something, which gives students a chance to talk with a partner about the gist of a story before they record it on a note-catcher.

Throughout, we will use annotations to draw your attention to instructional strategies that are described previously in this chapter or in previous chapters, particularly Chapter 3.

▶ Sample Lesson

Grade 3: Module 1: Unit 1: Lesson 3

Lesson Title: Reading for Gist and Determining the Message/Lesson/Moral:
Waiting for the Biblioburro

The Read-Think-Talk-Write Cycle in Action

Let's look "under the hood" at a lesson that features the read-think-talk-write cycle in action. In this lesson, students hear *Waiting for the Biblioburro*, a story about the struggles a girl named Ana faces with access to education in Colombia and the help she gets from the biblioburro, a librarian who travels around on a donkey with books. After listening to the story read aloud, students reflect on its message and create the Experiences with Overcoming Challenges anchor chart as a vehicle to share their reflections. Students also participate in a protocol called Say Something, which provides them with a structure to think, talk, and write about the gist of the story.

In Lesson 1 of this unit, students were introduced to the module topic and guiding question: *Why are education, reading, and books important?* In future lessons, students will follow a similar structure as the one in this lesson with other books that explore education around the world.

Opening

Strategic pairing: Teachers are invited to strategically pair students before the start of the lesson. This is an important decision point for teachers, since students will think, talk, and write with a partner throughout the lesson:

• *The Meeting Students' Needs section offers guidance for pairing English language learners (ELLs) with a partner with more advanced or native proficiency.*

• *Similarly, for other students who may need support, a partner who can act as a mentor is suggested. Mentors can be encouraged to share their thought process with their partners throughout the lesson.*

Framing purpose: Before reading, the teacher regrounds students in the guiding questions: "Why are education, books, and reading important?" and "How can I overcome learning challenges?" This situates their reading of this particular text within their larger arc of learning.

A. Reading Aloud: *Waiting for the Biblioburro* **(20 minutes)**

- Strategically pair students and invite them to label themselves partner A and partner B.

- Focus students on the **Guiding Questions anchor chart** and reread the questions aloud.

- Tell students that they are going to begin this work of overcoming challenges by hearing about a girl who faced challenges.

- Show students the cover of *Waiting for the Biblioburro* and explain that this story is set in Colombia. Focus students on the **world map**.

- Using a total participation technique, invite responses from the group:

  "Where is Colombia on the map?" (Responses will vary.)

- Place the **labeled pin** on Colombia and explain that it is on the continent of South America. Show students each of the continents on the map.

- Display the **Compass Points**. Tell students that they can use compass points to explain where places are. Read through each of the compass points.

- Point to the pin marking your location.

- Ask students to turn and talk, and cold call students to share their responses with the whole group:

  "Which continent do we live on?" (Responses will vary.)

  "Where are we in relation to Colombia?" (Responses will vary, but students should use the compass points.)

  "Has anyone had any experience with Colombia that you would like to share?" (Colombia or neighboring countries may be the country of origin for some students.)

Think: After the teacher reads Waiting for the Biblioburro *once all the way through, students have 5 minutes of silent think time to reflect on what the story made them think about. They may simply think, or they may write or draw. This processing time supports comprehension and is particularly important for quieter students or ELLs, who may need an opportunity to reflect before sharing orally.*

- While still displaying *Waiting for the Biblioburro*, complete a first read of the text, reading slowly, fluently, and with expression. Consider asking any Spanish-speaking students to pronounce the Spanish words (including the title) as you come to them. Refer to the glossary in the back of the text as necessary.

- After reading, invite students to spend 5 minutes reflecting silently. Reflection can include thinking or writing/drawing on paper. Students must be silent when they do this, though.

- Ask:

  "What did this story make you think about?"

- Invite students to begin reflecting.

- After 5 minutes, refocus whole group.

- Focus students on the **Working to Become Ethical People anchor chart** and remind them of the habit of character recorded, respect. Tell them that they need to be respectful as they listen to other students sharing. Explain that part of being respectful means treating others with care.

- Tell students they will now have the opportunity to share their reflections, if they would like to, with the whole group. Do not force anyone to share their ideas with the group, but provide those who desire it with the chance to voice their reflections.

- Invite students to share their reflections as they feel comfortable.

Talk: After students have had time to reflect on the story, they are invited but not required to share. Since they had think time, many students likely will feel ready to share. They may share about the challenges Ana faced in the story. Or they may connect to the guiding question and share their own experience overcoming challenges. The prompt is intentionally open-ended at this point, to invite students to bring their own real thinking to the group, rather than "guess what's in the teacher's head."

Note: We have excluded the prefatory material for this lesson, such as the Teaching Notes and materials list; instead, we start with the Opening section and go through the Closing and Assessment section.

Note: Lessons are for example only. They may look different than actual curriculum materials.

68

Overcoming Challenges anchor chart.

■ Ensure students recognize that this story is about one child and that not every child in Colombia faces the same challenge. Explain that some students go to schools and libraries just as they do. Explain also that just because this way of life is different, it does not mean it is any better or worse than the way that they live. It is just a different way of life. Take a moment to acknowledge and celebrate Ana's joy of reading and the hard work she and the librarian do in the name of reading, in a context that is different from what students experience in this classroom.

Meeting Students' Needs

■ For ELLs: Consider pairing students with a partner who has more advanced or native language proficiency. The partner with greater language proficiency can serve as a model in the pair, initiating discussions and providing implicit sentence frames, for example.

■ Provide differentiated mentors by purposefully pre-selecting student partnerships. Consider meeting with the mentors in advance to encourage them to share their thought processes with their partner. (MMAE)

■ If students are not familiar with Colombia, help build excitement about the country by sharing art, videos, visuals, etc., that provide background knowledge about the culture. (MMR, MME)

■ For ELLs and students who may need additional support with comprehension: Invite students who need heavier support to act out key sections of the text with you as you read. (Example: When reading "... her teacher moved far away, and now there is no one to teach Ana," act out packing your things and waving goodbye as you pretend to leave the classroom.) (MMR)

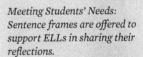
Meeting Students' Needs: Acting out a section of the text deepens comprehension and supports varied learning styles (multiple means of representation).

■ For ELLs and students who may need additional support with new vocabulary: Use word clusters and word maps and encourage students to explore translations, spelling and pronouncing aloud, various word forms, synonyms, definitions, translations, and collocations (words frequently used together) to develop knowledge of the word *challenge*. (MMR) Example:

— challenge=meydan okuma

— C-H-A-L-L-E-N-G-E

— challenger, challenging

— problem, difficulty

— a situation that tests someone's abilities

— face a challenge, overcome a challenge, a serious challenge

■ For ELLs and students who may need additional support with expressive language: Provide a sentence frame to bolster their participation. Examples:

— "This story makes me think about _____."

— "One challenge Ana faced was _____." (MMAE)

Meeting Students' Needs: Sentence frames are offered to support ELLs in sharing their reflections.

EL Education Curriculum   69

Chapter 6

Note: Lessons are for example only. They may look different than actual curriculum materials.

Academic vocabulary: Unpacking the academic vocabulary in the learning targets (e.g., gist, moral) prepares students for the work they will do in the lesson as they read, think, talk, and write about Waiting for the Biblioburro.

Total participation techniques: Students are introduced to equity sticks, which allow teachers to track who has talked/shared during the course of the lesson, promoting equity by making room for all voices.

Meeting Students' Needs: ELLs are invited to "say back" the learning targets in their own words and add translations of the academic vocabulary in the targets to the Word Wall, which further engages them in the work they are about to complete in the lesson.

Opening

B. Reviewing Learning Targets (5 minutes)

- Direct students' attention to the posted learning targets and select a volunteer to read them aloud:

  "I can determine the gist of Waiting for the Biblioburro."

  "I can identify the central message, lesson, or moral of Waiting for the Biblioburro."

- Underline the word *gist*.

- Explain to students that you are going to begin using **equity sticks** as a way of calling on them to share their ideas with the group. Each of their names is on a different Popsicle stick, and you will pull one at random. When you do, that student will share his or her ideas with the class.

- Ask students to turn and talk, and use equity sticks to select students to share their responses with the whole group:

  "What is the gist of a text?" *(what the text is mostly about)*

  "Why is it important to understand the gist of a text or what it is mostly about?" *(so you can retell it and remember the structure)*

- Focus students on the following bullet on the **Close Readers Do These Things anchor chart**, telling them that the strategies on this chart will help them when reading new texts:

  — "Read small chunks of text slowly and think about the gist (what the text is mostly about)."

- Underline the word *moral* in the second learning target.

- Ask students to turn and talk, and cold call students to share their responses with the whole group:

  "What is a moral?" *(a lesson)*

- Add the words *gist* and *moral* to the Academic Word Wall.

Meeting Students' Needs

- For ELLs and students who may need additional support with comprehension: Repeat and rephrase the learning targets. Say:

  "I know what the author of Waiting for the Biblioburro is trying to teach me." (MMR)

- When defining the word *moral*, provide an example from a familiar class text. (MMR)

- For ELLs: Invite students to add translations of the words on the Word Wall in their home languages, using a different color and placing them next to the target vocabulary.

Note: Lessons are for example only. They may look different than actual curriculum materials.

Work Time

A. Say Something: Reading for Gist and Determining the Message, Lesson, or Moral: *Waiting for the Biblioburro* **(30 minutes)**

▪ Distribute and display **Reading for Gist and Recounting the Story:** *Waiting for the Biblioburro.*

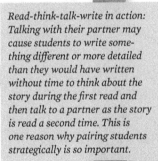

Technology & Multimedia

▪ Work Time A: Students complete their note-catchers in a word-processing document, such as a Google Doc, using speech-to-text facilities activated on devices or using an app or software like Dragon Dictation (http://www.nuance.com/for-individuals/mobile-applications/dragon-dictation/index.htm).

▪ Work Time A: Depending on the time you have available, consider showing students the following video about the real biblioburro: Ruffins, Ebonne. "Teaching Kids to Read from the Back of a Burro." *CNN.* Cable News Network, 26 Feb. 2010. Web. 14 Mar. 2016. <http://www.cnn.com/2010/LIVING/02/25/cnnheroes.soriano/>. Consider that YouTube, social media video sites, and other website links may incorporate inappropriate content via comment banks and ads. Although some lessons include these links as the most efficient means to view content in preparation for the lesson, preview links and/or use a filter service, such as www.safeshare.tv, for viewing these links in the classroom.

▪ Tell students they are going to hear *Waiting for the Biblioburro* read aloud again and use the Say Something protocol to complete this note-catcher.

▪ When prompted, they will turn and talk to an elbow partner—or "say something"—about a prompt or question. After sharing ideas with their partner, they will record them on the note-catcher.

▪ Read through each of the boxes on the Reading for Gist and Recounting the Story note-catcher and explain what students will record in each.

▪ Tell students that when they write on their note-catcher, they will write notes. Remind students that notes help them remember their thinking and do not have to be full sentences.

▪ Answer any clarifying questions.

▪ Show the cover of *Waiting for the Biblioburro* again and model writing the book title and author in the box at the top of the note-catcher.

▪ Reread *Waiting for the Biblioburro* aloud, stopping at strategic points for students to "say something" to their partner in response to a question.

▪ Refer to the **Reading for Gist Guide:** *Waiting for the Biblioburro* **(for teacher reference)** and **Reading for Gist and Recounting the Story:** *Waiting for the Biblioburro* **(example, for teacher reference)** for guidance.

The Say Something protocol: The teacher reads Waiting for the Biblioburro *again, stopping after key phrases, and asks a question (provided in the supporting materials). With their partners, each student then "says something" in response to the question and then records a response on their note-catcher. The questions are designed to help students determine the gist of the story. This protocol is a routine that is used in many of the 3–5 modules as an early, simple way for students to begin orally processing their reading.*

Read-think-talk-write in action: Talking with their partner may cause students to write something different or more detailed than they would have written without time to think about the story during the first read and then talk to a partner as the story is read a second time. This is one reason why pairing students strategically is so important.

EL Education Curriculum   71

Chapter 6

Note: Lessons are for example only. They may look different than actual curriculum materials.

Multiple modes of expression: Note that in addition to the required "talk," the lesson suggests an option of having students act out the story. Having students use their bodies, as well as language, to convey their understanding further deepens all students' learning and gives those with limited speaking skills another way to express their understanding.

- Consider inviting students to act out the story as you read, switching out actors after the strategic stopping points.

- After students have completed their notes, invite them to cover the questions and answers in the boxes at the bottom of their note-catcher.

- Explain that often when an author writes a book, there is an important message, lesson, or moral relevant to the real world outside of the book that he or she wants readers to take away. Tell students that sometimes the author explicitly states—or comes right out and says—the text's message, lesson, or moral. Other times, the message, lesson, or moral needs to be inferred from details in the text. Remind students that inferring means making a good guess based on evidence.

Discussion support: Another brief protocol, Think-Pair-Share, as well as a Conversation Cue are used to support students to think and talk about what they infer the message, lesson, or moral of the story to be, based on evidence from the text (which is captured on their note-catchers).

- Invite students to Think-Pair-Share, leaving adequate time for each partner to think, ask the question to their partner, and partner share:

"Use your Reading for Gist and Recounting the Story note-catcher to think about what happened in this story. What message, lesson, or moral relevant to the real world and outside of the story do you think the author wants you to learn from this story? What details make you think that?" (Responses will vary, but may include: Books are important.)

- If productive, use a Goal 1 Conversation Cue to encourage students to clarify the conversation about the lesson and the details that convey it:

"So, do you mean _____?" (Responses will vary.)

Synthesizing learning: Students' note-catchers serve as a form of evidence as they begin to think about the message, lesson, or moral of Waiting for the Biblioburro.

- Invite students to uncover the questions and possible answers in the boxes on the bottom of the Reading for Gist and Recounting the Story note-catcher.

- Read Question A and the possible answers. Invite students to turn and talk with an elbow partner:

"Which answer(s) do you think is definitely incorrect? Why? Cross it out."

"Which answer do you think is correct? Why?"

- Invite students to underline the answer they think is correct on their note-catcher.

- Using equity sticks, cold call students to share out and clarify any misconceptions. Refer to the Reading for Gist and Recounting the Story: *Waiting for the Biblioburro* (example, for teacher reference) as necessary.

- Repeat this process with Question B.

- Ask students to turn and talk, and cold call students to share their responses with the whole group:

"How did you answer these questions? What strategies did you use?"

Metacognition: After reading, thinking, talking, and writing, students identify strategies for answering selected response questions. While they are analyzing this specific text, they also are building transferable reading and test-taking strategies.

- If productive, use a Goal 1 Conversation Cue to encourage students to expand the strategies conversation:

"Can you give an example?" (Responses will vary.)

- As students share out, capture their responses on the **Strategies to Answer Selected Response Questions anchor chart**. Refer to the **Strategies to Answer Selected Response Questions anchor chart (example, for teacher reference)** as necessary.

- Direct students' attention to the Guiding Questions anchor chart.

- Invite students to Think-Pair-Share, leaving adequate time for each partner to think, ask the question to their partner, and partner share:

"From what you heard in **Waiting for the Biblioburro**, *why are books and reading impor-*

Note: Lessons are for example only. They may look different than actual curriculum materials.

tant to Ana?" (because she enjoys the stories)

"Are books and reading important to you? Why?" (Responses will vary, but may include: because reading helps me to learn about the world; it helps me to escape when I read fiction books about other people and other worlds)

- If productive, use a Goal 1 Conversation Cue to encourage students to expand the books and reading conversation:

"Can you give an example?" (Responses will vary.)

- Refocus students on the strategy on Close Readers Do These Things anchor chart practiced today. Ask students to turn and talk, and cold call students to share their responses with the whole group:

"How did this strategy help us to better understand this text?"

- Tell students that today they did part of a process called close reading, and that they will continue practicing this process throughout the year.

- Refocus students on the learning targets. Read each one aloud, pausing for students to give a thumbs-up, thumbs-down, or thumbs-sideways to indicate how close they are to meeting that target now. Make note of students who may need additional support with each of the learning targets moving forward. Repeat, inviting students to self-assess against how well they showed respect.

Meeting Students' Needs

- For ELLs and students who may need additional support with writing: Prepare sticky notes with prewritten words or drawings based on the gist of different sections of the text. As students listen to the story, they can match the gist represented on the sticky notes with each section of the read-aloud. (MMAE)

- For ELLs and students who may need additional support with comprehension: Invite students to turn to an elbow partner and retell *Waiting for the Biblioburro* in 1 minute or less. Have them share out and give them feedback on their language use and summarizing skill. Then, invite them to turn to their partner and summarize once again, this time in 30 seconds or less. Repeat the feedback process. (MMAE)

- For ELLs and students who may need additional support with comprehension: To ensure that the purpose of the Reading for Gist and Recounting the Story note-catcher is clear, ask:

"Why are we using this Reading for Gist and Recounting the Story note-catcher?" (to focus on the character, setting, motivation, challenge, and solution in Waiting for the Biblioburro, which will help us talk about overcoming learning challenges and succeed on the Mid-Unit 1 Assessment; to focus on how details convey the moral; the note-catcher format Someone/In/Wanted/But/So can be used as a sentence frame to explain the focus) (MMR, MME)

- For ELLs and students who may need additional support with expressive language: Students who need heavier support may have trouble verbalizing their thoughts when it is their turn to "say something." Help them identify key entries in their graphic organizer and allow them to repeat phrases and sentences that you model. (Example: If a student wrote *house* or drew a house in the "setting" row, point to it and the picture of the house on the first page of *Waiting for the Biblioburro* and say: "It takes place in Colombia, in a house on a hill behind a tree."

Revisiting purpose: Teacher questions invite students to connect the central message of this text to the big ideas of the module, as they think about why books and reading are important to Ana. Reading continues to build students' knowledge about the world.

Connecting to personal experience: Students connect the importance of books to the character Ana to the importance of books in their own lives. The teacher allows plenty of think time before students share their thoughts with their partner.

Checking for understanding: Students self-assess their progress toward the learning targets. Likely, the rich opportunities for reading, thinking, talking, and writing (note-taking) in this lesson supported almost all students to meet the targets. And even if not, students at least are coming to see that they will regularly have opportunities for interaction as they work to comprehend and analyze text.

Note: Lessons are for example only. They may look different than actual curriculum materials.

Encourage the student to repeat the sentence while pointing to the graphic organizer and the picture of the house in *Waiting for the Biblioburro*.) (MMR)

- For students who may need additional support with fine motor skills: Offer choice with Reading for Gist and Recounting the Story: *Waiting for the Biblioburro* by providing a template that includes lines. (MMR, MME)

- For ELLs and students who may need additional support with comprehension: Display, repeat, and rephrase the questions and answers on Reading for Gist and Recounting the Story: *Waiting for the Biblioburro*. (MMR)

- For ELLs, be aware that in some cultures the thumbs-up gesture may have a different meaning. Consider choosing a different way for students to show their learning against the targets or use it as a teaching point to explain what it means in the United States. Scan the responses and make a note of students who may need more support with this moving forward.

Closing and Assessment

A. Overcoming Learning Challenges (5 minutes)

▪ Focus students on the **Overcoming Learning Challenges anchor chart**.

▪ Invite students to Think-Pair-Share, leaving adequate time for each partner to think, ask the question to their partner, and partner share:

"What challenge did Ana face?" (no teacher and no access to books)

"How was the challenge overcome?" (A man brought a traveling library to the village on his burros.)

▪ As students share out, capture their responses on the Overcoming Learning Challenges anchor chart. Refer to the **Overcoming Learning Challenges anchor chart (example, for teacher reference)** as necessary.

Meeting Students' Needs

- For ELLs and students who may need additional support with comprehension/expressive language: In preparation for the Mid-Unit 1 Assessment, ask:

  "What is one thing you like about the book **Waiting for the Biblioburro?"**

  For students who may need heavier support, provide sentence frames:

  "One thing I like about **Waiting for the Biblioburro** *is _____."* (the beautiful pictures; the way Ana works hard to learn; how the librarian uses donkeys to travel to Ana) *(MMAE)*

- For students who are unsure of the answers to these questions, encourage them to repeat or paraphrase what their peers say. (MMAE)

Circling back to the guiding question: Students have a final chance to consider the guiding question and add to the Overcoming Learning Challenges anchor chart. Before sharing out, students Think-Pair-Share with their partner.

Meeting Students' Needs: Students who are unsure of what to say can paraphrase what their partner shares. There are many opportunities to talk: as a way to deepen understanding of the text and as a way to develop oral language (important for all students, but particularly critical for ELLs).

Note: Lessons are for example only. They may look different than actual curriculum materials.

Chapter 6C:
How Can Models, Critique, and Descriptive Feedback Strengthen Student Writing within and beyond the Curriculum?

In our curriculum, we use models and descriptive feedback (often in the form of peer critique) to not only strengthen students' writing, but also to help them develop habits of character and resiliency as learners. When students analyze models, they continue to build knowledge as readers and, as writers, they develop a clear understanding of the characteristics of quality writing in various formats and for diverse purposes. Understanding these criteria gives them a path to success. And descriptive feedback, often given through peer critique that is focused and specific, can have a powerful impact on student learning: Students who are taught to identify and correct their own errors are more likely to make long-term gains (Beach and Friedrich, 2006).

EL Education has written extensively on the use of models, critique, and descriptive feedback to support students to create high-quality work, including high-quality writing. Our book *Leaders of Their Own Learning: Transforming Schools through Student-Engaged Assessment* (Berger, Rugen, and Woodfin, 2014) includes a chapter on these practices that has greatly informed how we approach the writing process in our curriculum. Rather than reinventing the wheel, we have excerpted parts of the "Models, Critique, and Descriptive Feedback" chapter of *Leaders of Their Own Learning* for you here. We hope these excerpts will give you greater insight into how to approach these practices when teaching our curriculum and also generate excitement for how you might use the practice during other parts of your students' day, beyond the curriculum.[3]

It is important to note that we have excerpted portions of this chapter for you here because we feel that using models, critique, and descriptive feedback to help students improve the quality of their work can be a game-changer for students. Not everything in this chapter, however, is germane to our K–5 curriculum. But because we know that you teach other things in addition to our curriculum, we have included examples we think will prove useful. We want to keep encouraging you to see the curriculum and this book as a form of professional development. Rather than

---

[3] Full, formal group critique lessons, in which students and teachers use models to define the qualities of high-quality work in a specific genre, thus helping students build understanding of content and setting a standard for high-quality work, are not emphasized in our curriculum. However, these lessons are still a potentially powerful practice for your students and will be explored in this chapter as a "beyond the curriculum" extension.

thinking "this doesn't apply to the curriculum," think: "How can I bring this practice to my students during other parts of their day? How might these practices serve my students as mathematicians, athletes, or artists? What can I learn from this? How can it help me grow as a teacher?"

If you are just getting your sea legs with the curriculum, you may wish to wait to read Chapter 6C until you are feeling comfortable and confident. That's perfectly fine. Come back to it when you're ready to fine-tune these practices.

▶ How Can I Use Models, Critique, And Descriptive Feedback as Tools for Improvement?

It is a challenge to think of a skilled profession that does not rely on models, critique, and descriptive feedback to improve performance. Imagine fields such as medicine, journalism, or software development without clear models and continual critique and revision. Professionals in these fields know what a high-quality product looks like—whether it's a Pulitzer Prize–winning article or a software application with record-breaking sales—and these models provide them with a reference point for productive critique and feedback that will enable them to improve their own work. Professional dancers have watched thousands of dance performances and have them etched in their minds. Professional basketball players have watched thousands of games. They have a clear picture of where they want to go, and they need continual critique from coaches and colleagues to get there.

Picture a ballet troupe without someone continually adjusting posture and position, or a basketball team never critiquing strategies during halftime or analyzing their play on video. These ongoing feedback practices, which help us improve, are essential in nearly every field. Despite its prevalence in the world, this kind of on-the-job, on-the-spot feedback, based on strong models, is still strangely absent from many schools and classrooms. To be sure, grades and test scores abound, and occasionally students get assignments returned with comments, but these "results" are often thin and too distant from the moment of learning or effort to be useful.

Now more than ever, with the introduction of rigorous college- and career-ready standards, students need models of work that meets standards, and they need structured opportunities for critique and descriptive feedback so that they too can produce work that meets the standards. Students and teachers alike will benefit from seeing—sometimes even holding in their hands—examples of what they are aiming for. See the box: Defining Models, Critique, and Descriptive Feedback in the Curriculum and Beyond for brief definitions. Much more detail, including examples and videos, is provided in the pages that follow.

★ **Defining Models, Critique, and Descriptive Feedback in the Curriculum and Beyond**

Models. Models bring standards to life. They are exemplars of work used to build a vision of quality within a genre. Models are generally strong in important dimensions, which are discussed with students before they create their own work based on the model.

» **In the curriculum.** Models are provided for you in the curriculum. These models are always based on content students know and set expectations for quality work; however, they don't "give away" the thinking we want students to do in their own work. For example, if students need to write about a character in a story, the model will be about a different character in the same story.

» **In lessons beyond the curriculum.** Models can be drawn from current or prior student work or the professional world, or they can be created by the teacher.

Note: Models tend to be full drafts or completed work. They are artifacts that students examine. The curriculum also includes *modeling* (particularly for Grades K–2), when the teacher writes as students watch to show students how to apply a specific writing skill.

Critique lessons. In a critique lesson, students look at models together to develop criteria for quality work in a genre. The cognitive work they do to generate those criteria (by discovering and naming features that demonstrate quality) leads them to new learning and understandings about content. Critique lessons are standards-driven, with clear objectives, and are designed to support the learning of all students, not primarily to improve the work of one (as would a one-on-one peer critique).

> » **In the curriculum.** We don't typically include full critique lessons in the curriculum, but students do "unpack" models and "non-models," looking for attributes that make them high-quality work (or not).

> » **In lessons beyond the curriculum.** A full critique lesson, with clear objectives, is a powerful lever to kick off students' own efforts to create high-quality work and build understanding of content. Models, which serve as the reference point to generate criteria for quality work, are at the heart of critique lessons.

Descriptive feedback. Descriptive feedback may take place in the form of a teacher conferring with an individual student, written comments from the teacher, or a peer critique session. The constructive, precise comments that make up descriptive feedback specifically address a particular piece of work by a single student and are articulated in a way to raise the quality of the work toward the gold standard of the model. Feedback should lift up both positive aspects of the work as well as areas to grow and should always be kind, specific, and helpful.

> » **In the curriculum.** Descriptive feedback often takes the form of peer critique. As opposed to a critique lesson, which is designed to help all students take aim at high-quality work, a peer critique is designed for students to help each other improve their own individual work. (For a specific example of how the curriculum prepares students for peer critique, see Figure 6.13, which is an excerpt from a kindergarten lesson.)

> » **In lessons beyond the curriculum.** In addition to providing opportunities for students to give and receive peer feedback, honing your own skills at providing students with descriptive feedback will be an additional tool in your toolbox for helping students complete high-quality work.

What Makes These Practices So Effective?

Models, critique, and descriptive feedback are critical to helping students become leaders of their own learning. The practices help students meet standards by giving them the tools they need to answer the question that may paralyze them when they get their work back for revision: "Now what?" Often, students simply copyedit for conventions based on teacher corrections—grammar, spelling, and punctuation—and don't actually revise the work.

Instead, picture a student participating in a group critique lesson of a strong historical essay, chosen by his teacher as a model. The teacher has decided to focus only on the introductory paragraphs; each student reads and text codes the model for those paragraphs. The class then generates a list of the qualities that stand out as effective (e.g., thesis is clearly stated). Those qualities are discussed and written on chart paper in the front of the room.

When his teacher returns the first draft of his essay the next day, the student also receives a copy of the list of qualities that make for a good introduction to an essay that he and his classmates generated. He must now revise the introduction to match those qualities. He looks over his own paper and the need for revision is clear, as is the substance of what he needs to add and change. Critique, descriptive feedback, and the use of models are all practices designed to give students a vision of quality so that they know what they are aiming for.

Making Standards Real and Tangible

Standards do not create a picture of what students are aiming for. They are typically dry, technical descriptions. When a Common Core State Standard (CCSS) requires that students "use organization that is appropriate to task and purpose" or "use a variety of transitional words and phrases to manage the sequence of events," what does that mean? What does that look like?

Examining models and generating the criteria for success gives students a roadmap for meeting standards. They know what they are aiming for and how to get there. In addition to CCSS Writing standard W.5—*develop and strengthen writing as needed by planning, revising, editing, rewriting, or trying a new approach*—which speaks directly to the benefits of models, critique, and descriptive feedback, other connections to the standards include the following:

» Both the mathematics and literacy standards explicitly demand that students become independent learners who can "critique the reasoning of others."

» The need for students to evaluate the validity and quality of reasoning and craftsmanship permeates the standards. The strategies described in this chapter build students' skills to do so in a sophisticated way.

» Quality critique and descriptive feedback requires students to point to evidence to support their claims, a key to meeting the standards.

Starting with learning targets puts standards in concrete terms that students understand. Models then bring those learning targets to life and help students and teachers build a shared understanding of what success looks like.

Building a Mindset of Continuous Improvement

Critique and descriptive feedback help students understand that all work, learning, and performance can be improved. We can tell students that their potential to learn is great, but they won't believe it, especially in areas in which they don't feel confident, until they actually see themselves improve. There is nothing that does this more effectively than when students work through multiple drafts, rehearsals, or practices and end up creating work or performing at a level that is beyond what they thought possible. Participating in critique, developing the criteria for high-quality work, and giving, receiving, and using feedback promotes a growth mindset and teaches students the value of effort and revision. Figure 6.4 is a great example of the power of habits of character (e.g., *work to become effective learners*) and a mindset of continuous improvement.

Figure 6.4: Natalie's Grasshopper: Multiple Drafts

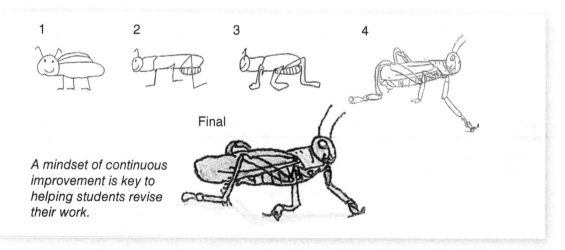

A mindset of continuous improvement is key to helping students revise their work.

Instilling Responsibility and Ownership of Learning

Critique and descriptive feedback emphasize skills of critical analysis and self-assessment and ask students to make important decisions about their work and learning. Because the path to meeting learning targets is clearly defined by a shared vision of what quality looks like, students can work independently and build skills confidently.

▶ How Can I Develop a Positive Classroom Culture That Will Allow Critique and Descriptive Feedback to Flourish?

To be effective, critique and descriptive feedback require a deliberate and sustained attention to emotional safety and depend on skills of collaboration. These practices help a classroom become a learning community dedicated to getting better together. An essential starting point for critique and descriptive feedback in any classroom is ensuring that the guidelines **BE KIND, BE SPECIFIC,** and **BE HELPFUL** are the backbone of every class. Formal and informal feedback and critique flow from these. Safety and encouragement, as well as structure and clear learning targets, will set students up for success.

Just about everyone has a feedback nightmare, a time when they felt hurt or judged by someone's feedback or criticism. Some students are particularly vulnerable, especially if they have not experienced much school success and have received many messages of negative criticism (both implicit and explicit). School and classroom guidelines must be carefully built and reinforced, but individual feedback also must be tailored and shaped with the particular student in mind. There is not a template or cookie-cutter approach that will work for every student.

"The conversations about habits of character have really impacted students. They focus more on their own learning than on 'getting it done.' Students work from the idea that although this is good, I can make it better and better. As they become more adept at giving and receiving feedback, they can become more critical of the feedback itself. They also become able to self-assess, which is a critical component of being college- and career-ready."

Tammi Bauschka

Literacy Program Specialist, Tucson, Arizona

This kind of safety can be hard to monitor. You must be vigilant and firm, especially when building a classroom culture with a new group. Very young students often don't realize that their comments may be perceived as mean. They can be candid even when it's hurtful to others and need to learn how to word things carefully. Sometimes older students may intentionally, but subtly, undermine a peer's work, such as complimenting work with a sarcastic tone or facial expression. It is imperative that you stop the critique the moment problems happen, deal firmly with unkind or untruthful comments or tone, and reestablish norms. Eventually, students will trust and reinforce the norms themselves. The curriculum's consistent emphasis on habits of character, particularly *work to become ethical people* and *work to become effective learners*, will both create the conditions for and reinforce these efforts. (Note: For more information on habits of character in the curriculum, see Chapter 7C.)

Establishing norms for critique is intimately tied to the work of building an active and collaborative culture described in Chapter 3C. If you haven't read that chapter yet, it's worth reading it before embarking on using models, critique, and descriptive feedback with your students. The Snapshot that follows offers a window into one teacher's work to build this kind of culture in his classroom.

📷 Snapshot: Building Culture with Fourth-Graders

"To build habits that establish a culture in which quality is the norm, I begin with a basic but demanding task that each student can accomplish, yet all can improve: the challenge of drawing freehand a straight line," says Steven Levy, EL Education school coach and former fourth-grade teacher at Bowman Elementary School in Lexington, Massachusetts. "I introduce standards of quality that guide our work throughout the year." Students develop the language, norms, and skills of describing quality through group critique as they analyze lines.

Levy assigns every student the task of drawing a straight line freehand and uses the work to demonstrate generating criteria, feedback and critique, revision, planning ahead, taking care of resources, and above all the norms of a safe, collaborative, and constructive classroom. "Practicing these drawings is a particularly effective way to begin the year because everyone has equal access to the assignment. No one can do it perfectly, so everyone is challenged," he says.

"When students have learned this process of producing quality work, they are ready to apply it to more complex tasks. We now go through the same process to develop standards for writing, for presentations, and for major projects. We do not follow the exact steps in the line exercises for everything we do. Sometimes I give more explicit instruction or direction at the beginning. At other times, depending on the effectiveness of the students' work, I recommend additional critique sessions or more practice of discrete skills between drafts. The steps are simply tools and processes designed to help students take more responsibility in producing quality work."

▶ How Can the Use of Models Improve My Students' Work?

Here, and throughout this chapter, we will consider the ways in which this practice is used within our curriculum and then offer guidance for those of you who may feel ready to extend the practice beyond the curriculum.

Using Models in the Curriculum

Models should show students where they are headed. They don't need to be perfect, but they must be good models of features that are connected to learning targets. Within the set of interrelated practices—models, critique, and descriptive feedback—models are the linchpin. They set the standard and the expectation from which critique and descriptive feedback flow.

In the curriculum, models have been provided. Often a model of strong work helps ground students in a vision of what excellent work on a particular task would look like. Sometimes, students also may analyze a model of weak work before beginning their own work. The models in the curriculum will be similar, but not exactly the same, as the work students will do independently.

Any time we ask students to analyze models, it is important to first give them time to think about the content and then ask them to analyze the craft. For example, if students are analyzing a Martin Luther King speech, we wouldn't first ask them "What rhetorical devices did King use?" Instead, we would bring them into the text by asking: "What was King trying to say? Why is it important?" Then we can move students to "How did King craft his speech to have the most impact on his readers?" First we want students to read as readers, and *then* to read as writers.

It is important that the model not give too much away in terms of the kinds of thinking we want students to do, but it should be familiar to them so that they can connect to it easily. For example:

> » In kindergarten Module 2, Lesson 7, before students draw in their weather journal, they examine one model and one non-model of similar work and share what they notice (see Figures 6.5 and 6.6). Often non-models are used to set expectations for craftsmanship. In this case, the non-model shows black clouds, a purple sun, and color extending outside the lines.

Figure 6.5: Kindergarten Model of Weather Journal

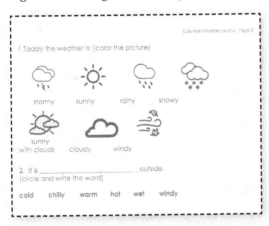

Figure 6.6: Kindergarten Non-Model of Weather Journal

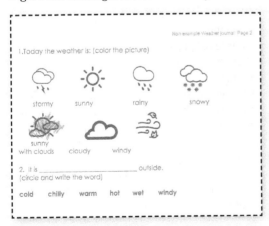

> » In Grade 2, Module 3, students research bees together as a class and then research other pollinators in expert groups. Before they write about the pollinators from their expert group, they examine a model piece of writing about bees (see Figure 6.7). Figure 6.8 is an excerpt from Unit 3, Lesson 1 in which students analyze the model and begin working on their own illustrations. (You can see a pollinator drawing resulting from this lesson on page 13.)

Figure 6.7: Grade 2 Pollinators Model

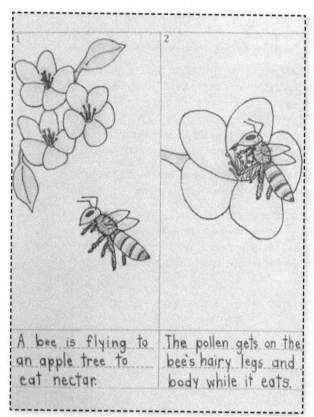

Figure 6.8: Analyzing a Model: Excerpt of a Grade 2 Lesson

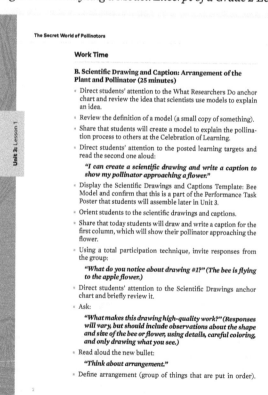

Using Models beyond the Curriculum

Models are provided for you in the curriculum, but if you want to extend this practice into other parts of your students' day, you'll need to gather your own models. Learning how to recognize and select powerful, generative models is important, and it takes practice. The more compelling the models are, the more powerful students' analysis will be. Ideally, you will begin building an archive of good work models that you gather and store for specific purposes. When you need to teach the format or genre of a research paper, for example, you have a file of research papers by former or other students to draw from.

You might also choose to create exemplary models yourself or find models from the professional world to set a high and authentic bar, especially for older students. If models of current student work are used, it is important to choose samples that represent different approaches to the same assignment, or different strong features, so there is little duplication in what is viewed and discussed. There should be a specific reason for each piece chosen. If the class is going to spend valuable, whole-class time considering a piece, there should be a clear reason and a connection to learning targets.

Using Weak Work as a Non-Example

Although it is most important to have exemplary models, it can also be useful to have examples of pieces that are poorly done in different ways, particularly in those areas that you feel your students may struggle. For example, to help students remember to be less repetitive with sentence structure in a composition, it can be powerful to have them critique an anonymous student composition that is fraught with repetitive language. The image of this weak work will stay with them and can be discussed regularly to remind the group to be careful to avoid its pitfalls.

When using weak work, there are some cautions. First, the work must be anonymous. Students should never be able to recognize it as the work of a current or former student. Second, the work must be treated respectfully. Modeling mean-spirited critique will promote an unkind classroom climate. Last, not all weak work is a good choice. Ideally, the work is compelling in its flaws. For example, if it is very strong in some areas but confusing in others, it can invite wonder and analysis. The best weak work is not an example of a student who wasn't trying, but rather a student who was putting in effort and created something interesting to consider, but had confusions that resulted in problems that are likely to crop up for many students.

▶ How Can I Build Standards-Based Critique Lessons around Models?

In the curriculum, we do not build entire lessons around models. Typically, the models (or non-models) are analyzed with students as one part of a lesson. However, designing standards-based critique lessons is a powerful practice that gives students a deep understanding of what quality looks like in a particular genre. The section that follows on critique lessons should be considered a "beyond the curriculum" practice—it will be well worth your time to read and practice when you are ready, willing, and able.

Conducting Standards-Based Critique Lessons, beyond the Curriculum

In a critique lesson, students look at models together to develop criteria for quality work in a genre. The cognitive work they do to generate that criteria (by discovering and naming features that demonstrate quality) leads them to new learning and understandings about content. A critique becomes more than a simple exercise in closely examining student work when it leads students to new learning, application of knowledge and skills, and meeting standards. It then becomes a standards-driven critique lesson. As with all lessons in our curriculum, standards-based learning targets are the foundation of every critique lesson. Critique lessons will not be effective without clear learning targets and models of what meeting the learning target looks like.

For those of you who are ready to try out this practice beyond the curriculum, we have included a sample in-depth critique based on a Grade 4 Common Core mathematics standard (see Snapshot: In-Depth Critique Lesson in a fourth-grade Mathematics Class). This example illustrates how effective critique can be as a lesson. Many concepts and areas of content that you might address in a more conventional lesson can be addressed more powerfully and concretely in a lesson connected to a critique of real work. Rather than *telling* students about the dimensions of good work in that genre, the students discover and name those features themselves. It is clearer, more engaging, and more memorable than a lecture-style lesson. Critique lessons like this actively involve students in analyzing work against learning targets and compel them to use academic vocabulary and cite evidence for their assertions. These are key skills for meeting standards.

> **📷 Snapshot: In-Depth Critique Lesson in a Fourth-Grade Mathematics Class**
>
> **Common Core Standard 4.MD.A.3**
>
> Apply the area and perimeter formulas for rectangles in real-world and mathematical problems.
>
> **Learning Targets**
>
> **1.** I can recognize when the formulas for rectangular areas and perimeters are used correctly in student work and can explain why, using evidence from the work.
>
> **2.** I can describe what a good solution to a real-world area and perimeter problem looks like and explain why.
>
> **Step 1: Choosing Work Samples for a Clear Purpose**
>
> The teacher has a collection of student work from prior years of students measuring rectangular spaces in the school, drawing labeled diagrams, and calculating area and

perimeter. From this collection, she creates a packet with four work samples—two samples are fully accurate (though different in approach); one is partially accurate; one is fully inaccurate. All of the work is anonymous, and there are no labels as to which samples are accurate and which are not.

Step 2: Individual Challenge (5 minutes)

The teacher hands a packet of the four samples to each student. Students silently and individually analyze the samples and try to make sense of them, determining which they think are accurate and why.

Step 3: Group Analysis (10 minutes)

The students are clustered into groups of four. Each group discusses which of the samples they feel are accurate and justifies their opinions with evidence from the work.

Step 4: Whole Group Critique (15 minutes)

The teacher leads the class in an analysis of the samples. First, she introduces the learning targets for the lesson. Next, she leads the class in analyzing each of the four student samples. She begins with what they noticed about the samples—without judgment—focusing on what strikes them about the work. She then focuses on accuracy, discussing which ones they feel are correct and why, citing evidence. After this, she leads the group in discussing which samples are good examples—those that are clear and correctly labeled and include well-explained reasoning.

Step 5: Small Group Brainstorm (5 minutes)

Small groups brainstorm a list of the attributes of a good solution—accurate and well presented.

Step 6: Synthesis: Building of Collaborative Criteria (15 minutes)

The teacher runs a whole class discussion, eliciting comments from each group. She charts their thinking about what a good solution to a real-world rectangular perimeter and area problem looks like.

Defining the Purpose for Each Critique Lesson

Critique lessons can have a variety of specific purposes: setting standards of quality and developing criteria for work (as in the example), supporting focused revision, or fine-tuning final presentations, products, or performances. It is important to make the particular focus of the critique clear from the outset. Frame the critique with learning targets so that you can keep track of guiding the inquiry to address them. Clarity about learning targets should not prevent the critique from producing unplanned discoveries, clarifications, and new ideas or directions, and it is important to celebrate and identify these.

Teacher-facilitated critique lessons that include looking together at models can be used to address learning in a variety of disciplines. The lesson could focus on the following:

» Content (e.g., simple machines, a historical timeline)

» Concepts (e.g., recurring themes in history, binary numbers)

» Skills (e.g., keyboarding, interpreting a bar chart, factoring equations)

» Product formats or genres (e.g., business letter, political map, watercolor portrait)

» Habits of character (e.g., group collaboration during fieldwork excursions, participation during literature circles, hallway behavior)

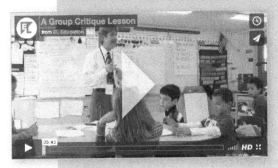

In the accompanying video, see EL Education's Ron Berger lead a group critique lesson with students from the Presumpscot School in Portland, Maine. The third-graders use a piece of student writing as a model from which to identify criteria for a quality story.

https://vimeo.com/44053703

Determining the Right Timing for a Critique Lesson in a Sequence of Curriculum

Depending on the goals and learning targets, critique lessons can be useful at a variety of times in a curriculum or long-term study:

- » **Introductory teacher-facilitated lessons using previously collected models:** to set a high standard for quality and to construct with students a framework of criteria for what constitutes good work in that domain or product format.

- » **In process, during the creation of work:** to support focused revision, clarify and tune student efforts to apply criteria for quality, refocus student concentration and momentum, and introduce new concepts or next steps.

- » **Just before final exhibition of work:** to fine-tune the quality of the presentation, display, or performance for an audience. Often final details and touches make a major difference in quality.

- » **After completion of an assignment:** to reflect on quality and learning and to set goals.

Depending also on the assignment or project being created, each of these points in the sequence of study suggests a different focus and style of critique lesson. Ideally a form of critique will be used at all points in the process.

OPPORTUNITIES TO CONDUCT CRITIQUE LESSONS IN THE CURRICULUM

The curriculum offers a number of logical opportunities when you might choose to conduct a critique lesson:

- » **K–5 Module Lessons.** You might choose to add a critique lesson during Unit 3 if you are noticing that students need more scaffolding with a specific aspect of the performance task.

- » **K–2 Module Lessons** (specifically when students do scientific drawing): You might conduct a gallery critique (see the section that follows for more information) so that students can identify techniques and strategies that they can use in their own work.

- » **K–2 Reading Foundations Skills Block**: You might choose to analyze a model of student writing that is particularly strong in the student's applications of certain spelling-sound patterns and ask students to identify the patterns.

As you become more familiar with the patterns of students' work in the curriculum, you can inject critique lessons at strategic points to scaffold toward clearer understanding of the expectations and more consistent high quality.

Chapter 6

Two Types of Critique Lessons

GALLERY CRITIQUE

In a gallery critique, all students post work for everyone to view closely. A gallery critique works best when the goal is to identify and capture only positive features in the selected work that can help everyone improve. Only a small set of the posted work may be cited. With work from the whole class, there is obviously going to be a lot of work with problems; this is not the time to try to point them all out. The point of a gallery critique is to find effective ideas and strategies in strong examples that students can borrow to improve their own work.

If the work is visual, it can be posted for viewing in a gallery style. If the work is written, it may be posted on a wall or copied and distributed. For written work, short pieces or a portion of a larger piece (e.g., a multistep word problem, the introduction to an essay, a poem) work best.

Clearly there are advantages to sharing every student's work, such as building accountability, excitement, shared commitment, and a realistic sense of how one's work compares with others. However, it is important to create safety for students whose initial performance on the assignment was weak. A protocol for a gallery critique might look something like this:

- » **Introduction.** Explain the steps of the protocol and the learning targets. Remind students of the norms of giving feedback: be kind, be specific, and be helpful.

- » **Step 1: Post the work (5 minutes).** Each student tapes his or her first draft to the wall.

- » **Step 2: Silent gallery walk (5 minutes).** Students view all of the drafts in a silent walk and take notes identifying strong examples of a predetermined focus (e.g., descriptive language, use of evidence, elegant problem-solving, experiment design).

- » **Step 3: What did you notice? (5 minutes).** Lead a discussion in which students are not allowed to make judgments or give opinions; they can comment only on things they noticed and identified.

- » **Step 4: What is working? (15 minutes).** Lead the class in a discussion of which aspects of the posted drafts grabbed their attention or impressed them. Each time students choose an example, they need to articulate exactly what they found compelling, citing evidence from the work itself. If they're not sure, draw them out until they can point to evidence in the work and name something specific. You should also point to examples you are impressed with and explain why. Chart the insights and codify specific strategies that students can use to improve their drafts.

IN-DEPTH CRITIQUE

A single piece of work (or set of related pieces) is used to uncover strengths or to highlight common areas in need of revision or gaps in knowledge that need to be addressed (e.g., use of evidence, descriptive language, topic development). Unlike a gallery critique, wherein the focus is exclusively on positive aspects in the collection of work, an in-depth critique analyzes a particular piece to determine which aspects are working and which are not. The goal is to recognize and name particular features that are effective or ineffective so that the class can learn from them. The Snapshot that follows describes one teacher's experience engaging her kindergarten students with an in-depth critique.

> 📷 **Snapshot: Using Critique and Descriptive Feedback to Create High-Quality Work**
>
> *This snapshot was adapted from a piece written by Jane Dunbar, kindergarten teacher at ANSER Charter School in Boise, Idaho, during her class's study of birds. Extensive fieldwork and research led students to their final product: beautiful, high-quality bird cards (see Figure 6.9 for an example of one student's bird card), which were sold throughout the state*

to raise money for bird habitats. The use of models and critique lessons were central to Dunbar's curriculum. (Note: This curriculum was created by the teacher and is not connected to our module on birds.)

Figure 6.9: Sample Bird Card

By February, we are ready to start the month-long project. Each child will research and draw a scientific representation of one bird. Although all kindergartners have the support of a fifth- or sixth-grade buddy for research, the drawings are all their own. Their exceptional drawings develop over time through carefully layered instructional practices and a classroom climate that makes all things seem possible to these young, impassioned learners. In a classroom community that supports strong character development (courage, compassion, respect, discipline, and integrity), children learn to challenge themselves, to give and receive constructive criticism, and to take risks as learners.

Steps to the Final Product

Best work: Kindergartners know that they must attend to lessons, practice, reflect on their work, and have the courage to take risks as learners and learn from their mistakes. I honor effort and intentions in this classroom each and every day. Kindergartners have been internalizing these behaviors since September.

A culture of quality: My role is to provide quality materials (paper, colored drawing pencils of every shade), exemplary photographs to work from, and modeling of how to visualize and then draw lines corresponding to the shape of a given bird.

Rubric. Students look at an exemplary bird drawing done by a former kindergartner. Next to this drawing is the photograph that was used as a model. "What do you notice?" I ask. Children look closely at similarities and differences. I help them tease generic comments into specific, explicit descriptions. After this close examination of work, I ask students what is important to notice when drawing a bird. The children develop criteria for the rubric. I use their words and add icons for each characteristic.

Collaborative Critique. Children continue to look closely at each other's work. This time, the rubric, the photo, and each draft of a peer's work is displayed. We focus our attention on the latest draft. I ask the children, "What do you notice?" I try to remind students that they only "notice" and that they do not make evaluative comments. I then ask the group, "What would you do on the next draft if this were yours?" And, "What would you change?" I challenge them for details. For example, "What about the eye?" and "What line, shape, color needs attention?" From this discussion, the child whose work is displayed makes his or her own decision about what will be the focus of the next draft and writes an intention on a sticky note. The child has been given many suggestions, but he or she has ownership of this next important decision of how to proceed. A collaborative critique of one child's work can take between 10 and 20 minutes.

Compliment Circle. A compliment circle follows the critique session. The student who has shown work calls on his or her peers for compliments. With both the critique and compliment circle, I have found it important to be sure each featured student gets the same number of constructive comments and compliments. Attention to balance saves any unintentional negative comparison between students and their work.

Sticky Notes. Each child, using the rubric as a guide, sets an intention for the focus of his or her efforts on the next draft. Writing the word or drawing the icon given on the rubric, the kindergartner focuses now on his or her own work and sets an intention. I place the

Chapter 6

sticky note above a new white piece of drawing paper and alert teachers and other adults present as to what the child is attempting to accomplish with this next draft. Adults can then support the child's intentions.

Doing More than They Thought Possible

Most children do four to five drafts before marking the rubric and formally assessing their own work. Each draft will take 30 to 40 minutes. At this point in the process, children decide if they have accomplished "best work" or if they wish to try again. A surprising number will want to try again. They are hooked. This process has led them far beyond what they ever thought possible.

Your Role during a Critique Lesson

Teachers must take an active role in facilitation throughout a critique lesson. This process works best when it looks organic (emerging entirely from student ideas) but is in fact skillfully shaped. Choose students strategically for comments, govern the flow of discussion and contribute enthusiasm, interject compelling comments to build interest and make key points, and reframe student observations when necessary to make them clear to the group and connected to the learning targets. Remember that this kind of critique is a lesson, with clear learning targets—don't hesitate to take charge of the flow to ensure that the session is productive.

BE A STRONG GUARDIAN OF CRITIQUE NORMS

Your most important role is to foster and sustain a critique culture that is emotionally safe for students and productive for learning. The critique rules, or norms, must be explicit and tracked vigilantly during the lesson to ensure that all students feel protected from ridicule (even subtle sarcasm or facial expressions) and that comments are specific and instructive. The critique rules should require participants to be kind, specific, and helpful in their comments. In the curriculum, during kindergarten Module 2, students are explicitly taught how to give kind, specific, and helpful feedback (see Figure 6.13 for an example).

In addition to guarding against any hurtful comments, this also means guarding against vague comments (e.g., "I like it," "It's good"). Students should point to specific features (e.g., "I think the title is well chosen," "Including the graph makes it much clearer to me") and stay connected to the goals for the critique lesson. Their comments should relate to the group effort to build understanding. Here are additional guidelines suggestions that can help to build a positive climate:

» It should always be clear that it is the work itself, not the author of the work, that is the subject of the critique.

» Use "I" statements (e.g., "I don't understand your first sentence" rather than "It doesn't make sense").

» Begin comments, if possible, with a positive feature in the work before moving on to perceived weaknesses (e.g., "I think the eyes in your portrait are very powerful, but I think adding eyebrows would give it more feeling").

» Frame ideas, when possible, as questions rather than as statements (e.g., "Why did you choose to leave out the illustration on this draft?" rather than "It was better with an illustration").

These norms are especially important when students are sharing their work with their classmates, but they apply even when the work is from outside of the class. Explicitly teaching and using critique rules will strengthen students' critique skills as well as their ability to hear and use descriptive feedback.

DISTILL, SHAPE, AND RECORD THE INSIGHTS FROM THE CRITIQUE

Many of the insights that you hope students will come to may arise from student comments, but you may need to jump on them, repeat them, reword them, or reframe them. Later they may even be codified for the class in the form of criteria or next steps. It is helpful to return to these insights during the critique, explicitly attributing them to the original student ("Tamika's theory" or "Jonathan's observation"), even though you have perhaps changed and deepened the original comment. If particular key insights don't arise, you shouldn't hesitate to seed them as questions or discovery challenges in viewing the work ("Did anyone notice...," "Can you see an example of...") or simply add them directly.

FOCUS ON NAMING THE SPECIFIC QUALITIES AND STRATEGIES THAT STUDENTS CAN TAKE AWAY WITH THEM

It is not useful for students to leave the session with the idea that "Aliya is a good writer" or "The book review we read was great," but rather, "Aliya used eight strategies that made her piece good, and now I know them and can use them." Naming the effective qualities and strategies must be explicit, openly discussed and negotiated, and must result in terms that students understand—in their language.

The more concrete the naming of features, the better. Charting the names of features and hanging them on the wall for reference helps. Vague insights put on a chart, such as "Use 'voice,'" are less helpful, particularly to weaker writers, than specific suggestions, such as "Include dialogue," "Use verbs other than 'said,'" "Use punctuation marks other than periods." Again, you should not hesitate to reshape student ideas into words that you feel will be clear and helpful, and to add to the list if students have omitted important qualities or strategies.

The process of naming qualities and strategies can also be a step in creating a rubric or a criteria list of what constitutes quality for this genre or skill, or it can refer to an existing rubric that the class uses, supporting that rubric with specific strategies. In the curriculum, the criteria for writing are held in writing rubrics that name specific qualities of high-quality writing in the genre (see Figure 6.10).

Figure 6.10: Sample Kindergarten Informative/Explanatory Writing Rubric

Opinion Writing Rubric: Grade K				
Use a combination of drawing, dictating, and writing to compose opinion pieces in which they tell a reader the topic or the name of the book they are writing about and state an opinion or preference about the topic or book (e.g., *My favorite book is…*).				
		4 – Advanced	3 – Proficient	2 – Developing	1 – Beginning
Knowledge and Understanding				
A	RL/RI.K.10	Demonstrates a deep understanding of topic or text	Demonstrates a clear understanding of topic or text	Demonstrates a limited understanding of topic or text	Does not demonstrate understanding, or shows a misunderstanding, of topic or text
Organization and Purpose				
B	W.K.1	**States** a relevant opinion and supplies a reason that supports the opinion	**States** a relevant opinion	Opinion is unrelated to task	Opinion is not stated
C		Briefly introduces the topic or text	**Names** the topic or text	Intended topic or text is unclear	Does not **name** the topic or text
Evidence and Elaboration				
D	L.K.6	Effectively uses domain-specific vocabulary	**Uses relevant words and phrases acquired through conversations, reading, being read to, and responding**	Uses a basic vocabulary	Uses a limited vocabulary

Note: Rubric is for example only. It may look different than actual curriculum materials.

TEACH THE VOCABULARY SO STUDENTS CAN TALK PRECISELY ABOUT THEIR WORK

Vocabulary is the foundation of effective critique. To use a metaphor, if critique is like surgery, carefully cutting into a piece of work to determine what is working well and what is not, then the surgical tools are the words we use to dissect the piece. If a student can use only simple terms to describe a piece (e.g., "It's good. I like it"), it's like attempting surgery with a butter knife. Students need sharp precision in their language to be effective surgeons (e.g., "I think the narrator's voice sounds too much like a kid our age and not like someone his character's age" or "Since you are writing a cause and effect essay, you may need to use more words that show causation"). The need for precision gives students an authentic reason and immediate application for learning new vocabulary and putting it to use. Critique lessons, peer feedback, and analyzing models together are all good opportunities for students to practice using precise academic and domain-specific vocabulary.

▶ Now That They Know What They Are Aiming for, What's the Best Way for My Students to Get Individual Feedback on Their Work?

Teachers give students feedback all the time. The question is, how much of this feedback is actually used by students to improve their learning? Figure 6.11 is a continuum of how a student might hear and use feedback.

Figure 6.11: Continuum of How Students Hear Feedback

Doesn't see it as feedback for him/herself. Blames other. "That teacher is mean."

⬇

Hears feedback, but ignores. Does what he/she wants to do anyway.

⬇

Hears feedback, would like to revise, but doesn't know how.

⬇

Receives feedback, revises, but does not meet the goal.

⬇

Receives feedback, revises, successfully meets the goal.

⬇

Receives feedback, revises, successfully meets goal, and can help others reach goal.

Source: Leaders of Their Own Learning: Transforming Schools through Student-Engaged Assessment. Copyright 2014 by John Wiley & Sons, Inc. All rights reserved.

Often the students most readily able to meet the final two points on the continuum are already the most capable, skilled, and successful. "Students can't hear something that's beyond their comprehension; nor can they hear something if they are not listening or are feeling like it would be useless to listen. Because students' feelings of control and self-efficacy are involved, even well-intentioned feedback can be very destructive ('See? I knew I was stupid!'). The research on feedback shows its Jekyll-and-Hyde character. Not all studies about feedback show positive effects. The nature of the feedback and the context in which it is given matter a great deal" (Brookhart, 2008, p. 2).

In this section, we propose that you think more analytically and strategically about the nature of the feedback you provide to students and that students provide to each other through peer critique. Descriptive feedback is distinguished by these features:

» The focus is on supporting the growth of an individual student or small group, improving a particular piece of work, performance, skill, or disposition.

» Feedback is focused on the work and is connected to clear criteria that students understand.

» It is typically an exchange between teacher and student, or student and student, and (unlike a critique lesson) it is not a public learning experience for the class.

» It is nested in a long-term relationship (e.g., teacher-student, student-student, coach-player, supervisor-worker). Maintaining a constructive relationship must be an implicit focus in all feedback conversations, whether spoken or written.

» Individuals are sensitive when receiving personal feedback. It is much more likely that strategic, positive comments will result in improvements than will criticism.

» Feedback ideally flows from strong knowledge of the student—knowing the student's strengths and weaknesses, knowing where she is in her growth and what she needs to spark the next step of growth.

It is most productive for students when descriptive feedback is connected to clear learning targets and helpful models, and when students have learned the language and norms of critique. In essence, when students are treated as partners in assessment from the outset, they will be in a much stronger position to make use of teacher and peer feedback.

Attending to How Feedback Is Given[3]

The good news is that like every other important instructional practice, feedback can be fine-tuned and improved through careful attention to its delivery and content. This is true for both teacher and peer feedback. Importantly, as students become more proficient giving and receiving feedback, they become more independent learners.

The Tone of Feedback

How words are used matters a great deal in giving effective feedback. Feedback should be understandable and user-friendly. Similar to learning targets, feedback should be framed in language students can readily understand.

» Effective tone:

- Be positive.

- Be constructive when critical.

- Make suggestions, not prescriptions or mandates.

» Ineffective tone:

- Finding fault

- Describing what is wrong but offering no suggestions

- Punishing or denigrating students for poor work

[3] Based on the work of Susan Brookhart and Connie Moss (Brookhart, 2008; Moss and Brookhart, 2009)

The Content of Feedback

Along with tone, the content of feedback is just as important. Assessment expert and author Grant Wiggins tells a useful story: "A student came up to [a teacher] at year's end and said, 'Miss Jones, you kept writing this same word on my English papers all year, and I still don't know what it means.' 'What's the word?' she asked. 'Vag-oo,' he said. (The word was vague!)" (Wiggins, 2012, p. 11). The following criteria for effective feedback will support students to use it productively:

» **Focusing on the work.** Feedback can be focused on the work or task, on the process of learning, or on the way a student self-regulates and uses his or her thought processes to accomplish a task. It should not be focused on the student personally, and personal comments should be avoided. Feedback should always be connected to the goals for learning and be actionable, offering specific ideas for what to do next and how to improve. (For example, "You have really persevered with getting the shape of this leaf just right! I notice that on your most recent draft the stem is colored green and doesn't look like the model. What can you try next?" will be more productive and actionable than "It looks like you got a little lazy on the stem.")

» **Comparing work to clear criteria.** Effective feedback compares student work or performance with criteria and with past performance, benchmarks, and personal goals. Norm-referenced feedback, which compares a student's performance with that of other students, is generally not useful. It doesn't help a student improve and often damages the motivation of unsuccessful students. (For example, you might tell a student, "You met the goal you set for yourself!" versus "This is the strongest work in the class!")

» **Helping students make progress.** The function or purpose of feedback is to describe how the student has done in order to identify ways and provide information about how to improve. Evaluating or judging performance does not help students improve. (For example, providing specific feedback tied to established criteria will help a student revise a draft, as opposed to stating that the work is simply "good" or "bad" or grading work in a draft stage, which tends to shut down motivation to revise.)

"If only using 'descriptive' vs. 'evaluative' feedback were simply a matter of wordsmithing! We could all learn how to write descriptive feedback just as we learned to write descriptive paragraphs in elementary school. Unfortunately, part of the issue is how the student understands the comment. Students filter what they hear through their own past experiences, good and bad" (Brookhart, 2008, p. 24). This brings us back to the importance of fostering a strong collaborative culture and building relationships with students. There are many strategies and techniques but unfortunately no shortcuts.

Preparing Students to Be Effective at Giving Feedback through Peer Critique

One of the most common structures for feedback and critique in classrooms is the use of peer critique. Often, teachers will ask their students to "find your writing critique partners and give them advice on their first draft" or something similar. In most cases, this practice is largely unproductive. Strategic, effective, specific feedback is a difficult enough practice for adults. For most students, it is impossible without guidance. Most of us have probably had the experience of listening into these peer feedback conversations among our students and finding the following common challenges:

» Students who can give only vague comments

» A confusing mix of copyediting (suggestions for spelling, grammar, and punctuation) with content or language suggestions. (Note: Helping students distinguish between these two types of feedback supports them in better understanding college- and career-ready language standards about conventions and grammar and writing standards about student thinking.)

» Students who finish their comments quickly and then engage in off-task discussions

Peer feedback can be effective when the conditions are right, when students are practiced in giving targeted feedback, and when they have clarity on the specific dimension of the work they are analyzing (see Figure 6.13 for an example of creating the conditions for productive peer critique).

Once students have learned the process of giving specific feedback effectively in these formal protocols, there is a positive phenomenon that can develop in which students begin giving each other informal critique, appropriately and respectfully, throughout the day.

▶▶ Video Spotlight

In the accompanying video, see how a strong skills focus, as well as appropriate vocabulary, helped students provide feedback to their classmate, Austin, which supported him to do exemplary work. Note that this video is actually embedded in lessons in the curriculum (specifically in Module 3 for Grades K–2, as students are learning how to do scientific drawing). Consider showing this video to students even earlier in the year so they understand what critique actually looks and sounds like. (See also the Snapshot: Peer Feedback in Small Groups).

https://vimeo.com/38247060

📷 Snapshot: Peer Feedback in Small Groups

At ANSER Charter School in Boise, Idaho, first-grade student Austin was preparing a scientific illustration of a Western Tiger Swallowtail, a local butterfly. The class had looked together at models of butterfly illustrations and had created criteria and a rubric for a strong illustration. In fact, they created two rubrics: one for the shape of the wings and one for the pattern inside the wings. Students were charged with using the eyes of scientists to examine a photograph and make sure its features and details were accurately represented in their illustration.

The problem was that Austin was just a first-grader, and when he began, he didn't look that carefully at the photograph; he defaulted to the icon of a butterfly shape that was in his head, and his first draft was a generic first-grade butterfly outline that looked nothing like a Western Tiger Swallowtail. Austin met with a small group on the carpet in front of the white board, and, using the criteria for wing shape, his peers gave him kind, specific, helpful suggestions of what he could change to make his drawing look more like the photograph (for example, they suggested that the wing shape in the photo was triangular, whereas his drawing had rounded wings).

Austin was happy to take their advice and quickly created a second draft that had more angular wings and included the "swallowtails" at the base of the wings, as his peers suggested. The growth in his second draft was appreciated by his peers, and they suggested he include both an upper and lower wing on each side, which he then did in his third draft. His peers again appreciated his growth but pointed out that he had "gotten round again" on the upper wings, and so on his fourth draft he made the upper wings more angular. His peers were delighted that the shape looked right now and suggested that he add the pattern, which he did for draft five. His sixth and final draft was a beautiful and accurate colored illustration and showed remarkable growth from his first draft, thanks to the help of excellent peer feedback (see Figure 6.12).

Figure 6.12: Austin's Butterfly Drafts

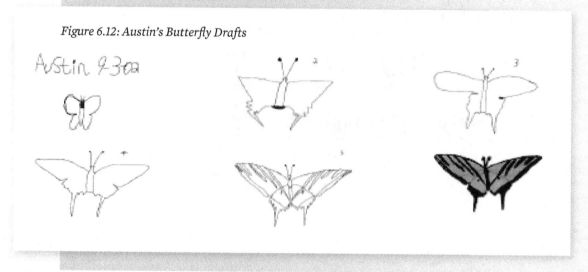

Peer Critique in the Curriculum

In the K–5 Module Lessons, peer critique is an integral part of scaffolding students' high quality work, which is grounded in CCSS W.5: *Develop and strengthen writing as needed by planning, revising, editing, rewriting, or trying a new approach.* Students learn the academic vocabulary associated with peer critique, such as what "feedback" means and what it means to "improve" one's writing. They also learn the criteria for feedback: It must be kind, specific, and helpful.

Often, the teacher will model giving a student feedback and then students give each other feedback, usually based on a specific criterion from the writing rubric. Students then debrief how well they gave and received feedback, which is connected to the habits of character *work to become effective learners* and *work to become ethical people* (e.g., using compassion when giving feedback). In many grades, students co-construct a High-Quality Work anchor chart, which helps them keep track, across the year, of what strong writing (or art) looks and sounds like. This groundwork is emphasized heavily the first time students engage in peer critique and then is reinforced throughout the year. Figure 6.13 shows an excerpt from a kindergarten lesson in Module 2 that highlights these points.

Figure 6.13: Learning to Give Peer Critique: An Excerpt from a Kindergarten Lesson

Weather Wonders

Work Time

C. Structured Discussion: Critiquing a Partner's Work (15 minutes)

- Refocus students whole group.
- Offer students specific, positive feedback on their writing. (Example: "I noticed that Octavia and Justice worked hard to tap out the sounds in the names of their characters so they could hear all the sounds in those words.")
- Tell students that they have been working very hard on their weather stories, showing a lot of perseverance through this challenging task.
- Tell students that another way that writers show perseverance is to work to improve their writing by asking others for feedback. Explain that feedback is giving useful information about someone's work.
- Direct students' attention to the posted learning targets and read the second one aloud:

  "I can improve my writing using feedback from a partner."

- Point out the word improve in the learning target and define it for students (to make better).
- Tell students that today they will share their work with their conversation partner. That partner is going to listen and then offer feedback by pointing out one thing they did well and one thing they might add to or change about their story.
- Tell students that when giving feedback to someone on their writing (that they have worked hard on), it is important to be kind and helpful at the same time. Tell students that they will want to give feedback to help their partner improve his or her writing, but that feedback should also not hurt their partner's feelings.
- Direct students' attention to the posted Peer Feedback anchor chart and read it aloud:

  "When we give feedback, we are: kind, specific, helpful."

- Define kind (gentle, good, and caring), specific (certain and exact, particular), and helpful (to be useful or of assistance) for students.
- Tell students that you are going to model giving feedback that is kind, specific, and helpful.
- Invite a student volunteer to help you model giving kind, specific, and helpful feedback:
  1. Invite the student volunteer to share his or her work with you.
  2. Model giving kind feedback by pointing out something that your partner did well using the sentence frame: "You did a good job of _____."
  3. Model giving helpful and specific feedback by pointing out something you think the partner could add to or change about his or her story using the sentence frame: "I think you should _____ because _____."
  4. Model referring to the High-Quality Work anchor chart to provide the criteria for your feedback.

▶ Putting Students on the Path to Success

Using models to show students what's possible can be magical. In the Austin's Butterfly video, you can see the amazement on the students' faces when Austin's accurate and beautiful final draft is revealed. Students lean in, look closer, and excitely gasp, "Oh, my gosh!" Their subsequent discussion, in which they develop the criteria for a quality final draft, is testament to the power of the practices described in this chapter to help students improve their work.

Despite the transformational power of these practices, teachers and school leaders must take care (and time) to develop the habits and skills students need to make the most of them. Nurturing a growth mindset is an essential foundation. Students must believe in their own power to improve their work; with this belief in place, the use of models, critique, and descriptive feedback will give them the skills they need to do so.

With time and practice, you will experience the power of these practices both within and beyond the curriculum. Analyzing models of high-quality work and critiquing the work of peers won't be special events; they will be a key part of teaching students content and skills and engaging them in thinking critically about their progress toward quality work. Hopefully, over time, you will gather and use a collection of student work to use as models in other parts of the school day and begin conducting critique lessons, and the practices will take hold in your classroom and throughout the school.

Chapter 6:
Instructional Leadership

Table 6.4: Chapter 6 Instructional Leadership

Questions to Ask Yourself and Your Staff
» Can you and your staff articulate the progression of the reading and writing standards and how they build toward college and career readiness? What additional professional learning may be necessary to reinforce the standards' emphasis on evidence?
» What is your staff's understanding of the relationship between reading and writing? How does this chapter connect to, extend, and challenge current paradigms and practices?
» How do teachers describe the connection between Writing for Understanding and the read-think-talk-write cycle? Is it clear that reading, thinking, and talking about text provide the fodder necessary for students' writing *and* that writing is another way for students to make meaning of what they read?
» How willing and comfortable are your teachers in helping students engage in rich conversation? Do they understand the importance of student discourse?
» What work have teachers done to lay the groundwork for active and collaborative classrooms where student talk can be productive and lead to new learning?
» To what extent are teachers ready to talk less so that students can talk more? Do they view learning from texts and peer conversations as equally worthy?
» How do teachers set expectations for high-quality work? Do they need more support to use models, critique, and descriptive feedback effectively? What schoolwide structures can you put in place to support these practices schoolwide, beyond the curriculum?
» What is the culture of feedback in your building? In what ways do you, or could you, model giving feedback to staff that is kind, specific, and helpful? In what ways might you support staff in doing the same with one another?
Evidence of Progress
» Teachers are talking about the relationship between reading and writing, reflecting their understanding of them as connected, not two separate subjects.

Cont.

» Writing instruction is well integrated with reading in lessons within and beyond the curriculum.

» Teachers are using the curriculum's K–5 Recommended Text and Other Resources List to help students "swim in text" on the module topic.

» Classrooms buzz with student talk. Students have opportunities to think and talk about text before and while writing.

» Teachers are making time to scaffold high-quality work, based on the Unit-at-a-Glance chart for every unit (but particularly Unit 3 for the performance task).

» Students give and receive feedback, based on models and clear criteria that help them improve their work. They can persevere through multiple drafts to create high-quality work.

» The use of models, critique, and descriptive feedback has taken hold in other subjects, beyond the curriculum.

» A schoolwide culture of feedback helps all staff see their own teaching practice as something that they can refine and improve.

Resources and Suggestions

» Common Core State Standards, Appendix A

» PD Pack: *Leaders of Their Own Learning: Transforming Schools through Student-Engaged Assessment* (ELeducation.org)

» EL Education Books that deepen understanding of the practices in this chapter:

  • *Transformational Literacy: Making the Common Core Shift with Work That Matters*

  • *Leaders of Their Own Learning: Transforming Schools through Student-Engaged Assessment*

» Book: *Writing for Understanding: Using Backward Design to Help All Students Write Effectively* by the Vermont Writing Collaborative

» Website: Models of Excellence: The Center for High-Quality Student Work (modelsofexcellence.ELeducation.org)

» Website: Vermont Writing Collaborative (vermontwritingcollaborative.org)

» Website: Fisher & Frey Literacy for Life (fisherandfrey.com)

» Article: "Writing Undergoing Renaissance in Curricula" by Diana Leddy

» Article: "Habits Improve Classroom Discussions" by Paul Bambrick-Santoyo

» Article: "Collaborative Conversations" by Douglas Fisher and Nancy Frey

» Resources on Protocols:

  • Classroom Protocols (Curriculum.ELeducation.org)

  • National School Reform Faculty website (nsrfharmony.org)

  • School Reform Initiative website (schoolreforminitiative.org)

Chapter 6:
Frequently Asked Questions

The shift toward reading for and writing with evidence feels important, but I miss all the stories and poems I used to read with my students and those that they would write. Is there time to bring in more stories and poems when teaching this curriculum?

Many literacy educators love fiction, and some of us may worry that the push on "evidence" has drowned out some of the sheer joy of reveling in a beautiful story or an elegantly crafted poem. In terms of our curriculum, it may reassure you to look at the grade-level curriculum map for the Module Lessons and see all the wonderful stories that do live in the curriculum (from *A Snowy Day* in kindergarten to *Peter Pan* in Grade 3 to *Esperanza Rising* in Grade 5). In Grades K–2, students also regularly play with poetry or sing songs about the topic they are studying (check out the song "Plants around the World" in Grade 2, Module 3). That being said, if you want to infuse even more fiction and poetry into the day, you can prioritize narratives during Storytime in the K–2 Labs or when helping 3–5 students select texts for their "free choice" reading. You also could incorporate more traditional read-aloud during other parts of the school day (e.g., morning meeting, the transition after recess or lunch). And of course, it is always inspirational to students for you to share what you are reading and your love of text—literature and nonfiction alike.

Where can I find more evidence-based protocols to use in my classroom?

There are many great resources for additional protocols. Once you get accustomed to how protocols work and the purposes they serve, you may wish to swap in new ones or bring them into other parts of your school day. You can find all of the protocols used throughout our K–5 curriculum on our website (Curriculum.ELeducation.org) or in our book *Management in the Active Classroom*. If you want to branch out and find totally new protocols, there are two websites worth checking out: The National School Reform Faculty (www.nsrfharmony.org) and the School Reform Initiative (www.schoolreforminitiative.org).

It's been really hard for me to "let the text do the teaching." I find myself still wanting to explain things to my students. What do you suggest?

If talking to your students about the texts they are reading, before giving them a chance to make meaning, is a habit you have been in as a teacher, one of the best ways to get into a *new* habit is to follow the lessons as they are written. The lessons are designed so that you talk less and students talk more so that they can learn from the text and each other. Spend some time intentionally following the lessons as written (i.e., with fidelity) and reflect on the results for you and your students.

I know it's important to give my students a chance to talk with each other about what they are reading and thinking, but they really struggle with partner and small group work. How can I make that time more productive for them?

The structures in the curriculum designed to foster student collaboration and discourse (e.g., protocols, total participation techniques, triads) recur over and over. The curriculum starts slow with these structures, offering guidance for introducing them and gradually building independence as time goes on. However, you know your students best. Just like anything you do in the classroom, these structures may require additional modeling, practice, feedback, and revision. Don't be afraid to take a pause, reinforce instructions or expectations, and start over if students struggle to work together independently.

Our school has used a Readers' and Writers' Workshop structure for many years. I understand that the EL Education curriculum uses the Writing for Understanding approach instead. What does this mean for me?

Many of us at EL Education also were trained in Readers' and Writers' Workshop, and there is much to value in that approach: Students have tremendous choice about what they read and myriad opportunities to express their voice as they write about passion topics. However, the challenge with the typical workshop approach is that students, as readers, often may not be "reading for evidence" and building knowledge on one topic, with teacher support, over time. Similarly, as writers, students may get stuck "writing about what they know" (e.g., my favorite sport, outer space, grandma) rather than building new knowledge and then writing to communicate that knowledge. Particularly given the emphasis on building world knowledge and tackling complex text, students need more shared experiences (so they can talk with others about the text) and scaffolded experiences (so they can process their reading and apply their new understanding in their writing).

Note that "free choice" reading still lives in the curriculum: in the K–2 Reading Foundations Skills Block independent work time, and in the Grades 3–5 Additional Language and Literacy Block. And students do still write narratives, albeit about a topic they have all been studying together. You can certainly add more free writing time if your schedule permits. But the emphasis on reading the same text and writing about the same topic is a shift toward equity; students don't have to rely on existing background knowledge or experiences, as they are all grounded in the same texts and content.

I'm interested in using models of high-quality work throughout the school day with my students, but it will probably take me at least a year to build up my own collection of high-quality work. Do you have any suggestions about where I can find strong models in the meantime?

Talking to your colleagues is a good first step. It's possible that there are others on staff who have strong examples of work that meets specific criteria. EL Education has a free online library of student work from all grade levels and content areas called Models of Excellence: The Center for High-Quality Student Work (modelsofexcellence.ELeducation.org). Work from this site can be downloaded and displayed or printed as models for your students. Ultimately, if you will be teaching the same curricula over multiple years, you will be better served by gathering your own models, but this is a good place to start.

How can I help my students develop a growth mindset about their work, especially their writing? So many of them feel that they just aren't good at it, and they have a hard time revising their work.

Using models and developing criteria for high-quality work with your students can be a powerful way to help them see that work isn't either *good* or *bad*, but, instead, that it meets criteria (or doesn't) in specific ways. Not every piece of work will meet all criteria equally well. When students see that there are specific ways for work to be improved, they suddenly have a path to success. Though the curriculum provides rubrics for quality writing, it may be useful to spend some additional time helping students set goals related to the rubrics that help them put the criteria in their own words. This can help them more easily see ways to improve their work. It will also be important for you to monitor the language you use when you give students feedback. It's important that they hear messages that emphasize their effort, such as "I like how you kept at this and used your feedback buddy's suggestion here," versus messages that make them feel that they did either a bad or good job, such as "needs work." The latter doesn't give them any information about how to revise their work now or in the future.

How can I help my students give each other more meaningful feedback?

Just like high-quality student work can serve as a model that helps students improve their own work, models of peer feedback, followed by feedback and revision of the process, will help students improve their ability to give meaningful feedback. They need criteria, practice, and support to do it well. Often a Fishbowl protocol is a useful place to start. With two volunteers giving peer feedback in the middle, students around the outside can observe their process and then provide feedback about its quality (e.g., "I like how Jalen gave a specific comment about maybe choosing a different transition phrase between paragraphs," "Carmen's comment 'I really liked it' won't give Jade a good idea of how to improve. Maybe next time she could use the checklist to point out the things Jade did well and say if anything is missing from the checklist in her paragraph"). For another example of a protocol that helps students give kind, specific, and helpful feedback, see the video "Praise, Question, Suggestion" at vimeo.com/84899365.

Chapter 6

Chapter 7:
Reflecting on Progress: Helping Students Grow as Learners and People

Chapter 7A:
How Will I Know If My Students Are Making Progress?

Classrooms and schools are *full* of evidence of how students are progressing toward standards, from daily exit tickets to year-end standardized tests and everything in between. There are a variety of ways for teachers, schools, and districts to make sense of this data, but no matter the approach, the goal is the same: to track progress, identify students at risk, pinpoint areas of instruction in need of improvement, and strategize solutions. Often teachers, led by school leaders, begin the school year by reviewing student data. They look at standardized test scores from the previous year or base-line test scores from the beginning of the year. Then they clump students into differentiated groups based on these scores.

Though this kind of data work has its place in schools, when we talk about using data to inform instruction in our curriculum, this approach is not exactly what we are talking about. Instead, we are focused on offering teachers opportunities throughout the year to look at evidence of student progress—from formative ongoing assessments gathered daily to summative mid- and end of unit assessments in the Module Lessons and benchmark and cycle assessments in the K–2 Reading Foundations Skills Block (Skills Block).

Evidence of student progress comes from a variety of sources, and all of it can be used to target instruction to best meet students' needs. But so much evidence can sometimes feel overwhelming. How should you collect it, and what should you do with it? How can you help students understand and track their progress so that they can become leaders of their own learning?

▷ How can you help students understand and track their progress so that they can become leaders of their own learning?

In this chapter, we will start out in Chapter 7A exploring the various sources of evidence of student progress in the curriculum. There is potentially a lot to gather, and we'll help you focus on the key evidence and some steps you can take to make sense of it. In Chapter 7B, we will look at how to turn that evidence into systematically collected data that will help you make instructional decisions to best support your students.

Chapter 7

And finally, in Chapter 7C we will turn our attention to an outcome for students for which it's difficult to collect data: habits of character. In Chapter 1, we introduced EL Education's Dimensions of Student Achievement. This seminal document (see Figure 1.2 for reference) captures our commitment to a definition of student achievement that goes beyond mastery of knowledge and skills to also include high-quality student work and character. We will explore how the curriculum is designed to help students make progress in this area as well.

▶ What's the Difference between Evidence and Usable Data?

Students' daily work from the learning activities in every component of our curriculum produces a great deal of direct and indirect evidence. Direct evidence is actual student work that reveals students' knowledge and skills (e.g., end of unit assessments). Indirect evidence is teacher perceptions of student performance (e.g., observation checklists). In the pages that follow, we will show you examples of direct and indirect evidence. Both are critical to assessing student progress.

When it comes to data, we use the term differently than you may be used to: We use it when referring to an organized subset of evidence that is systematically collected so that it can be used for analysis. To be considered data in this case, evidence must meet three criteria:

1. It must be systematically collected (e.g., you collect and score each student's work, versus "I feel like students are starting to get it").

2. It must be organized to aid its analysis (e.g., you create a spreadsheet to record all scores, versus a pile of completed assessments that are not organized in any way).

3. It must be based on a valid and reliable assessment.

Paul Bambrick-Santoyo, the author of *Data Driven Instruction: A Practical Guide to Improve Instruction* (2010), remarks that "if assessments define the ultimate goals, analysis identifies the strategy and tactics to get there." Helping all students meet the standards that form the foundation of assessments means we have to continually analyze student work and create effective action plans to change the outcome of students' learning. Using students' daily work as an important measure of their learning gives you an up-close-and-personal view of what enables a student's success. Using the analogy of watching a swim meet, Bambrick-Santoyo underscores the importance of seeing student learning in action, rather than just perusing their scores.

> *"Imagine a swimmer and her coach. The swimmer is a hard worker in practice, but when she goes to her first competition she finishes in third place. If the coach skips the meet and only reads the results in the newspaper, his advice will probably be that his student should focus on swimming faster. Had the coach actually gone to the pool, however, he would have seen that his swimmer was actually the fastest in the pool, and that her slow time was the result of her being the last racer off the starting blocks"* (Bambrick-Santoyo, 2010, p. 41).

The swim meet analogy illuminates an important point about analyzing student work. In this illustration, the coach analyzes the swimmer's performance in one type of race and creates an action plan—focus on the start—to improve her performance. Similarly, in the classroom, teachers frequently focus on one student's work and offer that student feedback in an effort to improve his or her performance the next time around. Gathering and analyzing the daily work of students in this way is the bread and butter of a teacher's job.

An essential next step is turning this evidence into data, which gives you the opportunity to analyze a collection of student work and organize it into data sets that may suggest bigger shifts in instruction for you, your grade-level team, or specialists who are assisting you with particular students or classes. To illustrate how evidence can become usable data, let's peek into a first-grade classroom in the Snapshot that follows.

Collecting Evidence

Mr. Bashir is a little nervous about teaching his first-graders about the sun, moon, and stars. In particular, he wonders whether his young students have the comprehension skills to make meaning of the complex texts in the second unit of Module 2. Unit 1 felt manageable. Students were able to access familiar narrative books and think, talk, and write about how the sun, moon, and stars inspire authors. But Unit 2 has been much more challenging. Students began with close read-alouds of informational texts to build their background knowledge about patterns of the sun, moon, and stars. Not only were the texts themselves challenging, but students were also expected to take notes and talk about their reading using evidence from the text.

In Lesson 6 of Unit 2, students used their notes from earlier lessons in which they read about (through read-aloud), thought about, and talked about complex text to prepare for their first Science Talk. Since Mr. Bashir has reviewed all of the unit assessments and he knows that the End of Unit 2 Assessment is a Science Talk, he decides that this is a perfect opportunity to gather some evidence of student progress (the Ongoing Assessment section of the lesson also offers this as a suggestion). He collects student notes and uses a Speaking and Listening Checklist aligned to Common Core State Standards (CCSS) to analyze his students' needs (see Figure 7.1).

The learning target for the Science Talk is "I can participate in a Science Talk about what makes day and night on earth using information from my notes as evidence." As a class, they determined that to meet this learning target, students would need to use their notes and should ask at least one question of a peer. After the Science Talk, Mr. Bashir asks students to reflect using Fist to Five to show their progress toward the learning target, with a fist representing no progress toward the target and a five representing that they had met the target. Most students raise four or five fingers. When Mr. Bashir asks why, students report that they shared their notes, listened to each other, and everyone shared. These were the exact steps that the class had determined would lead to success on the learning target, but Mr. Bashir is not certain that every student participated fully in the Science Talk.

Turning Evidence into Usable Data

When his students go to physical education class, Mr. Bashir decides to analyze his notes on the Speaking and Listening Checklist. He sees that 21 of 25 students did a great job taking turns and working in groups (CCSS SL.1.1: *Participate in collaborative conversations with diverse partners about Grade 1 topics and texts with peers and adults in small and larger groups*; CCSS SL.1.1a: *Follow agreed-upon rules for discussions*). However, when Mr. Bashir looks more closely at the Speaking and Listening Checklist, he notices that 14 of 25 students struggled with CCSS SL.1.1b: *Build on others' talk in conversations by responding to the comments of others through multiple exchanges*. Almost all of his students with speech and language Individualized Education Program (IEP) goals, as well as his English language learners (ELLs), struggled in this area.

Mr. Bashir also notices that almost all of his students (20 of 25) were proficient with regard to CCSS SL.1.4: *Describe people, places, things, and events with relevant details, expressing ideas and feelings clearly*. A few students did not clearly describe the patterns observed in the sky and instead either agreed with other students or had basic descriptions like "the sun is in the sky." A few of these students receive ELL support, so in addition to making his own instructional adjustments, he plans to talk to the English as a second language teacher to see if she can put additional supports in place.

Reflecting on this data leads Mr. Bashir to formulate two important adjustments to his instruction for succeeding lessons (leading up to another Science Talk in Lesson 8). First, he regroups his students, taking into consideration those who struggled with CCSS SL.1.1b. He decides that rather than working in triads, he will have students start off in pairs that will then join another pair to become a group of four for the Science Talk. He pairs two ELLs with similar language proficiency together, for example, because he knows that they work well together and are more inclined to share and discuss when they work together first. When they form a group of four, he will put this pair with another pair of ELLs with greater language proficiency. Based on past experience, Mr. Bashir also knows that giving partners an opportunity to discuss content first will encourage greater engagement when they are in groups of four for the Science Talk.

Figure 7.1: Mr. Bashir's Speaking and Listening Checklist

Second, Mr. Bashir decides to reteach how to use Conversation Cues[1]. Before lesson 8, he decides that he will model the Science Talk protocol a second time, this time with an emphasis on asking follow-up questions beginning with Conversation Cue question stems that the students have used previously. He identifies two Conversation Cues that students should definitely use during the Science Talk and that he thinks will best lay the foundation for them to be able to build on each other's ideas:

» "So, do you mean _____?" (Goal 1 Conversation Cue: Help all students talk and be understood; specifically "clarify")

» "S/he said _____" (Goal 2 Conversation Cue: Help students listen carefully to one another and seek to understand; specifically "paraphrase").

Mr. Bashir now feels confident that he has solid strategies to support more students to reach the learning targets of the lesson.

▶ There's So Much Evidence to Collect: What Should I Focus On?

When you collect evidence of students' thinking, talking, and writing, you are gathering information about what students know and can do. Looking at student work individually or with a teammate can guide minor course corrections for the daily journey of teaching.

There are many sources of evidence you will gather as you teach the curriculum. But the reality is that you probably won't have time for a careful analysis of all of it. Of course, you can and should focus on the summative assessments in the curriculum as a key source of evidence for further analysis, but beyond that it is up to you (hopefully in collaboration with your administrators, instructional coaches, and teaching teams) which of the ongoing/formative assessments to focus on more closely. Not every note-catcher, for example, will require analysis; however, those that ask students to demonstrate skills they have struggled with in the past, especially if they will be featured on an upcoming summative assessment, may be worth a closer look.

---

[1] For more information on Conversation Cues, see Chapter 2C.

We will spend some time in this section exploring all of the sources of evidence in the curriculum so that you have a better feel for what to expect[2]. And then in Chapter 7B, we'll explore more about what it means to turn this evidence into systematically collected data that is organized in such a way that aids analysis and is most useful to you. Because the key sources of evidence are a bit different at different grade levels, we have divided the evidence into Grades K–2 and Grades 3–5.

Sources of Evidence in the Grades K–2 Reading Foundations Skills Block

The Skills Block uses three primary forms of evidence: benchmark assessments, cycle assessments, and daily assessments (snapshots and exit tickets). These assessments are designed to help you first identify what microphase[3] of reading and spelling development a student is in so that you can target instruction, and then to help you monitor students' progress as they learn new skills through whole and small group instruction.

Benchmark Assessments

This collection of assessments includes Letter Name and Sound Identification, Phonological Awareness, Spelling, Decoding, and Fluency. The beginning-of-year administration helps you determine a student's microphase so that you can use this information to form differentiated small groups based on similar student strengths and needs. Ongoing administration (middle and end of year) helps you follow student progress through the phases so that you can continue to provide the most targeted instruction.

Cycle Assessments

Administered more frequently than benchmarks (approximately once per cycle starting in kindergarten Module 4 through Grade 1 and two or three times per cycle in Grade 2), cycle assessments are directly tied to what has been taught up to a given point in a module. These materials can also be differentiated based on student need. For example, if a small group of students in Grade 2 is mostly working in the late Partial Alphabetic microphase (below grade level), the cycle assessment materials can be differentiated to include measurement of letter sound recognition and spelling of CVC (consonant/vowel/consonant) words rather than more advanced words.

Daily Assessments

In Grades K–1, daily assessments are called "snapshot assessments," and in Grade 2 the daily assessment is in the form of an exit ticket. Each allows you to quickly check on mastery of daily learning targets.

Sources of Evidence in the K–2 Content-Based Literacy Curriculum

In the Module Lessons, formative assessment opportunities are explicitly identified in the Ongoing Assessment section of each lesson. Within the lesson, this section is adjacent to the Learning Target section so that you can easily see how progress toward learning targets will be assessed throughout the lesson. Though you will not formally assess students in the Labs, you may wish to use the assessment checklists from the Module Lessons, particularly the Speaking and Listening Checklist, to help you observe and keep track of student progress as they work in the Labs.

What follows are examples of summative and formative assessments in the K–2 content-based literacy curriculum (Module Lessons plus K–2 Labs [Labs]). This is not an exhaustive list, but it includes some of the more frequently occurring sources of evidence.

---

[2] See Table 2.5 in Chapter 2 for more information about the assessment system for the K–5 curriculum.

[3] For more information about the phases and microphases of reading and spelling development and the structure of the Skills Block overall, see Chapter 4.

K–2 Summative Assessments

END OF UNIT ASSESSMENTS

In Grades K–2, unit assessments occur once per unit. The format of the assessments varies and may include a written response, a completed graphic organizer, or a selected response. These assessments are on-demand, designed to give you an understanding of each student's knowledge and skills at that point in time. The end of unit assessments are designed so that students experience them as part of a typical lesson, rather than as a "test"; however, they are different from many other classroom experiences in that students must complete the work on their own, without peer collaboration.

ON-DEMAND WRITING

One end of unit assessment per module includes an on-demand writing task. Every module has an anchor writing standard—narrative, informative/explanatory, or opinion—and the end of unit writing task will assess this writing standard. As a summative assessment, these writing tasks are independent and on demand, with the exception of certain kindergarten standards, which call for students to write "with support." Sometimes, but not always, this on-demand writing task serves as a draft for the scaffolded performance task.

> ★ **Test-Drive Summative Assessments before Teaching the Lessons Leading Up to Them**
>
> The summative assessments in the curriculum are designed to assess students' progress toward standards. And the ongoing formative assessments that happen in every lesson offer you important evidence of how students are doing leading up to those summative assessments. Therefore, it will be an important part of your planning process within the content-based literacy curriculum to look ahead to the end of unit assessments (Grades K–2) and the mid-unit and end of unit assessments (Grades 3–5) and take them for a test drive.
>
> Doing the assessment yourself will allow you to identify the obstacles your students may encounter when they are given the task. During this step, be sure you know which standards are being assessed and how each question pushes you to demonstrate your knowledge and skills with reference to the specific standard. Connecting the dots between the standards, the assessment, and the flow of lessons leading up to it will guide you as you look for evidence of student progress in ongoing formative assessments.

K–2 Formative/Ongoing Assessments

ASSESSMENT CHECKLISTS

As we described in Chapter 1, the Characteristics of Primary Learners, which emphasize play, stories, and the arts, guided the design of our K–2 curriculum. When students play, sing, draw, and dramatize stories, they are learning. But how can these activities provide evidence of progress toward standards?

One way for teachers to gather evidence is through assessment checklists (see Figure 7.1 in the Snapshot from Mr. Bashir's first-grade classroom). In fact, in the primary grades, assessment checklists are required because some standards are *only* assessed through teacher observation; therefore, they are both formative and summative. You will use the following checklists throughout each module:

» Reading Literature Checklist

» Reading Informational Text Checklist

- » Opinion Writing Checklist
- » Informative Writing Checklist
- » Narrative Writing Checklist
- » Speaking and Listening Checklist
- » Language Checklist

TEXT-DEPENDENT QUESTIONS

In the primary grades, students' answers to text-dependent questions are most often assessed using the Reading Literature Checklist or Reading Informational Text Checklist because answers are given orally. In Grades 1 and 2, however, lessons and unit assessments begin to include selected response (multiple choice) or short constructed responses to text-dependent questions. Text-dependent questions will be a part of most lessons when text is read to or with students, most often during close read-alouds.

WRITING ROUTINES

In the K–2 curriculum, writing routines, such as research notebooks, journals, note-catchers, and graphic organizers, are repeated multiple times throughout a unit. For example, in kindergarten Module 2, students keep a weather journal in which they describe the day's weather, identify the type of clothing that would be most appropriate to wear, and write and draw about suitable activities based on the day's weather. Across Grades K–2, students keep research notebooks during Module 3. Each of these routines allows students to capture their thinking, record information, and synthesize their learning. They offer a rich source of evidence about their progress. (Note: At this age level, writing routines may also include sketching.)

Sources of Evidence in the 3–5 Content-Based Literacy Curriculum

In the Module Lessons, formative assessment opportunities are explicitly identified in the Ongoing Assessment section of each lesson. Within the lesson, this section is adjacent to the Learning Target section so that you can easily see how progress toward learning targets will be assessed throughout the lesson. Though you will not formally assess students in the ALL Block, students will continue to work toward the same learning targets as in the Module Lessons. You may wish to use the assessment checklists from the Module Lessons to help you observe and keep track of student progress as they work in the ALL Block.

What follows are examples of summative and formative assessments in the 3–5 content-based literacy curriculum (Module Lessons plus the Additional Language and Literacy [ALL] Block). This is not an exhaustive list, but it includes some of the more frequently occurring sources of evidence.

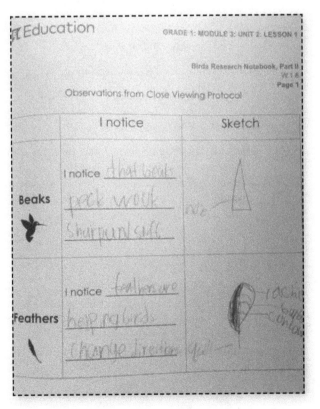

The use of research notebooks is a writing routine that allows students to capture their thinking, record information, and synthesize their learning.

3–5 Summative Assessments

MID-UNIT AND END OF UNIT ASSESSMENTS

Unit assessments occur twice per unit. The format varies, from written response to graphic organizers to multiple choice. These summative assessments are on-demand and often mirror a format from previous lessons (e.g., the assessment is a note-catcher similar to one students have completed previously).

ON-DEMAND WRITING

Every module has an anchor writing standard—narrative, informative/explanatory, or opinion—and each is taught and assessed twice over the course of the module. Students either write essays—to inform or to express a claim—or they write narratives. As a summative assessment, these writing tasks are independent and on demand. Sometimes, but not always, these on-demand writing tasks serve as a draft for the scaffolded performance task.

3–5 Formative/Ongoing Assessments

INFORMAL CHECKLISTS

Checklists in Grades 3–5 serve a similar purpose to those in Grades K–2. They are a tool to help you collect evidence of progress as you observe students working. However, unlike Grades K–2, where the checklists serve as formal assessments of certain standards, at this level the checklists are informal. They are designed to provide you with formative information that can inform instructional decisions going forward. The informal checklists in Grades 3–5 include:

- » Reading Fluency (used most frequently)
- » Writing Process
- » Collaborative Discussion
- » Presentation of Knowledge and Ideas
- » Speaking and Listening Comprehension

TEXT-DEPENDENT QUESTIONS

After reading Chapter 5, you know that text-dependent questions are an important part of close reading lessons. However, those text-dependent questions are not usually counted as formative assessment evidence because they are heavily scaffolded. Students also complete text-dependent questions beyond close reading lessons. These are done independently while reading additional sections of text—after practicing during a close reading—and can serve as formative assessment evidence.

WRITING ROUTINES

Writing routines, such as exit tickets, note-catchers, and graphic organizers, are repeated multiple times in a unit, often coinciding with chapters of an anchor text (see Figure 7.2 for sample writing). For example, the Character Reaction note-catcher is used repeatedly throughout Grade 5, Module 1, Unit 2. As students read each chapter of *Esperanza Rising*, they write a character reaction paragraph using evidence they have captured on their note-catchers. Routines like this appear frequently in Grades 3–5 because of the lengthy chapter books students read.

Figure 7.2: Grade 3 Sample Informational Writing

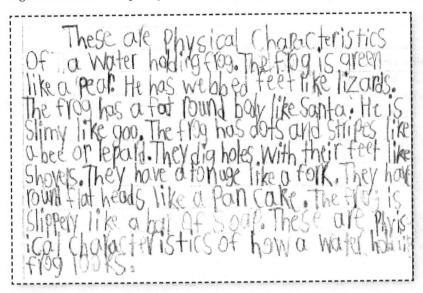

TRACKING PROGRESS FORMS

Tracking Progress forms are self-assessments that students in Grades 3–5 complete after each summative assessment. To complete these forms, students review their assessment for evidence of mastery of standards and add sticky notes to their work to point to this evidence. After students track their own progress, the teacher then reviews and adds to the form. At the end of the year, students review previous tracking progress forms and work to recognize the progress they've made throughout the year. Tracking progress forms include the following:

» Reading, Understanding, and Explaining New Texts

» Opinion Writing

» Informative Writing

» Narrative Writing

» Research

» Collaborative Discussion

★ What about the Performance Tasks?

Technically, the performance tasks at the end of every K–5 module are neither formative nor summative assessments. They are not formative since they come at the end of the module, concluding students' learning about the module topic and the literacy skills they have built over eight or nine weeks. However, they are also not summative because they are heavily scaffolded to help students create high-quality work, and so are not a strong measure of what students can do independently. For these reasons, we do not recommend analyzing performance tasks with the same lens you might use to analyze assessments.

Of course, performance tasks can give you amazingly rich insight into what your students are capable of with support and scaffolding. Consider looking at students' performance tasks through the lens of the attributes of high-quality student work (authenticity, complexity, craftsmanship) discussed in Chapter 6A. For more resources on analyzing high-quality student work, see Models of Excellence: The Center for High-Quality Student Work (www.modelsofexcellence.ELeducation.org).

▶ Now That I Have Collected the Evidence, How Do I Score It?

Knowing which sources of evidence are worth collecting and analyzing is one important step toward creating usable data. Next, it is important to score that work in ways that make progress toward standards clear and that will be useful to you when creating sets of data. To look at student work and its alignment to standards objectively, it is useful to use a systematic and consistent process. In the curriculum, each module includes an Assessment Overview and Resources document, which includes the assessments themselves and a variety of resources such as writing rubrics if applicable, checklists, and sample student responses at varying levels of proficiency. The scores you generate will help you compose data sets that you can analyze further to create an action plan for adjusting your instruction.

Often, especially for formative assessments (e.g., responses to questions on sticky notes; exit tickets), no tools are provided to support scoring student work. One of the best and simplest ways to approach scoring a collection of student work like this is to ask yourself the same question(s) about each student's work. This will allow you to gather all of the evidence from a group of students into data that you can use to adjust instruction if necessary, just as you would if you were using a rubric.

For ongoing formative assessments, what follows is a simple set of questions you can ask yourself:

1. What does this piece of student work indicate in terms of this particular student's progress toward the daily learning target?

2. What might this student need next?

3. Across this collection of student work, what patterns (of successes or struggle) am I noticing?

Figure 7.3: Grade 1, Module 3 Sample Research Notebook Page   *Figure 7.4: Sample Excerpt of Grade 5 Opinion Essay*

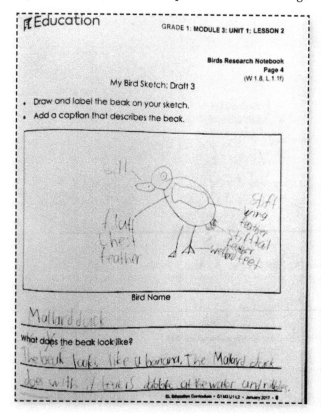

What does the work in Figure 7.3 tell us about this student's progress?[4]

1. What does this piece of student work indicate in terms of this particular student's progress toward the daily learning target?

   - Response: There are two standards that underpin the daily learning target (*I can create and label an observational drawing of a mallard duck*) for this particular lesson: CCSS W.1.8: *With guidance and support from adults, recall information from experiences or gather information from provided sources to answer a question*; and CCSS L.1.1f: *Use frequently occurring adjectives*. Based on this sample, this student is able to create a basic depiction of a mallard duck, use labels to identify important body parts (e.g., bill, tail feather, wing feather, chest feather, feet), and use adjectives to describe the body parts (e.g., stiff, webbed, fluffy). The student is also able to use similes as a sophisticated form of description ("The beak looks like a banana").

2. What might this student need next?

   - Response: This student needs support to use the provided source to add details to her drawing—specifically the shape of body parts—and to use appropriate language structures when forming a sentence. The student could benefit from oral rehearsal before writing or sentence stems to ensure that her writing shows correct grammar and usage.

What does the work in Figure 7.4 tell us about this student's progress?[4]

1. What does this piece of student work indicate in terms of this particular student's progress toward the daily learning target?

   - Response: There are three standards that underpin the daily learning target (*I can write an introductory paragraph for my essay giving context on the issue and clearly stating my opinion*) for this particular lesson: W.5.1a: *Introduce a topic or text clearly, state an opinion, and create an organizational structure in which ideas are logically grouped to support the writer's purpose*; W.5.4: *Produce clear and coherent writing in which the development and organization are appropriate to task, purpose, and audience*; and W.5.9b: *Apply Grade 5 Reading standards to informational texts*. When analyzing this sample against the Grade 5 Opinion Writing Rubric (see Figure 7.5), it is clear that the introduction provides context on the topic (information about who Jackie Robinson was and what he achieved), has a logical progression of ideas (introduces Jackie Robinson as a baseball player and then leads into his success as a leader of social change), and states an opinion (the most important factor in his success was support from family and friends).

2. What might this student need next?

   - Response: The introduction, while engaging, is long, with the opinion statement being only a very small part at the end. This student would benefit from support in summarizing information to provide context more succinctly and in linking the contextual information more purposefully to the opinion and the focus of the essay (e.g., providing more contextual information about the factors that led to his success before stating an opinion about which factor was most important).

---

[4] Note: For an individual student, only questions 1 and 2 apply.

Figure 7.5: Excerpt of Grade 5 Opinion Writing Rubric

Opinion Writing Rubric: Grade 5				
Write opinion pieces on topics or texts, supporting a point of view with reasons and information.				
		4 – Advanced	**3 – Proficient**	**2 – Developing**	**1 – Beginning**

Reading Comprehension					
A	RI.5.1￼W.5.9	Demonstrates a deep understanding of the topic or issue by developing an insightful opinion supported by logical reasons and well-chosen textual evidence	Demonstrates a clear understanding of the topic or issue by developing an opinion supported by logical reasons and textual evidence	Demonstrates a limited understanding of the topic or issue by developing an opinion weakly supported by textual evidence	Does not demonstrate understanding, or shows a limited understanding, of the topic or issue by offering an opinion unsupported by textual evidence

Organization and Purpose[1]					
B	W.5.1a	Opinion is introduced, clearly communicated, and the focus is strongly maintained	Opinion is clearly stated, and the focus is mostly maintained	Opinion may be somewhat unclear, or the focus may be insufficiently maintained	Opinion may be confusing or ambiguous; or the focus may drift
C	W.5.1a￼W.5.1d	Effective or engaging introduction and concluding statement or section	Introduction provides context on the topic or text￼Concluding statement or section is **related to the opinion presented**	Introduction and/or conclusion may be weak	Introduction and/or conclusion may be missing or unrelated to the opinion presented
D	W.5.1a	Logical progression of ideas from beginning to end strong connections between and among ideas with some syntactic variety	**Creates an organizational structure in which related ideas are grouped to support the writer's purpose**	Uneven progression of ideas from beginning to end; inconsistent or unclear connections between and among ideas	Frequent extraneous ideas may be evident; ideas seem to be randomly ordered or have an unclear progression
E	W.5.1c￼L.5.6	Consistently uses a variety of transitional strategies to clarify the relationships between and among ideas	Effectively **links opinion and reasons using words, phrases, and clauses**	Inconsistently or incorrectly uses transitional strategies and/or little variety in strategies applied	Few or no transitional strategies used

Note: Rubric is for example only. It may look different than actual curriculum materials.

Chapter 7B:
How Do I Turn Evidence into Usable Data?

Once you have scored each piece of student work, you are ready to begin thinking about the patterns you see and how those patterns will inform your instruction. Based on students' progress, what will you keep doing? What will you do more of, do less of, or do differently? What adjustments can you make to help more students reach standards? In short, how will you turn all of that evidence into usable data?

As a reminder, to be considered usable data, evidence must meet three criteria:

1. It must be systematically collected (e.g., you collect and score each student's work, versus "I feel like students are starting to get it").

2. It must be organized to aid its analysis (e.g., you create a spreadsheet to record all scores, versus a pile of completed assessments that are not organized in any way).

3. It must be based on a valid and reliable assessment.

For the most part, the ongoing formative assessments described in Chapter 7A, such as note-catchers and text-dependent questions, will not meet all of the criteria to be considered data. This is largely because you won't have time to systematically collect the data or organize it to aid analysis. There will be times, however, when you will want to pause on a formative assessment and turn that evidence into usable data, just as Mr. Bashir did in the Snapshot in Chapter 7A. He used evidence from his Speaking and Listening Checklist to adjust his instruction leading up to the summative end of unit assessment (a Science Talk) so that his students would have a greater chance for success.

▷ There's no sense collecting data if it doesn't inform actionable steps with direct benefit to students.

Formative assessments are a critical scaffold to help you prepare your students for the mid-unit and end of unit assessments, which is how you will assess their progress toward mastery of standards. Think of these assessments throughout the curriculum as rungs on a ladder your

Chapter 7

students are climbing. At the top of the ladder is mastery of standards. The information you glean from looking at your students' work and asking questions about what it shows about their progress on these lower rungs will ensure that you can adjust your instruction if necessary so that they can keep climbing.

We'll begin Chapter 7B by looking more closely at summative assessments in the content-based curriculum and the K–2 Reading Foundations Skills Block (Skills Block) and how evidence from these can be turned into usable data. We'll then look at evidence from formative assessments and explore under what circumstances you might want to analyze these more systematically. Finally, we'll conclude by unpacking more about what we mean by *usable* data. How can you use it to differentiate instruction to meet the needs of all of your students?

★ Using a Team Approach

It's important to consider how you will structure this work. In many schools, generating and looking at data happens collaboratively, through data-inquiry teams (or a similar structure by a different name). A collaborative structure supports teachers to analyze student work, build sets of data, and create specific action plans for changing their teaching practice to support all students' success.

Sheela Webster, principal of the World of Inquiry School in Rochester, New York, notes that her school's data inquiry teams, which involve all teachers, shift the focus of data from blaming teachers to supporting students. "In the past," she says, "it was very difficult to have conversations around data without it becoming a personal attack.... [Since we put in place regular data team meetings with an instructional specialist who is the keeper of the data], the data now belongs to the child, and it's not the teacher's fault.... We come together, know who this child is as a learner, and talk about instructional practice moving forward."

If your school doesn't have an official structure like this in place, we recommend that, at the very least, you sit down with a colleague or team, ideally with an instructional leader at the table, to set up systems for this work. As a team, you can look together at student work to assess progress and create structures to collect evidence and ensure that it becomes usable data. Making the data usable is key to this work: There's no sense collecting data if it doesn't inform actionable steps with direct benefit to students.

▶▶ Video Spotlight

In the accompanying video, Sheela Webster, principal of World of Inquiry School in Rochester, New York, discusses the value of data inquiry teams as a schoolwide structure.

https://vimeo.com/57527837

▶ When and How Should I Analyze the Evidence from Summative Assessments So That It Becomes Usable Data?

In the K–2 Module Lessons, students complete end of unit assessments approximately every two to three weeks (12 per year), and in the Skills Block they complete benchmark assessments three times a year and cycle assessments on average once per week. In the 3–5 Module Lessons, students complete mid-unit and end of unit assessments, which occur approximately every week and a half (24 per year). The frequency of these assessments offers you a great deal of evidence to turn into usable data.

The reality, however, is that you are unlikely to have time for a systematic analysis of all of that evidence, so how can you decide which of it to focus on?

> *"Using the right data to pinpoint exactly what students know and can do so that I choose the right next steps helps me avoid just putting a Band-Aid on a cut artery."*

Teacher
Atlanta

Choosing Evidence for Analysis in the Module Lessons

Each assessment generates information about student progress that can help you sharpen instruction and scaffold the success of all students. It's information to grow on, as well as information to go on. Keeping in mind that you won't necessarily have time for a deep analysis of the evidence generated from every assessment, you will want to make some choices about how to focus your energy. One way to do this is by reviewing your curriculum map and looking for assessments that meet the following criteria:

» The standards assessed are key standards of focus for your students (determined by performance on a pre-assessment or previous assessment). For example, if your students are struggling with reading informational text, choose an assessment for analysis that includes at least one Common Core Reading: Informational Text standard.

» You feel that your students have had enough practice to gain the context of the module topics and to practice the skills taught before being assessed. The curriculum builds in this time, which you can see in the Unit-at-a-Glance chart in the Unit Overview (this chart will help you see how a series of lessons leads up to an assessment). But you may feel that your students need more practice before you spend time analyzing the evidence from their assessments.

» The assessment requires students to demonstrate skills that they will need again on future assessments. (For example, can the mid-unit assessment be considered a pre-assessment (and scaffold) for the end of unit assessment?)

» The assessment allows you to compare data points and identify trends over time. For example, the Mid-Unit 1 Assessment in Grade 5, Module 1 includes questions on common prefixes. Students' acquisition of vocabulary is a data point that can be measured and tracked over time.

Now, while examining your assessments and using the preceding criteria, highlight those assessments that provide optimal opportunities for data analysis. Record your findings in a grid like that in Table 7.1

Table 7.1: Assessing Your Assessments for Further Analysis

Assessment	Assessment	Assessment
Description/How it's scored	**Description/How it's scored**	**Description/How it's scored**
Why is it optimal?	**Why is it optimal?**	**Why is it optimal?**

(Note: You may also be able to use a grid like this to assess formative assessments for further analysis).

Organizing the Evidence

Each module in the content-based curriculum includes an Assessment Overview and Resources document, which includes the assessments themselves and a variety of resources such as writing rubrics if applicable (see Figure 7.5), checklists where you can record your entire class's progress toward mastery of standards (see Figure 7.6) or where students can track their own progress against rubrics, and sample student responses at varying levels of proficiency. These tools are tailor-made for you to take evidence of progress and turn it into usable data that can help all students meet with success. We'll look at the important steps in this process in the pages that follow, which are followed by a Snapshot that will give you a sense of what the process looks like in action.

Figure 7.6: Grade 1, Module 1 Informative/Explanatory Writing Checklist

Informative/Explanatory Writing Checklist

This module focuses primarily on W.1.2. Instruction on this standard begins in Unit 1, continues in Unit 2, and is formally assessed in Unit 3. This checklist also includes L.1.2 standards that are taught and assessed in the Reading Foundational Skills Block but are included here for formative assessment purposes since students should be supported with applying these skills during their writing in the module lessons.

Module 1 Informative/Explanatory Writing Checklist																	
STUDENT INITIALS																	
COMPOSITION																	
Names a topic																	
Supplies some information about the topic																	
Provides some sense of closure																	
Piece shows solid understanding of content																	
WORD CHOICE																	
L.K.6 Use words and phrases acquired through conversations, reading and being read to, and responding to texts.																	
CONVENTIONS¹																	
L.1.2a Capitalizes the first word in a sentence, I, names, dates																	
L.1.2b Uses end punctuation																	
L.1.2c Uses commas in dates, words in a series																	
L.1.2e Spells untaught words phonetically																	
L.1.2d Uses conventional spelling— common patterns and high-frequency words																	

¹ Please note that all L.2 standards are taught and formally assessed in the Reading Foundations Skills Block. They are included here for formative assessment purposes.

Note: Checklist is for example only. It may look different than actual curriculum materials.

Identifying the Patterns and Trends That Can Inform Instruction

Tools like the checklist in Figure 7.6 will help you identify trends and patterns. Perhaps you will notice that nearly all of your students show an understanding of the content and use vocabulary that reflects this understanding, but that most students are struggling to provide a sense of closure in their writing. This is helpful and actionable information that can guide your planning for future lessons that you know will have more opportunities for practice writing paragraphs.

As you review sets of data like this, keep in mind these questions:

» In general, what do the students farthest from the standards most need to learn next?

» What is a generalizable "critical move" that could move the students who are close to meeting the standards into the next level? (You may want to revisit Teaching Notes in the particular sequence of lessons.)

» What instructional choices did you make that led to the success of the students meeting the expectation?

» What qualities does the work of the students exceeding the standards most exhibit?

» Finally, choose an "actionable" issue from the trends (e.g., a common challenge) that you can address to help students make meaningful improvement.

Table 7.2 shows how a kindergarten teacher answered these questions after students completed an assessment in Module 2 in which they identified story elements (characters, setting, and major events) in a literary text. In this example, the teacher noticed a trend of students having trouble distinguishing major events from less important story details.

Table 7.2: Asking and Answering Questions Based on Data: A Sample from Kindergarten, Module 2

Questions to Ask Yourself	Sample Answers from Kindergarten Module 2
In general, what do the students farthest from the standards most need to learn next?	*how to distinguish major events from less important story details*
What is a generalizable "critical move" that could move the students who are close to meeting the standards into the next level? (You may want to revisit Teaching Notes in the particular sequence of lessons.)	*more emphasis on major events when retelling stories read in the classroom; comparing and contrasting major events and minor details*
What instructional choices did you make that led to the success of the students meeting the expectation?	*identifying major events during read-alouds and recording them on an anchor chart; regularly using both the text and anchor chart as supports for retelling the story*
What qualities does the work of the students exceeding the standards most exhibit?	*the ability to not only identify story elements including major events, but also to explain why an event in a particular story is important*
Finally, choose an "actionable" issue from the trends (e.g., a common challenge) that you can address to help students make meaningful improvement.	*have the class work on sorting major story events from minor details and then explain their sorting decisions to their peers.*

Creating an Action Plan Based on the Data

Looking at data is only as valuable as the actions that result from your analysis. If you don't change your approach to instruction, you are likely to get the same results again and again. So, the next step in the data analysis cycle is to create an actionable plan for your classroom. Ideally this work will be done in teams. The Results Meeting protocol described in the box is a useful tool to help you and your team analyze data in your classroom and across classrooms. If you are unable to do this work in a team, you can still work through the protocol on your own.

RESULTS MEETING PROTOCOL[5]

Purpose

The goal of the results meeting is to analyze with your data inquiry team (grade level or department team) the results of the most recent assessment and determine an action plan that meets the needs of students in your grade/department.

Materials

Student data recorded on a checklist, Results Meeting protocol note-catcher (see Table 7.3), student assessments, assessment rubric, chart paper, markers

Time

Part 1, 40 minutes; Part 2, 45 minutes (Note: This protocol can be implemented as two separate protocols.)

Pre-work

Before engaging in a Results Meeting protocol, you will need to score your students' assessments and record the scores on a checklist.

Protocol Roles

Recorder (to record notes on chart paper); facilitator; timekeeper

Part One: Analyzing Student Data to Identify a Focus Standard (40 minutes)

Analyze: Individually read the checklist to determine areas of strength and struggle and trends related to student performance on standards. Record your individual findings on the note-catcher. (15 minutes)

Discuss and record on chart paper: Where did students do well? (5 minutes)

» Go around: Each person on the team names two areas in which he or she noticed students did well and cites evidence from the checklist.

» Group members ask "What evidence do you have?" as needed.

» The recorder takes notes on chart paper.

Discuss and record on chart paper: Where did students struggle? (5 minutes)

» Go around: Each person on the team names two areas he or she noticed in which students struggled and cites evidence from the checklist.

» Group members ask "What evidence do you have?" as needed.

» The recorder takes notes on chart paper.

Discuss and record on chart paper: What are the trends in the data? (5 minutes)

» Go around: Each person on the team names the top trend he or she noticed.

» The recorder takes notes on chart paper.

Discuss: Of the struggles identified, which should be prioritized (i.e., which standard)? (10 minutes)

» Open discussion: The team comes to an agreement about the top challenge to focus on right now.

» The recorder circles the selected challenge on the list on the chart paper.

Part Two: Acting on Student Data to Increase Achievement on a Focus Standard (45 minutes)

Sort (5 minutes): Physically place the student assessments into three piles based on the standard of focus: *met* or *exceeded* the standard of focus, is *approaching* meeting the standard of focus, is *not approaching* meeting the standard of focus.

Analyze (20 minutes): Each member of the team will now focus on one particular group of students. In pairs or alone, analyze the student work in your pile, focusing on the following questions and using the learning targets from Module Lessons as a guide.

» Student work: What are the trending strengths in your students' work? (refer to specific skills)

» Student work: What are the trending areas of struggle in your students' work?

» Unit arc: Based on the Unit-at-a-Glance chart (in the Unit Overview), will your group have an opportunity to revisit these standards? If so, in which lesson? If not, what are some high-leverage moves you can make to meet their needs?

» Unit arc: Based on the Unit-at-a-Glance chart, will your students be reassessed on this standard in the next assessment? If not, how will you assess their progress on the focus standard?

Share (10 minutes): Each group will have 3 minutes to share their notes about their pile of student work, focusing on their suggestions for re-teaching and reassessment.

Reflection (4 minutes): Which "high-leverage next steps" are most realistic, most helpful, and most effective?

» Silent think/write time: Each person silently assesses which solutions are doable/effective (1 minute).

» Each person on the team has 30 seconds to share his or her reflections.

Consensus and delegation (6 minutes): Which actions will teachers on our team take?

» Based on the reflections shared, the team discusses and comes to an agreement on a plan and dates for re-teaching and reassessing the focus standard for each group of students.

» The recorder writes the agreed-upon actions on the chart paper.

---

[5] Informed by Bambrick-Santoyo, P. (2010). Driven by Data: A Practical Guide to Improve Instruction. San Francisco, CA: Jossey-Bass.

Table 7.3: Results Meeting Note-catcher

	Notice	**Evidence**
Class strengths		
Class challenges		
Trends		
Standard(s) of focus		
High-leverage next step/ action plan		

The most important outcome of a Results Meeting protocol is a plan to support students who may need additional scaffolding or help to meet standards. Identifying feasible solutions is key. Once you have identified a feasible solution to an area in which students need improvement, consult your curriculum map and flag where skills and activities associated with this trend are targeted in future lessons. What new or different activities, grouping strategies, or supportive materials will you need to prepare in advance? Think back to Mr. Bashir's feasible solution to the problem of not having full participation in the Science Talk. He looked ahead for the next opportunity for his students to practice these same skills and made a plan for a different grouping strategy to best support them.

What does all this look like and sound like in practice? The Snapshot that follows, in which fourth-grade teachers meet regularly as a data inquiry team, provides another window into how data informs instruction.

Ms. Herrera, a Grade 4 teacher, and her team are partway through Module 2 of the curriculum, and students are building literacy and science skills as they study animal defense mechanisms. Throughout Unit 1, students have been using evidence from informational texts to make inferences and determine the main idea. All of the fourth-grade teachers are now looking ahead to the end of Unit 2 writing assessment, in which students will need to leverage all of their new reading skills to write an informative paragraph about the defense mechanisms of pufferfish.

Ms. Herrera has drafted her own exemplar response to this assessment and compared it to the example provided in the curriculum. Working from these two models, she and her teaching team can see that to score proficient or advanced, students will need to include specific evidence about how animals defend themselves in the air, on land, and in the water. Since they began Unit 1 looking ahead to all of the assessments in the module, they feel confident that they have supported their students to read for details with these tasks in mind.

Looking for Trends and Making a Plan

After the Mid-Unit 1 Assessment, the teachers met as a data inquiry team to look at students' performance on a series of text-dependent questions from the assessment.

They noticed three trends in the evidence from students' answers across all of their classrooms:

1. Almost all students were able to determine the meaning of unknown words and identify which details from the text supported their understanding.

2. Most students also correctly answered the selected response questions that asked them to find "right there" answers in the text.

3. In each class, however, five or six students got the third question wrong, which required them to infer.

Putting the Plan into Action

Based on these trends, the teachers put new strategies into action immediately to support students who struggled with drawing inferences and finding details. Ms. Herrera and her colleagues emphasized the importance of underlining the evidence in the text that helped them answer the text-dependent questions. Second, during the Additional Work with Complex Texts rotation of the Additional Language and Literacy Block, teachers spent more instructional time coaching students on how to determine the details that support the main idea. In particular, they co-constructed an anchor chart with students that would guide them through three steps in determining details:

1. Underline details in text that I think support the main idea (look for the key words from the main idea).

2. Ask myself: "Does this detail refer to the main idea? Does it confirm the main idea? What do I learn about the main idea in this detail?"

3. If it doesn't support the main idea, then it is not an important detail!

Reassessing Progress

At the end of the week, teachers reassessed students with an exit ticket to see if they were able to identify two details that supported the main idea. Based on this evidence, the teachers felt students were well on track to succeed in Unit 2, when writing would become the focus of their instruction.

A few weeks later, after students complete the Mid-Unit 2 Assessment, the fourth-grade teachers got back together in their data inquiry team. Using the rubric provided in the Assessment Overview and Resources document, Ms. Herrera scored her students' paragraph writing as follows:

2	Advanced
9	Proficient
13	Developing
4	Beginning

These were not the results she had hoped for, based on the progress students had made in Unit 1. Ms. Herrera knew that her students were able to identify supporting details, but now it seemed they had lost sight of the main idea. Most students who scored *developing* included evidence from the text about each animal, but they struggled to give an accurate or focused main idea. Her colleagues discovered the same thing in their classes. Perhaps they had overcompensated in their strategy for Unit 1, emphasizing finding details rather than articulating the main idea. Now, they determined, it was time to re-teach and give students time to practice again before the End of Unit 2 Assessment (also paragraph writing).

Refining the Plan

Since most students scored *developing* or below, the teachers determined that they would re-teach this to the whole class by modeling their expected response to this answer and analyzing two different answers with students. They also would have students analyze exemplar answers and determine which were best and why.

Even as these teachers followed the lesson plans, they grappled with how much to emphasize each element and how to support students who struggled with this new and more challenging curriculum. However, by meeting regularly to review assessment data—both formative and summative—these teachers were able to adjust their instruction and then readjust after further assessment. When instruction is driven by evidence, it is more likely to have a positive impact on student achievement.

Analyzing Evidence in the K–2 Reading Foundations Skills Block

Data drives instruction in the Skills Block. You will use benchmark assessments at the beginning of the year (BOY) to determine where each student falls in the phases of reading and spelling development (see Chapter 4 for more information on the phases). This information will help you determine the groups for small group differentiated instruction. Additional benchmark assessments administered in the middle (MOY) and at the end of the year (EOY) will help you track progress and adjust groupings if necessary. Evidence from cycle assessments, which occur at least once a week (approximately once per cycle starting in kindergarten Module 4 through Grade 1 and two or three times per cycle in Grade 2), can similarly be used to refine groups for small group differentiated instruction.

How exactly do you turn the evidence from these two kinds of assessments into usable data that informs groupings and instruction?

To effectively differentiate in the Skills Block, it is essential to know students' microphases from the outset and to continue to monitor students' progress (or lack thereof) through the microphases. Throughout a school year, you should take the following steps to gather this information and plan for differentiated small group instruction:

1. Administer BOY priority benchmark assessments.

2. Analyze benchmark results to determine a student's microphase and specific strengths and needs.

3. Group students in similar microphases together.

4. Use the Assessment Conversion Chart to determine appropriate cycles of instruction for each group.

5. Use Skills Block resources for differentiated small groups to plan targeted instruction (see the Independent and Small Group Work document for more details).

6. Monitor progress using cycle assessments and daily assessments (e.g., snapshot assessments and exit tickets); adjust grouping and instruction accordingly.

7. Administer MOY priority benchmark assessments to reassess students' microphase; continue to follow Steps 2–6 as needed.

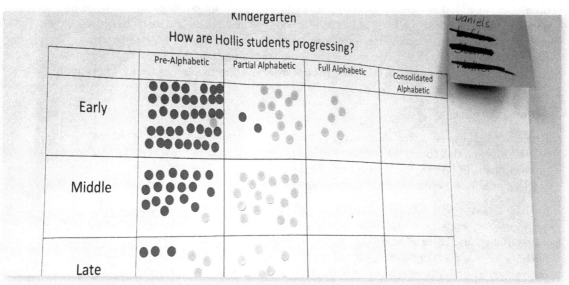

At Hollis Innovation Academy in Atlanta, Georgia, grade-level teams track Skills Block benchmark data throughout the school year and analyze how quickly students are progressing through the microphases.

Assessments in the Skills Block generate a lot of evidence; turning it into usable data is important work for teachers. To help make sense of the process, let's look at how a second-grade teacher worked with evidence in her classroom. The Snapshot that follows tells the story of Ms. Sisson and Jasmyn, her second-grade student. We'll look closely at the steps Ms. Sisson took after administering the initial benchmark Spelling assessment. (These steps also can be applied to the Decoding assessment, though that is not included in this example.)

📷 **Snapshot: Using K–2 Reading Foundations Skills Block Assessments to Identify Student Needs and Plan for Instruction**

Before the school year began, Ms. Sisson, a second-grade teacher, looked over Jasmyn's results from the Grade 1 end-of-year benchmark assessments. According to the assessments, Jasmyn had ended first grade below grade level, in the late Partial Alphabetic phase (which means she was using only partial alphabetic information to read and write).

Ms. Sisson knew that Jasmyn's first-grade teacher, Mr. Locke, had been monitoring Jasmyn closely throughout the year and that he, along with Jasmyn and her mom, was determined to accelerate her progress. Jasmyn's mom had signed her up for a summer reading camp at school and had asked Mr. Locke to give her extra work for the summer. Ms. Sisson was eager to get an accurate sense of Jasmyn's current strengths and needs.

Beginning-of-Year Benchmark Assessment

At the beginning of Jasmyn's second-grade year, Ms. Sisson administered Spelling, Decoding, and Fluency benchmark assessments. She and Jasmyn were thrilled to see that, based on the benchmark assessment results, Jasmyn's hard work over the summer had paid off. She was spelling and reading with increasingly more complete alphabetic information (early Full Alphabetic microphase). For example, in Grade 1 Jasmyn was able to read and spell words with short vowel sounds and some consonant clusters (e.g., *sit* and *trap*); now she was also able to read and spell some compound words (e.g., *cannot*) and some words with long vowel patterns (e.g., CVCe words like *rope*).

Cycle and Snapshot Assessments

During the first few months of school, Ms. Sisson checked in with Jasmyn individually about once per week during differentiated small group instruction. She administered a snapshot assessment on that day each week to check for mastery of that day's skill. Ms. Sisson used all of this evidence, along with Jasmyn's cycle assessment results, to track Jasmyn's progression through the Full Alphabetic phase, using a microphase tracker she created (see Figure 7.7).

Figure 7.7: Ms. Sisson's Microphase Tracker

	C1	C2	C3	C4	C5	C6	C7	C8	C9	C10	C11
		Late Partial Alphabetic					**Early Full Alphabetic**				
		Module 1					Module 2				
Standards covered											
Focus of Cycle	G1 intro	review: t,a,p,n,h,c,t h,s,m,r,v,g	review: i,ch,k,y,s h,z,d,l,f,	review: q,u	review: o,b,j,w, x	/e/ words	y as long e	wh - & -ck	-ll,-s s,-ff, -zz	bl-, cl-, fl-, gl-, pl-, sl-, sp-, spl-	-lt, -ft, -nd, -nk, -ng, -n -ed as /id/
yn	3		3	3	3	3	3	3	3	3	
wn	3		3	2	2	1	1	2	2	1	
nir	2		1	1	1	1	1	2	2	2	

(Left margin labels: automatic; with help or slowly 1=...et)

Middle-of-Year Benchmark Assessment

About halfway through Grade 2, Ms. Sisson followed the Grade 2 Assessment Path (suggested benchmark assessments to administer to a typical Grade 2 student; see Assessment Overview for more details) and administered the Spelling, Decoding, and Fluency benchmark assessments. In the steps that follow, we'll walk through her analysis and actions based on the Spelling assessment, one of the two priority assessments for Grade 2 (along with Decoding).

Step 1: Analyze results from a priority assessment.

For the Spelling assessment, since Jasmyn was most recently identified as reading in the early Full Alphabetic microphase, Ms. Sisson administered the Full Alphabetic list. Jasmyn correctly spelled 10 out of 12 words. Ms. Sisson knew this meant that Jasmine represented all of the sounds in the words accurately but not necessarily using the conventional spelling of the word. The only errors she made were *blingk* (blink) and *jumpping* (jumping).

Results	Analysis	Next Step
10/12 words correct	According to the Teacher Administration Guidance document, Ms. Sisson should administer the next, more difficult list because Jasmyn correctly spelled 10 or more words on the full alphabetic list.	Ms. Sisson administered the next spelling assessment using the Consolidated Alphabetic list.

Step 2: Use the scoring sheet guidance to determine a microphase.

Ms. Sisson continued on with the spelling assessment and next administered the Consolidated Alphabetic list. With this spelling list, Jasmyn incorrectly spelled a larger number of words (6 out of 12 were incorrect), making errors such as *claped* (clapped) and *oatmiel* (oatmeal). Ms. Sisson could see that Jasmyn still needed to learn and practice a number of spelling patterns (e.g., vowel digraphs such as *ea* and rules for adding suffixes to base words). Based on the scoring sheet guidance, she determined that Jasmyn was in the early Consolidated Alphabetic phase.

Results	Analysis	Next Step
6/12 words correct	Jasmyn correctly spelled six words. According to the scoring sheet, she is in the early Consolidated Alphabetic phase.	Ms. Sisson located the early Consolidated Alphabetic phase on the Assessment Conversion Chart. She identified a cluster of lessons that would address Jasmyn's needs (Grade 2, Module 2, Cycles 7–12).

Step 3: Group students in the same microphase together.

Ms. Sisson grouped Jasmyn with the only other two students currently spelling and reading in the early Consolidated Alphabetic phase.

Step 4: Use the Assessment Conversion Chart to identify cycles.

Ms. Sisson shared with Jasmyn that she had progressed to the early Consolidated Alphabetic phase. She emphasized and celebrated the tremendous growth Jasmyn had made in the last year and explained that she still had some work to do before she would read and spell on grade level and that she was confident Jasmyn would do it!

To round out the group of students in the early Consolidated Alphabetic phase (there were two students in addition to Jasmyn), Ms. Sisson looked for trends among all of her students. She added two additional students currently reading and spelling in the late Full Alphabetic phase because she knew that all of these students needed extra practice with many of the same spelling patterns.

Results	Analysis	Next Step
Jasmyn and two additional students are reading in the early Consolidated Alphabetic phase; two other students are reading in the Full Alphabetic phase.	This group seems to need practice with some of the same spelling patterns and has some other common strengths and needs (e.g., the *ea* and *oa* vowel teams).	Ms. Sisson looked closely at the late Full Alphabetic and the early Consolidated Alphabetic sections on the Assessment Conversion Chart. She examined the following cluster of cycles identified on the chart: » G1M4, Cycles 21–25 » G2M1, Cycles 1–6 » G2M2, Cycles 7–13

Step 5: Refine analysis.

The late Full Alphabetic and early Consolidated Alphabetic sections of the Assessment Conversion Chart include a large range of lessons. Ms. Sisson knew she should narrow down her choices by looking closely at the words each student spelled incorrectly.

She noticed that the following spelling patterns were represented consistently incorrectly across most of the students: *ea, oa, -tion, -sion,* and words requiring doubled consonants when a suffix is added. So she chose cycles with those specific patterns explicitly taught (G1M4C21; G2M1C3; and G2M2C9 and C12). She also noted that the *oa* and *ea* spelling patterns are some of the only long vowel patterns represented in the Spelling Assessments, so she also chose some cycles that include other /ā/ and /ō/ spelling patterns (G2M1C2–3 and C5; G2M2C7) in case the students need extra practice with these too and/or may find it helpful to compare and contrast the spelling generalizations for each.

Results	Analysis	Next Step
Students in these two phases consistently misspelled some of the same patterns.	The patterns consistently misspelled were: *ea, oa, -tion, -sion,* and words with doubled consonants in the middle.	Ms. Sisson looked closely at the spelling patterns and skills identified for each cycle of lessons, searching out and choosing the cycles with the specific patterns that were misspelled by most of the students (G1M4C21; G2M1C3; G2M2C9 and C12) and cycles with other /ō/ and /ē/ patterns (G2M1C2–3 and C5; G2M2C7). She used the Differentiation Pack materials for these cycles to plan small group instruction.

▶ What about Evidence from Formative/Ongoing Assessments? Is That Worth Analyzing and Turning into Usable Data?

Your main focus for systematically collecting and analyzing evidence of student progress will be the summative assessments in the curriculum. However, formative assessments offer a great deal of information about student progress, and there will be times when you'll want to take a closer look

It's important to pause here in the midst of this chapter about evidence and data to talk about judgment. As a teacher, you use your judgement all day long. Your students steer you in unexpected directions each day, and your judgment, based largely on your experience in the classroom, is what keeps things rolling. There's nothing wrong with using your judgment to guide you to the evidence you should analyze in a more systematic way, just as Mr. Bashir did when he suspected that his students hadn't all participated equitably in the Science Talk. This is what led him to pull out his observation checklist and start analyzing it for patterns.

Trust your instincts and use your judgment. If your students' discussions seem to be missing important understandings you had hoped they would have, if their pronunciation of letter-sound combinations is inconsistent, if their opinions are not backed up by evidence, or if you simply feel that a lesson didn't go well, it's time to hit the pause button. Gather their note-catchers or exit tickets or whatever ongoing assessment evidence was generated during the lesson and dig into some analysis.

In addition to your in-the-moment judgment, another indicator that a formative assessment is a good one for you to analyze further is students' past performance. If they struggled in a particular area on their mid-unit assessment and a subsequent lesson gives them a chance for further practice, that's a good time to look more closely at formative assessment evidence from that lesson.

In either case, ask yourself the questions described in Chapter 7A:

1. What does this piece of work indicate in terms of this particular student's progress toward the daily learning target?

2. What might this student need next?

3. Across this collection of student work, what patterns (of successes or struggle) am I noticing?

When working to turn evidence of individual students' progress into usable data, it's especially important to focus on Question 3. After identifying patterns, you can ask yourself an additional question:

4. What might groups of students who are struggling with this learning target need to reach success? How can this understanding inform my instruction going forward?

A simple way to think about what each group of students needs is to sort work into piles: work that is *beginning, developing, proficient,* or *advanced* for the given target/standard. From there you can consider upcoming lessons or interventions and what opportunities there are to differentiate instruction to better address students' needs.

▶ How Can I Use Data to Drive Differentiation and Best Support My Students?

Carol Ann Tomlinson, one of the leading experts on differentiated instruction, describes the difference great teachers make by seeing "humanity in every child; model(ing) a world that dignifies each child; and mak(ing) decisions to support the welfare of each child[6]." Recognizing and describing the strengths and challenges of your students allows you to tailor (i.e., differentiate) your instruction to meet their needs. Students' strengths and challenges are not static, however; students learn and grow all the time, and their struggles in one area (e.g., writing) do not necessarily mean that they will struggle in others (e.g., reading comprehension). This is why usable data, based on formative and summative assessments, is so important. Data allows you to select different instructional approaches and paths depending on the varying and changing needs of the students in your classroom.

After analyzing data for trends, you can select differentiated approaches that allow each student to work toward the same high standards. Sometimes a differentiated approach will be useful for one student, a small group of students, or your entire class. You want to be sure that the strategy you implement serves the right student(s) and doesn't impede those who are already succeeding.

As we described in Chapter 2C, the curriculum has been designed from the outset, based on the principles of Universal Design for Learning, to be supportive of students with varied learning needs. Also, extensive supports for English language learners (ELLs), such as Language Dives, are woven into every lesson to give students full access to the curriculum. Beyond these pillars of the design, considerations for differentiation are offered throughout the curriculum to best support all students. In the Module Lessons, the Teaching Notes, Supporting English Language Learners, Universal Design for Learning, and Meeting Students' Needs sections provide guidance.

---

[6] From keynote speech at the EL Education National Conference, 2011

However, despite the best-laid plans, sometimes students will need additional scaffolding and support. Table 7.4, which first appeared in Chapter 5, highlights differentiation options to consider based on the needs of your students.

Table 7.4: Scaffolding Options

	Scaffolding Options
Lesson calls for reading chunks of the text independently	» For students who might get overwhelmed by seeing the whole text on a page, format the text in "bite size" pieces (e.g., one paragraph at a time on index cards or one page as a separate handout). » Have students read with a buddy. » Have small groups read with you or another teacher (or via technology). » Provide structured overviews for some sections of text. » Reformat texts to include more embedded definitions or even picture cues. » Provide the text to students in a clear format, either on a handout or displayed clearly via technology. » Though K–2 students will not be reading the text independently during close read-alouds, it is still important to chunk the text for them to follow along with as you read. These chunks of text should be displayed for all to see or students should have their own copies.
Lesson calls for answering questions	» Start with concrete text-dependent questions before moving to the abstract. » Tackle small sections at a time. » Once students have tried the task, provide additional modeling for those who need it. » Provide sentence stems or frames. » Highlight key ideas/details in the text. » Modify graphic organizers to include picture cues or additional step-by-step directions.
	» Post directions and anchor charts. » Provide "hint cards" that give students more support with text-dependent questions (students access these only when they get stuck). » Indicate where students may find key information in the text or on an anchor chart by marking with sticky notes or highlights. » Give options for responding to questions with drawing, drama, or discussion before writing. » Make time for guided work with the teacher.
Lesson calls for writing	» Modify graphic organizers to include picture cues or additional step-by-step directions. » Provide sentence starters and sentence frames. » Use discussion, including Conversation Cues, to help students orally rehearse their answers before responding in writing. » Model writing using a similar prompt or a different section of the text. » Make time for small group guided work with the teacher. » Make time for more frequent conferring.

Cont.

	Scaffolding Options
Lesson calls for collaborative work	» Review norms for collaboration in advance and after group work. » Have small groups work with a teacher. » Form heterogeneous pairs (strategic partnerships). » Monitor specific students more strategically (e.g., seat them closer to a teacher). » Provide (and model) structured roles for group members.
Other literacy or intervention time	» Offer additional practice with fluency (e.g., oral reading, speaking with expression) and grammar rules. » Offer additional writing practice. » Offer additional work with structured phonics. » Pre-read with students the text used in the Module Lesson. » Have students read additional (easier) texts on the same topic or theme. » Have students reread texts used in Module Lessons. » Provide additional quality read-alouds, including via technology. » Pre-teach critical vocabulary. » Engage students in word study (e.g., structural analysis of specific words from the text).
Homework	» Provide students with read-alouds via technology (e.g., audiobooks). » Provide picture cues or additional directions. » Provide sentence starters or sentence frames. » Provide video or slides of class examples on a website. » Modify expectations of quantity.

Considering the Needs of English Language Learners

Chapter 2C offers an extensive description of the curriculum's supports for ELLs. Here we expand on that information with a few specific considerations for looking at ELLs' work for evidence of meeting learning targets. In addition to some of the general questions to ask yourself (described in Chapter 7A), consider these additional questions and differentiation options for ELLs:

» If assessment data and checklists reveal that the student is not yet meeting learning targets related to reading, does this reflect the student's *reading* level or the student's *English language* level? It can be easy to assume that a student who is learning English is a struggling reader. Yet, although the student may in fact "struggle" when reading in English, he or she may be a strong reader in his or her home language. Determining the cause of the struggle is important for planning the right next steps in supporting ELLs.

• Considerations for differentiation:

  ○ If the student is literate in a home language, ask him or her to read something in the home language for a teacher who also speaks that language and informally assess his/her fluency and accuracy.

  ○ Preview key story elements and vocabulary before the student reads.

  ○ Encourage the student to reread the text after they read related comprehension questions.

» If assessment data and checklists reveal that the student's performance on a particular task is inconsistent with his or her abilities (as demonstrated previously), were the instructions for the task represented in a clear and comprehensible way for students who are learning English? ELLs may benefit from additional scaffolds when receiving instructions.

- Considerations for differentiation:

  ○ Read assessment questions aloud to students.

  ○ Model the task and "think aloud" as you go.

  ○ Allow students to discuss the task in home languages before they complete the task independently.

  ○ Check for comprehension by inviting students to summarize the instructions for the task.

» If assessment data and checklists reveal that the student is not yet meeting learning targets related to writing, did the student have enough opportunities to talk before she was expected to write? As we know from Chapter 6, engaging in discourse before writing is an important scaffold for ELLs. Was the student given enough time to write? Writing in a second language may require more processing time. Before drawing too many conclusions from data, ensure that these scaffolds were in place prior to writing.

- Considerations for differentiation:
  - If the student can write in his/her home language, have a teacher who speaks the same language informally assess a written artifact for strengths in the home language.
  - Provide think time.
  - Provide oral processing time to plan writing with a teacher or peer in English or in the home language.
  - Model a sample written response and "think aloud" as you go.
  - Provide sentence frames.

» If assessment data and checklists reveal that the student is not yet meeting learning targets related to speaking and listening, did the student have sufficient think time? Was she asked probing questions to engage her thinking? Because ELLs may need additional language processing time, it may be difficult for them to participate in conversations even if they have mastered the content and are able to express their ideas.

- Considerations for differentiation:
  - Provide additional think time.
  - Use Goal 1 Conversation Cues to elicit more information and to promote equity (Conversation Cues are described in detail in Chapter 2C).
  - Empower students to advocate for themselves when they need more time to think or when they would like something repeated.

When determining appropriate action steps based on your analysis of the work of ELLs, a good place to begin is with the specific details in the K–5 Module Lessons: the language proficiency standards in the Supporting English Language Learners section and the ELL supports in the Meeting Students' Needs section. Identify which support you can integrate into your instruction to help students take ownership of the learning target and make progress. Consult with an English as a second language specialist to help identify individual students' strengths in English language development and to plan appropriate support for each student.

Chapter 7C:
Habits of Character Connect Students' Growth as Learners to Their Growth as People

As one of our three dimensions of student achievement, mastery of knowledge and skills is clearly a focus of our language arts curriculum, and our path to help students succeed in this area has been detailed throughout this book. High-quality student work, another dimension of student achievement, took center stage in Chapter 6, particularly in 6C, where we explored how models, critique, and descriptive feedback help strengthen student writing within and beyond the curriculum. Here we turn to the third dimension, character, which we call habits of character in the curriculum.

You may wonder why we have chosen to highlight habits of character in a chapter about assessments, evidence, and data. On the surface, it may not seem like it fits. However, for us, character development is as important an "outcome" for students as mastery of standards (albeit much harder to measure!). Additionally, one-third of our framework for character is about helping students *work to become effective learners*. One of the best ways we know to do that is to engage students in the assessment process. In this way, habits of character are both a means to help students master knowledge and skills and an important end in themselves.

▷ **...habits of character are both a means to help students master knowledge and skills and an important end in themselves.**

Three aspects of character are identified in our Dimensions of Student Achievement. Table 7.5 illustrates how each of these is taught in the curriculum. The right-hand column describes in student-friendly language some of the particular habits the curriculum works to grow.

Table 7.5: Habits of Character in the K–5 Curriculum

Aspect of Character	Habits of Character (in student-friendly language)
Work to become effective learners: develop the mind-sets and skills for success in college, career, and life (e.g., initiative, responsibility, perseverance, collaboration)	» I take initiative. This means I notice what needs to be done and do it. » I take responsibility. This means I take ownership of my work, my actions, and my space. » I persevere. This means I challenge myself. When something is hard, I keep trying and ask for help if I need it. » I collaborate. This means I can work well with others to get something done.
Work to become ethical people: treat others well and stand up for what is right (e.g., empathy, integrity, respect, compassion)	» I show empathy. This means I try to understand how others feel. » I behave with integrity. This means I do the right thing even when it is hard. » I show respect. This means I treat myself, others, and the environment with care. » I show compassion. This means I notice when people are sad or upset and reach out to help them.
Work to contribute to a better world: put their learning to use to improve communities (e.g., citizenship, service)	» I take care of and improve our shared spaces. » I use my strengths to help others grow. » I apply my learning to help our school, the community, and the environment.

In the pages that follow, we will explore the first aspect of our character framework: *work to become effective learners*. Specifically, we will address why it is so important to engage students in the assessment process, both as an end in itself (helping them develop the lifelong habits of effective learners) and as means to helping them master the literacy standards that the assessments in the curriculum measure. We will then explore how the other two aspects of our character framework—*work to become ethical people* and *work to contribute to a better world*—are an explicit focus of the curriculum.

▶ How Will Engaging My Students in the Assessment Process Help Them Become More Effective Learners?[7]

The most important assessments that take place in any school building are seen by no one. They take place inside the heads of students, all day long. Students assess what they do, say, and produce, and decide what is good enough. These internal assessments govern how much they care, how hard they work, and how much they learn. They govern how kind and polite they are and how respectful and responsible. They set the standard for what is "good enough" in class. In the end, these are the assessments that really matter. All other assessments are in service of this goal—to get inside students' heads, raise the bar for effort and quality, and foster a growth mindset (i.e., a belief that learning comes from effort and that making mistakes is a part of how we learn).

---

[7] This section is excerpted in part from the introduction to our 2014 book *Leaders of Their Own Learning: Transforming Schools through Student-Engaged Assessment.*

Engaging students in the assessment process is effective because it draws on these internal self-assessments that occur naturally for them. Unfortunately, students and teachers often don't know how to tap into this level of assessment and learn how to capitalize on it. Students frequently have widely varying internal standards for quality and aren't clear about what "good enough" looks like. Some students have internalized a sense that they don't have a value or voice in a classroom setting and that anything they do will be inferior to the work of the "smart kids." In other cases, they believe they have only one chance to do something and begin to work from a place of compliance and completion rather than working toward quality through a series of attempts.

Teachers frequently fall into the trap of simply saying "try harder" without giving students specific targets, feedback, time to revise, and a purpose for doing quality work. What students really need are tools and support to self-assess and improve their own learning and the motivation to do so. Knowing where they're headed and how to get there engenders responsibility and empowers students to take ownership of their learning. Unless students find reason and inspiration to care about learning and have hope that they can improve, excellence and high achievement will remain the domain of a select group.

▷ What students really need are tools and support to self-assess and improve their own learning and the motivation to do so. Knowing where they're headed and how to get there engenders responsibility and empowers students to take ownership of their learning.

Putting Students in the Driver's Seat

Often when we think of an assessment, whether formative or summative, we think of it as something that is done *to* students, rather than something done *with* students. A big part of our approach to assessment at EL Education is to reframe it as something that students do *with* their teachers. If we give students the tools to understand where they are headed with their learning, help them track progress along the way, and then debrief with them not only what they learned but how they learned it, we put them in the driver's seat. After all, students are the ones who are in control of their learning, not us. If they feel motivated to persevere when the going gets tough because they understand where they are headed and why, that will take them much further than our encouragement or admonishments.

Our curriculum is designed to build in students a sense of ownership over their progress, changing the main goal of assessment from evaluating and ranking students to motivating them to learn. From goal-setting and reflection to learning targets and tracking progress forms, students become leaders of their own learning, motivated internally to succeed. They learn the language of standards and metacognition, identify patterns of strengths and weaknesses, become self-advocates, and assess their own work.

Helping students be purposeful and skillful in their ability to reflect on what and how they learned is at the core of becoming a self-directed learner and thus is essential for college and career readiness. Reflection is built into every lesson in our curriculum, ensuring that students develop the skills to reflect deeply and concretely, beyond vague statements of preferences, strengths, and weaknesses. This process can begin in kindergarten. As kindergarten teacher Jane Dunbar describes in Chapter 6C, "I then ask the group, 'What would you do on the next draft if this were yours?' And 'What would you change?' I challenge them for details." Imagine the power of building this ability to reflect on drafts over years of practice.

Motivating Students to Care and Persevere through Challenges

Nothing is more important in fostering growth in students than the degree to which they care. Recent research suggests that student perseverance, grit, and self-discipline correlate strongly with academic success (Blackwell, Trzesniewski, and Dweck, 2007; Duckworth and Seligman, 2005; Dweck, Walton, and Cohen, 2011; Good, Aronson, and Inzlicht, 2003; Oyserman, Terry, and Bybee, 2002; Walton and Cohen, 2007). This will not surprise teachers or parents—it is common sense. But these "noncognitive" strengths are entirely based on the degree to which students care about their learning and their growth. If students don't care, they are not going to work hard.

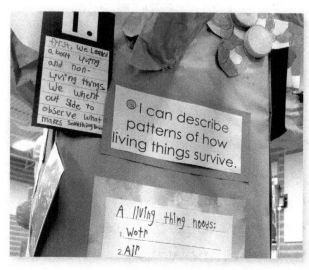

Collaborative, meaningful work and high expectations helped these students step up to challenges.

The apathy, disconnection, or lack of self-esteem that causes students to disengage in school—to stop caring—is not inherent. It is learned behavior. Kindergartners come to school excited to learn. In the course of their schooling, however, some students lose touch with their ability to thrive in a school environment. School becomes something that is done to them, something that they are not good at. They may feel they are good at sports, music, or video games, but school is just not a place where they succeed. Their test scores and grades make this clear.

In our curriculum, compelling topics, combined with meaningful tasks, collaboration with peers, and assessment practices that support students to do work that they are proud of, motivates them to step up to challenges.

▶ How Are the Other Aspects of Character (*Work to Become Ethical People* and *Work to Contribute to a Better World*) Taught in the Curriculum?

The first part of our framework for fostering habits of character is helping students become effective learners. One way we do this is by engaging them in the assessment process, as previously described, but there are many ways in which this is a focus in the curriculum. In kindergarten, this may mean something as simple as asking students to take responsibility when cleaning up in K–2 Labs (Labs). We also focus strongly on helping students be collaborative learners (see Chapter 3C).

Beyond our emphasis on helping students become effective learners, our curriculum gives them authentic opportunities to learn and practice each aspect of our framework for character (see Table 7.5), including *work to become ethical people* and *work to contribute to a better world*. The curriculum is unique in that it integrates an intentional focus on developing students' habits of character within the context of English language arts (ELA) lessons. No curriculum is values-free; every curriculum either explicitly or implicitly addresses how students are expected to behave, in addition to what they are expected to learn. We choose to be explicit about character strengths and how teachers can foster them.

At all grade levels, the curriculum is designed to give students authentic opportunities to understand how character is a part of—not separate from—their academic work. We don't tell students to "have good character," but instead give them chances to learn about or demonstrate good character and then reflect on it, often in the context of academic lessons. For example, students read about people (real or fictional) who embody certain habits and serve as compelling models

"One of the most noticeable differences the staff and I have seen throughout our entire school is the conversations students are capable of having with one another. The academic vocabulary, the respect, and the ability to be engaged in a conversation with minimal teacher guidance are impressive.

In one instance, I observed first-graders partner-editing their papers. As someone who used to be a fourth-grade teacher, I felt nervous for this teacher and expected to see tears at some point given the age of these students. But they amazed me! I watched them take the job of editing very seriously, and they did it in a way any teacher would hope for. I watched as students used their fingers to check each other's word spacing, mark words they thought may have been spelled incorrectly, and discuss the content of their sentences. The supportive and kind words students showed each other in expressing their concern over a possible mistake their partner made was really wonderful. In today's world, where people cannot have conversations on any difficult topic without feeling offended or upset, it was so encouraging to see how this curriculum facilitates habits of character. There's so much support and practice for students to learn to have respectful and difficult conversations with one another, while also challenging them academically."

Liz Freitag

Instructional Coach and Testing Coordinator, Valdosta, Georgia

for students' own aspirations. In Grade 5, students read about Jackie Robinson as an athlete who effected social change. Learning about the factors that contributed to his leadership may inspire students to take action in their own communities.

Students practice aspects of character as they work independently, collaborate with peers, and care for one another and their classroom. They reflect on habits of character individually as they evaluate their work, set goals for themselves, and engage in the assessment process with their teachers.

★ **Connecting the Curriculum's Habits of Character to Existing Character Frameworks**

Many common frameworks are used to help educators think about the development of character in the classroom: Character education, social-emotional learning, nonacademic factors, and the social curriculum are common examples. According to the U.S. Department of Education, the development of character is about helping "students and adults understand, care about, and act on core ethical values." We have our own language and approach to developing habits of character, but these can and should complement, not replace, existing frameworks, language, and routines for promoting social-emotional learning in your school.

For example, some schools focus on the five core competencies identified by the Collaborative for Academic, Social, and Emotional Learning, or others might be using Responsive Classroom or Caring School Communities, two programs designed to integrate social-emotional learning with daily classroom practices. Schools may have codified specific character words or habits to focus on (e.g., *self-discipline* or *kindness*). You can certainly continue to use these words; when using the curriculum, you can simply help students connect the language used (e.g., *perseverance*) to how your school may already talk about character (e.g., *tenacity*). Such connections will expand students' academic vocabulary and enrich their understanding of these important concepts.

Work to Become Ethical People

In Chapter 5A, we detail the complex considerations that went into our choice of texts in the content-based curriculum. In addition to choosing texts that ensure students will have the opportunity to meet ELA standards, we also prioritized texts that give students the opportunity to practice habits of character. We looked for texts that would offer students a chance to read, think, talk, and write about the human experience and reflect on how their actions impact others.

Every module has a habit of character focus that is woven into the lessons. As we designed the curriculum, we ensured that this habit of character focus was connected to the module topic, texts, and tasks so that students have an authentic and coherent experience. In Grade 3, Module 1, Unit 1, for example, students work to become ethical people, treating others well and standing up for what is right (e.g., empathy, integrity, respect, compassion). They practice and reflect on respect, compassion, and empathy in response to the potentially diverse views of different students as they learn about others who are facing challenges. After reading the texts, they practice and reflect on integrity when completing research reading for homework each night.

You may recall that the sample lesson in Chapter 6B comes from this same Grade 3 unit. In this lesson, students hear *Waiting for the Biblioburro*, a story about the struggles a girl named Ana faces with access to education in Colombia and the help she gets from the biblioburro, a librarian who travels around on donkeys with books. After listening to the story read aloud, students reflect on its message and create the Experiences with Overcoming Challenges anchor chart as a vehicle to share their reflections. Students not only share reflections about the character's experiences overcoming challenges, but are also invited to share their own experiences. This lesson opens the door for students to not only show empathy and compassion for the challenges children around the world face, but also for their classmates.

Later in this unit, in Lesson 6, students continue to add to a Working to Become Ethical People anchor chart. In this lesson, they focus on integrity because they are kicking off an Accountable Independent Reading homework structure. Their need to work independently gives students an authentic opportunity to consider what integrity means to them in the context of their own academic choices. Teachers help students understand that integrity means doing the right thing, even when it's difficult, because it is the right thing to do. In the context of homework, this means trying to do it each day, even when it is tough to do so, and if it isn't possible, being honest in recording the dates and pages read in their journals.

Work to Contribute to a Better World

The third part of our character framework is about contributing to a better world. Helping students consider their place in the world and how they can be of service is a part of the K–12 school experience for many students. In our curriculum we build off on this ethic by weaving service into ELA lessons so that students can put their learning to use to improve their communities.

Grade 2, Module 4 offers a nice example. In Unit 3, students are deeply engaged with this guiding question: "How can people take action to help butterflies?" They apply their knowledge about plants and pollinators to help one important pollinator: butterflies. Building on knowledge from Modules 3 and 4, students read about how planting wildflowers helps butterflies. For their performance task, students take action by creating a wildflower seed packet to then give away to a school or family member. The front of the wildflower seed packet includes a title and colored pencil drawing of a monarch butterfly. The back of the packet includes instructions for planting wildflower seeds and an opinion piece telling people why they should help butterflies.

As a culmination of the work of Module 4, students write letters inviting school and family members to a Celebration of Learning, where they share their reflections and give their seed packets to a guest. Creating work for an authentic audience motivates students to meet standards and engage in revision. Through the process, they develop perseverance and realize that they can do more than they thought they could.

This particular example of fostering habits of character is also a nice example of another dimension of student achievement: high-quality student work. The performance task for this module allows students to create high-quality work based on their deep knowledge of pollinators. Using the literacy skills built throughout the school year, knowledge built in Modules 3 and 4, and cycles of drafting, critique, and revision, students are able to create a high-quality product (the seed packet) that showcases their learning for the year.

Table 7.6 includes additional specific examples of how the curriculum integrates habits of character into the daily life of the classroom.

Table 7.6: Developing Students' Habits of Character in the K–5 Curriculum

Structures and Practices in the Curriculum	Explanation and Example
Provides structures that empower students to participate in a collaborative community; fosters a sense of belonging	Students consider how to collaborate effectively. For example, in Grade 3, Module 1, students generate norms for group work that are tied directly to specific habits of character: "I show empathy," "I behave with integrity," "I show respect," and "I show compassion."
Teaches the language of character explicitly and authentically in the context of lessons (not as a stand-alone "character curriculum")	Students learn how to talk about their interactions. For example, in Grade 1, Module 1, students do a collaborative challenge (stacking cups) to practice speaking and listening. During the Closing of the lesson, they reflect on how they used initiative (a habit of character) to complete the challenge.
Devotes time for students to regularly set and reflect on individual goals; students see they can succeed at this work	Students own their own learning, regularly self-assessing. For example, during the K–2 Reading Foundations Skills Block (Skills Block), students complete an assessment at the end of each weekly cycle. Each student then briefly confers with the teacher to reflect on progress and set a specific goal for the next week.
Devotes time for students to regularly set and reflect on group goals	Students frequently "step back" and consider how their interactions are going and what could be improved. For example, in Grade 3, Module 1, students work in small groups to discuss the books they chose for independent reading. After the discussion, they score themselves green (met the target), yellow (on our way), or red (not yet) based on how well they followed the discussion norms during their conversation.
Includes intentional grouping and protocols, so students interact with a wide variety of peers	Collaboration is a critical life skill explicitly named in the Common Core Speaking and Listening standards. In the Module Lessons, protocols—simple discussion routines—develop students' ability to have collaborative conversations with diverse peers.
Fosters collaboration as students work to create high-quality work; students see that this work has value to them	High-quality student work is one of our dimensions of student achievement. Collaboration is a key means to this end. For example, in Grade 1, Module 1, students read *The Most Magnificent Thing* and then work in small groups to design and then create a "magnificent thing" for their classroom.
Builds students' self-direction and independence	The curriculum helps students be leaders of their own learning. For example, in the K–2 Labs, across the eight weeks of a module, students are introduced to materials and activities, practice them with support, and then gradually increase their independent work. And in Grades 3–5, every day in the Additional Language and Literacy Block, students spend at least 20 minutes following a "task card" to guide their work with peers.
Builds students' ability to give and receive feedback that is kind, specific, and helpful	Students regularly critique one another's work, and they learn and practice how to give feedback. For example, in Grade 1, Module 1, students pair up and give each other one "star" (positive feedback) and one "step" (suggestion) on their draft "magnificent things," and then revise.

Cont.

Structures and Practices in the Curriculum	Explanation and Example
Challenges students to connect their learning with the broader world and help solve real problems	Students are most engaged when doing real work that matters. In many of the ELA and all of the Life Science modules, students are challenged to address an actual or simulated problem in their school or community. For example, in third-grade Life Science, they design a frog pond based on a scenario.
Repeated reading of texts allows students to make connections with the human condition and see other points of view.	Students read literary and informational texts that show many experiences and perspectives. For example, in Grade 3, Module 1, students read a true story about a young girl from Afghanistan who gains access to education by attending a "secret school" for girls.
Children are in the role of experts.	Children learn about the work that real professionals (such as meteorologists) do and take on those roles when possible.
Helps students see and celebrate how their ability is growing with their effort.	Growth mindset permeates the curriculum. For example, almost daily in the Skills Block, students notice how their effort to identify letter-sound patterns is helping them become better readers.

The Relationship between Habits of Character and "Academic Mindsets"

In her work "Academic Mindsets as a Critical Component of Deeper Learning," Camille Farrington suggests that one of the most basic foundations for increasing student achievement is the development of four academic mindsets ("the psycho-social attitudes or beliefs one has about oneself in relation to academic work"):

» I belong to this academic community. (Connection)

» I can succeed at this. (Confidence)

» My ability and competence grow with my effort. (Perseverance)

» This work has value to me. (Relevance)

Farrington's work has focused on high school students, yet we have found that this framework is powerful for elementary students as well. In explicitly addressing the habits of character described in Table 7.5 through the use of our curriculum, teachers can actively help develop these mindsets. When students develop a sense of belonging and engagement in an academic setting that engenders a sense of confidence, they are more likely to grow to become effective learners and ethical people. And contributing to their community helps students see firsthand the value of their work and feel satisfaction in their efforts.

EL Education believes that to prepare students for success in college, career, citizenship, and life, we must embrace a broader and deeper vision of what high achievement means. Good test scores are just a starting place. Mastery of knowledge and skills, character, and high-quality work are all critical for success.

Chapter 7: Reflecting on Progress: Helping Students Grow as Learners And People

Chapter 7A: How Will I Know if My Students Are Making Progress?

Chapter 7B: How Do I Turn Evidence into Usable Data?

Chapter 7C: Habits of Character Connect Students' Growth as Learners to Their Growth as People

▶ Instructional Leadership

Frequently Asked Questions

Chapter 7:
Instructional Leadership

Table 7.6: Chapter 7 Instructional Leadership

Questions to Ask Yourself and Your Staff
» What support does your staff need to understand the difference between evidence and data? Are they prepared to select evidence of student progress that is worthy of further analysis (i.e., worth the time to turn it into usable data)?
» Are systems and structures in place to help teachers organize and analyze data so that it can inform their instruction? For example, have you prioritized time during staff or team meetings for teachers to look at student work together? How might your instructional coach support this work?
» What best practices have you observed among those teachers who can respond to the needs of students (based on data) in ways that don't bog down their pacing? How can you ensure that all teachers can learn similar strategies?
» What support do teachers need to feel confident in knowing what they are seeing and hearing when they look at student work and listen to student conversation? What additional learning do they need to help them do this work effectively? For example, should you model the process of looking at student work and identifying what it tells you about student progress toward mastery of particular standards? Would this help your teachers develop consistent schoolwide practices? What do your teachers need most to be successful with this practice?
» What support have you given teachers to identify when and how to scaffold students who are struggling toward mastery of standards? What else do they need?
» In what ways do teachers see students as partners in the assessment process? What can you do to help teachers prioritize and master practices that put students in the driver's seat (e.g., learning targets, goal-setting, reflection)?
» Have you messaged the importance of habits of character? If not, why not? What are your own beliefs about how important habits of character are both as a means to help students succeed with this curriculum and as an end in themselves?

Cont.

Evidence of Progress

» Staff are not feeling overwhelmed by the amount of evidence of student progress (e.g., formative/on-going and summative assessments) generated by the curriculum. They feel confident in their ability to select which evidence is worthy of deeper analysis.

» Whole staff and team meetings have time dedicated to looking at student work together and calibrating analysis. Instructional leaders support teachers in this work.

» Teachers use Curriculum Maps and the Unit-at-a-Glance charts to determine if and when students will have additional chances to work toward mastery of standards. They are able to strategize what they will need additional time to re-teach and when they will do it (e.g., during built-in flex time). They stay on pace with lessons overall.

» Teachers understand the array of differentiation options available for students who need additional scaffolding, based on data analysis. They know how to scaffold students in ways that don't take away their access to high-level texts and high-level thinking.

» Teachers commit to engaging students in the assessment process. They ensure that students understand their learning targets and check their progress, and they make time for students to reflect on their learning. Even when time is tight, they don't skip time for students to reflect and track their progress.

» A focus on habits of character has allowed the curriculum to come to life in classrooms. Students are continually improving their abilities to work collaboratively, show respect for each other and their space, and connect their effort to their success.

Resources and Suggestions

» Resources available on our curriculum website (Curriculum.ELeducation.org):

- Assessment Overview and Resources (for every K–5 module)

- Checklists

- Writing rubrics

» Resources available on the main EL Education website (ELeducation.org):

- PD Packs

  ○ Using Data

  ○ Collaborative Culture

  ○ Leaders of Their Own Learning

» EL Education book that deepens understanding of the practices in this chapter:

- *Leaders of Their Own Learning: Transforming Schools through Student-Engaged Assessment*

» Book: *Driven by Data: A Practical Guide to Improving Instruction* by Paul Bambrick-Santoyo

» Website: Models of Excellence: The Center for High-Quality Student Work: resources available for teachers ready to do more in-depth analysis of student work (modelsofexcellence@ELeducation.org)

Chapter 7

Chapter 7:
Frequently Asked Questions

How should I record student grades? Does the curriculum have a progress monitoring system?

Our approach to assessment is standards-based, meaning that systems and structures within the curriculum are designed to reflect students' progress on each standard, versus giving letter grades or grading in more generic categories such as "writing." If your school already uses a standards-based grading system, it should be fairly easy for you to use that system for recording student grades from the curriculum. If not, you will likely need to develop your own systems for mapping scores from our rubrics, for example, onto your existing grading structure. EL Education currently does not have an official progress monitoring system for the curriculum. However, as is evident in this chapter and throughout the book, we have many resources in place to help you score student assessments and organize data.

I'm overwhelmed by the idea of analyzing my students' work. Is it really that important?

To thoughtfully and consistently analyze student work does take time, and you may feel overwhelmed by the pressure to cover material and stay on pace. This pressure may cause you to keep plowing through instead of pausing to take stock of how your students are making progress. This is not a good tradeoff. If you skip the step of looking closely at students' work in order to cover ground, you lose your most important lever to boost student learning: close understanding of how each student is doing and what he or she needs to work on next.

What should I do with evidence of student progress that I have decided not to analyze?

One option is to help students use their work to develop portfolios that show their progress toward mastery of standards and growth over time. Portfolios are a great way to deeply engage students in the assessment process. Helping them curate and analyze their own work as sources of evidence is valuable learning for them. Another option, harkening back to Chapter 6C, where we talk about using models as a way to help students identify the criteria for quality work, is to begin collecting your own models. In subsequent years, you can use actual models of student work from the curriculum, which will be powerful for your future students.

My school leaders haven't structured professional development time to allow teaching teams to gather to analyze data. Do you have any suggestions for how to do this work more independently?

First, we would encourage you to keep advocating with your school leaders for why you feel it would be more powerful to do this work in teams and the potential benefits you see both for teacher practice and student outcomes. But if that is not your current situation, you can still start by doing the work on your own or with a colleague who is willing to devote some time to working with you. Document your process and the impact it is having on your ability to meet students' needs. If your school leaders see the impact this work is having for you and your students, they are more likely to consider schoolwide structures. If a schoolwide structure is still not realistic, consider bringing your ideas for this work to team or grade-level meetings. You can start by having each team member bring in a sample or collection of student work for analysis and using the Results Meeting protocol. If you are the only teacher in your grade, you can do this in vertical team planning meetings or ask to include student work analysis in coaching sessions.

Where can I find resources for collecting evidence of progress in the K–2 Reading Foundations Skills Block?

The K–2 Reading Foundations Skills Block (Skills Block) includes benchmark assessments (administered three times per year), as well as weekly cycle and daily assessments. Each of these tools can help you determine students' strengths and areas of need and help you monitor progress. Refer to the Assessment Overview (in the K–2 Skills Resource Manual) for details about each type of assessment.

If my analysis of data shows that students need additional practice, how can I find time to re-teach lessons or parts of lessons?

Before considering how you will find time to re-teach, look at your Unit-at-a-Glance chart or Curriculum Map to see if there are already opportunities to address student needs built in to upcoming lessons. If you still feel that you need to spend time re-teaching a lesson, flex time is built in to the Skills Block, K–2 Labs, and 3–5 Additional Language and Literacy (ALL) Block for you to do this. Also, if you are a 3–5 teacher, the ALL Block is designed to deepen and enhance students' work in the Module Lessons, so there may already be built-in time to reinforce needed skills.

I love the curriculum's focus on habits of character, and I'm interested in putting more emphasis on how students can contribute to a better world. What else can I do beyond the lessons in the curriculum?

At all grade levels, contributing to a better world is an explicit focus of at least one module. Often, after students have had a chance to build knowledge about a compelling topic in the first two units of a module, they will have the opportunity to take action in Unit 3 (typically connected to the performance task). Students creating wildflower seed packets to support butterfly habitats (described in Chapter 7C) is one example. In the Module Lessons, each Module Overview also has a section called "Optional: Community, Experts, Fieldwork, Service, and Extensions." This is a good place for you to start thinking about opportunities for students to contribute to a better world (i.e., service) beyond their English language arts lessons but in a way that is connected to the module topic. For example in Grade 5, Module 1 ("Stories of Human Rights"), the Module Overview suggests reaching out to local immigration charities to find out whether students can participate in any charity events or raise funds for a specific cause. These optional (but no less important) extensions of the modules, which may happen during social studies or science time, are opportunities to give students holistic learning experiences.

I love the curriculum's focus on habits of character, but I'm not sure if I should be "grading" their growth in terms of character.

Our curriculum doesn't take a position on or provide resources for grading habits of character, largely since schools' grading systems are often already very complex, and schools may already have an existing approach to character. However, many schools in the EL Education network and beyond do grade certain aspects of character (sometimes called habits of scholarship or habits of work) that are in the "effective learners" category and have measurable components (e.g., I complete my homework on time) within a standards-based grading system. We do not suggest trying to grade students on their ethical character (e.g., compassion, respect), as it is difficult to quantify those habits and they may be most importantly exhibited when we are not watching students. However, students can certainly collect evidence of showing strong habits in ethical character.

Paramount to any effort to assess character is that character targets have clear criteria for success and are practiced, formatively assessed, self-assessed, and reported separately from academic grades. One of the easiest places to start with this work is the *work to become effective learners* aspect of our character framework. It can be powerful for students to see how their academic progress correlates with their progress toward the following criteria:

» I take initiative. This means I notice what needs to be done and do it.

» I take responsibility. This means I take ownership of my work, my actions, and my space.

» I persevere. This means I challenge myself. When something is hard, I keep trying and ask for help if I need it.

» I collaborate. This means I can work well with others to get something done.

Perhaps as part of your process of developing norms with your students, you could consider working with them to develop a rubric that will help them understand what it means to meet these criteria. This would provide you with a powerful vehicle to not only assess habits of character, but also to build and reinforce a positive classroom culture.

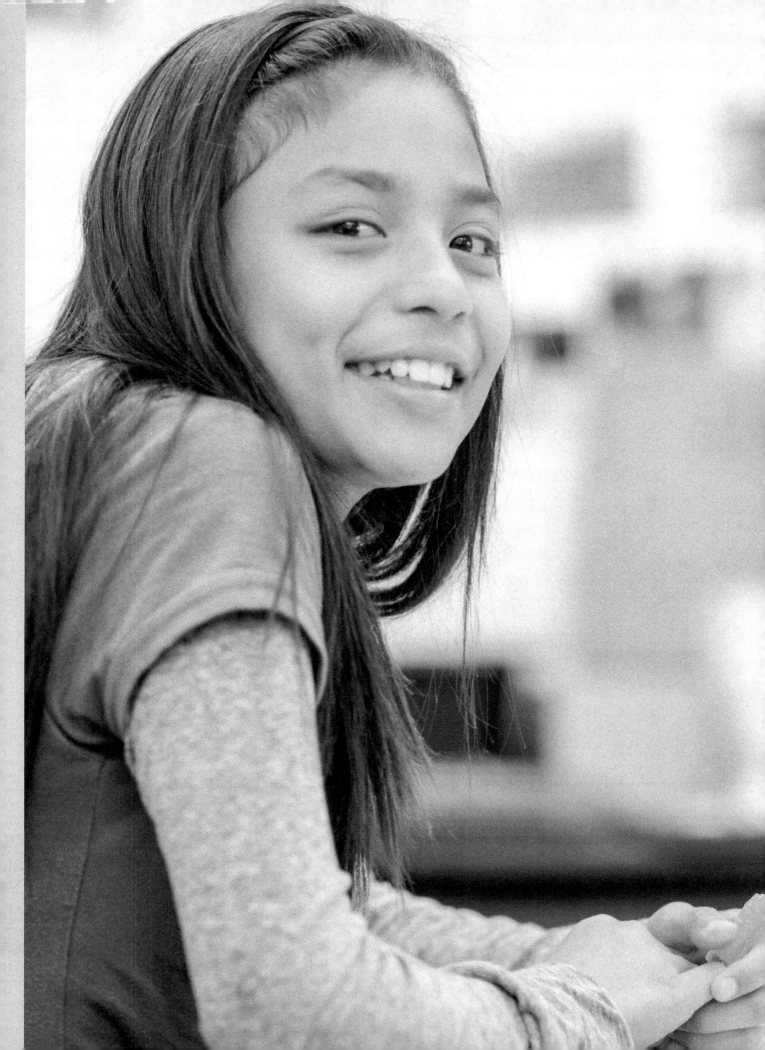

References

Abedi, J., & Linquanti, R. (2012). *Issues and opportunity in improving the quality of large-scale assessment systems for English language learners.* Stanford University. Retrieved fromhttp://ell.stanford.edu/sites/default/files/pdf/academic-papers/07-Abedi%20Linquanti%20Issues%20and%20Opportunities%20FINAL.pdf

Ackerman, D. (1999). *Deep play.* New York, NY: Vintage Books. ACT, Inc. (2006). *Reading between the lines: What the ACT reveals about college readiness in reading.* Iowa City, IA: ACT.

Adams, M. A. (1990). Beginning reading instruction in the United States. *ERIC Digest.* ERIC Clearinghouse on Reading and Communication Skills.

Adams, M. J. (1994). *Beginning to read: Thinking and learning about print.* Cambridge, MA: MIT Press.

Adams, M. J. (2009). The challenge of advanced texts: The interdependence of reading and learning. In E. H. Hiebert (Ed.), *Reading more, reading better: Are American students reading enough of the right stuff?* (pp. 163–189). New York, NY: Guilford Press.

Anderson, R. C., & Nagy, W. E. (1992). The vocabulary conundrum. *American Educator: The Professional Journal of the American Federation of Teachers, 16*(4), 14-18, 44-47.

Baldwin, R. S., Peleg-Bruckner, Z., & McClintock, A. (1985). Effect of topic interest and prior knowledge on reading comprehension. *Reading Research Quarterly, 20*(4), 497–504.

Bambrick-Santoyo, P. (2010). *Driven by data: A practical guide to improve instruction.* San Francisco, CA: Jossey-Bass.

Barnes, D. (1976). *From communication to curriculum.* Harmondsworth, UK: Penguin.

Beach, R., & Friedrich, T. (2006). Response to writing. In C. A. MacArthur, S. Graham, & J. Fitzgerald (Eds.), *Handbook of writing research* (pp. 222–234). New York, NY: Guilford Press.

Bear, D. R., Invernizzi, M. R., Templeton, S., & Johnston, F. (2003). *Words their way: Word study for phonics, vocabulary, and spelling instruction* (3rd ed.). Upper Saddle River, NJ: Prentice-Hall.

Berger, R., Rugen, L., & Woodfin, L. (2014). *Leaders of their own learning: Transforming schools through student-engaged assessment.* San Francisco, CA: Jossey-Bass.

Berger, R., Strasser, D., & Woodfin, L. (2015). *Management in the active classroom.* New York, NY: EL Education.

Berger, R., Woodfin, L., Plaut, S., & Dobbertin, C. (2014). Transformational literacy: Making the Common Core shift with work that matters. San Francisco, CA: Jossey-Bass.

Berger, R., Woodfin, L., & Vilen, A. (2016). *Learning that lasts: Challenging, engaging, and empowering students with deeper instruction.* San Francisco, CA: Jossey-Bass.

Berk, L. E. (2013). The role of make-believe play in the development of executive functioning: Status of research and future directions. *American Journal of Play, 6*(1), 98–110.

Biemiller, A. (2010). *Words worth teaching: Closing the vocabulary gap.* Columbus, OH: SRA/McGraw-Hill.

Blackwell, L. S., Trzesniewski, K. H., & Dweck, C. S. (2007). Implicit theories of intelligence predict achievement across an adolescent transition: A longitudinal study and an intervention. *Child Development, 78* (1), 246–263.

Bloodgood, J. W., & Pacific, L. C. (2004). Bringing word study to intermediate classrooms. *Reading Teacher, 58*(3), 250–263.

Brooker, L., & Woodhead, M. (Eds.). (2008). *Developing positive identities: Diversity and young children.* Milton Keynes, UK: The Open University.

Brookhart, S. (2008). *How to give effective feedback to your students.* Alexandria, VA: ASCD.

Bunch, G. C., Lotan, R., Valdés, G., & Cohen, E. (2005). Keeping content at the heart of content-based instruction: Access and support for transitional English learners. In D. Kaufman & J. Crandall (Eds.), *Content-based instruction in primary and secondary school settings* (pp. 11–25). Alexandria, VA: Teachers of English to Speakers of Other Languages.

Bunch, G., Kibler, A., & Pimentel, S. (2012). *Realizing opportunities for ELLs in the Common Core English language arts and disciplinary literacy standards.* Stanford University. Retrieved from http://ell.stanford.edu/sites/default/files/pdf/academic-papers/01_Bunch_Kibler_Pimentel_RealizingOpp%20in%20ELA_FINAL_0.pdf

Cervetti, G. N., Jaynes, C. A., & Hiebert, E. H. (2009). Increasing opportunities to acquire knowledge. In E. H. Hiebert (Ed.), *Reading more, reading better: Solving problems in the teaching of literacy* (pp. 79–100). New York, NY: Guilford Press.

Cervetti, G. N., & Hiebert, E. H. (2015). The sixth pillar of reading instruction: Knowledge development. *Reading Teacher, 68*(7), 548–551.

Chall, J. (2005). Diagnostic assessments of reading, 2nd ed. Austin, TX: PsychCorp, A brand of Harcourt Assessment, Inc.

Charney, R. S. (1992). *Teaching children to care: Management in the responsive classroom.* Turners Falls, MA: Center for Responsive Schools, Inc.

Christison, M. A. (1999). *A guidebook for applying multiple intelligences theory in the ESL/EFL classroom.* Burlingame, CA: Alta Book Center.

Clark, C., & Rumbold, K. (2006). Reading for pleasure: A research overview. *National Literacy Trust.* Retrieved from http://files.eric.ed.gov/fulltext/ED496343.pdf

Collier, V., & Thomas, W. (2004). The astounding effectiveness of dual language education for all. *NABE Journal of Research and Practice, 2*(1), 1–20.

Cunningham, A. E., & Stanovich, K. E. (1997). Early reading acquisition and the relation to reading experience and ability 10 years later. *Developmental Psychology, 33,* 934–945.

Duckworth, A. L., & Seligman, M.E.P. (2005). Self-discipline outdoes IQ in predicting academic performance of adolescents. *Psychological Science, 16,* 939–944.

Dweck, C. S., Walton, G. M., & Cohen, G. L. (2011). Academic tenacity: Mindsets and skills that promote long-term learning. White Paper. Seattle, WA: Gates Foundation.

Eberle, S. (2011). Playing with multiple intelligences: How play helps them grow. *American Journal of Play, 4*(1), 19–51.

Edreports.org. (n.d.). *Grades 6-8 summary of alignment and usability.* Retrieved from http://www.edreports.org/ela/reports/series/engage-ny.html

Erikson, E. H. (1959). *Identity and the life cycle.* New York, NY: International Universities Press.

Ferris, D. R., & Hedgcock, J. S. (2013). *Teaching L2 composition: Purpose, process, and practice.* New York, NY: Routledge Press.

Flanagan, J. (2009). *Sensory processing disorder.* Retrieved from http://www.kennedykrieger.org/sites/kki2.com/files/08-09.pdf

Fletcher, J. M., & Lyon, G. R. (1998). Reading: A research-based approach. In W. M. Evers (Ed.), *What's Gone Wrong in America's Classrooms.* Stanford, CA: Hoover Institution Press. Retrieved from http://arthurreadingworkshop.com/wp-content/uploads/2012/06/10-FletcherLyonResearchBased.pdf

García, O. (2009). *Bilingual education in the 21st century: A global perspective*. West Sussex: UK: Wiley- Blackwell Press.

García, O., & Walqui, A. (2015). What do educators need to know about language as they make decisions about Common Core standards implementation? In G. Valdés, K. Menken, & M. Castro (Eds.), *Common Core bilingual and English language learners* (pp. 47–50). Philadelphia, PA: Caslon Publishing.

Gay, G. (2000). *Culturally responsive teaching: Theory, research, and practice*. New York, NY: Teachers College Press.

Gibbons, P. (2010). Classroom talk and the learning of new registers in a second language. *Language and Education, 12*(2), 99–118.

Gomez, K., & Zywica, J. (2008). Annotating to support learning in content areas: Teaching and learning science. *Journal of Adolescent & Adult Literacy, 52*(2), 155–164.

Good, C., Aronson, J., & Inzlicht, M. (2003). Improving adolescents' standardized test performance: An intervention to reduce the effects of stereotype threat. *Journal of Applied Developmental Psychology, 24*, 645–662.

Gough, P. B., Alford, J. A., & Holley-Wilcox, P. (1981). Words and contexts. In O.J.L. Tzeng & H. Singer (Eds.), *Perception of print: Reading research in experimental psychology* (pp. 85–102). Hillsdale, NJ: Erlbaum.

Gough, P. B., Juel, C., & Roper-Schneider, D. (1983). A two-stage model of initial reading acquisition. In J. A. Niles & L. A. Harris (Eds.), *Searches for meaning In reading/language processing and instruction* (pp. 207–211). Rochester, NY: National Reading Conference.

Halvorsen, A-L., Duke, N. K., Brugar, K. A., Block, M. K., Strachan, S. L., Berka, M. B., & Brown, J. M. (2012). Narrowing the achievement gap in second-grade social studies and content area literacy: The promise of a project-based approach. *Theory & Research in Social Education, 40*(3), 198–229.

Hart, B., & Risley, T. R. (2003). The early catastrophe: The 30 million word gap by age 3. *American Educator, 27*(1), 4–9.

Hayes, D. P., Wolfer, L. T., & Wolfe, M. F. (1996). Sourcebook simplification and its relation to the decline in SAT-Verbal scores. *American Educational Research Journal, 33*, 489–508.

Hernandez, D. J. (2012). Double jeopardy: How third grade reading skills and poverty influence high school graduation. *The Annie E. Casey Foundation*. Retrieved from http://www.aecf.org/m/resourcedoc/AECF-DoubleJeopardy-2012-Full.pdf

Hiebert, E. H. (2012). Core vocabulary: The foundation for successful reading of complex text. *Text Matters*. Text Project, Inc.

Himmele, P., & Himmele, W. (2011). *Total participation techniques: Making every student an active learner*. Alexandria, VA: Association for Supervision & Curriculum Development.

hooks, b. (2000). *Feminist theory: From margin to center*. Cambridge, MA: South End Press.

Howard, S. (2006). What Is Waldorf Early Childhood Education? *Gateways, Fall/Winter*. Waldorf Early Childhood Education Association.

International Dyslexia Association. (n.d.). Multisensory structured language teaching. Retrieved from https://dyslexiaida.org/multisensory-structured-language-teaching/

Juel, C. (1998). Learning to read and write: A longitudinal study of 54 children from first through fourth grades. *Journal of Educational Psychology, 80*(4), 437–447.

Kintsch, E., & Hampton, S. (2009). Supporting cumulative knowledge building through reading. In S. R. Parris, D. Fisher, & K. Headley (Eds.), *Adolescent literacy, field tested: Effective solutions for every classroom* (pp. 47–57). Newark, DE: International Reading Association.

Kohn, A. (2015). Who's asking? *Educational Leadership, 73*(1), 16–22.

Landauer, T. K., & Dumais, S. T. (1997). A solution to Plato's problem: The latent semantic analysis theory of acquisition, induction, and representation of knowledge. *Psychological Review, 104*(2), 211.

Larson, K. (2004). The science of word recognition, or how I learned to stop worrying and love the bouma. *Advanced Reading Technology, Microsoft Corporation*. Retrieved from https://www.microsoft.com/typography/ctfonts/WordRecognition.aspx#top

Lesnick, J., George, R. M., Smithgal, C., & Gwynne, J. (2010). Reading on grade level in third grade: How is it related to high school performance and college enrollment? *The Annie E. Casey Foundation*. Retrieved from http://www.chapinhall.org/sites/default/files/Reading_on_Grade_Level_111710.pdf

Liben, David. (2010). *"Why text complexity matters" in Common Core state standards for English language arts and literacy in history/social studies, science, and technical subjects. Appendix A: Research supporting key elements of the standards*. National Governors Association Center for Best Practices, Council of Chief State School Officers: Washington, DC.

Long, M. H. (1996). The role of the linguistic environment in second language acquisition. In W. C. Ritchie & T. K. Bhatia (Eds.), *Handbook of second language acquisition* (pp. 413–468). New York, NY: Academic Press.

McNamara, D. S., & O'Reilly, T. (2009). Theories of comprehension skill: Knowledge and strategies versus capacity and suppression. In A. M. Columbus (Ed.), *Advances in psychology research, volume 62*. Hauppauge, NY: Nova Science Publishers, Inc.

Metsala, J., & Ehri, L. (1998). *Word recognition in beginning literacy*. Mahwah, NJ: Erlbaum.

Michaels, S., & O'Connor, C. (2012). Talk science primer. Cambridge, MA: TERC. http://inquiryproject.terc.edu/shared/pd/TalkScience_Primer.pdf. Based on Chapin, S., O'Connor, C., & Anderson, N. (2009). *Classroom discussions: Using math talk to help students learn, grades K–6* (2nd ed.). Sausalito, CA: Math Solutions Publications.

Morgan, A., Wilcox, B., & Eldredge, J. (2000). Effect of difficulty levels on second-grade delayed readers using dyad reading. *Journal of Educational Research, 94*(2), 113–119.

Moss, C., & Brookhart, S. (2009). *Advancing formative assessment in every classroom*. Alexandria, VA: ASCD.

Nagy, W., & Anderson, R. (1984). The number of words in printed school English. *Reading Research Quarterly, 19*, 304–330.

Nagy, W., Herman, P., & Anderson, R. (In press). Learning words from context. *Reading Research Quarterly*.

Nagy, W., Anderson, R., & Herman, P. (1987). Learning word meanings from context during normal reading. *American Educational Research Journal, 24*, 237–270.

National Center for Education Statistics. (2012). *The nation's report card: Vocabulary results from the 2009 and 2011 NAEP reading assessments*. Institute of Education Sciences, U.S. Department of Education, Washington, DC.

National Center on Universal Design for Learning. (n.d.). *The three principles of UDL*. Retrieved from http://www.udlcenter.org/aboutudl/whatisudl/3principles

National Governors Association Center for Best Practices, Council of Chief State School Officers. (2010). *Common Core state standards*. Washington, DC: Author.

National Governors Association Center for Best Practices, Council of Chief State School Officers. (2010). *Common Core state standards (appendix A)*. Washington, DC: Author.

National Institute of Health. (n.d.). *National reading panel*. Retrieved from https://www.nichd.nih.gov/research/supported/Pages/nrp.aspx

Nelson, J. (2011). Positive discipline: The classic guide to helping children develop self-discipline, responsibility, cooperation, and problem-solving skills. New York, NY: Ballantine.

Nelson, J., Perfetti, C., Liben, D., & Liben, M. (2012). *Measures of text difficulty: Testing their predictive value for grade levels and student performance*. Council of Chief State School Officers, Washington, DC.

O'Connor, R. E., Swanson, H. L., & Geraghty, C. (2010). Improvement in reading rate under independent and difficult text levels: Influences on word and comprehension skills. *Journal of Educational Psychology, 102*(1), 1–19.

Oyserman, D., Terry, K., & Bybee, D. (2002). A possible selves intervention to enhance school involvement. *Journal of Adolescence, 25*, 313–326.

Parke, R. D., & Gauvain, M. (2009). Gender roles and gender differences. In *Child psychology: A contemporary viewpoint* (7th ed.) (pp. 475–503). Boston, MA: McGraw-Hill.

Pinter, A. (2006). *Teaching young language learners*. Oxford, UK: Oxford University Press.

Rasinski, T. (2004). Creating fluent readers. *Educational Leadership, 61*(6), 46–51.

Rasinski, T. V., Padak, N. D., McKeon, C. A., Wilfong, L. G., Friedauer, J. A., & Heim, P. (2005). Is reading fluency a key for successful high school reading? *Journal of Adolescent & Adult Literacy, 49*(1), 22–27.

Recht, D. R., & Leslie, L. (1988). Effect of prior knowledge on good and poor readers' memory of text. *Journal of Educational Psychology, 80*(1), 16–20.

Rodgers, C. R., & Raider-Roth, M. B. (2006). Presence in teaching. *Teachers and Teaching: Theory and Practice, 12*(3), 265–287.

Scholastic. (2007). Guided reading indicators. In *Fountas and Pinnell Continuum for Literacy Learning*. Retrieved from www.scholastic.com/teachers/sites/default/files/posts/u133/pdfs/text_level_indicators.pdf

Shanahan, T., Fisher, F., & Frey, N. (2012). The challenge of challenging text. *Reading: The Core Skill, 69*(6), 88–62.

Shaywitz, S. (2003). *Overcoming dyslexia: A new and complete science-based program for reading problems at any level*. New York, NY: Vintage Books.

Snow, C. E., Burns, M. S., & Griffin, P. (1998). *Preventing reading difficulties in young children*. Washington, DC: National Academy of Sciences.

Staehr Fenner, D. (2013). *Overview of the Common Core state standards initiatives for ELLs*. TESOL International Association.

Stanovich, K. E. (1986). Matthew effects in reading: Some consequences of individual differences in the acquisition of literacy. *Reading Research Quarterly, 2*(4), 360–407.

Stanovich, K. E. (1992). Speculations on the causes and consequences of individual differences in early reading acquisition. In *Reading Acquisition* (pp. 307–342). Hillsdale, NJ: L. Erlbaum Associates.

Stanovich, K. E., & Cunningham, A. E. (1993). Where does knowledge come from? Specific associations between print exposure and information acquisition. *Journal of Educational Psychology, 85*(2), 211.

Tedick, D., & Wesely, P. (2015). A review of research on content-based foreign/second language education in U.S. K–12 contexts. *Language, Culture, and Curriculum, 28*(1), 25–40.

The Nation's Report Card. (n.d). *National Results Overview*. Retrieved from https://www.nation-sreportcard.gov/reading_math_2015/#reading?grade=4

Tyre, P. (2012). The writing revolution. *Atlantic*. Retrieved from https://www.theatlantic.com/magazine/archive/2012/10/the-writing-revolution/309090/

United Nations Educational, Scientific and Cultural Organization. (1996). Universal Declaration of Linguistic Rights. Declaration presented at the World Conference on Linguistic Rights, Barcelona, Spain.

Vermont Writing Collaborative. (2008). Writing for understanding: Using backward design to help all students write effectively. Vermont: Author.

Walqui, A., & Van Lier, L. (2010). *Scaffolding the academic success of adolescent English language learners: A pedagogy of promise*. San Francisco, CA: WestEd.

Walton, G. M., & Cohen, G. L. (2007). A question of belonging: Race, social fit, and achievement. *Journal of Personality and Social Psychology, 92*, 82–96.

Weisberg, D., Zosh, J., Hirsh-Pasek, K., & Golinkoff, R. M. (2013). Talking it up: Play, language development, and the role of adult support. *American Journal of Play, Special Issue, 6*, 39–54.

Whipple, G. M. (1925). *Report of the national committee on reading*. Bloomington, IL: Public School Publishing.

Wiggins, G. (2012). Seven keys to effective feedback. *Educational Leadership, 70*(1), 10–16.

Wiliam, D. (2014). The right questions, the right way. *Educational Leadership, 71*(6), 16–19.

Williams, J. P., Stafford, K. B., Lauer, K. D., Hall, K. M., & Pollini, S. (2009). Embedding reading comprehension training in content-area instruction. *Journal of Educational Psychology, 101*, 1–20.

Wong Fillmore, L., & Fillmore, C. (2012). What does text complexity mean for English learners and language minority students? Paper presented at the Understanding Language Conference, Stanford, CA.

Index

NOTE: Page numbers in **boldface** indicate primary discussion. Figures are indicated by f and tables by t following the page number. Footnotes are indicated by n and the note number, e.g., 27n4.

A

academic courage, building, 164

"Academic Mindsets as a Critical Component of Deeper Learning" (Farrington), 427

Accountable Independent Reading, 223, 231, 319

activity, in self-managed classrooms, 176

Additional Language and Literacy (ALL) Block, **83–92**

    Additional Work with Complex Text, 321

    assessment system, 72t

    components, 65, 83–85

    evidence-based components, 333

    independent and free-choice reading, 83t, 87t, 319

    key features, 65–66

    promoting proficiency and growth, 83t–85t

    reading and speaking fluency, 84t, 87t

    reinforcing and extending Module Lessons, 65, 86, 87t, 118

    rotations and student groupings, 88–90, 89t, 90f, 113t

    structure of, 86, 86f

    word study and vocabulary, 85t, 87t

    work with complex texts, 84t, 87t

    writing practice, 85t, 343

Alphabetic Principle, 201

anchor charts

    building, 171–172

    as evidence-based instructional strategy, 333

    function of, 171

    supporting students with, 172

anchor/central texts, 33, 263–264

anchoring phenomenon, in Life Science modules, 67

Anholt, Laurence, 263

annotating, protocols for, 168

argument writing, 331–332

Arlon, Penelope, 264

assessments

    benchmark assessments, K-2, 391–393

    checking for understanding, 158–161, 194

    checklists, 392–393, 394

    in curriculum design, 30–31

    formative assessments, 392–393, 394

    Fountas and Pinnel Benchmarking System, 208, 217, 218, 219, 249

    Grades 3-5 curriculum, 66, 71t–72t, 393–395

    K-2 Module Lessons and Labs, 62, 70t–71t, 391–393

    K-2 Skills Block, 217–218, 218t, 249–250, 391, 409–413

    K-5 curriculum, 69–72

    key features, 69

    quick checks, 159–160t

    standards-aligned, 32

    student engagement in assessment process, 420–421

    student progress in meeting learning targets, 155–156, 156t

    summative assessments, 392, 394

    writing, in Module Lessons, 342–343

    writing and reflection, 158–159t

authenticity, 12–13

B

background knowledge, building, 67–68

Back-to-Back and Face-to-Face (protocol), 282, 341

Bambrick-Santoyo, Paul, 388, 406n5

"Baseball Study" (Recht and Leslie), 258

Bauschka, Tammi, 105, 361

Beckhard and Harris Change Equation, 38

belonging, sense of, 15–16

benchmarks

    benchmark assessments, K-2, 391–393

    Fountas and Pinnel Benchmarking System, 208, 217, 218, 219, 249

Benton, Katie, 174, 203, 224

Berger, Ron, 7, 9, 151, 152, 153, 155, 161, 167, 259, 263, 276, 276, 340, 357

Birds (Scholastic Discover More) (Arlon and Gordon-Harris), 264

Brookhart, Susan, 373n3

C

Caring School Communities framework, 424

CBAM (Concerns-Based Adoption Model), 38

Center for Applied Special Technology, 109

central/anchor texts, 33, 263–264

challenges

    building academic courage, 164

    fostering culture of grappling, 163–164

    as motivation for academic success, 422

change of curriculum, **36–45**

    assessing readiness for teacher support, 40–41

    Frequently Asked Questions, 49–51

    implementation complexities, 41t–45t, 413

    instructional and operational leaders, 38–39

    Instructional Leadership, 46n5, 46t–48t

    laying groundwork for, 37–38

    managing complex change, 37–39

    maximizing potential for success, 36–37

Charney, Ruth, 184, 187

checking for understanding, *See* understanding, checking for

Cicero, Stacey, 229

classroom culture

    allowing critique and descriptive feedback to flourish, 361–362

    building, 179–188

    snapshot, 362

    structures and strategies for building, 184–188

classroom management, **173–189**

Elkonin Boxes (Sound Boards), 207
ELLs. *See* English language learners (ELLs)
empowerment of students, 148, 149t–150t
Engineer Lab, 76t, 77
English language arts (ELA) standards
    central to Life Science modules, 69
    compliance with Common Core State Standards, 9, 50
    in K-5 curriculum, 55
English Language Development (ELD) Standards, 97, 120
English language learners (ELLs), **93–108**
    challenging curriculum for, 94
    close reading/read-alouds support for, 283, 284
    conversation and language learning, 96–97
    Conversation Cues, 27n4, 97, 100–102t
    data analysis and differentiated instruction for, 414, 416–418
    developing and honoring home language, 98
    discourse in read-think-talk-write cycle, 340
    educator responsibility for success of, 95–96
    English Language Development (ELD) Standards for, 97
    ESL teacher involvement with, 120
    as fastest-growing student population, 93–95
    flexible grouping of students, 113t, 340
    honoring diversity and inclusion, 98, 104
    instructional strategies, 99–108
    K-5 curriculum support for, 4, 108t, 119–120
    Language Dives, 22, 25n3, 97, 99–100, 347, 414
    language usage and error correction, 107–108, 348
    learning English not barrier to learning, 95
    levels of support, 103–104, 347
    modeling productive conversations, 103
    multiple modes and intelligences for, 105–106
    oral language and K-2 Labs, 75
    peer feedback for, 348
    plagiarism considerations, 348
    principles underlying support for, 95–99
    second language development, 96
    snapshot, 94
    structured phonics benefits, 209–210
    translations, cautions in using, 98–99
    vocabulary and phrases in context, 106–107
    vocabulary routines, 34
    writing practice, 106, 348
    writing supports for, 347–348
Equity sticks, 163t
ESL teachers, involvement with ELLs, 120
Esperanza Rising (Ryan), 263, 278
evidence of student progress
    criteria for, 388
    evidence vs. usable data, 388–390, 430
    Frequently Asked Questions, 430–432
    Grades 3-5 curriculum, 393–395
    Instructional Leadership, 428t–429t
    K-2 Module Lessons and Labs, 391–393
    K-2 Skills Block, 391, 409–413, 431
    scoring of evidence, 396–398, 396f, 398t, 430
    sources of, 387–398
    student work in first grade (snapshot), 389–390, 390f

tracking progress forms, 395
turning evidence into usable data, **399–418**, 430
evidence-based learning, **327–348**
    adding stories and poems to curriculum, 380
    building culture of evidence in classroom, 334–336
    curricular structures, 332–333, 336–341
    curriculum addressing reading and writing standards, 332–334
    deepening student learning, 327–328
    Frequently Asked Questions, 380–382
    Instructional Leadership, 378t–380t
    instructional strategies, 333–335
    protocol sources, 380
    reading standards, 328, 329t
    read-think-talk-write cycle, 337–341, 337f
    sentence frames supporting collaboration and discussion, 335–336
    writing for understanding, 336–337, 337t
    writing standards, 329–331, 329t
executive functioning skills
    K-2 Labs and, 74
    providing options for (UDL Principle 2), 110
exploration
    Explore Lab promoting, 76t, 77
    primary learners and, 16
expression of ideas
    primary learners and, 18
    providing options for (UDL Principle 2), 110

F

Farrington, Camille, 427
feedback. *See also* critique and descriptive feedback; peer critique
    characteristics, 373
    content of, 374
    individual feedback on student work, 372–377
    tone of, 373
feedback loops, 39
Finn, Richard, 4
fluency
    definition, 22
    reading and speaking, in ALL Block, 84t, 87t
    research and curriculum development, 22t–23t
    teacher fluency, 321
formative assessments
    as evidence for usable data, 399–400, 413–414
    in Grades 3-5 curriculum, 394
    in K-2 curriculum, 392–393
Fountas and Pinnel Benchmarking System, 208, 217, 218, 219, 249
Four T's, 131f, 257
Freitag, Elizabeth, 37, 423
Fundamental questions about teaching and learning, **5–18**
    Common Core State Standards, 9
    content-based literacy, 13–14
    elevating student achievement beyond test scores, 11–13, 11f
    equitable access to high-level work for all students, 8–10
    helping students stay active and engaged in learning, 14–18

motivation of students, 6–8

G

gallery critique, 368
global language errors, 107
goal-setting and reflection, 61, 66
Godwin, Laurie, 8
Gordon-Harris, Tory, 264
Grades 3-5 curriculum, **63–69**
    Additional Language and Literacy (ALL) Block, 65–66, 83–92
    backward design of modules, 64
    comprehensive literacy curriculum, 63f
    content-based literacy, 63–66, 65f
    key features of Module Lessons and ALL block, 65–66
    Life Science modules, 66–69
    module, unit, and assessment structure, 64f
    Module Lessons, 63–64
    practice of skills, 66
    scaffolded high-quality writing in, 344–346
    unit assessments, 63
    writing structures in, 343
grading, curriculum change and, 45t
Graham, Steve, 328
grammar, usage, and mechanics (GUM), 84t, 87t
grappling, fostering culture of, 163–164
grouping of students
    ALL Block, 88–90, 89t, 90f, 113t
    flexible grouping, 112–113, 113t
    K-2 Labs, 81, 113t
    snapshot, ALL Block, 90–92
growth, in self-managed classrooms, 176
growth mindset, fostering, 8, 382
guided play, in K-2 Labs, 75
guided practice, 187
guiding questions, 30

H

habits of character, **419–427**
    academic mindsets and, 427
    connection to existing character frameworks, 424
    contributing to a better world, 425, 431
    Frequently Asked Questions, 430–432
    in Grades 3-5 curriculum, 65, 66, 424–425
    grading rubric, 432
    Instructional Leadership, 428t–429t
    integration into curriculum, 422–427
    in K-2 Module Lessons and Labs, 61, 425
    in K-5 curriculum, 419, 420t, 426t–427t
    motivating students through challenges, 422
    student achievement and, 12, 419
    student engagement in assessment and effective learning, 420–422
    working to become ethical people, 424–425
Hesse, Karen, 261f
Higgins, Dolly, 257
high-level work, equitable access to
    elevating student thinking, voice, and work, 10
    ensuring, 8–10
    honoring diversity of learners, 9–10
    incorporating Common Core standards, 9

high-quality writing, defined, 344–345
Himmele, Persida and William, 161
Holyfield, Annie, 74

I

IES (Institute for Educational Science), 203
Imagine Lab, 76t, 77
improvement, continuous, 360, 360f
independence, primary learners and, 16
independent reading
    Accountable Independent Reading, 223, 231, 319
    in ALL Block, 83t, 87t
    in K-5 curriculum, 269–270, 270t
Institute for Educational Science (IES), 203
instructional practices. *See* teaching curriculum
Interactive Word Wall, 266
interest of students
    in central/anchor texts, 263
    providing options for recruiting (UDL Principle 3), 110

J

judgment, in student assessment, 413–414

K

K-2 curriculum. *See also* structured phonics
    backward design of modules, 60
    close read-aloud in, 60
    content-based literacy, 55, 58, 59–60
    evidence-based learning in, 335
    key features of Modules and Labs, 61–62
    Labs (*See* K-2 Labs)
    module, unit, and assessment structure, 59f, 71t
    Module Lessons (*See* K-2 Module Lessons)
    overview of, 58, 59f
    performance tasks, 60
    scaffolded high-quality writing in, 345
    Skills Block (*See* K-2 Reading Foundations Skills Block)
    writing structures in, 342–343
K-2 Labs
    about, 60–61, 61f
    assessment system, 71t
    daily schedule, 80n2, 80t
    evidence-based approach to, 333
    function of, 73–74
    grouping of students, 81, 113t
    key features, 60–61
    meeting developmental needs of primary learners, 74–75
    promoting proficiency and growth, 76t–77t
    reinforcing and extending Module Lessons, 77
    Skills Block complementing, 234–235, 235t–236t
    snapshot, 81–83
    stages unfolding over course of module, 78–81, 79f
    structure of, 78, 78f, 79
    time requirements and scheduling, 117
    writing in, 343
K-2 Module Lessons
    about, 59–60
    assessment system, 59f, 70t
    key features, 61–62

Printed in the USA
CPSIA information can be obtained
at www.ICGtesting.com
LVHW012034121023
760310LV00011B/11